About the Author

William J. Morgan, Jr., is currently a Professor in the School of Hospitality Management at Florida International University at Miami.

He received his B.S. from the School of Hotel Administration at Cornell University, his M.S. in Business Administration from the State University of New York at Albany, and his Ph.D. in Hotel Administration, with minors in Hospital Administration and Industrial and Labor Relations, from Cornell University.

The author has broad experience in food service and hospital administration positions, and has held management positions in hospitals and clubs. He has taught in hotel and restaurant programs in community colleges in both New York and Florida and has served as lecturer and instructor in charge of the Basic Food Program at the School of Hotel Administration, Cornell University.

He has also taught in Switzerland, South America, and the Caribbean and has undertaken specialized instructional work for the United Nations.

He has done research in the use of fats in food service work and in the role of attitudes in the retention of food service workers. His articles have been published in the *Cornell Hotel and Restaurant Administration Quarterly* and other industry periodicals. He has also served as a consultant to educational institutions and operating establishments in matters related to food service.

Dr. Morgan was awarded a National Restaurant Foundation Fellowship in 1970. He has been a member of the Cornell Society of Hotelmen, the Council on Hotel, Restaurant and Institutional Education, the Food Service Executive Association, and the American Society for Hospital Food Service Administrators.

THIRD EDITION

Supervision and Management of Quantity Food Preparation

PRINCIPLES and PROCEDURES

William J. Morgan, Jr.

Professor, School of Hospitality Management
Florida International University

McCutchan Publishing Corporation
P.O. Box 774
Berkeley, California 94701

First edition published 1974. Second edition, 1981.

Library of Congress Catalog Card Number 88-60453

ISBN 0-8211-1260-0

Printed in the United States of America

Preface

The operation of any food service preparation and service facility is fast becoming more than developing a specialized recipe and then determining the proper cooking procedures and the appropriate delivery of food to the guest. Although it is, of course, all of these and more, present-day quantity food preparation is a complex process that probably involves more of the science of management than the art of food preparation and presentation.

This third edition of *Supervision and Management of Quantity Food Preparation* has been written to address the many new developments, both technological and philosophical, that were first considered in the second edition in 1981. Since then, these changes have become driving forces in the food service industry.

In the seven years since the second edition, issues such as smoking in dining areas and health concerns in dietary decisions have joined other issues, including the grocery or convenience store as a restaurant competitor and the home microwave combined with the VCR and take-home meals as new patterns that have influenced almost every form of food service. In addition, other pressing issues such as legal liability and litigation (particularly as these apply to guest safety and matters related to the dispensing of alcoholic beverages) have also concerned today's food service managers.

The use of computers for more efficiency and greater profitability, new forms of cooking equipment and preparation methods to meet diminishing labor availability, and new consumer trends all influence managerial decision making. The resurgence of the front of the house or service aspect as an important part of the total food experience challenges today's management and shakes the foundations of any parochial food service professional.

Although some community colleges and technical and vocational schools have recently moved to develop the chef, or cook practitioner, as an important position, the technology of the discipline, changing consumer tastes, and the new ownership forms and resulting control methods all continue to place greater emphasis on the need for the well-prepared food service manager rather than for the journeyman chef. Of course the master chef, the journeyman cook, the individual food service entrepreneur, the storefront, and the *prix fixe* operation will all continue to exist, as will elements of classical cuisine. The recent history of the discipline, however, and the projections for trends to come suggest that the emphasis will be shifting from food service as a major art form catering to sophisticated consumers to the science of managing more diversified food service operations. As an illustration, the National Restaurant Association schedule for presentations throughout the United States during 1987 covered twenty-five differing management topics while offering only three concerned with culinary skills.

Food-related trends appear, flourish, and expire as diverse tastes and consumer concerns dictate the operation of food service facilities. Through all these changes, though, an emphasis appears on various environmental conditions that influence when, what, and how the food is accepted. These multifaceted concerns require a technically capable generalist as a manager who can create and orchestrate synergistic food service systems into an experience the guest will find desirable.

Hotels, private clubs, classical restaurants, and so on will still remain as the last bastions of the classical, extensive, and esoteric cuisine in the United States (although in fewer numbers), but even here, given the changes in consumer tastes, the current rules on business-expense meals, and the loss of adequate revenue on some profit and loss statements, we find a reduction in the scope of offerings and more establishments using prepared, frozen, or convenience food items.

Mergers, chain acquisitions, and cross-industry associations have resulted in industry hybrids more attuned to marketing concepts than to classical food preparation techniques. The fast food segment and ethnic food offerings in the industry continue to enjoy major sales, with much of the preparation at these facilities being done by nonprofessionals. These people are technically competent in a specialized area but are supervised by a more competent food service manager who, as a generalist, is able to foresee trends and develop marketing techniques to influence sales.

This third edition thus maintains its major emphasis on educating the university, community college, or vocational student in the multiple and complex duties of the quantity food service manager (or the general manager of an operation dealing with food service managers). As stated, the industry requires fewer and fewer professionals who will have to practice the art forms of classical cuisine due to lack of consumer demand, changes in taste, the inability or unwillingness to expend time and/or money for this experience, or the fact that the industry can provide a greater return with a comparable product using centralized or alternate production methods. All food service operations do, however, require managers and/or supervisors who are not only conversant with food preparation principles and practices but also possess the tools to be able to make precise and correct managerial decisions.

This new edition has been revised to keep students current by providing the materials for this mission. The food preparation chapters have been updated to consider changes in menu, equipment, foods, and consumer choices. The major concerns about dietary health—particularly regarding saturated fats, cholesterol, and fiber—have been addressed. This third edition also covers more widely used equipment forms such as microwave and steam-convection ovens. In addition an enlarged segment on fish (one of the leading topical issues) has been included. The present volume also addresses newer findings on sanitation, including AIDS and some of the psychrophilic pathogenic bacteria.

Finally, this edition presents entire new chapters on quality assurance and legal liabilities of the food service operation. The issues of corporate culture and social responsibilities have also been considered. The sections on computers and financial controls have been expanded, and the chapter on service has been given special attention in order to incorporate the present concerns of managers and diners alike.

Using the valuable managerial tools this text provides, the present-day and future manager of any food service operation should be able to anticipate problems and thus either prevent them from appearing or solve them as they emerge in the areas of food preparation or in any of the many related environmental concerns found in almost any quantity food service operation today.

William J. Morgan, Jr.
Montreux, Switzerland

Contents

Figures

Tables

Part I

Management

1 *Volume Food Service: Past, Present, and Future*

Objective: To acquaint the student of volume food management with the history of the subject, to outline the multiplicity of functions within the scope of quantity food service supervision and management, and to suggest opportunities available in the industry.

History of Volume Food Service

The feeding of large numbers of people by means of a centralized procurement, preparation, and service system is a relatively recent innovation. Some primitive civilizations, in attempting a division of labor, delegated the preparation of food for the tribe (or other sociological group) to a particular segment of the population. These food preparers often were lower in status than others in the community, and as a result the work was not considered "worthy" of those who could accomplish other duties.

Primitive attempts to feed people under quantity conditions were in the minority, however. The family unit has been the chief sociological group throughout the ages and has remained the principal source of food for people of all cultures. While the male members generally provided the raw food materials by hunting, fishing, trapping, or agricultural pursuits, the female members tended the home fires and prepared the items that would later be served to the family unit.

The economic base of most primitive and ancient civilizations was agricultural. The people lived from the land, eating what was available in an area, and they were ready to move, on short notice, to more lucrative hunting areas or lands not depleted of basic natural food materials. This ecological habit has continued until the present day; now attempts are being made to recycle, conserve, and maintain supplies of many scarce materials and animals.

Some references to food being prepared and served in common areas are found in writings about the inns of ancient Egypt and the courts of Greece and Rome. The coffeehouses of Constantinople in the 1500s and the English coffeehouses of the seventeenth century have also been noted as places where food and drink were prepared in quantity. The cookshops of France that prepared classical ragouts for take-home use and the famous Monsieur Boulanger, who added other items to his cookshop offerings, are further examples of early volume food service units. In the main, however, most food was eaten at home by family groups.

Figure 1a. The first inns, located on European travel routes, were among the earliest establishments to offer quantity food service. (From *Stock and Custom Menus,* p. 9; copyright 1966, Ad Art Litho, Cleveland, Ohio; reprinted by permission.)

First Volume Food Service Units

The first real volume food service units in any number arose in Europe. These operations developed as a result of the increased desire and ability of people to travel, and they were closely associated with inns.

In feudal times, travel was very limited in the civilized world. The economy had an agricultural base; a majority of the people resided on large farms and furnished food and military service to their feudal lord, while receiving protection and the other necessities of life from the manor house. Little in the way of outside social intercourse was required, and travel, such as it was, was limited to selected trips between feudal centers. Some quantity food preparation was carried out in feudal castles in connection with social events or during times of danger, when vassals found it necessary to retreat to the safe confines of the castle.

Other early attempts at quantity food service occurred in religious communities, where food was grown, prepared, and served to the cloistered residents. As population centers developed, food in quantity was also made available in college hostels and in the infamous poorhouses, precursors of present-day hospitals. But preparation and service of food to large numbers of people remained the exception, rather than the rule, until the advent of extended travel.

In the early modern period newly designed transportation routes made it possible for more people to travel. The fear of highwaymen decreased, and people began to undertake journeys of some distance—to visit centers of religious influence, to transact business, or for pure adventure. Because of the nature of the transportation methods available and the limited distances that could be covered in a day, it was necessary to make nightly stops. At these stops travelers relaxed and refreshed themselves with food and drink. The facilities that provided these services were known as inns. Preparation of food and drink in quantity became an integral part of their operation, along with the other major elements of hospitality—lodging and protection of the weary traveler.

Evolution of the Inn

As travel expanded and trails developed into stage routes and post roads, increased numbers of people became mobile. Trips were taken between centers that developed into cities, as the feudal system broke down and a restless population began to seek employment opportunities. Additional facilities outside the home—inns—were needed to feed and house these mobile guests.

An inn was usually owned and operated by an innkeeper assisted by his family. In many cases the innkeeper's wife served as the early counterpart of today's volume food service manager. She applied her previously learned cooking methods to quantity food situations and taught these skills to her children and employees. The manner in which the food was offered created phrases such as "room and board" and "cold shoulder" that are still in our language. (The large table offering foods in buffet style for the arriving guests was the "board." The innkeeper who dispensed with the traditional greeting and hot food for the late arrival, and offered only a previously cooked, and now cold, shoulder to eat, gave us a term that still connotes lack of hospitality.)

As time passed, travel became more widespread; new roads were constructed to meet the increased demand, and new inns followed. When colonization of America started, the new residents introduced these facilities in their adopted land. The eventual movement of pioneers to the western frontiers caused a need for and development of inns in these remote areas. The tradition that had begun in Europe was continued in the new United States.

The inns that started in the developing centers of population, in both Europe and the United States, served somewhat different public needs from those located on highways. Although they continued to provide the common law requirements of lodging, food, and protection, they also began to serve as group meeting places, social gathering spots, and, in some cases, centers of revolt. They continued to be closely tied to the communications networks, however, because they were located in the central areas of towns or villages, where stage coaches, and later trains, first reached the community.

In the more remote areas of the United States, the horse-borne traveler—eating a freshly killed rabbit beside a campfire and sleeping wrapped in a blanket under the stars —first gave way to the pioneer family, eating a female-prepared meal served from the tailgate of a Conestoga wagon, as greater numbers of people moved west. Eventually towns and way stations were formed along the route, and inns sprang up to provide an alternative to the family-prepared meal.

The ratio of prospective customers to available facilities was often greatly out of balance. In the 1800s, some of the more primitive mining colonies of the West had to institute a novel form of volume food service in order to feed the large numbers demanding this service. The self-service group feeding system they began is still in use today: it is known as the cafeteria.

During this period of expansion and metamorphosis of the inn, some entrepreneurs decided to break with the common law tradition of providing three basic services and to provide only food to the consumer. These operations were started first in urban centers where other facilities were available for lodging. Among the first of these food enterprises was Delmonico's, founded in New York City in 1827. Building on the type of institution begun by Monsieur Boulanger, the first pure table service restaurant form of quantity food operation, separate from the inn, was opened. Others followed in short order.

Current Status of Volume Food Service

Ever since the invention of the automobile the American people have exhibited a high level of mobility. The present "air age" has contributed further to this development. A highly mobile population requires numerous inns (hotels and motels). The shift in the population from rural to urban areas, the decrease in home-produced food, and changes in work habits have all acted to increase the demand for volume food service units apart from their transportation-linked counterparts. Factory workers moving from one section of the city

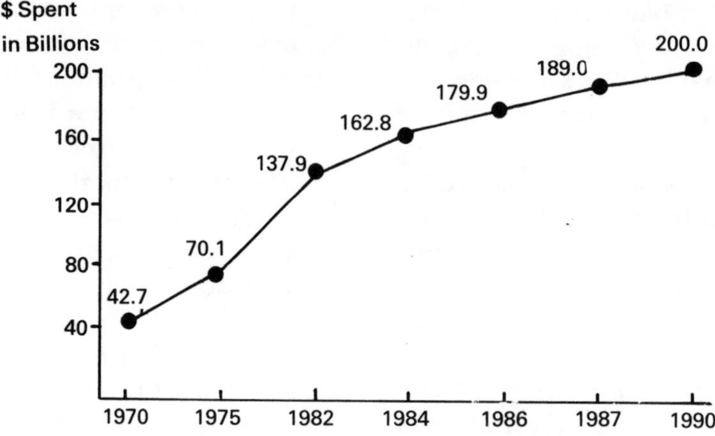

Figure 1b. Food Service Historical and Projected Sales. Other forecasts, such as *Restaurants and Institutions*, are less conservative and suggest sales of $206.8 billion in 1988, well before the $200 billion forecasted for the 1990s in this chart. (Data based on material in *Hospitality*, April 1987, p. 12, and National Restaurant Association Food Service Industry Fact Booklets.)

to another to work an eight-hour day, college students living in boarding institutions, housewives working to supplement family income, military personnel assigned to remote bases or ships, businessmen courting customers at meals, and families who use the dining out experience as a form of entertainment have all helped to provide an expanding market for the business of volume food service.

Whether operated as a component of a hotel or as a free-standing separate facility, the food service operation has become indispensable to American life. The average individual eats a meal away from home 3.7 times a week, and 40.5 percent of all dollars spent for food are spent in food service facilities. Food-away-from-home sales in 1986 were calculated at $185.8 billion, and the projections for 1987 were approximately $197.5 billion—roughly 5 percent of the gross national product.

Feeding large numbers of people is no longer merely an adjunct to the business of industrial production or of educating the young. No longer just a part of the travel sector or the general hospitality field, volume food service has become an independent factor in almost all socially oriented functions.

Fast food outlets and ethnic operations—primarily Italian, Chinese, and Mexican—currently account for the majority of present-day food sales. However, except for the Italian and Chinese sectors, which have maintained constant popularity for many years, other trends are likely to appear, flourish, and disappear. The overall growth trend of the industry as a whole, though, is expected to remain strong with an 8 percent growth per year projected. (One example of such a trend is *nouvelle cuisine*, which has about disappeared as of this writing).

Total employment in the food service industry today is more than 8 million persons. Most food service operations are small, with 70 percent having sales under $500,000 per year and being operated by an individual owner, but chain operations with twenty-five or more units each, account for more than 25 percent of all food service sales.

Heavy movement has shown up in the take-out market, with 42 percent of all food service establishments now offering some form of off-premises meals. These run the gamut from the fast-food hamburger carried in a paper bag or styrofoam insulated container (microwave proof, of course) to the supermarket deli sandwich counter, soup and salad dispensing bar, or the signature gourmet-type cryovacted item the classical restaurant dispenses.

The industry today provides a continuum of varied services: at one end is the specialized fast food operation, offering breakfast, a noonday meal, or a snack to a market caught in the confines of both an accelerated sociological clock and a restricted budget; at the other extreme is the ***haute cusine*** gourmet restaurant, serving an extensive offering of traditional menu items. Although fast food and full-service restaurants both are presently doing well, the number of classical operations continues to decline. Even in the top-rated and well-positioned hotels, where diversity of the classical concept has always been the normal order of business, and multiple outlets are offered the clientele, we find a retrenchment. Many of even the finest hotels now offer only one classical or French-style room, one general-purpose dining room with a contemporary style and menu, and an all-purpose coffee shop. Some hotels have gone to the extreme of contracting out the food service operation, or else they have introduced the specialized food service of an already established restaurant group into their operation. Some hotels and many motels have given up food service completely and have built their facilities next to a free-standing restaurant operation.

A number of the more popular chain operations catering to the younger group have offered a more eclectic menu based on the "grazing" concept. (Grazing is practiced by diners who use dining out as more of a social event with meals giving way to small amounts of desired foods at any and all times of the day according to desire rather than to a set meal pattern or period.) These places offer such foods as stuffed potato skins or fried chicken wings as well as filet mignon with bernaise butter.

A relatively new experience in the food service industry has been takeovers and mergers. In an attempt to gain a greater share of the market, grow with fewer growth-related problems, increase profits, correct past experiences, and/or venture in new directions, food service operators practice either a friendly or hostile takeover or merger. These takeovers are either vertical—where the new element is necessary to the production of the original business; for example, a food processor might take over a restaurant chain that uses its food—or horizontal—where a competitor is absorbed or another type of business entirely is taken over.

Many mergers or takeovers are executed when the stock of the taken company is selling well below its true value. The taken company may lose its autonomy, have its corporate culture changed, or be operated as a separate entity to remain in friendly competition with its new owner. In 1985–86 seventy-one takeovers or mergers took place in the food service industry, and twelve in the hotel field during the same period.

Most growth has occurred at the fast food end of the scale, while many of the gourmet establishments are finding it difficult to continue their operations. The original Delmonico's restaurant offered 300-odd menu items; the average restaurant today has reduced its menu to more manageable and limited scope, offering closer to 12 items.

The number of classical restaurants continues to decline as these establishments fight the encroachment of specialization and changes in consumer tastes. The 21 Club of New York, for example, has survived for over fifty years, but other well-known New York haute cuisine establishments, such as Le Voisin and Le Pavillon, have closed their doors in the face of declining sales. The traditional gourmet market has eroded, and many a gourmet establishment has changed its decor, its image, or its menu, trying to remain in business by redirecting its efforts toward another market.

Of course, there are restaurants that still operate in the classical manner, providing fine service and outstanding food, but many have instituted new procedures and controls in order to ensure success. Typical remaining classical establishments are found in the country's most cosmopolitan cities, particularly New York, San Francisco, and New Orleans. Among these, the restaurants usually found on lists of classical establishments are Antoine's, New Orleans; the Bakery, Chicago; Cafe Chauveron, Miami; Bookbinder's, Philadelphia; Brennan's, New Orleans; the Brown Palace, Denver; Ernie's, San Francisco; Lutèce, New York; Four Seasons, New York; Loche Obers, Boston; Pier 4, Boston; and Scandia, Hollywood-Los Angeles. Among the more traditional hotel food service operations might be included the Greenbrier, White Sulphur Springs, West Virginia; the Palmer House, Chicago; the Pierre, New York; the Shoreham, Washington; Stanford Court, San Francisco; and the St. Regis, New York. Foreign restaurants and hotels offering similar service and fare include such operations as the Claridge, London; Dorchester, London; the Imperial Hotel, Tokyo; the Mandarin, Hong Kong; Bellevue Palace, Berne; Société des Bains de Mer, Hôtel de Paris, Monte Carlo; and the Ritz, Paris.

Related Disciplines

The production of food in quantity requires the expertise of a chef, cook, or other culinary worker who can transform raw agricultural products into palatable and nutritious meals for the particular consumers being served. This process uses a certain body of technical knowledge. The amount of information required depends on several factors: the form in which the food is received; the extent and complexity of the menu; the equipment and facilities available; the delivery system used to get the food to the consumer; and the financial requirements under which the operation functions. Although specific problems may relate to only one particular operation, there remains a common body of information that applies to any food operation and that is shared by all personnel involved in preparation of food in quantity.

This culinary information is fundamental for the operation of any unit, but it is not the only requirement for a properly functioning establishment. It must be coupled with knowledge in other disciplines that relate to food preparation and service. The food service manager or supervisor must be cognizant not only of techniques for the preparation of food, but also of important principles in fields such as mathematics, psychology, chemistry, physics, and microbiology.

Mathematics. The food service manager or supervisor uses mathematical computations to ensure that the correct amounts of ingredients are included in recipes and that the quality-control standards of temperature and pressure are maintained. The need to achieve a satisfactory yield/cost ratio and the construction of a proper pricing structure on a particular product also require mathematical applications. Supervisors make mathematical computations to determine what use of labor and what productivity considerations will enable the production of food in quantity to result in a successful financial venture.

Mathematics is also applied to the accounting functions required by government regulations and by accepted business practices. It enables managers to administer budgets and cost-control centers, which are so important to a successful quantity food production operation. The management of payrolls, the application of percentages to trade discounts, and unit pricing are also important applications of this subject. Other uses may be found in the determination of break-even points, the control of food costs and sales, and the proper determination of purchases.

Psychology. Significant psychological principles must also be utilized by the supervisor of a quantity food operation in his attempts to supervise food service workers properly. Increased productivity must be realized, and the manager or supervisor should be able to relate this to such factors as the employee's internal motivation and work satisfaction. This same discipline may also be useful to the volume food service manager in projecting, meeting, or creating the needs of the consumer market.

Psychological considerations that affect the

preparation of food items in a professional manner include:

(a) status problems among kitchen workers that cause production problems;

(b) the effect on consumers of having to wait in line for food or at tables for service by waiters;

(c) the effect of color, sound, and general decor on consumer acceptance of food items;

(d) the relationship of the size of the serving plate or the number of pieces in equal-sized portions to the acceptability of a menu item by guests; and

(e) the importance of the ego in guest and worker relationships.

Many of the problems experienced by a food service operator are not related to food, but rather are psychologically based and related to service and decor. An operation that offers mediocre food with outstanding service and decor will probably succeed. An operation with excellent food and poor service and decor may well fail.

Many service problems have their origins in the food preparation section of the operation and involve preparation personnel. The supervisor must properly identify the problems and integrate the preparation and service sections into a system that produces the desired results. The psychological implications inherent in attempting to do this must be recognized, because much of the business has become highly dependent on personnel: this is a people business even more than a food business.

Physics. A working knowledge of physics must also be applied to the preparation of food. Only by means of this discipline is it sometimes possible to explain problems that may develop in a product. The effectiveness of a range or the differences between convection and conventional ovens may be explained only by the laws of physics. Principles from this discipline are often needed to understand the operation of specialized equipment, such as refrigeration and air cooling systems, and to understand some of the processes of food preparation, such as why food cooks faster in steam cooking equipment.

Chemistry. The science that deals with the composition and structure of matter in the universe and the changes that may take place in relation to these structures is an important tool for the food service manager or supervisor. Reference to this subject enables him to understand such complex food-related procedures as the hydrogenation of fat, the action of baking powders in producing carbon dioxide, and the changes that take place in food colors after cooking.

Microbiology. Microbiology is of extreme importance to the food service manager or supervisor because sanitation problems may develop in any volume food operation. Microbes are encountered all the time; they may be found in any part of the food service facility. Some are unimportant from a health standpoint, but some agents may cause spoilage of food, changes in the taste of food, or even illness in customers who partake of the food exposed to them.

Microbiology teaches recognition, growth habits, and methods of control of the microbe. It enables those responsible for food production operations to train their workers in the correct measures of controlling harmful bacteria in the food preparation and serving areas.

It should be apparent that the scope of volume food service management encompasses much more than the preparation of specific food products and the transformation of unprocessed food items into palatable delicacies. The subject couples technical knowledge with information from other disciplines to give the student full understanding.

Those who use this book will have been exposed to varying amounts of these related subjects. Some will have completed courses in each of these disciplines before studying quantity food preparation. Others will have had the main principles of other disciplines stressed during other food service course work. It is not the intent of this work to present a synopsis of all material related to food preparation but, where a procedure from another field explains a process that takes place in food preparation, it will receive attention. Sufficient information will be presented to enable the potential manager or supervisor to explain the reasons for a specific action both to himself and to his employees.

Importance of the Subject

Why study volume food preparation? Why has it been considered important in every curriculum developed for both the two-year and the four-year colleges of hospitality education in the United States and elsewhere?

Volume food service has become recognized as an indispensable part of the field of hospitality. An individual hotel, restaurant, or institutional management student who aspires to a management position in accounting, finance, sales, condominiums, or hotels, in most cases will have some relation to volume food service functions. He or she may well be charged with accounting for or controlling inventories of food or constructing or implementing methods to control food costs. A personnel manager may be asked to recruit workers for a food service operation and be required to construct job specifications for each position. A sales manager attempting to explain the merits of a particular convention facility to a group contemplating a meeting must know the type and scope of food service to be offered.

In every case, a worker in a seemingly unrelated area of the hotel and restaurant field is better able to accomplish his task if he is conversant with the specialized problems of the volume feeding unit. No matter what his area of interest within the field of hospitality or related fields—hospital administration, club management, or travel agency management—he will be concerned with the preparation and service of food in quantity. It is seldom that a person travels, is housed, is hospitalized, is entertained, or is incarcerated without food playing a major role.

Advantages and Disadvantages of the Work

The work of the volume food service supervisor may be arduous and at times racked with problems. Food service may be high on the list of topics that consumers complain of and may serve as the "whipping boy" for other problems the guests are not able to express. Work hours are sometimes long, and weekend and holiday work may be the rule rather than the exception, in the early days.

The supervisor of a hospital food service operation may find that many patients identify the food as a problem. A bedridden patient has little knowledge of much that happens to him in the hospital. Reluctant to question a physician, nurse, or medical procedure, he may well question and complain about the food he is offered. His fear of illness or uncertainty about the course of a particular disease may be the real cause of the complaint, but the food is accused.

The student away from home for the first time and the military recruit suffering frustration under a newly imposed regimentation, may also direct their displeasure at the food they are served, because the real sources of problems are either unrecognized or insulated against complaint. An inanimate object such as food, with which they are familiar, can easily take the brunt of their complaints, allowing them to vent pent-up emotions.

Of course, in many cases complaints are justified about the food, service, or atmosphere offered in these captive situations. I submit, however, that many apparently legitimate problems have other unrelated causes.

Does this indicate that hospitality students should attempt to steer clear of these situations and find more placid positions in areas unrelated to food? This may seem the best approach for some, but, as noted before, there is really no area unrelated to food. If an individual aspires to a management or supervisory position in the hospitality industry, food is going to be of concern to him. The more he knows about food preparation, the fewer problems he will have.

Despite the problems, the work of the food service supervisor or manager is exciting, creative, and indispensable to all other phases of hospitality work. His skill is in great demand by employers. This profession gives an individual the opportunity to express himself; it provides both personal and monetary satisfactions and in many cases opens avenues to rapid advancement.

Many college students who express a preference for other hospitality-related positions realize on graduation that volume food service management may be "where the action is." Industry recruiters visiting colleges suggest that in this field an individual can find many openings offering liberal benefits.

Approach to the Subject

The principal approach of this book is to provide the student with the necessary tools for him to organize, supervise, and administer a volume food service operation properly, regardless of the type or size of the enterprise.

This is not a cookbook or a manual for culinary workers, cooks, or food preparation technicians. Rather, it is an attempt to provide the student with a body of knowledge from a managerial viewpoint that will prepare him for placement in the management hierarchy.

The student must be ready to follow before he may lead. In order later to supervise and make management decisions that affect culinary practitioners, he must be familiar with the tools and equipment used and know the jargon of the industry. He should be exposed to the principles of food preparation at each important station of the kitchen and have enough experience to step into an operating position and carry out the tasks effectively when conditions make this necessary. During emergencies, peak periods, and at times of unusual labor demands the supervisor should be able to hold his own in carrying out the actual production procedures followed in a particular establishment. But, more than this, he must gain the respect of his subordinates and superiors by speaking the language of the discipline and understanding the limitations placed on workers by their facilities, equipment, and assigned tasks.

The successful quantity food service supervisor must be realistic in what he requires of his workers and what he provides to his customers. He need not be able to do every task better than his subordinates, but he must be able to make constructive suggestions and recommendations. He should know what constitutes quality in a specific product and be able to suggest why a procedure did not produce the planned results. He must guide his subordinates toward activities that will result in satisfaction for the individual worker, the accomplishment of customer goals, and the realization of financial objectives for the company.

Recent changes have occurred in the food service industry. Processed foods in convenience forms have gained broad acceptance. Shortages of skilled labor have occurred in food preparation positions, particularly at the lower skill levels, such as assistant to the cook and food service worker positions. The quantity food service industry is now as much, or more, concerned with problems relating to labor costs as with food. This dramatic shift requires those involved in supervision to be conversant with subjects formerly considered alien to the proper operation of a food service facility.

It is the objective of this book to present the broad base of knowledge the student will need to make decisions in the management of any volume food service operation.

Education of Managers and Supervisors

Not too many years ago the food service manager gained his position only after an extensive period of training and experience. Individuals began at the apprentice level doing routine culinary tasks under the tutelage of a practicing chef. They progressed through the various kitchen stations into the journeyman ranks when they had gained the necessary skills, and some arrived at the master chef position after a number of years. It was assumed that the kitchen supervisor had completed a tour at every station in the kitchen, and that he had been exposed to almost every situation, problem, and procedure.

Although this route has been effective in producing supervisors for quantity food operations, the number of persons undergoing this form of training has sharply diminished in recent years. Despite government assistance, apprenticeship training programs have had only limited success in attracting and retaining entrants who successfully complete the program and find placement as food managers or supervisors. As the industry has expanded in response to the growing market, even the producing stations of the kitchen have experienced problems in attracting and retaining sufficient numbers of personnel.

Many young people who in the past were a major source of applicants today seek swifter gratification of their aspirations. They are unwilling to put in the long hours and extensive training that are required to produce efficient culinary workers. The workers who once emigrated from Europe have also diminished. Other workers who are eager to be hired lack the specialized knowledge required.

Coupled with this labor shortage at all levels has been a dramatic change in the food habits of a major segment of the American market. Fast food takeout operations with limited menus have expanded as people allow less time for dining. Changes in the technology of food production have resulted in centralization of production skills and procedures at commissary-type operations, while fewer skilled personnel are needed at the user facilities. The "mein host" philosophy exemplified by the gracious innkeeper of previous times has been eroded. Division of labor for more efficiency has taken over. Chain and franchise operations centralize not only culinary talent but also many of the managerial duties previously delegated locally or jealously held by individual entrepreneurs.

In recent years managerial applicants have come mainly from the expanding technical institutes, trade schools, and colleges. A limited number of schools specializing in food preparation and some government-sponsored programs have also provided graduates to fill the producing stations. Students from these latter groups, however, often lack supervisory skills; they are forced to neglect this area of study in order to complete their specialized instruction in the preparation and service of food within the established training time.

Colleges and technical institutes offer the best hope for providing the industry with the managers and supervisors it needs. A program that combines basic instruction in technical knowledge, some practical experience in laboratories, summer, part-time, and cooperative work, and exposure to management principles should produce individuals well suited for supervisory positions in the industry.

Recent Changes and Expected Trends

Food and beverage sales have increased some 80 percent in the past fifteen years. One-fourth or more of the population now eats at least one daily meal away from home. A youth market has become important in all food sales, and militant consumerism and a health food movement have surfaced. Businessmen have replaced chefs in many successful food operations as attempts are made to control costs. Fast food outlets, which provide low-cost food items at convenient locations, have come to stay, replacing many a restaurant whose pricing structure and turnover would not provide the necessary level of sales or profit.

The leisure patterns and eating habits of a major segment of the population have changed. People travel more during times formerly taken up by work, and snacks have replaced many of the more formal meals.

The cities, plagued by crime and transportation problems, have experienced decay, and a number of restaurants have opened in the suburbs to serve their newly arrived residents. Many previously successful city restaurants have ceased to operate.

Traditional food service systems consisted of culinarians converting raw agricultural materials into serviceable products. In modern systems major procedural steps are often centralized at remote locations in order to increase efficiency or to conserve scarce man-

Table 1-1. Colleges Offering Hospitality Management Training

Alabama
Auburn University, Auburn*
Bessemer State Tech College, Bessemer
Carver State Technical College, Mobile
Community College of the Air Force, Maxwell Air Force Base
Enterprise State Junior College, Enterprise
Jefferson Junior College, Birmingham
Lawson State Community College, Birmingham
S.D. Bishop State Junior College, Mobile
Tuskegee Institute, Tuskegee*
Wallace State Community College, Hanceville

Alaska
Alaska Pacific University, Anchorage*
Anchorage Community College, Anchorage
University of Alaska, Fairbanks*

Arizona
College of Ganado, Ganado
Navajo Community College, Tsaile
Northern Arizona University, Flagstaff*
Phoenix College, Phoenix
Pima City Community College, Tucson
Scottsdale Community College, Scottsdale

Arkansas
Arkansas Tech University, Russellville*
Southern Arkansas University, Camden*

California
American River College, Sacramento
Bakersfield Community College, Bakersfield
Barstow College, Barstow
Cabrillo Community College, Aptos
California Polytechnic State University, San Luis Obispo*
California State Polytechnic University, Pomona*
California State University, Chico*
Canada College, Redwood City
Cerritos College, Norwalk
Chabot College, Hayward
Chaffey Community College, Alta Loma
Citrus College, Azusa
City College of San Francisco, San Francisco
Columbia College, Columbia
Contra Costa College, San Pablo
Cypress College, Cypress
Diablo Valley College, Pleasant Hill
El Camino College, Torrance
Feather River College, Quincy
Glendale Community College, Glendale
Golden Gate University, San Francisco*
Grossmont College, El Cajon
Hartnell Community College, Salinas
Lake Tahoe Community College, South Lake Tahoe
Lassen College, Susanville
Loma Linda University, Loma Linda*
Long Beach City College, Long Beach
Los Angeles City College, Los Angeles
Los Angeles Trade-Technical College, Los Angeles
Los Angeles Valley College, Van Nuys
Merced College, Merced
Mesa College, San Diego
Mission College, Santa Clara
Modesto Junior College, Modesto
Monterey Peninsula College, Monterey
Mount San Antonio College, Walnut
Ohlone College, Fremont
Orange Coast College, Costa Mesa
Oxnard College, Oxnard
Palomar Community College, San Marcos
Pasadena City College, Pasadena
Porterville College, Porterville
Questa College, San Luis Obispo
Saddleback College, Mission Viejo
San Bernardino Valley College, San Bernardino
San Diego Community College, San Diego
San Joaquin Delta Community College, Stockton
San Jose State University, San Jose*
Santa Barbara City College, Santa Barbara
Shasta College, Reading
U.S. International University, San Diego*
University of California, Berkeley*
University of California, Davis*
University of the Pacific, Stockton*
University of San Francisco, San Francisco*
Ventura College, Ventura
Victor Valley College, Victorhill
Western States University, Fullerton*
Yuba Community College, Marysville

Colorado
Aims Community College, Greeley
Colorado Mountain College, Steamboat Springs
Colorado State University, Fort Collins*
Community College of the Air Force, Lowry AF Base
Metropolitan State College, Denver
University of Denver, Denver*

Two- and four-year colleges that are members of the Council of Hotel, Restaurant, and Institutional Education. (From *Directory of HRI Schools;* copyright 1972, CHRIE, Washington, D.C.; reprinted by permission.)

*Four-year college.

Table 1.1. (continued)

Connecticut
Manchester Community College, Manchester
South Central Community College, New Haven
University of New Haven, New Haven*

Delaware
Delaware Technical and Community College, Georgetown
Widener University, Wilmington*

District of Columbia
George Washington University, Washington*
Howard University, Washington*

Florida
Broward Junior College, Fort Lauderdale
College of Boca Raton, Boca Raton*
Daytona Beach Community College, Daytona Beach
Florida International University, Miami*
Florida Junior College, Jacksonville
Florida Keys Community College, Key West
Florida State University, Tallahassee*
Gulf Coast Community College, Panama City
Hillsborough Community College, Tampa
Manatee Junior College, Bradenton
Miami-Dade Junior College, Miami
Okaloosa-Walton Junior College, Niceville
Palm Beach Junior College, Lake Worth
Pensacola Junior College, Pensacola
St. Petersburg Vocational Technical Institute, St. Petersburg
St. Augustine Technical Center, St. Augustine
St. Leo College, Saint Leo*
St. Thomas University, Miami*
Santa Fe Community College, Gainesville
Seminole Community College, Sanford
Valencia Junior College, Orlando

Georgia
Dekalb Community College, Ft. McPherson
Georgia State University, Atlanta
University of Georgia, Athens*

Hawaii
Cannon's International Business College of Honolulu, Honolulu
Hawaii Pacific College, Honolulu
Kapiolani Community College, Honolulu
University of Hawaii, Honolulu*

Illinois
Chicago State University, Chicago*
Chicago City Wide College, Chicago
College of DuPage, Glen Ellyn
Culinary School of Kendall College, Evanston*
Elgin Community College, Elgin
Frontier Community College, Fairfield
John A. Wood Community College, Quincy
Joliet Junior College, Joliet
Kennedy-King College, Chicago
Lexington Institute of Hospitality Careers, Chicago
Northern Illinois University, Dekalb*
Shawnee Community College, Ullin
Southern Illinois University, Carbondale*
Triton College, River Grove
University of Illinois, Urbana*
Western Illinois University, Macomb*

Indiana
Purdue University, Lafayette*
Purdue University at Indianapolis*
Purdue University at Calumet Hammond
Vincennes University, Vincennes

Iowa
Iowa State University, Ames*
Iowa Western Community College, Council Bluffs

Kansas
JohnsonCounty Community College, Overland Park
Kansas State University, Manhattan*

Kentucky
Jefferson Community College, Louisville*
Morehead State University, Morehead*
Transylvania University, Lexington*
University of Kentucky, Lexington*
Western Kentucky University, Bowling Green*

Louisiana
Nicholls State University, Thibodaux*
University of New Orleans, New Orleans*
University of Southwestern Louisiana, Lafayette*

Maine
Beal College, Bangor
Southern Maine Vocational-Technical Institute, South Portland
University of Maine, Orono*

Maryland
Baltimore's International Culinary Arts Institute, Baltimore
Community College, Baltimore
Essex Community College, Baltimore County
Hagerstown Junior College, Hagerstown

Montgomery College, Rockville
Prince Georges Community College, Largo
University of Maryland, College Park*
University of Maryland, Eastern Shore*
Wicomico Vocational Technical Center, Salisbury
Wor-Wic Community College, Salisbury

Massachusetts
Berkeshire Community College, Pittsfield
Boston University, Boston*
Bunker Hill Community College, Charlestown
Cape Cod Community College, West Barnstable
Chamberlayne Junior College, Boston
Endicott College, Beverly
Framingham State College, Framingham*
Holyoke Community College, Holyoke
Laboure Junior College, Boston
Massasoit Community College, Brockton
Newbury College, Brookline
Northern Essex Community College, Haverhill
Quincy Junior College, Quincy
Quinsigamond Community College, Worcester
University of Massachusetts, Amherst*

Michigan
Andrews University, Berrien*
Central Michigan University, Mt. Pleasant*
Davenport College of Business, Grand Rapids
Eastern Michigan University, Ypsilanti*
Ferris State College, Big Rapids
Genessee Community College, Flint
Gogebic Community College, Ironwood
Grand Rapids Junior College, Grand Rapids
Grand Valley State Colleges, Allendale
Henry Ford Community College, Dearborn
Kalamazoo Valley Community College, Kalamazoo Valley
Lake Michigan College, Benton Harbor*
Lansing Community College, Lansing
Macomb Community College, Mt. Clemens
Michigan State University, East Lansing*
Muskegon Community College, Muskegon
Northwestern Michigan College, Traverse City
Northwood Institute, Midland
Oakland Community College, Farmington
St. Claire Community College, Port Huron
Schoolcraft College, Livonia
Siena Heights College, Adrian*
Washtenaw Community College, Ann Arbor
Wayne County Community College, Detroit
Western Michigan University, Kalamazoo*
West Shore Community College, Scottville

Missouri
Central Missouri State University, Warrensburg*
Crowder College, Neosho
Forissant Valley Community College, St. Louis
St. Louis Community College at Forest Park, St. Louis
University of Missouri, Columbia*

Mississippi
Copiah Lincoln Junior College, Wesson
Hinds Junior College, Jackson
Meridian Junior College, Meridian
Northeast Mississippi Junior College, Booneville
University of Southern Mississippi, Hattiesburg*
Utica Junior College, Utica

Minnesota
College of St. Scholastica, Duluth*
Mankato State University, Mankato*
Normandale Community College, Bloomington
Rochester Community College, Rochester
Southwest Minnesota State College, Marshall*
University of Minnesota Technical College, Crookstone
University of Minnesota-Twin Cities, St. Paul*

Nebraska
Nebraska Central Community College, Hastings
McCook College, McCook
Southeast Community College, Lincoln
University of Nebraska, Lincoln*

Nevada
Clark County Community College, North Las Vegas
Southern Nevada Vocational-Technical Center, Las Vegas
Truckee Meadows Community College, Sparks
University of Nevada, Las Vegas*

New Hampshire
New Hampshire College, Manchester*
University of New Hampshire, Durham*

New Jersey
Atlantic Community College, Mays Landing
Bergen Community College Paramus
Brookdale Community College, Lincroft
Fairleigh Dickinson University, Rutherford*
Hudson County Community College, Jersey City
Middlesex Community College, Edison
Montclair State College, Upper Montclair*

Table 1.1. (continued)

New Mexico
New Mexico Highlands University, Las Vegas*
University of New Mexico, Albuquerque*

New York
Cornell University, Ithaca*
Culinary Institute of America, Hyde Park
Erie Community College, Buffalo
Fiorella H. LaGuardia Community College, Long Island City
Herkimer County Community College, Herkimer
Hofstra University, Hempstead*
Hudson Valley Community College, Troy
Jefferson County Community College, Watertown
Monroe Community College, Rochester
Nassau Community College, Garden City
New York City Community College, Brooklyn
New York Institute of Technology, Old Westbury
Niagara County Community College, Sanborn
Niagara University, New York*
Onandaga Community College, Syracuse
Paul Smith's College, Paul Smiths
Pratt Institute, Brooklyn*
Rochester Institute of Technology, Rochester*
Schenectady Community College, Schenectady
State University of Agricultural and Technical Colleges at
Alfred
Cobleskill
Delhi
Morrisville
State University of New York, Canton
State University of New York, Farmingdale*
Suffolk County Community College, Riverhead
Sullivan County Community College, South Fallsburg
Tompkins Cortland Community College, Dryden
Tri-County Area School, Bartlesville
Villa Maria College, Buffalo
Westchester Community College, Valhalla

North Carolina
Appalachian State University, Boone*
Asheville-Buncombe Technical College, Asheville
Barber-Scotia College, Concord*
Central Piedmont Community College, Charlotte
East Carolina University, Greenville*
Fayetteville Technical Institute, Fayetteville
Guilford Technical Community College, Jamestown
Lenoir Community College, Kingston
Southwestern Technical College, Sylva
Technical College of Alamance, Haw River
University of North Carolina, Greensboro*
Wake Technical College, Raleigh
Wilkes Community College, Wilkesboro

North Dakota
North Dakota State School of Science, Wahpeton
North Dakota State University, Fargo*

Ohio
Ashland College, Ashland*
Bowling Green State University, Bowling Green*
Cincinnati Technical College, Cincinnati
Clermont General and Technical College, Batavia
College of Mount St. Joseph, Mount St. Joseph*
Columbus Technical Institute, Columbus
Cuyahoga Community College, Cleveland
Hocking Technical College, Nelsonville
Jefferson Technical College, Steubenville
Kent State University, Kent*
Miami University, Oxford*
Ohio State University, Columbus*
Owens Technical College, Toledo
Rio Grande College, Rio Grande
Sinclair Community College, Dayton
Stark Technical College, Canton
Terra Technical College, Fremont
Tiffin University, Tiffin*
University of Akron, Akron*
University of Toledo, Toledo*
Youngstown State University, Youngstown*

Oklahoma
Carl Albert Junior College, Poteau
Oklahoma State Technical, Okmulgee
Oklahoma State University, Stillwater*
Oscar Rose Junior College, Midwest City
Tulsa Junior College, Tulsa

Oregon
Central Oregon Community College, Bend
Chemeketa Community College, Salem
Lane Community College, Eugene
Linn-Benton Community College, Albany
Oregon State University, Corvallis*
Portland Community College, Portland

Pennsylvania
Bucks County Community College, Newton
Butler County Community College, Butler
Community College of Allegheny County, Monroeville
Community College of Philadelphia, Philadelphia
Delaware County Community College, Media

Drexel Institute of Technology, Philadelphia*
East Stroudsburg State College, East Stroudsburg*
Keystone Junior College, La Plume
Luzerne County Community College, Wilkes Barre
Mercyhurst College, Glenwood Hills*
Montgomery County Community College, Blue Bell
Mount Aloysius Junior College, Cresson
Pennsylvania State University, University Park*
Pierce Junior College, Philadelphia
Westmoreland County Community College, Youngwood
Williamsport Area Community College, Williamsport

Rhode Island
Bryant College, Providence*
Community College of Rhode Island, Lincoln
Community College of Rhode Island, Warwick
Johnson and Wales College, Providence*
University of Rhode Island, Kingston*
Woonsocket Skill Center, Woonsocket

South Carolina
Horry-Georgetown Technical College, Conway
University of South Carolina, Columbia
Winthrop College, Rock Hill*

Tennessee
Shelby State Community College, Memphis
Southern Missionary College, Collegedale
State Technical Institute at Memphis, Memphis
University of Tennessee, Knoxville*

Texas
Central Texas College, Killeen
Del Mar College, Corpus Christi
El Centro College, Dallas
El Paso Community College, El Paso
Hill Junior College, Hillsboro
Huston-Tillotson College, Austin*
North Harris County College, Houston
Northwood Institute-Texas Campus, Cedar Hill
St. Philip's College, San Antonio
San Antonio College District, San Antonio
San Jacinto College, Pasadena
San Jacinto College-North Campus, Houston
South Plains College, Lubbock
Southwestern Adventist College, Keene
Texas Tech University, Lubbock*
Texas Women's University, Denton*
University of Houston, Houston*
Wiley College, Marshall

Utah
Brigham Young University, Provo*

Vermont
Champlain College, Burlington
Ethan Allen Community College, Manchester Center
New England Culinary Institute, Montpelier
University of Vermont, Burlington*

Virginia
James Madison University, Harrisonburg*
John Tyler Community College, Chester
J. Sargeant Reynold Community College, Richmond
Northern Virginia Community College, Annandale
Thomas Nelson Community College, Hampton
Tidewater Community College, Virginia Beach
Virginia Polytechnic Institute and State University, Blacksburg*
Virginia State University, Petersburg*

Washington
Clark College, Vancouver
Edward-Brodsky-Porges Highline Community College, Midway
Everett Community College, Everett
Lower Columbia College, Longview
Seattle Community College, Seattle
Shoreline Community College, Seattle
Skagit Valley College, Mount Vernon
Spokane Community College, Spokane
Washington State University, Pullman*

West Virginia
Fairmont State College, Fairmont*
Marshall University, Huntington*
Potomac State College of West Virginia University, Keyser*
Shepherd College, Shepherdstown*
West Virginia State College, Institute*

Wisconsin
Fox Valley Technical Institute, Appleton
Madison Area Technical College, Madison
Milwaukee Technical College, Milwaukee
Nicolet College and Technical Institute, Rhinelander
University of Wisconsin, Madison*
University of Wisconsin-Stout, Menomonie*
Wisconsin Indianhead Technical Institute, Ashland

power. Responsibility for a particular preparation step may be transferred completely to another enterprise by the use of convenience or ready food forms and by changes in purchasing or menu structure.

Closed convenience food systems, in which portions of food products are processed, frozen, and held for service as needed at meal periods, have been tried. Food has been prepared conventionally but in great quantities at central locations, containing equipment capable of mass producing the items, and then delivered to a number of user locations.

Industry literature predicts that additional changes will be made necessary by shortages in labor, increases in prices, and the failure of productivity to keep pace with increases in benefits paid to workers. Some experts see a return to the small, individually owned and operated food establishment, in which labor costs are not a major problem and the entrepreneur uses his or her personal cooking experience to provide the labor, satisfy the guest, and make a profit. This does not seem to be easy to accomplish, however, in view of the shortage of skilled personnel and the erosion of the work ethic among young people.

A more plausible trend is the continued increase in productivity made possible by further refinement of food service systems and by greater utilization of automation, newly designed equipment, and new food forms.

Increases in productivity may be realized more easily if more attention is paid to employer-employee relationships, so that the goals of workers may be made congruent with the goals of the organization and the returns from increases in productivity are shared with those who carry out production.

Although efficiency, productivity, centralization, speed, and technology may be the important words to meet the growth projections for the industry, they must be worked into systems that have been developed with a view to the consumer. The food service customer will not compromise his desire for value, and more and more he looks for showmanship and merchandising when he dines out. Consumers may be willing to accept fast foods and convenience items, but they also appear to be demanding more from a dining experience in the way of decor, style, and flair on the part of the front of the house.

In addition, workers must be protected against the dehumanization that may accompany the use of productivity tools, such as computer-assisted menu planning systems, assembly lines, and other hardware designed to increase efficiency. Workers may become more specialized and fewer in number, but they will remain an important element in the food delivery system of the future. Additional labor problems cannot be tolerated in this service industry, in the interest of increased efficiency.

Future Prospects for Managers

At present the volume food service industry finds it difficult to recruit and retain adequate numbers of supervisors. Yet it is more than ever dependent on managers and supervisors who have the basic technical knowledge and managerial ability to direct culinary staffs with only limited technical backgrounds. By relying on these supervisors, the industry has been able to expand to meet demand. But with the average food service establishment experiencing employee turnover rates of approximately 101 percent and the average age of the food service worker at twenty-three, the industry finds itself with an average worker who is in a declining proportion of the population due to a declining birthrate and an aging population. In 1987 the NRA identified the possible problems facing the industry (see *Restaurants and Institutions*, May 13, 1987, pp. 26–27): a move to increase minimum wages (always seen as a forecast of doom); an increase in liability insurance rates due to greater concern for injury to guests or others by former guests served alcoholic beverages and then driving; smoking issues by a health-conscious society that desires clean air in both working and recreational environments; the new immigration laws that "dry up" many sources of employees unscrupulous employers once used or that require a potential employer to ascertain the legitimacy of a potential employee or else face stiff fines for noncompliance; the takeout of food with its inherent problems of food quality and temperature control, transportation, costs, and so on; challenge of providing quality service to consumers who know more, desire more, and are quite ready to change allegiances if unsatisfied. Many of these concerns are, of course, ongoing (such as the minimum wage and use of immigrants or newly arrived workers), but some are new and topical.

The food production industry has attempted to fill the labor shortage by supplying new foods and equipment to simplify the work. But the tasks still require many food service workers.

In many operations an accounting approach to management has been superimposed on the food production requirements. Although this philosophy cannot be accepted in its entirety, it does have some merit in view of the industry's need to control both productivity and food costs. However, the food problems remain, and accounting is only another management tool.

Successful quantity food service appears to be a question of marketing: providing the foods and services that consumers want at the times and places they need them. The consumer and his desires are important elements in the education of culinary workers. The workweek of the average American is rapidly decreasing and his disposable income is increasing, giving him both the time and the money to eat out more often and to travel more. These trends project an attractive picture for the quantity food producer.

Accompanying these developments are apparent changes in consumer tastes and food habits. More people are eating meals at hours other than the traditional mealtimes, and many new types of foods and preparation methods—fast foods, takeouts, and disposable containers and utensils—are popular. The "baby boom" generation is currently reaching its peak of earning power, growth of children, and so on at ages thirty-five to fifty-five. With more working couples and thus more disposable family income as well as a propensity to use either the dining-out experience or its most noticeable alternative—the home entertainment concept—food service will keep on changing. Research has shown that 52 percent of all American homes own a microwave oven, and thirty-five percent own a VCR (videocasette recorder) that can play movies or prerecorded shows. Moreover many families are disposed to use these with takeout food to create their own "dining-out" facility. In fact 62.4 percent of the people sampled stated that they had taken food home last month and used these specialized pieces of equipment as their dining-out experience. This, of course, creates a much greater technological, marketing, and management challenge for the food service industry.

The modern food service manager must still be efficient in producing quality food, but his problems are much different from those of the classical chef who meticulously produced a sauce and put it to the side of a cluttered range to be held for later service, or who created stocks from cracked bones and less tender meat cuts, simmered and rafted in his own kitchen. There still are enterprises that call for this attention to culinary detail, but there are infinitely more that use convenience food items to replace more complex and time-consuming preparation methods. For these operations, the major problem is the proper functioning of the system rather than the production of a particularly difficult culinary masterpiece.

It is interesting to note that in the food service industry, most problems are not related to food itself or its purchase, preparation, storage, and so on. These areas are usually the minimum concerns, and this is relevant to those who train and educate only for the preparation of the food: This does not seem to be where the problems lie.

Changes are also apparent in the competition the manager faces. Local grocery outlets now provide many food forms not unlike those offered by operating restaurants. A ready-to-eat food item in an individual- or multiple-serving throwaway container offers many consumers a most acceptable alternative to a restaurant portion of a similar item at a much higher price. The takeout, fast food outlets have attempted to capture this market and have parried the thrust of grocery stores in many locations. Other more conventional forms of food operations may also have to meet this challenge. With the extensive use of cryovac and irradiation, resulting in longer shelf lives and protection of quality, it is conceivable that kiosk-type facilities will supplement the drive-in forms that have until now been attached to many fast food and other food-dispensing facilities such as restaurants and supermarkets. These will dispense take-home foods at the expense of full-service dining in a facility.

But if these trends suggest that the manager or supervisor needs somewhat different culinary abilities and somewhat less specialized knowledge today, they suggest an equally important reason why he needs to know even more about food preparation. In many establishments it was basic policy to delegate full responsibility to the chef in all food matters, and some general managers hesitated even to enter the sacred domain of this culinary artist. With the present lack of trained chefs, managers and supervisors must have the technical knowledge to supervise and direct the work of culinary workers who know much less about food preparation techniques and who look to their supervisor for assistance.

The chain and franchise enterprises that have centralized purchasing, menu preparation, and commissary food operations have also felt the lack of knowledgeable labor in the field. It takes technical knowledge for management to design and administer centralized systems that will produce the desired results.

As the forms of quantity food systems become more sophisticated and as the business becomes more concerned with effective labor utilization, the manager takes on even more importance. Without a pool of adequately trained manpower to meet the projected expansion of the industry, supervisors become indispensable in training workers and integrating all elements of the operation into a smoothly functioning system.

The future looks bright and busy for the world of hospitality. Consumers (despite warnings to the contrary) are apparently willing to accept something less than the traditional gourmet food forms and service. They are, however, unwilling to subsidize inefficient management by paying increased prices.

Facilities continue to expand, and chains are entering new fields, such as feeding operations in hospitals, colleges, nursing homes, and factories. New menus are constructed and organizations developed to provide the type of food desired by a particular market. Whether it is in traditional operations where extensive menus and impeccable service are provided, or in fast food operations offering limited menus of grilled and deep-fried items, the industry stands ready to welcome the potential manager.

But the future is not without its problems. A Delphi projection reported in a *Current Issue Report* of the National Restaurant Association (1987) discussed the conditions and concerns in the food service industry of the 1990s: personnel shortages with fewer potential rank and file workers and fewer good and experienced management personnel; a need to turn more to women, senior citizens, and the handicapped to staff the ever-expanding facilities of food service; the emergence of more labor-saving equipment in reaction to this personnel shortage and ever-increasing labor costs; large increases in liability insurance costs, particularly as they relate to dispensing alcoholic beverages; a rise in the minimum wage and thus the overall cost of labor; more use of prepared foods due once again to the problems with labor and the changes in consumer tastes. It is worthy to note that many of the "baby boomers" who are now an important segment of food service consumers were reared on the tastes and delivery methodologies of the fast food outlet. Thus it should not be too difficult to accept the demise of classical cuisine in a restaurant where men must wear a coat, the average check might be $50 to $60, and it takes three hours to eat the meal. For one thing, the Internal Revenue Service no longer permits writing off the full amount as a "business expense," and many other changes will affect this type of dining. (The Delphi concept, first used by the Rand Corporation in the 1960s, is a think tank method involving the subjective judgment of experts who are asked to respond in group fashion based on their experience. These experts give their best estimates rather than an objective evaluation based upon analytical, empirical, or mathematical computations or computer projections.)

The person who combines basic culinary skills with related supervisory expertise will be courted by companies attempting to meet customer demands. The experience the student gains in laboratories and work situations should be coupled with the information in this academic presentation of quantity food service management and supervision. To be successful, he needs both experience and technical knowledge. Experience may be a great teacher, but only if it is experience in correct procedures. Academic knowledge also is useful only if it can be applied to real life situations. It is the objective of this book to help make the experience phases of the student's education more meaningful. In so doing, I hope that the student will be provided the best of both worlds.

2 *Management Structures and Functions*

Objective: To introduce the student to the elements of food service management, this chapter includes a consideration of the organization of a food production facility, stresses the composition of the major forms of food service operations, and explores the supervisory tools of staffing, training, supervision, sales analysis, cost controls, and budgets.

The Elements of Management

The management of food production, like all other forms of management, requires sufficient knowledge of all elements of the system to be able to relate each to the others so as to obtain the major objectives of the company. It is more than knowing how to cook an egg. It is also knowing what type of egg to use; the sanitary conditions to be maintained; the yield to be realized from an egg; the storage conditions to be followed; the best equipment to use in processing a particular egg dish; the quality of performance to be expected of an employee producing that dish; and the pricing structure applicable to the item.

Not long ago, an individual could hope to become a manager of a food service operation only if his father owned a restaurant, or if he undertook an apprenticeship leading to qualification as a chef. Today, as chapter 1 noted, the form of the food service enterprise is changing. The individual owner is being replaced, in many instances, by a chain or franchised operation. These larger companies have begun to use some of the scientific approaches to the accomplishment of work proved effective in industry. These methods have increased profits and allowed further expansion. With centralized controls instituted in many of the larger companies, new management opportunities have been created at every level.

Food service management, like other management situations, consists of carrying out the function of an establishment to satisfy the needs of the consumer and either earn a profit for investors or, in nonprofit institutions, keep within the budget allocation. To accomplish this objective, a food service manager must formulate the goals of the enterprise, consider the methods available to achieve them, weigh these alternatives, and select the most appropriate ones.

In carrying out these procedures, the manager will be concerned with *planning* the action to be taken by the enterprise, *coordinating* the various assets of the operation so that the men, materials, equipment, facilities, and time may be used to reach the goals in the desired way; *staffing* the organization so that sufficient personnel and those with the necessary talents will be available; *controlling* the operation of the organization by the proper methods to ensure efficiency and keep costs down; *reporting* the results of operations to higher management, stockholders, or others concerned with this information; and *budgeting* for both short- and long-run goals so that the means to accomplish the planned objectives can be provided.

Of course, the lower levels of management, such as the first level supervisor or the middle level manager, have fewer opportunities to formulate goals and select alternatives, because many of these decisions have already been made on a higher level. However, some decisions remain at each level.

In making these decisions and progressing toward the goals, the process of management is one of control. The food service manager controls the resources made available to him. The capital, plant, raw materials, and equipment are all utilized within a plan designed to meet the needs of the consumers. The most important resource available to the manager is the skill of his subordinates.

Management of resources is carried out within a structure that imposes many constraints on the manner of operation. Other constraints, dictated by government agencies, competition, and general economic conditions, determine the type of structure—the organization—that is to be formed.

Organizational Structure

An organization provides for the personnel, equipment, facilities, funds, supplies, and procedures to carry out a planned movement toward a predicted goal. Management directs this movement within the limits imposed.

Every establishment engaged in producing food in quantity has an organizational structure. Refinements in the structure are made to meet the particular requirements of each type of facility, but a common core exists. Whatever the organizational unit, location, and scope of the operation, it usually is built around a structure that requires a relatively small capital investment per worker. Less money is allocated to facilities and equipment than in most other production and manufacturing concerns. Greater numbers of workers are required to maintain the continuous flow of production to meet consumer demands.

The production rate of the average food preparation and service worker is quite low compared to those of workers in other industries. Although equipment assists the workers in the production of food, few new machines or tools have been introduced, and many facilities prefer to use hand work.

In an attempt to make the industry more attractive to prospective employees, to increase production, and to meet the requirements of federal and state minimum wage laws, wages for food preparation workers have increased some 48 percent in the past decade. The productivity of the workers has increased only minimally, however.

Despite the recent trend toward corporate ownership, a majority of quantity food service operations are still small restaurants owned by single individuals or families, like the original inns. Many of these owners pride themselves on their food preparation and do not consider mass-produced items equal in quality to food they prepare locally.

A large number of small organizations consider themselves locked into traditional food delivery systems, such as table service or cafeteria service, and they give little thought to change. The quality and service standards guests are assumed to demand have remained untested. Many organizations are reluctant to accept scientific management principles that have been used by other industries.

Table 2-1. Sales Leaders in Food Service

Name	Sales	# Units
McDonalds	$11 Billion	9,460
Burger King	4.5 Billion	5,108
Kentucky Fried Chicken	3.1 Billion	6,729
Wendys	2.69 Billion	3,842
Hardee's	2.4 Billion	2,835
Pizza Hut	1.8 Billion	5,200
Marriotts	1.5 Billion	2,580

Notice that the first six are fast food outlets, and all are chain operations. Although there are more "smaller" operations, the larger chain operators generate most of the sales. (Source: *Standard and Poor*, Industry Survey, March 26, 1987.)

Table 2-2. Employee Size of Food Service Operations

Number of Employees	Number of Operations		Percentage of the Industry		
	1964*	1980*	1964	1980	Change
0-4	196,000	98,146	59.0	35.1	-23.9
5-9	64,000	63,834	19.0	22.8	+3.8
10-19	22,000	54,183	6.0	19.3	+13.3
20-49	10,000	43,345	3.0	15.5	+12.5
50-99	2,000	11,471	.5	4.1	+3.6
100 or more	500	3,660	.14	1.3	+1.16
Information not available (seasonal operations)	—	—	10.00	1.9	-8.1
Total	375,000	279,496	100	100	

* Columns do not add up because seasonal operation data is not available.

From *Dun's® Census of American Business™, 1980 Eating and Drinking Places* SIC 58, p. 19, reprinted by permission.

A comparison of employees in Food Service Operations from 1964-1980. Worthy of note in this comparison is the reduction in the total number of operations (a 25.4 percent reduction) from 375,000 to 279,496 from 1964 to 1980 and a comparable increase in operations above the 0-4 employee levels, particularly in the 10-19 and 20-49 employee ranges. This supports the projections of changes in ownership forms from individual owners to the chain operation and a comparable reduction in the small "Mom and Pop" operations of yesterday, which had few if any hired employees.

Recently, some organizations (particularly the chains) have begun to change the basic organizational forms for the first time since the industry began. But the major form of organization remains the table service restaurant delivering a hand-produced product to the guest, and the major problem remains a relatively unproductive worker.

Certain trappings of the past that create unacceptable working environments also persist in many operations. Symbols of rank, such as the height of a cook's hat, the style and color of uniforms, or the type of food permitted to be prepared at a particular station, remain. Unacceptable "back of the house" environmental conditions—affecting facilities, equipment, temperature, and humidity—exist in many units. Turnover rates among workers are very high, and many positions go unfilled because management is unable to attract and retain sufficient numbers of workers.

A few forward-looking, and successful, leaders in particular segments of the industry have attempted to identify organizational problems and institute changes recently. Examples include profit sharing for workers, to increase productivity; shopping center layouts and scramble exits, replacing the cafeteria line, to increase turnover and sales; and the growth of the fast food business, to meet changes in consumer desires. These fresh and often daring approaches to management can be the salvation of quantity food production. If the conditions that currently exist in many units remain unchanged, little hope can be held for these facilities: they must change to meet changes in demand and conditions.

Some operators have attempted to change

the entire concept and structure of their organizations. They have given up the dual role of producer and retailer, which created many organizational problems as the facility had to perform a variety of functions and fulfill a variety of goals. They have restructured their organizations around the delivery aspect alone and have used proper purchasing or reorganization of physical layout to reduce the need for physical facilities, technical equipment, and expert personnel.

Such a change in organizational form results in some change in the quality and type of food produced. The customers' desire for speed, however, makes them willing to accept something less than the classical cuisine concept, and this has resulted in success for many establishments adopting these new approaches to organization. But there is still a sufficient number of potential consumers who demand chef-produced items served with a flair to support facilities willing to supply this offering.

Operations that are seeking something less than the item produced laboriously by hand are using new concepts such as the open kitchen, where the kitchen is located in the dining room for showmanship and entertainment value, and the equipment-centered theme, where limited specialized equipment is used to provide a small selection of fast food menu items. Most food service operations, however, are variations on a theme. They may be described in terms of how they differ from the traditional organizational structure.

The first consideration of a food service manager must be the organizational setup under which he will operate. He must be cognizant of its parameters, which dictate certain managerial methods. Local conditions may require deviation from the norm and incorporation or omission of specific factors.

At the heart of the organizational structure of a particular operation is the food production system. Some systems that have been in existence for many years reflected only the relationships among the various components of the operation—purchasing, receiving, storage, production, portioning, and serving. More recent systems stress that these are components of a whole and study the various subsystems within the whole.

Systems should be varied to meet the individual needs of an operation. They may be "open," receiving food from outside sources that have already performed some of the production procedures, so that only reconstituting, tempering, or final preparation is required at the receiving facility. Or the system may be "closed," accomplishing all processes and procedures internally, often using down times to prepare, freeze, and hold foods for future meal periods. Or it may be a "hybrid" form, using both external and internal facilities, personnel, and equipment to provide, produce, and serve the products.

Whatever its form, the up-to-date system should reflect the peculiar needs of the establishment. Most systems today use specialists where possible, rely heavily on new technology in the area of convenience food items, and use new forms of equipment, in their attempt to improve productivity.

Traditional Structure

Most quantity food service organizations are structured in a *line* hierarchy, supported by a *staff* group. The line personnel are those primarily concerned with preparation and service of the food. The line supervisor traditionally was a professionally trained culinary worker, who had experienced a long period of training at every kitchen work station before assuming his supervisory position. More recently, however, because adequate numbers of new workers are not entering the field, the line personnel in many organizations have limited experience and training.

The executive chef with long professional experience and training was prepared to step into any work station in the kitchen. With his *toque blanche* (white cap) as a symbol of authority, he had the time and the talent to experiment, create, and learn the intricacies of a new dish that would then be recreated, named, and delivered to guests with the required flair. Labor and food costs were generally low; time was of no concern; and the chef was an artist who took a personal interest in everything in the kitchen, from the ordering to the service. He supervised the operation, supported by a sous chef. This professional assistant possessed similar training experiences, but was still in a position of upward mobility and not yet ready to assume control of his own kitchen. Each station in the kitchen was staffed by a specialized technician (roast cook, vegetable cook, fry cook, breakfast cook, etc.) who performed specialized duties under the direction of the sous chef or executive chef. Each worker had sufficient technical knowledge to perform the work of the station and produce the desired results. A rounds or swing cook was usually available to fill in during periods of emergency and to replace workers on vacation days and days off. This group of highly professional workers was supported by culinary workers at each station who performed the more repetitive and less glamorous tasks.

The staff support provided to this line was minimal. The chef directed all food preparation procedures. He often planned the menu, ordered the food, supervised the cost procedures, and determined the work hours of his subordinates. A like supervisor, the maitre d'hotel supervised all service functions related to the guest, carried out "beyond the swinging door."

The manager of the operation was often a "front of the house" individual who relegated food preparation procedures to the more talented chef. He depended upon the chef to produce items in a form, quality, and quantity that pleased the guests and at a price that generated a profit. Although the manager might have risen from the food production ranks, he hesitated to produce friction by stepping into the kitchen or superimposing his

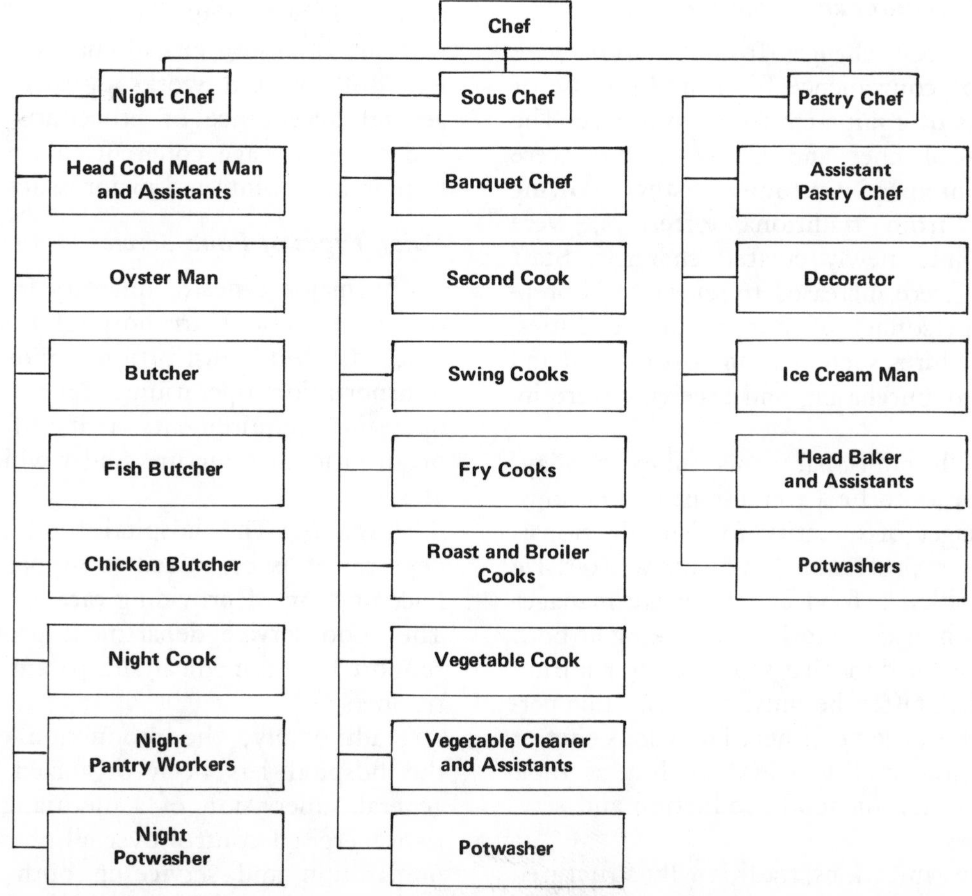

Figure 2a. Organization of a "traditional" kitchen. (From Donald E. Lundberg and James P. Armatas, *The Management of People in Hotels, Restaurants and Clubs,* rev. ed., p. 24; copyright 1964, William C. Brown Company, Publishers, Dubuque, Iowa; reprinted by permission.)

decisions on those of the chef. In most cases, he only handled accounting decisions and personalized the guest greeting, seating, and service.

This was an acceptable arrangement as long as well trained and experienced personnel were available, the food produced was acceptable to the consumers, and the profit desires of management were met. However, an expanding market and a lack of experienced technical help have dictated organizational changes. Executive chefs have become in short supply as new facilities have opened and older chefs have retired. Fewer workers have started the long periods of training required to produce the traditional managerial and operating personnel. Production and profit problems have appeared, and organizational changes have been made to meet the immediate need of providing food to the guests.

Modern Variations and Principles

The greatest changes from tradition were the use of convenience foods and the use of new types of equipment to speed service. The functions of chef and maitre d'hotel were often combined. Customer tastes, evolving naturally from traditional offerings, were prodded into newly created channels. Staff functions were increased to relieve food preparation personnel of nonproductive duties, and procedures such as food cost control and centralized purchasing and receiving were instituted.

Although traditional forms still exist today, there appears to be a trend in new directions. The manager of quantity food production is often not a professional culinary worker. He is often titled a food and beverage manager and finds himself, like Janus, looking at both sides from the door that separates preparation and service. Often he must supervise line personnel who have never heard of a sous chef or rounds cook, and who look to him as their only authority on food production and service matters.

In all organizations, traditionally structured or more up to date, certain structural principles must be followed. The organization should be as flat as possible, that is, there should be a limit on the number of supervisory levels, in order to increase supervisory effectiveness and improve communications. Authority and responsibility should be delegated to the lowest possible levels, in order to increase the job satisfaction of employees and give the higher level supervisors more time to consider planning and policy decisions. Final responsibility can never be delegated to subordinates, however, but rests with management.

The organization should assign responsibility for each task to only one unit. There must be a reasonable span of control in terms of supervisor-subordinate relationships. Seven to ten employees reporting to each supervisor is considered acceptable at the lower levels. Higher level supervisors may have jurisdiction over more workers, since less direct supervision by them is required.

Line people should control the organization, and staff should be able to advise them without violating normal channels of authority. Both should work together to achieve general acceptance of procedures and goals and to encourage coherent thinking and action on key points and major issues.

Major Types of Food Service

The major types of quantity food production organizations are hospital, hotel, restaurant, fast food, institutional, industrial, and transportation operations. Each has specific operating requirements that influence the organizational structure under which it operates.

Hospitals. The hospital food production department is organized to support the basic line function of providing care to the patient. The food service department provides staff support to the medical and paramedical practitioners.

Traditionally, the production of food in the hospital has been organized under the general supervision of a dietitian. The dietitian exercised control over all phases of food preparation and service in both the therapeutic and the administrative areas. As organizational units became larger, dietary personnel were assigned to either administrative, teaching, or patient-related functions. The most recent innovations are the use of contract feeding companies and food managers. The patient-care duties—instruction of patients, construction of special diets, and consultation with physicians—are given to professional dietitians. The production and service of food and the related administrative and financial concerns are assigned to the food service manager. This arrangement permits more effective use of dietary personnel, who are in such short supply, and the employment of specialized food managers.

Hospital food service departments may take either a centralized or a decentralized form. Under the centralized form, food is prepared and served to each patient's designated tray in the production area. Ward personnel just transport and deliver it. This arrangement gives dietary personnel more control over the food and financial aspects. It usually results in monetary savings and fewer errors. In decentralized operations, bulk food is sent in heated carts to the ward or floor where it is served in portions and distributed to each patient by a nurse or dietary aide.

Food preparation in hospitals was generally divided into house or general foods and therapeutic foods. Special diet kitchens, staffed by different workers, prepared the therapeutic diets, while the food for ambulatory patients, patients eating regular diets, and staff members was prepared in a separate area. A combination of these areas has since taken place in most hospitals, and some have instituted central-commissary-type operations. In these, the food is prepared in one place for a number of hospitals. After it is delivered, final preparation, heating, and serving are done at the particular hospital. Some institutions have switched to convenience food trays for all patients, on both regular and special diets: frozen or chilled items are delivered to a particular ward or room to be heated by microwave or reconstituting equipment and served to each patient. Disposable dishes and utensils are often used with this form of service.

The projected development of the health campus, in which all forms of medical care are centralized, suggests further changes in food production organizations. It seems to call for even greater use of central-commissary-type personnel, equipment, and cost-control procedures.

Nursing Homes. Another major medical facility that is also concerned with the production and delivery of food in quantity is the nursing home. Although many sociologists call them the "warehouses" of the old, great strides have been made in improving nursing homes since the almshouses of Elizabethan days. These facilities have expanded rapidly in recent years as a result of increased medical care coverage for the aged. This growth may be only a beginning, as socialized forms of medicine are reaching the discussion stage in Congress.

The food problems and organizational requirements of the nursing home are much like those of the hospital. The therapeutic concerns are directed by a dietitian—often a visiting professional because of the shortage of these specialists. The other functions—purchasing, food production, and the like—are administered by food managers and their personnel or contract food service companies.

Hotels, Restaurants, and Clubs. Of all the types of food service organizations the ones that still follow the traditional form most closely are the hotels, restaurants, and clubs. Although there are many variations, the traditional approach is so widely applied that its consideration is appropriate here.

Long the front-runners in providing gourmet food and service, hotels often remain the last bastions of traditional food production organization, although many exclusive and expensive clubs have also retained the traditional approach. Despite the on-site employment of a resident manager or general manager, the chef still holds sway in these enterprises. The traditionalist seeking gourmet food and service at a snap of the fingers will find it in these two types of operations—in grand hotels, such as the Ritz of Paris, or in prestigious city clubs.

Many hotels have been reluctant to accept

ready or convenience foods, because they are considered inferior in quality and may thus be unacceptable to the guests. Other hotels have been prevented from using these labor-saving items because of provisions in union contracts that are written to protect the jobs of their food service workers.

Much of the resistance to convenience foods is attributable to the quality of the first convenience items. Previously most of these foods were sauced to protect the protein items from excessive drying during reconstitution. The available items were unacceptable for many hotel menus. Improvements in food forms and new methods of reconstitution have made these objections less valid.

Some hotels and clubs have tried in-house closed systems of mass producing prepared recipes, but sanitation concerns have presented problems in this process. As labor costs became even greater and the availability of culinary talent was reduced, more hotels have joined the movement to use labor-saving items. More production now takes place outside these establishments, as butchers and bakers disappear from the labor scene and cooks are reduced in number. The role of the hotel as both manufacturer and retailer is being supplanted by its function as retailer only.

Many hotels have assigned their food service operations to chains specializing in the restaurant business. Most have also reduced the scope of their menus and have specialized operations in two or three food service rooms to supplement the general grill or coffee shop menu offerings. Typical of these, for example, are the Hilton hotels, which have operational arrangements with Trader Vic's restaurants, and the Marriott Motor Hotel in Philadelphia, one outlet of a fast-growing and successful chain, which has the following food facilities: a room offering South Seas cuisine; one offering charcoal-broiled steaks; a room with nautical decor offering seafood; a coffee shop with a fast food menu; an outdoor room for luncheon and cocktails; and a family-style room offering a general menu twenty-four hours a day.

Most restaurants today are single proprietorships, and, like other food establishments, face rising labor costs and limited operating funds. Chain-operated restaurants, also facing these problems, have streamlined with combination food and beverage supervisors and have begun to use more convenience food items. This cuts labor costs by using fewer and less skilled workers.

Leading chain-operated restaurants have achieved the maximum use of labor by centralizing food production in commissaries. This permits centralized purchasing and centralized control of mass-produced items, which are then shipped chilled or frozen to the user units or, in some cases, sold to others outside the chain.

Productivity outputs of food service workers (averaging $12,000 to $13,000 of sales per employee in the United States) have been almost doubled by some chain-operated restaurants using these innovative procedures and systems. The Marriott chain, for example, presently reports $24,766 of sales per worker.

Fast Food Operations. A relative newcomer to the field of quantity food service is the fast food operation. It is organized around the concepts of speed and control. Offering a very limited menu, these enterprises are able to prepare the desired items with a minimal number of employees and pieces of specialized equipment. By using paper products, other disposables, and convenience or preprepared items, the operation is turned into a form of food assembly line. Only final procedures are carried out, and customers appear willing to help with the work in the interests of speedy service and low prices.

A working unit manager serves as the mainstay of these operations. He is assisted by a small number of food preparation personnel, many of whom possess few culinary skills. By the use of effective prepackaging and prepreparation, they are able to keep the guests moving at a rapid rate.

Institutional and Industrial Feeding Units. The main food delivery systems used in institutions and industries are the cafeteria and the scramble shopping center system. The short order and quick turnover requirements of these operations require specialized work stations capable of fast production. Some enterprises provide vending by machines, and others offer table service in specialized dining areas, such as college faculty clubs or supervisors' dining rooms in plants. However, the typical institutional or industrial food operation provides only quickly produced items. The organization is built around a unit manager or food production manager who supervises the cooks, the short order stations, and the salad, dessert, and (in many cases) baking areas.

Transportation Food Service. Airlines, trains, and ships are the last group of organizations using quantity food preparation and are in many ways a compendium of all the other forms. Although passenger trains are presently in financial difficulty, the advent of Amtrak suggests that use of this form of transportation may increase in the future. The few trains now serving passengers are organized either as chef-controlled operations stressing customer service in dining cars, or as product-controlled vending operations in snack or tavern cars. The latter are used on short runs or the "piggyback" runs operated in some sections of the country to carry both passengers and their automobiles.

Ships are fast disappearing as a major form of transportation, but they have found increased business in cruises. For these, the traditional form of food and service are offered.

Airlines, the darlings of the transportation field, have attempted to recapture a chef-centered organizational approach. Many operate under an executive chef who supervises central-commissary production of food that is delivered to the aircraft. Many chefs, limited only by lack of extensive on-board equipment and available space, provide menus that border on the full traditional offering. Some airlines have recently been forced to curtail their previously lavish menus because of cost factors. One American company, apparently sensing a change in customer tastes, has recently returned to offering sandwiches. This box lunch approach has also been used by many European airlines on short haul, high density flights of less than ninety minutes' duration.

Also worthy of note are the life-care systems, the armed forces, and the recreational segments of the food service industry.

Life Care. As the life expectancy of the American population increases, longevity results in an aging population who often find themselves detached from grown children who have moved to other areas. Although financially independent, these retired persons in many cases do not desire to live

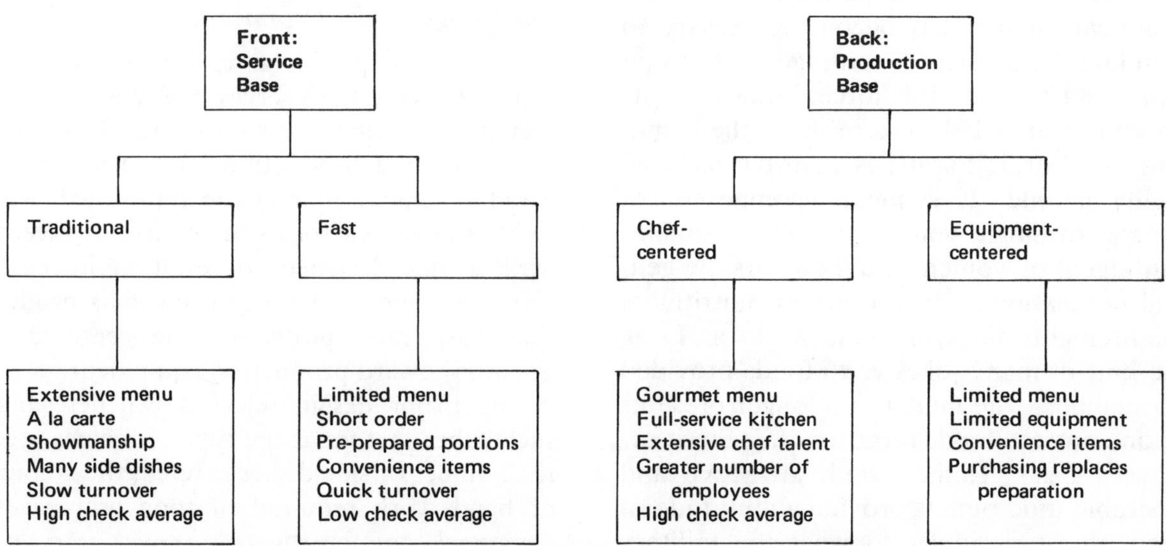

Figure 2b. Organizational bases for front and back of the house

alone, or may not be able to accomplish the chores and duties home ownership requires. Although not physically or emotionally incapacitated, they prefer to be with peers for socialization and to have their physical and psychological needs fulfilled. This has resulted in the new life-care industry, which consists of facilities that provide readily available medical care, security, housing, recreation, and food service facilities to its residents. Many hotel companies have entered this financially lucrative area and either operate existing facilities under a contractual arrangement or build and maintain the facilities themselves. Residents usually precontract for meals provided in these environments, with a requirement that one main meal be taken under normal circumstances. Other meals required or meals required by visitors or guests are paid for as usual in a commercial restaurant facility. The menus offered in such facilities usually follow the nutritional requirements of the elderly and are in a financial range that suits the clientele being served. As the aging of the U.S. population increases, it is foreseen that these types of facilities will increase as will a similar form of condominium or time-sharing hotel facilities in which food service operations provide for or supplement meals prepared by residents and/or guests.

Armed Forces. Despite a desire for peace, it appears that it has become necessary to maintain large armed contingents both at home and abroad. This force, initiated at its present level in 1941 as a result of the beginning of World War II, is multifaceted and highly mobile. It is mainly composed, of course, of single young men and a smaller contingent of women, and it mirrors the general population as to age group, nutritional requirements, likes, dislikes, and so on. Long the butt of many jokes as to foods provided its members, the military no longer presents a one-entree food form on a take-it-or-leave-it basis. Rather, both attractive and desirable food outlets provide a multitude of food offerings similar to what the military person would find in most civilian facilities. On some bases, both here and abroad, there are, in fact, contractual arrangements between civilian-operated fast food companies and the government to provide the regular fast food fare that is so desirable to civilians in this age group. The navy has also made some attempts to provide the same fare to personnel at sea. To supplement the general meal pattern, clubs are also maintained by the military for both officers and enlisted men (NCOs and others) that cater to their tastes in a recreational and off-duty mode.

Recreational. Recreational food service and vending facilities at sports events, parks, theatres, trailer and recreational vehicle parks, theme parks, and the like comprise a very substantial segment of the food service industry. In fact, many innovative food service procedures—such as the centralized commissary and the prepare, chill, and deliver concept—were pioneered at these types of facilities. Comprising some $15 billion in sales, this segment provides products to its consumers that are generally quickly prepared; easy to transport, hold, and consume; and easy to serve. Of course at some locations where circumstances dictate, such as at theme parks with attached lodging or hotel facilities, the menu offered can compete with the range of food normally offered in the average commercial dining room.

The Design of the Organization

Within the particular requirements of the type of market it serves the volume food preparation department is organized on either a service or a production base. The service-based organization may be traditional, with lavish and showy forms of service, or speedy, with service designed to result in increased turnover. Operations organized on a production base may be either chef-centered or oriented toward production equipment.

The major design selected will determine such other factors as the type of recipes used, the number of side dishes offered, the amount of hand work required of food preparation personnel, the customer turnover rate, and the lead time for preparation of an item.

Chef-centered production is compatible with traditional service and usually results in a more elaborate menu, much hand preparation, and showmanship in both preparation and service. The menu form is usually a la carte (although table d'hote forms are used in hotels and resorts), the turnover rate is slow, and the check average is high. Conversely, equipment-centered production, which may be based on deep fryers, grills, or atmospheric steamers, for example, calls for a more limited menu and more moderate check average, necessitating increased turnover and scant attention to service.

Although chef-centered production and traditional service appear to go together, many chains have been successful in combining equipment-centered production with the traditional form of service. Using preportioned frozen food items that can be boiled in the bag or reconstituted by microwave equipment, they achieve a high rate of consumer satisfaction with a minimum amount of equipment and kitchen talent. Major efforts are expended on decor and service. This combination offers opportunities for success in the future to many operations facing labor problems in the production area.

Once the major organizational structure is determined, it must be related to the goals of the organization, the company environment, and any special considerations that exist.

Goal Orientation

An organizational plan must be constructed within the parameters of the company's major objectives. The financial condition and longevity of the concern may impose special requirements on the design. There are three general stages in the life of a company—survival, expansion, and leadership in the field—and each may require a different approach to organization.

Survival Stage. A company that recently began operations may well find itself attempting to survive the competition it is experiencing. In an industry that suffers a mortality rate of up to 80 percent during the first five years of operation, this is a very real problem to a new restaurant of any type, and it will certainly be a major consideration in designing the organization.

During this first stage the food company will be attempting to reach a position where an adequate cash flow is realized, debts are paid, and reserves can be built. Many food operations use much of their money to buy or rent facilities, equipment, and other materials. Then the short-term loans that have been advanced on food products, the utility bills, and the payroll become due.

While the company is experiencing these financial problems, it must also try to attract a clientele and achieve a steady rate of growth. The food production unit will be hard pressed to meet performance standards and to share, pare, and combine if necessary. Innovation will be restricted but resourcefulness will be a necessity. Managerial acumen will be thoroughly tested, retested, and refined as the organization attempts to become a popular and profitable venture. Here management will probably find its biggest challenge in the preparation of quality food. The correct combination of elements must be maintained.

Expansion Stage. The second goal of a company may be to expand. Once a unit has achieved the first plateau of survival and found general acceptance from the market, it may desire to grow. If its managerial talents have resulted in the dividends of increased sales, the company may attempt to capture larger segments of the market. Many organizations at this stage suffer severe setbacks, because organizational forms and procedures that were successful during the period of consolidation and conservation break down under the stress imposed by expansion.

Recipe enlargement, dilution of supervision over increased staffs or several locations, and attempts to increase the number of guests served in a particular time period may well result in disaster. It behooves the manager to plan and consider all aspects of the growth pattern, often in increments, before actual expansion is attempted. Many who have found success in a one-unit venture find chaos in the multiple-unit operation. It is comparable to the difference between food service provided at a leisurely pace to a well satisfied clientele on Tuesday and a product rushed to a capacity crowd, to increase turnover on a Friday or Saturday.

Leadership Stage. The third phase of goal orientation and managerial concerns occurs at the leadership level in the life of an organization. If the food and service have been well received and the operation has gained a sufficient clientele to provide an acceptable rate of return, it may remain at the status quo, continue to expand horizontally or vertically, or attempt to become a leader in a particular field. Innovation, attention to detail in both preparation and service, and effective public relations must be accomplished if this goal is to be realized. A prestigious unit that experiences a reduction in standards may be bolstered by its name alone for a period of time. This will not continue for long, however; if the shortcomings are not corrected, the organization may find itself back at the first plateau of survival again.

These different goal orientations at the three stages of development must be considered by the manager when he plans his food production organization.

Product Life Cycle. Another factor in the history of almost any product or organization is its life cycle because these depend upon the wants and needs of potential consumers, its competition, and the particular environment in which they operate. Even trend setters of the day have a life cycle, with an inevitable end. This may apply to an organization, but it most certainly relates to certain trends in the industry. Witness mesquite wood cooking, blackened redfish, *nouvelle cuisine*, and so on. The life cycle of tends follows a pattern: introduction, growth, maturity, and decline. This can explain how it is that many organizations grow very quickly, expand extensively, and then disappear.

The introductory phase represents the identification of some new idea, concept, or need that results in the organization entering an environment or providing a new product or service. A large market is created by marketing trend or physical or psychological need. E.M. Statler, the late and great hotelier, answered when asked what was needed for the success of hotels, that there were in fact three reasons for success—location, location, location. This implies that if a hotel is in the right location that is all it needs and it will not fail. Many food service operators operate their facilities in somewhat the same manner, treating customers with disdain because after all no other place is nearby and they happen to have the "right" location.

If indeed the organization or product has been well received and is successful, the company attempts to maximize its success through growth, usually by expanded hours, building, offering more of the same, and so on. Then the service or product usually grows quite rapidly, effortlessly, and sometimes without the much-needed adequate planning. When market saturation has been achieved or others have entered the field as competitors to help to satisfy the needs and wants of the consumers, the maturity stage is at hand. This can also happen when the trend has slowed and is no longer the "in thing." Then, unless a new need is generated for the product or service or a change is made, the organization or product disappears.

This is why today there is the "catch phrase" of positioning or repositioning an operation to meet current need. This represents an attempt by many restaurants, hotels, and other establishments to recapture the market by offering something different—a new concept or trend. It is the reason steak house management might think of offering chicken or ethnic food or why a restaurant is redecorated to capture a differing or redirected clientele.

Sometimes such actions merely exacerbate the problem and speed up the operation's demise. However, on occasion this does gain larger market segments for a time, although in doing so, the establishment is only emulating the actions of competitors or leaders in the field that have been able to provide the "correct" facility, product, or service.

Management must give some concern, however, to an analysis comparing the goals of the organization and any "repositioning" suggested to change how things have been progressing. Should goals come first, or do goals follow the attempt to reposition? Sometimes repositioning is a dangerous game. In reality, it is difficult to be everything to everyone.

Market and Menu Requirements

When the major objectives of the organization have been determined, and its goal orientation is clear, a marketing matrix should be constructed.

A marketing audit or analysis should be conducted to determine specific factors of the operation, such as the speed of the service (which determines the equipment and layout to be selected). The menu that will meet the tastes and needs of the consumers and the organizational structure that will meet the particular requirements of the unit must be considered.

In this evaluation the following questions must be answered: For *whom* are we trying to do *what*? *When* is it to be accomplished? *Where* is it to be done? *How* is it to be done? And *why* is it being done in this manner?

Detailed answers to these questions will ensure that the organization proposed and the goals set will be compatible with both the functions to be carried out and the market to be served. The marketing analysis chart in figure 2c is a management aid for considering the major factors of any preliminary marketing plan.

Identification of the consumer's needs, values, and self-image, and a compilation of socioeconomic and demographic data for the market area are needed in order to determine site location, menu form, and pricing structure. These are as important to the food production supervisor as the actual preparation of the food.

An important part of the supervisor's duties is development of a method of identifying the customer and his wants and establishing the ability to make the customer aware of his needs and of how the particular operation can satisfy them. A continuous flow of information must be maintained to ensure that changes in attitudes, trends, and tastes are properly evaluated. These consumer changes may dictate changes in restaurant operation to retain or capture a market.

Marketing research that is able to identify the potential or present customer, determine the frequency of his eating out, and learn how he decides to use a particular facility is a never-ending need of the food service operator. For this he may use government agencies, trade associations, industry periodicals, and marketing research firms or consultants.

With data on the consumers' wants, images, and disposable or discretionary incomes, an operator may construct the name, logo, average check, location, theme, and menu that will make the his food facility acceptable to the particular market he wishes to attract.

Organizational Environment

The organizational environment of the food production facility must be constructed so that all elements of the system will function properly. Location, accessibility to the market, and outside and inside decor are all important to the success of the venture. For example, many downtown restaurants that used to be very successful are today experiencing extreme financial difficulty because customers feel unprotected and fear dangers in the parking lots at night. Bright lights in the parking area, valet parking, fences, security patrols, and the like may be more important parts of the organizational plan of these restaurants than use of convenience food items or an a la carte form of menu.

The organizational environment also includes such variables in the food production areas as the tasks being performed, the size of the work group, the style of leadership, and the physical and psychological environment. An in-depth analysis of the organization and the site are important elements. Traffic counts and flow, road patterns, and access routes as well as parking facilities will help determine if a guest can easily get to or use a planned or operating food service facil-

IDENTIFY AND EXAMINE YOUR OPERATION'S BASIC REVENUE OPERATING PERIODS AND CHARACTERISTICS

SERVICE OFFERED	DAYS AND HOURS OFFERED OR OPERATED	WHO BUYS/HOW OFTEN? WHY FROM YOU?	DESCRIBE TYPICAL ORDER SOLD IN THIS SERVICE TYPE	APPROXIMATE REVENUE PER SALE? NET PROFIT?	DESCRIBE SERVICE METHODS USED	HOW COULD YOU INCREASE NUMBER/SIZE OF SALES? (ANY CARRY-OUT IDEAS?)
• BREAKFAST BUSINESS	Typical Number of Sales per day? (Customer Count)			Daily/Weekly Gross: Net:		
• MORNING SNACK BUSINESS	Typical Number of Sales per day? (Customer Count)			Daily/Weekly Gross: Net:		
• LUNCHEON BUSINESS INCLUDING "BRUNCH"	Typical Number of Sales per day? (Customer Count)			Daily/Weekly Gross: Net:		
• AFTERNOON SNACK BUSINESS	Typical Number of Sales per day? (Customer Count)			Daily/Weekly Gross: Net:		
• DINNER BUSINESS (FIRST SEATING) (MAIN SEATING) (LATE SEATING)	Typical Number of Sales per day? (Customer Count)			Daily/Weekly Gross: Net: Gross: Net: Gross: Net:		
• LATE SUPPER BUSINESS (AFTER SHOWS, ETC.)	Typical Number of Sales per day? (Customer Count)			Daily Weekly Gross: Net:		
• EVENING						

Figure 2c. Marketing analysis chart. (From "Marketing Management Guide," a pamphlet developed by Kelley Rodgers and Company, Chicago, for the National Restaurant Association's 49th Annual Restaurant-Hotel-Motel Convention and Educational Exposition, Chicago, May 20-23, 1968.)

ity. One-way streets, construction, no left turn signals, no lead arrows on traffic lights, and heavy oncoming traffic can all do as much to ruin a proposed or operating restaurant as a poor menu can. As noted previously, collecting data on existing and planned competition is essential and should include their menu, offering prices, portion sizes, marketing processes, hours and scope of operations, and so on. If you plan on taking competitors' business share, it is well to know what is available.

Work Force

The most important element in the organization, and the one affected by all these variables, is the staff. These are the people the food service supervisor must hire, train, assign, supervise, and discipline, if necessary. Through them the organizational goals are achieved.

Job applicants are found through union organizations in some sections of the country, or by advertising in newspapers or trade journals. Many businesses use the federal and state employment services and school vocational counselors. Friends of present workers may be another source of applicants, but care should be taken to ensure that this does not become the sole source; if it does, unofficial leaders may develop among the employees and challenge the organizational leadership.

Because of labor shortages, hiring has become all too often a perfunctory process, in which anyone who appears for a job will be hired. This is an unsatisfactory procedure, and attempts should be made to match the individual who applies to the job available.

Supervisors must realize that employees have aspirations; when these are not satisfied in a particular job, a competing establishment that offers an additional five cents per hour may induce the employee to change jobs.

Realistic efforts should be made to determine the workload of each employee, and a fair reward should be given for his efforts. If employees participate in determining both toil and rewards, turnover will be reduced and employee productivity increased. Then hiring will be less of a problem.

Studies have shown that workers reduce their production to equate with what they feel they are receiving in benefits, if they believe the return is unfair. Other studies show that job satisfaction is the most important element in worker stability or turnover. With productivity and turnover so important to the supervisor of quantity food production, these are crucial facts to keep in mind.

Two tools that can be used in the hiring process are the staffing table and the job description.

Constructing a Staffing Table

The staffing table outlines the numbers and types of workers the organization requires to carry out its functions. In many industries there is a direct linear relationship between the units of work produced and the number of workers required. For example, if a machine shop started business with five manually operated lathes, which would produce a set amount of work, it would need five workers. If at a later date two additional lathes were put into service, two more workers would be required to staff them.

This direct relationship does not exist in the average food service operation. When a restaurant or other walk-in food facility is opened, it requires a certain number of workers to handle the potential business, even if no customers actually come in. Breakfast production requires a different number and type of workers from lunch or dinner, and different food delivery systems have different requirements at each meal. Thus, the hours of operation, menu offered, and type of service provided affect staffing. In addition labor regulations promulgated by government agencies and contracts negotiated with unions make staffing specifications. A union may require a certain number of workers to perform a task or may limit the weight to be lifted by one worker. Government regulations on the number of rest periods that must be allowed to women employees may also influence staffing.

Many guides are available to assist the manager concerned with staffing. Among the best

Table 2-3. Meals Produced per Man-Hour of Labor

Type of Institution	Number of Meals
Hotel	1.25 to 1.50
Restaurant	1.50 to 1.87
Cafeteria	3.60 to 8.75
School lunchroom	5.45 to 15.00
College dormitory	3.38 to 9.07
Hospital	4.76

From Donald E. Lundberg and James P. Armatas, *The Management of People in Hotels, Restaurants and Clubs,* rev. ed., p. 131; copyright 1964, William C. Brown Company, Publishers, Dubuque, Iowa; reprinted by permission.

are those presented in tables 2-3 to 2-5 While table 2-5 discusses school lunch facilities, it is applicable to other types of food delivery systems with good results.

Whatever guide is used, the manager must consider the individual problems of his operation in arriving at the number of workers to be included in the staffing table.

In designing any staffing table, the manager must consider the relationship of staffing to the amount of income generated. This will tell him whether the staffing table he has constructed is valid. If it is not, the hours of operation could be changed, employee work hours could be adjusted, new food forms could be utilized, the scope of the menu could be changed, or the physical layout of the kitchen could be altered. Since the worker is the most important element, his actions and complaints are among the most important factors to be considered.

Drafting Job Descriptions

A second important tool in the hiring process, and an aid in determining whether the staffing table is adequate, is the job description. It outlines the *what, why,* and *how* of the duties to be performed by the worker. With this detailed description of the responsibilities and requirements of each position, a manager can hire more effectively and staff more realistically.

Job descriptions for the hotel and restaurant industry are available from the United States Government Printing Office, Washington, D.C. Assistance in constructing job descriptions and a *Dictionary of Occupational Titles* (an aid in determining the scope of industry jobs) are available at offices of the United States Employment Service and at many state employment service offices. Additional assistance in constructing job descriptions and in other matters of an organizational nature may be secured from the National Restaurant Association. Particularly useful is the NRA's *Profitable Food Service Management through Job Analysis, Job Description and Specifications* (1966).

Table 2-4. Staffing Formulas

Type of Institution	Formula
Hotel or club	y = 2.34 + 2.2x
School	y = 6.44 + .92x
Hospital	y = 4.01 + 1.08x
Cafeteria	y = 2.99 + .82x

y = required number of full-time employees working 206 hours per month
x = thousands of meals served per month

From Paul Richard Broten, "Controlling Restaurant Costs" (thesis, Cornell University, 1953), appearing in J. William Connor, *Food and Beverage Merchandising,* p. 149; copyright 1958 by Cornell University, Ithaca, N.Y.; reprinted by permission.

Table 2-5. Staffing Requirements of School Lunch Facilities

Size of Operation and Worker Assignment	Duties	Number of Workers	Regular Working Hours From	Regular Working Hours To	Total Man-Hours per Day
350-500 meals per day					
Head cook	Planning, supervising, and participating in kitchen work; inventory control; general administration.	1	7:30 a.m.	2:00 p.m.	6
Assistant cooks	Preparation of food, cooking, baking, serving (1 person at cash register during serving hours); general cleaning, receiving goods, storeroom maintenance.	3-4	7:30 a.m.	2:00 p.m.	18-24
Kitchen and lunchroom helpers	Setting up serving line; dishwashing; and general cleaning.	2-4	10:30 a.m.	2:00 p.m.	6-12
Janitor	Cleaning lunchroom and kitchen floor; disposing of trash.	1	Intermittent		2
Total		7-10			32-44
700-1,000 meals per day					
Lunchroom supervisor	Administrative duties, planning and supervising school lunch operations.	1	Intermittent		3-4
Head cook	Planning, supervising and participating in kitchen work; inventory control; maintaining records.	1	7:00 a.m.	2:30 p.m.	7
Assistant cooks	Preparing food, cooking, baking, serving, and general cleaning; receiving goods; storeroom maintenance; operating cash register during serving; wiping tables in lunchroom as needed.	6-9	7:30 a.m.	2:00 p.m.	36-54
Kitchen and lunchroom helpers	Setting up serving line; wiping tables in lunchroom; general cleaning.	1-2	10:30 a.m.	2:00 p.m.	3-6
Dishwashers	Washing dishes, pots, pans; general cleaning.	3-4	10:30 a.m.	2:00 p.m.	9-12
Janitor	Cleaning lunchroom and kitchen floors; disposing of trash; assisting in heavy lifting when needed.	1	Intermittent		3-4
Total		13-18			61-87
1,400-2,000 meals per day					
Lunchroom supervisor	Administrative duties; planning and supervising school lunch program; central purchasing of food and supplies.	1	Intermittent		4-5
Head cook	Planning, supervising, and participating in kitchen work; receiving goods; inventory control; maintaining records.	1	7:00 a.m.	3:30 p.m.	7-8
Assistant cooks	Preparing food, cooking, baking, serving, and general cleaning; receiving goods; storeroom maintenance; operating cash register during serving; wiping tables in lunchroom as needed.	10-15	7:30 a.m.	3:00 p.m.	70-105
Kitchen and lunchroom helpers	Setting up serving line; wiping tables in lunchroom; general cleaning.	3-4	9:30 a.m.	2:00 p.m.	12-16
Dishwashers	Washing dishes, pots, pans; general cleaning.	4-5	10:30 a.m.	3:00 p.m.	16-20
Janitor or maintenance supervisor	Cleaning lunchroom and kitchen floors; disposing of trash; assisting in heavy lifting when needed.	1	Intermittent		3-6
Total		20-27			112-160

From Konrad Biedermann, O. Wilhelmy, Jr., and M. R. Dull, *Layout, Equipment and Work Methods for School Lunch Kitchens and Serving Lines,* p. 44, Marketing Research Report no. 753, United States Department of Agriculture, Washington, D.C., 1966.

In drafting job descriptions, food service managers should consider alternative procedures or arrangements that might affect the position. New pieces of equipment, a change in the location of a work station, or a change in worker hours may make an operation more effective and alter the job description. Changes in menu, hours of service, and numbers of consumers may also dictate revisions in job descriptions.

Trade periodicals and food and equipment representatives should be consulted for new approaches to old problems. Just because a procedure is accomplished in a certain manner does not mean that a new, more efficient manner has not been found. Thought should therefore be given to a periodic review of all job descriptions.

The job description not only is a tool for achieving proper utilization of labor, but is also invaluable in determining a proper salary schedule, simplifying jobs, and lessening confusion within the organization.

It may be drawn up by a supervisor or consultant who analyzes what is being done in a particular position or by the worker himself after giving adequate thought to what he does.

A preliminary introduction of the process to the worker and a combination of worker-manager construction of the form appear to give better results than if the description is completed by a manager, worker, or outside consultant alone.

The example in figure 2d is part of an investigative package that consists of a job analysis, a job description, and a production worksheet, which translates the job tasks into a form specifying the time period for performing each duty. The employee may then follow this schedule, and the supervisor may use it to check his performance.

Training

When new workers are hired, procedures are changed, new equipment is purchased, or new facilities are opened, training of some form must take place. This is a function of the food service manager. Today's new foods, new techniques, and changes in consumer requirements, necessitate more training than ever before.

Training is designed to change the way an individual carries out a procedure. In order to be effective, the learner must see a need for the change and demonstrate a desire to have

Vegetable Cook Job Description

Job Summary: The vegetable cook directs the preparation, cleaning, and cooking of all vegetables. He does the following:

1. Requisitions the vegetable supply and rotates the preparation.
2. Receives clean vegetables from vegetable room.
3. Schedules and times the cooking according to daily menus, including parties and banquets, and the type of service the establishment maintains.
4. Arranges and maintains the cooking of vegetables in rotation to assure a fresh supply at all times.
5. Determines the style of preparation and method of cooking.
6. Is responsible for the seasoning as directed by the chef.
7. Is responsible to keep the vegetables hot and maintain standard color, texture, thickness, and appearance.
8. Is responsible for the size of serving whether on luncheon, dinner, or a la carte.
9. Serves vegetables as ordered on luncheon, dinner, or a la carte.
10. Determines the use of leftover vegetables and schedules the use along with his other work.
11. At the end of his shift, returns any uncooked vegetables to the vegetable room and frozen vegetables to the freezer.
12. Keeps the station and refrigerator in order.
13. Turns his station over to his alternate or relief man.

Figure 2d. A typical job description. (From *Hospitality Education Program Newsletter,* Florida State University, Tallahassee, June 1972, p. 9; reprinted by permission.)

this change take place. Only the person who does the task has the power to make the change occur, and no amount of training will accomplish the change unless he sees the need.

A previously trained worker may have to be moved out of his former function before a change to a new method may be taught. Because of this, many managers would rather hire only inexperienced workers in order to make the training process easier.

Once the benefits and advantages of learning the new procedure have been accepted by the trainee, his past experiences must be determined so that a jumping off point for the learning process may be constructed. Unless it is necessary for him to unlearn a poor procedure, he can simply build the additional learning on his previously learned facts, without the necessity to relearn facts already known.

People will tend to repeat the pleasant and avoid the unpleasant. The teacher should therefore stress the positive and pleasant aspects with praise and ego-building procedures. Some minimal amount of tension should also be maintained in the learning process as an incentive. The tension should be quite low, however, for when too much is applied no learning takes place. A marking system, an attendance record, and questions asked about reading assignments are all forms of minimal tension.

The instruction in technical skills, which is most often used in food preparation work, is best presented in periods of no more than fifteen to twenty minutes. If possible it should be related to an immediate application. There should be goals that can be reached easily by the trainee, and the teaching units should be kept small. If possible, a complete task or job should be taught in one session.

Workers will learn at various speeds in accordance with the normal distribution curve. In skill learning, the more difficult the job, the greater the improvement possible as a result of training. This improvement will be most noticeable at early stages.

Tasks should be taught in the order in which they are completed. Key points and the *why* of each process should be stressed.

Table 2-6 presents the training procedure developed for the manpower development program of one large company. It has proved effective.

Supervision

Supervisors of food service workers must know what is considered acceptable performance at particular work stations and what actions can be taken to achieve this performance.

Duties and tasks should be combined where possible and work station arrangements located to maintain maximum efficiency of production. Tracing the movement of each menu item from purchasing to service should enable the supervisor to determine the number and kinds of tasks to be performed, the amount of work space necessary, and the best placement of equipment.

An organizational chart of the food production facility should be prepared so that

Table 2-6. Training Procedure

Step 1. Prepare the Employee for Instruction
Put him at ease
Explain the job and its importance
Get him interested in learning the job

Step 2. Present the Job
Follow your breakdown
Explain and demonstrate *one step* at a time
Tell why and how
Stress *key points*
Instruct clearly and patiently
Give everything you will want back but no more

Step 3. Try Out Performance
Have him do the job
Have him tell why and how and stress *key points*
Correct errors and omissions as he makes them
Encourage him
Get back everything you gave in step 2
Continue until *you* know *he* knows

Step 4. Follow Through
Put him on his own
Encourage questions
Check frequently
Let him know how he is doing

the lines of communication, authority, and responsibility are well defined. Organizations should be kept as flat as possible, with the minimum number of supervisory levels, while maintaining a manageable span of control, so that workers are neither oversupervised nor undersupervised.

Supervisors should have empathy with workers and be able to create conditions that motivate them to produce the results desired by the organization. Goals and needs of individual workers should be identified and, where possible, made congruent with goals of the company. Then motivation of workers becomes a very minor problem.

The rules of the operation should be made known to all workers. Violations of these rules should result in speedy investigation of the circumstances, and, if warranted, decisive disciplinary action should be taken.

Supervisors must be fair and consistent in their actions. They should attempt to use rewards for motivational purposes. With certain individuals, and under certain circumstances, punishment will sometimes be necessary. When used, it must follow an expected pattern.

Each worker should be considered an individual as well as a member of the working unit. Supervisors must realize that workers have other interests in addition to their jobs.

Tasks should be structured to reduce or eliminate unproductive times, and workers should be permitted to share in the rewards of increased productivity.

Supervisors must make proper use of workers, materials, equipment, and time, within an acceptable financial framework, so that maximum effectiveness is derived from scarce resources.

When the organizational structure has been completed to accomplish these ends, the manager needs three main continuing tools: (1) up-to-date knowledge of the market; (2) knowledge of the product being served; and (3) a properly functioning system of controls.

Market and Sales Analysis

In order to offer a type of food to a particular consumer market, managers and supervisors must keep abreast of the market's ever-changing requirements. Do the items offered meet the current needs of consumers? Are the products following the overall plans of the operation?

Market reaction information must be gath-

Sales Analysis Form

Day: Wednesday
Meal Period: Lunch
Weather: Cloudy, cold

Date: February 11, 1970
Special Events: None
Special Problems: Breakdown of deep fat fryer midway in meal period

Items (in order of menu position or cafeteria serving line)	1 Ground Steak	2 Sweet and Sour Pork	3 Fried Chicken	4 Etc.
Price	$ .95	$1.05	$1.00	
Number forecasted	15	25	28	
Number served	20	25	8	
Number remaining	–	–	20	
Time ran out	–	12:30	–	
Disposition of leftovers	–	–	Finished in oven, used for evening special	
Comments	–	Could have sold more because of chicken problem	Unable to keep up with orders because of equipment failure	

Figure 2e. A sample sales analysis to be used in future menu planning.

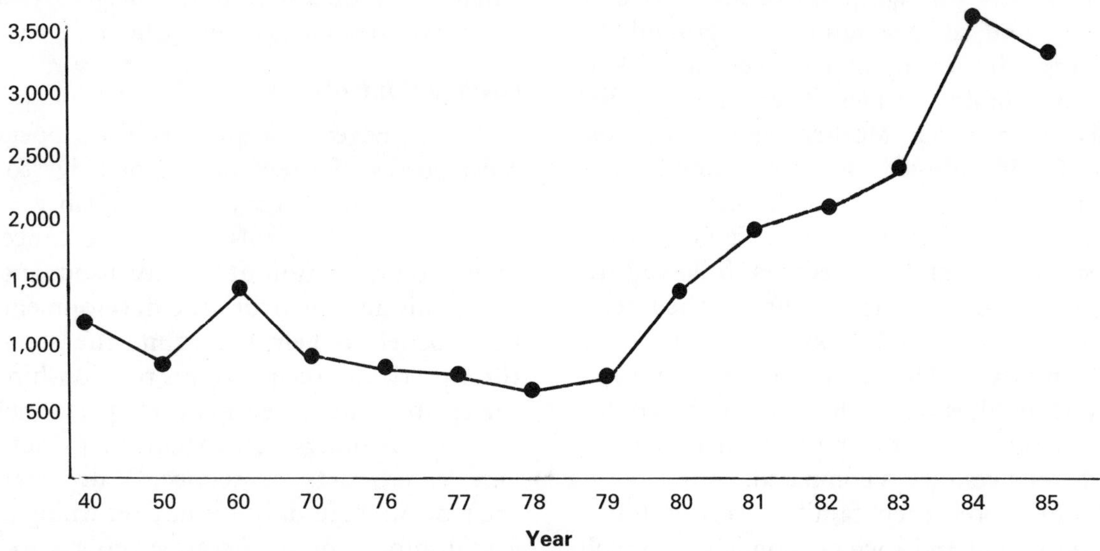

Figure 2f. Eating and Drinking Place Failures: 1940–1985. Rates of failures of eating and drinking places (second only to apparel and accessory stores) is, according to Dun and Bradstreet, attributable nine out of ten times to poor management. Other causes noted are poorly developed concepts, over capitalization, high operating costs, and overzealous expansion. (Source: *NRA News*, April 1986, pp. 37–38, 311 First Ave. NW, Washington DC 20001.) Steven Rockwell of Alex Brown and Sons reports that 50 percent of all new restaurants fail the first year, and half of the remainder fail the second year. (Source: Standard and Poor, *Industry Survey*, March 26, 1987.)

ered from sales history records. The sales analysis form in figure 2e shows the amount of each menu item sold, the weather on the date of sale, specific events that may have contributed to or detracted from its planned sales, the time at which the item ran out (if applicable), a list of the competing menu items, and the pricing structure in effect.

This type of information, gathered from sales records such as waiters' checks or multicounters, can be supplemented with data from desirability sampling of consumers that are available through trade associations or in government or industry publications.

In its efforts to capture a market or to improve on service to its present market, a food service operation usually should not try to be "all things to all people." Considering factors of age, sex, economic level, and ethnic background, it should identify a market with unfulfilled needs and then develop an operating policy and organizational structure that will meet these needs. The policies and structure will cover such elements as the menu to be offered, type and speed of service, location, pricing, decor, entertainment offered, hours and days of operation, and employees hired. Although many of these factors are outside the scope of this book, the food preparation policies—type of menu and service—are considered in later chapters.

Product Expertise

The second continuing tool of the quantity food service manager is his knowledge of the product offered. Although the market may be defined, with special considerations identified and integrated into the operating plan, this information must be related to the main products to be served. The serving of food to guests is the raison d'etre of the quantity food operation.

The quantity food manager should realize that he is operating in a realm where every consumer believes he is an expert. (After all, hasn't he eaten food all his life?) Individual experiences have constructed norms for him, and the consumer views the food presented to him from the vantage point of his particular age, sex, and socioeconomic background. In most cases his eating experiences have taken place in family settings where love is dispensed with food. Mothers and wives purchase foods enjoyed by their families and prepare them by the methods accepted by a majority of the family group. Serving hours are scheduled and procedures followed to bring the food to the consumer when temperature, color, and texture are at their optimum level. The family receives its food the way it likes it, to the best of the cook's ability, and it is to this performance that the commercial venture is compared.

Furthermore, each family, even within a specific ethnic and socioeconomic group, will have deviations from the group norm. Italian spaghetti and German sauerbraten may have many local inflections. Even in purely Americanized foods variations exist. The food operator must be able to offer varieties to meet the tastes of most segments of his market or one version that will satisfy most customers in a particular market segment. As an alternative, he may offer a specialty item that will be accepted by smaller numbers of people but from several large market segments.

In addition to these factors, the operator is dealing with a product that has many complex forms, each with special purchasing, storage, and preparation requirements. He must handle these products from purchasing to service, using many different pieces of equipment. Often he must accomplish his goals with a minimum number of well trained personnel. Limited menu policies, specialty restaurants, and fast food operations have attempted to solve some of these problems by reducing the number of food types offered, the equipment employed, or the effort spent on preparation. These measures reduce the need for skilled personnel.

Whatever the type of facility, certain common characteristics create problems. Of note is the labor shortage, which results from the unusual hours of operation and low status of the occupation. These factors make it difficult for any quantity food manager to attract and retain sufficient culinary help.

Quality Controls

The manager of a quantity food operation must possess the technical knowledge to construct and administer effective quality, quantity, and cost controls. His prime concern is with the production of quality food, and this guides his actions, from the development of a taste panel to help determine the standards for a particular recipe, to his relationship with the establishment's cost-control personnel.

Few customers call attention to deficiencies in products or service. Many manifest their displeasure only by not returning to the establishment or by negative reports to their friends. This after-the-fact reporting may produce sales problems before management can take adequate corrective action. In view of this, the manager must be able to judge for himself what is an acceptable standard for a particular food or service, so that corrections can be made before the guests complain.

The tools of quality control are recipe, recipe development, temperature, time, purchasing, preparation, and portioning standards. In addition to overt controls, which the employees know exist, the manager must use some covert controls, such as sampling. He might take the inventory of a food item at an off hour, use a "shopper" to sample and report on a menu item, or weigh and taste every *n*th portion. These samples or observations must be judged against benchmarks or standards. In establishing valid criteria, the manager uses his greatest technical expertise.

Cost Controls

The food preparation manager must be able to utilize cost-control systems. He needs to know the food cost percentages and standard and potential costs if he is to maintain a satisfactory cost/sales relationship. This is necessary in both profit-making and nonprofit operations, since even the latter must break even and not spend more than the budgeted allowance.

Food Cost Percentage. The basis of the cost-control system is the food cost percentage. This is the ratio of the cost of a food item to its selling price or of the cost of all items to the establishment's total sales. It is found by the formula:

$$\frac{\text{cost of food}}{\text{selling price}} = \text{food cost \%}$$

If the food cost percentage is fixed, and the cost of the food is determined, it is possible to determine the selling price by the formula:

$$\frac{\text{cost of food}}{\text{food cost \%}} = \text{selling price}$$

If the food cost percentage is fixed, and the selling price has been set, it is also possible to determine the price that should be paid for a food item by the formula:

$$\text{food cost \% x selling price = cost of food}$$

The composite food cost percentage of overall costs to total sales may be used in a small operation; a breakdown of departmental costs to total sales may be suitable for a medium-sized operation; and a commodity cost to commodity sales percentage may be used in a large operation or one on a very small margin (such as a cafeteria).

Managers may also use precost or standard cost control systems and comparisons made of actual versus potential sales. (These are discussed in the next sections of this chapter.)

Whatever system is selected, it is important that the manager use the information to guide his future actions and change conditions before irreparable damage is done. The system must not be too complex and should provide data within a reasonable period of time. A manager or owner who is on the premises most of the day would find the simple total cost to total sales percentage quite sufficient, since he probably has already pinpointed the problem area. A more detailed system might be necessary in a larger or multiple-unit operation, where changes in percentages tell very little without some indication of the specific department or food item involved.

Actual Food Cost														
Date		Beginning Storeroom Inventory	Storeroom Purchases	Total	Issues	Direct Purchases	Total Cost	Less Transfers	Net Cost	Sales	Month to date		
											Cost	Sales	%
3	1	4000 –	200 –	4200 –	270 –	50 –	320 –	10 –	310 –	800 –	310 –	800 –	38.8
3	2	3930 –	240 –	4170 –	290 –	60 –	350 –	20 –	330 –	870 –	640 –	1670 –	38.3

Figure 2g. A summary food cost record, such as this, may be compared to the operation's previously determined food cost percentage. Direct purchases are items that are sent directly to the kitchen after purchase, without being issued through the storeroom. Transfers are food items used by the bar or in other nonfood situations. A cumulative monthly food cost percentage gives more accurate results than a daily percentage.

Standard Food Cost (Precost)

Menu item	1 Chicken, Fried	2 Beef, Roast	3 Fish Sandwich	4 Etc.
Purchase unit	2 lbs.	8 lbs.	2 lbs.	
Market price	.28/lb.	1.00/lb.	.70/lb.	
Portion size	8 oz.	4 oz.	4 oz.	
Portion cost	.14	.25	.18	
Surrounding item cost	.20	.25	.08	
Total portion cost	.34	.50	.26	
Menu price	1.10	1.30	.80	
Number sold	40	20	15	
Weighted cost	13.60	10.00	3.90	
Weighted sales	44.00	26.00	12.00	
Food cost percentage	30.9	38.5	32.5	

Figure 2h. The standard or precost method determines what the food cost percentage has been in a test period. The surrounding items are garnishes and other food materials served with the menu item and not charged for separately. The weighted cost is the total portion cost multiplied by the number sold. Weighted sales are the menu price multiplied by the number sold. The food cost percentage is the weighted cost divided by the weighted sales. The total food cost percentage for all menu items for the period is found by dividing the total weighted cost by the total weighted sales. This percentage may then be compared with the actual food cost percentage realized at later periods to check efficiency and cost control.

The cost of food is found by a number of different methods, depending on the size of the operation, the storeroom and issue system used, and the type of purchasing done.

The simplest way to determine the cost of food for an operation is by the formula:

cost of beginning inventory + cost of purchases – cost of ending inventory = cost of goods sold

This formula may be used in any type of organization, but lends itself best to the small one. An inventory of the food is taken on the last day of each month. It serves as both the ending inventory for one accounting period and the beginning inventory for the next. Purchases are recorded by a receiving record, voucher system, or some other means.

There could be much confusion about what the items were used for, in what department they were used, and whether, in fact, they were not wasted or stolen. This simple system just states that food of a certain value has been used; no attempt is made to suggest how.

In larger operations or where more detailed controls are necessary, issue forms from the storeroom, identifying the department and in some cases the specific menu item requiring the material are used to trace each item. Additional inventories also check on end use or direct issue food—items received by an establishment and sent directly to the kitchen for use rather than being issued through the storeroom. Transfers of food to the beverage department and of wine to the food department are also accounted for. All of these refinements give the manager a more realistic picture of the cost of food.

Selling price under any of these systems is taken from the sales records of menu items. This may be a cash register tape or, in more detailed systems, an analysis of restaurant checks showing how much money was brought in by each menu item.

Precost or Standard Cost System. In the precost or standard system of cost control, the ideal cost of each menu item is calculated, based on the assumption that every procedure in purchasing, storage, preparation, and service is being carried out properly. This standard is then applied over a period of time. The sales generated by the item are used to establish a precost or standard food cost percentage. The actual food cost and sales generated by each item may then be compared with the standard to determine whether production is within the tolerances set.

Potential Sales Method. In the potential sales method, a form commonly used in cost control of alcoholic beverages, purchased food items are translated into potential sales of the menu items realized from their use. Control of food costs is then based on a comparison of the potential sales dollars and the amount of sales actually generated by the used material (computed from differences in beginning and ending inventories).

This form of control is often used in fast food operations where limited menus and preportioned foods are common. These enterprises can identify each menu item with a cash register key code so that the register keeps both inventory and sales records. Then it is easy to match potential sales estimates to cash register totals of actual food used and sales generated.

Interpreting Cost-Control Data. In any of the systems, standardization must be maintained in recipes, portions, specifications of purchase, and yields realized after preparation. Only if these procedures are maintained at standard levels, do changes in percentages indicate an actual food cost change.

Changes in the food cost percentage or figures outside the precosting or potential sales tolerances are then reliable symptoms that managerial attention is needed. The food service manager still has to identify the specific problem, however.

Some common reasons for a percentage increase are: portions larger than usual, waste in the use of leftovers, dishonest personnel, failure to use standard recipes, or slipshod receiving.

Decreases in percentages arise from: portions smaller than usual, high use of leftovers, an increase in business without increased issues, or errors in overpricing the menu.

Budgets

A final function of all managers and supervisors is concern for the budget. The budget encompasses all the elements previously considered, since every decision made in planning or accomplishing food service tasks may be expressed in quantitative financial terms.

A budget is a systematic financial plan, in which all aspects of an operation (such as food, equipment, personnel, utilities, and supplies) are given a common denominator—the dollar.

There are many forms of budgets. The cash budget provides for monetary liquidity within an operation so that sufficient sources of cash are available to meet payment obligations. Capital budgets plan for expansion, replacement, and acquisition of necessary capital assets to meet future commitments. The most important to the manager or supervisor, however, is the operating budget.

An operating budget is usually based on one calendar or fiscal year. It determines the business's operations, matching responsibilities and requirements, expressed in financial terms, against projected income.

Many tools are used in the construction of a budget: break-even points, demographic data, and pro forma balance and income statements. But, for the food service operator, the base points are the forecasts of the sales of each menu item, its food cost and menu price, the customer turnover, and the required personnel, utilities, supplies, time, and equipment.

Some budgets, particularly in governmental organizations and in some highly structured chain operations, use a line item approach. In this form, statistical and internal forecasts are translated into costs, which are assigned to specific headings, such as personnel, or food costs. The operator has little chance to take money from one heading and assign it to another requiring higher expenditures. Most budgets, however, are more flexible, and permit managers to juggle total funds so that savings in one area may be applied to requirements in another.

This appears to be a more realistic approach, since it follows the way budgets are first constructed. If a supervisor plans to use a convenience food in producing a menu item, it may increase the portion cost of the raw food material but it should also reduce labor costs, since fewer man-hours will be required to prepare the item for service.

An important tool in the administration of the budget and in the successful operation of any food production facility is the break-even analysis. Expressed in the volume of units to be produced (i.e., the number of meals or covers), it determines the point at which total costs will equal total sales. This point is found by measuring income to be realized against fixed and variable costs.

To construct this information, by either graph or formula, a manager or operator projects his income from sales, based on the check average, turnover, and size of dining facilities, and compares this against the total of his fixed costs (such as rent and taxes) and his variable costs (such as the cost of food materials, utilities, and labor) (see figure 2i). This information will enable the supervisor to make adjustments in his operating policies to achieve the desired level of profit or (in the case of nonprofit or government organizations) the break-even point.

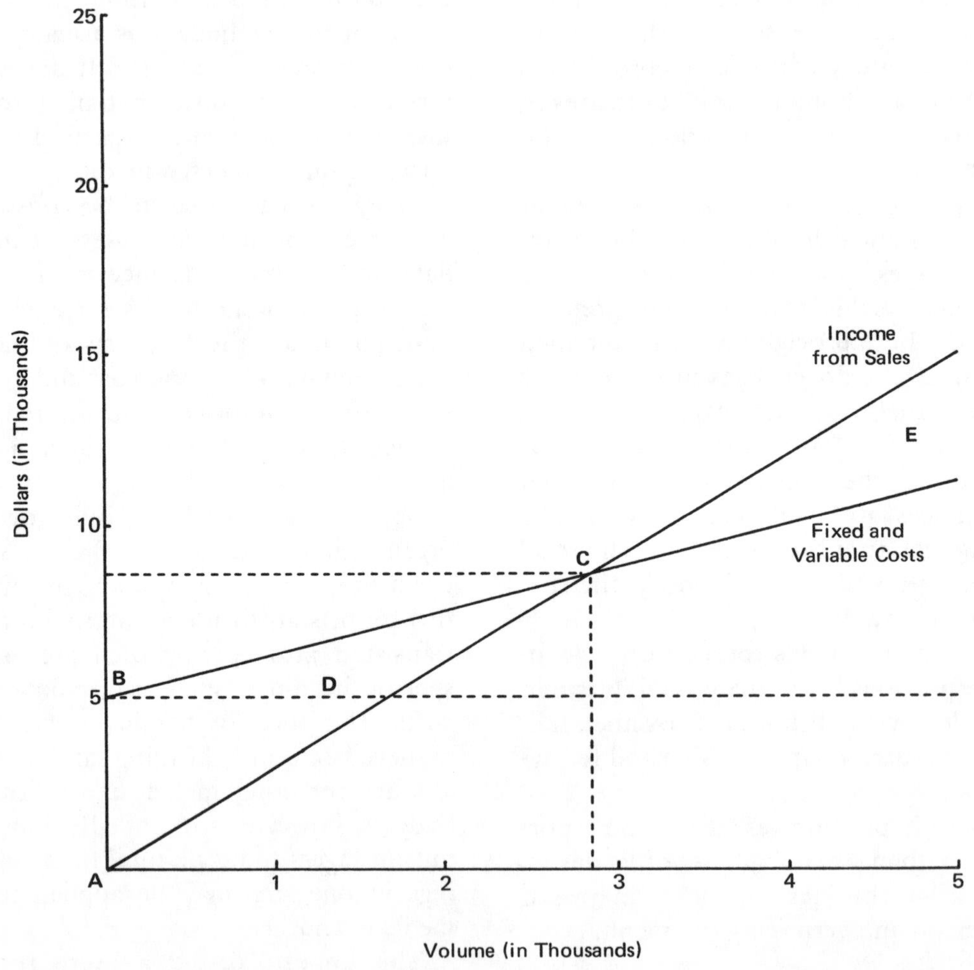

Figure 2i. A graphic presentation of a break-even analysis. Point A represents no income (zero sales). The income-from-sales line rises as sales volume increases. Point B is the amount of fixed costs ($5,000) at zero sales. The costs line increases (due to variable costs) as sales increase. Point C is where total costs equal total income—the break-even point. Expressed in volume, it is 2,800 covers. Area D, before the break-even point is reached, indicates the enterprise is operating at a loss, as costs exceed income. Area E represents profitable operation, since sales income exceeds total costs.

Construction of the Budget

In order to construct a satisfactory budget the manager or supervisor must know the following basic facts about the operation:

a. The amount of food needed to feed the projected number of consumers. This information must include knowledge of the yields to be expected, of market pricing considerations, and of the purchasing procedures that give maximum returns.

b. The amount of personnel time required for the preparation and service of the menu items. Personnel must be scheduled so that highly paid workers with more talent are used to accomplish the most technical duties, while less complex tasks are assigned to workers receiving lower wages.

c. What controls on preparation, storage, supplies, portioning, and the like exist and whether they are effective. A manager or supervisor needs to know the operation's standards of performance before he can reasonably project that x number of dollars in labor and food costs will generate y number of dollars in sales. After the budget goes into effect these controls should provide management with information on a daily basis, so that problems are spotted and corrective actions taken before they become magnified and cause budget failure.

d. What the staffing tables, production schedules, standard purchase specifications, portions, and recipes are. This knowledge enables the manager developing a budget to be reasonably sure that he can meet the operating requirements with the amount of funds requested.

Budgets are prepared in many forms for different types of operations. A hospital budget may be expressed in projected portion costs and beds occupied during the period. In a restaurant the number of covers to be served is the base.

The cornerstone of all budgets is the forecast. Upon this base all budget considerations are built.

It has been reported that engineers working on a structural design problem generally compute the necessary material requirements, and then routinely add a safety factor to ensure that the strength of the material will meet the computed loads and stresses. Some budget planners also add "fudge factors" or overruns to ensure that sufficient funds will be available to meet projected demands, particularly when they believe the budget will be reduced by those reviewing it at higher levels.

I cannot speak to the validity of the report about engineers, but in food service establishments there should be no need to carry out such a procedure. If a budget planner knows his operation, and keeps cognizant of daily practices by using the proper controls, this safety factor will not be necessary.

Changes may occur during a budget operating period. Work schedules may have to be revised; certain foods may have to be removed from the menu because of excessive increases in their market prices; leftovers may have to be worked into subsequent menu offerings. But this is what supervision is all about: a supervisor's ability to solve these difficulties and keep the budget viable is what makes him valuable. When an operation is running according to a predetermined schedule, a manager or supervisor is less in demand. Of course, uncontrolled events will take place, and supervisory action will then be needed to keep the operation active while staying within the budget.

If budgets and other planning procedures are properly constructed, managers and supervisors will experience more enjoyable work periods with fewer crises.

Computers

Electronic computations of data according to a binary system were developed as a result of World War II and the search for the atomic bomb. They have since become an important element in procuring, producing, and accounting for food and beverages in quantity food preparation facilities. After World War II it was believed that only six computers would be needed to accomplish all the computations required by all the industries of our country. Today we have thousands, including desk-top microcomputers, computers in most commercial aircraft, and computer applications for the home.

Computers are most effective when used with repetitive computations. For example, in payroll applications where the constants of pay rate per hour, number and rate of deductions, tax percentages, and so on are maintained, only the number of hours worked are changed. This is an easy calculation for the computer to make and then it will print the payroll and the checks needed to pay employees.

Computers in our industry were first used in repetitive types of applications. However, with the appearance of more sophisticated equipment, greater storage capacities, and the development of new systems, the applications or uses for computers have been expanded. Among the most widely used applications in our industry are the following:

(1) Maintaining payrolls and other personnel records.

(2) Accounting office applications, such as construction of budgets, cash and sales controls.

(3) At point-of-sale terminals in connection with cash registers in order to provide a current inventory, sales record, and cash control.

(4) In computer-assisted menu planning applications (CAMP) for the planning of menus to determine costs, nutritional levels, and so on.

(5) In the issuing of foods and other materials from storerooms. Standard recipes only require the number to be served in order to have computers determine the amount of issue needed.

(6) In cost control systems for food and/or beverages based upon a system of actual versus potential or standard sales or costs.

(7) In the preparation of alcoholic drinks in service bars or in standard applications where speed and control are more important than atmosphere or procedure. Computers preprogrammed with drink recipes pour and account for beverages requested.

(8) An automated restaurant in the fast food sector has been tried with a computer preprogrammed with standardized recipes. The computer prepared food items by "issuing" the necessary amount of food and activating the preparation equipment.

(9) Marketing problems as to trends, cycles, projections, and so on can be determined by computers.

(10) Checks and the clearance of credit cards as to validity and available balance can be made by computers.

It has been suggested that in 1987 some 19 million microcomputers were in operation (quite a difference from the originally forecasted 6) performing a number of functions that they can do faster than humans are able to do them; making fewer errors (if programmed correctly); providing quicker flow of information; and permitting the operation to be more productive.

Computer systems are currently used in about 74 percent of all food service operations, with the fast food segment maintaining the highest usage rate of approximately 88 percent. This, of course, is due to standardization of menu, portions, price, method of service, and so forth, which all lend themselves readily to computer applications.

As was noted previously, computers can be used in almost any area of the operation, but the ability to provide sales information and to analyze this information quickly appears to be the biggest benefit of computers. In fact, cash registers have widely been replaced by point of sales computer terminals, and it is forecasted that computer terminals now under development, which will be able to recognize voice signals (even of differently spelled but similarly pronounced words such as *two, too*, and *to*) may soon be the main restaurant ordering device. Customers or waiters may use them to order meals. Some restaurants now use handheld computer terminals on which waiters and waitresses record the orders of guests at tableside; others use a menu screen and a computer pen or "mouse" to have guests order their food items directly from the chef's computer in the kitchen.

The networking of computers in multi-establishment companies also permits one computer to communicate with another to collect information, check accuracy, and provide collated sources of data. Computers can be programmed with proper software to maintain control over operations, markets, menus, accounting procedures, labor costs, production, service, settlement of accounts, pricing, settlement, and inventory. Management can virtually control any and all aspects of the coordination between production and service using computers. Elements can be (as noted) a handheld terminal, touch screen, typewriter key, or voice recognition device. They can be used to answer a phone, dial a number, activate a tape, adjust a thermostat, or start or stop a cooking process.

Computers should be "user friendly," requiring little training or indoctrination for those who use them so that it is easy to enter information and have the information displayed for easy checking or use. (Computer programs could be better written to make use easier, but certain computer "experts" like to keep programs difficult to enhance either their own egos or their financial rewards.)

The receiving of goods, for example, may be made more efficient and effective by utilizing computers to scan UPC codes (universal product codes) imprinted on canned goods and other containers or by using voice-activated terminals to enter information rather than using a pen or pencil to enter the data.

As with other management tools, the computer remains just that—a tool. Although some computers are programmed to recognize auditory signals and respond by "talk" from a prestored set of taped human words, it is still necessary for the supervisor or manager to use the computer in the proper applications. The computer can only assist in the decisions made by managers and supervisors.

Computers operate under programs designed by humans, and they base any decisions upon comparisons between sets of data stored and sets of data entered into the computer by humans. As the acronym GIGO states—"Garbage In, Garbage Out"—the computer only contributes to the magnification of problems when errors are made by humans. But given the correct data and the program necessary for the appropriate computation, computers can do a lot to make the management and supervisory functions more pleasant and efficient. Routine computations and comparisons can be given to the computer to handle, while the more esoteric or theoretical concepts and decisions can be reserved for the human intellect—a capacity so immense that the computer pales when compared to it.

Corporate Culture

Every food service company (as well as every other type of business) will have its own corporate culture. It may be one that is planned for or that has just happened—but in any case a corporate culture exists. It is a way of doing things, an interest, a set of values. It is also a character, a trust or lack of trust, a nebulous "thing" that may be felt not in totality but only as signals emitted that, like shots from an expert marksman, tend to produce a close pattern when scrutinized.

The corporate culture is not something the company says about itself (although this can be part of it). The culture is more what an outsider, a customer, a competitor, or a critic might say about the company. It is a set of parameters that dictate specific actions on the part of those who work within it, with it, or through it. The culture dictates the dress, the language, the mission, and the values and goals the company seeks, attains, or misses. It helps to maintain and attract a certain work force, and it is one of the reasons that a certain type of customer chooses to do business with that company.

A culture may be noble, true and straight as the laws of nature, or it can be phony, distorted and convoluted. The important element to keep in mind is that it is not important what the culture is (unless you work in a certain organization); what is important is what the culture appears to be. The best politician does not always win the election, nor is the best person always promoted within a company. Conversely the most incompetent is not always the first to be fired—in fact, due to political actions, he may be the last.

People tend to gravitate towards those who are like themselves and with whom they have an affinity and feel comfortable. Certain groups, therefore, reward the values and behaviors they find compatible with their own needs. When this is done often enough, and at enough levels in the company, it sets the tone for the development of a company culture. If we apply the term *culture* to the society as a whole and determine its meaning there, it will be easier to see why it is essential to know the culture of a company or an organization.

Culture in sum and substance is developed over time in society. It is the value system, the language, the religion, the dress, and the emphasis given to work, truth, or a thousand other values, beliefs, rituals, and actions. Whole cultures change, but usually very slowly, and when this happens the new values are superimposed upon its members so that a norm or standard is produced. The goals of a culture serve as the causes or reasons for its existence, and when a person is introduced into a culture far different from his own, we use the term "cultural shock." The outsider cannot understand the language, enjoy the food, accept the values, practice the religion, or understand the actions of its members.

Extrapolating to an organization, a similar situation exists, and each potential manager, supervisor, or worker needs to be able to dissect the culture of the organization with which he or she will be associated and to determine if compatability exists between the corporate culture and personal needs.

When a company is first organized, the culture is often nothing more than a mirror image of its founder. Since "he's the boss," his values prevail. Others hired generally attempt to emulate the boss (often to a disgusting extent), and only after there is growth, differing levels of authority, new locations, and so on, do any great changes take place. Even then when culture is talked about, it is often necessary to return to the founder to find out what he or she was like and did in order to determine why something is done in a certain manner today.

In cultural analysis then, we must look for the signals that indicate the company culture and character and then use these to develop a pattern that guides our actions. For example, if one enters an elevator in a building, one is expected to behave in a certain way. If the person enters a car, a train, or an airplane, he might behave quite differently in each situation. So it is with a culture; we must know it in order to know how we are expected to behave in all its situations.

Look at some of the signals—the design used for the building, the materials from which it is made, where it is located—these all indicate the emphasis a company places on prestige, status, rank, and so on. Is the design traditional? Is the type of construction expensive? Does the building blend gracefully with its surroundings? All these concerns indicate some of what the organization is attempting to portray.

What about the name, the logo? What do these suggest? Are we faced with tradition here or is it something new and innovative? How about the people who work there? Where do they come from? How are newcomers greeted? Who gets the greatest rewards? Who has the largest office or the nearest parking space? What is the turnover?

What does the company say about itself? What kind of publications does it produce? What quality of paper does the company use? Is the publication believable? What items does it stress—profits, personnel, customers?

What type of organization does the company have? Is it flat or bureaucratic? What are its goals? Who makes the decisions? What kind of communication exists? What types of facilities are provided for employees? What kind of price structure is evident? Who are the major customers? Questions like these can go on indefinitely exploring a company's culture.

It should be evident that from these types of signals it is possible to learn a lot about a company. Supplemented by financial reports, brochures, newspaper articles, and personal observations, a person can determine what the company culture might be and what the overriding concerns are. Is it profits, the bottom line, creativity, the work ethic, paternalistic management, customer satisfaction, worker equity, glitz, "bull," or "fluff"? What the company says is not always what it is, and to be an effective supervisor or manager within a particular company, it's important to know the "real" culture.

3 *Personnel Management*

Objective: To consider the elements involved in personnel management within the food service organization. This chapter surveys planning, hiring, training, and evaluation. The uses of discipline and wages are discussed as are the functions, tools, and styles of supervision.

Manpower Planning

Before anything can be accomplished in a food service operation or specific tasks be completed with any degree of excellence, timeliness, and effectiveness, some attention must be given to the number of workers needed to staff the operation. Of course, this is necessary before completion of tasks is possible in any organization, be it manufacturing or service, but the nature of a typical food and beverage operation creates a personnel situation unique to this industry.

Because of the type of service provided in a food service operation, at least a skeletal staff is always required regardless of the volume of sales or the hours of operation. As long as a food and beverage establishment is open, a staff sufficient in number and in the skills necessary to provide the offered service must be available. Both front and back of the house personnel must be on hand to cover every aspect of the operation, from seating the guest through cooking and serving the meal and on to the collection of the money.

Of course, some of these tasks and procedures can be combined; in slack periods, a waitress may also act as hostess, or she may mix a drink at a service bar. Yet despite this possibility, the fact remains that as long as the doors of the establishment are open, there must be a minimum of personnel and talent available to meet consumer needs.

Attempts have been made to alter this basic requirement by building changes into the system. Procedures such as reducing the scope of the menu or changing the preparation method of particular foods have made it possible to staff an establishment during operating hours with individuals who are not highly trained or talented. Foods purchased in ready-to-use form, with only the final tempering and portioning required, or the use of standard labor time, where the food is cooked by more technically competent people and then chilled or frozen and stored for use at a later time, have both been used. These procedures enable an establishment to stay open at less busy times by using less skilled personnel to deliver a menu product that is comparable to that provided when the more highly skilled staff is on hand.

Design changes in the layout of the establishment to combine production services or communication centers in order to make it easier for minimal staff to carry out multiple functions have also been used. Sometimes even consumers have been "designed" into a system and "required" to carry and bus their own trays in a cafeteria design or to ladle their own soup and make their own salad—all to achieve staff reduction (although the marketing for these procedures has convinced consumers these are added attractions for their benefit).

Combinations

Combinations of a change in menu as well as design changes in both layout and equipment have also been used in manpower planning, especially in the fast food segment of the industry. Here limited preportioned, premeasured, listed menu items are coupled with specifically designed equipment, timers, and built-in customer assistance to provide an acceptable product with a minimum of labor expense.

Staffing Table

Regardless of the philosophy adopted or the type of staffing alternative used, the basic component of providing manpower for any food or beverage operation is the staffing table. Of course, much of the critical detailed work required to compile the staffing table will be performed by personnel specialists. However, line supervisors should be familiar with the basic requirements because personnel matters are the primary concern of the line supervisor in each department of the operating establishment.

Tasks and Productivity. Tasks serve as the basic element in any staffing table. Every goal of the establishment must be identified, and the tasks required to accomplish those goals have to be determined. This is the way to start constructing a staffing table. Once the tasks have been identified and matched up with the personnel necessary to accomplish them, the list can then be refined into productivity categories so that a proper staffing table can be made up. For example, it may initially be determined that guests will be served prepared food in a table service system by a waitress who can also provide wine service, mix a limited range of cocktails, and operate the cash register. It must then be decided how many guests this waitress can serve per hour under the following conditions:

(a) Serving table alone

(b) Serving table with wine service

(c) Serving table with wine service and mixing drinks

(d) Serving table with wine service and handling guest seating

(e) Handling guest seating and using cash register

It should be obvious that a waitress handling duties as outlined in (a) above would be able to accommodate many more guests than she would under the conditions of (e) or even (c). But many establishments give little attention to tasks and operate staff on a simple time and customer count alone—a process that is completely wrong. At some point, with the increase of customers and the proportional increase in tasks, additional qualified personnel must be added to the staffing table.

Part Time versus Full Time. The use of full-time personnel should of course be the cornerstone of the well-run food or beverage operation. Well learned and mastered procedures as well as strong positive attitudinal relationships between employees, employers, and organizations can do much to make an operation a financial and gastronomic success. But in the interest of financial control, it has also been standard policy to use procedures such as a split shift or part-time workers to augment and/or replace permanent full-time workers.

The split shift, which requires a regular employee to work a breakfast meal period, punch out for a period of time due to a slacking off of business, then return for a heavy lunch period has, I believe, little place in our manpower planning. A much better arrangement to handle the peaks and valleys of business would be to use part-time workers with overlapping scheduled periods at peak sales times or else to redesign processes or menu forms in order to assist in handling peak periods.

A complete inventory of ready-to-serve foods prepared by a cook on a regularly scheduled workday of 7 A.M. to 3 P.M. or the use of part-time workers, who may only work from 11 A.M. to 2 P.M. on X number of days per week, are much more effective means of handling manpower planning than the process of overburdening regular workers with additional duties they are unable to perform adequately or use of the split shift, which requires them to waste time until the next shift period is due.

Hiring Process

Once it has been determined what the hours of work are, how many workers will be required, and what their qualifications will be, the next thing is to decide where the workers will be found. The personnel departments of large operations will of course be extremely helpful in location, prescreening, and providing specialized services in the selection process, but the main responsibility for hiring needed personnel belongs to the line supervisor.

Personnel sources are many and varied with unions, schools, friends, employment agencies, and advertising media among the most commonly used. In some heavily unionized cities, it is not possible to hire an employee without reference to the union representatives, while in other cities that have a less formal unionized structure, any source may be used.

Although good workers can come from many sources, it seems that for a particular operation in a specific location some services turn out to be better than others. Witness the attention that some colleges or universities receive from industry recruiters as they attempt to fill their management ranks. Harvard Business School graduates often receive considerably more attention than do the graduates of a less prestigious institution. The same process often holds true for the supervisory review of workers, with some attention given to where current workers come from, as well as how they are doing in their assigned duties.

The government has barred the use of some questions on application forms so that such factors as race, religion, national origin, and so on may not be used to discriminate against applicants. This is in essence good for the supervisor because he or she should only be involved in matching task requirements with an individual's ability to meet them and should not permit those extraneous elements to influence a personnel decision.

Application forms do contain many important questions, however, and valuable inferences can be made by the supervisor from the applicant's answers. Such information as places worked, duties handled, salary level, training received, and languages spoken can be significant in matching candidates to tasks.

It is important to note here that a far-reaching immigration bill prohibiting the hiring of illegal aliens, while offering residency to aliens already domiciled in the United States, was passed in October 1986. Employees are now required to maintain records (I-9 forms) showing that they have verified each applicant's employment eligibility by proper means that may include a passport, a birth certificate, and so on. The failure to maintain adequate records or the act of hiring non-documented "illegal" aliens can result in heavy fines—$100 to $1,000 for lack of the proper paperwork, and $250 to $2,000 for each "illegal" hired (first offense) up to $3,000 to $10,000 and six months in jail for subsequent offenses.

Interviews and Testing. If an applicant is generally qualified for the position under consideration and worthy of additional consideration, the next and final step in the selection process is interviewing and testing. Interviews permit supervisors to observe, question, and judge attitudes, qualifications, and conditions that are not readily discernible through application forms or other printed media.

When used to give the applicant information about the job or the company or to answer specific questions, the interview procedure also permits supervisors to gain additional insight into areas covered but not fully explained in the application form. If need be the interview can be used to place the applicant under stress in order to see how he or she might react to a customer complaint or criticism; it might also be used to look for any personal mannerisms that might disturb a guest or contribute to a guest's displeasure.

The polygraph examination or the psychological stress evaluator or indicator has often been used during this period to determine if the prospective employee is trustworthy, is telling the truth, and is to be trusted with handling money and other valuables. At this writing, however, many states have passed legislation to prohibit the use of these devices, and the U.S. Congress is currently considering legislation that may outlaw these procedures since many consider them to be both unreliable and an invasion of privacy.

Testing can be used as part of the internal process or as an adjunct to it to determine an applicant's qualifications in a particular area of the operation. That way, supervisors in each area would be able to judge the ability of a potential worker to open a bottle of wine, type a letter, or operate a particular piece of equipment.

The physical examination is another form of test that has been used for many years to determine whether a prospective employee is physically able to accomplish the work. In the field of food service, where transmission of communicable disease is such a serious issue, detecting a transmittable disease has been an important part of this test. In many states, specific tests for food handlers are required on a regular basis after hiring as well.

A new condition has appeared recently, however, and in these days of constant litigation, problems have come up in both the preemployment physical and the discharge "for cause" of certain employees as related to their physical condition. One of the major public health concerns of the last thousand years has been plagues in general. In particular, the appearance of AIDS (acquired immune deficiency syndrome), a viral-type disease first diagnosed in 1981, has alarmed the population. Though originally more common in homosexual males and drug addicts who use contaminated needles, AIDS is quickly spreading to the general population. The prognosis is very poor since a diagnosis of AIDS means death at this point.

So intense has been the fear of this disease and so concerned are people about contracting it, that hysterical behavior by some members of society has caused an unnecessary panic. Although the consensus among medical practitioners is that AIDS can be transmitted only through sexual contact or exposure to infected blood, many companies have instituted procedures to pretest job applicants for the virus or to discharge those who have been identified as being carriers of the virus. Although this may appear to be a prudent course of action to take in the field of food service management, it seems to have presented legal problems.

Legal research has shown that since AIDS is transmittable only through sexual or hematological means and since infected persons can be considered as handicapped, there are impediments to discharging employees with the AIDS virus. For example, the Rehabilitation Act of 1973 would prohibit any action against employees with AIDS (if they are able to do the job) if the organization is receiving any federal funding. The same law would also prevent management from refusing to hire or from firing such an individual based on the illness or virus itself. Since the disease has been found to be not transmittable except as noted, it would not be communicable in the general methods related to food service. Second, many states have passed specific legislation preventing discrimination against the handicapped in hiring or firing, and people with AIDS or the AIDS virus apparently fall into this category.

At this writing, the AIDS issue appears to be a major problem for the food service manager who must, in many cases, hire a person who might be infected with this virus or this disease and must then educate fellow workers with the information that they will not be unduly exposed to infection. What if this employee cut his finger or had an open cut and was handling salad or some other food not to be later cooked?

Realistically, of course, it would be better to find other reasons not to hire a worker with this affliction (if it were known prior to employment) and to be supportive to anyone found to have developed the disease, while keeping the information low key from fellow employees and customers.

In view of recent Supreme Court rulings (see U.S. Supreme Court 85–1277), it appears that even though a contagious disease is present, there may not be summary dismissal, and that there must be probable cause for any testing of present employees because of employees' rights.*

At this time it seems inconceivable that any restaurant would want to publicize the fact that, "We have an AIDS person working in our kitchen, but medical research has shown he is not able to infect anyone." This would end the restaurant's operation.

As with many other questions one needs to take a long reflective look at this problem. Many more clear minds than present legal experts need to address this problem. Maybe the near future will present a cure, but currently the management of a food service establishment appears to be on the horns of a dilemma if a person with AIDS applies for a job or if a current employee develops it.

When all the information of a preselection process is put together, the supervisor working independently or with the personnel department of a large operation may either approve the applicant or find the applicant unfit for the open position. Remember, it is within the power of the supervisor to refuse to hire any applicant for any reason so long as that reason is not forbidden by law in areas such as discrimination based on sex, age, religion, race, and national origin.

*There may, however, be an opportunity to use the customer preference defense, which generally states that "although I am not taking the action, the customer would not patronize such an establishment with such an opportunity to be exposed to this disease, and therefore I must not employ such individuals." An attorney, of course, should be consulted to explore all options.

Orientation

Once the applicant has been accepted and a decision made to employ that person in the establishment, there must be some process of orienting the individual to the organization. This function, as well as most other functions required in the employee-organization relationship, rests with the line supervisor in charge of a particular segment of the operation.

General Orientation. Although in larger organizations the personnel departments are available to assist in a general orientation to the company, and in the small organization the owner or manager may be able to provide a similar service, most of the orientation is the direct supervisor's function. The particular function and goals of that section or department and how these relate to the overall goals of the organization must be stressed to the new employee.

Questions about pay, promotion, and benefits must be answered, and information in general areas must be provided. The new worker should be made to feel comfortable in the surroundings of the organization which has now become his or her working home. Disciplinary rules, procedural policy, and management philosophy must also be presented so that a proper orientation to the more specific requirements of the department can take place.

Task Orientation. Along with the general orientation, the supervisor must undertake a more detailed exposure to the tasks, duties, and requirements of that particular department, section, or job. This permits no opportunity for a fellow worker to teach the new employee in areas he is not sure of himself, and so there is no chance for the blind to lead the blind. If proper and effective performance is to be received, the supervisor must see that the new worker starts off knowing the job expected and that all of her or his questions are resolved. The employee must know what is

Table 3-1. Employee Traits

Attribute	All Companies: Total Points	All Companies: Average Rating	By Industry Segments: Lodging	Restaurants: Table Service	Restaurants: Fast Food	Institutional	Other*
Work Experience	914.0	17.6	20.4	16.4	18.6	17.9	13.4
Verbal Skills	693.0	13.3	12.8	13.4	12.7	12.1	12.9
High Level of Ambition	658.0	12.7	10.8	11.4	19.3	15.0	11.1
Preparedness & Enthusiasm in their Company	569.0	10.9	12.1	10.0	8.1	12.1	11.0
Personal Manner	542.0	10.4	10.1	10.6	9.7	10.0	11.5
Grooming & Appearance	538.0	10.3	12.5	11.4	5.4	9.7	9.8
Supervisory Experience	530.0	10.2	7.6	12.5	17.1	6.4	10.8
University/HRI Extra Curricular Activities	391.5	7.7	6.7	8.4	4.7	8.6	12.5
Grade Point Average	364.5	7.0	5.9	5.9	4.6	8.1	10.3
TOTALS		99.9**	99.9**	100.0	100.2**	99.9**	103.3**

*Includes: Airline, Cafeteria, Consulting Firms, Contract Food Service, Food Sales, Retail Department Store
**Does not equal 100 due to rounding

Recruiters were also asked to rate the following questions on a scale of 1-10 (1 = low; 10 = high):

	High Importance (8-10)	Medium Importance (4-7)	Low Importance (1-3)	Average Rating
How important is a faculty member's recommendation in selecting a new hire?*	51%	45%	4%	8.2
How important is the HRI degree compared to another college program degree?**	72%	26%	2%	7.9%

*49 respondents **50 respondents

What recruiters at schools of hospitality management look for in students (Source: *Career Paths*, Jan. 1986, p. 17, published by *Nation's Restaurant News*).

to be done, why it is done, when it should be done, how it is done, and what relationship that task has to the overall integrated functions of the other sections and the entire establishment.

Training. As part of this orientation process and occurring either before, during, or after the general and specific orientation procedures have taken place is the possibility of specific training. Training permits an individual to do something which she or he could not do previously, or it permits the individual to accomplish tasks more efficiently than before the training was instituted. Training may be an ongoing part of any operation.

Of course, if we are able to hire an individual for a particular job and the individual possesses all the requisite qualifications to perform the tasks required, no training is necessary. But this is more often the exception than the rule. Even with very technical jobs, training is often required to orient the new worker to the process used in a particular establishment as well as to outline the specialized requirements imposed upon a general practice of the skill involved. For example, an engineering department worker would have to learn specific features of different models of equipment or a highly trained pastry chef must learn the specialties of the house.

Although teaching is a profession in itself with many individuals who spend their entire lives perfecting their practice, all supervisors have to spend some time in teaching others to accomplish required tasks. In the food and beverage operation, most of the teaching will take the form of skill training. There are four types of training processes generally available for use in any operation.

1. *Vestibule* is training that occurs before the worker starts the job. It usually takes

place in a classroom situation with mockups of work situations, laboratories, and so on.

2. *Apprenticeship* training is used to expose the student to all aspects of a particular skill so that by doing all tasks from the very menial to the most sophisticated, the apprentice can eventually progress to the status of journeyman.

3. *On-the-job* training is the form that will probably be most commonly used in the average food and beverage operation. It permits an inexperienced worker to accomplish the tasks in some form while still receiving some constructive guidance from someone with greater skills.

4. *Programmed* training is a self-controlled and administered program. The student receives immediate corrective action and reinforcement as he or she progresses through a series of steps at a self-imposed pace toward an operational goal.

Most food and beverage establishments use very little vestibule training. Some use apprenticeships at the level of cooks, bakers, and chefs, but most establishments use on-the-job training with some reinforcement provided by the programmed route as well.

Supervisors responsible for training can follow the procedures previously outlined but should also be guided by the following considerations:

(a) People learn at different rates.

(b) The learning of skills first results in a dramatic improvement, then a leveling off, and finally small increments of further improvement up to a maximum level.

(c) People learn best because they want to after having seen the reason for what they are learning. People can learn under negative pressures such as fear of punishment, but they never learn as well this way.

(d) The more of the senses used in the learning process and the more repetitive it is, the better the skills are learned.

(e) Learning must take place in manageable segments and be put to immediate use if possible.

Evaluation of Workers. Most organizations have some form of evaluation process to insure that workers are performing at desired levels, to inform the employees of their levels of competency within an organization, and often to meet the demands of unions, governmental agencies, courts, or else to justify actions taken vis-à-vis employees. We all evaluate people, conditions, or events even though the process may be completely informal, and so we all possess some ability to make evaluations. Many of us, however, evaluate from a purely subjective standpoint and only judge others as to how they relate to our own needs, goals, or aspirations. Supervisors in an operating establishment must be more objective in making evaluations and must be able to evaluate workers according to their effectiveness in meeting section, department, and finally organizational goals.

Given a fair and adequate evaluation process, we will have better workers who will know how they are doing. Furthermore, the organization will be able to compensate adequately those who are instrumental in achieving organizational goals while correcting or dismissing those who are not. Although supervisors are not generally charged with designing the evaluation methods used in a particular organization, most supervisors will be required to participate in evaluating their subordinates and in their turn will be evaluated by their own superiors.

Types of Evaluations. Most companies that use formal evaluation methods choose from a variety of approaches. The factor check list presents the evaluator with a series of statements that suggest either positive or negative aspects of work behavior. These statements have been assigned positive or negative numerical values and enable the evaluator to assign an employee a total grade and to compare that employee with others. Graphic ratings rather than numerical ratings can also be used with the statement form; they have a graduated degree range or a continuum of "always to never" or some series of comparative evaluation. As with the factor check list based upon qualities of predetermined value to the organization, an employee can receive a total grade with a graphic rating system as well.

A forced distribution evaluation system requires the supervisor to place each employee into some category of comparison such as top quarter or bottom half and so on. This avoids the numerical computations, but does require a more detailed comparison of employees within the same job classification.

Management by objective is a more personalized supervisor-employee form of evaluation in which employees select goals upon which the evaluation will be based in conjunction with their superiors. Success in achieving these goals becomes the basis for later evaluation.

Regardless of the form used, supervisors must be meticulous in maintaining their objectivity when completing the evaluation instrument. Diaries of employee activity kept since the last evaluation that list both positive and negative events will enable the supervisor to give a fair and effective evaluation. Any supervisor's desire to be a good guy or to please everyone by interpreting "halo items" (the use of "Sir" by the employee or an employee's good looks) as outstanding performance only makes evaluations a waste of everyone's time.

Form constraints and differing standards between supervisors in separate departments will greatly influence the fairness and effectiveness of the evaluation process. A concerted effort by each supervisor to properly consider each factor as objectively as possible and to be able to substantially support any rating given will tend to make the evaluation system more acceptable to both the employee and the company.

Although the word *discipline* is often considered a negative factor or punishment that is applied to an individual to correct negative behavior, it is in reality a positive behavioral pattern, a choice that comes from within an individual. Discipline is needed within an organization for it to function properly and maintain standards. These accepted standards permit each individual to count on certain conditions which in turn enable him to achieve what is expected of him. Given the norm required and the behavior expected, most individuals will try to perform at the required levels. There will be some, however, who need an externally imposed guideline or reminder. Some examples might be that "X" number of portions have to be prepared within a certain time period or employees are only permitted to be late once a month.

Though internal satisfactions and rewards usually motivate the required levels of behavior, negative punishment is sometimes needed for those who violate accepted levels of behavior. Supervisors are responsible for any discipline needed in their departments. It is much easier to maintain high operational performance when employees understand the reason for a rule and follow that rule without power or threats being imposed from outside that particular department.

In creating the rules for a department, it might be wise to remember that it took only ten commandments to establish a guide for all society to follow. Many organizations have far too many written and verbal rules, and as a result many are either forgotten or disobeyed. Rules that relate to discipline should be relevant, fair, clear, flexible, reasonable, important, necessary, and promulgated.

Employees should be expected to observe the rules without too much outside influence or pressure; but when necessary, violations of rules must be addressed in a fair, efficient, and expeditious manner. Supervisors should not make statements, take action, impose punishment, or otherwise act until a complete investigation of the circumstances has been made and all parties heard.

When this has been done, the course taken should result in corrective action vis-à-vis the violated rule as well as insure that a similar action will not occur again. The severity of the infraction, any extenuating circumstances involved, and the past record of the individual should all be considered. Due process for appeal or review of the imposed penalty should be available to the employee involved. The approach of using a more positive discipline where the worker is treated as being responsible for his own performance and made to think over his obligations and course of action has become very successful in achieving results. This strategy involves less need for punishment and generates less employee resentment. Punishment often results only in antagonism and resentment rather than in correcting the inappropriate behavior. With a more highly educated and more highly motivated work force, this is even more the case. Workers treated like adults will act like adults. This doesn't apply to *every* worker, of course, but most managers will be able to correct the problem without the need for discipline being *imposed* if they share "why we can't do something" or the reason for the implication of a rule violation. Some attempt should be made to ensure that offenses punished and unrepeated do not continue to plague the employee for his entire tenure with the organization or even beyond. This can be done by eliminating the misdeed from the records after a period of time. Most procedures include an understanding of infractions or offenses and punishments; and most hospitality organizations consider offenses against a guest or offenses involving fighting, drinking, or stealing to be the most serious and those subject to dismissal.

Wages

One of the most frequent topics discussed anywhere, particularly among the lower level operational workers in the hospitality industry, is the subject of wages. Wages are based upon an operational philosophy of what the organization has decided to pay its employees after considering such items as geographical location, the size and nature of the company, the time and type of work to be performed, and its value to the company. Wages are the management's payment given in exchange for workers' hours and efforts.

Wages can be given to employees at a certain rate per hour or in an incentive form at a rate that equates to particular levels of production. In the hospitality industry wages also come from the consumer in the form of the *tip* (to insure promptness) or from restaurant management in the form of a substitution for money wages such as free meals or meals at a reduced price.

The amount of money received in wages has a great influence on the overall life style of the individual, and, as a result, wages are of great concern to workers. Wages have been used to motivate workers with rewards for high performance or service, and they have also been used as negative motivators, such as when merit or promotional wages are withheld from an employee to indicate supervisor displeasure. One theorist on the subject whom I tend to agree with is Frederick Herzberg. He classifies wages as a hygienic factor only, which can cause worker dissatisfaction if too low but can never cause satisfaction.

The hospitality industry appears at the lower levels of wage income as far as most employees' salaries are concerned. This is despite the fact that some service personnel receive in tip income considerably more than many managers receive as salaried employees.

Often a wage policy will look good on a profit and loss statement and will be able to be translated into a low labor cost percentage, but the policy results in a higher labor turnover (and the net costs of this are not always reflected on the profit and loss statement in the cost of errors, training, hiring, procedures, lower productivity, etc.) This happens because the worker does not view the salary as equitable and either reduces output to compensate or leaves as soon as something more opportunistic appears. At $3.35 per hour and assuming a 50 percent productivity rate (not too unusual in the food service industry at the present time), the labor cost per hour for this employee is really $3.35 times 2, or $6.70 per hour, since he is *really* working only half the time. Does it not make more sense to sometimes pay a higher rate to fewer employees who are more highly motivated and who gain higher productivity rates and are likely to stay longer at the establishment they consider to be a good employer?

Food service management often use staff reductions, part-time workers, split shifts, and the like to control the labor-cost-percentage figure in a yo-yo form. The worker is treated as an expense rather than as an asset and not surprisingly usually acts accordingly. Really a shortsighted solution to a long-standing problem. Looking at the literature today compared to twenty-five or thirty years ago, one can see it is much the same. The industry has said things like, "If we raise the minimum wage, we'll go out of business because we'll have to pass the cost on in raising menu price." Of "if we raise the minimum wage, we'll have to fire some of the workers because they won't produce enough to merit that increase." In fact the industry is still strong despite many raises in the minimum wage. Moreover, it is possible to raise the wage without passing on the increase to the consumer if the worker becomes motivated to do the work (see below). Too many times, increases in productivity result only in bonuses for the managers and better looking labor costs percentages with no real benefits to the workers who actually increased the productivity. No wonder workers choose not to produce. Since service and labor-intensive activity make up the backbone of our industry despite convenience foods, new equipment, and part-time workers, we had better find a way of treating workers fairly. What we have been doing isn't working for us or them.

Table 3-2. Wages and Pricing

If a worker receives $2.00 per hour for 40 hours of work, he earns a total salary of $80.00 per week.

If he contributes during this time 200 units of work, his output per man hour is 5 (200 divided by 40).

The unit-labor cost under these circumstances is 40 cents (80 dollars divided by 200).

If the worker is able to increase his output 3 percent to 206 units within the same number of hours (200 times .03), the output per man hour now is 5.15 (206 divided by 40).

Thus it would be possible to raise the wages of this worker an additional 3 percent to 2.06 dollars per hour or a total weekly of 82.40 dollars without raising the prices charged to the consumer.

The labor cost remains the same .40 cents per unit (82.40 dollars divided by 206).

Note: The figures used in this example are only for illustrative purposes. The idea is to show that it is possible to sell an item at the same price even if the wages to the worker are increased to reward an increase in productivity. Of course, under normal circumstances both the worker and the company would benefit from any increase in productivity levels.

If fairness and equity are important in overall supervisory activity, they are particularly necessary in administering wage and salary programs in an organization. Five to ten cents an hour difference may not be considered of much importance to many managers and supervisors at the higher levels of income, but these amounts can seem very large to workers who are at minimum wage scale, and many workers change jobs and organizations within a geographical area because another establishment offers ten cents more per hour. Internal equity between levels of jobs, hours of work, degrees of responsibility, and so on must also be maintained, as well as fair wages, if supervisors are to avoid problems while they administer their departments and the monetary factors involved.

Supervisory Styles

Supervisors are the middle level between an organization's policy planners and the workers, and they serve to direct the employees toward specific goals so that the organization achieves its objectives. Responsible for all aspects of personnel direction, hospitality supervisors walk a narrow line in a variety of organizational environments while integrating policies and administering programs. Workers see the supervisors as representatives of management, and management regards the supervisors as spokespersons for these workers.

There are only two ways to have tasks accomplished in an organization and so achieve the organizational objectives and goals—either the workers accomplish the tasks or the supervisors and management do. The particular style of supervision practiced within an organization may vary from very autocratic, with little concern for the worker, to laissez faire, with a hands-off policy in which external forces—upper management, the consumer, other workers, and so on—are assumed to be operational.

Most studies have shown that in order to meet the organizational production goals, some attention has to be given in a humanistic manner to the feelings and needs of employees. A generally supportive posture and some participation by the workers in their own destinies, task assignments, and methods of reaching goals seem to bring about more positive tangible results than do orders dictated by an autocratic leader or policies and rewards offered by a benevolent paternalistic supervisor.

The beginning of the Industrial Revolution led to a scientific management approach in supervision which resulted in a division of labor and a detailed span of control. But the growth of unions, which appeared as a result of management and supervisory errors as well as improved communication and information, demonstrated the advantages of a more humanistic style of management.

Although some individuals and some cultures require the autocratic approach by a supervisor, most supervisors are able to achieve greater productivity, more employee satisfaction, and less necessity for disciplinary action with some style of participative management.

Unions began as social organizations. They have managed to become powerful because of management and supervisory policies that have violated the wants, needs, and goals of their workers. Writers who practice a style of crisis management as they suggest methods to thwart a union or to parry its thrusts would be better advised to suggest alternative and more enlightened methods of supervision that would make the union unnecessary to the average hospitality worker.

The relationship of the autonomy permitted to the worker to conduct his or her own affairs and to make decisions accordingly is inversely proportional to the amount of control exercised by the supervisor over the worker in these matters. This relationship also has a great influence on increased productivity realized.

Utilizing McGregor's Theory X and Y and Ouchi's Z, supervisors would be well advised to consider the needs of the workers totally involved in production and to compare these with possibilities for the workers to make suggestions from below instead of receiving orders and policies from the top down. The days of the autocratic chef are gone in most situations (though they linger in some European and Third World countries). He is no longer the sole authority on hiring, firing, menu construction, purchasing, pricing, and so on.

Projections for 1995 show the need for 126,000 cooks, 141,000 managers, 584,000 service personnel, 304,000 kitchen helpers, 116,000 bartenders, and so forth. We presently staff our food service operations with a work force made up of 60 percent in the sixteen-to-twenty-four-year age group. Forecasts state that this age group will be reduced by some 13 percent by 1995. In addition, new legislation will reduce the influx of illegal aliens into the United States and penalize establishments that employ undocumented workers (a practice many operators followed because it allowed them to hire and treat workers poorly, knowing that they would not complain and be exposed to deportation). As in the past, many operators see the need to employ more women, senior citizens, and the handicapped to make up for these shortfalls, but might it not be a better move to hire fewer of these "prime" workers in the youth group, pay them more, and thus get better allegiance and higher productivity?

After all, supervisors (and owners as well) are judged not so much on what they do but on what their subordinates do. Guests see a waiter or waitress much more than they will see the owner, supervisor, maitre d', or chef (even if the chef has been put into a display kitchen in the dining room, an old arrangement currently being practiced as a new trend). Do operators really want part-time workers who give part-time allegiance and part-time production, or do they want the worker to feel a part of the team and to be able to share in the benefits?

Tools

The function of the supervisor as she or he relates to subordinates and superiors is one of managing the following tools.

Motivation. This is not something that can be applied to the worker, rather it is something the worker already possesses. It is the desire or degree of movement to do something that will result in satisfying some want or need. It is the supervisor's job to present an environment in which this feeling can readily occur for the individual employee, so that as the worker progresses towards his or her goal, major objectives of the company are fulfilled as well. You really can't have the latter without consideration of the former.

Communication. The supervisor is also concerned with communicating ideas, changes, plans, policies, directions, and so on, not only to her or his subordinates but from them to her or his superiors. She or he also must maintain open lines of communication with fellow supervisors in other departments and sections so that a properly integrated and functioning system exists. The worker must feel that he is a valuable part of the organization, worthy of being informed as to the whys, hows, when, and so on, if organizational objectives are to be achieved. These objectives are, after all, only achieved through the workers.

In the absence of accurate information, workers tend to make up information that may be erroneous and may eventually cause problems for both the supervisors and the organization as a whole. In communication, a good adage to follow is "It's not what is that is important—it is what appears to be."

Attitude. A knowledge of worker attitudes toward the job and the causes of satisfaction and dissatisfaction are also important to supervisors as they attempt to channel worker efforts toward the successful operation of an organization. Workers who are dissatisfied with their jobs and have poor attitudes toward their work will—given the opportunity—try to avoid the unpleasant conditions, which in turn results in turnover rates that are excessive. Although some companies create turnover when workers cease to smile or to move smoothly, the expenses of high recruiting costs, training costs, breakage, customer dissatisfaction, and so on would suggest a more creative and economical approach. It would be well to check attitude concerns periodically, in order to prevent disruptive personnel situations before they start.

Concerns of the Future

Changes in systems design, new foods, new equipment, and the like will of course require differing trade-offs between personnel, money, materials, and time within organizations. However, those who project the future suggest that there will be larger and more efficient hospitality organizations requiring more and more skilled supervisors to meet the organizational objectives.

More technology and a greater upgrading of society in the form of education and personal aspirations will result in hospitality workers who are more sophisticated and more knowledgeable in their wants and desires. Better informed and better qualified supervisors will be needed to administer these workers.

A more affluent clientele with more leisure time will lead to expansion of the industry and result in more positions for supervisors in the food and beverage area. This expansion will in turn result in more technology to meet consumer demand, but the industry will remain service oriented with the personal delivery of services. Service in general will become an important segment of many industries, and workers displaced in one area by technology will gravitate toward service-centered activities and locations. Service means people, people mean production, and that means supervisors—qualified ones who can achieve both results for organizations and employee satisfaction.

Some new companies have appeared and offer to relieve food service operators of many of their personnel-related problems by providing employees on a contractual basis. These companies screen, test, and hire employees for a general personnel pool and then furnish them when and where needed to the smaller food service operations. These companies can better control the costs involved in administering personnel programs and are able to provide more personnel benefits such as medical insurance and retirement.

This appears to be a program similar to the "fee for service" concept that has been used for many years in such areas as window washing or restaurant plant and floristry maintenance. However, despite the advantages these companies offer, I would caution against replacing all food service employees with such an arrangement, except for those in the most elementary positions. It would, I feel, be incorrect to have employees give their allegiance to an outside personnel company and feel that they are only temporary employees of a particular food service operation.

4 *History, Composition, and Functions of Food*

Objective: To acquaint the student with the history of food and the various food families. Food classification according to chemical makeup is explained, and the nutritional value of foods and the psychological and sociological implications of food usage are explored.

What Is Food?

Food is as old as life itself. It is nature's way of maintaining the species and providing for a complete cycle in its "no waste" or "dust to dust" continuous chain. Food is used as fuel for the body (calories), as an agent for the repair of body tissue, and as a regulator of body functions.

Many common elements of chemical construction are found in the vegetable, animal, and mineral worlds, because nature has constructed a food chain from earth to plant, to animal, to man, and back to earth again. This cycle maintains all forms of life and recaptures expended materials.

Of greatest importance in this food chain is the nitrogen cycle. Nitrogen is a necessary element for the maintenance and repair of body tissue and is introduced into the body in the form of protein. In a never-ending cycle, nitrogen is liberated from the air by means of lightning and dropped on the soil in rain, or is deposited in the ground in the form of chemical fertilizers, or results from the decay of plant or animal tissue in the earth. It is then converted into plant protein. The plants are eaten by animals and/or human beings. Man gains further supplies of nitrogen in protein from the flesh of animals that he eats. The discharges of animals and people are returned to the soil, becoming a source of nitrogen again. And when people, animals, or plants die, soil bacteria convert their cells into nitrogen substances. These substances then find their way into the cycle once again.

The food man eats—the prime concern of this book—is produced by the earth in various forms of plant life and secured from lower forms of animal life of the air, sea, and land.

History of Food

Food history is congruent with the history of man. According to Judeo-Christian teaching, man was cast into his present fate, which requires a constant fight for survival, because of his interaction with a particular fruit that had been forbidden him.

From the earliest days of recorded history, man and lower animals have been concerned with the collection of food to survive. In prehistoric times, man apparently had to spend much of his time hunting, trapping, and fishing in order to meet his requirements for food. Many times he found it necessary to risk his life in his attempt to satisfy his appetite. Early man developed behavioral patterns paralleling the habits of lower animals. He hunted for food, ate great amounts, and then rested, allowing his body to digest. This cycle was repeated once the food was utilized as a fuel source for his body, and he became hungry again.

Individuals who were able to capture animals or uncover forms of plant life became stronger than those who were less fortunate in their food hunting experiences. Darwinian theory suggests that those successful in maintaining a proper intake of food survived, while those who, because of age, infirmity, or ineptness, were unable to gather food disappeared.

This basic biological function of man's relationship with food continued as more sophisticated forms of social behavior developed. Cultural evolution in the form of better weapons, early tools, and the discovery and use of fire changed the methods by which a particular animal, fish, or bird was subdued or prepared for eating, but basic appetites and fare remained quite constant. The discovery and development of agriculture—capturing seeds in the life cycles of fruits and vegetables, and planting, cultivating, and harvesting them—led to greater variety in the diet.

Through experience man found that certain food types were more important than others in his quest for survival. Many religious sects found it necessary to incorporate specific food controls into their religious laws to protect their communities from illness and death. Some foods still have religious taboos attached to them, probably because certain cultures experienced sanitation problems in using them.

Food forms have been used as currency and as evidence of wealth. The lack of food has caused great sociological upheavals, such as the mass emigration from Ireland to America resulting from the Irish potato famine. Nations have gone to war in attempts to feed their people. Food has influenced national boundaries such as the sea limits set by maritime countries to protect fishing rights.

Whatever the time, the place, or the culture food has been a ubiquitous human commodity. The bones left after man has devoured an animal and the utensils used to prepare his meals have often been the only evidence of ancient life styles that man has left. Barring ecological catastrophe, or complete chemical synthesis, food will continue to be an important indicator of man's life, while providing him with the means to exist, procreate, and enjoy.

Food Families

Foods used by man may be classified either generically or according to their main functioning units. I will consider them in both basic classifications:

(1) Family groups: meats, poultry, fish, vegetables, fruits, cereals, fats, spices and herbs, and beverages.

(2) Functioning units: proteins, carbohydrates, fats, sugars, vitamins, minerals, and additives.

Meat. Meat is defined as the flesh of an animal that lives on the land. It may be from the main body structure or from the organs or glands of the animal. It has been used as food by people in most parts of the world. The forms most often used are those of animals indigenous to an area that are easy to capture or domesticate and relatively free from disease. The most important food animals in the United States are cattle, hogs, and sheep—yielding beef, veal, pork, and lamb. (For further discussion of meat, see chapter 14.)

In each animal, individual cells join to form specialized tissues, organs, and systems. There are some variations even within a species, however, due to age, sex, and type and amount of activity.

The bones form the skeletal structure of the animal and protect such vital parts as the heart, lungs, and brain. They assist in the manufacture of certain elements (such as blood corpuscles) in the life support system.

Bones are composed primarily of calcium phosphate. The structure of the bone may indicate the animal's age. At tender years the bones remain unfused at certain points (such as the break joint of a young lamb) and are moist and somewhat pliable. As the animal matures they fuse, becoming hard and more brittle. This condition can be used to identify the type of meat when it is purchased. Aside from this use, bones have little importance in food preparation work, except for the extraction of gelatinous material from the marrow for stocks.

Another part of the animal is the connective tissue. This binds muscle to muscle or bone to bone, to give the animal mobility. A connective tissue that joins muscle to muscle is called a tendon, while that joining bone to bone is called a ligament. Connective tissue may also be found within a muscle where it holds individual groups of muscle fibers together.

Connective tissue is an important factor in food preparation. There are two main types: the white form, called *collagen,* may be softened by cooking; the yellow form, called *elastin,* remains unaffected by cooking.

Muscles are the most important food component of animals from a food standpoint. Muscle tissue is made up of fibers grouped into bundles called *fasciculi.* They are held together by coverings of connective tissue and are anchored to bones or other muscles.

Muscles are composed of the proteins *myosin* and *myogen.* They also have liberal amounts of *glycogen,* a form of carbohydrate. The muscle pigment *myoglobin* gives each species of animal flesh a characteristic color, although age, sex, and type of food influence the particular shade.

Each type of animal has a characteristic muscle configuration. The use of the muscle, the age of the animal, the type of feed eaten, and hereditary factors dictate the preparation methods for a particular cut of meat. Generally, high age and activity levels give muscle tissue greater taste and less tenderness. The amount of activity of a muscle may be considered inversely proportional to the tenderness. The less tender cuts are generally more flavorful than the more tender ones.

Meats are generally composed of water (47 to 73 percent), protein (12 to 20 percent), fat (5 to 30 percent), and traces of carbohydrate and ash.

Organs and glands are specialized types of tissue that perform specific biological functions in the animal. For example, the brain and heart control action, the lungs and liver purify blood, and the stomach aids in digestion. Many of these organs are eaten and provide particular tastes and variety to the diet. They are often rich sources of vitamins and minerals, notably vitamins A, B, and D, and iron. Muscle tissue, however, remains the most important part of the animal used as meat.

Poultry. Poultry may be defined as the flesh of birds—both wild and domesticated. The most important types used for food are chickens, turkeys, ducks, and geese.

Similar in structure to the land animals that provide flesh foods for man, all forms of poultry have the same muscle, bone, fat, and connective tissue configurations. Some of their organs, such as the liver and the gizzard, are also used for food.

The tissue found in poultry is usually less coarse than that found in other animals. Age, activity, and type of feed affect such factors as taste, tenderness, and method of cooking, as in other animals. The aerodynamic design of birds produces some major changes in bone formation, musculature, and bone density, which result in quite different flesh yields. The foods eaten by birds and their unique digestive processes also require some different organs and glands.

From a nutritional standpoint and for preparation purposes, poultry is akin to the other flesh-producing animals. It is also a complete protein and furnishes the same general nutrients as other types of meats.

A major food that is a by-product of poultry is the egg. Chicken eggs are most important in man's diet. Like their parents, eggs furnish water, protein, fat, and ash to the diet, with abundant amounts of vitamins A and D and iron.

Fish. Fish, the third major form of protein food used by man, is the flesh of vertebrate and invertebrate cold-blooded animals that live in salt or fresh water.

Similar in structure to the other classes of flesh foods, fish are made up of muscles, connective tissue, bones, and fat in various amounts depending upon the class. Generally their flesh is much more fragile than that of warm-blooded animals, and thus more prone to bruising. Spoilage occurs more readily unless the fish are kept at cool temperatures like those of the water where they were caught. Age, sex, and type of feed have less influence on the tissue structure and eventual use of fish.

The major difference between varieties of fish seems to be in their fat content. Fish that live in colder water generally have more fat and suggest different cooking methods than those from warmer areas. Also the type of muscle fiber found in vertebrate fish differs from that in shellfish.

No major form of organ or glandular food is provided by fish, except the roe of certain species. The coral roe of lobster and its liver are also eaten as delicacies.

Fish provide comparable nutrients to those of the other flesh foods. Some provide greater amounts of iron, and salt water varieties are an important source of iodine.

Vegetables and Fruits. Although somewhat different in their biological makeup and preparation, vegetables and fruits are so closely related in structure, use, and function that they can be included under one heading. They are the whole plants or parts of plants that are used as food, and they comprise one of the four basic classifications of foods deemed necessary for proper nutrition. A broad spectrum is available, varying with climate and geographical considerations.

Vegetables may be classified into families, such as legumes, mustards, and goosefoots, or by the part of the plant that is eaten, such as roots, bulbs, leaves, stems, flowers, fruits, seeds, and tubers. In each classification, a wide range of textures, tastes, colors, and nutrients is available.

Vegetables are relatively easy to grow and are available in some form all year. Most are priced quite reasonably compared to the flesh foods. As a result, they form the major part of the diet in many countries and cultures, and they are an important part of the quantity food service picture.

Vegetables and fruits are available in fresh, frozen, canned, and dehydrated forms. The specific amounts of their components differ somewhat according to the form. The major component is generally *cellulose.* Some forms of it may be eaten raw; some can be made edible by cooking; and others are removed before or after cooking as refuse. The cellulose is held together by a substance called *protopectin.* The tenderness, type of use, and cooking methods of fruits and vegetables depend on the basic form of the product and are closely related to its cellulose type and content. Older fruits and vegetables usually develop a more solid and unyielding form of cellulose.

Vegetables and fruits also contain varying amounts of carbohydrates, minerals, vitamins, and flavoring substances. The moisture (water) content varies from 70 to 90 percent.

Vegetables serve primarily as regulatory agents and sources of energy, moisture, and nutrients.

Cereals. Cereals are part of the vegetable kingdom and one of the major foodstuffs required for adequate nutrition. Cereals were among the first foods cultivated and used extensively by ancient civilizations. They remain an important part of the quantity food scene.

Cereals are basically the seeds of grain from families of grasses. They are utilized in the food chain both as feed for the lower animals that later become sources of protein for man and, in processed forms, as food for man himself. Among the more widely used cereals are wheat, corn, rice, oats, rye, and barley.

Grains are all similar in structure, composed of like molecular arrangements that vary depending on the type of grain and the part utilized. There are three main parts of cereal grains: (1) the outer coating, called *bran,* which is basically cellulose but rich in protein, (2) the central part, the *endosperm,* which contains most of the cereal's starch, and (3) the *germ,* which contains most of the fat, protein, and vitamins.

Cereals are a widely used food, valued for their supply of energy at low cost. They may be used as breakfast foods or processed into flours, breads, or a variety of other starch forms. They store easily and find wide application in all forms of food service work.

Specific milling procedures are used to process grains. Grains planted at certain times of the year or in particular sections of the country have peculiar characteristics that suggest special uses. (These are discussed in detail in chapters 16 and 17.)

Fats. Fats occur naturally in animals, between groups of muscle tissues, or surrounding vital organs. Animal fat is used to protect or cushion vital organs from external injury and to store reserve energy that accumulates when the animal eats more than his metabolic requirements. Fats are an important part of many vegetables and are extracted for use in food preparation. Fats are also found in the milk of animals and the eggs of birds. In eggs, fat is in the yolk, and in milk it is the cream.

Fats come in two main forms, solid and liquid, depending on the degree of saturation. Animal fats are generally highly saturated and stable, while vegetable fats tend to be liquid and basically unsaturated. See page 75.

Food processors combine fats to suit specific purposes. For example, a combination of animal fat, vegetable fat, and cream makes oleomargarine. (The word *oleo* is derived from *olein,* which is a basic fat found in beef.) They also combine fats with additional hydrogen, in the presence of nickel (which acts as a catalyst to the chemical reaction), to make hydrogenated fats. These are solid, more stable, and more plastic. They are used in baking and certain other forms of food preparation.

Fats give variety to the diet. They lengthen the period required for digestion and remain in the stomach longer than other foods, thus making the satisfaction of eating last longer. Fats also contribute to the satisfying taste of foods, and they tenderize foods such as meat when they melt during cooking.

Fats may be used as shortening agents in pies and cakes, tenderizing the gluten strands in the moistened flour and making it more palatable. They also serve as the cooking medium in procedures such as sautéing and deep frying.

Spices, Herbs, and Flavoring Agents. Originating in many different parts of the world, spices, herbs, and other flavoring agents are parts of plants, flowers, or complete agricultural products, used to add zest to a dish. Although they often were used in the past to mask a taste generated by spoilage or decay of a food, they are presently used (in most cases) to enhance the flavor of a culinary work or to give unusual stimulation to a traditional dish.

Spices are available in whole form (best used in long, slow cooking processes) and ground. Quality spices provide superior levels of flavor, color, and strength. Volatile flavor oils contribute specific aromas and flavors. Care must be taken to add these items at a time in the cooking process that will give the best results. Ground spices are added near the end of the cooking period, while whole spices are added early in the process.

Dehydrated spices, in the form of salts and flakes, and blends of spices that are routinely combined in certain dishes are also available. Some common blends are apple pie spice mix, poultry seasoning, and Mexican chili spices.

Beverages. Running the gamut from pure extracts of fruits or vegetables to synthetic drinks utilized to cool, refresh, or stimulate, beverages form an important part of the food picture.

The traditional coffee, tea, and milk, brewed from tropical beans or leaves or processed by the dairy industry, have been supplemented by nectars, punches, ades, and other drinks in an effort to provide variety, and zest to meals. Some beverages made with milk, such as malts, provide nourishment in the form of protein, fat, carbohydrate, vitamins, and minerals. Most other beverages, however, provide only traces of these substances. They do produce stimulation, primarily from the caffeine or closely related substance they contain. Some manufactured beverages have stimulants such as caffeine added, and some provide caloric "instant energy" in the form of simple sugars.

For further discussion of beverages, see chapter 12.

Classification by Chemical Composition

Almost all foods utilized by man contain a combination of nutrients. Certain foods, after long periods of satisfactory use, have become accepted as furnishing essential nutrients. Of course, it is now possible to analyze foods to determine the validity of this assumption. The food service manager needs to know the major nutrients that have been identified, that enable foods to be classified by chemical composition and function.

Protein. Proteins are the most important classification of foods. They are chemical compounds that contain carbon, hydrogen, oxygen, and nitrogen, plus lesser amounts of sulfur and phosphorus. Proteins aid in the growth and repair of body tissue. They may also be used for energy if other sources are not available, although this is an inefficient use of them, because they can perform more specialized functions that other energy sources cannot fulfill.

The major constituents of proteins are substances called amino acids. Some twenty amino acids have been identified, and eight of them are known to be essential to normal tissue growth and maintenance. Foods that provide all eight amino acids are said to contain complete proteins; the foods in this category are meat, fish, poultry, eggs, milk, and cheese. Other foods rich in protein, although lacking some amino acids, are cereals, gelatin, nuts, and some beans. Since these foods furnish proteins that are insufficient alone to build or repair tissue, they are said to contain incomplete proteins.

During the digestion of protein substances, the body absorbs the amino acids for use in its major functions. The main chemical structure of the protein molecule is called the peptide linkage. This linkage is broken during digestion and the amino acids are liberated. Although both complete and incomplete proteins are eaten, once the amino acids are freed the body selects and uses the ones it needs in particular cells for specific purposes.

If more proteins are absorbed than are required by body tissues, they may be used as sources of energy and consumed as calories. (A Calorie or large calorie [Cal] in food technology is the amount of heat that will raise the temperature of one kilogram of water one degree centigrade. A small calorie [cal], used in other disciplines, is the heat applied to a gram of water to raise it one degree.) Proteins furnish four Calories per gram. They may also be converted into a substance closely resembling carbohydrate or fat in chemical composition and be stored for later energy use, or they may be discharged from the body in urine.

Carbohydrates (Starches and Sugars). Carbohydrates are chemical compounds of carbon, hydrogen, and oxygen. They are contained primarily in starchy or sugary foods, but are found in lesser amounts in almost every food.

The carbohydrate group includes all sugars, starches, and cellulose-type foods. The major difference between the three is in the number of monosaccharides ($C_6H_{12}O_6$) they contain.

The basic forms of carbohydrates are manufactured by plants in the chloroplasts of the leaves by a process known as photosynthesis. Carbon dioxide in the air, in the presence of the chlorophyll of the plant, produces forms of glucose by the following reaction:

$$6\,CO_2 + 6\,H_2O \xrightarrow[\text{chlorophyll}]{\text{light}} 6(CH_2O) + 6\,O_2$$

The $6(CH_2O)$ is best expressed as the classical $C_6H_{12}O_6$

Carbohydrates are classified as *monosaccharides,* or simple sugars, when they contain one basic sugar unit ($C_6H_{12}O_6$); as *disaccharides* when they contain two; and as *polysaccharides* when they contain many. Only monosaccharides can be used by the body, and all other carbohydrates are broken down to this form before use. Examples of monosaccharides are glucose ($C_6H_{12}O_6$) and fructose ($C_6H_{12}O_6$). Some disaccharides are sucrose ($C_{12}H_{22}O_{11}$), lactose ($C_{12}H_{22}O_{11}$), and maltose ($C_{12}H_{22}O_{11}$). A polysaccharide is starch [$(C_6H_{10}O_5)_x$].

Sugars are carbohydrates with chains of twenty-four or fewer carbon atoms. Those with greater amounts of carbon are called dextrins or starches.

Carbohydrates are chiefly used as sources of energy, furnishing four Calories per gram.

Fats. Fats are both a generic classification of foods and a classification by chemical composition. Chemically they are glycerol esters of fatty acids or triglycerides. This means that they are substances formed by the combination of one part glycerine and three parts fatty acids, and they contain carbon, hydrogen, and oxygen.

Fats are found in both animal and vegetable forms. They are either solid or liquid, according to the degree of saturation of the carbon molecules, and provide the body with nine Calories per gram.

Fats are chemical compounds based on chains of carbon atoms in lengths from two to twenty-four. These carbon atoms are chemically joined either by sharing their valence electrons with other atoms of the molecule and thereby achieving a steady state or saturated condition, or by a double bond from one carbon atom to another, thereby achieving a more unstable or unsaturated condition.

Fats that have many double bonds are unsaturated, are usually liquid, and require protection against oxidation and rancidity during storage. Saturated fats do not usually require this protection.

In the hydrogenation process, the carbon bond is broken so that each carbon atom can accept the single valence electron of a hydrogen atom. This changes the fat into a saturated one and permits it to become more solid and plastic.

Emulsifiers are often added to hydrogenated fats that are used as shortening agents in cakes or sweet doughs. An emulsifier incorporates air into the fat.

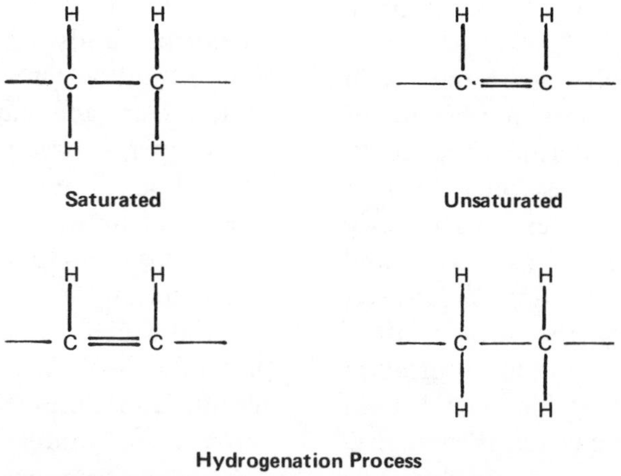

Saturated **Unsaturated**

Hydrogenation Process

Figure 4a. Saturated and unsaturated fat molecules illustrating the double bond. In the hydrogenation process, the carbon bond is split and each carbon atom accepts one additional hydrogen atom.

The melting point and smoking temperature of a fat also depend on its degree of saturation and the length of its carbon chains. The more unsaturated a fat, the lower the smoking temperature. The longer the carbon chain, the higher the melting point.

The body appears to need three essential fatty acids that it is not able to manufacture from other substances. Some authorities have identified these as *linoleic, linolenic,* and *arachidonic.* Others question the latter as essential and claim it may be manufactured within the body. In any event, a normal diet that includes vegetable fats generally contains sufficient amounts of all three to satisfy the body requirements.

Vitamins. Certain substances inherent in food are important in the regulation of body functions and the maintenance of its physical condition. Vitamins are one group of these substances.

A vitamin is an organic compound important or essential in some life process. It may be provided by a food or produced within the body from a food. The most important vitamins are discussed below.

Vitamin A is a substance necessary for normal night vision, growth, and resistance to airborne infections. It is found in yellow-colored vegetables, in animal products with a yellow cast and a fat base (such as butter, cream, and egg yolk), and in many green vegetables.

Vitamin B is a complex substance with many components, the most important of which are thiamine, niacin (nicotinic acid), and riboflavin. This vitamin is found in both animal and vegetable sources, particularly milk, lean meat, whole grains, liver, and greens. The lack of B vitamins generally results in a breakdown of the use of other foodstuffs by the body. This may result in diseases such as beriberi and pellagra or in symptoms such as digestive upset, mental anxiety, and skin problems.

Vitamin C is a substance generally found in citrus and other fruits and in green vegetables. It is an important element in the prevention of infection, and some recent research has related it to the prevention and treatment of common colds. A lack of this vitamin results in lowered resistance to infections and problems with teeth, bones, and gums.

Vitamin D is a substance required for development and maintenance of sound bones and teeth. Insufficient supplies of this vitamin may result in a bone malformation condition called rickets. The body gains most of its vitamin D from sunshine (where available), but significant amounts are also found in fish oils, such as cod liver oil, and in egg yolks. Irradiated vitamin D is added to most forms of whole milk.

Vitamin E is a substance found in certain oils and cereal grains. It has recently been promoted as a deterrent to heart attacks and as a necessary component for a normal sex life. It does appear to have antisterility properties and to aid in regulating metabolism. In foods it acts as an antioxidant.

Vitamin K is a substance that assists the coagulation of blood. It is available in liberal amounts in leafy green vegetables and eggs.

Other vitamin substances have been identified (e.g., folic acid, biotin, pantothenic acid, and pyridoxine, among others of the B group), but the above are the most important for food service managers to consider.

Minerals. A mineral is a basic element furnished by food that has been found essential to normal body functions. Minerals are present in the body in small amounts. They aid in building an adequate skeletal framework, in the proper functioning of the blood, and in other body life support systems. The most important minerals are discussed below.

Calcium and *phosphorus* are used in the construction of bones and teeth. They also assist the mechanism of blood clotting. *Copper* and *iron* are needed for the hemoglobin of blood, and *iodine* is used in thyroid gland functions. *Sodium* assists in maintaining the electrolyte balance of body fluids. The body also contains trace amounts of such minerals as *cobalt, fluoride,* and *sulfur,* all of which perform certain body functions.

A properly balanced diet, selected from the four basic groups pictured in figure 4b, is believed to provide the minerals to maintain adequate levels in the body. Specific foods or dietary supplements may be used at times to ensure adequate ingestion of a particular mineral, required, for example, by nursing mothers, young children, or people with special problems.

Additives. A plethora of substances have been added to foods in varying amounts to provide adequate amounts of particular nutrients to a cross section of consumers. Examples are the enrichment of white flour, the irradiation of whole milk with vitamin D, and the iodizing of salt. Other substances, such as calcium propionate, are added to improve the keeping quality or shelf life of products by reducing oxidation and retarding spoilage. Still other additives are used to increase taste sensitivity and thereby enhance the attractiveness of a food product. Such a substance is monosodium glutamate, which stimulates the taste buds.

All substances added to foods must be approved by the United States Food and Drug Administration. If classed as GRAS ("generally regarded as safe") or as previously approved, these substances may be used as antimicrobial agents, antioxidants, agents to change or improve the color, flavor, or texture of foods, or agents to preserve, stabilize, or bleach foods.

The GRAS substances, having been used for many years with no apparent injurious effects, were not examined closely until recently. Prior to 1958, and before passage of an amendment to the Pure Food, Drug, and Cosmetic Act, the burden of proof that the use of an additive posed a danger was on the government. The burden now has been placed on those wishing to add a substance to prove its safety. Even the GRAS items are being reexamined, and some have been removed from the approved list in view of new evidence. Notable among these is the purple dye that was used for years to mark meat products approved by federal inspectors. Other types of dyes in orange, red, and brown hues are now being used for this purpose.

Although the safety of some long-used additives has been questioned, many experts suggest that the majority remain safe at the level of intended usage; evidence that questions the safety of these substances arises only in tests at consumption levels far above normal.

Recent interest has focused on the use of additives to make meat products more tender. Proteases of bromelain and papain (enzymes from pineapple and papaya) have been injected into animals ready for slaughter. The enzyme then circulates through the bloodstream of the animal and is dispersed throughout the meat. After slaughter, it assists in tenderizing the tissue. Enzyme tenderizers may also be applied locally at the time of preparation, but the injected tenderizers appear to give better results.

Other additives are using during preparation. Polyphosphates are added to meats that have been cooked and refrigerated, to prevent the development of a warmed-over flavor upon reheating. Textured vegetable proteins that have been made to resemble bacon, sausage, turkey, and the like are also used.

Another element that is not strictly an additive but is of concern is the amount and type of drugs given to animals during raising that remain in the meat when eaten by consumers. About four out of every five animals are given drugs for growth development or to cure or prevent disease. Because some drug residues can remain after slaughter, there has been the danger of allergy problems or, in extreme cases, of anaphylactic shock in consumers. A good example is the growth stimulant DES (diethylstibestrol), previously used in beef animals and found to be detrimental to humans; it was banned by the Food and Drug Administration (FDA) in 1979. The two most widely used drugs in animals are penicillin and tetracycline. These continue to be used even though the FDA petitioned the Secretary of Health and Human Services in 1985 to discontinue their use in animals. The request was denied.

The FDA banned sulfites in August 1986 on all raw fruit and vegetables (except potatoes), and effective January 1987, sulfite labeling was required on all packaged foods with concentrations over 10 parts per million.

Biological Implications of Food

In any consideration of food it is imperative to discuss the nutritional aspects and food's relationship to the proper functioning of the human body. The public's great concern today with such matters as caloric control and regulation of food additives gives these subjects even greater importance.

Of course, the manager of an institution or other facility in which the consumers are a captive group and depend on the foods offered as their only source of nourishment will be more concerned with furnishing an adequate and nutritious diet to his guests than a restaurant or transportation facility manager.

To help determine an adequate diet, the United States Public Health Service, the Council on Foods of the American Medical Association, the American Institute of Baking, and others in the quantity food service industry have constructed and promulgated guidelines, listing the major nutritional elements and suggested food groups that will provide adequate nourishment.

One of the earliest of these was the *basic seven wheel,* which suggested seven classifications of foods that give a balanced diet and provide all the essential nutrients: (1) butter and fortified margarine with added vitamin A; (2) green and yellow vegetables; (3) oranges, tomatoes, and grapefruit; (4) potatoes and other vegetables and fruits; (5) milk and milk products; (6) meat, poultry, fish, and eggs; and (7) bread, flour, and cereals. The number of servings of each class that were necessary to meet the daily nutritional requirements was suggested, and adjustments were made for the particular requirements of children, adults, and expectant or nursing mothers.

A more recent revision of this basic list, and the form generally used now, was suggested by the United States Department of Agriculture. This listing consists of four basic food groups and includes all other foods in a fifth category. The groups are displayed in figure 4b.

Coupling this list with the recommended daily dietary allowances suggested by such organizations as the National Academy of Sciences (see table 4-1) a food service supervisor should be able to construct a menu and provide food offerings that will meet the nutritional requirements of his specific consumer group.

Calories appear to be one of the most important factors and of great concern to many consumers. The need for calories, an energy source available in food, varies with the individual's age, sex, body structure, and degree of physical activity. All calories consumed above the basal metabolism rate (the rate at which calories are used up simply to maintain the body at rest) must be expended in activity or they will be stored as fat for future use. A reduction in weight is realized when more calories are used by the body than are being supplied by current food intake. Unless the body is misfunctioning, the mechanics of weight control are as simple as that.

Caloric, vitamin, and mineral standards are the major guides used for general consumers. Particular adjustments may be necessary in hospitals or programs dealing with undernourished or infirm persons. In such cases, certain foods may have to be increased or avoided to meet specific needs of the consumers.

Food today serves man's basic biological functions even more efficiently than in the past. Scientific research has revealed new food components, particular needs for certain components, and methods of synthesizing substances to gain the desired nutritive results.

It is a prime concern of the food service manager to ensure that the foods produced in his establishment fulfill these basic biological requirements. Although the consumer does not always depend on a particular establishment to provide all the necessary nutritional

Eat Vital Foods Every Meal Every Day
a selected variety from each group

Group 1. Breads and Cereals

4 or more servings daily:

enriched, whole grain or restored breads and cereals; other baked foods made with enriched or whole grain flour; enriched macaroni, spaghetti, and noodles.

Group 2. Milk and Milk Products

children—3 to 4 cups; teenagers—4 or more cups; adults—2 or more cups:

to drink and in cooking; cheese and ice cream may replace part of the milk.

Group 3. Vegetables and Fruits

4 or more servings daily:

include a citrus fruit or tomato, a dark-green or yellow vegetable, and other vegetables and fruits, including potatoes.

Group 4. Meat Group

2 or more servings daily:

beef, veal, pork, lamb, fish, poultry, eggs; with dry beans, dry peas, nuts, and peanut butter as alternates and for variety.

Plus: other foods to complete meals and to provide additional food energy and other food values; and a regular program of activity, rest, and hygiene.

Figure 4b. The four basic food groups that must be included in each day's diet for adequate nutrition. (Adapted from *From Wheat to Flour,* p. 73; copyright 1965, Wheat Flour Institute, Chicago; reprinted by permission.)

Table 4-1. Recommended Daily Dietary Allowances[1]

							Fat-Soluble Vitamins			Water-Soluble Vitamins							Minerals					
	Age (years)	Weight (kg)	Weight (lb)	Height (cm)	Height (in)	Protein (g)	Vitamin A mg.	Vitamin D mg.	Vitamin E mg.	Vitamin C mg.	Thiamin mg.	Riboflavin mg.	Niacin mg. NE	Vitamin B_6 mg.	Folacin mg.	Vitamin B_{12} mg.	Calcium mg.	Phosphorus mg.	Magnesium mg.	Iron mg.	Zinc mg.	Iodine mg.
Infants	0.0-0.5	6	13	60	24	kg x 2.2	420	10	3	35	0.3	0.4	6	0.3	30	0.5[2]	360	240	50	10	3	40
	0.5-1.0	9	20	71	28	kg x 2.0	400	10	4	35	0.5	0.6	8	0.6	45	1.5	540	360	70	15	5	50
Children	1-3	13	29	90	35	23	400	10	5	45	0.7	0.8	9	0.9	100	2.0	800	800	150	15	10	70
	4-6	20	44	112	44	30	500	10	6	45	0.9	1.0	11	1.3	200	2.5	800	800	200	10	10	90
	7-10	28	62	132	52	34	700	10	7	45	1.2	1.4	16	1.6	300	3.0	800	800	250	10	10	120
Males	11-14	45	99	157	62	45	1000	10	8	50	1.4	1.6	18	1.8	400	3.0	1200	1200	350	18	15	150
	15-18	66	145	176	69	56	1000	10	10	60	1.4	1.7	18	2.0	400	3.0	1200	1200	400	18	15	150
	19-22	70	154	177	70	56	1000	7.5	10	60	1.5	1.7	19	2.2	400	3.0	800	800	350	10	15	150
	23-50	70	154	178	70	56	1000	5	10	60	1.4	1.6	18	2.2	400	3.0	800	800	350	10	15	150
	51+	70	154	178	70	56	1000	5	10	60	1.2	1.4	16	2.2	400	3.0	800	800	350	10	15	150
Females	11-14	46	101	157	62	46	800	10	8	50	1.1	1.3	15	1.8	400	3.0	1200	1200	300	18	15	150
	15-18	55	120	163	64	46	800	10	8	60	1.1	1.3	14	2.0	400	3.0	1200	1200	300	18	15	150
	19-22	55	120	163	64	44	800	7.5	8	60	1.1	1.3	14	2.0	400	3.0	800	800	300	18	15	150
	23-50	55	120	163	64	44	800	5	8	60	1.0	1.2	13	2.0	400	3.0	800	800	300	18	15	150
	51+	55	120	163	64	44	800	5	8	60	1.0	1.2	13	2.0	400	3.0	800	800	300	10	15	150
Pregnant						+30	+200	+5	+2	+20	+0.4	+0.3	+2	+0.6	+400	+1.0	+400	+400	+150	–[3]	+5	+25
Lactating						+20	+400	+5	+3	+40	+0.5	+0.5	+5	+0.5	+100	+1.0	+400	+400	+150	–[3]	+10	+50

From Food and Nutrition Board, National Academy of Sciences, National Research Council, *Recommended Dietary Allowances*, p. 43, Government Printing Office, Washington, D.C., 1980.

1. The allowances are intended to provide for individual variations among most normal persons as they live in the United States under usual environmental stresses. Diets should be based on a variety of common foods in order to provide other nutrients for which human requirements have been less well defined.

2. The recommended dietary allowance for vitamin B-12 in infants is based on average concentration of the vitamin in human milk. The allowances after weaning are based on energy intake (as recommended by the American Academy of Pediatrics) and consideration of other factors, such as intestinal absorption.

3. The increased requirement during pregnancy cannot be met by the iron content of habitual American diets nor by the existing iron stores of many women; therefore the use of 30-60 mg of supplemental iron is recommended. Iron needs during lactation are not substantially different from those of nonpregnant women, but continued supplementation of the mother for 2-3 months after parturition is advisable in order to replenish stores depleted by pregnancy.

factors in his diet, the reason man eats is to achieve this end. Despite the lack of a legal mandate requiring that food provide the maximum in nutritional benefits, it remains a social obligation of the manager to attempt to meet this requirement.

The Digestive Process

To gain the maximum benefit from the food he eats, man's body must act on it in a process called digestion. The food is introduced in the mouth. Through the action of the teeth, the tongue, and the palate, it is subdivided into minuscule pieces and constantly mixed with the salivary juices. This action prepares the food for swallowing, by lubricating it and reducing it to suitable size. Enzymes contained in the saliva change the chemical components of the food into simpler sugars that are more readily used by the body (e.g., the enzyme ptyalin changes starch into maltose).

The food is then passed through the esophagus and into the stomach. Contractions of this organ break it up into still smaller pieces, while it is mixed with gastric juices consisting of hydrochloric acid and enzymes (notably pepsin). These produce protein forms that can be readily used by the body. The mixing process continues until the food is reduced to a semiliquid form called chyme. This is passed through the pyloric opening (a muscular constrictor that keeps solid food in the stomach while it is being digested but allows liquid food to pass) into the small intestine.

The small intestine, a relatively narrow, tubelike organ, serves as a reservoir for the reception of numerous effluents from such organs as the pancreas, the liver, and glands located in the intestine itself. These liquids are mixed with the food mass as it is moved through the intestine by means of peristaltic waves. During this process, enzymes in the various digestive juices reduce proteins, carbohydrates, and fats into more basic substances that can be absorbed by the body or acted on further by other enzymes in the intestine.

Table 4-2. Major Digestive Enzymes

Name	Where Found	Function
Ptyalin	Mouth	Digests starch
Pepsin	Stomach	Digests protein
Rennin	Stomach	Curdles milk
Amylopsin	Pancreatic juice	Digests starch
Steapsin	Pancreatic juice	Digests fats
Trypsin	Pancreatic juice	Digests protein
Amylase	Intestines	Digests starch
Lipase	Intestines	Digests fat
Lactase	Intestines	Digests lactose
Maltase	Intestines	Digests maltose
Sucrase	Intestines	Digests sucrose

As the food is changed into usable forms, passing along the small intestine from the duodenum to the jejunum to the ileum, it is absorbed through the intestinal wall into the blood and lymphatic systems of the body. There it is either immediately consumed as fuel or stored for later use.

With the digestion of most of the food mass completed, and usable nutrients largely removed, the remainder passes into the large intestine. There a large amount of moisture is absorbed from the semiliquid mass. A marked increase in bacterial growth occurs, resulting in the formation of fecal matter, which is discharged in more solid form through the anus.

As the digestive process continues, the food substances are carried by the bloodstream to specific tissues needing nourishment or to organs, such as the liver, for conversion into other forms for storage. In some cases, excess amounts of nutritive substances are carried to the kidneys for discharge from the body.

Thus, digestion converts food into substances that furnish the body with fuel, regulate body functions, and maintain its systems in working order. Food furnishes a ready source of energy in the form of glucose, carried in the blood. Extra amounts of this fuel are converted into a substance called glycogen and stored for use in the near future. Reserves in excess of those needed for relatively immediate use are converted into fat.

Fats are handled much the same as carbohydrates in the digestive process. Although they may undergo other processes generating amino acids, they basically serve as sources of fuel. The body's fuel needs are measured in calories. If food intake exceeds caloric consumption by the body, fat is generated and deposited in the tissues.

Protein is circulated in the blood as amino acids, which either repair or replace tissue. If fuel from carbohydrates and fats is inadequate, protein may be converted into a form of glucose to be used as fuel. This is, of course, an inefficient use of this important body building substance.

Nothing in food is useless in the biological processes. Even the largely indigestible cellulose serves to stimulate the intestinal tract and provide for normal elimination of body wastes.

Psychological Implications of Food

Closely allied to the biological functions that are the prime purposes of food are those of a psychological nature. In effect, the body's way of demonstrating a need for food is both biological and psychological. As the sugar level of the blood decreases and the digestive process empties the stomach, this organ emits pressure, bowel sounds, and feelings of emptiness. The whole body feels tired from a lack of readily available energy sources.

Lower forms of animal life react to these conditions by searching out food sources, satisfying their cravings, often eating to excess, and then going without food for days until hunger feelings reappear.

Man, although possessing these same biological needs, appears able to regulate them and to gear them to psychological and sociological considerations. He is able to refrain from eating for a specific period of time and to select certain foods to the exclusion of others in satisfying his hunger. After eating, he achieves a sense of well being, like other animals. Many primitive societies closely follow animal behavior and sleep off heavy eating.

As the society becomes more sophisticated, however, psychological factors become more important. Food is selected and eaten not only to satisfy energy needs and hunger, but also on the basis of factors such as color, texture, temperature, and sound. The natural color of the food affects its acceptability, and a change of color due to poor preparation or merchandising gimmicks will often deprive a dish of its ability to satisfy. Green beans heated to a temperature that destroys their natural chlorophyll color may be less acceptable to a consumer than those that carry the true green. Whipped potatoes tinted green with food coloring to celebrate St. Patrick's Day will generally find low consumer acceptance.

Some exceptions to this theory do occur. Consumers who are accustomed to canned vegetables may find olive-colored green beans more acceptable than fresh green ones. It is the operator's job to know the food habits of his clientele.

The textures and temperatures of foods also have psychological aspects. A serving of foods all of the same consistency—whether rough, soft, or slippery—will generally satisfy the appetite less than a mixture of textures, which gives variety and interest to a meal. The temperature of an item affects the ability of the body to discern its particular taste. Ice cream served too cold may be tasteless; if too warm, it may seem too sweet. Thus incorrect temperature may make it difficult for a consumer to differentiate between an average and an outstanding meal.

Sound and odor also play important parts in the psychological acceptance of foods. The sputtering of butter or steak drippings on a hot sizzle platter delivered to a dining room guest and the accompanying odor of the same item on a charcoal grill do much to make the dining experience psychologically as well as biologically satisfying.

Foods may have heavy or light connotations and even exhibit sexual characteristics. Meats that are pale in color, such as chicken, are considered light food, while red meats are considered heavy and associated with masculine characteristics. (Fat content probably plays a role in this also, as fat remains in the stomach longer and is digested more slowly.) Greens appear cool (probably by association with grass and water) and are accepted best in that manner. Hot foods go best with red surroundings, although the color contributes only psychologically to heat. Foods such as soufflés and whipped desserts are considered feminine, while the purer and simpler dishes and those with higher caloric values are associated with men.

A four-ounce portion of meat offered to a guest in one piece may seem less satisfying to the appetite than the same size portion offered in three slices. Food is indeed a psychological as well as a biological experience.

Sociological Implications of Food

If the food service manager is to succeed, he must recognize many sociological implications of food.

New Englanders find it difficult to accept white-shelled eggs (probably because they are used to raising a particular type of hen), while New Yorkers suspect the brown-shelled varieties of being unfit for table use. Jews and Muslims are forbidden to eat any flesh of certain animals and certain parts of others.

Status and economics are also factors. For example, flour is bleached in the United States to distinguish it from the dark flour used by peasants in Europe, and caviar is served at parties as a symbol of wealth and status.

The amount of food eaten has had sociological implications, as an indicator of prosperity. Barons and earls of old ate to excess; their rotund shapes were considered signs of their financial worth and the availability of food in their households. Currently many people restrict their intake of calories to achieve svelte silhouettes in an attempt to project a youthful, "swinging" image.

Food implies love or devotion in the Jewish family: witness the chicken soup given to heal the ills of a child. In primitive societies animal hearts or other glands are thought to give strength or sexual prowess to the human consumer. Some people consider milk and cheese constipating. Others believe that hot bread leads to indigestion or that use of sugar results in diabetes. These are often culturally perpetuated beliefs.

Food service, therefore, is more than satisfaction of the body's biological requirements. A food manager must also recognize psychological and sociological factors and taboos if he wants to give consumers complete satisfaction from the food he offers.

Environmental and Psychological Influences on Food Selection

The customer's environment (the decor, heat, and lighting provided in conjunction with the food) does much to determine how he will accept the food that is offered. The individual consumer's self-image, mores, and background guide his acceptance or rejection of a particular food. This process begins when he seeks out a food operation whose style, decor, menu, form of service, and price will meet his self-image requirements. It continues when he chooses a food with a particular color, taste, name, and method of preparation.

Although, in furnishing an establishment, form should follow function, an operator must keep in mind that the decor selected for the service areas of his facility and the type and intensity of heat and light provided will greatly influence how any food will be accepted. The major design principles of proportion, balance, rhythm, harmony, and emphasis must be interwoven into a theme that is followed from the outside of the establishment to the inside, encompassing the menu, glassware, uniforms, music, etc. The use of checkerboard tablecloths, maple or mahogany furniture, and copper or pewter utensils portends the attraction of a customer seeking foods such as steak or roast beef. The scrubbed, white, and brightly lighted downtown cafeteria suggests speed, efficiency, and cleanliness, attracting a different type of customer and offering food of a different character.

The colors and materials used may also affect customer comfort. While the use of greens and blues in the salad or seafood area may sell more of these foods, it may also cause the customers to complain that the room is too cold. The same green that makes fish look appetizing may only meet with failure when used on a sign or other merchandising effort for a steak or beef item, whereas red will do that job much better.

The level and type of lighting also affect the appeal of food. Filament lighting or color-improved cool white fluorescents both do better in emphasizing meats than standard warm white fluorescent light, which better emphasizes yellow foods. This factor can substantially affect sales of a particular item.

Lighting intensity will also influence restaurant operation. The level of light appears to be directly related to turnover: high intensity lighting leads to a higher turnover rate, and lower level lighting is associated with more leisurely dining and higher check averages.

The use of a new neodymium gas light, which shows both skin tones and most foods to good advantage, is discussed by Eino Lampi in "Hotel and Restaurant Lighting," *Cornell Hotel and Restaurant Administration Quarterly,* February 1973, pp. 58-64, along with further information on the use of lighting in food service establishments. Additional work in this area has been done by Dr. Frank Borsenik of Michigan State University and Professor Richard Penner of Cornell University.

5 *Newer Forms of Food Preparation*

Objective: To consider recent changes in quantity food preparation by overviewing the history of food, discussing the development of convenience foods, and surveying current and future trends that include the natural foods movement and the evolution of special dietary foods.

Food and life are synonymous in the history of man. Providing energy to the human organism has always been one of the basic human needs. But beyond this, people have also always associated foods with religious practices, economic relationships, or current fashions. Foods that were found to cause problems to a people or tribe were often forbidden by religious decree, while foods that were rare or difficult to produce were accorded a high economic position and reserved for the rich because of the monetary expenditure involved.

Some foods had powers of sexuality, strength, beauty, or longevity attributed to them, and people would seek out particular food items for the temporal benefits these foods could provide. There were also accidental discoveries of the connections between food and disease prevention, such as the British Navy discovering that sauerkraut prevented scurvy. Food, as a necessary part of life, was first eaten just when man was hungry and when it was found; later food became part of various social rituals: meeting with friends, being entertained, or as a prelude to another event or part of a religious holiday.

This chapter traces some of the changes and trends that have taken place in the preparation and service of food. It is imperative that those responsible for food service planning, management, and supervision be aware of the trends that are currently taking place. In this way they will remain effective as agents in meeting the needs of a volatile market that continues to change and grow as it has throughout man's history.

Civilized man first ate food prepared in the home by members of an individual family. The food consisted of items available in a particular geographical area, and selected, prepared, and eaten in accordance with local religious practices, economic relationships, and current fads and tastes. Those who traveled away from home for brief periods of time carried their food with them. As travel became more general and the distances traveled became greater, the roadside inn or village restaurant developed to serve the food needs of the individual traveler. These establishments were generally utilitarian in nature, and the functional need of basic nourishment was considered most important, just as it was in the home.

Later, however, the inn (which later became the hotel) and some restaurants generated a new style of food service—the classical or traditional form, used for entertainment, relaxation, or diversion. Many hours and talents were used to produce different, interesting, and attractive food forms as diners "oohed" and "chewed" their way through copious quantities of colorfully arranged, aesthetically proper, and gastronomically correct foods.

Marzipan modeling, sugar pulling, *saucier* inventiveness, or *sommelier* and *gueridon* procedures were all used to enhance foods. Not only were numerous hours spent by butchers, bakers, chefs, their apprentices, and kitchen helpers to produce these foods in a way that had become traditionally correct, but these preparations were also wedded to the functions of the wine steward, captain, or maitre d' hotel who presented the food to a guest in the traditionally correct manner—a manner well-suited for a king. The silver, gold, and copper, and the flames and flashes of the table service added full measure to the food form being offered as the diner was entertained and fully engaged in a two- to four-hour dining experience.

The procedures used to produce these results are the precursors of the food preparation principles that are used today when raw agricultural products are converted into edible culinary offerings. The technical expertise of many historical practitioners, by a process of talent and trial and error, has produced for us the Coq au Vin, Lobster Thermidor, Caesar Salad, and Lady Baltimore Cake. But the qualities needed to produce intricate and exciting dishes and to present them in a stimulating manner require talented and trained culinary workers; enough time to produce and serve the menu items; and customers with the time, the tastes, and the money to enjoy an elaborate meal.

But as previously suggested (see Chapter 1), the kitchens offering classical cuisine, with their skilled chefs, detailed hand-done methods accomplished in house, and minutely segmented technical functions, began to diminish in number. Yet this tradition remains an important element in the finer continental-style restaurants, the private clubs, and the highly rated hotel. In other segments of the industry, however, the traditional kitchen with its own butcher, baker, saucier, fish cook, sous chef, and so on has slowly given way to newer organizational forms. These changes have been dictated by a concern for costs, a lack of sufficient technical personnel, and changing consumer tastes. The first step in the movement from a haute cuisine food offering toward the forms of today, which are more functional, was the movement toward convenience foods.

Convenience Foods

Convenience foods consist of any food form in which some procedure, process, or preparation, on a continuum from minimal to total, has already been completed. A canned food item is a convenience food; a prepeeled potato is a convenience food; and a preportioned, fully cooked and frozen shrimp dinner is also a convenience food item.

The first real work in preparing quantity convenience food was during the Napoleonic era, when canning procedures were developed to provide safe and acceptable foods for Napoleon's advancing armies. Some work had, of course, already been accomplished in home food preparation where procedures for drying and curing meats had been in use for years. However, the Industrial Revolution served to make convenience foods not only broadly tolerated but also necessary. The necessity of feeding large numbers of people as an adjunct to the business of industrial production and the concern for cost containment really started the convenience food movement.

To begin with, there was some initial experimentation, then additional work was done on frozen vegetables and entrees in the 1920s, but the basic concept was not accepted by the general population. Food service professionals said that the products being developed were inferior in quality, taste, and texture (which in the early days appeared to be true). With the woman available full time in the home to raise the family, cook the meals, and maintain the house, even the concept of convenience was unacceptable. Sociological research has indicated that those who used a convenience item—such as instant coffee—instead of a made-from-scratch item were originally considered lazy or unorganized. (See Mason Haire, "Projective Techniques in Marketing and Research," in *Marketing in Progress*, ed. H.C. Barksdale [New York: Holt, Rinehart, and Winston, Inc., 1964].) In addition, the great majority of the population did not travel much, ate most of their meals at home, and when they were away during a meal period at work or school, they carried food with them.

With the outbreak of World War II, the need for full employment to meet war production needs, including the employment of many women, changed the attitude of most Americans towards fast and convenience foods. The full employment and lack of manpower as well as the increased mobility of our population all contributed to more people eating out. Foods that were pre-prepared, precooked, and prepackaged saved manpower, and were now considered desirable items. With time so important, new delivery systems to get food out to a more mobile population were also needed, and this developed into the fast food operation.

Of course the troops in the field who needed combat rations were also an important element in this development. The government spent millions of dollars developing ration systems that would be convenient to use, light to carry, and an acceptable substitute for home cooking.

The experiences of those war years were built upon in the postwar era as convenience foods in every form from juices to completely processed and plated individual meals, were brought into most homes. Fast food outlets, which used these convenience items in the form of the preportioned hamburger patty or the precut French fry or the apple pie portion, contributed to this growth. Families with members who used to carry lunches to school or to places of employment or on picnics and had eaten most of their remaining meals at home, now ate more convenience foods away from home as fast food outlets and sit-down restaurants attracted more of the meal dollar.

Today, with more working wives and mothers and more extra money available, more than one in three meals is eaten outside of the home. Eating establishments that commanded some 20 percent of the total money spent on food in 1960 now account for some 40 plus percent of the dollars spent on food items. Within the area of public food service, the fast food segment now accounts for 45 percent of all eating places and approximately $38 billion sales per year. Convenience food sales continue to grow, as the average sit-down restaurant employs more convenience foods to substitute for professional food preparation personnel, and fast food operators supplement their limited burger and French fry menus with more ambitious offerings such as quiches and crepes. In fact, the use of convenience foods by chain operators exceeds the total commercial segment as may be seen in Table 5–1. Over 50 percent of chains now use the major convenience food forms of vegetables and portion-controlled meats, poultry, fish, and potatoes. Fast food has found its way even to Paris, the epicurean center of the world, with the Boulevard St. Michel on the Left Bank near the Sorbonne filled with fast food outlets.

A full 50 percent of the grocery stores in the United States (19,000 out of 38,000) now have deli or bakery outlets with takeout food service in direct competition to the free-standing total service restaurant. This, compared with 37 percent in 1981 and 17 percent in 1973, shows that the trend is toward grocery outlets becoming ever more formidable competitors. Soup and salad bars, drive-through facilities for take-home foods, and in-store sit-down cafes are also found in many grocery outlets. Convenience or "C" stores that started with wrapped cake or

Table 5-1. Chains Are Fervent Fans of Frozen Foods

Chain usage of frozen food is higher than the commercial segment as a whole in more than half of 38 different product categories, reflecting the convenience, consistency, and ease of preparation of frozen foods.

Item	% using product among . . . Chains	Total
Frozen French fries	89.2	89.8
Frozen fish steaks and fillets	69.8	68.0
Breaded fish portions	64.2	62.1
Chicken fillets/breast strips	60.5	56.4
Frozen pies/pieces	55.9	50.3
Juice concentrate	52.8	61.9
Frozen portioned meats (steaks)	52.5	51.7
Frozen vegetables	50.8	57.6
Frozen potato specialties	50.5	47.6
Onion rings	48.5	47.7
Sausage patties	48.5	45.8
Frozen turkey	47.5	57.2
Frozen cakes	47.0	49.1
Sausage links	46.0	48.2
Chicken strips and nuggets	44.6	42.5
Peeled and deveined shrimp	43.7	55.0
Chicken patties	43.2	36.3
Frozen formed potato products	43.2	37.7
Fried chicken/pieces fully cooked	42.9	46.8

Item	% using product among . . . Chains	Total
Precooked portion beef patties	41.7	55.
Whole frozen chicken and parts	41.4	42.
Breaded shrimp	37.4	49.
Breaded vegetables	32.8	37.
Frozen danish	32.3	28.
Frozen biscuits and muffins	31.8	30.
IQF chicken unbattered	30.0	33.
Frozen soups	27.7	24.
Frozen dough	25.7	34.
Frozen entrees (non-Italian)	24.2	28.
Frozen pancakes and waffles	22.6	19.
Veal (primal cuts)	20.6	34.
Frozen Italian entrees	19.2	22.
Frozen processed eggs	18.6	17.
Frozen cookie dough	17.9	15.
Frozen cherries	14.9	18.
Frozen avocado pulp	13.6	10.
Frozen Mexican specialties	12.1	11.
Frozen quail/Cornish hens	11.1	18.

(Source: *Restaurants and Institutions,* Oct. 2, 1985, p. 108.)

cookies and coffee in styrofoam cups are also becoming strong competitors as they start to offer a full range of ready-made or made-to-order deli sandwiches, cold plates, salads, microwaved soups, pizzas, and so on.

Local home delivery of pizza, hamburgers, and the like are sometimes coupled with air delivery over great distances for such nostalgia or signature items as the White Castle Burger from Columbus, Ohio, and fish from Legal Seafood in Boston. Of course with take-home deliveries, concern must be given to surcharges, the amount of the average check that would warrant this service, plus the delivery costs, the insurance coverage, and labor costs for the delivery personnel, as well as the crime rate in certain areas that would set delivery personnel up as easy marks for robberies.

Convenience food use has received even more impetus with the introduction into many food service establishments of the ready food concept, as they attempt to produce the entire food package in house. By using a minimum of talented professionals according to a standardized schedule, it is possible for a facility to prepare, chill, or freeze food items for later service. These items may then be tempered, portioned, and served by less technically qualified personnel without the need to maintain highly skilled people at a high payroll rate on duty during all serving periods. By cooking, chilling, and rethermalizing four hundred meals in 18 minutes, one hospital was able to reduce labor by twelve full-time employees and cut energy costs $6,000. Of course this same process could be used in the home as well, but most homemakers appear to choose the complete convenience food item totally prepared outside the home. A vacuum machine cooking process (*sous vide*) first developed in Europe in the 1970s has also begun to find extensive usage. Foods are blanched or partially cooked, vacuum packed, and kept chilled for future use. They are recooked in low-temperature ovens, pressureless convection ovens, steamers, or microwave ovens. A recent FDA letter to the NRA, however, cautions against on-premises pouch preparation and cooking as a violation of the serving of "home canned" foods in commercial establishments and, if enforced, could result in only commercially prepared *sous vide* products being utilized. (See *Nation's Restaurant News*, February 15, 1988, page 1.)

Comprising foods that are minimally, partially, or completely processed, convenience foods may find utilization in almost every form of operation from the sit-down to the fast food outlet. The main concerns in their use, regardless of the outlet, relate to their speed of preparation, cost and labor, quality, flexibility or utilization, acceptability by the consumer, consistency, and nutritional concerns.

Speed of Preparation. The need for saving time, or speed, was of course one of the original factors leading to the production and use of convenience foods. From minimally pre-prepared foods, such as potatoes that are peeled or salad ingredients that are cut, mixed, and bagged, to such items as the partially prepared breaded fish sticks or the completely mixed salad dressing, a convenience food item is available in a minimum amount of time. With convenience foods, there is less need to forecast exact portions or to have excessive lead times between preparation and service. This reduction in time also reduces labor and, by increasing customer turnover, contributes to a more efficient delivery system.

Cost and Labor. The cost of convenience food must be compared with the from-scratch version of the same item in the following areas: the cost of a servable portion of the product; the cost of the labor needed to prepare the convenience form of the item compared with the cost of the labor needed to prepare the unpreprocessed form; the cost of storage, including the space to be allocated to this function; and the cost of inventory counts of each form of the item.

Quality. The quality of convenience foods was, in many cases, at a very low level in the early days of the industry. Items of a protein nature were difficult to reconstitute or bring to serving condition and had to be enhanced and protected by sauces, gravies, and so on. The thickening agents used in those sauces and gravies often "broke" when heated, and people noticed a distinct reduction of quality.

At the present time, however, almost all of these major problems have been corrected, and the quality of the product is equal to the made-from-scratch item. It is important to make an evaluation of the taste and appearance of the product by operating personnel. This can be done by means of taste panels and the like. A detailed analysis of the product's acceptability by the consumer is also essential. A product that is inexpensive in relation to labor costs and is easy to store but is not accepted as a quality product by the consumer is a product that should not be used.

Flexibility. The use of convenience foods in an establishment can give great flexibility in food preparation and storage, as well as aiding in the area of future forecast. Convenience foods are less bulky than the fresh products from which they are made. They are easier to receive, inventory, and issue. Because of their ready availability, they give the menu forecaster more latitude and allow the chef or cook to order close to the exact amount of food forecasted to meet particular customer needs.

The overall menu can be expanded in scope without the necessity of actually preparing the items. Late in the meal period, items can be allowed to run out without the need to replenish them or prepare a substitute item. The convenience of having a food item available in a brief period of time by use of a microwave oven or boil-in-the-bag preparation offers great flexibility to an operation.

Consistency. The consistency of the convenience foods used must also be considered by the operator. Despite the use of grading standards on fresh food items, there is still a great deal of latitude because we are dealing with people and food, and neither lend themselves to machine-like standards. The ability to be able to get a product from the purveyor on a regular basis which consistently meets the establishment's standards is of great importance to an operator if a convenience food item is to be used.

In the convenience food form, however, and particularly in items that are completely processed, it is easier to control consistency:

a meat patty must always weigh "X" ounces, be covered with a sauce of a certain thickness, be garnished by a certain count of fruit, and so on.

Nutritional Concerns. An area in which convenience or fast food is said to be weakest has traditionally been that of nutrition. This is particularly true of the fast food hamburger bun, French fries, and soda meal. Despite this concern, most of the worries have been either disproved or dismissed as being unimportant.

In the area of convenience and fast foods, the lack of vitamins A and C seems most widespread, and many operations use additives to make up for the lack of these vitamins in convenience food items. With the Type A school lunch, which has stringent government requirements for a balance of nutritional elements and vitamins, some operators have been able to comply with the nutritional regulations by adding vitamin C to the French fries and using a fortified milk shake instead of a soda.

Delivery Systems. The use of convenience foods can be blended into the classical food preparation system if either minimally, partially, or completely processed items are used. But the best use of all types of convenience food forms occurs in a fast food type of delivery system.

From prepeeled or precut French fries to a completely processed individual or 5-ounce portion beef stroganoff dish, the food items contrast sharply with that of the conventional food form of delivery and suggest new approaches. With the emphasis shifting from bulk preparation to batch or, in fact, unit preparation, and with much of the preliminary work accomplished outside of the establishment, a new design is necessary. Items such as freezers, refrigerators, convection ovens, pouch cookers, and steamers may have to be purchased or increased. Such areas as vegetable preparation, butcher shops, stock pots, ranges, and the like may have to be replaced.

Labor retraining, rescheduling, or reutilization may also be necessary to compensate for the work that has already been done on the product outside of the facility. Receiving, storage, and issuing procedures will have to be varied to meet the needs of the new items as well.

Specific Preparation Changes. In making a shift to maximize the use of convenience foods, the major emphasis will be away from such preliminary steps as measuring, mixing, breading, portioning, cutting, and related activities and toward those functions that relate to tempering, holding, portioning, and serving. The first direct result of this change in direction will be a reduction in the labor used as well as a reduction in the talent needed to produce a particular food item. An item can be mass produced at a time convenient for the preparation personnel; the item is then subdivided, portioned, and either chilled or frozen for later use, with only holding facilities needed from preparation to serving time.

Health, Organic, and Natural Foods

Rebelling against a society that they felt neglected the human aspects of mankind and questioning organizationally imposed parameters and mores, the counterculture of the 1960s was probably the first to turn against the fast and convenience food revolution. Championed by humanistic and environmentally oriented consumers and urged on by people like Adelle Davis and Dr. Roger J. Williams, an idea was born that inspired the founding of many new restaurants and motivated some established operations to include "organically" grown and processed foods on the menus. *Pure, safe, healthful,* and *natural* are adjectives that proponents use to describe this new food concept.

The early environmental and naturalistic movements of the 1970s have become incorporated into consumer attitudes and are the health food and organic food advocates of the present. The use of megavitamins to increase sexual potency or to reduce the aging process and the quest for organic foods grown only with natural fertilizers and without the use of pesticides or other chemicals have been challenges to the chemical analogy industry, which has come up with soybean fibers that are spun and chemically altered to taste like turkey or look and taste like beef.

Although some faddists have carried health and organic concerns to excessive lengths, both government and the general citizenry have at least partially embraced this philosophy of whole or natural foods. The government has reoriented itself to vitamin research and nutritional concerns neglected since the 1950s and, with the color additive amendment of 1960, has begun to look at the two thousand or so substances that can be added to the food we eat to make it more attractive, tastier, better textured, and last longer. As mentioned, the vitamin contents of fast food items have been evaluated, measured, and challenged, with suggestions made for the addition of vitamin C or other nutrients to bring the food up in value to current nutritional standards.

Within the corporate segment of our society, such companies as Hilton Hotels are apparently tuned to the messages being sent. This company has undertaken a massive campaign of promoting healthful foods for the fitness conscious traveler. (See "Hilton's Healthy New Promotion Fits Food to Fitness," *Institutions* 1 [July 1980] : 29-33.)

Although some research projects have questioned the relationship between cholesterol, lipoproteins, and heart disease (and some of these appear valid), the preponderance of evidence suggests a positive relationship. In addition the medical community and a large proportion of the consuming public have embraced this health-food–disease link.

On the other hand, some foods used in attempts to improve one's health and nutrition have actually been the cause of major medical problems; for example, bone meal was found to contain lead, and deaths were caused by the use of dolomite or protein powders in 1977. (See "Diet Crazes," *Newsweek* 19 [December 1977] : 67-77, and Ronald H. Smithies, "Health Foods, Are They Safe—Are They Natural?" *Good Housekeeping* [May 1978] : 214.)

With the words *organic, health,* and *natural* as rallying points, the proponents of this type of food preparation take issue with the problems caused by lack of proper nutrition, additives, and disease-producing elements. They are critical of fats, sugars, salt, additives, chemicals, and the like. They have also called for menus and foods resulting in the vegetarian menu item, the salad bar, the slimline menu of the cuisine minceur, and such food items as granola, bone meal, and Tofu made of soybeans and sea water. Some changes in preparation methods and in the raw food materials used, as well as in menu planning, are necessary with health and nutrition as a desired objective.

Although most food fads tend to run their course within a five-year period, good nutrition and concern for health in diets appear to be concerns that are here to stay and will have to be dealt with for a long period of time. As covered thoroughly in Chapter 8 on menu planning, the jogging, aerobics, and food choices of those concerned with health are important elements that the food service operator needs to recognize. Sugar-free, caffeine-free, and fat-free dietary foods are more and more popular with the general public. Beef is staging a mild comeback after a heavy advertising push to keep it the number one protein meat choice, but even here "light" forms with less fat or less fatty cuts are being featured and selected.

The Heart Association guidelines of serving margarine in lieu of butter; skimmed milk in place of whole milk; broiling, baking, steaming, or poaching items in place of frying or sauteeing them are valued by many consumers. Reducing salt and other sodium and using less cholesterol and fat in diets must be important to menu planners in the commercial food service sector since a significant number of consumers follow these guidelines when they eat out or choose a particular restaurant. Surveys have shown that health and nutritional concerns are number one and two with consumers, and these concerns are reflected in reduced use of beef, eggs, butter, and alcohol. The need for foods rich in fiber to prevent problems in the digestive tract has also received wide attention and has led to a popular resurgence of vegetables, salads, and the cereal grains. So much has been made of fiber's value that some producers have added pure wood or vegetable fibers to their products in order to elevate the fiber percentage and be better able to merchandise their product. Cooking methods have also changed considerably including the quick stir-frying of vegetables (the wok-type Chinese methods) and baking, broiling, poaching, steaming as methods of choice to reduce fat.

Availability and Cost. Due to the recent increases in demand, more natural and organically grown foods have become available on the food market, although some of the foods advertised as such do not actually meet the standards for these kinds of foods. Foods meeting the requirements of the health, natural, or organic groups must always be purchased from reliable and ethical purveyors; it has been shown that some foods advertised as organic have in fact been labeled that way just for the sake of sale. In 1972 the Office of Consumer Affairs of the President's Office offered guidelines for foods lableled as *natural, organic,* or *health* foods, but these are by no means universally accepted or adhered to.

One should expect to pay higher prices for organically grown natural foods but should not expect that the cost will automatically result in higher nutrition. Although organic meat may have less fat, it does take longer to produce and is therefore more expensive. It still gives the same amount of calories per gram, and the protein still carries out the same restorative functions.

Preparation and Delivery Methods. Stir cooking, lightly or partially cooked, or whole-unit foods are the catch phrases of the organic or natural food follower. Change in menus to reduce levels of red meat consumption, fat, sugar, and salt usage and increase in the use of whole grain and other whole foods will contribute to new preparation methods. There will be more broiling of fresh fish and more fast stir cooking as done in the wok or on the Chop Suey range. Food processors with their specialized blades, cutters, and attachments can grate, blend, puree, dice, or grind whole foods quickly to achieve the totality of nutrient, bulk, and taste desired by modern health-conscious consumers.

New menu forms cater to this market as vegetarian plates are provided, and fast food hamburger outlets provide salad bars. Even the government is considering banning foods such as candies, soft drinks, and so on from schools so as not to allow "junk foods" to compete with the nutritionally adequate Type A school lunch.

The slimness desired by the follower of cuisine minceur or the healthfulness sought by the health food client must be considered an important element in the food preparation picture of today, something the food operator should be aware of. In addition, many adherents of this school follow a theory of lighter flavors, finer textures, and less concern for standardization of presentation; they look to the operator to provide high levels of inventiveness in service forms. They are not, however, easily swayed by the use of such phrasing as "a dining out experience" if used to overcome a lack of imagination in either the food or preparation methods. In fact, many seem to be avoiding restaurants completely.

More couples and families well able to afford the funds necessary to eat in restaurants or fast food outlets are now undertaking gourmet cooking at home, using new types of equipment or food processors that claim maximum vitamin retention and pureness of taste and nutritional content. Food service has come full circle in this case, with people staying home to eat.

Of major concern to the food service supervisor are the changes in food preparation techniques and delivery systems. Individuals in the supervision and management sections of a quantity food operation must be familiar with the specific advantages, disadvantages, equipment requirements, preparation variances, and delivery system changes. Only through this familiarity is it possible to adjust planning or preparation methods in order to meet the needs of an ever-changing food service industry.

Dietary Foods

Although probably serving as background for the health or organic food follower, dietary foods have long been used as an adjunct to other medical procedures. The pure dietary food proponent is the latest wave in the evolution of the newer food concepts. They believe that dietary foods possess curative, preventative, or catalystic powers, and under such banners as orthomolecular medicine, they criticize conventional medical processes as they join with the health and natural food proponents in attacking many of the convenience and fast food procedures.

This type of food preparation has the most formally established background of any of those under discussion and has seen an entire profession grow up around it, as it has been practiced in hospitals and nursing homes throughout the country. While many of the inventive practitioners of the classical school were creating, garnishing, and serving food to appreciative customers, they were also guilty of destroying the survival value of the food as they leached out minerals and destroyed vitamins. Today we see more traditional, industrial, and other forms of food preparation beginning to use the methods proposed by the dietary segment of the food service industry, with the knowledge gained from a long scientific history.

An English nurse named Florence Nightingale was shocked by the unsanitary conditions that existed in military hospitals during the Crimean War. She started an attempt to introduce order and cleanliness to these facilities and to the foods being provided. Her efforts served as a catalyst and resulted in the first dietary kitchens and specialized dietary food being established in the mid 1850s.

At about the same time the first scientific understandings about the makeup of food items and their specialized use were being made. Building upon the work of ancient alchemists, scientists developed the use of quantitative experimental techniques. In 1828 the German chemist Wohler (1800-1882) disproved the vital force concept and synthesized the organic compound urea, and the German chemist Liebig (1803-1873) demonstrated that proteins, fats, and carbohydrates are burned by the body.

Despite the early theories of men like Hippocrates, emphasizing the proper dietary treatment of disease, and the scientific studies of men such as Réaumur (1683-1757), who established the chemical nature of digestion, and Lavoisier (1743-1794), who developed the theory of metabolism, the experiments of Liebig were the first real beginnings of organic chemistry. Following these early experiments there were other scientists, such as McCollum with his discovery of vitamin A in 1917 and Osborne and Medel with their work in 1918 on the inorganic mineral, who added to the basic information upon which the dietary profession has been founded.

Used as curative or restorative agents by physicians in hospitals or in outpatient treatment, foods have been a widely accepted form of therapy. With growing knowlege of the organic and inorganic components of food, it became possible to attack or maintain compatibility with such conditions as diabetes, gout, or heart disease. Dietary food became a necessary and desirable adjunct to the practice of medicine. But beyond this, since these elements were found to be of such importance, the necessary components were added to the foods eaten by everyone as a preventative measure.

An example is the addition to table salt of iodine in order to prevent goiters from growing in people who did not live near the sea and seafood sources with their rich supply of iodine. White flour, which had already been bleached to remove the peasant stigma of dark bread, was enriched with essential nutritional elements that had been destroyed or removed in the bleaching process.

Some additives to food items, however, were attempts to improve quality and palatability levels and were less concerned with the nutritional aspects of food. Harvey W. Wiley, chief of the Bureau of Chemistry of the

U.S.D.A. from 1883 to 1912, was probably most important in helping to control adding some of these elements; he might be considered the precursor of the present health food orientation toward eating. It is fortunate that men such as Wiley did appear in nineteenth century America as part of the organic approach to eating because borax and salicylic acid were being added to foods as preservatives, while alum was added to white flour to make it finer. Copper sulfate was added to pickles to make them greener, and lead salts to cheeses for better color.

Serving as a major segment of hospital regimen from the standpoint of costs, treatment, and patient concern, dietary food involves simply the service of food to patients and staff within a hospital environment. The unique difference from other food service procedures, however, is that in dietary food, specific foods are withheld from a patient, preparation methods are varied, or other foods are augmented—all to aid in disease correction or containment from the perspective of nutrition.

The newer followers of the dietary approach to foods, the orthomolecular school, suggest that dietary treatment is not necessarily just a part of hospital treatment. By the scientific analysis of hair and blood, some people propose treating the individual by means of injections, oral tablets, and later by foods that contain the minerals and other substances the individual needs. Could this be the start of the pill meal? It is difficult to say; at this writing there appear to be disagreements among some members of the medical and dietary professions.

Delivery Systems. Neither food types used in the dietary approach nor the preparation and delivery systems vary much from the classical restaurant or fast food outlet, though perhaps they are most like an airline food facility. Convenience foods are currently being developed to meet the specialized needs of hospitals. These pre-prepared foods plus the problems of labor cost and maintaining heat levels have led to the use of microwave units at locations dispersed throughout the hospital facility. The food can be cooked and served just for the local unit. This centralized type of delivery system has been adopted by many hospitals in order to match the quality and control demands that existed with the previous decentralized systems. With the possible implementation of a national health insurance plan and the excessive rates of hospitalization costs, more attention will probably be paid to the food service segment of hospitalization costs.

Preparation Variances and Consumer Acceptance. With every consumer a self-appointed expert in the way food should taste or be prepared, dietary food is often criticized by patients as the only part of their hospitalization which was not up to par. Confronted by a food tray lacking the expected condiments or with foods prepared in an unfamiliar way, a patient with a painful or uncomfortable condition often vents his anger against the food since that patient is often reluctant to criticize or challenge the medical establishment. He has placed his body in their control and while he may know nothing of the involved medical procedures or the terminology, he does know food. Dietary food remains the whipping boy of the hospital experience and will probably remain so due to the individual preferences and psychological complications of an uncomfortable and ill consumer.

Future Food Concerns

In an attempt to reduce costs, speed turnover, and provide adequate profit many operators hire unqualified workers, change systems, and attempt to use the flambée as a substitute for quality. Many consumers have seen through this and have returned to family-prepared food where better controls are maintained on price, quality, service, sanitation, and so on.

Just over the horizon, as a compromise between the fast food concepts dictated by speed and leisure and the restorative and generative eating style pursued by health food advocates, is the movement toward gourmet cooking at home where attempts are made to recapture some of the style, form, and finesse of former days. Even fast food outlets are attempting to individualize their service and expand their menus as they see the consumer revolt in some of the areas. More concern can be expected as the average age of the general population increases in the United States and a more sophisticated consumer appears in the market.

Freeze-dried instant meals of steaks, omelets, and fruits that require only the addition of water and some final heating are currently available for home or institutional use. These, plus compressed foods, the retortable pouch developed for the space program, and the multipurpose food based on the simple-cell protein concept where food items are produced from micro-organisms acting upon wood or agricultural wastes are also being made the subjects of current in-depth experimentation. But this is for the future—for today the food service operator must deal with the realities of the fast foods, convenience foods, health foods, and dietary foods that have augmented, modified, and varied the classical food preparation and delivery systems of the past.

In a direct response to the new dietary requirements, and probably to keep up the interest of tired menu planners and curious consumers as well, many new and/or unusual foods have found their way into the mainstream "grazing pastures" of the contemporary food service operation and even the standard menu of many average families. Some of these are natural foods that have come from other parts of the world, having remained local and thus unknown until recently in the United States. Other foods have been known here for years but have been used only by small segments of the population or in local regions. The remainder of these new foods have been "created" by technology to resemble or replace a food that is in short supply or that has become poorly accepted because of health concerns associated with it. Some have been replaced due to cost concerns. Certain imitation or substitute foods have, however, later received criticism for not containing the necessary nutritional elements for which they were identified or for lacking the necessary parts to provide the intended functions. Examples of the first group are lemon grass—a grass from Vietnam that can be used as a tea or a cooking spice; ivy gourds—a cucumberlike vegetable from India; malanga—a root starch; calabaza—a squashlike vegetable from Cuba; and dasheen—a tarolike vegetable from the West Indies. These foods have all been introduced into the United States recently. Cherimoya from Mexico, green and nicknamed the custard apple; jicama also from Mexico, a chestnut-tasting salad fruit; loquats from Chile; the kiwi from New Zealand; monkfish, the cheaper lobster substitute; shark steaks; and radicchio, the red wild chicory, are all foods now known and widely used that not too long ago were considered exotic. But what of the manufactured, imitated, or created foods—the egg and sugar substitutes and the crablike products made chemically from washed and denatured whitefish, the new protein krill made from seaweeds, or the edible seeds of amaranth containing lysin mixed with incomplete protein flours such as cornmeal to make complete proteins? Or what of the botanical arrangements where pear trees are bred to need only 200 hours of winter dormancy so that pear season, which normally runs from mid July to the first part of September, may now last from the latter part of June to early October? Another example is the calorieless foods of nondigestible polysaccharides with sucrose esters that simulate fats in taste and texture, have bulk but no calories, and cannot be digested? Are these acceptable foods to use? Should food service operators include them in their offerings?

For example, turkey can replace frankfurters, salami, bologna, or pastrami with no problem so far as protein content goes, but it does reduce the fat content. And even though scientists can duplicate the flavor code of the twenty-one chemical components that give us the taste of fresh-squeezed orange juice or the flavors of the vanilla bean or cherries, or can weave textured vegetable soy protein into items that look like, cook like, and taste like beefsteaks, are they the same? Some nutritionists, such as Dr. George Briggs, make this point: "It's not what is in a substitute but what is not." As stated, many lack the minerals, vitamins, proteins, and other nutrients of the foods they replace. Still other new forms of producing or processing foods (covered more completely in Chapter 6), such as irradiation, have been accused of creating possible undesirable by-products in foods that might harm the consumer. In this age of health, coupled with the high use of litigation, controversial products or processes might not be acceptable in a commercial food service operation.

6 *Preparation Techniques and Terminology*

Objective: To acquaint the student with the essential procedural steps necessary for the delivery of food to guests and the decisions and tools involved with each of these steps. To consider major food preparation methods, terminology, and the variables that affect these techniques.

Procedural Systems

The production of food in quantity requires a system in which a number of individual procedures are interrelated to give the desired results. Most often all procedures are carried out under one roof. Some recent food production system designs, however, have centralized certain steps in locations remote from the main preparation areas, in an effort to gain better use of facilities, manpower, and equipment. Centralization also permits specialized functions to be carried out in one location for a number of consuming units.

Whatever its physical location, each procedure is an important element in the food delivery system. All food served in quantity facilities, whether hotel, restaurant, club, hospital, school, ship, or plane, goes through a series of eight steps, by which preparation personnel transform the raw agricultural products into menu items that will satisfy the needs of consumers. These steps consist of ordering, receiving, storing, measuring, manipulation, processing, portioning, and serving. They are blended into a mosaic pattern that enables an enterprise to provide the type of food that satisfies its market and meets its financial objectives.

These system components are further interrelated with other systems external to the operation. The ordering of a food item may be well planned in a facility but if it does not relate to the marketplace, it will not provide the necessary raw materials. It is important, therefore, that managers and supervisors of these major internal steps be fully cognizant of the external operating systems on which they depend.

Ordering

The first step in the food preparation system is the ordering or purchasing of food. This function may be carried out by the manager of the food operation, by a subordinate assigned to the task, or by a centralized purchaser in a remote location who orders for a number of operations. Whatever system is used the manager or supervisor of the facility that will ultimately use the materials must be concerned with this important phase and how it is carried out.

Foodstuffs ordered must be matched to the requirements of the particular clientele and delivery system. For example, the pricing structure of one operation may dictate the grade of a food and the portion size, which in turn may dictate a particular count or size of the food item ordered. Speed of service in another location might require ordering preportioned or ready food items.

If ordering is to meet the needs of the system it serves, the manager must be familiar with the use to be made of each food and the various types, grades, classes, and forms of foods available. He can then match the items available with the requirements imposed by his particular operation. This information is blended into a word picture called a specification. It provides both buyer and seller with a common body of knowledge about what is to be provided and the tolerances of acceptable quality. The specification becomes the minimum buying standard for each food item. It should result in purchase of the best quality for a specific use at the lowest price. (Specifications are discussed in depth in chapter 9.)

This is considered a rational purchasing system, based on specific need and price considerations. It varies considerably from the emotional buying practiced by many operators, predicated on the personality or presence of a particular salesman, the exterior packaging of a product, or the level of trade advertising.

Using specifications as overriding standards of quality, type, and price, the buyer next considers the amount needed to meet estimated demands. Forecasts of the popularity of menu items, yields from purchased food units, and common packaging and container sizes (see figure 6a) must all be considered. The buyer must also know the lead time necessary from ordering to delivery so that adequate supplies will be available when needed by the food production unit. Usage rates, safety levels, and ordering points should be established for each item, so that a normal replenishment schedule is maintained and sufficient amounts are kept available to meet demands.

The lack of these computations may result in ordering foods too often or too infrequently. Ordering too often results in excessive ordering costs and the possibility of running out of an item. Not ordering often enough produces excessive inventory costs, increases the chances of spoilage or theft, and contributes to excessive inventory taxes (where applicable).

Forecast Method. Many operations determine the amount of an item to be ordered by applying the forecast of monthly or weekly servings, the portion size, and the number of portions in the common containers that are available. After adjusting the amount to meet case lot sizes, they are ready to order. For example, suppose canned peaches were to be offered on a menu five meal periods during the month, and 200 people are expected to be served. One peach half is the portion size, and a number 10 can usually yields twenty-five halves. The ordering would be determined as follows:

Forecast: 200 servings
Servings per unit: 25 per no. 10 can
Units needed: 8 no. 10 cans
Size of case lot: 6 no. 10 cans
Order: 2 cases

Usage Rate Method. Where a cyclical or standard menu is used and the same items are offered in a meal pattern, it may be possible to order on the basis of past usage. This is particularly appropriate in institutions, where a constant forecast is maintained, but it may easily be applied to commercial operations where weekly or monthly averages indicate that similar amounts of materials are used during each period.

This method of ordering is also used in facilities where certain minimum amounts of material are required to be kept on hand to meet emergency situations, such as hospitals, military commands, or areas subject to extremes in weather that make deliveries impossible. The manager needs to establish the following:

Usage rate: number of units used per average day
Lead time: number of days from time of order to receipt of material (expressed in usage units)

A Guide to Common Can Sizes

Can	Contents	Use
6 oz.	Approximately ¾ cup 6 fl. oz.	Used for frozen concentrated juices and individual servings of single strength juices.
8 oz.	Approximately 1 cup 8 oz. (7¾ fl. oz.)	Used mainly in metropolitan areas for most fruits, vegetables and specialty items.
No. 1 (Picnic)	Approximately 1¼ cups 10½ oz. (9½ fl. oz.)	Used for condensed soups, some fruits, vegetables, meat and fish products.
No. 300	Approximately 1¾ cups 15½ oz. (13½ fl. oz.)	For specialty items, such as beans with pork, spaghetti, macaroni, chili con carne, date and nut bread—also a variety of fruits, including cranberry sauce and blueberries.
No. 303	Approximately 2 cups 1 lb. (15 fl. oz.)	Used extensively for vegetables; plus fruits, such as sweet and sour cherries, fruit cocktail, apple sauce.
No. 2	Approximately 2½ cups 1 lb. 4 oz. (1 pt. 2 fl. oz.)	Used for vegetables, many fruits and juices.
No. 2½	Approximately 3½ cups 1 lb. 13 oz. (1 pt. 10 fl. oz.)	Used principally for fruits, such as peaches, pears, plums and fruit cocktail; plus vegetables, such as tomatoes, sauerkraut and pumpkin.
46 oz.	Approximately 5¾ cups 46 oz. (1 qt. 14 fl. oz.)	Used almost exclusively for juices, also for whole chicken.
No. 10	Approximately 12 cups 6 lbs. 9 oz. (3 qts.)	So-called "institutional" or "restaurant" size container, for most fruits and vegetables. Stocked by some retail stores.

Figure 6a. Average container sizes. One no. 10 can equals two no. 5 cans, two 46-ounce cans, four no. 2½ cans, or five no. 2 cans. (Courtesy of American Can Company, Greenwich, Connecticut.)

Safety level: amount of material required to be maintained on hand
Order point: level of units at which an order for replenishment should be made
Maximum stock level: maximum amount that can be kept on hand (dictated by storage capacity and replenishment frequency—weekly, monthly, etc.)

For example, if records indicated that 60 number 10 cans of peaches were routinely used each month, the usage rate would be 2 cans per day. If the time from order to receipt of material is four days (a typical period in many locations or operations using centralized purchasing), the lead time usage is 8 cans (2 cans x 4 days). If ordering is done monthly, the maximum amount to be kept on hand would be 60 cans (2 cans x 30 days).

Using the usage rate method of ordering, peaches should be replenished when the amount on hand drops to 8 cans. The order should be made for 60 cans. The 8 on hand would be used up during the lead time, and receipt of the order would then bring the amount to the maximum level on the fourth day.

If a safety level is imposed, the order point must be increased by this minimum amount that has to be kept on hand. For example, if a four-day supply (8 cans) has to be maintained for emergency purposes, the order point should be set at 16.

This method bases ordering on past usage without reference to menus. It can, of course, be used only if the menus to be offered and the number of covers to be served reasonably reflect those in the past.

Whatever form is used, it is imperative that the enterprise not operate on a hand-to-mouth basis. The hand-to-mouth method places storage costs and the possibility of losses on the purveyor. However, it also permits purchasing and delivery problems to develop that may prevent an establishment from serving a particular item on the date planned.

In large metropolitan areas, where adequate supplies and purveyors are available, the amount of material kept on hand can be reduced and orders made more frequently—even daily. But some backup items should be kept in storage. A frozen preportioned item that duplicates the menu item being produced gives insurance in case of changes in forecast and avoids spoilage of excess items.

Ordering Record (Forecast Method)

Item	Forecast of Servings	Unit	Servings per Unit	Units Needed	Size of Case Lot or Pack	Order
Peach halves	200	No. 10 can	25 per no. 10 can	8	6/10	2 cases

Ordering Record (Usage Rate Method)

Item	Unit	Servings per Unit	Usage Rate (Units per Day)	Lead Time (Units)	Safety Level (Units)	Maximum Stock Level (Units)	Order Point (Units)
Peach halves	No. 10 can	25 per no. 10 can	2	8	8	60	16

Figure 6b. Two forms of records that may be used to determine amounts to be purchased. The forecast form requires the manager to consider the forthcoming menus in order to estimate his needs. The usage rate form may be made a part of the stock record cards; then orders are instituted when posting operations show that the order point has been reached.

Receiving

Attention to purchasing and ordering will be wasted, if the second step of the food delivery system is not properly administered. The attention given to constructing proper specifications to meet menu needs must be followed by a realistic receiving and inspection procedure. Only this ensures that the desired item is received not only at the price ordered but also in a usable condition and quality.

At the inspection and receiving step, foods are matched with written specifications, using such tools as scales, thermometers, counts, and can cutting tests to check that quality, quantity, and other standards have been met. A standard weight chart for the commonly

Chart of Average Weights

Item	Purchase Unit	Approximate Number per Unit	Gross Weight
Fresh fruits and vegetables			
Apples	Bushel box	56-163	48 lbs.
Asparagus	Crate	12 bunches	30 lbs.
Apricots	Western crate	60	22 lbs.
	Bushel	144	48 lbs.
Bananas	Box	100	40 lbs.
Beans, green or wax	Bushel		28-30 lbs.
Carrots	Bag		50 lbs.
Cabbage	Bag		50 lbs.
Celery	Crate	2-3 doz.	
Cucumbers	Bushel	8-12 doz.	48-50 lbs.
Lettuce	Box	2 doz.	48 lbs.
Lemons	Carton	190 count	
Mushrooms	Basket		1 lb.
Onions	Bag		50 lbs.
Oranges	Carton or box	Cal. 48-180	77 lbs.
		Fla. 82-100	90 lbs.
Potatoes, baking	Bag	90 count	
Potatoes, other	Bag		50 or 100 lbs.
Peaches	Bushel		48 lbs.
Peppers	Bushel	8-10 doz.	25 lbs.
Tomatoes	Box	by size, 5 x 5, 6 x 6, etc.	28-32 lbs.
Canned fruits and vegetables			
No. 10 cans	Case	6 cans	46-49 lbs.
No. 2½ cans	Case	24 cans	50-57 lbs.
No. 303 cans	Case	24 cans	40-50 lbs.
Eggs			
Jumbo	Case	30 doz.	56 lbs.
Large	Case		45 lbs.
Small	Case		34 lbs.
Frozen Foods			
Vegetables	Case	12 2½-lb. boxes	30-35 lbs.
French fried potatoes	Case		30 lbs.
Fruit	Can		30 lbs.
Eggs	Can		30 lbs.
Ready foods	Case	Varies with manufacturer (for example, 4 4-lb. cakes per case; 24 6½-oz. individual entrées per case)	12-30 lbs.

Figure 6c. A sample chart of average weights, used to aid in the receiving of food materials. Each operation should construct a set of these charts for its own geographical area and specific purchases, since packs vary.

ordered units of foods and a realistic familiarity with quality standards are needed by the manager or supervisor to assure that this step properly contributes to the system.

The manager must recognize dating codes on foods to know whether fresh items are being delivered and are being checked by his personnel. Weight checks and knowledge of standard weights also help to uncover delivery shortages in particular products.

Storage

When the material has been delivered and receiving procedures have been completed to the satisfaction of the manager, the next step is storage. Since all food, whether animal or vegetable, is composed of living tissue, exceptional care must be taken to maintain it at high quality until it is used. In addition, foods must be protected against loss through theft or misuse.

To carry out these functions, the manager must be familiar with potential spoilage agents and their control. He must institute an issue control procedure to ensure proper use of items. Storage time, temperature, and ventilation must be geared to each food and attempts made to protect the items from vermin. Both issue and replenishment procedures must ensure correct use of items and guard against depletion before new supplies are received.

The selection of storage locations and their proper maintenance are also concerns of the food service manager. Use of adequate shelving, pallets for case lot storage, and easily maintained construction materials will aid this step in making a fair contribution to the food delivery system.

Measuring

Once foods are ready for use and have been properly identified for issue, they must be measured. When possible, units of purchase should correspond to the units of issue used in production recipes. This will reduce the need to measure many items.

One of the most efficient methods of carrying out measurement is use of an "ingredient man." This procedure, first attributed to Katherine Flack of the New York State Department of Mental Health, uses a division of labor according to specialized work methods. The ingredients of recipes are weighed or measured by less technically skilled personnel; cooks receive the correct amounts of raw food items and practice their art without wasting their expertise on routine measuring tasks.

Tables of equivalency and of common container capacities make these procedures much easier.

Such refinements as tare weights for containers, volume measuring gauges on water supply hoses over kitchen kettles, and contoured stainless steel measuring sticks for large steam-jacketed kettles may also facilitate measurement with a minimum amount of effort and increase efficiency in production.

Manipulation

The next step in the delivery of food to the guest is manipulation. This may be nothing more than opening a container or arranging the food in an appropriate serving device, or it may involve more sophisticated actions, such as cutting, chopping, peeling, or dicing. Specialized equipment and hand tools and a particular expertise may be required for these manipulative procedures.

If the process is determined and the volume to be produced is computed, the manager can decide whether to dispense with certain manipulative steps by changing the form of items purchased. Hand work may be reduced if alternative goods can be purchased. Although preparation work performed at another location may cost the user higher prices than unprepared items, the specialized purveyors may perform the manipulative processes for a lower cost. This not only reduces total costs but also permits in-house preparation personnel to be used more effectively. Typical examples of alternative goods are prepeeled potatoes, prepackaged salad

Cost Comparison of Convenience or Ready and Conventional Food

Cost Factor	Product A Time	Product A $	Product B Time	Product B $	Product C Time	Product C $
Initial cost						
Cost per serving portion						
Pre-preparation						
Storage space						
Refrigeration						
Equipment and utilities						
Lead time from preparation to service						
Spoilage percentage						
Cleanup						
Total real cost						
OTHER CONSIDERATIONS						
Quality						
Nutritional value						
Preparation skills required						
Availability						
Flexibility in usage						

Figure 6d. A guide for realistic consideration of the financial and other merits of convenience (ready) and conventional food items

greens, and presectioned fresh fruits. A realistic assessment by the manager of the comparative money time, and equipment requirements of these products may indicate that it is desirable to purchase the ready product.

In some cases, however, it may be more advantageous to process the item after purchase. This is particularly true when preparation personnel are idle during nonpeak periods. Portioning of such items as jellies and dressings from larger containers and sectioning of fruits and salad ingredients may be done by personnel who are not otherwise occupied. Only a realistic comparison of costs will enable the manager to make the proper decision.

Processing

The heart of the system is the processing step. Transformation of raw products into end products is the main element of this procedure.

Processing usually necessitates combining the ingredients in a recipe, exposing them to other manipulative processes, and use of heating or cooling equipment. More technical knowledge and greater attention to detail are necessary at this stage than at any other. If proper procedures have been followed during previous steps, however, and all elements of the system are integrated, it may be possible to achieve dramatic results with minimum effort and talent. A large number of successful operators produce sophisticated menus with a minimum of equipment, using personnel who have a minimum amount of technical training and experience.

At the processing point, a division of food operations occurs. All operations carry out the elements up to this stage within a narrow range of variation. It is here that the separation of gourmet from ordinary food begins to take place.

With technical personnel in such short supply, and the expansion of the industry making still greater demands on those who are available, it is imperative that this part of the system operate as efficiently as possible. The manager must hire and train his workers wisely to produce the desired food items. He must be ready to step into any void that develops due to the illness of a worker or a peak period demand. The interrelationship of personnel, product, and equipment must be maintained to obtain maximum efficiency with minimum effort. This is the main theme of this book, and great attention will be given to the subject.

Portioning

To distribute equal amounts of food to consumers under a fixed pricing policy and to gain the proper yield from a product, food must be portioned for service.

The item may be portioned by count (for example a fixed number of shrimp to an order, or a set number of pieces in a preportioned item). It might be portioned by weight, using portion scales to ensure proper division of the product. Volume portioning is another method, using a tool, implement, or container to measure the amount to be dispensed.

In any form of portioning, care must be taken that both the customer and the company receive a fair share from the product. Too large a portion means a monetary loss to the food operator, while too small a portion results in consumer dissatisfaction and loss of business.

The portioning process is a tool of food preparation, not an indispensable element in the system. Quantity food operations (with the possible exception of limited menu, fast food operations) may not require exact measurement of each portion served. If measurement is not done, however, a periodic sampling of weight or volume must be undertaken to check that a reasonable portioning standard is being maintained. The periodic "eyeballing" of a carved meat item on a cafeteria or buffet line by trained personnel may be an acceptable practice, although portioning devices are available in the form of concealed portion scales.

Where volume is the measure, care must be taken that the physical cuts of the item are consistent with the portioning unit and that differences in preparation styles do not result in different yields. Items composed of both juice and solids and meat items with gravy or sauce bases must be specially controlled to ensure that standard amounts of solids and juice or meat, sauce, and vegetables are portioned under a volume system.

Particular portioning problems arise with roasted meats. A rest period of fifteen to twenty minutes must be provided for most meats after removal from the oven. During this postoven rise period, the internal temperature of the meat continues to rise before the heat begins to dissipate from the mass, and final firming takes place. If cutting is done prior to this, the meat will tend to shred, resulting in portioning difficulty and a reduction of yield.

The tools used in portioning must be selected for size, form, and type. A slotted spoon gives a very different portion than a solid one, while a knife that is not properly honed or of the wrong type may destroy portioning attempts.

Although portioning is important and necessary for the food operator, the diner should not be made aware of it. Mounds of vegetables, salads, and the like all neatly stacked on a plate in the shape of the food scoop, with no variation in appearance, make the portioning process detract from the service part of the system. Portioning should be done as unobtrusively as possible, as an adjunct to the preparation and service functions.

This particular step is often transferred out of the house by purchasing preportioned food items. This not only reduces one step in the food production system but also ensures that a standard portioning system will be followed so that the manager or supervisor can maintain a better control on costs.

A variety of items ranging from meats (in steak or patty form) to milk, sauces, vegetables, condiments, and jams are all available in preportioned form. The supervisor should realize, however, that, since another enterprise has done the portioning, the process will be paid for in higher purchasing costs. The

Table 6-1. Portioning Tools

Tool	Size or Description	Amount
Food scoops	no. 6	2/3 cups or 6 ounces
	no. 8	1/2 cup or 4 ounces
	no. 10	3/8 cup or 3 ounces
	no. 12	1/3 cup or 2.5 ounces
	no. 16	1/4 cup or 2.25 ounces
	no. 20	3-1/5 tablespoons or 2 ounces
	no. 24	2-2/3 tablespoons or 1.5 ounces
	no. 30	2-1/5 tablespoons or 1 ounce
	no. 40	1-3/4 tablespoons or 0.75 ounce
Ladles	1-ounce	1/8 cup
	2-ounce	1/4 cup
	4-ounce	1/2 cup
	6-ounce	3/4 cup
	8-ounce	1 cup
Glassware	5-ounce	3-4 ounces
	8-ounce	6-7 ounces
Counts and preportions	Fresh fruits*	
	Apples	56-163 count per box
	Oranges, California	48-180 count per box
	Oranges, Florida	82-100 count per box
	Lemons	95-235 count per box
	Canned fruits and vegetables, no. 10 cans	
	Apricots, halves	65-151 count per can
	Cherries	248-522 count per can
	Pears and peaches	25-40 count per can
	Potatoes	200-375 count per can
	Olives, no. 1 to no. 9	128 (no. 1) to 32 (no. 9) count per pound
	Butter pats	72-110 count
	Cream cheese, individual packs	3 ounces
	Cereals, individual packs	1 ounce
	Juice, individual size	6 ounces
	Sugar and salt, individual packets	1 teaspoon
	Saltines and crackers, individual packs	Varies with type; 7/8 to 1 ounce, average
	Tea, individual bags	28, 35, or 46 grains
	Entrée items, boil-in-the-bag pouches	4-10 ounces
	Convenience items, jams, jellies, sauces, etc.	1/2 ounce, usually
	Milk, individual containers	8 ounces

*Counts for fresh fruits, which originally represented the count in the box, may actually stand for the *size* of the fruit, since box sizes vary from one locality to another.

extra cost must be compared with in-house labor costs, control procedures, equipment, and time considerations, to see whether preportioned purchases are justified for the particular facility.

Serving

The last, but certainly not the least, part of the quantity food system is service of the food to the consumer. Whether it is done at a table service restaurant, at a cafeteria line, or in a plane flying at 30,000 feet, this represents the entire food system to the consumer. Meticulously followed food preparation principles may be completely negated by service that is slow or slovenly. Temperatures of foods may be changed by poor serving techniques, or hot foods may be received in an unsatisfactory condition. The lack of an accompanying vegetable, sauce, or condiment may make an entrée unacceptable to the guest. Conversely, the use of a rechaud or flames at the table, in even a modified form of French service, may do much to increase the acceptability of an otherwise routine meal. The location of an item on a cafeteria line, the amount and kind of color it has, and the light or ice surrounding it might mean the difference between poor and excellent acceptance.

All types of restaurants use foods of the same basic form and from a very narrow range, except for differences in grade. It is mainly in the methods of preparation and serving that differences are noted.

A close relationship must be maintained between preparation and serving of the food, with procedures and schedules interrelated to achieve consumer satisfaction. If status problems arise between front of the house (waiters and waitresses) and back of the house (preparation personnel), attempts must be made to resolve them and to instill a team approach to food service. Depending on the particular operation, service may be under the control of a maitre d'hotel or a hostess. It is carried out by waiters, waitresses, and busboys.

All service personnel should know the major ingredients and general preparation methods of menu items to be able to answer the questions of guests. As many implements, tools, and replenishment items as possible should be kept in the dining room so that service people spend less time returning to the kitchen for butter, water, silver, and the like. Many items can be portioned by the service personnel themselves to increase speed of service and achieve better use of preparation personnel. Soup in bains-marie for service portioning, salads kept ready in pass-through refrigerators, and garnishes placed on sandwich or breakfast plates make service a team effort and produce better results than service of a product totally prepared and portioned in the back of the house, out of the guest's sight.

Basic Principles of Food Preparation and Processing

Although each element of the food service system is important, the main focus of this book is on the processing or preparation of food. The first and most important consideration for this element is knowledge of the methods and principles of food preparation. The principles discussed next are the basis for the major procedures and in many cases explain other techniques as well.

Transfer of Heat

Food may be prepared by the use of heat or the absence of it. In cooking, heat is used to make items more palatable, easier to digest, and safer for human consumption. Heat removal permits longer storage of the product or changes the form (as in ice cream).

Heat is a form of energy or molecular motion. When applied to foods it produces a physical state in which the substance's molecules vibrate at an accelerated rate. This results in changes, such as a different color, coagulation of protein, vaporization of water, and volatilization of acids or flavor agents. The rapidity of the molecular motion is measured in temperature variations.

Heat may be transferred from or to a product in three basic ways: conduction, convection, and radiation. All three are used in food preparation work.

Conduction. In the conduction method of heat transfer, heat is passed from one molecule to another that is touching it. Conduction is exemplified by a metal rod with one end in a fire: the other end transmits heat to the hand of a person holding it. Conduction is used in range-top cookery and, in combination with other methods, in oven and steam cooking. Different metals have varying rates of conductivity. Highly conductive metals such as copper find wide use where heat by conduction is desired.

Convection. In convection transfer, heat is transmitted through liquid or gas from the source to the recipient. Although convection is used in many forms of food preparation, it is best demonstrated in the convection oven, which transmits heat by an attached fan to decrease cooking time.

Radiation. Radiation is the transfer of heat

from the source by means of radiant waves. Ceramic broiler material that radiates heat to a meat product on the grid below is a good example of this form.

Heat transfer types can be combined in order to decrease cooking times and/or increase quality. Examples include slow-cooking procedures, convection or pressure fryers, and combination ovens using convection and microwave or conventional heat with convection and steam.

Heat always flows from a high heat source to cooler recipient. Increases and decreases in temperature indicate this transfer. A major exception is latent heat, which can cause a substance to change in state with no increase in temperature, a principle applied in making ice cream and in refrigeration.

Heat is measured in Btu.'s (British thermal units). One Btu. is the amount of heat necessary to raise the temperature of one pound of water one degree centigrade. It is also measured in a succession of stages called degrees on both a centigrade and a Fahrenheit scale. The centigrade equivalent of a Fahrenheit temperature may be found by the formula:

$$C. = 5/9(F.-32)$$

The Fahrenheit equivalent of a centigrade temperature may be found by the formula:

$$F. = 9/5C.+32$$

The temperatures of foods are measured with thermometers. Temperature levels are indicators of completion of a cooking procedure. Temperatures are also used to measure the efficiency of equipment and to determine when a cooking process should begin.

For a discussion of cooking equipment, see chapter 7.

Microwave Cookery

Another form of "heat transfer" used in food preparation is electromagnetic radiation in the form of microwaves. Magnitron tubes produce microwaves that pass through food products enclosed in special equipment. The microwaves radiate at great speeds and from many directions. This causes a rapid agitation of all the molecules in the product and results in heating the food.

Because of the penetration of the waves and the lack of a cumulative heating effect on the outside surface of the food, no characteristic browning takes place. Unless an additional browning unit is employed, the food will not display the normal cooked appearance.

Microwave cookery is very swift, often cooking a product in a fraction of the time required by other methods of heat transfer. In addition, it will not heat any substance that does not contain moisture, so that paper cooking containers may be used, for example.

Generation of Gases

A second basic principle of food preparation is the generation of gases in products. The gas steam is generated by heat acting on water; carbon dioxide (CO_2) is generated by heat acting on baking powder in the presence of water, or by a combination of baking soda and an acid, or by yeast acting on sugar in a fermentation process.

In all applications, the gas that is generated is used as a leavening agent for the particular product.

Use of Chemicals

Chemicals in various forms are used in food preparation work. They produce carbon dioxide (as noted above), produce specific tastes, maintain colors, or retard spoilage.

Most of the chemicals in foods are added by a food processor for specific taste, firming, coloring, nutritional, or preservative purposes. Three major types of chemicals are most commonly used.

Monosodium Glutamate (MSG). This chemical additive has long been used to stimulate the taste buds and make tastes more acute by accentuating the flavor. Long a favorite in Oriental cooking, it was identified as a cause of the "Chinese restaurant syndrome," a condition characterized by headaches, facial pressure, and chest pain. Clearing this obstacle, it has recently been identified with other injurious effects on consumers, but continues to receive governmental approval. Recent research (1985) by Dr. R. Kenny showed, by a double-blind testing method, that the Chinese restaurant syndrome could not be supported in a sample of thirty individuals who claimed to be affected. (See *Food and Chemical Toxicology*, Nov. 12, 1986, p. 234.)

Sodium Bisulfite and Sodium Acid Pyrophosphate. These substances are used as anti-oxidants and whitening agents for potatoes. Note that as of August 1986 sulfites are forbidden to be added to fresh vegetables except potatoes. In prepared foods, sulfites in amounts greater than ten parts per million must be noted on the label as of January 1987. This FDA regulation is a result of persons who were allergic to the substance suffering allergic attacks after consuming foods with sulfites in them.

Tartrate, Phosphate, or Sodium Aluminum Sulfate Baking Powders. These products are used to generate carbon dioxide gas in baked and other products.

Microorganisms

Microorganisms are also used in the preparation of some foods. The use of yeasts in baking is one of their most important applications. The traditional story is that wild yeasts were introduced accidentally into an unleavened grain product and produced the first loaf of leavened bread. Microorganisms are also important in the manufacture and/or aging of cheeses, wines, and meats. Microorganisms are currently used as a part of a spray for tender products such as strawberries to prevent frost development during the cold nights of the growing season.

Combining Procedures

Basic principles of food preparation also apply to the physical procedures used before or during cooking. These procedures are manipulative and concern the combining or dividing of food. They are as important to good food preparation as any other steps, and if not carried out properly they may prevent satisfactory completion of cooking.

Blending. This is the thorough mixing of one product with another, usually in a liquid or semiliquid state. It suggests a complete intermingling of the substances so that a new, third form is produced. The process is carried out with less vigor than beating.

Beating. Beating is more vigorous mixing of food products usually of a more solid type.

Mixing. Mixing is the joining together of two food items of like or unlike consistency, by agitation, shaking, stirring, or the like. It may be done with either liquid or solid substances.

Creaming. Creaming is a procedure in which a fat or shortening is mixed with sugar so that the softened fat intermingles with sugar granules.

Whipping. Whipping is the combination of two products, or the manipulation of a single product, by a process of rapid agitation that incorporates air. It suggests fluffiness, lightness, and delicate texture. The process is usually applied to dessert items, but it may also be used for vegetable products such as potatoes.

Dividing Procedures

Food may be divided before, during, or after other steps of food preparation. Dividing is classified according to the type, shape, and size of the resulting pieces. Although there are many variations, the following are considered the major forms of division that the food manager must know.

Cutting. Cutting is usually carried out with a knifelike implement or equipment attachment. The product is divided into smooth-surfaced pieces, with size and shape depending on the particular use to be made of the food. The term may also apply to a quasi-mixing process, in which fat is divided ("cut") into pieces in flour during the preparation of pastry.

Dicing. Dicing is the dividing of a product into small cubes. The term *mincing* is also used, but suggests finer division.) The dicing process may be carried out with a knife, by specialized machines designed for this function, or by attachments to other machines such as mixers.

Tearing. Tearing is a process of division using opposing power sources to separate a product. Salad greens that suffer injury or discoloration from the action of iron-based implements usually are divided by this procedure. (Labor considerations, however, dictate use of a knife or machine as a substitute for this time-consuming process, in many cases.)

Chopping. Chopping is the nondirected cutting of a solid product into a great number of pieces. It may be done by hand, with a knife, or by machinery using rotating blades and a rotating bowl. The term is often used interchangeably with *grinding*, in which food is put through a worm-gear-driven machine into a plate-type cutter for division.

Preserving and Curing Procedures

Food may be cured or preserved if it cannot be used immediately, or if the marketing channels used supply an inferior product for fresh use, or to give variety tastes to a standard product.

The basic forms of preserving are drying, curing, smoking, freezing, and canning. In each, an attempt is made to remove one or more of the basic conditions that cause spoilage, aging, or decay of the product, and thus prolong its life.

Particular foods lend themselves to certain methods of preservation. The appropriate methods for specific foods are covered in more detail in the discussions of particular food types (chapters 12-18).

Drying. In the drying process, a great amount of moisture is removed from the product in order to hinder the growth of bacteria, which need moisture to multiply. Depending on the type of food, the moisture may be removed by spraying the substance in droplet form and exposing it to a heat source; subjecting a solid product to a combination of smoke and heat; applying salt-base substances to dehydrate the product; or exposing the product to a combination freezing and drying procedure.

The removal of moisture from a product permits easier storage: either no refrigeration is required, or the product has an extended shelf life under refrigerated conditions. It requires only rehydration for later use.

Many freeze-dried products have excellent quality upon rehydration. Fruits and vegetables have been prepared in this manner for many years. Some products, however, never reconstitute to their original consistency, taste, and appearance. They possess the basic nutritional and functional requirements, however, and may be used in recipes, combined with other ingredients, to achieve results that equal use of the fresh product at a lower price. Dried milk is a good example.

Most of the products in this classification are received in the dried form. Little drying is carried out by the average food service establishment.

Canning. Canning has long been an acceptable method of preserving foods to use at a later date. It enables the producer to ship perishable products great distances without refrigeration. The canning process requires removal of air and heating the product to temperatures that cook it and kill the spores of pathogenic organisms.

Despite a few recent incidents of botulism that resulted in deaths, the commercial canning industry has generally maintained a highly acceptable safety record in processing canned foods.

Food subjected to the temperatures required for canning never approximates its fresh condition in color (particularly the green varieties), texture, or taste. Many consumers, after long exposure to canned foods, prefer the canned product to the fresh. Foods containing acids or sulfur may interact with the steel or tin of the can, despite the addition of protective enamels to the container, and some discoloration or taste change may be noted after shelf storage. Many consumers have come to accept these changes, too, as usual and reject other methods of processing. (A recent taste panel selected a canned tomato juice, in which an acid/can reaction had taken place, over a glass-processed juice. The tasters considered the can-generated taste the "normal" one for tomato juice.)

Canning is a procedure to be carried out by the producers of food and generally is not done in a user establishment.

Smoking. Smoking is a form of drying to a level less than complete dehydration. It is usually carried out on meat or fish, more to impart flavor than to preserve. A number of additive substances have been introduced to give a smoked flavor to products that have not been so processed.

Depending on the degree of smoking and the internal temperature reached, the process may produce a smoked taste only, a partially cooked or tenderized product, or a fully cooked and ready-to-eat product.

Although some food service establishments do have smokehouses to process specialty meat items, most smoked products come from meat processing plants.

Freezing. Freezing is a relatively recent method of processing, compared to most others. It was made possible when a method of moving products quickly through an ice-crystal-forming range was developed. (Newly developed "freeze flow" products remain soft in the freezer and are ready to use without defrosting. Products such as pie fillings and puddings fit into this category.) Previously the uncontrolled exposure of foods to low temperatures usually resulted in ice formation that ruptured the cells, loss of cell fluid, and reduction of texture and taste. The new process produced an acceptable product very close to the fresh form in taste and texture.

The food is first blanched by means of a short cooking period, in order to inactivate the enzymes and partially sterilize it. Then it is exposed to low temperatures in a flash freezing technique, using liquid nitrogen at a temperature of approximately minus 300 degrees Fahrenheit or immersing the product in liquified Freon at a temperature of approximately minus 35 degrees Fahrenheit.

Most freezing is carried out in food processing plants. The food service facility with a blast freezer that goes to minus 5 degrees Fahrenheit and below may effectively use freezing as a form of food preparation on the premises, however. The blast freezer not only stores foods ordered and received frozen but also holds leftovers and processes foods prepared in large quantities during slack periods and held for later service. Many foods offer no freezing problems, but operators must make sure that the correct starches are used in sauces, to prevent separation upon reconstitution, and that strict sanitation is maintained in all preparation procedures to prevent bacterial contamination. (Both these subjects are considered further in chapters 10 and 12.)

Curing. Curing is a term usually applied to meats. There are two major forms, a dry cure and a brine cure. In the dry cure a salt and sugar mixture is rubbed on the surface of the meat and it is stored for six to seven weeks at a temperature below 40 degrees Fahrenheit. In the brine cure, the meat is soaked in a brine composed of a mixture of salt, sugar, and saltpeter, using a ratio of nine pounds, three pounds, and three ounces, respectively, for each hundred pounds of meat. Techniques of stitch pumping or artery pumping are sometimes used to increase penetration of the brine and decrease the time required for processing.

All cured meats achieve a characteristic, heat-stable, red color (i.e., the color is not affected by cooking), because of the action of the saltpeter (potassium or sodium nitrate) on the myoglobin of the meat. The normal protein pigment, myoglobin, combined with oxygen when the meat is cut, gives oxymyoglobin; when cooked, this gives metamyoglobin, a brown-colored substance. If the meat is cured, the myoglobin plus potassium or sodium nitrate gives nitrosomyoglobin, also called nitric oxide myoglobin, a heat-stable red pigment.

Irradiation. Work has been done in preserving foods by both ionizing and nonionizing radiation so that bacteria are destroyed and enzymes inactivated. Some twenty-four countries including the Netherlands and Japan are currently using irradiation to ster-

Table 6-2. Foods Approved by FDA for Irradiation Treatment

Food	Purpose	Dose Limit	Date Approved
Fruits and vegetables	To slow growth and ripening and to control insects	Up to 1 kilogray (kGy)	April 18, 1986
Dry or dehydrated herbs, spices, seeds, teas, vegetable seasonings	To kill insects and control microorganisms	Up to 30 kGy	April 18, 1986
Pork	To control *Trichinella spiralis* (the parasite that causes trichinosis)	Minimum 0.3 kGy to maximum of 1 kGy	July 22, 1985
White potatoes	To inhibit sprout development	50 to 150 gray	Aug. 8, 1964
Wheat, wheat flour	To control insects	200 to 500 gray	Aug. 21, 1963

Source: *FDA Consumer*, July/August, 1986, p. 13.

ilize foods by killing insects and bacteria, retarding sprouting times, and increasing shelf life. The FDA, which had permitted the usage of cobalt 60 on spices and grains in 1985, issued an order to permit the use on pork, fruits, and vegetables of cesium 137, a by-product of plutonium extraction. Dosages below 100 kilorads are permitted, and a long-time nemesis like trichinosis in pork is destroyed. Some critics, however, question the safety of this process and state that the regrouping of molecules and the breakdown of the natural chemical balance will result in radiolytic compounds dangerous to humans.

Aseptic Packaging. Aseptic packaging, approved by the FDA in 1981 after being used many years throughout Europe, is a sterile packaging technique with no refrigeration required of a product, which contains no preservatives and no additives. The process reduces the cost of distribution, storage, and energy. Products are stored in paper containers with laminated polyethylene liners and an aluminum shield barrier that keeps light and oxygen out. The products are heated to 140 degrees Celsius or 284 degrees Fahrenheit for 2 to 4 seconds to kill bacteria and then piped through a sterile system into sterile containers. Up to now only 1 liter and individual 250 milligram sizes have been available, but new sizes are being developed. Research is also under way on how to package products containing particulates, such as soup with chunks of food in it, to supplement foods currently packaged under a system that handles liquids such as milk, fruit juices, salad dressings, clear soups, and the like.

Inert Gas Storage. Inert storage of meats and vegetables, that is, putting foods in impermeable bags with a ratio of air to carbon dioxide of two: three, has been used in food preparation. This atmosphere slows the bacterial growth that causes spoilage, permitting refrigerated storage of fish for four weeks and chicken for six weeks. It also slows the ripening of fruits and vegetables by limiting the amount of carbon dioxide that can be generated and the amount of oxygen to which the food can be exposed.

Cooking

The final process carried out before food is portioned and served to the guest is cooking. Taking foods that have already been partially prepared, the culinary worker applies external conditions to complete the processing.

The term *cooking* refers to the application of heat to achieve the desired results. (The principles of heat transfer were discussed earlier in this chapter.) Cooling, brewing, and reconstituting are other methods of the food preparation process. The most important method is cooking, however. It may be subdivided into two major classes: dry and moist.

Dry Methods

In dry cooking, heat is applied to the food product without any additional liquid. This method uses transfer by radiation, convection, or conduction. The process is usually carried out in an oven, in a broiler, in a radiating heat source such as a toaster, or by exposure to direct flame.

The dry methods of cooking usually produce dramatic changes in exterior color of the product, relatively great amounts of shrinkage (in relation to temperatures employed), and taste changes that are considered highly desirable.

The basic dry heat cooking methods are:

Baking. The food is heated in an enclosed space, usually by convection with some radiation and conduction heat transfer.

Broiling. The food is exposed to a direct heat source with most heat transfer taking place by radiation. Some heating by conduction is realized from a hot grid.

Searing. In searing direct short-term exposure to flame is used, destroying tissue. This method is incorporated in most broiling.

Toasting. The food is exposed to a heating element producing a browning effect. Toasting is usually used for dextrinization of grain products such as breads and muffins.

Roasting. Roasting is the same as baking. It usually applies to meats.

Frying. Frying is the cooking of a product in a fat. If a small amount of fat is used, the process is referred to as sautéing or grilling; when a larger amount is used, it is called pan frying or deep frying. The process usually gives a distinctive exterior color and imparts characteristic tastes. In all types, but most often in deep fat frying, a coating of bread crumbs or other substances may be placed on the food to protect it from excessive fat absorption.

Moist Methods

The moist methods of cooking are usually used to protect a product during the application of heat, to prevent excessive shrinkage, to produce variety in taste, or to tenderize an item.

Moist cooking methods usually protect an item's surface color. They may result in loss of acceptable texture or loss of nutrients if proper procedures are not followed to control the rate of cooking and the liquid generated.

Most moist cooking is done by convection, using the liquid as a vehicle for heat transfer, and by conduction, passing the heat through the product from molecule to molecule.

The major moist cooking methods are:

Scalding. The product is heated to just below or just at the boiling temperature. Scalding is usually carried out on products that are liquid and tender (owing to their sugar content). Whole milk is an example. Scalding may be done on the range or in a steam-jacketed kettle, but is more properly accomplished in a double boiler where the substance is protected from extremes of direct heat by a water bath.

Boiling. Boiling is the most common method of moist cooking. The product is included in a liquid, usually water, and a rapid agitation of the liquid molecules heats and cooks it. Boiling may be accomplished in a steam-jacketed kettle or on a range. Great attention must be paid to the amount of the boil. For example, a rolling boil may cause the physical breakdown of a tender product.

Poaching and Simmering. In both poaching and simmering, foods are cooked just at the base level of boiling. A delicate fish item may be poached to maintain its texture and color. Simmering is used for long periods of cooking of less tender meats or for blending and concentrating a completely liquid item by reducing its volume through evaporation of part of the liquid. Both methods are usually accomplished on a range or in a steam-jacketed kettle and rely on convection heat transfer.

Braising. Braising is exposure of a solid food product to a liquid fat or combination of fat and other liquid in two stages of cooking: it is actually frying in the early stage, for exterior color change, and simmering or stewing in the later stage, for tenderizing. It usually requires a long period of cooking.

Stewing. Stewing is similar to simmering. It is usually reserved for a mixture of vegetables and meats, cooked in a liquid and in their own extracted juices. It is done at low temperatures for long periods of time to achieve tenderness of the product and intermingling of the flavors.

Blanching. In blanching, boiling water or hot deep fat is used to partially cook a product. It may be used to assist in the removal of skins from fruits (for example, tomatoes immersed in boiling water for a minute are easily peeled), as a preliminary to the freezing process, or to precook items in order to make more effective use of equipment or personnel during meal periods (for example, if French fried potatoes are blanched, they require only heating and browning during a peak period).

Steaming. Steam may be used in a variety of ways in food preparation work, in either direct or indirect contact with food. It is most often referred to as a moist form of cookery, however. Steam, placed in direct contact with food items in a steamer, speeds cooking, maintains maximum color, and helps to retain nutrients. It is best used in this manner for the preparation of vegetables from a frozen condition.

Brewing

Brewing may also be considered a food preparation technique. It is usually the leeching out of flavor and color from a minutely divided substance into a liquid. This may be accomplished in the presence of heat, as with coffee, or the absence of it. Heat appears to give more desirable results, although products such as iced tea may be made with either hot or cold water.

Reconstituting

The final method of food preparation to be considered is reconstitution. It is defined as bringing a food back to its original form. Generally it involves the transfer of heat to a frozen or chilled product in order to bring it to serving temperature. Foods that are frozen usually require about twice the heating time that the chilled form of the same food would require.

A number of methods may be used to reconstitute foods. A freeze-dried product may be immersed in a water bath; alternating refrigeration and convection heat cycles may bring a previously cooked and frozen item back to an acceptable use level; or a dry steam injector system may defrost and reheat an item for service.

Reconstituting a ready or convenience product may use the following heat forms: dry heat of convection or conventional ovens; moist heat of water baths or steamers; radiant heat of quartz-type ovens; or microwave heat.

Reconstitution may entail just heating a fully prepared food or finishing and fully cooking a convenience item that was shaped, breaded, or blanched prior to final in-house preparation.

Originally, the regularly available food service equipment (conventional and convection ovens, steam-jacketed kettles, microwave ovens, and steamers) was used for reconstituting convenience or ready food items. More recently specialized equipment has been developed for this specific task. Notable are reconstituting units powered by combinations of infrared energy and refrigeration, infrared energy, convection heat, and refrigeration, or microwave energy and convection heat. Each of these pieces of equipment was developed to overcome major problems that arose when basic food service equipment was used for reconstitution. These problems included scorching, surface drying, uneven heating, and sogginess of the food, and the necessity of using different pieces of equipment to reconstitute different foods.

Although some operating procedures have been devised to correct certain reconstitution problems (see chapter 14), a key factor is the human operator and his attention to the procedure. More work is needed to make this process consistently deliver a high quality item to the consumer. Due to labor and productivity considerations, major emphasis is being placed on this area, and rapid improvements in equipment methodology are expected.

7 *Facilities, Tools, and Equipment*

Objective: To explore the factors that influence the physical plant and choice of equipment, including menu, productivity, and focus of the unit. To discuss the range of specific equipment available in the areas of food preparation and storage, and how to make the work flow most efficiently.

Factors Affecting Facilities and Equipment

Among the major variables that influence the production of food in quantity are the physical plant, the tools, and the equipment of the operation. The food facility may be likened to a food factory, in that it is a complex organization performing many varied and specialized tasks. It differs from most other manufacturing facilities, however: for example, a car is built in one plant, assembled in another, and sold at a third location, but food is often stored, cooked, served, and consumed in one place. This diversity of operations requires many different pieces of equipment and an integration of the functions performed so that maximum efficiency may be obtained.

The functions to be performed are the governing feature. The food preparation facility must provide adequate space to accomplish these tasks. Necessary storage, processing, and serving areas and adequate equipment must be provided. Consistent with the profit desired or other considerations, the facility must be able to accommodate the consumers to be served and offer an appealing menu. It must be flexible enough to meet minor changes in demand and supply and keep pace with the turnover required by profit considerations.

The facility should allow each department some autonomy, to provide for worker satisfaction and uncrowded work space. Provisions must also be made for the sharing of equipment or work space, where feasible, in order to conserve funds and to interrelate the departments into a smoothly functioning unit.

Specialized requirements of the type of food facility must be considered in determining its size and form. The overall layout of the operation must provide for these specific features.

Pressing labor shortages, unusual peak periods, the need for mobility or speed, and the form of service must all be considered, if the physical layout is to accommodate the required performance in the time allowed.

The most important factor in determining the adequacy and arrangement of the facility and equipment is the menu. Coupling the extent and form of menu to be offered with

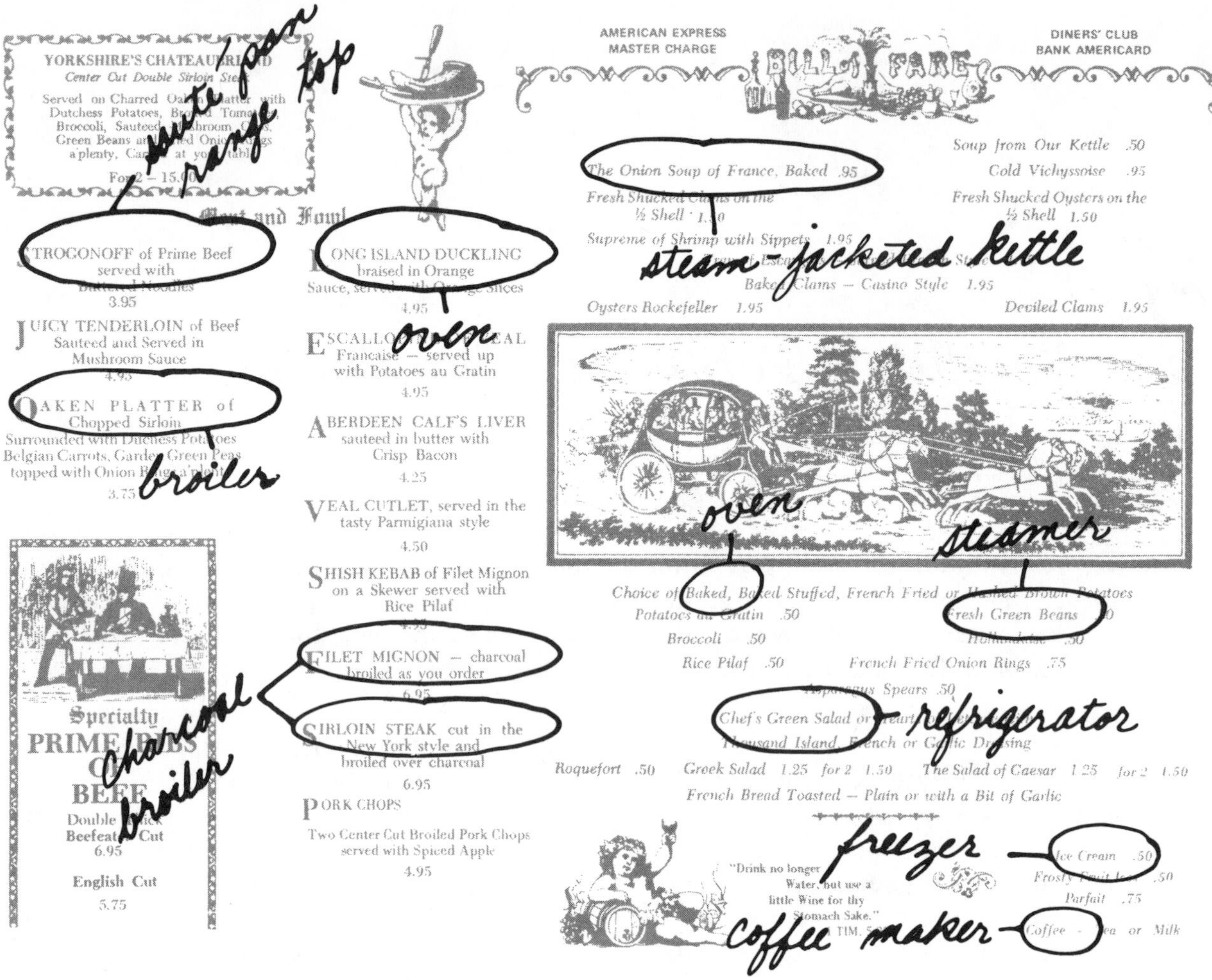

Figure 7a. Analysis of a menu to determine equipment needs in planning a food production facility. (Adapted by permission from "Equipment Purchasing Systems," *Volume Feeding Management,* March 1967, p. 30; menu courtesy of the Yorkshire Inn, Miami.)

the forecasts of consumption of each item and the turnover rate of patrons, it is possible to determine the required size of the facility and the type and amount of equipment. Then flows of work, layout schemes, and overall space requirements can be set.

Other factors to be considered are the sizes of the portions to be served; the number and size of the batches to be prepared; and the times specific pieces of equipment will be in use. Figure 7b shows a form that may be used in determining these facts.

In selecting and placing pieces of equipment, the operator should consider sharing possibilities, changes of work hours, and new production methods as possible alternatives. If conflicts arise over the use of a machine, alternative preparation methods using other pieces of equipment or even hand labor might be considered. Equipment should be kept as mobile as possible so that it can be used in different sections of the operation. If it is modular in design it can be used with other equipment with a minimum of effort. A pan that fits refrigerator, oven, and steam table so that an item can be stored in, cooked in, and served from the same modular unit, saves the time and labor of changing equipment.

The Physical Plant

Since the physical plant is so important and limits the amount and type of food production that can be carried out, a complete evaluation of requirements should be made before facilities and equipment are considered. The following are important factors:

(a) Geographical area—nearest city, population, etc.

(b) Description of the clientele served.

(c) Menu, extent of service, rate of turnover, expected check average, and other service factors.

(d) Purchasing and storage factors, such as frequency of deliveries and items to be purchased.

Equipment and Space Requirements per Item

Menu item:

Total forecast:

Forecast by time period:

Equipment needed:

Preparation time:

Number of batches to be prepared:

Size of batches:

Time of equipment use:

Serving and holding equipment needed:

Time of serving and holding equipment use:

Plating or assembly area utilized:

Special problems:

Figure 7b. This form can be used for an in-depth equipment and space utilization survey for each menu item to be served in a meal period.

(e) Additional services to be provided—catering, banquet business, takeout service, etc.

(f) Special requirements—cart storage in hospitals, multiple use of dining rooms in colleges, large storage areas for prepared foods and assembly-line preparation for airlines, etc.

Once these specific factors have been determined and the requirements made known to the operator, the adequacy of the preparation area may be judged. Many operators use as a rule of thumb an assignment of 60 percent of the space to the dining area and 40 percent to the kitchen facilities. More realistic space allocations may be made based on the numbers of consumers to be served in a time period. Table 7-1 lists three of the most popular methods of calculating the space, based on the rental factor, the profit factor, and the footage per number of consumers served per hour.

General Standards of Equipment Selection

Once the parameters of the physical plant have been decided, particular pieces of equipment may be selected. The first questions to settle are the total amount of an item to be prepared; the piece of equipment needed to produce the item; the capacity of the equipment; the time required for preparation; the number of batches to be prepared; and alternative methods of preparation. Then it is necessary to consider three of the most important factors:

(1) Need for equipment in terms of the labor or costs that may be saved;

(2) Fuels available and desirable; and

(3) Cost.

Need

The first, need, has already been determined in relation to menu form, number of consumers to be served, etc. The operator now must determine whether the piece of equipment will either improve the quality of the product; increase the quantity produced; reduce errors; replace another piece of equipment that is not functioning properly and

Table 7-1. Methods of Determining Kitchen Space Requirements

A. Rental Factor Method

1. The ratio of rent to sales, expressed as a percent, is divided into the yearly rent to get the amount of annual sales needed:

$2,400 ÷ 5% = $48,000

2. The sales per year are translated into sales per day by dividing by the number of days in operation:

50 weeks x 6 days per week = 300 days in operation
$48,000 ÷ 300 days = $160 per day

3. The daily sales are allocated among the meal periods according to the percent of business expected:

Breakfast:	10% x $160 = $16
Lunch:	50% x $160 = $80
Dinner:	40% x $160 = $64

4. The meal period sales are divided by the expected check averages to arrive at the number of people to be served:

Breakfast:	$16 ÷ $ .50 check average = 32 guests
Lunch:	$80 ÷ $ .75 check average = 106 guests
Dinner:	$64 ÷ $1.50 check average = 43 guests

5. The meal period with the largest number of guests is then used to find the number of seats required. The turnover rate for the meal period is divided into the number of guests. (A turnover rate of 2 per hour means that each guest occupies a dining room place 30 minutes on the average.) Then 20 percent of this figure is added to it, to account for unoccupied seats that occur when the size of a party does not match an available table arrangement.

106 guests ÷ 2 per hour = 53 + (20% x 53) = 63 dining room seats

6. To determine the size of the dining room, an industry standard of 10 to 20 square feet per seat is used:

63 seats x 15 square feet = 945 square feet

7. If the 60/40 dining room/kitchen ratio is used, the kitchen area is:

(945 square feet ÷ 60) x 40 = 630 square feet

The 60/40 ratio must be revised to meet convenience and ready food kitchen requirements.

B. Footage per Meal Served Method

Using a rule of thumb, the largest number of guests to be served per hour is multiplied by a square footage factor based on industry averages, to get the kitchen size. An allowance of 5 square feet per meal served per hour is accepted:

106 meals served per hour x 5 square feet per meal = 530 square feet

C. Rate of Profit Method

1. The ratio of profit to sales, expressed as a percent, is divided into the annual net profit to arrive at the sales required:

$10,000 ÷ 10% = $100,000

2. The annual sales are translated into sales per day:

50 weeks x 5 days per week = 250 days of operation
$100,000 ÷ 250 days = $400 per day

3. The check average is divided into the daily sales to get the number of guests expected to be served:

$400 ÷ $1.50 check average = 266 guests per day

4. The guests are then divided according to the meal period. Assuming two meals, lunch and dinner, and a 50 percent spread:

50% x 266 guests per day = 133 guests per meal

5. The rule of thumb factor, 5 square feet of kitchen space per meal served, is used to determine kitchen area (turnover rate is assumed to be 1 per hour):

133 guests x 5 square feet = 665 square feet

Adapted from Arthur Dana, *Kitchen Planning for Quantity Food Service;* copyright 1949, Harper Brothers, Publishers, New York; reprinted by permission. Although this book is now out of print it is an important reference source on space allocation for food service planners.

Table 7-2. Labor Saving Required to Justify Equipment Cost

Cost of Equipment	Annual Labor Cost $3,000	$3,500	$5,000	$6,000	$8,000
	Minutes Required to be Saved per Day				
$100	2	1	1	1	1
$300	5	4	3	2	2
$500	8	7	5	4	3
$700	11	10	7	5	4
$900	14	12	9	7	5
$1000	16	14	10	8	6
$1500	24	21	14	12	9
$2000	32	27	19	16	12
$3000	48	42	28	24	18

Courtesy of Toledo Scale, Toledo, Ohio

Note: Figures are based on 10 percent depreciation per year and on 2,000 working hours per year (250 eight-hour days). Labor savings result only when the employee is doing other work, not watching the equipment perform the task while he remains idle.

requires expensive repairs; or help to reduce labor costs.

The labor cost considerations are probably the most important, since the equipment has to assist workers and conserve labor. It must permit workers to produce more. They must be able to carry out other functions while the machine completes tasks previously assigned to them. Predicted savings in man-hours must be compared to the amortized cost of the equipment. Table 7-1 gives some guidelines as to the savings that are required.

It is well to remember that changes in production methods or purchase of a food item in a different form may be alternatives to purchase of a new piece of equipment. These choices should be considered before equipment is purchased.

Fuel

The fuel used to operate the equipment is part of the true cost of the equipment. The availability of a particular fuel or power source in a particular geographical area may greatly influence the selection. However, some general considerations may be listed here.

Food service equipment is generally operated by steam, electricity, or gas. Each power source is discussed below.

Steam. Steam is a product obtained by heating water to the boiling point (212 degrees Fahrenheit) and above, confining the exudate, and continuing to heat it. Water in an open container will never reach a higher temperature than 212 degrees, but if its vapor is captured after the water is heated to this temperature, it may be superheated to higher temperatures and pressures.

Two common pressures are used in food service work: low pressure, five pounds per square inch (psi), and high pressure, fifteen pounds per square inch. Steam units are designed to operate on a psi scale, with a direct relationship between pressure and temperature. Table 7-3 shows the relationship between temperature and pressure in steam equipment. The superheated temperatures are the reason food cooks much faster in steam equipment than in containers open to the atmosphere.

Steam may be used either in direct contact with the food or in a surrounding jacket or container. It may be generated by a boiler incorporated in the equipment or produced in a larger and remote boiler and then piped to the equipment.

Steam equipment prepares food more rapidly than cooking in water or in a dry medium. Its major advantages are this speed,

Table 7-3. Steam Pressure and Temperature Relationships

	Pounds per Square Inch	Boiling Temperature of Water (° F.)
Normal atmospheric pressure	0	212
Steam pressure	5	228
	10	240
	15	250

the conservation of nutrients, and the retention of moisture in the food.

Heat that is added to water in an open container is all used to vaporize the water into steam, and, since the atmospheric pressure remains constant, the water boils away as steam with no increase in the temperature of the remaining water. When some constraint is placed on the steam, however, increased pressure is applied to the surface of the water. This requires an increase in the water temperature before full boiling takes place. As a result, cooking takes place much more rapidly. There is approximately six times as much available (latent) heat in steam as in water boiled at atmospheric pressure. This latent heat is released when the steam contacts food in the cooking compartment of a steamer or steam-jacketed kettle.

Steam may be used in steamers, steam-jacketed kettles, food warmers, reconstituting equipment, urns, and proofing cabinets. Some steam is also used in ovens, to control surface crusts on baked products. Dishwashing equipment, of course, uses steam too.

This source of power usually requires an extensive piping system, hooding for exhaust, and some form of pit or draining area. Some self-contained units have been designed to reduce these requirements, particularly in smaller steam-jacketed kettles.

Electricity. Electricity is used to operate food service equipment with motor driven components. It may drive a food mixer motor, a chopper motor, or the compressor on a refrigerator. It may also be used to heat an oven or range or to heat the water in a self-contained, electric, steam-generating unit.

Electricity is clean, safe, and flexible in use, but it sometimes lacks the pinpoint control of temperature desired in range-top cooking and the like. Electricity is usually generated at a central power plant, using water, coal, oil, or nuclear materials as power sources. It is then transmitted through circuits to the facility.

The unit of electrical power is the *volt.* This is similar to the psi in steam. Its rate of flow along electrical circuits is called the *ampere.* When it reaches a use area, the electricity enters a transformer, and the voltage is stepped down to a more manageable level for use. Commercial cooking equipment requires voltages of 208, 220, 230, or 240. The more conventional 110- or 115-volt supply may be used only for smaller pieces of equipment such as toasters and coffee makers.

Electric motors operate on the principle of repulsion of like poles and attraction of opposite ones. Electric current, flowing through a magnet in a motor assembly, sets up polarity fields and causes the motor shaft to spin. In units that provide heat, an electric current flows against levels of resistance (expressed as *ohms*). This heats the wires or elements in such units as toasters, ovens, and ranges.

The use of electricity is measured in *watts* (Amperes x Voltage): 1,000 watts (1 kilowatt) equals 56.883 Btu.'s, and 1 kilowatt hour (1 kilowatt working 1 hour) equals 3,413 Btu.'s.

Gas. Gas is the third major fuel used in food preparation work. It may be either natural or manufactured and is piped by pressure through transmission lines from the producing or capturing source to the user location.

Gas is sold by the cubic foot. Manufactured gases, used primarily on the eastern seaboard and made from coal, coke, and oil, provide heating values ranging from 500 to 550 Btu.'s per cubic foot. Natural gases provide between 960 and 1150 Btu.'s per cubic foot, while liquified petroleum gases may provide from 550 Btu.'s per cubic foot (when supplied as air-gas mixtures) to 2500 Btu.'s per cubic foot (when supplied in undiluted vapor form). One study equates 550 cubic feet of natural gas with 100 kilowatt-hours of electricity.

Gas is considered to give better pinpoint control on ranges, with instant heat generation and stoppage. It usually requires venting of the equipment and some safety measures because of its explosive capabilities. It must also be equipped with such protective devices as safety cutoffs and pilot lights.

Gas may be used with any type of food service equipment but finds its best application in direct heat equipment such as ranges, ovens, and broilers.

Cost

The final major factor in equipment selection is the cost of the unit and of the fuels it uses. Other incidental costs include installation expenses, cost of additional equipment required, such as hoods, draining, wiring, and ducts, and the cost of financing the equipment purchase.

Energy Costs

Many articles have been written about energy costs, methods of saving energy, and forecasting methods to determine energy needs. Government regulations have been imposed on organizations to control temperatures, and companies have changed equipment and adapted equipment to reduce the use of energy. Switches have been installed to turn off equipment, logs have been instituted to track times and temperatures, and loops for hot waste water have been made permitting heat transfer to incoming fresh water. All of these measures are, of course, important, and managers and supervisors should continue to research the periodical literature for ways to conserve on this significant expenditure in any food service operation. But, at the present time, the most important element in energy conservation in the food service operation is the efficient management of the output of food service equipment.

One of the most effective means for accomplishing the proper energy management of food service equipment is found in a method proposed by Dr. Frank Romanelli of the Anderson Mayfair Properties. (See "Energy Management in Food Service Systems," *Cornell Hotel and Restaurant Administration Quarterly* [August 1978]: 4-5). The procedure proposed by Romanelli involves a management audit for all kitchen equipment to determine what it really costs to prepare an individual menu item in a particular way and what quality results are attained. In this way it then becomes possible to price menus realistically, including the energy costs, or to change menu items or preparation methods in order to reduce energy costs.

His method is to determine the kilowatt hour (kwh) consumption for each piece of equipment without the need to install expensive meters. He suggests the following method:

1. Begin measuring the on-time of the thermostat signal light immediately after food is placed in the equipment.
2. Record the total on-time of the thermostat signal light during the cooking process.
3. Conduct five different tests with all factors the same: the same piece of equipment, the same cooking temperature, food product of the same size, shape, weight, and temperature.
4. Calculate the arithmetic mean of the on-time of the thermostat signal light for the five tests.
5. Divide the mean on-time by 60 to determine the percentage of one hour.
6. Multiply this percentage by the electrical

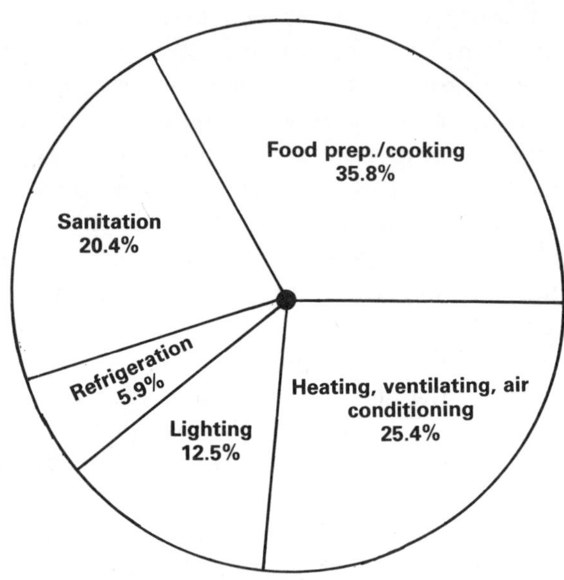

Figure 7c. Major portions of energy costs of a typical food service operation. Suggestions for saving on these percentages offered by Florida Restaurant Association director of information and education services include calibration of thermostats, closing of areas not in use, staggering turn-on times for heavy-duty equipment, turning air conditioning up to 85 degrees at night, and establishing an employee award system for energy-saving ideas. (Source: *Florida Restaurant Association Bulletin*, Aug. 1, 1987.)

rating of the equipment. The result is the kwh consumption for the food product prepared in this manner using this equipment.

For example, a mean of 30 minutes of the five tests in which the thermostat light is on divided by 60 minutes in one hour equals .50 part of one hour the thermostat light is on during this procedure. This multiplied by 12 kw, the rating of the equipment being used, equals a rate of consumption of 6 kwh.

With this information available for every menu item, it is possible to adjust, change, or vary menu or preparation procedures to achieve the minimal use of energy for the item produced or else the proper pricing of a menu item to include the necessary energy costs. When these procedures are wedded with other conservation measures, some meaningful reductions of excessive energy costs can be realized. This technique can serve as a stopgap measure until more extensive conservation measures can be undertaken when a new facility is constructed or major alterations are made or new equipment is purchased.

Maintenance and Safety Factors

Maintenance and safety considerations are also important in selecting equipment. If spare parts are available within a reasonable period of time and easily installed, this can make a significant difference. Information should be gathered on the availability of the manufacturer's representatives in the area and the need for special materials to maintain effective operation of the equipment. The adequacy of plans furnished with the equipment and the manufacturer's reputation are also important.

The operator's ability to maintain the equipment and keep it sanitary is a key factor. A maintenance care record should be kept for each piece of equipment, listing all expenditures made for care, repair, and upkeep. The procedure and schedule to be followed in maintaining the equipment should be included. This promotes the most effective and economical use of the equipment. If preventive maintenance procedures are adequately followed, repairs should be kept to a minimum, and machines that require constant repair or replacement of parts may signal the need for replacement.

Taking all these factors into consideration, another guide for the purchase of equipment was developed by Brother Herman E. Zaccarelli of Purdue University based on a formula that contained (A) labor savings, (B) savings in products as a result of buying the equipment (for example, the differences in

Maintenance Record Card

Name of Equipment:	**Identifying Number:**
Model Number:	**Manufacturer:**
Date of Purchase:	**Guarantee or Service Period:**

Maintenance

Service to Be Performed	Date to Be Done	Done By

Repairs, Adjustments, or Service

What Was Done	Date	By Whom	Cost

Figure 7d. A maintenance record card that can be kept for each major piece of equipment, to ensure that adequate upkeep and service procedures are carried out and that major repairs are recorded, so that the need for replacement can be determined.

shrinkage rate and resulting costs with old and new equipment), (C) the cost of the equipment installed, (D) the cost of utilities over the life of the equipment, (E) the cost of maintenance and repair over the life of the equipment, (F) the interest that could have been earned on the purchase money, and (G) the salvage value when the equipment is discarded after the average life of the equipment has passed.

$$\frac{A + B}{C+D+E+F-G}$$

If the answer is 1 or more, it is a good buy.

The life of equipment ranged from twenty years for range hoods to twelve years for ice machines; fourteen years for broilers, slicers, scales, and carts; and fifteen years for dishwashers, ovens, ranges, and refrigerators. (See *Culinary Review*, April 1983, p. 21.)

Employees should be instructed in the proper use of the equipment. Operating instructions should be posted at all equipment locations to guard against incorrect operating procedures that may damage the machine.

One of the major techniques of preventive maintenance is use of a user inspection form. This often uncovers and corrects minor problems before major ones develop. An operator conversant with the problems that may develop in a machine may be able to spot a condition that requires only a minor adjustment before it develops into a major replacement problem. More extensive inspections, adjustments, and repairs should also be scheduled regularly to ensure that the equipment performs the work for which it was designed.

The major pieces of food service equipment are discussed below.

Ovens

Ovens are units of equipment that provide dry heat methods of food preparation. They may be fired by either gas or electricity and are available in either conventional or convection types. The latter have additional fans to increase air current circulation. Large rotary or reel-type ovens and reconstituting ovens including a refrigeration unit are also available.

Figure 7e. **A reconstituting oven. Food may be stored frozen in the unit until reconstituting time or transferred from frozen storage to the unit for heating. No previous thawing is necessary, and any container may be used.** (Courtesy of Foster Refrigerator Corporation, Hudson, New York.)

Conventional Gas Ovens. The gas oven is fired by gas logs located under the oven compartment. It should contain a safety device to cut off the flow of gas in case of pilot light failure, and a pilot light that burns a small amount of continuous gas and fires the logs when the "on" control is activated.

Gas ovens have a temperature indicator and usually have a damper to control the emission of moisture from the oven compartment. They generally require a long period of preheating, and they tend to concentrate excessive heat at the bottom of the oven compartment.

Electric Ovens. Electric ovens usually have heat sources at both the top and the bottom of the compartment. They also have heat concentration controls and compartment temperature controls. Many have Thermopane windows for viewing products during cooking.

Reconstituting Ovens. The reconstituting oven has a combination heat and refrigeration cycle that alternately heats and cools the product to prevent external drying while the food is being prepared from its frozen state. Quartz units inject pulsating radiant heat into the product and refrigerated cycles then capture the convected heat. This permits rapid defrosting and reconstitution of an item with only minor losses of moisture and flavor.

Convection Ovens. Convection ovens contain a fan in the oven space to transfer heat to the product at a much more rapid rate through convection currents. This produces more rapid cooking of the product, so that more trays can be included in each production run than would normally be possible in a conventional oven.

Convection ovens usually have Thermopane doors, interval timers for control, interior vapor-proofed lights, and dual controls for fans and heating elements.

Rotary Ovens. Rotary ovens have movable trays that generally operate on a "ferris wheel" principle around a heat source. They lend themselves best to large operations, giving maximum oven potential in a minimum of space. The oven may have four, six, or eight trays, and each can be rotated to the single door for loading and unloading. Rotary ovens are available in gas, electric, and oil-fired models.

Combination Ovens. Combination ovens, which combine a convection oven with a pressureless convection steamer, have been used in Europe and have recently been introduced into the United States. They may function as a regular dry fast-cooking convection oven or with controlled humidity. Humidity can be varied from 5 to 30 percent, and such ovens can be used for oven frying or baking or for making crusty products. To gain a product comparable to the slow-cooking oven, they do a job in 2.5 hours that would take approximately 8 in the slow-cooking oven.

They are currently available only in electric models, but gas models should be available in the near future. A steam generator within the oven requires a water-line hookup and a drain to carry out condensate. Temperatures average from 100 to 550 degrees, and everything from meats to bakery products to pouches can be cooked in this equipment. The modes of steam, combination, or convection can be varied while the product is being cooked and as the surface condition or the degree of browning requires. For example, the steam and oven modes are used for crusty breads.

Available options include a temperature probe to shut off the cooking process at the right temperature, a holding temperature mode, a rapid-cooling mode, and glass windows for observation. Sizes vary from six half-size pans to forty full 18 by 26 pans in size.

Cleaning combination ovens is speeded up with the use of the steam cycle. The boiler unit must receive the same attention as any steam equipment to prevent boiler scale buildup (see steam equipment).

Slow Cooking and Hold Ovens. Slow cooking and hold ovens are available in either gas or electric models in modular bun pan models. These may be stacked or decked, as with ordinary ovens, and require no venting although hoods are usually available. They are available in the high-humidity model 90 to 95 percent with ordinary heat or in 30 to 60 percent humidity with convection currents at lower temperatures. Dials allow programs for cooking times or internal temperature by means of a probe; cooking temperatures approximate 200 to 225 degrees, and holding temperatures are at 140. Shrinkage can be reduced to as much as 5 to 10 percent (versus 30 percent in some convection ovens) in these ovens. Since cooking is slow, it can be done at night during off hours and be ready

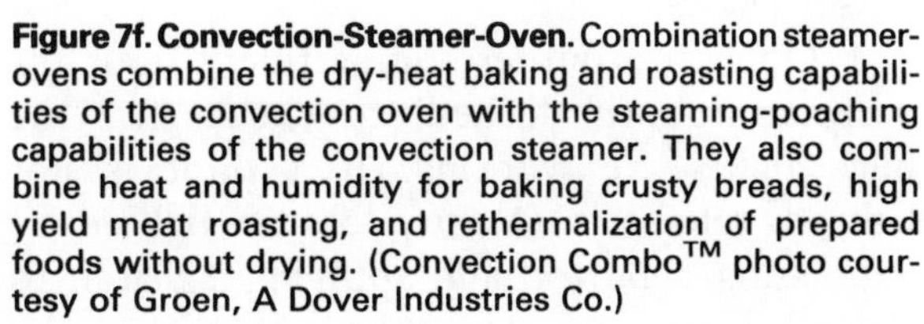
Figure 7f. Convection-Steamer-Oven. Combination steamer-ovens combine the dry-heat baking and roasting capabilities of the convection oven with the steaming-poaching capabilities of the convection steamer. They also combine heat and humidity for baking crusty breads, high yield meat roasting, and rethermalization of prepared foods without drying. (Convection Combo™ photo courtesy of Groen, A Dover Industries Co.)

for a meal or banquet the next day. The slow-cooking process takes approximately seven to eight hours, and meats can be held for twenty-four hours at the 140-degree range.

Some bacterial concerns must be observed because of the low temperatures. Raw meat should not be handled by forks to prevent introduction of bacteria into a sterile environment. Also the temperatures of meat being held must be monitored to avoid danger zones. Reheated meat must be heated in an ambient oven temperature of 250 degrees to an internal temperature of at least 130 degrees for two hours to kill any surface bacteria.

Cleaning the unit is very easy. Most units are solid metal pieces that need only be wiped with detergent water and then dried.

General Specifications

Ovens are usually measured by standard pan size capacities (18 inches by 26 inches), such as a two-pan oven or a three-pan oven. They may be single units, included with other pieces of equipment (such as a range), or decked with other ovens (such as the model in figure 7g).

The height of the door opening usually indicates the basic purpose of the oven: a four-inch to eight-inch opening for a baking oven, and a twelve-inch to fifteen-inch opening for an oven used to roast larger pieces of meat. In stacking oven decks, thought must be given to the use of each oven in relation to its position. For example, if three roasting ovens are stacked in one deck, reaching and removing heavy food items from the top oven may be very difficult.

Quartz-type ovens, which operate at temperatures from 650 to 750 degrees Fahrenheit are available for rapid heating, particularly of convenience foods. They operate either by infrared radiant heating or by conventional conduction and convection methods.

All ovens should have venting systems in order to remove the heat they generate from the kitchen preparation areas. A Thermopane door is desirable (if possible) to permit viewing of the product without having to open the door. The door should be flush with the oven bottom and counterbalanced to permit it to remain open in any position desired. Quick recovery ability (the ability to return quickly to the preheated temperature after the door has been opened or a product placed in the compartment) is an important feature for an oven to have.

Some models have thermocouples that sample the internal temperature of the product and can shut off the power supply to the unit when the temperature reaches a certain level. Others have interval timers. An internal light source and removable and adjustable shelving are also desirable features.

Location and Use. Ovens should be located in areas large enough to permit use of a peel (a flat wooden implement used to remove products from an oven), and they should be close to a table or other landing area where heavy, hot products can be placed after removal.

Ovens must always be preheated prior to use. Some models of electric ovens have intensity controls that reduce the heating time. An oven thermometer can supplement the built-in temperature controls to ensure a satisfactory temperature level.

Products to be placed in ovens must be protected against any direct heat sources that may be found in some gas or electric models. Time and temperature indicators must be used only as guides to cooking. Specific food processing determinants are the true indications of completion of the cooking cycle.

It is desirable to protect against excessive oven spillage from products such as fruit pies by use of spill pans or aluminum foil. These measures save major cleanup.

Operating Instructions

Gas Ovens

1. Open the burner compartment door for each section (if decked) to check that the pilot lights are working. If a pilot is not lighted, relight it. (Most pilots are lighted by depressing a button and applying a match to the pilot opening. After the pilot lights, the button must still be held down for a short

Figure 7g. A gas-fired oven decking arrangement with two bake decks. Each is a two-pan oven. Better use of space may be gained by including a roast deck under two bake units. (Courtesy of South Bend Range Corporation, South Bend, Indiana.)

period of time. Then it may be released, and the pilot will remain lighted.)

2. Turn the thermostat control to the highest setting (450 to 500 degrees).

3. Turn the gas control to "on."

4. Check that the gas log has lighted. Then close the burner compartment door.

5. Turn the thermostat control to the desired temperature, and permit the oven to preheat. Keep the oven door open for the first five to ten minutes of preheat time to ensure adequate venting. Test with an oven thermometer that the desired temperature has been reached. Insert the item to be cooked.

6. To discontinue operation, when the cooking is completed, turn the gas control to "off" and the thermostat to the lowest setting.

Special Instructions

1. Do not operate a gas oven if the pilot light is out. Follow the safety relighting instructions.

2. Space all pans away from each other and away from the sides of the oven.

3. Open the oven door as seldom as possible during use.

4. To give products a strong bottom and a light top, set the oven temperature 25 degrees above the desired baking temperature before loading the oven. Then turn it down to the baking temperature after loading. To give a strong top, turn the thermostat to 25 degrees above the baking temperature for the last ten minutes of baking.

Electric Ovens

1. Turn on the power.

2. Preheat by setting the control switches (if provided) to "high." Turn the thermostat to the desired temperature.

3. Test the temperature with an oven thermometer, and turn the control switches to "medium" after preheating.

4. Load the oven quickly, and avoid opening the oven door during cooking.

5. To discontinue operation, turn the electric power switch, control switches, and thermostat to "off" or the lowest setting.

Cleaning

All ovens should be cleaned regularly; a weekly schedule is suggested. Grease coating and sugar spillage contribute to smoking, odor, and taste problems in subsequent products and may result in lower oven efficiency. All ovens should be cooled before cleaning.

Then the interior is scraped with a metal scraper or brush. Washing the interior surfaces is usually not necessary or desirable, but exterior surfaces may be washed with a solution of detergent and water. Highly polished surfaces such as stainless steel must be polished with a nonabrasive stainless steel cleaner. Windows must be kept clean and free from deposits both inside and out by scraping and cleaning with detergents. The burner compartment of a gas oven should be kept free from dust and/or debris by brushing. Racks should be scraped with a metal brush or pad and washed in detergent water. Thermocouple units (if provided) should be cleansed of carbonized deposits to ensure proper sampling of temperatures, and peels should be scraped and wiped with a damp detergent cloth. Some electric ovens may provide for the removal of hardened food spills by sprinkling salt on the spill, turning the oven to 500 degrees, and charring. The spill can then be scraped easily from the oven floor. Oven cleaners are not generally used in commercial ovens.

Ranges

Ranges are flat-top heat sources used for preparing pots of food, making sauces, sautéing, and the like. They may be operated by gas or electricity and are built for either heavy, light, or special use. Some special models are the chop suey range, the range-griddle combination, and the range-oven grouping. The surface of an electric range may be solid plate or coil top. Gas models may have open burner, solid, or ring top surfaces. Much research is being done on a magnetically cooled induction-type range that would generate heat through cool tops directly into the pan and the food with little or no excess heat and no requirements for hoods or makeup air. For this type of range, steel magnetic utensils must be used as food containers.

A range is purchased for specific functions. Its heat sources relate to the size and number of units to be carried on the top, and the temperature controls relate to the heat concentrations desired on specific range parts.

Rounded fronts, toe spaces for workers, and adequate overshelving and reach areas are desirable features of ranges. Gas models should contain pilot lights and automatic cutoffs in case of pilot light failure. Adequate hooding and venting are required for effective range operation, and nearby work space and landing areas are helpful.

Pan and utensil storage should be provided nearby to reduce excessive travel by workers. Overhead lighting should be available at the range. It should be vaporproof, to prevent grease collection on fixtures and possible breakage into food products being prepared.

Ranges should be lighted at the beginning of a food preparation period so that heat is available when it is needed. Some gas ranges and fast-cycling electric units produce instantaneous heat, but solid top models of both kinds require preheat periods.

Sauce and stock pots must not be dropped on range surfaces or roughly dragged over the tops, and spillage should be kept to a minimum. Handles of pans must be turned in or set even with the range edge to protect against accidental spilling of hot products. Adequate potholders must be available and used by personnel at every range station.

Operating Instructions

Gas Ranges

1. For models equipped with pilot lights, lift the top cover to ascertain that the pilot is activated. Then turn the gas control knob to the temperature desired.

2. If the pilot light is inoperative, relight it. In most models this is done by depressing a spring-type button nearby, holding it down, and applying a match to the light. After thirty seconds, the button can be released, and the pilot should stay lighted. If not, wait five minutes and repeat the process.

3. On models without pilot lights, a taper is used to light the gas logs that serve the range top. First light the taper; then turn on the gas and apply the flame.

4. To stop operation, turn off all gas controls.

Figure 7h. A gas-fired range, with four open burners, a 36-inch griddle/broiler combination, high back shelf, and two ovens underneath. (Courtesy of Garland Division, Welbilt Corporation, Maspeth, New York.)

Electric Ranges

1. To start operation, turn the control to the temperature setting desired.

2. To stop operation, turn off all controls.

Cleaning

Ranges should be cleaned daily to ensure efficient operation and the maintenance of satisfactory sanitation. The range should be turned off and cool before cleaning. The top surface may then be scraped with a stiff brush to remove food stains or caramelized food deposits. A rust preventive solution should be placed on all outside surfaces.

Grills or Griddles

A griddle or grill may be either part of a range top or a separate piece of equipment, usually located close to the range. Grills are fired by either gas or electricity. The top is usually made of cast iron or highly polished steel. It has a top baffle to prevent spillage and an underneath spillage or grease collector pan connected to the grill top. All grills require venting or hooding.

Grill surfaces must be seasoned before use and kept free from food deposits and excessive oil. Before use, the grill's heat source has to be activated (the lighting procedures for ranges apply) and the surface brought to the right temperature for the item being prepared. A light covering of oil and an impervious surface prevent food from sticking and burning. During cooking, the surface should be scraped periodically with a spatula, steak turner, or similar tool to remove residue materials into the drip pan. Generally, pans and pots should not be placed on the grill; the range should be used for heating them.

Cleaning

A grill should be cleaned each day after use. First the heat source is inactivated; then the grill is scraped and wiped clean with paper towels or a cloth. While the surface of the grill is still warm, a pumice or griddle stone may be used with a little grease to bring back a highly polished surface. The stone should be rubbed with the grain of the metal, not against it. After use of the stone, a thin coating of oil must be left on the grill surface for proper seasoning and prevention of rust deposits. The drip pan must be removed, washed in a detergent solution, and dried. All exterior surfaces must be kept free from food, grease, or caramelized food deposits by periodic scraping and cleaning. Use of steel wool on grill surfaces should be avoided, however.

Steam-Fired Equipment

Steam-fired equipment generally takes two forms: (1) that in which the steam is in direct contact with the food, and (2) that in which the steam surrounds the food compartment in a jacket, and is kept out of direct contact with the food.

Steam equipment may be self-generating, having its own boiler to produce steam for the system, or it may be connected to an exterior source, using steam generated at some remote location. The steam used may be released as exhaust at the end of the cooking cycle, or it may be recaptured in a steam condensate return line and brought back to the boiler to be reheated for future use.

The water in steam equipment may be heated by gas or electricity, or the electrical system may be used for control purposes only.

All steam equipment should have adequate safety features: pressure-reducing valves (PRVs), to handle the delivery of higher steam pressures than are to be used; safety valves that are periodically tested and remain unhindered, so that any dangerous increase in steam pressure is exhausted without damage to the equipment or injury to operating personnel; and a pressure indicator and a safety lock if the equipment has steam in a cooking compartment, to tell the operator the steam level and prevent him from opening a door while superheated steam is in the compartment. Gas units, of course, must have safety cutoffs and should have pilots.

On self-generating models, a low-water cutoff is needed to stop the generation of heat when the water gets below a safe level. Most models have a sight glass to indicate the water level in the boiler at an inspection before operation begins. A blowout device for the periodic cleaning of the boiler unit is also necessary on self-generating models.

Some models have drying devices to supply "dry" steam in the compartment for reconstituting prepared products. All steam used in direct contact with food must be "clean," with no boiler additives or the like in steam that comes from a remote generating source. A unit that has a steam exhaust system at the end of the cooking cycle must have a pit for

Figure 7i. A high-pressure steam cooker with a freezer for food storage underneath. The unit has a defrost cycle before each cooking cycle begins. It operates on a remote steam supply. (Courtesy of the Hobart Manufacturing Company, Troy, Ohio.)

Figure 7j. A dry-steam atmospheric steamer for heating precooked foods and making hot sandwiches. Jets of water become steam when they contact the heater plate. The steam is superheated to "dry" condition before entering food compartment. (Courtesy of Wear-Ever Food Service Equipment, Fort Wayne, Indiana.)

draining that is gapped from the equipment to the atmosphere to prevent backup sanitary problems. Small trunnion kettles should have tilting devices that lock the kettle into place if the handle is released, and larger steam-jacketed kettles should have either winding units to hold the containers for filling or unloading spigots on the bottom that can be disassembled for cleaning. Very large units may have mechanically operated stirring rods and unloading devices. All steam equipment must be located under hoods for heat and vapor exhausting.

Steamers

Where steam is to be included in the food compartment, a perforated food container will give the best cooking results. Blocks of frozen and preblanched products should be separated before heating to ensure more uniform cooking. Foods with different flavors should not be prepared together in a steamer.

Forced convection steamers that hold up to three standard cafeteria counter pans have an included convection blower, and the door can be opened at any time in the cycle. Other pressureless steamers allow different foods to be cooked at the same time because with a vent at one end, odors, tastes, and colder layers of water vapors are constantly being blasted out of the cooking compartment.

Both self-generating and other steamers usually require a preheating period in order to generate the required steam. If a model has an adequate supply of ready steam, this of course is not necessary.

Before operating any unit with active steam in the food compartment, the worker must first place the food in the compartment, have the door "dogged down" (secured with metal latches against opening), and then activate the steam control.

Operating Instructions

1. Turn on the boiler and wait until the pressure rises to the proper level (five or fifteen pounds).

2. Place the food in the proper pan, and put it in the unit.

3. Close the door and lock it by placing the tongue of the door lock under the roller on the casting and pressing downward until the lock comes to a firm stop, or, on low-pressure models, by closing the door hasp and turning the wheel on the jacket to the right until it is tight. (On high-pressure models, when steam enters the compartment its internal pressure against the door makes an additional seal.)

4. Turn on the steam control (or the control interval timer on some models). This puts steam in the jacket and begins the cooking process.

5. After cooking has been completed push the steam control to exhaust the steam. High pressure models will exhaust steam automatically.

6. After all steam has been exhausted, open the door part way for a few seconds to allow the vapor to clear. Then open it fully and remove the food.

Cleaning

Steamers should be cleaned at the end of every day by washing the inside of the unit with detergent and water, rinsing, and wiping dry. The bottom drain must be clean and free of food. The door gasket should be inspected regularly and replaced when evidence of hardening or damage is noted.

Steam-Jacketed Kettles

Steam-jacketed kettles are available in sizes from ten quarts to eighty gallons. Steam is kept in an outside compartment completely separated from the food being prepared. The kettle may have a full or a two-thirds jacket. It requires only activation of the steam valve to get steam into the jacket. (In self-generating models an additional preheating period is necessary in order to generate sufficient steam for operation.) An overhead water hose with a measuring device on the line is a desirable addition near a steam-jacketed kettle.

Operating Instructions

1. Turn on the boiler and wait for the pressure to reach the necessary level (if applicable).

2. Open the water valve and fill the kettle according to item being prepared.

3. Adjust the speed of cooking by adjusting the valve in the steam line.

4. After cooking is completed, turn off the steam and remove the item from the kettle.

Cleaning

Steam-jacketed kettles should be filled with water and brought to boiling after each use to make later cleaning easier and to prepare the kettle for other use during the meal period. Scrubbing with a stiff brush will help to remove food from the interior of the kettle. A later rinsing is all that is needed. Steel wool is not recommended for cleaning steam-jacketed kettles. In fact it should never be allowed in food service establishments, because it may be easily introduced into foods being prepared.

In self-generating steam equipment it is usually necessary to "blow down" the boiler unit once a week, to remove boiler scale, the mineral deposits that form and collect as a result of heating water. Safety valves on steam equipment should be "lifted" daily to ensure that they are operative.

Coffee Makers

Coffee makers are available in manual and automatic forms and in urn or individual container models. Urns may be operated by electric, steam, or gas power. The larger models include a battery of urns plus a boiler to supply sufficient hot water.

Urns operate on a jacket principle similar to a steam-jacketed kettle. The inside container, which carries the coffee brew, is made of glass or stainless steel, and the outside jacket contains hot water to keep the brew warm. Urns require water or steam sources, drainage systems, and hoods. The automatic, individual pot, coffee maker requires only a filtered water supply and a heat source (usually an electric hot plate). In some automatic models, water may be poured into the unit, so no connected water supply is needed.

Operating Instructions

Urns

1. Place the coffee in the filter or leaching unit. The filter may be made of muslin, metal, or paper. (Muslin filters should be kept in water between uses to inhibit the oils collected from the coffee as it brews from becoming rancid.)

Figure 7k. An automatic, individual container, coffee brewer that operates electrically with an outside water supply, premeasured coffee, and disposable filters. The unit keeps the coffee at the correct serving temperature after it is made. (Courtesy of Bunn-O-Matic Corporation, Springfield, Illinois.)

2. In the manual models, draw water from the hot water source, and pour it over the grounds. The resulting brew is collected in the inner container. In the automatic or siphon type, press a button to start the water spraying over the grounds automatically. A major problem in the manual urns has been safety. The worker usually has to pour hot water while perched on a ladder, stool, or chair, because of the height of the urns, and the possibility of spillage is great.

Cleaning

Urns must be kept meticulously clean. The inside of the container, the sight glass, the filters, and the faucets must be cleaned every day. Filters and faucets can be removed for cleaning. Water should always be left in both the urn and the jacket at the end of the cleaning period, to prevent damage to the unit if heat should be applied accidentally. Water in the urn also stops oil oxidation, but if the unit has been properly cleaned, there will not be oils to oxidize.

Operating Instructions

Individual Pot Models

1. Place the filter and premeasured coffee container in the coffee reservoir and lock it in place.

2. Put the container under the spout and press the button to start the filtered water spraying over grounds. In nonautomatic models pour water of the correct temperature into the unit.

Cleaning

Individual pot units require only detergent cleaning at regular intervals and changing of the water line filters. Hot plates used for holding pots should be cleaned with a damp cloth and dried. Coffee pots may be run through the dishwashing machine for cleaning. Water should be kept in pots that are left sitting on hot plates, to prevent accidental burnout in case the heat is on in the hot plate element.

Mixers

Mixers are used to mix food items or, with attachments, to perform functions such as slicing, knife sharpening, grating, or grinding. They are available in a variety of sizes and in both table and floor models. Most mixers are vertical models with the beater shaft perpendicular to the floor, but some larger models used in baking operations are horizontal in design.

Mixers operate on electric current. Various speeds and attachments enable them to per-

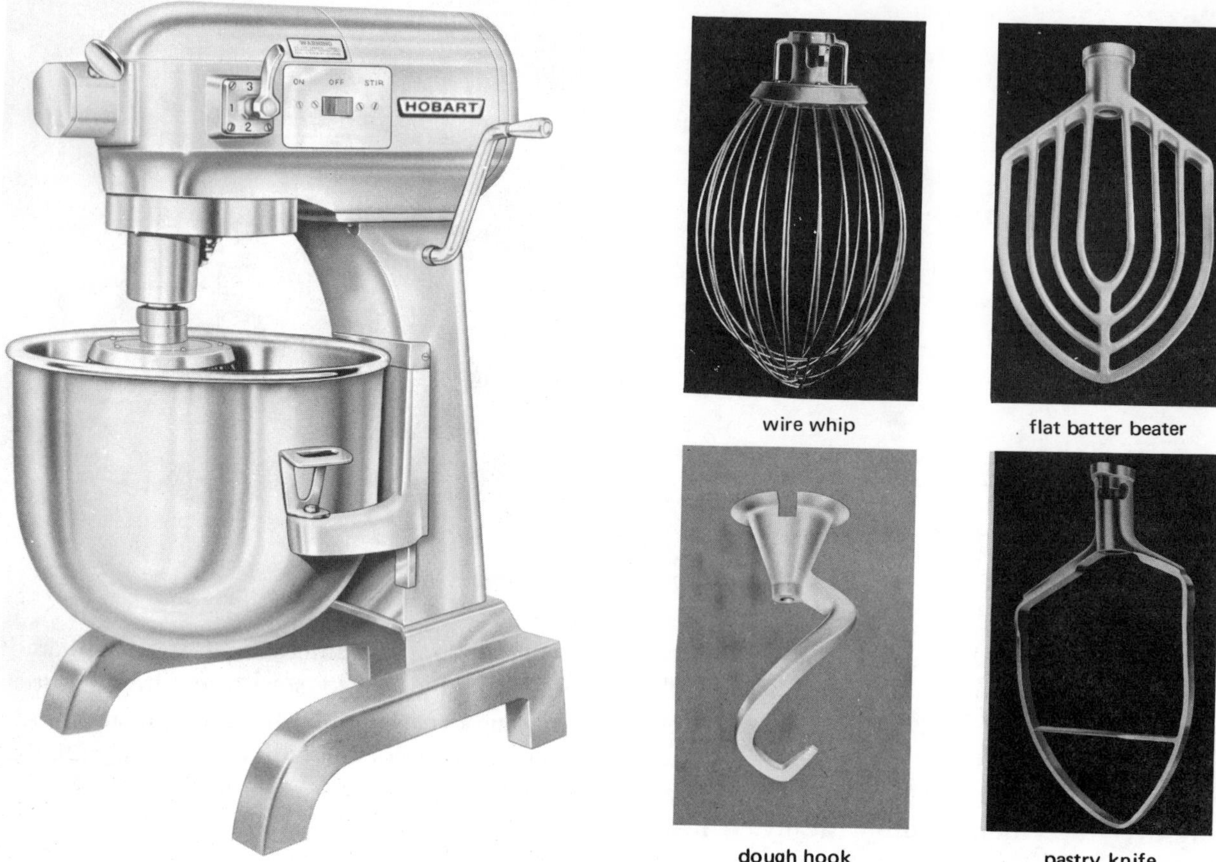

Figure 7/. A twenty-quart capacity electric mixer and its major agitators. This model also has a gear-drive mechanism for use of attachments such as choppers, dicers, and graters. (Courtesy of Hobart Manufacturing Company, Troy, Ohio.)

form a multitude of functions. There are four major attachments: (1) the whip, which is used to incorporate air into products, (2) the batter beater, which mixes heavy batters, (3) the pastry knife, which cuts fat into flour, and (4) the dough hook, which mixes heavy doughs. Many mixers have attachments to raise the bowl into the mixing device and dollies or adapters to handle heavier bowls.

The drive shaft of a mixer may be used to operate juice extractors, knife sharpeners, food slicers, graters, and grinders.

Operating Instructions

1. Select the appropriate attachment and bowl size. Special care should be taken to identify bowls and beaters, particularly where a number of mixers are used, to avoid incorrect use that may cause machine damage.

2. Put the attachment in the bowl, place the bowl on the mixer, and fasten it in place. Most units have a three-point fastener; be sure all three are engaged.

3. Raise and fasten the attachment to the mixer shaft.

4. Put the food item to be mixed in the bowl. (For ease of operation food may be put in the bowl before the bowl is placed on the mixer cradle.)

5. Start the mixer. Mixers are usually started at slow speed, with the bowl located at the lowest position. The food is gradually brought into contact with the beaters so that excessive strain is not suddenly placed on the motor. Speed changes are possible on some models during operation; on others speed must be changed only when the machine is switched to "off." It is important that the

correct procedure be followed, to prevent damage.

6. Carry out the required mixing procedure. Scraping the bowl while the mixer is in operation presents a safety problem. It is better for the operator to stop the blades while this is done.

7. At the completion of the mixing process, stop the machine and remove the bowl and mixer blade. Leave the bowl holder in the lowest position and the speed at the lowest setting for the next use.

Cleaning

Bowls and mixers should be washed with a detergent solution. Particular attention should be paid to the shaft and the shaft seal during every cleaning. Leaks in this seal may cause damage to the mixer or adulteration of a mixed product.

Cutters, Choppers, and Grinders

Cutters, choppers, and grinders may be individual pieces of equipment or attachments to food mixers. Cutters and choppers are machines that cut vegetables and other products by pressing them against one or several rotating blades or a rotating blade and a rotating bowl. Grinders are worm-driven gear assemblies that propel food items toward and through grinding plates or blades. A combination cutter and mixer, called a vertical cutter/mixer or Schnell cutter, cuts and mixes foods at the same time in a very brief period.

Operating Instructions

1. Check for proper assembly of equipment. Many models have electrical safety cutoffs, which prevent the equipment from operating until all safety guards are in place.

2. Either insert the items to be processed and turn on the equipment or reverse this procedure, depending on the specific unit. In equipment that cuts foods in a variety of ways, experiment to learn what pressure to exert and what size item to introduce. Care must be taken with foods that contain bones and with very soft foods that may stall the

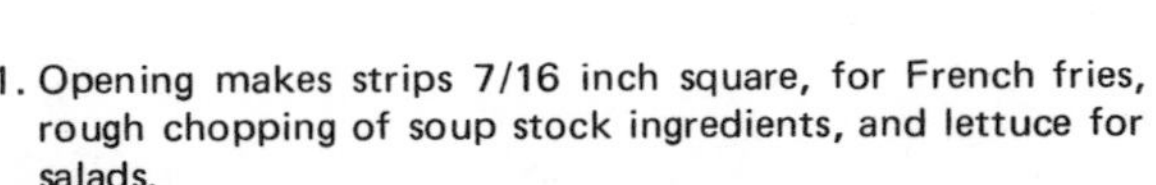

1. Opening makes strips 7/16 inch square, for French fries, rough chopping of soup stock ingredients, and lettuce for salads.
2. Opening makes 3/16 inch strips, for juliennes, carrot and beet sticks, fine chopping of celery for chicken salads, etc., and ingredients for soup stocks.
3. Opening does bias slicing, for cabbage slaws, chips, celery, and shredding lettuce. Slices are variable from 1/64 inch to 3/8 inch.
4. Opening does straight slicing for carrots, celery, cucumbers, pepper rings, etc. Slices are variable from 1/64 inch to 3/8 inch.

Figure 7m. A vegetable cutter and slicer, used for a variety of vegetable preparations. Additional shredder plates are available for more versatility. The machine has a safety electrical cutoff, which prevents operation when the cover is lifted. It may be cleaned by pouring water through the feed openings while the machine is running. (Courtesy of Qualheim, Inc., Racine, Wisconsin.)

machine motor. Use a tamper to push the food against the blades.

3. When the whole batch has been processed, turn off the control, allow the blades to stop rotating, and remove the food.

Cleaning

All machines should be unplugged and disassembled for cleaning. Caution must be exercised when handling sharp blades and removing the blades from the machine assembly. All parts should be washed in detergent and water, rinsed, and dried. The unit is then reassembled with all guards, locknuts, and cutoff units reengaged as before. Some food cutters may be cleaned by pouring water through them while they are in operation, but in these too additional cleaning is necessary.

Microwave Equipment

Microwave units, commonly called ovens, are used either to prepare food or to reheat already prepared items. A magnetron tube changes electrical energy into microwave energy that is reflected by metals but passes through paper or glass and is absorbed by water, fat, and sugar. These waves strike the food at varying angles, causing rapid heating, but they are influenced by the shape of the items to be cooked, and the density and amount of food in the oven; the same number of waves are emitted each time. For example, one potato cooks in approximately 3.5 to 4 minutes, 2 potatoes take 7 minutes; three take 8 to 9 minutes; and four cook in 10 to 12 minutes. The microwave energy is absorbed into only the top 1.5 inches of the materials to be cooked or heated. From then on, the item is cooked from the inside out. Thus thin items cook faster than thick ones, and thicker parts of food items should be placed to the outside while thinner parts are put in the center. A round or donut-shaped item is the best form since it has no corners to overcook and no center to be underdone. Lighter foods absorb waves faster than more dense food, and heavily sugared items may be hotter within a muffin than the muffin itself.

Microwave ovens vary from 500 to 2000 W with capacities of 1 cubic foot (15 inches wide by 8 inches high by 12 inches deep) to 2 cubic feet and over. Stir fans, rotating antennae, or turntables are available for even cooking. Since microwaves cannot give the typical brownness to food, additional browning units are also available as are temperature probes.

Some of the newer models can use aluminum-foil trays without damage although generally metal should not be used in the unit. Ionizing radiation is a problem if the unit has any leakage. Therefore a safety cutoff should be available, and operators should carry out periodic testing for leakage.

Figure 7n. A microwave electronic oven with push-button cooking cycles. A dial timer with settings up to twenty-one minutes and six preset timers are available. The unit is ready to operate in ten seconds. (Courtesy of Litton Industries, Minneapolis.)

Operating Instructions

1. Turn on the power switch to heat the unit to operating levels.

2. Insert the item to be cooked in the compartment, close the door, set the timer for the desired cooking period, and press the control button.

3. At end of the cooking period, remove the food item and turn off the unit. Many operations keep a glass of water in the unit during down times to ensure that the equipment is not damaged if it is turned on accidentally without food in the compartment.

Cleaning

Cleaning the unit is very easy. Most units are solid metal pieces that need only be wiped with detergent water and then dried. A cup of water in the oven steamed for 30 to 45 seconds will assist with the cleaning process.

Refrigerators and Freezers

Refrigerators and freezers both work on the same principle of removing heat from products and insulating them against further heat gain. They are available in various sizes, and generally operate by means of a compressor with a Freon fill.

Desirable features include pass-through doors, giving access from either side of the unit to save steps, and pan slides to hold modular trays or sheet pans, which eliminate the need to load and unload items from trays to shelves. Magnetic latches and concealed heating wires to reduce ice buildup will prolong the life of door latches and gaskets of freezers. The units should also have temperature indicators. Thermopane glass doors may cut down on the heat gain that occurs from opening doors for viewing the contents.

Walk-ins and units that accept modular roll-in carts will give flexibility to an operation large enough to warrant them (400 to 500 meals per day). Locks should be provided for control, and shelving (if included) should be adjustable and removable for easy cleaning.

An alarm system and/or an easy escape method should be provided for every walk-in refrigerator or freezer in case of accidental entrapment. All refrigerators need drains for ease of cleaning, and they should be air-gapped to prevent backup from faulty drainage lines. Reverse-cycle compressors can make defrosting the units easy.

Operating Instructions

1. If possible, separate the items to be stored according to desirable temperature and humidity.

2. Stack foods for maximum circulation of air, using duck boards in walk-ins.

3. Cover all materials to prevent spoilage or contamination from items on higher shelves. Wrap all items to be frozen to prevent freezer burn (dehydration).

4. Use air locks, where possible, to cut down on extreme temperature differentials between the freezer and the storeroom or kitchen.

5. Maintain a log of temperatures to check on the performance of the equipment.

Cleaning

Refrigerators and freezers must be defrosted on a regular schedule for maximum efficiency. All reach-in units should be cleaned daily by removing and sorting items and washing walls and surfaces with detergent water. On a weekly basis all shelving should be removed and the unit washed with soda water.

Walk-ins may be cleaned weekly and freezers cleaned when defrosted (usually once a month).

Slicers

Slicers are designed to slice meat items but they may be adapted to handle vegetables and other products. Slicers may be manually operated or automatically controlled. They may slice items by count or on a continuous basis.

The food to be cut rides in a movable carriage that brings it in contact with a rotating blade. A dial adjusts the depth of the cut,

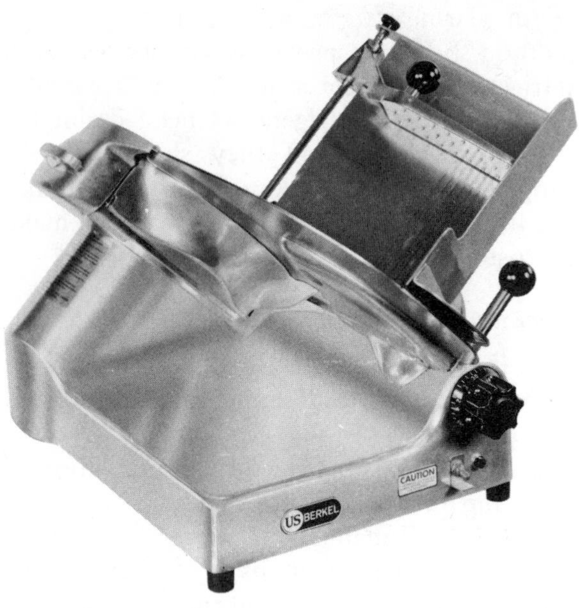

Figure 7o. A gravity-feed slicer with an attached knife sharpener. The knife diameter is 12½ inches and the thickness of the cut adjusts up to 5/8 inch. A vegetable chute is available for quantity slicing of fruits and vegetables. (Courtesy of U.S. Slicing Machine Company, La Porte, Indiana.)

and additional attachments such as portion scales, infrared light to keep items warm, and knife-sharpening stones are available with the equipment.

If possible the slicer should be on a mobile stand, to give it greater flexibility in operation.

Operating Instructions

1. Plug in the unit, and lock the wheels if it is on mobile stand.
2. Place the items to be cut on the carriage, and set the slicing control gauge.
3. Activate the "on" switch, and use the gravity-feed tamper handle to push the food against the blade. Allow the slices to fall on the platform of the unit without attempting to catch them. (An angled blade and carriage arrangement is desirable for cutting items that tend to fold and crumble.)
4. When the items have been cut, turn the machine off, and return the slicing control to the closed position.

Cleaning

Protein foods are routinely cut on this piece of equipment and tend to collect between the blade and the guard. The machine must be completely disassembled to be cleaned at least daily and, in cases of intensive use, more often.

The unit must first be unplugged. Then the knife guard is removed and all parts washed with detergent water. On some models the guard and holding carriage may be removed for repeated washing during the day's operation.

Great care must be taken with the blade. A narrow object or cleaning cloth should be run between the guard and the blade to remove all food deposits. Blades may be removed, but this is considered unnecessary if adequate time is spent on other cleaning procedures. A baffled table with drain and water hose connections will make cleaning easier, since on most models all parts are protected against water damage.

Peelers

Peelers come in various sizes and are either stationary or mobile. The peeler contains an uneven abrasive rotary disc that tumbles the vegetables to be peeled against its surface or against the sides of the peeler compartment. This causes the skin or peel to be rubbed off. A steady stream of water washes the skins of the vegetables from the peeling compartment into a drain and deposits them in a trap at the bottom of the machine.

Peelers must be located close to both a drain and a water source. They benefit from proximity to a table or deep sink at which later procedures, such as eyeing potatoes, can be done. Although potatoes are the major item peeled in this equipment, carrots, turnips, and others may be also processed.

Operating Instructions

1. Be sure that the peeling disc, door, peel trap, and strainer are in place.
2. Adjust the flow of water into the peeling chamber.
3. Turn on the motor and put in the vegetables. (Sort vegetables according to size before introducing them into the peeler, to ensure uniform peeling.)
4. At the end of the peeling time, open the door. The peeled vegetables will be deposited on the peeling table or in the deep sink. Then shut off the machine.

Cleaning

At the end of each day, the peel trap should be removed and cleaned. The disc should be removed and all parts of the peeler washed down with water. A bag of closely knit material tied to the drain of the peeler may catch some of the minute peels and starch deposits that could cause drainage problems.

Figure 7p. A potato and vegetable peeler with both abrasive disc and cylinder sides, self-locking discharge door, and peel trap. Thirty to thirty-three pounds can be peeled in one to three minutes' time. (Courtesy of Hobart Manufacturing Company, Troy, Ohio.)

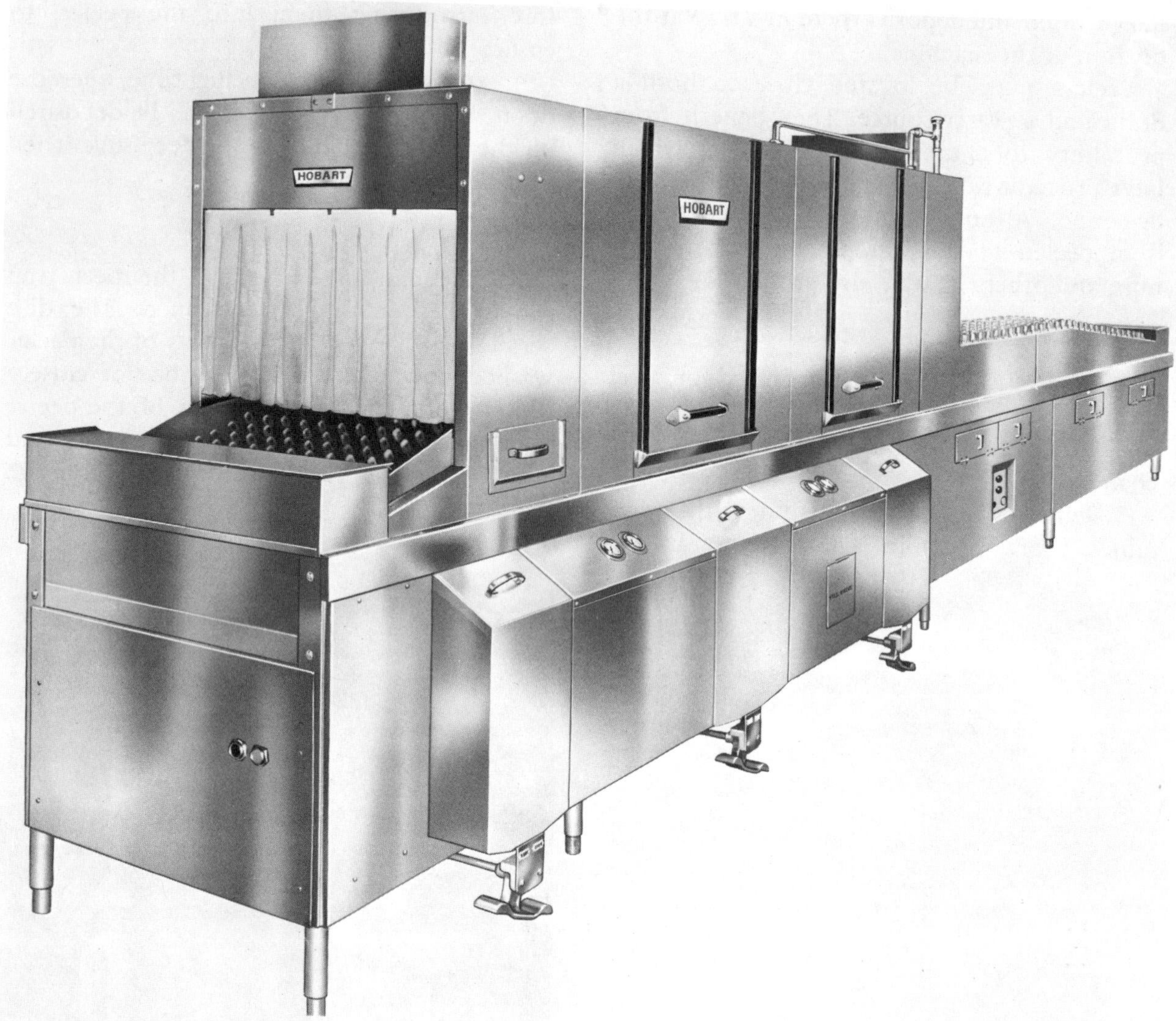

Figure 7q. A flight-type dishwasher, with prewash and final drying section. It is conveyor fed, requiring no racks or containers except for silver. The conveyor speed is five to eight feet per minute. (Courtesy of Hobart Manufacturing Company, Troy, Ohio.)

Dishwashing Machines

Although not strictly a part of food preparation equipment, dishwashing equipment is an important implement of the food facility.

Dishwashers may be either rack models or automatic flight models in which no racks are used and the dishes move through the machine on a continuous belt. Rack types may also have conveyors to move the dishes through a series of tank sprays. Low-temperature dishwashers and warewashers are available that operate at the 120- to 140-degree Fahrenheit range in conjunction with a chemical agent for sterilization. This results in great energy savings compared to the 120-degree prewash, 140- to 160-degree wash, and 180-degree rinsing cycle of other machines that (particularly the flight type) consume substantial amounts of energy.

Dishwashers may have automatic detergent dispensers and drying agents. Some models, particularly the flight units, may require booster heaters and larger drains.

These machines are purchased according to the number of dishes to be processed per hour. The average table service restaurant can expect to use seven dishes per customer meal.

Hard water in dishwashers wastes detergent and leaves dishes and glasses spotted. Where extremely hard water is found, a water-softening unit might be worth employing.

Operating Instructions

1. Fill the machine tanks, add detergent (if necessary), and bring the temperature up to the operating levels according to the directions for the type of machine.

2. Separate dishes, silver, and glasses before racking to prevent breakage. Presoak the silver and rack it business end up. Scrape other dishes to avoid excessive use of detergent and fouling of the wash tanks.

3. Put the dishes through the machine according to type, so that detergent levels and temperatures can be adjusted to the needs of the loads.

Cleaning

Machines should be cleaned after every meal period by emptying and flushing all tanks, removing spray arm heads, cleaning all scrap trays, and generally cleaning both inside and outside surfaces.

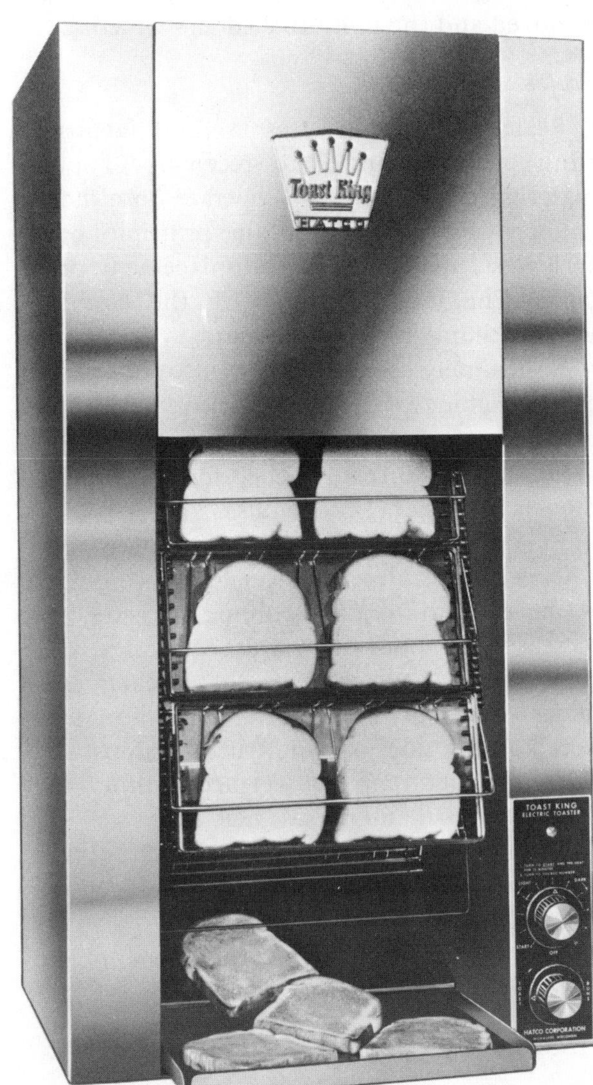

Figure 7r. A conveyor-type bread and bun toaster, with variable speed and toaster controls. It can toast up to 720 bread slices or bun halves per hour. (Courtesy of Hatco Corporation, Milwaukee.)

Toasters

Toasters are machines that brown breads, rolls, and sandwiches. They are available in either gas or electric models and in either slot or conveyor form. Conveyor types usually require clips on each tray for sandwiches, muffins and the like, and a drawer to hold processed items.

Operating Instructions

Simply feed the items to be toasted into the machine using the control to achieve the degree of toasting desired.

Cleaning

To clean the toaster, crumb trays should be removed and the unit brushed and wiped.

Scales

Scales have many uses in food facilities, from portion control to receiving of bulk materials. They generally operate on either a counterweight, sliding beam principle or a springless, dial face, dash displacement principle. The most accurate are the counterweight, sliding tare beam scales.

Scales may be imbedded into floors for easy weighing of hand truck loads in the receiving area; they may be part of other equipment, such as slicers; or they may be counter models for general kitchen use.

In quantity food work, scales are used whenever possible, since weight measurement is more accurate than volume measure. To increase efficiency in the use of scales, tare (or unloaded) weights for the kitchen containers normally used in weighing should be noted on the sides of hand trucks, scoops, etc. Then products can be weighed without the need to unload and reload their carriers.

Scales should be checked, calibrated, and sealed, particularly where purveyors may raise disputes about weights.

No specific operating instructions apply to scales.

Cleaning

Scales should be brushed and washed with detergent water. Steps to prevent rust should be taken where necessary.

Broilers

Broilers are equipment units that cook foods by radiant heat. They are available in gas, electric, or charcoal models and may be separate pieces of equipment or backshelf models called salamanders.

The cooking principle is that heating a ceramic material causes it to emit radiant energy to the food. Normally the food is cooked below the heat source in broilers, but some models, particularly those fired by charcoal, cook it above the heat source.

Many models provide an overshelf holding oven. Gas models, of course, have the standard pilot and safety cutoff controls. Most models have grid-level controls to position the food in relation to the heat source. All broilers must be protected by hooding and should, if possible, have a fire-control system of carbon dioxide ducting.

Operating Instructions

1. Preheat the broiler before use. For gas models, check the pilot light and gas "on" control. A fifteen-minute preheating period is normal. (To keep the broiler on standby, the switch may be kept on the low setting.)

2. Pull the grid out, and place the item to be broiled on it. Adjust the grid to the correct height for the item being prepared and the degree of cooking desired. Normally the closer to the heating element the faster the outside browning and the rarer the inside cooking of the product. For example, meat placed at positions far from the element will be well done before its surface browns.

3. If broiler trays or sizzle plates are used, watch closely to prevent grease fires and flare-ups from fatty items. Wipe the grid periodically with an oiled cloth and remove carbonized food with a wire brush to prevent excessive sticking.

Figure 7s. A gas-fired, single-deck, infrared broiler. The infrared heat decreases preheating time and increases broiling efficiency. (South Bend Range Corporation, South Bend, Indiana.)

4. At the end of the cooking period turn the heat source off.

Cleaning

The broiler should be cool before cleaning. The grid should be removed and wire brushed on both sides. Then a thin layer of oil is applied. Grease and burned-on food particles must be scraped from the unit. In charcoal models, ashes must be removed from the tray. Where grease traps are provided, these must be removed and washed to clean them.

Deep Fat Fryers

Deep fryers are available in electric or gas models and in conventional or pressure-cooking types. They come in many sizes and are normally selected to handle 1.5 to 2 times the weight of the fat in each batch that is to be fried.

Fryers require hooding, and there should be loading and landing areas nearby. They should be protected against fire by carbon dioxide systems in hoods or hood dampers, or by keeping fire extinguishers nearby.

Some fryers have automatic timing mechanisms. Some may have a cold zone to trap food particles. Convection fryers pump the oil through heat exchangers that absorb heat from the burner and transfer it to the oil. This reduces energy and heat loss as well as the possibility of scorching the oil. The same process constantly filters out impurities. Fryers should have two sets of baskets, so that one set can be loaded while the other is being processed. They should have either a siphon or a manual filtering device and be protected by two thermostat fails. Recovery rate is important in fryers to prevent excessive grease absorption.

Figure 7t. An electric deep fryer with a fat capacity of twenty-eight pounds and an extra fat container underneath. It has temperature controls, a dual thermostat, and swing-up heating rods for burn-off cleaning and easy fat removal. (Courtesy of General Electric, Chicago Heights, Illinois.)

Operating Instructions

1. Place the fat in the container. It must cover the highest elements of the electric models to prevent flash fires and fat breakdown. If solid fats are melted and used pack them closely around the elements and melt them at low temperatures.

2. For gas models, light the unit by the procedure for all other gas equipment (see gas ovens above). For electric models, activate the unit with the control dial.

3. Set the thermostat at the operating temperature. Electric models usually have two lights, one to indicate current flow and the other to indicate that the desired temperature has been attained. A separate thermometer to indicate that the fat frying level has been reached, is recommended.

4. Remove excess moisture and breading from the food, and load it into the baskets. Do not overload them. Lower the baskets into the fat.

5. When the cooking is completed, remove the baskets from the fat, drain them, and tip the food out on the landing surface.

Special Instructions. Salt, water, particles of food, excessive heat, and certain metals such as copper are enemies of fat. Therefore, the frying baskets should be loaded and unloaded at the side of the fryer, not over the fat. Salting should also be done away from the fat. Items in the baskets should be quickly immersed and shaken before removal from the fat. The fat should be filtered after each day's use and stored in a cool, dark place for better results. Blanching or partial cooking prior to peak periods will enable more efficient use of the fryer at mealtimes.

Cleaning

The fryer should be turned off and the fat filtered before cleaning. The fryer should then be filled with a detergent solution, brought to a boiling temperature, and drained. The process is repeated twice more with clear water. Heating elements of some electric models may be set to burn off carbon deposits. Care must be taken to ensure that the gas logs are clean under gas-fired units. All exterior parts of the fryer should be washed with detergent solution and dried.

Warming, Holding, and Serving Equipment

Special equipment is used to hold and serve foods before or during meal periods. These units do not contribute quality to any food item, and they should be avoided if at all possible by processing and serving food at once.

If necessary, however, this equipment may be bought in either wet or dry forms, fired by either electricity or steam. The bain-marie, or water bath heated by steam, is probably the oldest form used in the serving area. The steam serving table, the electric serving table, the roll warmer, and the infrared heated landing area are other types. Ovens, steam-jacketed kettles, proofing cabinets, and the back shelves of ranges are also used for holding purposes.

Heat and humidity are important considerations in this kind of equipment. A proper combination must be maintained for the foods involved.

By the use of batching procedures to schedule cooking, products can be prepared as close to serving time as possible, in order to reduce the need for much of this type of equipment. Cooks do not like to run out of foods, however. They may use warming and holding equipment to prevent this from happening. But the larger amounts of items they then prepare contribute to leftovers. Adequate scheduling and forecasting by management will reduce the use of holding equipment. A change to a different form of delivery system, such as from cafeteria to a la carte, can greatly affect the need for this equipment.

No specific operating procedures are required save the setting of temperature and humidity controls.

Cleaning

Spilled food should be wiped from the equipment as soon as possible to prevent caking. Food deposits are scraped off and surfaces washed with detergent water. Steam tables and bains-marie are boiled out. The operator must be sure that the water level stays above the heating elements (where appropriate). Use of soft water in wet units will reduce boiler scale and make cleaning easier.

Other Equipment Considerations

While a piece of equipment is generally selected on the basis of need, cost, size, and fuel, some other general factors must also be considered, such as type of construction, materials used, and organizational approval.

Most food service equipment is made of metals, with stainless steel, aluminum, cast iron, and chromium-coated or enameled steel the most common. Each material available should be considered from the standpoint of use, price, and care required before a piece of equipment is purchased.

Stainless steel is usually the most expensive. It has an excellent appearance, is durable, is practically immune to stains, and will not react with foods.

Aluminum is also a good metal for food equipment. It is strong (and may be made stronger by being anodized), but it is also light and lends itself readily to mobile equipment. Aluminum conducts heat very well, and is available in a variety of finishes. It is less expensive than stainless steel.

Cast iron is a porous, inexpensive iron that is used for the legs or bearing members of some pieces of equipment, notably tables. It breaks very easily, and costs relatively little. It has few applications in the types of equipment considered above although some grill surfaces made of this are seen.

Chromium- or enamel-covered steel is used for such items as refrigerators, ovens, and toasters, among others. It is relatively inexpensive and forms a serviceable covering, although the enamel form is prone to chipping and cracking.

Whatever material is selected, the equipment should be well constructed, easy to clean, resistant to wear, and not reactive with the foods that are to be in contact with it. The design should avoid corners, welds, and cracks for ease of cleaning.

The functioning food zones of equipment (those that will be in normal contact with food) should be examined to make sure that the materials and construction are smooth, corrosion resistant, nontoxic, and nonabsorbent.

All electrical equipment should be grounded to prevent accidental injury to operators from electric shock. The required safety devices to prevent both electrical and other injuries should be installed.

The gauges and finishes of the metals should be consistent with the functions the equipment will perform. Form, too, should follow function. Money should not be wasted in purchasing luxury finishes or unnecessary thicknesses of material when these are not important for the function being considered. Conversely, attempts to reduce purchasing costs by cutting corners in the strength of materials, the type of construction, or the form of finish may result in false economy for the operation.

Certification of acceptability by the Underwriters Laboratories, the National Sanitation Foundation, or the American Gas Association Laboratories, indicated by the seals in figure 7u and the letters UL, NSF, and AGA, respectively, should be used as a guide in selecting equipment. The seal indicates that the equipment has been evaluated under the criteria of the agency involved. The National Sanitation Foundation tests equipment for design, construction, and materials acceptable for use in food service facilities. Parts of the equipment that will be in contact with food receive more attention than other structural parts, but all are examined to see whether they are well constructed, easy to clean, and free from possible difficulties in food service use. Food zones, splash zones, and non-food-contact zones are evaluated according to specific standards.

The UL and AGA seals indicate the safety of equipment powered primarily by electricity and gas, respectively. Acceptance by these agencies indicates that all possible measures have been taken by the manufacturer to ensure that the equipment is safe, has been properly constructed to prevent injury, and may be used with confidence.

Hand Tools of Food Service Workers

Some of the more common utensils, pots, pans, and hand tools used in food facilities are illustrated in figures 7v and 7w. The captions note the standard or usual sizes where applicable.

If possible, minor equipment should be related to major equipment in modular arrangements so that production efficiency may be increased, and fewer transfers and transportations will be required to accomplish tasks. This makes it possible to store, cook, and possibly serve a food from the same pan. It reduces the hand work required to transfer food

Figure 7u. The seals of approval of the American Gas Association, the National Sanitation Foundation, and the Underwriter's Laboratories, indicating the acceptance of a piece of equipment by these organizations.

from one container to another and reduces the number of pans to be washed by the pot washer.

Pots, pans, and other utensils are available in steel, aluminum, copper, cast iron, and stainless steel. Each manager must relate particular selections to his own needs. Such factors as type of menu, desirable weight, feasible cost, and desirable capacity are considered. Heat conduction ability, method of construction, and reaction with foods are also important. The sanitation maintained in construction of the utensil and the ability of the material to withstand chipping, warping, and crazing are further factors. The equipment should be able to endure the treatment it will receive in use and be particularly adapted to the function it will be asked to perform.

Stainless steel and aluminum pots and pans are good general materials for most food service use. Aluminum is considered by many to be the best for pots, pans, and utensils. Plastics are now being used in food service work particularly for such items as dish racks, dish bussing boxes, and trays. They can be used in most situations that do not require exposure to high cooking temperatures. Because of their relatively low cost and their inert nature in food preparation use, they are finding wider and more general acceptance in the industry.

A manual pot washer or mechanical washing equipment, if possible, should be used to keep the pans and other utensils completely sanitary. Copious amounts of hot water and detergents are necessary to remove food deposits, grease, and stains from these pieces of small equipment. If no mechanical equipment is available and hand labor must be used, a steam line insert in a deep sink will do much to increase worker efficiency and provide clean pans and utensils to the preparation personnel. Steel wool should be avoided here, as in all other parts of the food establishment. A steel ring cleaner or an abrasive plastic pad may be used instead.

Hand tools originally purchased and maintained by the journeyman cook have come to be shared in many locations. If at all possible, management should issue a personal set of these utensils to each preparation worker. This will usually induce workers to take better care of their tools. Instruction in the proper sharpening and honing of knives is, of course, recommended. (For example, see figure 19d.)

Color coding the handles to identify utensils quickly can be very helpful in locating and using knives and other hand tools. Storage of each tool in a particular location will ensure that the tool is available when needed and will keep search time to a minimum.

The size and the shape of the handle are important factors in choosing tools that are to be held for any length of time. The tool should be comfortable to use efficiently without unduly tiring the worker or causing safety problems. Hand equipment must be constructed so that it is easy to clean as well as efficient for its intended purpose.

Knives must be selected with particular care. Costs must not be permitted to dictate a cheap grade of steel that will not hold an edge. Cutting surfaces must then be provided that will not dull the knife edge by their unyielding nature. Knives should be selected for particular applications. Chopping, peeling, boning, and slicing utensils are of most importance (see examples in figure 7v).

The Management of Efficiency

All the equipment that is necessary and all the tools that are available will not, of themselves, provide efficiency in any food production area. With the exception of the automated restaurant, most food service operations still require manpower, and efficient production flows from these workers. The tools and equipment provided only enable managers to achieve the desired results with a minimum of manual effort. But this saving will actually be gained only if managers realize that a waste of effort is taking place. Whether it is called work simplification, layout analysis, or systems engineering, managers should make an effort to view their produc-

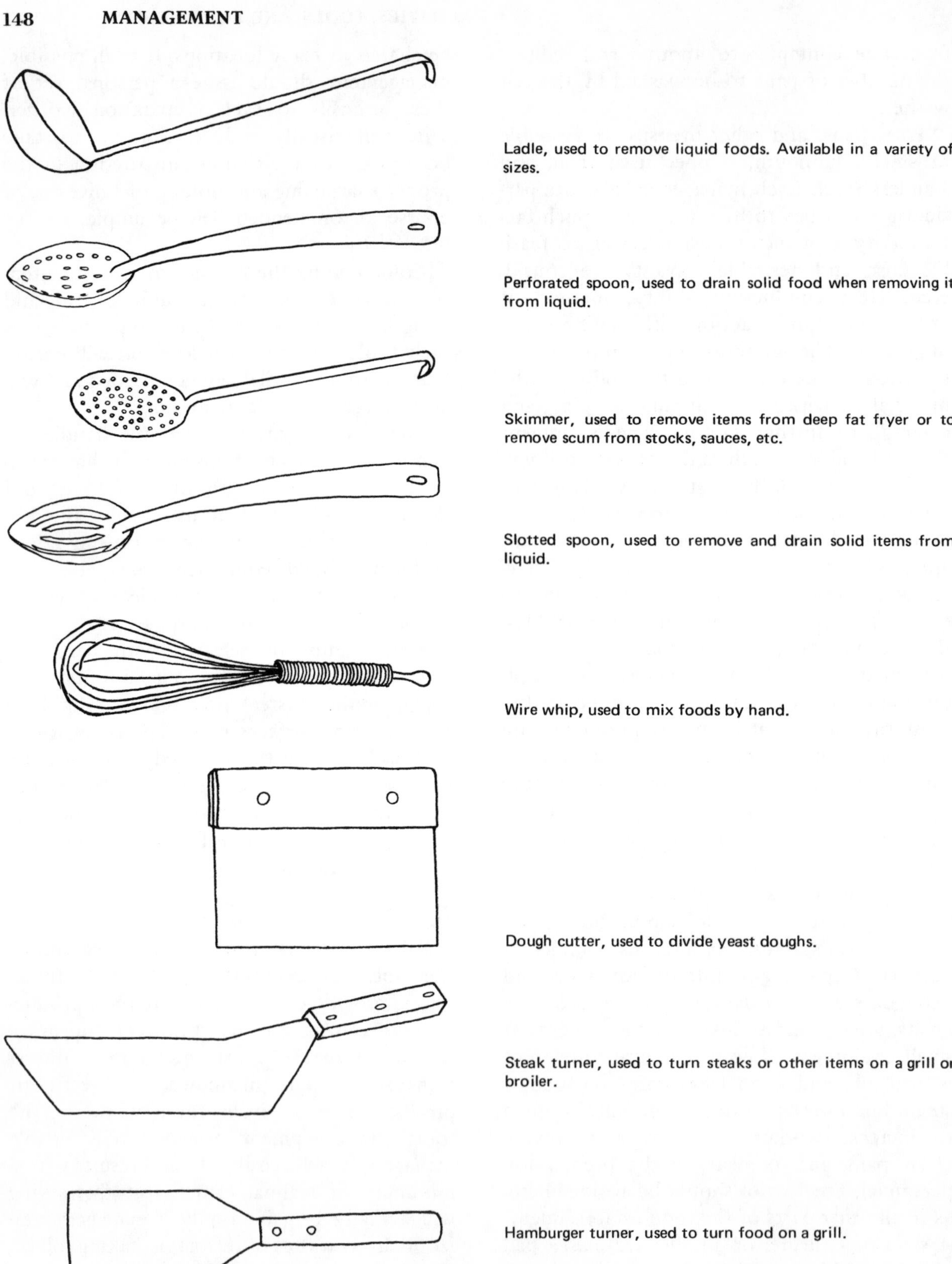

Figure 7v. Some of the common hand tools used in quantity food preparation work.

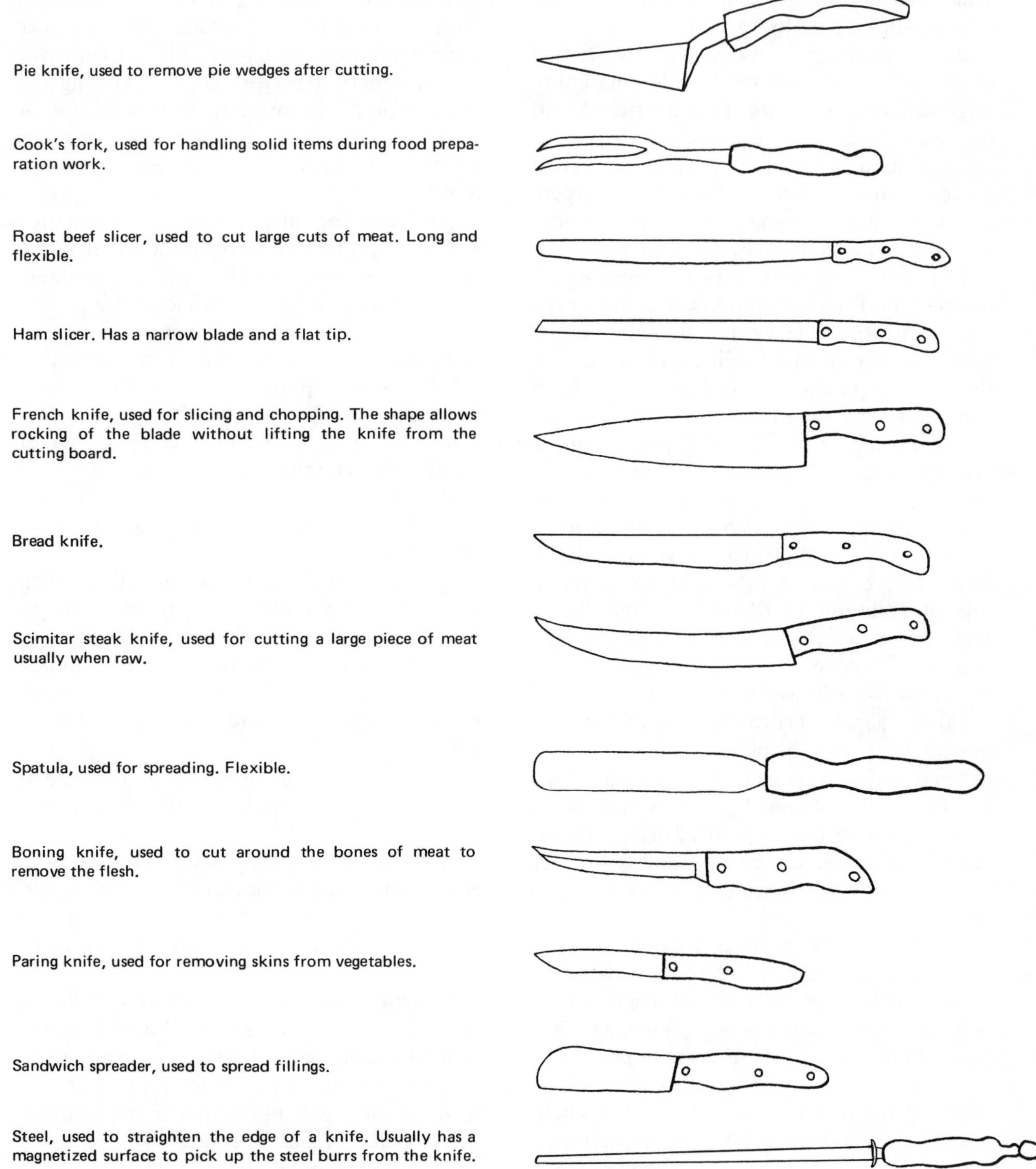

Figure 7v. (continued)

tion areas with an eye to increasing efficiency. This must be done in order to gain a proper relationship of men to machines.

Electrical energy is available at one or two cents per kilowatt-hour, while minimum wages for employees are approximately $1.60 per hour plus benefits. One kilowatt-hour equates with about 200 man-hours, which makes manpower some 1,000 times as expensive as machinery power, even when the original cost of the equipment is considered.

It is true that only man can accomplish certain food service procedures, but, even among these, efficiency may be improved by better layout of the facilities, better use of the available equipment, or better menu form and purchasing methods.

It is estimated that 20 to 25 percent of the average food service worker's time may now be wasted due to inefficiency. Whether to follow the spartan efficiency line of Taylor, a foreman of a steel plant who was a leader in efficiency, or the work simplification methods of Gilbreth, of *Cheaper by the Dozen* fame, remains an individual decision for each manager. However, the following general principles may be followed in most cases:

(a) Construct benchmarks against which performance may be judged. Use a statistical or engineering approach that considers past records, results obtained in similar operations, or mathematical models, if available. In the absence of these, at least use some subjective rule of thumb against which to judge performance.

(b) Taking the menu as a point of departure, analyze each item produced with a view to what is being done, who is doing it, how it is being done, when it is being done, why it is being done, and where it is being done.

(c) Look at the whole picture as it relates to the processing of each individual product. Examine the relationships of all departments and personnel in the production process.

(d) Consider whether down times for equipment and personnel could be used by incorporating other tasks, changing schedules, or combining functions.

(e) Search out procedures that require excessive travel or carrying items great distances, both of which are unproductive. Consider using equipment on wheels, moving the place of the function performed, or changing the departmental design. Put related pieces of equipment or related equipment and materials together. Consider pass-throughs to reduce travel.

(f) Look for fatigue-causing factors, such as the weight of equipment to be handled, the height of working surfaces, and the availability of opportunities to sit while working.

(g) View the efficiency of each worker from the standpoint of linear work space provided, tools required and provided, reach range, and search and assembly time. Consider color coding of tools and stacking storage of supplies and equipment.

(h) Aim for modular use of equipment.

(i) Store items where they will be most often used.

(j) Consider the flow of materials through the kitchen. Emulate the assembly-line or straight-line approach when possible.

(k) Prepare the menu items in batches, where possible, to achieve better use of small pieces of equipment and better quality products.

(l) Consider prefabrication of food items to reduce problems in food handling or preparation.

(m) Look for true work simplification equipment, such as measuring pumps for dispensing water at ranges or steamer stations or conveyor belts for tray return or food delivery.

(n) Anticipate obsolescence by keeping up with trends in food service. Some hospitals now use only coffee makers, refrigerators, freezers, and microwave heating equipment to feed all their patients with pre-prepared and preportioned regular or special diets.

(o) Place the greatest emphasis on the higher skilled and better paid employees. Use these workers as focal points for layout and equipment placement. Surround them with the equipment, materials, and space they re-

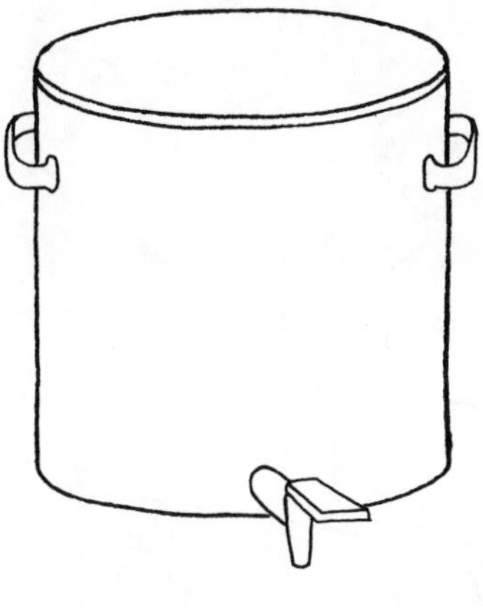

Stock pot with spigot, used for making stocks or soups or for range-top cooking of other items, such as vegetables. Available in a variety of sizes from 10 to 120 quarts.

Sauce pot, used for general range-top cooking of a variety of products. Available in a variety of sizes from 6 to 60 quarts.

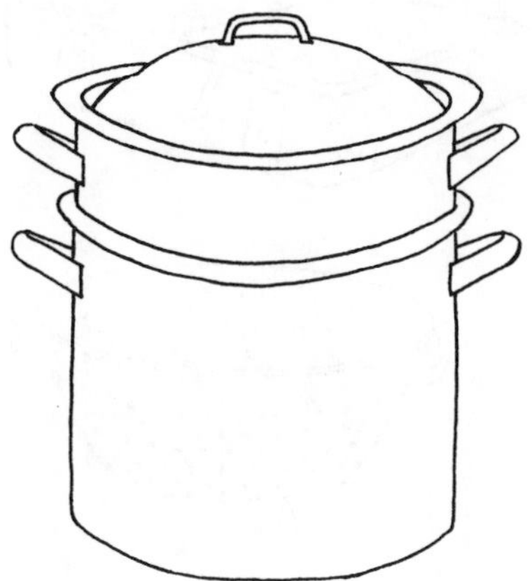

Double boiler, used to heat tender foods while protecting them from the direct and extreme range-top temperatures. The bottom container holds water and the upper container food. Available in sizes from 4 to 40 quarts.

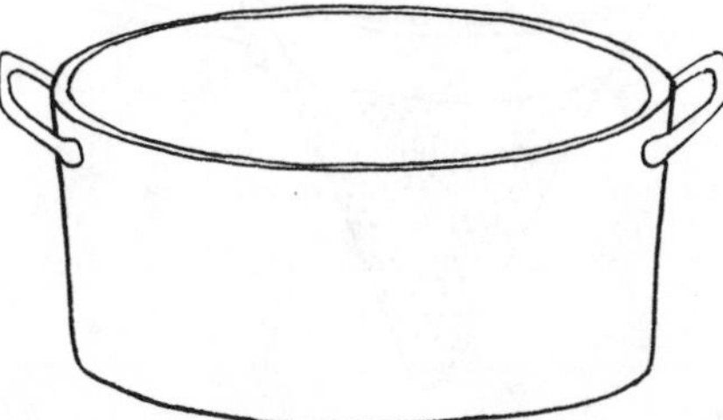

Braiser, used for braising and stewing. Available in sizes from 15 to 28 quarts.

Figure 7w. Some of the common pots, pans, and utensils used in quantity food preparation work.

Sauce pan, used for making sauces or other range-top work. Available in sizes from 1 to 10 quarts.

Sauté or fry pan. Some models are Teflon-coated to reduce sticking. Diameters from 7 to 14 inches.

Heavy duty sauté pan.

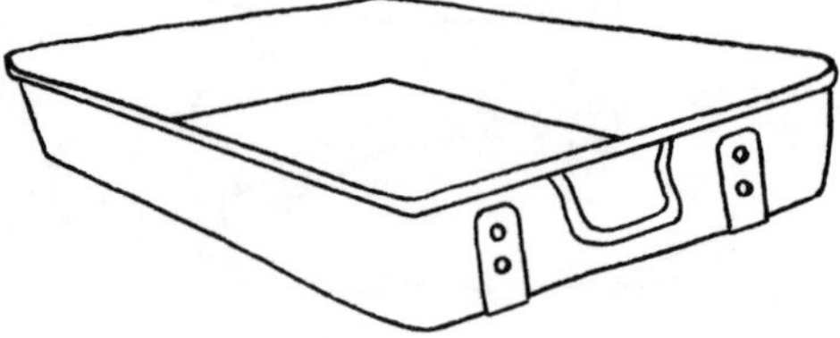

Oven roasting pan. Most common sizes are 16 x 20 and 18 x 24 inches.

Colander, used to drain products or wash items with water. Available in a variety of sizes.

China cap strainer, used to strain food items. The hook fits over the side of a stock pot or other container. Most common sizes are 2 to 5 quarts, although others are available.

Figure 7w. (continued)

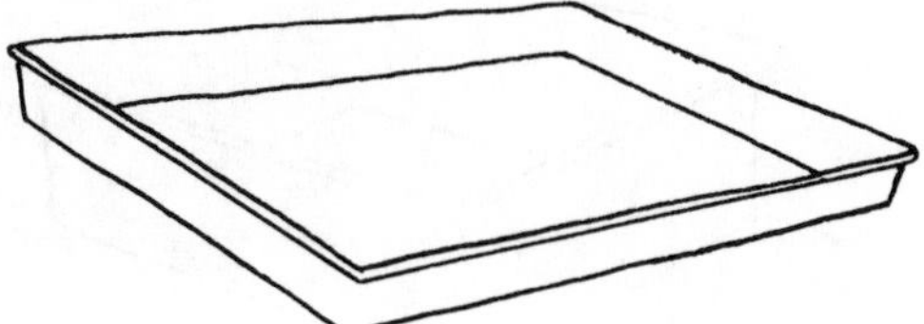

Standard sheet pan, used for baking sweet products or meat items and for refrigerator storage on a file-shelf arrangement. Most common size is 18 x 26 inches.

Layer cake pan, used for baking cakes. Most common diameters are 7 to 9 inches.

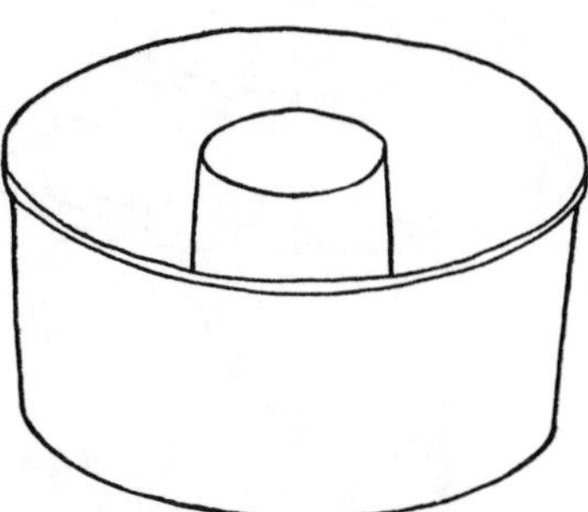

Tube cake pan, used for baking air-leavened cakes such as angel food. Available in a variety of sizes, with removable or nonremovable inside tubes.

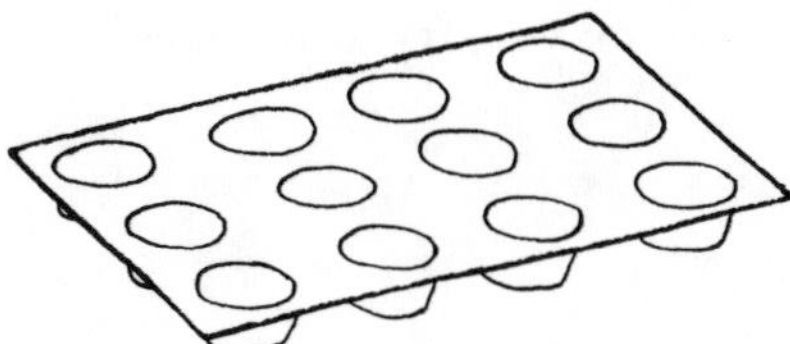

Cupcake pan, used for making cupcakes or muffins. Available in one, two, and three dozen sizes.

Measure, used for measuring dry or wet ingredients. Available in sizes from 1 pint to 1 gallon.

Figure 7w. (continued)

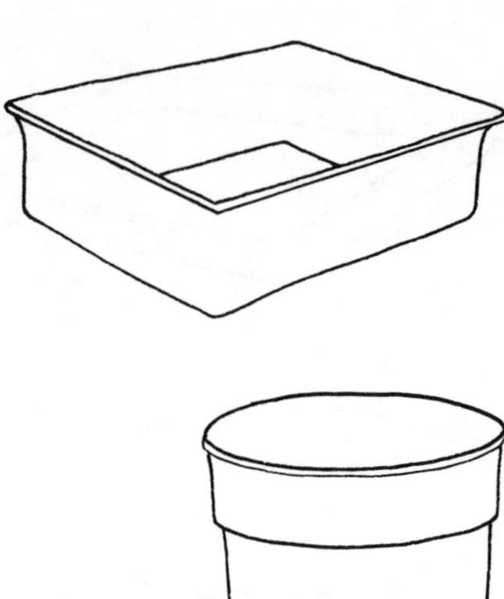

Steam table counter pan, used for both preparing and serving food. Available with adapters for steam table openings in a variety of sizes (full, half, one-third, etc.)

Steam table round pan (commonly referred to as a "boot-leg"), used for serving soups and other liquid foods from a steam table or bain-marie.

Banquet ring, used to cover a dinner plate before service or used with a container and hot pellet for hospital tray service. Available in sizes to fit most plates.

Figure 7w. (continued)

quire to accomplish their assigned tasks more effectively. Support these stations with lower paid workers, who may carry out travel, assembly, and collection tasks that do not require the expertise of higher paid personnel.

8 *Menus and Recipes*

Objective: To introduce the student to the importance of menus and recipes in the supervision of quantity food service operations. The determining factors of a menu and its forms and parts are discussed in terms of planning, pricing, and layout. The history of recipes introduces their use and value.

The menu offered in a particular facility may be considered the operational game plan for the establishment. It is the blueprint that influences many other factors, such as the size of the physical plant, the tools and equipment needed, and the personnel required.

Many food operations construct menus after the facilities and personnel have been provided, but it would be infinitely better if the menu were constructed first. On the other side of the coin, an operation that constructs a menu without considering the elements necessary to produce it may find itself in a chaotic condition.

Consumer Requirements

The first consideration in planning the menu and the recipes necessary to present it is what the consumer requirements are in the specific market segment that has been identified. The more knowledgeable the manager is about these unique requirements, the more likely it is that the operation will be a success. The menu planner must determine both the characteristics of the potential consumer and the specific demands he brings with him. Factors that influence these demands are discussed below.

The feasibility study that is done to identify the market and establish the goals and objectives of the food service facility will help to determine the name, location, theme, decor, and pricing structure to be used. The menu reflects these decisions and is the merchandising tool that will result in the necessary sales. It must be built on the answers to two questions: who are the customers, and what are their particular desires?

Food of a certain type or quality may be the major reason consumers will seek the service provided by an establishment. Or price and convenience may be the most important elements. A desire for relaxation, entertainment, or atmosphere may be the primary reason the customer appears, and food sales may be only a secondary effect of the satisfaction of these needs.

Whatever the major reason or desire, the market must be identified and analyzed to determine it before the menu is constructed. Many important marketing surveys made by and for specific segments of the industry have been published in the periodicals of the trade. Trade associations will also assist in securing this information. Of course, individually constructed surveys may be commissioned from marketing consultants or research firms. Excellent marketing studies have been completed for the International Food Service Manufacturing Association and definitive work also done for and available from the National Restaurant Association, 311 First St., North West, Washington, D.C.

Studies have been done on both regional and national levels to determine what is being eaten, by whom, and where. A few have been done by national research sampling firms, but most have used the question-and-answer approach to determine likes and dislikes. One of the most complete studies on a national scale, representing all segments of the population from a geographical, education, and economic standpoint, was completed by the United States Army in 1960 and is available from the Quartermaster Food and Container Institute for the Armed Forces, 1819 West Pershing Road, Chicago, Illinois. It has been tested statistically and is still quoted as a valid source on food preferences.

An important source of information demonstrating the changes in food consumption that have taken place for the American consumer and the resulting food preferences can be found in *The Changing American Diet* by Letitia Brewster and Michael Jacobson published in 1978 by the Center for Science in the Public Interest, 1755 S Street N.W., Washington, D.C.

The writers Brewster and Jacobson, calling attention to the data presented in Table 8-1, suggest that many of these changes in preference and usage are probably due to a combination of factors, such as better productivity, changes in food preparation methods, more affluence among consumers, and changing life styles. They also note, however, that in terms of the total calories consumed by the average American, the calories derived from fats have increased by 31 percent from 1910-1976; those derived from the complex carbohydrates have decreased by 45 percent in the same time period; and those derived from sugars have increased by 50 percent. They link this change to possible problems and noted increases in the rates of diabetes, heart disease, stroke, and tooth decay among Americans.

The recently instituted CREST Reports (Chain Restaurant Eating Out Share Trends), published by the National Restaurant Association, and other industry periodicals are important research tools that indicate current consumer requirements, preferences, and activities.

Other important studies in this area may be found in the ***Cornell Hotel and Restaurant Administration Quarterly*** or in the periodical Gallop Surveys, which are accomplished, and published, in the trade press. The U.S. Army Natick Laboratories, Natick, Massachusetts, also maintains an active participation in this field and publishes periodical reports in this area.

Age

The age of the typical consumer is an important element in construction of the menu. Different age groups have major differences in tastes, caloric requirements, suitable portion sizes, acceptable prices, desire for speed of service, preferred types of foods, and preferred methods of preparation.

Younger consumers generally require foods with higher caloric content and purer taste. They are less likely to accept many sauces or spices and more concerned with the true taste of the food. Older diners, probably because of maturation and sophistication of the taste buds, are more likely to accept sauces, seasonings, variations in food types, and different methods of preparation.

A young diner will generally be more concerned with the speed of service and the price of the menu item being offered than an older

Table 8-1. Daily Food Consumption and Changes in Food Consumption

Approximate Daily Food Consumption

Food	1910	1950	1976
Total, all foods	4.4 lbs.	4.1 lbs.	4.0 lbs.
Beef	2.4 oz.	2.2 oz.	4.2 oz.
Butter	4.8 tsp.	2.8 tsp.	1.2 tsp.
Cheese, hard and cottage	0.2 oz.	0.5 oz.	0.9 oz.
Chicken	0.6 oz.	0.9 oz.	1.9 oz.
Coffee, 6-ounce cups	1.3 c.	2.2 c.	1.9 c.
Corn syrup	1.0 tsp.	1.7 tsp.	6.0 tsp.
Cream	.8 tsp.	1.0 tsp.	.5 tsp.
Fish	.5 oz.	.5 oz.	.6 oz.
Flour, wheat	9.4 oz.	5.9 oz.	4.9 oz.
Flour and other cereal products	12.9 oz.	7.3 oz.	6.3 oz.
Fruit, fresh	5.4 oz.	4.7 oz.	3.6 oz.
Fruit, fresh and processed*	6.3 oz.	8.2 oz.	9.5 oz.
Frozen dairy products	.3 Tbs.	3.0 Tbs.	4.4 Tbs.
Margarine	0.4 tsp.	1.6 tsp.	3.3 tsp.
Meat, red fresh	6.0 oz.	5.9 oz.	7.3 oz.
Milk, low-fat	0.3 c.	0.2 c.	0.5 c.
Milk, fresh whole	1.3 c.	1.5 c.	.9 c.
Potatoes, fresh	8.7 oz.	4.2 oz.	2.2 oz.
Potatoes*, total	8.7 oz.	4.6 oz.	5.1 oz.
Poultry	0.8 oz.	1.1 oz.	2.3 oz.
Soft drinks	0.4 oz. (1909)	3.5 oz.	10.8 oz.
Sugar, refined cane and beet	3.3 oz.	4.4 oz.	4.2 oz.
Sweeteners, total calories	3.9 oz.	5.2 oz.	5.9 oz.
Tea, 6-ounce cups	.5 c.	.3 c.	.4 c.
Vegetables, fresh	3.5 oz. (1920)	4.3 oz.	4.6 oz.
Vegetables, fresh and processed*	4.9 oz. (1920)	7.9 oz.	9.5 oz.
Calories	3490	3260	3380
Protein	102 gms.	95 gms.	103 gms.
Fat	124 gms.	145 gms.	159 gms.
Carbohydrate	495 gms.	402 gms.	390 gms.

Changes in Food Consumption

Food	Years	Change in consumption (per person)
Apples, fresh	1910-76	-70%
Beef	1910-76	+72%
	1950-76	+90%
Butter	1910-76	-76%
Cabbage, fresh	1920-76	-65%
Candy	1968-76	-18%
Chicken	1910-76	+179%
Coffee	1910-76	+22%
	1946-76	-44%
Corn syrup	1960-76	+224%
Fish, fresh and frozen	1960-76	+42%
Food colors (certified dyes)	1940-77	+995%
Fruit, fresh	1910-76	-33%
Grapefruit, fresh	1910-76	+800%
Margarine	1910-76	+681%
Potatoes, fresh	1910-76	-74%
Potatoes, frozen	1960-76	+465%
Soft drinks	1960-76	+157%
Sugar and other caloric sweeteners	1909-76	+33%
Tuna, canned	1926-76	+1,300%
Turkey	1910-76	+820%
Vegetables, frozen	1960-76	+44%
Wheat flour (including flour used in bread, spaghetti, and so on	1910-76	-48%

Reprinted from "The Changing American Diet" by Letitia Brewster and Michael Jacobson, which is available from the Center for Science in the Public Interest, 1755 S Street, N.W., Washington, D.C. 20009, for $2.50, copyright 1978.

Changes in Food Consumption 1970–1984

	Pounds Eaten in 1984	Change Since 1970
Animal products	**576**	**– 6.3%**
Red meats	153	– 7.3%
Beef, veal	79	– 8.1%
Pork	61	– 1.6%
Poultry	63	+ 28.6%
Eggs	253*	– 15.4%
Dairy products	303	– 9.8%
Crop products	**819**	**+ 4.7%**
Cereals, baked goods	150	+ 5.6%
Vegetable oils	47	+ 14.6%
Fruits, melons	163	+ 1.9%
Vegetables	288	+ 1.4%
Sugar, sweeteners	135	+ 11.6%
All foods	**1,395**	**– 0.1%**

*Number of eggs.

Americans are eating less red meats, more poultry and more vegetables. Compare with the date 1910–1976 Source for data from 1970–1984, *US News and World Report*, April 30, 1984 p. 20.

*Fresh equivalents of processed weights are used; that is, the weight of frozen or dehydrated produce is converted to the weight of its fresh equivalent.

consumer, who may be more concerned with the tenderness of a meat product, the taste sensation experienced, the decor, and the form of service. Older diners usually demand more variety in vegetables and salads, and they consume more of these. Younger customers choose more protein and carbohydrate foods.

Sizes of portions may be reduced for older consumers, while the number and type of embellishments may have to be increased. Younger married couples with children look for child-sized portions and corresponding price reductions, in selecting a restaurant.

Dessert sales will usually be high among very young and very old customers, and fewer

SLATER SCHOOL & COLLEGE SERVICES

FOOD PREFERENCE QUESTIONNAIRE

INSTRUCTIONS

1. Menu items on this page are part of a comprehensive Food Preference Survey.
2. Use a soft black pencil to completely blacken that space best describing your choices and opinions. DO NOT USE PENS. DO NOT USE OTHER CHECK MARKS.
3. Mark only one choice for each item.
4. If you want to change a response be sure to completely erase your first answer.

EXAMPLE:

1	CORNED BEEF	▬		
3	PINEAPPLE UPSIDE DOWN CAKE		▬	

		LIKE	DO NOT KNOW	DISLIKE			LIKE	DO NOT KNOW	DISLIKE
1	CORNED BEEF				2	BEEF BISCUIT ROLL			
3	PINEAPPLE UPSIDE DOWN CAKE				4	CLAM CHOWDER			
5	GRILLED SAUSAGE				6	VEAL CUTLET PARMIGIANA			
7	BUTTERSCOTCH PUDDING				8	MUFFINS			
9	BUTTERED GREEN PEAS				10	CAULIFLOWER			
11	ROAST TURKEY				12	SALISBURY STEAK			
13	BAKED APPLE				14	BLUEBERRY PIE			
15	GRILLED CHEESE SANDWICH				16	ORANGE SHERBET			
17	FRIED RICE				18	BARBECUED PORK			
19	MILK				20	KALE			
21	BREAD PUDDING				22	CHICKEN CACCIATORE			
23	TOSSED GREEN SALAD				24	HOT BISCUITS			
25	SWEET POTATOES				26	LETTUCE AND TOMATO SALAD			
27	WATERMELON				28	LIMA BEANS			
29	STUFFED PEPPERS				30	TOMATO JUICE			
31	GRAPEFRUIT HALF				32	BOSTON CREAM PIE			
33	FRIED SCALLOPS				34	MEAT LOAF			
35	COLD CEREAL				36	PARSLEY BUTTERED POTATOES			
37	GRILLED HAM STEAK				38	BROWNIES			
39	ASSORTED COLD CUTS PLATTER				40	FRANKFURTERS			
41	TUNA SALAD SANDWICH				42	BAKED CHICKEN			
43	PIZZA				44	ANGEL FOOD CAKE			
45	PEACH COBBLER				46	SCRAMBLED EGGS			
47	ROAST LEG OF LAMB				48	BEEF STEW			
49	HOT CAKES AND SAUSAGE				50	WHOLE KERNEL CORN			

YOUR SUGGESTIONS FOR ADDITIONAL MENU ITEMS YOU WISH TO HAVE SERVED

THANK YOU FOR YOUR PARTICIPATION

Figure 8a. **A food preference survey form used to determine the food likes and dislikes of college students.** (Courtesy of ARA-Slater School and College Services, Philadelphia.)

will be ordered by the moderate age groups.

In a facility catering to all age levels, every factor must be considered, and provisions should be made to meet the unique requirements of each group. Most operations, however, identify a particular age group as their predominant market.

Sex

Generally speaking, a man requires a higher caloric intake than a woman because of his biological makeup and the kind of work he usually performs. Many older females, however, choose copious amounts of filling foods, particularly in the dessert area.

Fruits, salad plates, and other combinations that cater to the artistic and economical side of women will generally be well received. Calorie-counter entrée plates and some low calorie dessert offerings should also be provided for those who are attempting to limit their caloric intake.

Soufflés and other foods with light, frothy textures may have feminine or "sissy" connotations, particularly to adolescent consumers. If young men dominate the market of an operation, this factor must be considered.

Women generally spend less for their meals and eat at a slower rate than men do. Menu planning should reflect these pricing and turnover conditions, if women are to be the predominant market.

Religious, Ethnic, and Geographic Requirements

Three closely related factors, religious, ethnic, and geographic needs, must be considered in planning the menu and recipes. Religious taboos as to types of food, methods of preparation, foods to be offered on particular days, or foods acceptable at certain times of the year must be taken into account by the menu planner.

Members of a particular nationality or residents of a certain section of the country may have been cultured to accept specific foods or manners of preparation. The use of spices might have to be drastically reduced for a New England clientele or increased for a southern or southwestern one. Catering to the habits of the group and serving foods familiar to them has always been a proper procedure for the menu planner. The mobile nature of the United States population and the cosmopolitan makeup of many city populations make this less of a problem than it has been in the past, but it must still be given some consideration.

Life-Style Considerations

The economic level of the consumers, the percentage of disposable income they have, and the usual price they pay for a meal all dictate particular requirements for the menu planner. The type of work the consumer does, the time he or she has available for dining, and his or her quality versus quantity expectations also assist the menu planner in devising a proper offering. A typist with one hour for lunch will require quite a different menu from

Appetizers
Chicken/seafood nuggets
Melon
Nachos
Fruit cup

Soups
Vegetable
Chicken
Beef
New England clam chowder

Seafood Entrees
French-fried shrimp
Shrimp, nonfried
Seafood platter
Flounder

Poultry Entrees
Roast turkey
Fried chicken
Turkey breast
Chicken tenders

Meat Entrees
Prime rib/roast beef
Steak
Chili
BBQ spareribs

Sandwiches
Cheeseburger
Hamburger
Gourmet hamburger
Club sandwich

Salads
Tossed green
Special house salad
Taco salad
Chef's salad

Beverages
Cola soft drinks
Orange juice
Regular beer
Coffee

Entrees: Tacos and Pasta
Tacos
Pasta with sauce
Spaghetti with sauce
Pizza

Desserts
Apple pie
Cookies
Chocolate cake
Cream-style cheesecake

Side Dishes
French fries
American fries
Baked potatoes
Mashed potatoes

Figure 8b. Top four most popular overall menu items in each food category for 1987. (Source: 1987 Menu Census, *Restaurant and Institutions*, Feb 18, 1987, pp. 28, 30, 36, 38, 40, 46, 50, 56, 62, 68, 74)

an executive entertaining a client at a combined dining and selling meal or a construction worker expecting to put in four more hours of strenuous manual work after his meal.

We are what we eat, or we try to appear to be what we eat. Many years ago it was thought chic to be portly because that suggested one had enough to eat or at least enough disposable income to be able to buy desirable foods. No longer is this true. To be fat or even overweight now is to be "gross." One must be svelte to play a better tennis game, go to a health spa, or at least own leg warmers. This means people eat lightly and healthily. One may drink beer, but it should be "light," and it is best to avoid beef for fear of cholesterol. Of course the wine cooler is the alcoholic drink of the day to replace the mineral water, which seems to have had its day and disappeared, as have the "stiffer drinks" of yesteryear.

A Gallup survey conducted in 1986 showed that 40 percent of the people surveyed had changed their eating habits to reflect nutritional concerns, and lighter menus are being offered by just about every one of the Restaurant and Institutions 400. But more than this is happening, including a movement toward exotic or strange food or unusual or fun items. The "yuppies" (young upwardly mobile professionals), the DINKs (double incomes, no kids), and the YMCAs (young married childless achievers) are what the writers of the media write about and the consumers many restaurant operators cater to. But let's not forget the ULTRAs (the 55 to 60 age group with considerable disposable income and more time in which to spend it). Whatever the age, the clever term, or the conditions, we are dealing here with trends, fads, and conspicuous consumption. This exceeds what is "good" or what is "healthy" to focus on what is "in." Menu planning can reflect this complexity. It can seem contradictory sometimes, but a good menu planner is also able to anticipate, lead, and market if the proper information has been collected.

A chef makes blackened redfish, which quickly becomes "in" rather than just burned. Soon a moratorium has to be declared on fishing for this species before it becomes endangered due to its popularity. But soon another trend will come along to save this species from extinction. (By the way, what happened to mesquite cooking? Have all the trees been burned up or has that trend passed?)

Quiche was the "in" luncheon item until someone discovered that eggs contained cholesterol, and the *nouvelle cuisine* fad lasted long enough for people to realize that it was pretty, well arranged and presented, but they were hungry fifteen minutes after eating or had to eat six or so different courses to be satisfied.

Adding to all this frenzy, fast food hamburger outlets publish nutrition guides, while "grazers"—interested in health, harmony, and happiness—eat deep-fat fried vegetables and chicken wings, which (many times) are probably fried in animal fats, and consume the now ubiquitous potato skin (previously thrown away) that is full of vitamins, minerals, and a high-fat substance used as a filler. Children raised on fast food hamburgers are now adults looking for Mexican fajitas or tacos, stir-fried vegetables, chicken nuggets, Peking wings, or a haystack of rice noodles covered with chocolate sauce.

Menus compete with the trends and the competition, but it remains a basic operating tenet that these trends usually last five years at the most as they race from California to New York or from New Orleans to Chicago. It remains the challenge of each operator to cater to his own market and the tastes of that market. To do what he does best and to provide the quality, consistency, and convenience that this market demands is essential. Not everyone is eating sushi or sliced kiwi. A good number still eat the "unhealthy" hamburger, spaghetti and meatballs, and bread pudding, even some YMCAs, DINKs, or yuppies after jogging or before their wine coolers.

External and Internal Restrictions

Certain restrictions are imposed on the menu planner by his competition, by government regulatory bodies, and by the makeup of his facility.

Many food operations are located in a cohesive marketing area and either share potential customers or exist on customer spinoff from other operations. As a result, many of their menu decisions are based on what the competition is doing. Although "the better mousetrap" philosophy may well result in increased sales for a brief period of time, this market strategy will probably cause the competition to make similar improvements, and soon erode the gains from the first menu policy changes.

Regulatory bodies can also affect menu planning. The regulations governing type "A" school lunch menus, the military Standard Subsistence Law, and the dairy products labeling and use acts of major dairy-producing states often determine what a menu can offer to a particular market.

Augmenting these consumer requirements and external restrictions are others that are internal in nature. The facilities must meet particular space, layout, storage, and equipment needs. An adequate number of personnel with sufficient technical knowledge must be available to produce the menu items planned. Finally, the raw materials must be readily available in the amounts necessary to produce the items.

Sufficient profit must be generated from the menu to make the venture worthwhile. The relationship of an item's popularity to its profitability must be uppermost in the mind of the menu planner.

Form of Menu

Many years ago it was considered necessary to provide an almost limitless number of menu items from which the guest could choose. Classifications ranged from hors d'oeuvres through soups, fish, entrées, roasts, salads, desserts, and beverages, and in each category extensive numbers of items were offered to satisfy every palate. Although a similar range is still provided in some gourmet establishments, resorts, and shipboard dining rooms, the trend appears to be in the direction of a limited menu.

The limited menu offers six to twelve main entrées to the guest, plus a selection of appetizers, soups, and desserts. This form of menu produces savings in storage space, required types and amounts of equipment, and control expenditures. In addition, purchase specifications can be better standardized, and culinary workers can become more proficient in producing the limited number of items. From the limited menu concept the specialty house and the fast food operation have evolved. In these, an even more restricted offering has resulted in greater specialization, greater control possibilities, and more efficient production.

Another menu policy that has reduced extensive offerings is use of a cyclical menu. A

The Inaugural Luncheon

of

ABRAHAM LINCOLN

Willard Hotel, March 4, 1861

Mock Turtle Soup

Corned Beef and Cabbage — Parsley Potatoes

Blackberry Pie — Coffee

Figure 8c. The menu for Lincoln's inaugural luncheon indicates that the desires of the consumers took precedence over the grandiloquence of the event.

cyclical menu offers a number of items on a revolving basis, so that the same items are repeated regularly. Cycles are selected according to weekdays, weekends, or seasons of the year. The best basis is usually a two- or three-week package. Measures generally should be taken to ensure that the same food does not repeat on the same day every week, although some restaurants capitalize on a weekly routine and regular customers come for the "Tuesday pot roast," for example. Table 8-2 shows the quarterly pattern of a cyclical series of eighteen daily menus plus three Friday and three Sunday menus that avoid repetition on the same days.

Cyclical menus enable specialization in the buying, preparation, and serving of food. They may emphasize the items that are both popular and profitable. The cycle period can be geared to the movement or habits of the customers. For example, a general hospital with a five-day average patient stay might call for a different cycle from that of an orthopedic hospital with a fourteen-day average patient stay.

The du jour menu is another form. The items selected are either specialty foods of the restaurant or generally popular items. Although the form means "of the day," or "ready," the same menu items may be repeated every day, with only the daily special varied. This menu achieves specialization in purchasing, storage, training of workers, and selection of equipment. Pricing and the work of service personnel are also made easier. However, a facility using this form of menu must have a market of sufficient scope to support it.

The use of convenience food items, kept pre-prepared and frozen in individual or limited portions and reconstituted in a very short period of time, gives flexibility to the menu planner who wants to present a more elaborate offering. These ready foods may also be used to supplement regularly prepared amounts of the same menu items, and thereby enable supervisors to be more daring in making forecasts, since backup items are readily available. Or they may constitute the complete menu offering.

Whatever its form, the menu must meet the particular needs of the consumers and give the profit desired by the establishment. It is planned around the entrées, meat items, or meat substitutes that are offered. Other foods and courses are provided to produce the proper balance in terms of nutrition, caloric requirements, color, taste, texture, variety, and method of preparation.

Entrées

Entrées are the most difficult part of the menu to balance and to plan. They make up some 25 to 40 percent of the total meal cost and dictate which other foods are to be offered.

Table 8-2. A Quarterly Menu Cycle

Week	Mon.	Tues.	Wed.	Thurs.	Fri.	Sat.	Sun.
1	1	2	3	4	1F	5	1S
2	6	7	8	9	2F	10	2S
3	11	12	13	14	3F	15	3S
4	16	17	18	1	1F	2	1S
5	3	4	5	6	2F	7	2S
6	8	9	10	11	3F	12	3S
7	13	14	15	16	1F	17	1S
8	18	1	2	3	2F	4	2S
9	5	6	7	8	3F	9	3S
10	10	11	12	13	1F	14	1S
11	15	16	17	18	2F	1	2S
12	2	3	4	5	3F	6	3S
13	7	8	9	10	1F	11	1S

From John M. Welch, *Analyze Your Food Cost,* p. 4, Circular no. 723, Agricultural Extension Service, University of Missouri, Columbia, July 1960; reprinted by permission.

Entrées vary, depending on the meal period and other factors. They should provide a proper balance in price, taste, type of food, method of preparation, and "psychological" weight. Beef, lamb, veal, pork, red pastas (spaghetti, ravioli, etc.), and most heavily sauced items are considered heavy, while chicken, most fish, and salad plates are considered light.

Beef, chicken, pork, veal, and lamb are usually accepted by a majority of consumers in that order. Lamb and veal have more ethnic connotations than the other meat forms. Shrimp and tuna are high on the list of fish selections, although other types of seafood are increasing in popularity owing to new methods of processing and better transportation procedures.

A limited menu that would find good acceptance from most classes of consumers might include:

—a roast item from the beef, pork, or lamb category

—a variety of steaks and chops from these three categories

—a poultry item prepared by a method other than roasting or grilling

—two fish items prepared by methods varied from those of the other foods offered

—A casserole, slurry, meat extender, or convenience food item to round out taste, texture, and preparation method varieties.

The menu planner must decide on garnishes, relishes, and accompaniments to the entrée items offered. He should try to avoid the trite except in traditional dishes. Lamb and mint jelly or pork and applesauce may have been used for years, but could well gain interest, new flavor, and pleasing results if varied. Cranberry sauce and turkey might be required on a holiday menu, however, to satisfy the consumers.

Appetizers and Soups

Appetizers and soups are the least expensive part of the meal pattern, but some attempt should be made to offer an adequate variety in this classification.

Juices and soups should be offered, at the very least. Juice selections should include at least one fruit and one vegetable variety. Soups should be offered in both the lighter or clear types and the heavier forms such as creamed or pureed soups.

Color, flavor, and texture should be considered in this course offering. In complete dinner menus, light appetizers or soups should accompany heavier entrée items and vice versa. Seafood items, in many forms, provide variety and customer satisfaction at this course.

Vegetables

Vegetables should be selected in which the caloric content, color, texture, taste, and method of preparation complement the entrée they accompany.

At least four should be available in most operations, with at least one from the 20 percent classification and one from the 5 percent group (see table 8-3). It is desirable to include potatoes, rice, and/or noodles on every menu. Little extra preparation or cost is necessary to provide two forms of potatoes, and this is suggested.

Differences in cutting vegetables, preparation changes, or combinations of vegetables will make this course a much more inviting one. In plate combinations or dinner offerings that provide vegetables without a consumer selection, great care must be exercised to make sure the vegetable contributes to the entrée and does not clash with other items provided.

Desserts

The dessert is the most difficult course of the meal to provide. The menu should offer as broad a range as possible. Selections from both heavy items (pies, cakes) and light (gelatin, fruits, ices) should be available. At least six desserts should be offered in each menu.

Beverages

Using the traditional coffee, tea, and milk as the point of departure, most menus can be

Table 8-3. Carbohydrate Content of Fruits and Vegetables

	Carbohydrate Content			
	5 Percent	10 Percent	15 Percent	20 Percent
Vegetables	Asparagus	Beets	Artichokes, globe	Beans, kidney
	Bean sprouts	Brussels sprouts	Oyster plant	Beans, lima
	Broccoli	Carrots	Parsnips	Beans, navy
	Cabbage	Dandelion greens	Peas	Corn
	Cauliflower	Leeks		Horseradish
	Celery	Olives, green		Potatoes
	Chard	Onions		
	Chinese cabbage	Rutabagas		
	Cucumber	Winter squash		
	Eggplant			
	Endive			
	Greens, beet			
	Greens, mustard			
	Kohlrabi			
	Lettuce			
	Okra			
	Olives, ripe			
	Peppers			
	Pumpkin			
	Radishes			
	Spinach			
	String beans			
	Summer squash			
	Tomatoes			
	Turnips			
	Watercress			
Fruits	Avocado	Blackberries	Apples	Bananas
	Honeydew melon	Cranberries	Apricots	Cherries, sweet
	Muskmelon	Currants	Blueberries	Figs, fresh
	Rhubarb	Gooseberries	Cherries, sour	Grape juice
	Strawberries	Grapefruit	Grapes	Prunes, fresh
	Watermelon	Lime juice	Huckleberries	
		Oranges	Loganberries	
		Orange juice	Mulberries	
		Peaches	Pears	
		Tangerines	Pineapple	
		Lemon juice	Plums	
			Raspberries	

enhanced by greater variety in beverage offerings. Steak houses and other specialty houses find wide acceptance of alcoholic beverages such as beer, while in fast food operations and others, carbonated drinks, milkshakes, and frappes may outsell the traditional drinks.

Here again attempts must be made to balance the beverages with the entrées and the form of menu provided.

Specialty Restaurant Menus

Specialty restaurants and multiple restaurant operations housed under one roof, such as in a hotel, an airport, or an entertainment complex, have menus that vary somewhat from the traditional general offering.

Many specialty operations have achieved success providing a very limited selection of preportioned items, such as steaks and lobster tails. This enables the operation to control production and costs, reduce the needed equipment and employee talent, and yet increase turnover. Other parts of the menu are often restricted also to salad offerings, one or two soups, and two or three desserts. Vegetables are limited, and many are offered only under an a la carte pricing system.

Multiple operations under one roof generally specialize according to price, decor, and type of food. A group of facilities may include a fast food equipment-centered outlet, a specialty restaurant, and a traditional dining

R.M.S. "QUEEN MARY"

LUNCHEON

Tuesday, August 4, 1964

Juices: Grape Fruit   Clam   Pineapple   Tomato

HORS D'ŒUVRE

Shellfish Cocktail, Russian Dressing
Smoked Irish Salmon with Capers
Salade à la Russe   Herrings in Tomato   Œufs, Gribiche
Chou-fleur à la Grecque   Salade Hermine
Portuguese Sardines   Pickled Lambs' Tongues
Saucisson: Cervelat, Salami, Liver, Lyon, Arles and Mortadella
Olives—Green, Ripe and Farcies
Salted Mixed Nuts

SOUPS

Consommé Célestine   German Lentil Soup
Cold: Crème Vichyssoise   Jellied Turtle Soup

FISH

Fried Fresh Codling, Orly
Fillet of Brill, Mornay
COLD: Lobster Salad, Mayonnaise

EGGS

en Cocotte, Diplomate   Scrambled, Princesse
Omelettes (to order): Savoyarde, Espagnole and Fermière

ENTREES

Fresh Calf's Liver sauté, Lyonnaise (Cole Slaw Salad)
Curried Chicken, Madras (Oriental Aromatic Condiments)

CONTINENTAL SPECIALITY

Sauerbraten Kartoffelklösse

Fresh Round of Beef, previously marinated with Salt, Vinegar, Sliced Onions, Lemon, Sugar and Spice, braised and cooked with the addition of chopped Raisins and Ginger and White Wine. Served with German Potato Dumplings and Braised Red Cabbage

GRILL (to order, 15 mins.)

Pork Cutlet, Chesapeake   Chopped Tenderloin, Tyrolienne
Spatchcock Diablé, Saratogas

JOINT

Boiled Corned Round and Brisket of Beef
with Vegetables and Dumplings

SUGGESTED MENU

Jus de Pamplemousse

—

Consommé Célestine

—

Filet de Barbue, Mornay

—

Foie de Veau sauté, Lyonnaise
Haricots Verts   Pommes Frites

—

Gâteau Monte Carlo

Fromage   Café

Red and White Wine on request

—

Your individual selection of Wine may be purchased from our comprehensive Wine List

—

The Chef invites you to give him an opportunity to prepare your own favourite dish — whether it be a speciality of American, European or Eastern cuisine. He merely asks that you give the Head Waiter sufficient notice to enable your order to be prepared to perfection. The Head Waiter will also gladly offer suggestions and advice on dishes to suit your personal taste, and if you are on a restricted or special diet, to see that your requirements are met

—

Speciality Foods for Infants available for ready service on request

VEGETABLES

French Beans sautées   Fried New Parsnips
Green Peas with Mint   Braised Pascal Celery
Spaghetti, Marinara

POTATOES

Baked Jacket   Sautées   French Fried   Creamed-Purée

COLD BUFFET

Roast Ribs and Sirloin of Beef, Horseradish Cream
Roast Lamb, Mint Sauce   Roast Duckling, Apple Sauce
Rolled Ox Tongue   Galantine of Chicken   Baked York Ham
Roast Turkey, Cranberry Sauce   Veal and Ham Pie

SALADS

Hearts of Lettuce   Casanova   Cole Slaw   Nina
Scarole   Fresh Fruit

DRESSINGS

Russian   Vinaigrette   Roquefort   French

SWEETS

Chocolate Custard Pudding   Apple Pie
Pineapple Mousse, Chantilly
Compote of Apricots, Pears and Plums—Whipped Cream
Gâteaux: Banbury   Monte Carlo

ICE CREAM

Vanilla   Biscuit Tortoni   Chocolate   Peach

SHERBET

Raspberry

CHEESES

Danish Blue   Camembert   Stilton   Gorgonzola
Caerphilly   Cheddar Loaf   St. Ivel   Brie   Gruyère
Philadelphia Cream

FRESH FRUIT

Pears   Plums   Oranges   Apricots   Nectarines   Tangerines
Apples   Grapes   Greengages

Tea (Hot or Iced)   Coffee (Hot or Iced)

Figure 8d. A traditional menu. (Courtesy of the Museum of the Sea aboard the Queen Mary, Long Beach, California.)

Table 8-4. Fiber Rich Foods

FRUIT
• **Prunes, dried** 4 medium, 5 grams* • Blueberries ½ cup, 5 grams • **Pear** 1 medium, 4 grams • **Apple** 1 medium, 4 grams • **Strawberries** 1 cup, 3 grams • **Banana** 1 medium, 3 grams • **Raisins, dried** ¼ cup, 3 grams • **Orange** 1 medium, 3 grams • **Peach** 1 medium, 3 grams • **Grapefruit** ½ fruit, 3 grams • **Apricots** 3 medium, 2 grams • **Nectarines** 2 medium, 2 grams • **Canteloupe** ¼ small, 2 grams • **Watermelon** 1 cup diced, 2 grams • **Plum** 1 medium, 1 gram • **Pineapple** ¾ cup, sliced, 1 gram • **Honeydew melon** ¼ small, 1 gram • **Cherries, red** ½ cup, 1 gram • **Grapes, white** ½ cup, 1 gram

RICE AND PASTA
• **Brown rice, cooked** ½ cup, 2.5 grams • **White rice, cooked** ½ cup, 1 gram • **Spaghetti, white flour** 1 cup, cooked, 1 gram • **Macaroni, white flour** 1 cup, cooked, 1 gram

FLOURS
• **Oat bran** 1 cup, 40 grams • **Corn meal, whole wheat** 1 cup, 28.5 grams • **Bran, 30–40%** 1 cup, 18–22 grams • **Whole meal** 1 cup, 19 grams • **Whole wheat** 1 cup, 9 grams • **White** 1 cup, 4 grams • **Wheat germ** ¼ cup, 2.7 grams

VEGETABLES
• **Corn, sweet** 1 medium ear, 8 grams • **Spinach** ½ cup, 6 grams • **Yam** 1 medium, 5 grams • **Peas, green** ½ cup, 5 grams • **Sweet potato** 1 medium, baked, 4 grams • **Romaine lettuce** 1½ cups bite-size pieces, 3 grams • **Endive, escarole** 4 large leaves, 3 grams • **Swiss chard** ½ cup leaves, 3 grams • **Cabbage, cooked** 1 cup, 3 grams • **Cabbage, raw** 1 cup, 2 grams • **Broccoli** ½ cup, 3 grams • **Brussels sprouts** ½ cup, 3 grams • **White potato** 1 medium, 3 grams • **Summer squash** ½ cup, 2 grams • **Tomato, raw** 1 medium, 2 grams • **Beets** ½ cup, 2 grams • **Beans, green** ½ cup, 2 grams • **Carrots** ½ cup, 2 grams • **Asparagus** 6 spears, 2 grams • **Zucchini** ½ cup, 2 grams • **Cauliflower** ½ cup, 1 gram • **Mushrooms** 5 medium, 1 gram • **Pepper, green** ¼ cup, chopped, 1 gram • **Onions** ¼ medium, 1 gram

BREADS
• **Whole wheat** 1 slice, 2.4 grams • **Brown** 1 slice, 1.4 grams • **White** 1 slice, 1 gram

CEREALS
• **Fortified whole-bran cereal** ⅓ cup, 9 grams • **Bran flakes** 1 cup, 4 grams • **Corn flakes** 1 cup, 3.5 grams • **Whole-wheat flakes** 1 cup, 3.5 grams • **Shredded whole-wheat biscuit, 100% natural** 1 large biscuit, 3 grams • **Toasted oat cereal** 1 cup, 2 grams • **Crisp whole-wheat nuggets** ¼ cup, 2 grams • **Granola** ¼ cup, 2 grams • **Oatmeal, cooked** 1 cup, 2 grams • **Malted wheat cereal** ¾ cup, 2 grams • **High-protein rice & wheat cereal** 1 cup, 1.5 grams • **Puffed rice** 1 cup, 1 gram

BEANS AND PEAS
• **Soybeans, cooked** ½ cup, 21 grams • **Chick-peas, cooked** ½ cup, 8 grams • **Split peas, cooked** ½ cup, 6 grams • **White, canned with tomato sauce** ½ cup, 6 grams • **Northern beans, cooked** ½ cup, 5 grams • **Kidney beans, red, cooked** ½ cup, 5 grams • **Pinto beans, cooked** ½ cup, 5 grams • **Lima beans, cooked** ½, 4 grams • **Lentils, cooked** ½ cup, 4 grams • **Barley, cooked** ½ cup, 2 grams

NUTS
• **Almonds** ½ cup, 10 grams • **Peanuts, roasted** ½ cup, 6 grams • **Sunflower seeds** ¼ cup, 5 grams • **Walnuts, shelled** ½ cup, 3 grams • **Cashews** 1 oz. (26 small), 3 grams • **Peanut butter** 2 tablespoons, 2 grams

To take advantage of the desires for high-fiber foods, operators should attempt to make liberal use of these foods in appropriate menus. (Source, *Redbook*, June 1984, p. 130. Original source: Adapted from *The Composition of Foods*, Elsevier/North Holland, 1978, and *Plant Fiber in Foods*, Diabetes Research Foundation, Inc., 1980.)

room offering a more complete menu. A few combination facilities offer multiple types of foods from a centralized core production facility or from a series of specialty kitchens. These multiple operations are often structured on an international theme, with such countries as Germany, China, and Mexico represented by menu offerings.

The general menu planning principles previously considered apply to specialty restaurants as well, and the only additional requirement facing the specialty operation is the need to ensure that an adequate market seeking such limited offerings exists to support the operation. In most population centers this is no problem.

Other Selection Factors

In every course of the meal or section of the menu being considered, the operator should make sure that basic nutritional and caloric requirements are being followed. The basic four food groups must, of course, be offered in almost all menus, but this is particularly crucial in facilities serving a captive audience that is dependent on the food they offer for proper nutrition. Less concern may be shown by the restaurant serving one meal to a casual guest, although it too should offer items that permit the diner to select a proper nutritional balance if he so desires.

The colors of foods must be considered by the menu planner. All foods should produce pleasant plate combinations, and garnishes and other accompaniments should be selected for contrasting colors to achieve consumer acceptability. If colors are varied within each part of the menu and among the selections from a particular food class, they add to consumer satisfaction.

Mouth feel (texture) and taste of menu items must also be kept in mind by the menu planner. Variety should be offered in these areas so that every item eaten does not feel the same in the mouth or give the same taste. The sauces or types of foods used in a plate combination should not be all smooth, all coarse, or all grainy. If uniformity does occur, other parts of the meal should provide variety in texture.

Acid and tart tastes should be varied with sweet and bland items for stimulation. Acid and tart items belong at the start of the meal period to stimulate the appetite, while sweeter items should be served at the end.

Variety in the forms of foods and the methods of preparation should also be offered. Items may be sliced, quartered, whole, diced, etc., to vary the form. Attempts can be made to provide broiled, baked, grilled, fried, and boiled selections.

In specialty houses where only one form of food preparation is utilized, variation in this factor is sacrificed, although it is of no less importance. The effect of sameness may be overcome by varying the offerings in other parts of the meal.

Plate makeup topography must also be studied by the menu planner to select variety in the heights and forms of the items presented. This increases eye appeal and consumer acceptability.

Pricing Forms

There are two major systems of pricing menus: the a la carte system and the table d'hote system. Many nuances, combinations, and branches of the two have also been constructed to fit particular operations.

The a la carte (from the list) system in its pure form is the menu on which each item is given a separate price. In the eyes of the consumer it appears to reduce the price of foods, but in reality it results in a higher check average and lower food costs for the operator. It is easier to price and to control from a cost standpoint, and it can change the eating habits of consumers—they select fewer soups and desserts than they would eat under other menu forms.

If a la carte service is used properly, food should be prepared to order and should arrive at the customer in top quality. By the nature of the pricing system, the amount of food should also be greater than if the same item were ordered under a table d'hote pricing system.

A la carte pricing is also used in most cafeteria operations, but with very different preparation and service methods.

At the opposite end of the continuum is the table d'hote menu, which was the traditional pricing system. In this form, a number of courses from a more extensive menu are provided to the consumer at one price.

Because the menu is extensive and the costs of all the offered foods must be covered, one-price menus are more difficult to construct. Table d'hote has been rejected by many facilities in favor of marketing strategies that can vary to meet the demands of consumers.

Many food operations have developing pricing systems to combine some advantages of each major type of menu. A combination a la carte and dinner menu is offered in some establishments, while others use a table d'hote form in which the price of the individual entrée determines the price of the dinner. Some establishments set a price for the entrée

Table 8-5. Methods of Menu Price Determination

A. Operating Expenses Plus Profit

1. Determine the operating costs, from either past history or future projections. Divide the total by past or projected sales to get the operating cost percentage. Profit may be included at this step or added as a markup on specific menu items using method B. The latter is suggested.

total operating expenses ÷ total sales = operating cost %

2. Subtract this percentage from 100% (total sales) to get the overall food cost percentage. Multiply the total sales dollars by the food cost percentage to get the dollar amount of food cost.

100% (sales) – operating cost % = food cost %
$ of sales x food cost % = $ of food cost

3. The entire menu must realize an average of this food cost percentage. Find the total cost of each menu item (including surrounding item costs). Divide the total cost by the food cost percentage to find the menu price for that item. Adjust individual menu prices according to their base cost to maintain a realistic menu price spread.

raw cost of menu item + surrounding item costs = total item cost
total item cost ÷ food cost % = menu selling price

B. Profit Markup per Item

1. Assign markups to individual menu items, based on the following standard:

Type of Item	Markup
High-priced items	10%
Fast-moving items	15%
Slow-moving items	20%
Appetizers	50%
Desserts	40%

2. For each menu item, subtract the operating cost percentage plus the markup from 100% (sales) to get the food cost percentage.

100% (sales) – (operating cost + markup) = food cost %

3. Add the raw cost of the item to the surrounding item costs, and divide the total by the food cost percentage to find the menu price. Be careful to keep a realistic range from the highest to the lowest priced menu item.

raw cost of menu item + surrounding item costs = total item cost
total item cost ÷ food cost % = menu selling price

and vegetable plate, while assigning additional charges to desserts and appetizers. Others give choices of vegetables but use the same pricing form.

Whatever the system, the food preparation department must anticipate the end result. For example, at noon meals most people will order completely a la carte (if available), while on Sundays table d'hote pricing seems to be most popular in operations offering both types. Such differences in customer selection may determine how many soups or desserts are to be prepared and what percentage of the guests will require salads. All these are related to the pricing system used.

The prices of menu items should include the costs of making the item plus provisions for garnishes, breads, condiments, and other surrounding items that accompany a major food. For two methods of setting prices, see table 8-5. Food cost percentages should not be applied "across the board" to all items on a menu in arriving at prices. Items with higher raw costs might be priced off the menu if this were done, while lower cost items would become difficult to resist. A realistic price spread between highest and lowest priced items should be maintained, to ensure adequate profit margins. It is dollars, not percentages, that are earned and deposited in the bank. Applying a smaller markup to a higher cost item than to a lower cost one may still result in a higher check average and more income, although the food cost percentage will be higher.

The labor involved in preparing each menu

item must be taken into account in setting the price. Such items as stews, casseroles, and spaghetti require much more hand labor than higher cost items such as steaks or chops, which need only be placed on a broiler grid.

Plate combinations and specials should also be devised, but loss leaders are not generally possible in food service work and should be avoided. A product sold at or below cost may work well in a grocery store, where the consumer may select other items to increase his total bill; but, if applied to an entrée in a food establishment, it usually results in a satisfied customer and an operator in financial difficulty.

All menu pricing must be related to the turnover in the operation. Quick turnover usually means a lower check average and smaller markup percentage. Turnover is expressed in the number of customers who will occupy a dining room seat per hour. A deluxe table service restaurant may have a turnover rate of from 0.25 to 1, an average table service restaurant about 1, and a cafeteria or counter operation from 2 to 4.

Effect of Menus on Food Preparation

The menu type, pricing system, and style have a decided effect on all facets of a food facility. The factors most closely related to the menu are discussed below.

Personnel. A menu designed to meet the requirements of a particular market segment will, of necessity, offer foods that vary in the complexity of their preparation. The technical knowledge of the preparation personnel has a direct bearing on the food a facility can offer and the quality of the items prepared. Offering products beyond the abilities of the culinary workers available will result in disaster for the operator, no matter how good the menu looks on paper. However, a manager may be able to purchase food in semiprepared or ready forms that augment the skills of his workers and enable the establishment to offer more elaborate items.

Items that require large amounts of hand work by culinary workers may contribute to frequent crises during meal periods when a sufficient number of workers is not available to meet customer demands. If there are enough workers to meet the need, slack periods may find them available to work but unassigned to tasks because the menu items require numerous workers only at peak periods.

Specialty menus, limited menus, and use of central-commissary-type food processing seem to offer the most relief to an industry lacking a sufficient number of adequately trained workers. However, careful selection of types of food and preparation methods to be used and use of labor-saving devices and equipment will permit the menu planner to offer a more extensive choice. By trying to reduce the amount of hand work required in producing menu items and using down times to prepare for peak periods, the operator can improve the productivity of personnel. To accomplish this, he must analyze the menu being offered.

Timing. The timing requirements imposed by menus are also an important consideration for the food production manager. An a la carte menu that requires complete preparation of food only after the guest has ordered (or even just reconstitution of an item after ordering) may result in labor or equipment problems that cause delays, conflicts, and eventual customer dissatisfaction.

A menu that allows for pre-preparation can alleviate delays. The inclusion of an additional course before the entrée or an accessory item that is readily available, such as a relish tray, may reduce the timing problems encountered with a hastily assembled menu.

Cost Factors. Cost factors are a major consideration in planning a menu, but they must not be permitted to be the sole consideration. If costs are interrelated with the numerous other limiting factors the menu planner faces, these other factors may solve a problem imposed by costs alone. For example, timing and personnel problems may often be solved by the decision to purchase an item in a different form. Considering cost alone might argue against the use of this food type. Conversely, the change of a potato menu item from French fried to baked or the preblanching of the French fries before peaks of service may be all that is needed to solve a menu-staff-time problem, rather than buying a preprepared potato item that meets the menu offering but costs considerably more.

Costs may suggest complete removal of an item from a menu. For example, excessive purchase costs may make an item profitable only at a menu price that widens the spread among items offered and is more than the customers normally pay.

Equipment and Facilities. To create the most satisfactory relationship of menu to equipment, the menu should be planned first and then the equipment purchased and the facilities designed to meet its needs. Even in this situation, many operators buy equipment that is not justified, or they overtax existing pieces of equipment by the methods of preparation the menu calls for.

In any operation, the menu must be examined from the standpoint of overutilization and underutilization of equipment and facilities. Ovens that are used both to prepare an item (such as a baked potato) and to hold it at serving temperature may not be available for preparing other required products. Equipment of a certain size may not be capable of producing the amount of food called for on a menu.

The menu should call on specific equipment and tax it in ways that utilize personnel efficiently, and the equipment available must be able to support the menu offered.

The browning of bacon may be done more effectively in an oven when the grill and range areas are required for egg cookery. A siphon coffee urn may release a food worker who would be required to pour the water over the coffee in a manual type. Adequate numbers of dishes, casseroles, or other specialty plates must be available for the menu items offered so that preparation personnel can serve an item when requested without searching for a suitable dish because every item on the menu is using the same kind of plate.

Facilities too must be related to menu requirements so that adequate work space, assembly areas, and flows of products are maintained.

Equipment used by a particular employee must not only meet menu requirements but also be located near the worker, and adequate accessory materials and equipment must be nearby. Planning a portion size to fit a platter rather than a small plate might eliminate some side dishes and simplify work for service personnel, while reducing the plating up work for preparation personnel as well.

A table d'hote menu that offers soup with every meal might use a bain-marie to advantage in an area accessible to service workers for ease of service by themselves rather than holding soup in a trunnion and requiring food preparation workers to portion it.

Only a realistic appraisal of the menu, its form, pricing structure, garnish requirements, and the like will allow a satisfactory relationship of personnel, facilities, and equipment to develop.

Forecasting. The forecast of menu acceptability imposes specific demands on food preparation personnel. No cook likes to run out of an item, and many managers echo this philosophy. But overpreparation causes cost problems and uses holding and storage equipment to satisfy unexpressed demands. Menu changes and realistic forecasting can avoid these problems. In addition, equipment such as microwave or convection ovens can be used to provide quick backup items for the menu, if forecasts turn out to be low.

A menu item that is not popular because of its price or method of preparation is properly eligible for removal. Only an adequate forecast and supplemental sales history records will indicate if an unpopular item is causing unnecessary storage, waste, or equipment utilization.

A sales history record, such as the analysis form in figure 2e (see chapter 2), showing the date, meal, day, weather, competing menu items, featured specials, and special events in the area will provide the data needed to make forecasts more realistic. Separate records should be maintained for weekends and holidays, since these present different patterns from weekdays. The record shows the number sold of each item, from which the percentage of the total in that category can be computed. An adequate collection of these data forms the basis of future forecasts. Menu planning will then come closer to reality, producing fewer leftovers and a more satisfied clientele.

Specialty operations using limited menus and preportioned items that are cooked to order find forecasting less of a problem. It is also of less concern to the food operation serving a captive group, such as the hospital or university service. It remains a major concern, however, of the free-standing restaurant offering a complete menu, and managers and supervisors should make early attempts to collect valid sales data on their customers. (For further discussion, see chapter 2.)

Physical Makeup of the Menu

The menu presented to the guest may take many physical forms, from the cafeteria menu board with individual pricing of every item to the waiter who recites the complete menu to a guest.

The menu form must reflect the establishment and its philosophy. From it the customer surmises the attitude of the facility and the quality and price of its food. It is one of the most important sales tools available, for it reaches the customer when he wants to read it. Although this is one of the few things that has not been recently tested in court, the menu is considered by many to be a form of contract of what the operation has to offer the guest.

Materials and Size. A tough text type of cover stock that will resist wear and staining should be selected for the menu. A hard-wearing outside cover with a removable insert is less expensive than a cover with the menu printed on it and may be particularly useful if the menu changes daily. It is best to avoid slick plastic covers, however, unless the patrons come to the table from work experiences that would actually cause menu stain. Varnished menu covers should also be avoided, because, although they do not stain, the varnish cracks rather easily and gives a poor appearance to the menu.

The cover should follow the theme presented by the exterior of the establishment, the decor, and the type of food offered. Covers may also be changed at different seasons of the year, or a series of covers showing scenes such as local buildings, birds, or local views may be produced. Variety in covers is particularly important where repeat business is routine, rather than the exception.

A folding menu from six by eight inches to nine by twelve inches, or a single-sheet menu nine by fourteen inches is an acceptable size for most establishments. Particular care must be taken to ensure that the size blends with both the table size and the general area available for dining. The size of the menu should be manageable in terms of printing considerations also. It is not wise to see how many items may be printed on it in order to impress the guest.

A 90-pound paper stock has been found to meet the requirements of most restaurants. This weight will give good service at a reasonable cost.

The menu printing colors should be chosen carefully to blend with the decor of the establishment. Contrasting colors make reading easier, but the operator must be careful to avoid colors that might psychologically diminish hunger (such as purple or olive gray) or colors that become washed out in a dimly lighted room (such as red printing on a white background in a red, dimly lighted room).

Format. The appearance of the menu must suit both the offerings and the clientele. The size of the print should be legible to the readers. Those who need glasses but hesitate to wear them because of vanity will seek out a restaurant more often if they can read the menu easily with the naked eye. With a clientele primarily over forty, this is worth some consideration.

The distance between an item and its price should be kept as short as possible. Use of dotted lines, double spaces, and indentations will make reading easier.

The operator should make sure there are no spelling errors on the menu (unless an error is used as a deliberate form of merchandising) and that menus stained with grease from previous meals are, of course, discarded.

Text. For merchandising purposes the menu should list the name of the restaurant, the phone number, and the hours of operation. If the menu is a popular one and impressive but expensive, smaller ones on less expensive stock can be provided for guests to take as mementos.

If possible, a separate menu should be provided for breakfast in a restaurant that offers three meals. Customers should not be asked to review their previous dinner meal as they start a new day. The customer's attitude, and the decor required to meet it, cannot be the same at breakfast as it would be at other meals.

Menu items should be arranged in the order in which the meal will be ordered and eaten. The item explains how a dish is to be prepared and how it will arrive at the table. It is best to use English, if possible, and only use French or other foreign terms if they are easily understood. If a foreign word must be used, the menu should explain what it means in English, so that the diner will not be surprised. Many a wine or meal sale has been lost because the customer was unsure of what the item would be and was fearful of making an error. Some foreign words, such as consommé and au gratin, are acceptable, but others should be avoided unless it is certain that the guest will understand them. Terms such as en brochette may conjure up unpleasant images in the minds of some guests and make the item unpopular, creating a false sales history for that item. In traditional gourmet operations, of course, French is acceptable and, in fact, desirable.

The menu can use expressive words to make the offerings attractive to guests but it should avoid becoming so flowery in language that the words become unbelievable. In fast food operations the wording should be limited, in order to make ordering easier and to increase turnover. The use of descriptive words can inform and instill confidence in the customer. Listing methods of processing, such as "sugar-cured" or "candied," brand names, and places of origin are acceptable and effective. Avoid such words as "plain," "boiled" or

New York Sirloin Steak 6.50
Filet Mignon 6.50
Top Sirloin with Mushroom Cap 5.50
Ground Sirloin Steak with Onions 4.00
Roast Prime Ribs of Beef Au Jus 5.00
Center Cut Pork Chops 3.25
Premium Ham Steak with Pineapple Ring 3.50

New York SIRLOIN STEAK 6.50

FILET MIGNON 6.50

Top SIRLOIN with Mushroom Cap 5.50

Ground SIRLOIN STEAK with Onions 4.00

Roast PRIME RIBS of BEEF Au Jus 5.00

Center Cut PORK CHOPS 3.25

Premium HAM STEAK with Pineapple Ring 3.50

Figure 8e. Two menu listings showing how a better designed arrangement is easier to read.

"mashed." A "plain omelet" is better described as a "fluffy" one, while "whipped" or "snowflake" potatoes sound much more attractive than "mashed."

In no event should the menu contain such phrases as "Order by number," or "Do not ask for substitutes." The facility is operated to serve and please the guest; procedures that require the guest to serve the establishment have no place.

"Screwball" merchandising, such as the use of words with the double meanings or spelling errors, can backfire. These devices often have the effect of alienating customers.

The top right-hand corner of the menu and the first and last places of columns can be used for emphasis of particular items. Clipons, table tents, and the suggestions of serving personnel may also serve this purpose.

Color photography is an effective merchandising tool to use on menus, if it is good. If the colors give a poor indication of the true appearance of the food, it should be avoided. A ham with a blue tint or a roast that looks like it needs a blood transfusion does not help merchandising.

Special Meal Menus

Although certain basic considerations affect all menus in every type of facility, different meal periods make some different demands on menu makeup.

Breakfast menus lend themselves to fewer traditional foods. The items presented should be ones that can be rapidly prepared. Many consumers are not really hungry at breakfast time, and therefore are more difficult to sell. Attempts must be made to provide the new and unusual items as well as the traditional.

Luncheon menus offer lighter foods. Sandwiches are a great favorite. Plate combinations can be developed that increase turnover, increase speed of service, and offer price specials that increase check averages. As many items as possible should be prepared in advance and kept available, but sanitation and quality-control requirements prevent advance preparation of some menu offerings.

Luncheons lend themselves to the use of leftover foods (although these should be avoided wherever possible by proper forecasting), grilled foods, and other short order items. In many operations, alcoholic beverage sales adequately supplement the luncheon menu and increase check averages.

Dinner menus support the heavier foods that are eaten more leisurely. Because higher check averages can be anticipated, it is possible to increase courses, permit more time for dining, and offer more cooked-to-order items.

Future Trends in Menus

On-demand meal menus are being seen more today, as the life-styles of many people change. It is foreseen that they will be an important factor in the future. Precursors of this form of meal are the Sunday brunch (a breakfast and luncheon combination) and the menu offerings of many diners, cafeterias, and transportation terminals, where a consumer may order a meal at an odd time of the day or out of sequence with other diners.

Restaurants must make provisions to furnish meals at all hours and to offer food forms that lend themselves to selection at more than one meal. The stringent hours for meals previously accepted by consumers and operators alike may be giving way to new requirements of an active and mobile clientele with ever-changing tastes. Convenience food forms and new pieces of equipment, such as the microwave oven, will assist the menu planner in meeting this challenge.

Changes in working hours or increases in the hours worked per day in order to provide longer weekends may well require new meal periods to replace the 10:00 a.m. and 3:00 p.m. coffee breaks that are now customary. Ecological considerations may require staggering work hours to reduce the level of pollution or to maximize transportation facilities. In view of these possibilities, a combination lunch and dinner meal period might be just over the horizon, or additional main meal periods may be instituted to meet the requirements of society.

Recipe History and Development

No one really knows, but recipes could have been first developed when early man had an unproductive hunting trip and was instead forced to collect various types of foods and combine them to make a satisfying meal. They may also have been developed by an efficient food preparer who sought to make more effective use of his fire, time, and utensils. Whatever their origin, recipes are now used extensively.

A recipe is a formula by which a number of ingredients are combined in a particular way, in order to give desired results. Old time chefs, who served long periods of apprenticeship working under masters of cooking, developed technical talents that enabled them to combine foods in new ways, varying the amounts of food materials, the types of seasonings, or the methods of preparation, to produce different tastes. When a chef had sufficient skill to work without supervision, he would submit a recipe of his own creation to a group of master chefs. This product became his masterpiece and gained for him the opportunity to work on his own.

A great many recipes have become common knowledge in the culinary field, through long usage and application in a number of establishments throughout a geographical area. Some, however, were jealously held by those who developed them. These special combinations of foods, flavorings, and procedures were the private property of a practicing chef, known only to him, and the product of his talents, taste, and professional ability. A chef would become well known for a food item produced in a special way. Often it carried his name or the name of the establishment in which he worked.

Talent, secrecy, and taste were the basic elements in making these products. As one chef tried to outdo another in attempts to produce something new and different, exotic ingredients and complex procedures were often employed in developing particular recipes.

In most establishments the chef was on duty daily and played a very personal part in producing the menu items presented to the guest. His acceptance was the final step before the food was served. If a particular combination did not meet his taste requirements, changes were made before the food was served. Most chefs guarded their taste buds by not smoking. Each tried to develop acute tastes to evaluate the products of his kitchen accurately. A good chef could do this with few written notes and with little fear of outside interference.

The Accounting Approach to Recipes

Although the chef approach to recipe development and control still exists in some quantity food operations, the number is increasingly limited. A new trend began in the United States in the early 1920s, after prohibition of the sale of alcoholic beverages. Many facilities that produced outstanding foods, with little concern for either material or labor costs and little management control over the chef, found that, because the supporting sales of liquor were no longer available, some cost controls in the food area were necessary.

In addition, changes in work habits and a reduction in the number of workers entering apprenticeship training for chefs began to cause some minor shortages of traditional chefs. Managers and owners who had been reluctant to enter the kitchen for fear of losing the chef's services now found it necessary to step into the "back of the house." Costs had to be watched more closely, and standards of foods had to be controlled: it was no longer acceptable to offer guests only those foods that reflected the personal tastes of the cook who had prepared them.

In an attempt to control both costs and tastes, an accounting approach, in the form of standardized recipes, found its way into the food preparation areas of restaurants, hotels, and clubs. The items to be used in a particular product were standardized, and cost considerations were constantly watched. Portion sizes, the quality of raw materials purchased, and preparation methods were also made standard. This enabled the owner to control product taste and costs more closely. The standardized recipe also helped to maintain customer satisfaction and made the shortage of chefs and the turnover of personnel less of a problem. With a standard recipe, it was easier to duplicate the product despite changes in workers.

The need for this kind of control has become even greater. Many recipes today are provided by food processors who price them according to their own costs, making the task of the manager easier. It is the rare chef who creates his own recipe and holds it in his head.

If food must be served the same way every time and meet standard costs for every ingredient, it should be the rare manager who will permit a recipe to be followed from memory.

Truth in Menu

Although the first reference to truth in menu by the National Restaurant Association occurred in 1923, much more attention has recently been given to this concept. Led by California, many of the more heavily industrialized and socially responsible states, some fifteen in number, have either passed legislation or discussed measures to control truth in menu procedures. Moreover, since 1977, the Federal Trade Commission has been involved with proposals for nutritional disclosure and labeling requirements which would be comparable to that required on container labeling by the Food and Drug Administration.

Although many bills have been tabled, defeated, or changed, the legislation in effect in Los Angeles County remains an example of what may come about in other jurisdictions in the country. In this legislation fines up to $2,500 per violation can be levied for violations of the truth in published menus.

This truth-in-menu movement is not new to our industry. Some agricultural states have always been interested in assuring that their butter production was protected, thus requiring a menu notification when margarine was served. But interest and activity in the area of menu control has become more widespread with consumer movements.

With some research showing a causal relationship between cholesterol consumption and coronary heart disease, many consumers became interested in what saturated fats were included in the foods they were eating. Others were interested in knowing the geographical source of the product, if frozen food had been used, if meat substitutes were added to the product, or the nutritional components of the menu being offered. However, almost all consumers and many states became concerned about substitutions in food, reductions in quality, changes in methods of preparation, and the amount of food being served. A quarter pound of a product—if merchandised that way—had to be a quarter pound; Vermont turkey had better not come from South Carolina; and "fresh fish" could not be frozen.

Some of these consumer concerns may seem unreasonable. For example, some authorities suggest that it really does not matter if a food product such as fish is fresh or frozen as long as the product satisfies the guest. Although this may be true, the fact remains that consumers have demonstrated an interest in this area, and—as with all broadly based consumer requests—the astute operator will try to meet these demands.

The menu serves as a form of contract between the food service establishment and the consumer. It is important, therefore, that it properly reflect the type, form, style, amount, condition, and method of preparation of the food item that is being offered.

Unmet consumer demands will result in the intervention of governmental agencies requiring the inclusion of additional information on menus and the provision of products in the form they have been proffered. At the very least, consumers will only patronize those establishments that provide this type of information and service. Surprise is not a word that goes well with a menu. The menu serves to represent the food item the guest will later see and consume. Consumer groups, governmental regulatory bodies, and even industry

Broiled Salmon Patties

Yield: 40 or 20 4-oz. portions (no. 8 scoop size) **Recipe No.:** 207
Time Required: Pre-preparation time, 30 minutes; cooking time, 10 minutes
Utensils Required: 20-qt. mixer; portion scale; 2 baking sheets
Method of Serving: Serve on dinner plate with 1/2 oz. of tomato sauce

	Weight		Measure		
Ingredients	**40 Portions**	**20 Portions**	**40 Portions**	**20 Portions**	**Directions**
Salmon, drained and flaked	6 lbs. 12 oz.	3 lbs. 6 oz.	1-1/4 gals.	2 qts. 1 pt.	Mix. Shape into 4-oz. round patties.
Cracker crumbs	1 lb.	1/2 lb.	1-1/2 qts.	3 cups	
Eggs	2 lbs. 10 oz.	1 lb. 5 oz.	24	12	
Lemon juice			1 cup	1/2 cup	
Salt			4 tsps.	2 tsps.	
Pepper			1 tsp.	1/2 tsp.	
Bacon slices			40	20	Wrap each patty with a bacon slice. Secure with a toothpick. Broil 5 mins. on each side. Remove toothpicks. Serve on dinner plate with 1/2 oz. of tomato sauce.
Toothpicks			40	20	

Figure 8f. A complete standardized recipe listing all required information. (Adapted from a recipe by Bernice Olds, Cafeteria Supervisor, Oscoda Area Schools, Oscoda, Michigan; reprinted by permission.)

self-regulating bodies are ready to insure that "what the customer sees on the menu is what he or she gets on the plate."

Recipe Development

Recipes are available from many sources: government agencies, trade associations, food purveyors, cooperative food agencies, and trade periodicals. Whatever the source, it is imperative that they be tested at the particular operation where they will be used, to ensure that they are clear, practical, and suitable for its personnel, equipment, guests, and pricing structure.

When tested and accepted, a recipe should provide an unequivocal plan for producing the required item. Small-quantity recipes cannot often be multiplied by a factor to build them into larger yields without testing and varying the ingredients, particularly the seasonings. Nor can substitutions be made in a recipe without evaluating the results before offering the product to the guests.

Recipes should be available for preparing all types of foods—leftover items as well as fresh materials. Recipes can tell how to process leftover vegetables, for example, in salads, gelatins, or soups; meats in stews, pot pies, or a la king dishes; and items such as chicken livers in combination products.

Recipes should be used by specific workers, and these workers should be kept in mind as the recipe is being selected and tested. Workers must understand what is required and be trained to carry out the processes if the recipe is to work.

The following general considerations should be helpful in writing, testing, changing, and using recipes:

1. Use a recipe form that tells the user (the employee):

    a. what is to be produced,

Recipe Cost

Recipe No.: 207
Yield: 40 portions

Ingredients	Amount Used	Market Price	Cost of Amount Used
Salmon	6 lbs. 12 oz.	$1.20/lb.	$ 8.10
Cracker crumbs	1 lb.	.30/lb.	.30
Eggs	2 lbs. 10 oz.	.60/lb.	1.57
Lemon juice	1 cup	.04/cup	.04
Salt	4 tsps.	.001/tsp.	.004
Pepper	1 tsp.	.002/tsp.	.002
Bacon slices	40 (20 wide strips/lb.)	.90/lb.	1.80
Toothpicks	40 (700/box)	.20/box	.012
Tomato sauce	20 oz.	.01/oz.	.20
Total recipe cost			$12.028
Portion cost			$.3007

Figure 8g. A recipe cost form used to determine the portion cost for the recipe in figure 8f.

b. the amount to be produced,

c. the equipment, utensils, and tools required to produce it,

d. the time required,

e. the yield expected,

f. the portion size and serving method.

2. List the ingredients in the order and form in which they will be used. If preliminary steps, such as preheating an oven, are necessary, list them at the beginning of the recipe.

3. Make all measurements by weight, where possible. This is the easiest and most accurate method.

4. Do not abbreviate, if possible (except for standard measurement abbreviations); it may lead to errors.

5. Ingredients to be mixed or manipulated together should be listed together.

6. Use accepted culinary terminology that the workers will understand. If English is not their native language, translate the recipes using the correct idioms, not literal translations.

7. List procedures next to the ingredients that are involved in the procedure.

8. Be as specific as possible about seasonings. Avoid such phrases as "season to taste."

9. Outline a specific test to tell when a product has been completed.

10. List the sources of original recipes for future checks.

11. Provide for fifty, twenty-five, and ten portion yield increments, so that cooks will not have to calculate amounts of ingredients on the job.

12. Number the recipe, type it on a card (approximately five by eight inches in size), and enclose it in some sort of protective cover.

13. Always list the item first and the form later (e.g., beef, ground).

14. Key the production sheets to the recipe number to be used.

15. Attach a wire and clips over production tables to facilitate the use of recipes.

16. Check, review, and update recipes periodically.

17. In enlarging recipes, first test the recipe as presented and have key personnel and/or a taste panel evaluate:

a. appearance,

b. taste,

c. amount of manipulation required,

d. labor involved,

e. cost.

Then build the recipe to fifty portions by changing all measures to a common denominator of weight, dividing the new yield by the old, and multiplying each ingredient by the factor obtained. Redo the recipe, and test it with the panel as before. Make variations as necessary. Seasonings will usually need to be increased less than the mathematical computation suggests; start by using three-fourths of the computed amount, and work up if required.

Recipe Costing

Each ingredient in a recipe must be costed out: the purchase price for the amount used to produce the number of portions desired must be calculated. A cost per portion should then be determined, to use in fixing menu prices.

Although recipe yields set the purchasing parameters and establish menu prices in relation to purchasing costs, each recipe must be costed to include the basic raw market price of every ingredient used without reference to yield. Yield-cost considerations are discussed in chapter 9. These relate the purchasing costs to the number of portions realized from recipes in which the particular foods purchased are utilized.

No matter what the yield on a particular recipe or what the menu price required to generate the desired profit percentage, the recipe cost is a function of the price paid for each item used, divided by the yield realized to get the portion cost (see figure 8g).

9 *Purchasing and Storage*

Objective: To expose the student to the workings of the market system and the specifications, including government standards, that affect it. To discuss ordering, receiving and storage, and issuing procedures that ensure high quality, efficiency, and good inventory control.

Whatever the type of organization, the menu, and the equipment, personnel, and tools, quality food will not be produced by a facility until quality food is purchased.

"Good food is not cheap, and cheap food is not good," has long been accepted as a truism. However, even if a reasonable price is paid for food, errors committed by managers, supervisors, or workers in purchasing and storage, can cause raw materials to reach preparation personnel in a quality or condition that harms production.

Many organizations have attempted to centralize the control of purchasing, by requiring the food preparation department to submit orders to a purchasing agent. In large metropolitan operations, such as schools and hospitals, centralized purchasing may cover a number of unrelated organizational units. This gives the organizations benefits in purchasing that would not be available to an individual unit, including (a) decreases in price because of increases in amounts ordered, (b) better rapport with purveyors who keep in closer contact with larger customers, and (c) greater knowledge of food types, standards, and packaging through specialization of the larger purchasing staff needed when more items are ordered.

In any purchasing situation—centralized or decentralized—the supervisor of the food preparation department must be cognizant of good purchasing techniques. He must be able to maximize possible benefits, so that they can contribute to the production of quality food.

The Market System

The first requisite for the manager is an appreciation of the marketing system, its sources of supply, its seasonal pricing, and its other unique characteristics.

Marketing is a process that establishes the time and place utility of an item. Marketing permits an item to be available in a particular location at a particular time. It permits an exchange to take place between a raw food producer and a consumer who will use the food to construct a menu item.

The farmer, rancher, or fisherman located at some distance from the consumer delivers his product to a food processor or middleman who makes it ready for use by a food service establishment. The raw agricultural product is processed, divided into smaller lots, and delivered to distribution centers in marketing areas throughout the country by middlemen. Among the most important in the food industry are wholesalers, who take ownership of food materials and arrange for final distribution from their own warehouses, and brokers, who act only as agents between buyers and sellers without the restrictions or problems imposed by ownership of the commodity.

Transfer of these often perishable agricultural commodities is dependent upon the forces of nature, the methods of transportation available and selected, and the demand generated by consuming establishments in view of the amount of materials available and the price.

Foods have varying degrees of perishability, from reasonably stable canned or dried products to fresh milk, meat, and fish, which deteriorate rapidly unless treated with care. Elements in the marketing structure are designed to maximize profit by protecting these perishable items and delivering the full 100 percent for use. Although they do a commendable job, the axiom *caveat emptor* still prevails, and those responsible for purchasing must know how to order and receive quality food.

Most marketing procedures are carried out in an environment controlled by government agencies or self-regulatory cooperative marketing bodies. But the budgets of these organizations usually do not provide for enough regulatory personnel to offer complete control. Some purveyors, if given the opportunity, may take advantage of any lack of control and furnish items of less than acceptable quality or measure.

It is important, therefore, that food service managers, supervisors, and purchasing agents be cognizant of food regulations and regulatory bodies, so that they can use these to make purchasing procedures more effective.

Some of the more important government regulations the food purchaser should know are listed in table 9-1. He must also become familiar with local ordinances and rules. Many federal laws have been enacted to protect both the ultimate consumer and the restaurant operator against unsatisfactory procedures. These and other locally prepared regulations should be reviewed to check that stan-

Table 9-1. Government Food Regulations

Federal Laws

Pure Food, Drug, and Cosmetic Act—regulates the preparation, processing, sanitary standards, labeling, and additives of foods.

Perishable Agricultural Commodities Act—regulates dealers in fruits and vegetables engaged in interstate commerce.

Agricultural Marketing Act—regulates inspection and grading of all processed foods and fresh foods other than meat and poultry.

Federal Meat Inspection Act—regulates inspection and grading of all meats and meat products, including establishment of standards of identity and labels.

Poultry Products Inspection Act—regulates inspection of fresh, frozen, canned, and ready-to-cook poultry products.

Egg Products Inspection Act—regulates all egg products and maintains continuous inspection procedures.

U.S. Public Health Service Milk Ordinance and Code—regulates the inspection and grading of milk and dairy products.

Imported Meat Act—regulates the labeling of meats and meat products imported into the United States.

Federal Agencies

Quality standards for foods in interstate commerce are regulated by the Food and Drug Administration, the Department of Health, Education, and Welfare, the Bureau of Commercial Fisheries, and other agencies. For example, the Department of the Interior issues seals of inspection for fish and fish products.

State and Local Laws

State and local health codes or sanitary regulations may govern packaging, production, and storage of all forms of foods.

New York City Wholesale Fruit and Vegetable Report

United States Department of Agriculture

FRUIT and VEGETABLE MARKET NEWS
4-A Hunts Point Market
Hunts Point and East Bay Avenues
Bronx, New York 10474-7355
Recorder Phone No. (212) 542-3564
Telephone (212) 542-2225

Agriculture Marketing Service

Fruit and Vegetable Division

VOL: LXXIII

NO: 135

DATE: FRIDAY, JULY 17, 1987

NEW YORK CITY METROPOLITAN AIR, BOAT AND TRUCK ARRIVALS IN STANDARD PACKAGE COUNT UNLESS OTHERWISE STATED SINCE LAST REPORT
****

APPLES: AG 2121 CL 3210 WA 4616 NZ 3308
APRICOTS: CA 4619 WA 2740
ASPARAGUS: MX 5111
ARTICHOKES: CA 2615
AVOCADOS: CA 4684
BANANA: ZZ 3615
BEANS: NJ 1466 NY 1219
BEETS: NJ 1010 OH 1260
BROCCOLI: CA 3892
CABBAGE: CA 3010 NJ 1561
CANTALOUPS: CA 6646 TX 5492
CARROTS: CA 5133
CAULIFLOWER: CA ...

UNLOADS

BROCCOLI CA 3 CARROTS 2 POTATOES CA 5 ID 9

TOTALS: ON TRACK 30 ARRIVALS 21
UNLOADS 19

RAIL AND BOAT SHIPMENTS FOR JULY 16, 1987: AMOUNTS SHOWN ARE IN 10,000 POUND UNITS:
****

APPLES: WA RT 32 TOTAL 32
AVOCADOS: S-CA RT 8 TOTAL 8
BROCCOLI: C-CA 14 RT 35 TOTAL 49
CABBAGE: C-CA RT 5 TOTAL 5
CANTALOUPS: C-CA RT 84 TOTAL 84
CARROTS: AZ 10 C-CA 150 RT 9 TOTAL ...

****
F.O.B. SHIPPING POINT INFORMATION FOR JULY 16, 1987:
****

W A S H I N G T O N

YAKIMA VALLEY SUNNY 53-76

APPLES:
DEMAND RED DELICIOUS VERY LIGHT, GOLDEN DELICIOUS GOOD MARKET ABOUT STEADY Controlled Adtmosphere Storage traypack cartons Red Delicious wide range in price and condition WA Extra Fancy 72s 12.00 few 13.00-...
10.00 ...

Fresh Fruit and Vegetable
NATIONAL SHIPPING POINT TRENDS
FEDERAL-STATE MARKET NEWS

EASTERN RELEASE
ISSUED
PHILADELPHIA, PENNA.

U. S. DEPARTMENT OF AGRICULTURE, AMS
FRUIT AND VEGETABLE DIVISION
261 PRODUCE BLDG., 3301 SO. GALLOWAY STREET
PHILADELPHIA, PENNSYLVANIA 19148

COOPERATING WITH VARIOUS STATE DEPTS. OF AGRICULTURE
Area code 215 Tel. 597-4536-39 inclusive

VOL. XXIX
NO. 28
DATE: WEDNESDAY
JULY 15, 1987

NATIONAL SHIPPING POINT TRENDS

UNLESS OTHERWISE STATED SHIPMENTS ARE TO FRESH MARKETS FOR THE WEEKS ENDING JUNE 27, JULY 4, AND 11, IN THAT ORDER IN THOUSAND HUNDRED WEIGHT (CWT) UNITS. EXPECTED MOVEMENT IS FOR THE WEEK OF JULY 14-20. TRADING IS FOR THE WEEK OF JULY 7-13. PRICES ARE FOR MONDAY, JULY 13 COMPARED TO MONDAY JULY 6 AND REPRESENT F.O.B. SALES AT SHIPPING POINT OR PORT OF ENTRY. PROTECTIVE SERVICES ARE EXTRA UNLESS OTHERWISE STATED.

ONIONS, DRY

SOUTHERN NEW MEXICO---Shipments 215-165-136---Movement expected to decrease slightly as most shippers finishing direct seeded stock. Trading on Yellow Early fairly active, Late slow following increased volume from other competitive areas. Prices lower. 50 lb sacks Yellow Grano and Ben Sheman repacker size 8.00-9.00, medium 8.00-9.00, jumbo 12.00-13.00; White jumbo 12.00-16.00; medium mostly 10.00.
NORTHERN SAN JOAQUIN VALLEY, CALIFORNIA---Shipments 144-155-182---Movement expected to decline slightly as harvest is completed in some fields. Heavy rail-truck movement as trucks remain in short supply. Trading active for jumbos, moderate for others. Prices jumbo steady, mediums ...f-state competition, ...

spray programs underway in southwestern Idaho to control the carriers of leafroll virus. Overall crop continues to do excellent, about 1 week-10 days ahead of normal.
LAST REPORT
KERN DISTRICT, CALIFORNIA---Shipments 670-590-467---Movement expected to decrease with few more shippers finishing this week. Trading non size A moderate, others fairly slow. Prices non size A unchanged, others slightly lower. U.S.#1 size A cwt basis in sacks unless otherwise stated. Centennials 100 lb non size A 7.00 and 50 lb cartons 70-80s 15.00-16.00. Shipments to continue. LAST REPORT
STOCKTON-DELTA, CALIFORNIA---Shipments 0-4-...
Movement expected to increase as additional ... start during coming ... No F.O.B. ...

Figure 9a. The "Fresh Fruit and Vegetable Market News," outlining the availability of produce. It is published by the U.S. Department of Agriculture, Agricultural Marketing Service, as an aid in determining prices and market supplies. The area editions, such as the top example, cover a particular marketing area. The bottom example shows how some agricultural states, such as Florida, combine these reports into a federal-state publication to indicate supplies from major producing areas.

dards are being followed by purveyors and processors.

Daily marketing reports from the Department of Agriculture, news from trade publications, and information from salesmen may all be used to determine what is available, the prices being asked for items, and the relative firmness or softness of the market in a particular food form. Menus may then be varied or changed to take advantage of plentiful items and to avoid items in short supply, at high prices, or of low quality.

Only by using all possible sources of information will the person responsible for purchasing be able to do an efficient job and buy the product that best relates to a particular need. This information may then be matched to the requirements dictated by the menu, customer tastes, the ultimate use of the item, the available storage facilities, and the desired profit margin.

Purchasing Specifications

After making an extensive survey of all food items available in the area, the food service manager or supervisor would be well advised to draw up a concise description of every food form he has to purchase to meet the specific needs of his operation. The specification should be based on characteristics of the food product that are important in producing the menu item using that product.

All available industry sources should be used in arriving at these specifications, and individual testing should be done to learn how a particular food form reacts in local recipes, with local equipment and personnel. These tests also establish the usable portions or yield to be expected.

The Information Service of the U.S. Department of Agriculture's Consumer and Marketing Service offers information on specifications. It can also provide a food acceptance service, in which a USDA inspector officially certifies that the foods delivered from a purveyor meet the specifications of a participating operation. Of course, this service costs money, usually in the form of higher unit prices on all foods ordered. It is, however, available for use by those who believe it to be warranted.

Most operations should be able to construct their own specifications if a few general factors are included. The factors considered important in any specification are discussed below.

Grades. Grades are classifications of foods by a descriptive term or a number, to ensure uniform quality and to give an indication of desirable use. Most grades are assigned by governmental agencies, according to very strict criteria. Some are assigned by food producers or processors. These are called packer grades, and, because of their origin, they are not considered as objective as government grades. Because the government does not produce or sell the foods, and its prime mission is protecting the public, its grades are considered to be more reliable.

Grades refer to such characteristics in foods as visual appearance, color, uniformity of size, degree of ripeness, and wholesomeness. Most managers or supervisors of food operations are not able to recognize the various standards of quality of the numerous foods they use. Grades should be used to provide this information. If they are not used, supervisors must possess specialized knowledge about every food form used or depend on the honesty of a purveyor to provide the quality required. Since the grading procedure is financed by tax dollars, all operators should put the results to good use.

Unfortunately, there is no standard system of grades, nor are all foods required to be graded. But the grades that do exist should be known and used as an element of specifications. Grades for meat are discussed in chapter 14. Egg grades are discussed in chapter 16.

The grade desired will not always be the highest grade available. A lower grade, with a less attractive exterior appearance, may well be selected if a product is to be cut up or combined with other ingredients in a dish. Price savings may be realized when exterior condition is not considered important. Every

Table 9-2. Average Monthly Availability of Fresh Fruits and Vegetables

Commodity	Percentage of Total Annual Supply												Annual
	Jan. %	Feb. %	Mar. %	Apr. %	May %	June %	July %	Aug. %	Sept. %	Oct. %	Nov. %	Dec. %	Total (million lbs.)
Apples, all	9	9	10	9	8	5	3	3	10	12	10	11	3,890
Washington	10	11	12	12	12	8	4	2	5	7	8	11	1,643
New York	10	10	11	10	8	5	2	2	8	12	11	10	483
Michigan	12	11	11	8	5	1	*	1	6	15	13	15	321
Apricots					6	60	32	2					20
Artichokes	4	8	15	20	11	5	4	5	5	8	7	7	62
Asparagus, all	*	5	23	34	23	13	1		*	1	*		104
California	*	6	31	45	12	4	*			*	*		75
New Jersey				7	54	38	1						17
Avocados, all	9	8	9	8	9	7	7	8	7	8	9	10	166
California	9	9	11	10	11	10	8	8	6	6	6	7	132
Florida	12	3	*				4	7	10	17	24	23	31
Bananas	8	8	9	9	9	9	8	7	7	8	8	9	3,623
Beans, all	6	5	6	9	10	12	11	10	9	8	6	7	331
Florida	13	11	13	20	13	3	*		*	2	11	14	135
Beets	4	4	6	7	6	12	14	13	12	11	6	4	83
Berries†					2	31	43	13	4	4	2		4
Blueberries					2	31	38	26	3				36
Broccoli	11	10	12	10	7	6	4	4	6	9	10	10	62
Brussels sprouts	15	14	9	6	4	1		1	6	12	17	14	20
Cabbage, all	9	8	10	9	9	9	8	7	8	8	8	8	1,718
Florida	17	16	20	22	14	2	*				1	8	398
Texas	15	15	18	14	6	2	2	2	2	2	7	16	245
California	10	11	11	10	11	10	7	5	5	6	7	7	229
New York	12	8	6	3	1	1	7	9	12	14	14	14	153
New Jersey	*	*	*		*	19	27	16	14	14	7	2	106
Cantaloupes, all		*	2	5	8	20	25	24	12	4	1		1,394
California					*	14	28	33	17	6	2		854
Mexico		*	12	35	43	9	*						174
Texas					19	53	16	10	2	*			155
Arizona					1	44	52	*		2	1		118
Carrots, all	9	9	10	9	9	8	7	7	8	8	8	8	1,366
California	8	8	8	8	10	11	12	8	6	6	7	8	726
Texas	13	14	17	15	10	4	2	3	3	4	6	9	346
Cauliflower, all	9	7	8	7	5	5	4	5	10	17	13	9	145
California	12	10	11	11	8	7	5	5	5	6	9	12	90
New York						*	2	7	19	43	26	3	27
Celery, all	9	8	9	8	8	8	8	7	7	8	10	10	1,346
California	7	7	7	6	6	9	10	7	7	9	13	11	840
Florida	15	14	17	16	14	9	1			*	3	11	360
Cherries					6	43	45	6					124
Chinese cabbage	9	9	8	8	7	7	7	7	8	9	10	9	41
Coconuts	8	7	8	8	6	5	4	4	10	11	12	18	29
Corn, sweet, all	2	2	3	6	14	18	17	16	10	5	4	3	1,470
Florida	4	3	5	12	27	27	5	*		4	7	6	724
California					6	21	28	20	12	7	4	2	150
Cranberries, all									8	24	50	18	40
Massachusetts									12	18	45	24	25
Wisconsin									1	29	60	9	13
Cucumbers	5	5	5	7	11	14	13	10	9	9	7	6	620
Eggplant	8	8	7	8	7	7	8	10	10	10	8	8	83
Endive, Belgian	10	12	15	11	12	3			4	9	9	12	3
Escarole-endive	9	8	9	9	8	8	8	8	8	8	8	8	145
Garlic	6	9	10	9	7	7	10	10	11	7	7	7	83
Grapefruit, all	12	12	13	12	9	6	3	2	2	8	10	10	1,677
Florida	13	12	14	13	9	4	1	*	1	11	11	11	1,133
Western	7	6	7	8	13	16	13	13	8	2	3	4	292
Grapes	5	3	4	4	3	6	10	15	18	15	10	8	497
Greens	10	9	11	11	9	7	6	6	7	8	8	9	237
Honeydews	1	3	7	6	5	12	12	20	21	11	2	1	315

*Supply is less than 0.5% of annual total.

†Mostly blackberries, dewberries, and raspberries.

Commodity	Jan. %	Feb. %	Mar. %	Apr. %	May %	June %	July %	Aug. %	Sept. %	Oct. %	Nov. %	Dec. %	Annual Total (million lbs.)
	Percentage of Total Annual Supply												
Lemons	7	6	8	8	9	11	11	10	8	7	7	7	373
Lettuce, all	8	8	8	9	9	9	9	9	8	8	7	8	4,264
California	8	9	8	6	9	10	10	9	9	9	6	6	2,881
Arizona	9	5	12	26	9	2	*			2	14	20	683
New York					*	10	40	30	16	3	1		83
New Jersey					10	35	12	7	6	24	7		77
Limes	5	5	5	5	7	14	15	12	9	7	7	8	40
Mangoes		1	6	11	17	23	22	14	5	1			19
Mushrooms	9	8	10	9	8	8	7	6	7	8	9	10	59
Nectarines	2	3	1		*	11	35	34	13	1			124
Okra	1	2	4	6	9	16	20	18	12	7	3	2	36
Onions, dry, all	8	7	9	9	9	9	9	8	8	8	8	8	2,400
Texas	*	*	5	27	31	13	11	8	3	1	*	*	494
California	3	1	1	2	11	20	23	17	9	6	4	3	387
New York	11	9	11	6	2	1	1	8	14	12	12	11	358
Onions, green	6	6	8	9	10	11	10	9	8	7	7	7	193
Oranges, all	11	12	13	11	10	7	4	4	4	5	7	11	3,250
Western	9	10	12	12	10	7	5	6	6	6	6	10	1,900
Florida	16	15	14	10	10	6	3	1	*	3	9	13	1,155
Papayas, Hawaii	7	8	8	8	9	9	10	8	7	9	9	8	20
Parsley and herbs‡	7	6	9	8	7	8	7	7	8	9	12	12	73
Parsnips	13	12	10	9	9	4	3	3	8	11	10	9	26
Peaches, all	*	*	*		3	21	32	28	14	1			1,139
California					5	23	35	25	8	3			259
South Carolina					2	20	49	28	1				235
Georgia					4	45	42	8	*				207
Pears, all	7	7	8	6	4	2	4	13	16	16	10	7	393
Oregon	14	13	11	7	3	*		*	4	17	16	14	117
California	1	1	1	*			13	32	29	19	4	1	116
Washington	9	9	7	5	3	*		10	17	16	14	11	99
Peas, green	8	13	12	13	13	13	10	9	6	1	1	2	40
Peppers, all	7	7	7	6	8	10	11	10	10	9	8	7	455
Florida	15	11	12	13	16	14	1			*	4	13	159
Persimmons	4	1							1	29	46	19	4
Pineapples, all	6	8	10	13	14	12	8	6	5	5	7	7	145
Puerto Rico	6	7	11	17	15	11	7	5	5	5	5	6	71
Hawaii	7	8	8	8	12	10	9	10	5	5	10	8	53
Plantains	7	7	8	9	9	10	9	12	10	7	6	7	109
Plums-prunes	1	1	1		*	13	29	31	20	3			290
Pomegranates									11	68	20	*	9
Potatoes, all	9	8	9	9	9	9	8	8	8	8	8	8	12,150
California	5	4	4	4	8	23	25	10	5	4	4	4	2,162
Idaho	12	11	13	13	13	6	1	1	2	6	10	11	1,452
Maine	11	11	15	20	18	10	1	*	*	1	5	7	1,318
Pumpkins	1	2	3	4	3	2	1	1	4	74	2	2	43
Radishes	7	7	9	10	11	10	9	8	6	7	7	8	227
Rhubarb	6	13	16	19	26	12	3	1	1	1	*	1	17
Spinach	10	10	12	10	9	8	6	5	6	8	8	8	83
Squash	7	7	6	7	8	9	9	9	10	11	9	8	339
Strawberries	3	5	8	19	26	19	8	4	3	1	1	3	352
California		*	4	22	33	18	10	6	4	2	*	*	237
Mexico	21	24	24	6						*	6	18	50
Florida	10	22	41	25	1							1	15
Sweet potatoes, all	9	8	9	7	5	2	3	5	9	12	18	13	766
Louisiana	9	8	9	7	4	1	4	8	11	12	15	12	256
North Carolina	9	9	10	9	7	4	1	2	6	10	19	15	138
California	8	8	9	7	5	4	3	3	6	10	20	16	111
New Jersey	11	10	11	11	9	5	2	1	4	7	15	14	70
Tangelos	16	3	*	*					1	10	30	40	125
Tangerines	24	8	4	1	*					3	20	39	228
Tomatoes, all	7	6	7	8	10	12	11	10	8	8	6	6	2,153
California	1	*		*	1	7	17	17	16	23	14	4	643

*Supply is less than 0.5% of annual total.

‡Includes parsley root, anise, basil, chives, dill, horseradish, and others.

Commodity	Percentage of Total Annual Supply Jan. %	Feb. %	Mar. %	Apr. %	May %	June %	July %	Aug. %	Sept. %	Oct. %	Nov. %	Dec. %	Annual Total (million lbs.)
Tomatoes (cont.)													
Florida	13	10	11	13	19	14	1			*	5	14	577
Mexico	14	16	21	21	16	5	1	*	*	*	1	5	464
Ohio	1	*	1	8	19	21	16	8	4	7	9	5	99
Turnips-rutabagas	12	10	10	7	5	4	4	5	9	11	13	11	198
Canada	12	11	10	6	3	1	*	4	11	12	17	13	78
Watermelons	*	*	1	2	10	29	31	20	6	1	*	*	2,690

Courtesy of the United Fresh Fruit and Vegetable Association, Washington, D.C.

*Supply is less than 0.5% of annual total.

food item must therefore be considered in terms of how it will be used, so that realistic grades may be required in the specifications.

The grades applicable to specific food items are discussed further in the chapters on preparation of the particular foods.

Use of the Product. In setting the specification, the end use of the product must be determined. The purchaser may be able to reduce the in-house pre-preparation or preparation procedures by varying the form or type of the item. As noted above, the use may also permit purchase of a lower grade product at a price saving.

An a la carte dinner plate will require a larger canned fruit item to serve as a garnish than will a table d'hote offering. Using a fancy grade tomato to cut up in a salad would mean excessive costs, when a lower grade tomato would have been as acceptable.

Yields. Yields are an important consideration in any specification. They are determined by tests made to find the ratio of usable portions to the total amount of a product that is purchased. Standard yield averages, based on practices in the industry, are available for most food forms. However, testing must be done in each food operation to ensure that the results fit its unique requirements. Only by using its own equipment, personnel, and recipes can a facility be certain that the yields listed will actually be achieved.

Yield testing must be conducted on a number of occasions under controlled conditions to make sure that the results give a true picture of what to expect "on the average." The personnel who will normally use or prepare the item should handle it with the usual equipment under a normal production run. A yield produced in a test kitchen might not reflect the yield that will be realized in the main kitchen.

Examination of yields might indicate that it is desirable to purchase a lower grade of meat with less fat. Prime cuts of meat may not yield properly in some situations, and taste considerations would have to give way to cost factors.

Table 9-3. Food Acceptance Service Procedure

1. Buyer decides what is needed, based either on USDA grades and standards, on specifications available for some commodities, or on specifications tailor-made to meet specific needs. Supplier is selected or bids are requested from several suppliers.
2. Contract with supplier is signed providing for inspection of all deliveries by USDA inspector or grader.
3. USDA inspector or grader examines food before delivery, to see that it meets specifications, and stamps each product or sealed package as "accepted" or "certified." Buyer is assured on delivery that each stamped package or product contains what was specified at time of order.

Further information on acceptance service program is available from:

Consumer and Marketing Service
U.S. Department of Agriculture
Washington, D.C. 20250

Prime beef is the top quality, produced from young and well-fed beef-type cattle. Meat from such animals has liberal quantities of fat interspersed with the lean (marbling) and is juicy, tender, and flavorful. Prime rib roasts and loin steaks are consistently tender. Little prime grade beef is found in retail markets because most of it is sold to hotels and restaurants.

The inspection mark, a circle, may be used only on ready-to-cook poultry that has been examined by a government inspector and passed as wholesome food. This mark denotes wholesomeness only —not grade (quality). It may be used without the grade mark.

The grade mark, a shield, tells the quality (U.S. Grade A, B, or C). Poultry may carry the grade mark only if it has been inspected for wholesomeness. The shopper who buys ready-to-cook poultry bearing this mark is assured of a high-quality, wholesome product.

The official grade mark for eggs is in the form of a shield. It always carries the grade name (such as U.S. Grade A), the letters "USDA," and the words "Federal-State Graded" or a similar term.

Figure 9b. Some of the more common grade or quality indicators used by federal inspectors or agencies for food products. Specific seals and grades are discussed under each food type in later chapters. (Courtesy of the United States Department of Agriculture.)

Table 9-4. Cooked Yields of Meat

Type of Meat	Net Servable Cooked Yield	Type of Meat	Net Servable Cooked Yield
Beef		**Lamb**	
Roast sirloin (boneless)	70%	Roast leg	45%
Pot roast	60%	Roast loin	40%
Chopped beef	75%	Lamb stew (boneless)	75%
Short ribs (bone in)	60%		
Corned beef (brisket)	60%	**Veal**	
Beef liver	75-90%	Veal cutlet (boneless)	80%
Stew (boneless)	75%	Calf's liver	75%
Swiss steak	70%	Roast leg	50%
Tenderloin steak	90%	Roast loin	50%
Sirloin steak (boneless strip)	75%	Veal loin chop (bone-in)	75%
Sirloin steak (bone-in strip)	80%	Veal rib chop (bone-in)	75%
Minute steak (boneless butt)	80%		
Boneless top and bottom round roast	70%	**Pork**	
		Breaded tenderloin	100%
Knuckle butt roast	65%	Sausage patties	55%
Shoulder clod roast	70%	Breaded pork chop (boneless)	90%
Oven-prepared beef rib	50%	Pork chops (bone in)	80%
Chef's delight beef rib	60%	Spareribs	65%
Boneless round	60%	Roast pork loin	50%
Fresh bone-in beef brisket	45%	Ham steak (bone in)	80%
Hotel special rib steak roll	75%	Baked ham (bone in)	65%
Beef round, rump and shank off	50%	Roast fresh ham	50%
		Poultry	
		Fried chicken, 2 lbs.	100%
		Turkey, 18 lbs./up	40%

Courtesy of Swift and Company, Chicago.

All yields are general averages based on many hundreds of tests. They allow for waste in trimming the meat, cooking, shrinkage, and small-end waste. Determination of exact shrinkage for each meat item cooked is advisable.

The yield test is a good method of keeping tabs on the pricing structure used in buying food materials. A cheaper item may not be the best buy, and yield testing will help to determine if this is so.

The method of yield testing described in table 9-5 may be used to determine the yield and portion cost of almost any food item, from bulk ice cream to whipped potatoes. If an item must be subdivided before preparation (for example, a primal meat cut must be butchered first), the method in table 9-6 will give better yield and pricing results. A number of yield tests should be made under similar conditions to establish the portion cost.

Financial Factors. Price, of course, must always be considered in purchasing. It makes up a major part of the specification. The menu form and the usual price paid for an item may dictate its removal if the price goes above a certain level. But price must be related to the other factors that make up the specification. It may never stand alone.

Although there is a clear relationship between the availability of food products and the seasons of the year, this fluctuation creates fewer pricing problems today because of changes in processing methods. Of course, most animals raised for slaughter are still born in the spring, and more eggs are still laid in spring than in winter. Harvests of fruits and vegetables follow the northward path of the sun in the United States, from Florida's first harvest in March to upstate New York's harvest in September. The fishermen who brave the Grand Banks of Newfoundland bring home larger catches in May, June, and July than they do in ice-laden trawlers in December and January, and the price of tomatoes in the Northeast in midsummer is quite different

Table 9-5. Yield Testing of Bulk Items

1. Multiply the amount of the product purchased by the market price per unit of purchase to get the total purchase price.

quantity purchased x market price per unit = total purchase price

2. Determine the standard method of preliminary and final preparation. Weigh or measure the product after every procedure to learn where and how much material is being lost. Determine the standard portion to be served. Weigh or measure each serving and count how many are yielded.

3. Divide the number of portions served under normal standard conditions into the total purchase price to get the raw food cost per portion.

total purchase price ÷ number of portions = raw food portion cost

from the price of the same product in February.

But canning, freezing, drying, and other processing of foods make their prices less subject to seasonal fluctuations. The more processing is done, the less effect the seasons have on the price, usually.

Demand generated by seasons of celebration, holiday, religious feast days, and the like may cause prices to spike at a particular time, but these occasions pass, and prices usually return then to their normal curve.

Prices of some fresh produce may vary some 50 percent from highest to lowest around an average yearly price. (See table 9-2 for the supply history of fresh produce items.) Thus it is important for managers and supervisors to plan menus and purchases that take advantage of desirable prices and that use processed items instead (where available) when fresh ones are in short supply.

The cheaper product is not always the best, nor is the most expensive always the most desirable. Although the base price per unit or per pound seems to be the most important consideration, the cost per servable pound and the comparative quality are the key factors.

A food may be available in ready form, requiring a minimum amount of reconstituting or heating; as a convenience item with some preliminary preparation done; or in its

Table 9-6. Yield Testing of Items Requiring Subdivision before Preparation

1. After all pre-preparation, cooking, and portioning has been completed, divide the usable weight of the product by the original weight to determine the percentage of the item that is usable.

usable weight ÷ original weight = usable % of original weight

2. Divide the original price per pound by this percentage to find the cost per servable pound.

price per lb. ÷ usable % = cost per servable lb.

3. Divide the cost per servable pound by the original cost per pound to get a constant cost factor.

cost per servable lb. ÷ price per lb. = cost factor per lb.

This factor may be used to determine the cost per usable pound of the item at any market price. Simply multiply the market price by the cost factor.

market price x cost factor = cost per servable lb.

4. To find the portion cost, (a) determine the number of ounces per portion and portions per pound, (b) divide this into the cost factor per pound to get the factor per portion, and (c) multiply this factor by the market price.

16 oz. (1 lb.) ÷ number of oz. per portion = portions per lb.
cost factor per lb. ÷ portions per lb. = cost factor per portion
market price per lb. x cost factor per portion = portion cost

Assuming adequate yield testing and a uniform portion size, any change in market price of the original food item can be reflected in the portion cost by multiplying the price by the portion cost factor.

natural, raw state, requiring complete preparation. Each must be considered from the standpoint of overall serving cost, including labor and time required to prepare the item, yield realized, and equipment and storage facilities necessary. Whole potatoes that must be peeled may be purchased at a lower price per pound, but they may result in a more expensive servable portion than prepeeled and oxidation-protected products that cost more initially. A less expensive tomato puree with a lower specific gravity may more than balance the saving with excessive waste as a sauce is reduced to the desired thickness.

Within like grades or standards of quality, price variations of more than 10 percent should be viewed with caution. The buyer should attempt to learn why such high or low prices have been set, since the food market works on nearly pure competition, and great variation in price is not to be expected.

Container Sizes. The specification should give some indication of the size container or package in which the food is to be provided. This should have a direct relationship to the portion size and the number of portions to be prepared at one time.

It does little good to achieve a saving by purchasing a number 10 can or a 100-pound sack in lieu of a smaller container, if only a portion of the item is used and the remainder spoils in a refrigerator or storeroom. Foods purchased in larger units than needed also require measuring before they may be used, require additional storage space, create inventory problems, and increase inventory taxes in some states.

Other Considerations. A specification should also indicate such items as count, size, pack, style, and degree of ripeness, if applicable to the food.

Whatever the specification arrived at, it must be realistic and related to the needs of the operation. It may be as detailed as the individual operator finds consistent with his policy, or as broad as he sees fit. The more definitive it is, however, the more likely it is

Table 9-7. Common Containers for Ready Foods

Size Container	Type of Food
no. 10 cans, 6 to a case no. 303 cans, 24 to a case no. 300 cans, 24 to a case	Most canned vegetables and fruits (most are purchased by weight, but such items as peaches, pears, onions, and potatoes are purchased by count), prepared foods, soups, convenience foods, jellies, pickles
no. 3 cylinder (51-oz.) cans, 12 to a case	Condensed soups
1-gal. glass containers, 4 to a case	Mayonnaise, salad dressings, sweet relish, mustard, olives, vinegar, beverage bases to make juice
4-lb. glass jars, 12 to a case	Jellies, cherries, honey
13-oz. to 1-lb. cans, 12 to a case	Spices
10-lb. or 20-lb. case (bulk)	Noodles, spaghetti, macaroni
50-lb. blocks	Shortenings
1-lb. bags, 24 to a case	Coffee
24-oz. boxes, 12 to a case	Gelatine dessert products
100-lb. bags	Rice, flour, sugar
14-oz. boxes, 24 to a case	Wild rice, brown sugar, confectioners sugar, cornstarch
24-oz. to 46-oz. bottles or cans, 12 to a case	Juices (most in 46-oz. size)
2,000 units to a case	Individual sugar and low-calorie sugar packs
5-oz. bottles, 24 to a case	Sauces (A-1, 57, Worcestershire, etc.)
no. 5 can, 6 to a case	Mints, tuna, salmon
no. 1 tall (16-oz.) can, 24 to case	Salmon

that the product will meet the needs of the establishment.

At the least, the specification should contain the following factors, based on a preliminary testing of the item against others, in relation to the menu, and in the manner in which it will be used:

(a) The specific name of the product desired. Use common names, brand names, trade names, or trademarks to properly identify items.

(b) The quantity desired in the normally accepted measure. If the size of the container is important, specify it.

(c) The condition in which the item is to be shipped and received. Wrapping or other protection and temperature considerations are important here. If time of delivery is important, specify that too. The purveyor is in business to serve his buyers; a buyer need not accept food at any time and in any condition.

(d) The grade wanted, if grades are available.

(e) Any other factors that are important to the food, such as count, size, geographical area of origin, or style of pack.

It is not enough for a food service operator to order "Ground beef—50 pounds," or "Canned peaches—1 case." The order must be specific enough to ensure that the ground beef has a limited fat content (or half the product may vanish when it is cooked) and that the peaches have the desired syrup density, size, style, and cut.

Well constructed specifications will make the job of food preparation workers a little easier. Copies of the specifications should be provided to purveyors, purchasing agents, and receiving clerks, so that adequate information is available to those who provide, order, and receive the materials. If purveyors are given a copy of the specifications, they will usually be able to supply the material requested each and every time.

Projected Changes in Grading

As in the past when the USDA held public hearings in 1981 or responded to the results

Table 9–8. Grade Change Options Under Consideration During the Period 1981–1983

Options Under Consideration	Meat	Poultry	Eggs	Dairy		Fruits and Vegetables	
				Butter, Cheese	Instant Non-Fat Dry Milk	Fresh	Processed
Current grade names	Prime, Choice, Good	A, B, C	AA, A, B	AA, A, B	Extra	Fancy, No. 1, and No. 2*	Fancy or A, Choice or B, and Standard or C**
Option A	Prime, Choice, Good	A, B, C	A, B, C	A, B, C	A, B, C	Fancy, No. 1, No. 2	A, B, C
and Option B		AA, A, B	AA, A, B	AA, A, B	AA, A, B		AA, A, B
Option C	A, B, and C or AA, A, and B				For all graded foods		
Option D	Develop separate consumer grade system using different color U.S. grade shields to signify different quality levels.				For all graded foods		
Option E	Keep present grade names and require mandatory retail grade labeling of a product if it is officially graded.				For all graded foods		

Courtesy of the United States Department of Agriculture, Food Safety and Quality Service, Washington, D.C.

NOTE: Where applicable, grade designations given indicate the top three official USDA grade names.

*These are primarily the grade names. There are numerous exceptions to this order and these names.

**Currently, either the descriptive or letter grade is in use. However, the grade names are gradually being changed to A, B, and C exclusively.

of a survey conducted during 1979–1980, there is presently some movement in Congress to change the grading standards. However, there is some doubt whether this interest will actually result in changes because action taken in 1983 to change the grades was subsequently abandoned, and the same standards remain in effect today. Proponents of these changes suggest that the current grades, which were first used in the early 1900s, have become too complex and are really not meaningful for the average consumer.

Worthy of note here is that many grades are based upon pure surface concerns. The cosmetic appearance of a fruit depends on its appearance or the lack of a bruise or an imperfection, and this may be the major determining factor in the grade assigned. This is despite the fact that from a purely nutritional standpoint, two specimens could be equal, except for a surface bruise.

A number of options were offered but were also rejected. (See Table 9–8.) As with other forms of change in the area of food service—from the use of equipment, to utensils, and convenience food forms—the housewife and retail consumer will probably determine what, if any, changes will be made. The quantity food service operator will then be required to operate under the grading system that has been selected. With the current concerns for low-fat diets, however, still others are making attempts to produce and identify lean or low-fat meat animals and poultry and to label produced foods with other standards accordingly. As a result, the grading standards for meat and many other foods remain in a state of flux and confusion.

I do not believe that it really matters what system or recommendation is finally decided upon. The important element is that some standard grading system is used, that purchasing agents know what the grading requirements are, and that some relationship be maintained between intended use, price, and the grade that is purchased.

Ordering

Although many buying methods are available, the most frequently used forms in food preparation work are the competitive bid and direct or open market buying.

The competitive bid is used most often by government agencies and large operations to ensure that an adequate consideration is given to price. It is used mostly for equipment and supplies but also for some foods. A monthly or yearly milk or bread contract may well be offered by a city or county school board based on competitive bids.

A detailed specification must be included in every invitation to bid submitted to purveyors at the start of negotiations. These specifications must not be so restrictive that only one company can bid on the item, for this would destroy the main advantage of bidding. The specification must include in detail all information that may relate to the order, including such facts as delivery times, penalties for nondelivery, and bacterial counts of products. Most bid buying is done by centralized purchasing departments or offices that develop the specifications from technical information received from the user facilities.

In open market or direct market buying, no formal bidding procedure is used. However, quotations are often obtained from at least three competing companies to ensure that the item is being obtained at the best price.

Receiving

When the order is delivered, items that are purchased by count must be counted, while those purchased by weight must be weighed. Where purchasing is done by volume but a weight determination can be made, such as for fresh vegetables purchased by the crate, box, lug, or bushel, weighing must be carried out.

If grade indicators are used, they must be matched against the order. Style, pack, count, size, and fill must all be checked. A count of the number of cases of a canned order is only

SUBMIT BIDS TO: Florida International University Purchasing Services P.C. Bldg., Room 519 Tamiami Trail Miami, Florida 33199 (305) 554-2161	FLORIDA INTERNATIONAL UNIVERSITY **INVITATION TO BID** Bidder Acknowledgement
BIDS WILL BE OPENED and may not be withdrawn within 45 days after such date and time.	BID NO.
MAILING DATE: / PURCHASING AGENT	BID TITLE
All awards made as a result of this bid shall conform to applicable Florida Statutes.	DELIVERY WILL BE ____ DAYS after receipt of Purchase Order
VENDOR NAME	REASON FOR NO BID
VENDOR MAILING ADDRESS	
CITY-STATE-ZIP	F.E.I.D. NO:
AREA CODE / TELEPHONE NUMBER	Certified or cashier's check is attached, when
TOLL-FREE NUMBER	required, in the amount of: $
I certify that this bid is made without prior understanding, agreement, or connection with any corporation, firm, or person submitting a bid for the same materials, supplies, or equipment, and is in all respects fair and without collusion or fraud. I agree to abide by all conditions of this bid and certify that I am authorized to sign this bid for the bidder.	______________________ AUTHORIZED SIGNATURE (MANUAL) ______________________ AUTHORIZED SIGNATURE (TYPED) TITLE

GENERAL CONDITIONS

BIDDER: To insure acceptance of the bid, follow these instructions.
SEALED BIDS: All bid sheets and this form must be executed and submitted in a sealed envelope.
(DO NOT INCLUDE MORE THAN ONE BID PER ENVELOPE). The face of the envelope shall contain, in addition to the above address, the date and time of the bid opening and the bid number. All bids are subject to the conditions specified herein. Those which do not comply with these conditions are subject to rejection.

1. EXECUTION OF BID: Bid must contain a manual signature of authorized representative in the space provided above. Bid must be typed or printed in ink. Use of erasable ink not permitted. All corrections made by bidder to his bid must be initialed.
2. NO BID: If not submitting a bid, respond by returning this form, marking it "NO BID", and explain the reason in the space provided above. Failure to respond 3 times in succession without justification shall be cause for removal of the supplier's name from the bid mailing list. NOTE: To qualify as a respondent, bidder must submit a "NO BID", and it must be received no later than the stated bid opening date and hour.
3. BID OPENING: Shall be public on the date and at the time specified on the bid form. It is the bidder's responsibility to assure that his bid is delivered at the proper time and place of the bid opening. Bids which for any reason are not so delivered, will not be considered. NOTE: Bid tabulations will be furnished upon written request with an enclosed, self-addressed, stamped envelope. Bid files may be examined during normal working hours by appointment.
4. PRICES, TERMS AND PAYMENT: Firm prices shall be bid and include all packing, handling, shipping charges and delivery to the destination shown herein. Bidder is requested to offer cash discount for prompt invoice payment.
   (a) TAXES: The State of Florida does not pay Federal Excise and Sales taxes on direct purchases of tangible personal property. See exemption number on face of purchase order. This exemption does not apply to purchases of tangible personal property made by contractors who use the tangible personal property in the performance of contracts for the improvement of state-owned real property as defined in Chapter 192, F.S.
   (b) DISCOUNTS: Bidders are encouraged to reflect cash discounts in the units prices quoted; however, bidders may offer a cash discount for prompt payment. Discounts shall not be

Figure 9c. A sample bid sheet for a formal bid, outlining the conditions for bidding. (Courtesy of Florida International University, Miami.)

considered in determining the lowest net cost for bid evaluation purposes.

(c) MISTAKES: Bidders are expected to examine the specifications, delivery schedule, bid prices, extensions, and all instructions pertaining to supplies and services. Failure to do so will be at bidder's risk. In case of mistake in extension, the unit price will govern.

(d) CONDITION AND PACKAGING: It is understood and agreed that any item offered and shipped as a result of this bid shall be a new, current standard production model available at the time of this bid. All containers shall be suitable for storage or shipment, and all prices shall include standard commercial packaging.

(e) SAFETY STANDARDS: Unless otherwise stipulated in the bid, all manufactured items and fabricated assemblies shall comply with applicable requirements of Occupational Safety and Health Act and any standards thereunder.

(f) PAYMENT: Payment will be made by the buyer after the items awarded to a vendor have been received, inspected, and found to comply with award specifications, free of damage or defect and properly invoiced. All invoices shall bear the purchase order number. An original and three (3) copies of the invoice shall be submitted. Failure to follow these instructions may result in delay of processing invoices for payment. The purchase order number must appear on bills of lading, packages, cases, delivery lists and correspondence.

5. DELIVERY: Unless actual date of delivery is specified (or if specified delivery cannot be met), show number of days required to make delivery after receipt of purchase order in space provided. Delivery time may become a basis for making an award (see Special Conditions).

6. MANUFACTURERS' NAMES AND APPROVED EQUIVALENTS: Any manufacturers' names, trade names, brand names, information and/or catalog numbers listed in a specification are for information and not intended to limit competition. If bids are based on equivalent products, indicate on the bid form the manufacturers' name and number. Bidder shall submit with his proposal, cuts, sketches, and descriptive literature, and/or complete specifications. Reference to literature submitted with a previous bid will not satisfy this provision. The bidder shall also explain in detail the reason(s) why the proposed equivalent will meet the specifications and not be considered an exception thereto. Bids which do not comply with these requirements are subject to rejection. Bids lacking any written indication of intent to quote an alternate brand will be received and considered in complete compliance with the specifications as listed on the bid form.

7. INTERPRETATIONS: Any questions concerning conditions and specifications shall be directed to this office. Inquiries must reference the date of bid opening and bid number. Failure to comply with this condition will result in bidder waiving his right to dispute the bid conditions and specifications.

8. CONFLICT OF INTEREST: The award hereunder is subject to the provisions of Chapter 112, Florida Statues. All bidders must disclose with their bid the name of any officer, director, or agent who is also an employee of the State of Florida, or any of its agencies. Further, all bidders must disclose the name of any State employee who owns, directly or indirectly, an interest of the five percent (5C) or more in the bidder's firm or any of its branches.

9. AWARDS: As the best interest of F.I.U. may require, the right is reserved to make award(s) by individual item, group of items, all or none or a combination thereof; to reject any and all bids or waive any minor irregularity or technicality in bids received. When it is determined there is competition to the lowest responsive bidder, then other bids may not be evaluated. Bidders are cautioned to make no assumptions unless their bid has been evaluated as being responsive.

10. ADDITIONAL QUANTITIES: For a period not exceeding ninety (90) days from the date of acceptance of this offer by F.I.U., the right is reserved to acquire additional quantities up to but not exceeding those shown on bid or $3,000 for commodities at the prices in this invitation. If additional quantities are not acceptable, the bid sheets must be noted "BID IS FOR SPECIFIED QUANTITY ONLY."

11. SERVICE AND WARRANTY: Unless otherwise specified, the bidder shall define any warranty service and replacements that will be provided during and subsequent to this contract. Bidders must explain on an attached sheet to what extent warranty and service facilities are provided.

12. SAMPLES: Samples of items, when called for, must be furnished free of expense on or before bid opening, time and date, and if not destroyed may, upon request be returned at the bidders expense. Each individual sample must be labeled with bidder's name, manufacturers' brand name and number, bid number and item reference. Request for return of samples shall be accompanied by instructions which include shipping authorization and name of carrier and must be received with your bid. If instructions are not received within this time, the commodities shall be disposed of by F.I.U.

13. INSPECTION, ACCEPTANCE AND TITLE: Inspection and acceptance will be at destination unless otherwise provided. Title and risk of loss or damage to all items shall be the responsibility of the contract supplier until acceptance by the ordering agency, unless loss or damage results from negligence by F.I.U.

14. DISPUTES: In case of any doubt or difference of opinion as to the items to be furnished hereunder, the decision of the buyer shall be final and binding on both parties.

15. GOVERNMENTAL RESTRICTION: In the event any governmental restrictions may be imposed which would necessitate alteration of the material, quality, workmanship, or performance of the items offered in this proposal prior to their delivery, it shall be the responsibility of the successful bidder to notify F.I.U. at once, indicating in his letter the specific regulation which required an alteration. F.I.U. reserves the right to accept any such alteration, including any price adjustments occasioned

thereby, or to cancel the contract at no expense to F.I.U.

16. LEGAL REQUIREMENTS: Applicable provisions of all Federal, State, county and local laws, and of all ordinances, rules, and regulations shall govern development submittal and evaluation of all bids received in response hereto and shall govern any and all claims and disputes which may arise between person(s) submitting a bid response hereto and F.I.U. by and through its officers, employees and authorized representatives, or any other person, natural or otherwise; and lack of knowledge by any bidder shall not constitute a cognizable defense against the legal affect thereof.
17. PATENTS AND ROYALTIES: The bidder, without exception, shall indemnify and save harmless F.I.U. and its employees from liability of any nature or kind, including cost and expenses for or on account of any copyrighted, patented, or unpatented invention, process, or article manufactured or used in the performance of the contract, including its use by F.I.U. If the bidder uses any design, device or materials covered by letters, patent or copyright, it is mutually agreed and understood without exception that the bid prices shall include all royalties or cost arising from the use of such design, device, or materials in any way involved in the work.
18. ADVERTISING: In submitting a bid, bidder agrees not to use the results therefrom as a part of any commercial advertising.
19. ASSIGNMENT: Any Puchase Order issued pursuant to this bid invitation and the monies which may become due hereunder are not assignable except with the prior written approval of F.I.U.
20. PUBLIC PRINTING (APPLIES ONLY TO PRINTING CONTRACTS):
    (a) PREFERENCE GIVEN PRINTING WITH THE STATE: F.I.U. shall give preference to bidders located within the state when awarding contracts to have materials printed, whenever such printing can be done at no greater expense than, and at a level of quality comparable to that obtainable from a bidder outside the state.
    (b) CONTRACTS SUBLET: In accordance to Class B Printing Laws and Regulations, "Printing shall be awarded only to printing firms. No contract shall be awarded to any broker, agent, or independent contractor offering to provide printing manufactured by other firms or persons."
    (c) DISQUALIFICATION OF BIDDER: More than one bid from an individual, firm, partnership, corporation or association under the same or different names will not be considered. Reasonable grounds for believing that a bidder is involved in more than one proposal for the same work will be cause for rejection of all proposals in which such bidders are believed to be involved. Any or all proposals will be rejected if there is reason to believe that collusion exists between bidders. Proposals in which the prices obviously are unbalanced will be subject to rejection.
    (d) TRADE CUSTOMS: Current trade customs of the printing industry are recognized unless expected by Special Conditions or Specifications herein.
    (e) COMMUNICATIONS: It is expected that all materials and proofs will be picked up and delivered by the printer or his representative, unless otherwise specified. Upon request, materials will be forwarded by registered mail.
    (f) RETURN OF MATERIALS: All copy, photos, artwork, and other materials supplied by the purchaser must be handled carefully and returned in good condition upon completion of the job. Such return is a condition of the contract and payment will not be made until return is effected.
21. LIABILITY: The seller agrees to indemnify and save F.I.U., its officers, agents, and employees harmless from any and all judgements, orders, awards, costs and expense including attorneys' fees, and all claims on account of damages to property, including loss of use thereof, or bodily injury (including death) which may be hereafter sustained by the seller, its employees, its subcontractors, or F.I.U. employees, or third persons arising out of or in connection with this contract and which are determined by a court of competent jurisdiction to be a legal liability of the seller.
22. FACILITIES: The University reserves the right to inspect the bidder's facilities at any time with prior notice.
23. ANTI-DISCRIMINATION CLAUSE: The Bidder shall comply with the provisions of Executive Order 11246, September 24, 1965, and the rules, regulations and relevant Orders of the Secretary of Labor.

NOTE: ANY AND ALL CONDITIONS ATTACHED HERETO WHICH VARY FROM THESE GENERAL CONDITIONS SHALL HAVE PRECEDENCE.

SUPPLEMENTAL CONDITIONS

VENDOR'S RIGHTS TO PAYMENT

"Pursuant to section 215.422(3)(b), Florida Statutes, a state agency shall mail the vendor's payment within 45 days after receipt of an acceptable invoice and receipt, inspection and acceptance of the goods and/or services provided in accordance with the terms and conditions of the purchase order contract. Failure to mail the warrant within 45 days shall result in the agency paying interest at a rate of one percent per month on the unpaid balance. The interest penalty shall be mailed within 15 days after mailing the warrant."

OCCUPATIONAL HEALTH AND SAFETY (TOXIC SUBSTANCES)

In compliance with Chapter 442, Florida Statutes (Florida Right-to-Know Law) any chemical substance or mixture in a gaseous, liquid, or solid state, which substance or mixture causes a significant risk to safety or health during, or as a proximate result of, any customary or reasonably foreseeable handling or use and is delivered to the University as a result of the attached purchase order must be accompanied by a Material Safety Data Sheet (MSDS). The MSDS must be reproducible and include the following information:

Figure 9c. (continued)

(a) The chemical name and the common name of the toxic substance.
(b) The hazards or other risks in the use of the toxic substance, including:
   1. The potential for fire, explosion, corrosivity, and reactivity;
   2. The known acute and chronic health effects of risks from exposure, including the medical conditions which are generally recognized as being aggravated by exposure to the toxic substance; and
   3. The primary routes of entry and symptoms of overexposure.
(c) The proper precautions, handling practices, necessary personal protective equipment, and other safety precautions in the use of or exposure to the toxic substances, including appropriate emergency treatment in case of overexposure.
(d) The emergency procedure for spills, fire disposal, and first aid.
(e) A description in lay terms of the known specific potential health risks posed by the toxic substance intended to alert any person reading this information.
(f) The year and month, if available, that the information was compiled and the name, address, and emergency telephone number of the manufacturer responsible for preparing the information.

Any questions regarding this requirement should be directed to: Department of Labor and Employment Security, Bureau of Industrial Safety and Health, Toxic Waste Information Center, 2551 Executive Center Circle West, Tallahassee, Florida 32301-5014, Telephone: 1–800–367–4378."

PRISON REHABILITATIVE INDUSTRIES (PRIDE)

Chapter 85–194, Laws of Florida, effective June 18, 1985, amended Section 946.15, Florida Statutes, to provide in part, that any service or item manufactured, processed, grown, or produced by the private nonprofit corporation which manages correctional work programs, which corporation is currently Prison Rehabilitative Industries and Diversified Enterprises, Inc., may be furnished or sold to any contract vendor for any state agency or to any subcontractor of the contract vendor. Therefore, it is expressly understood and agreed that any articles which are the subject of, or required to carry out this contract shall be purchased from the corporation identified under Chapter 946, F.S. in the same manner and under the procedures set forth in Section 946.15(2), (4), F.S.; and for purposes of this contract the person, firm, or other business entity carrying out the provisions of this contract shall be deemed to be substituted for this agency insofar as dealings with such corporation.

The provisions of this law only apply if PRIDE produces a product covered by this agreement and can satisfy the terms of the agreement with respect to quantity, quality and time of delivery.

Any questions concerning PRIDE's ability to provide products or services should be directed to Prison Rehabilitative Industries and Diversified Enterprises, Incorporated, Corporate Offices, 611 Druid Road East, Clearwater, Florida 33516, Telephone: (813) 441–1950.

SPECIAL CONDITIONS

1. ASSEMBLY AND/OR PLACEMENT:
   All items must be completely assembled when delivered to the University.
   NOTE: Special Instructions:
   It is important that the equipment be delivered on site, assembled and put in place ready for immediate hook up.
2. AVAILABILITY OF FUNDS:
   The obligations of the University under this award are subject to the availability of funds lawfully appropriated annually for its purposes by the Legislature of the State of Florida.
3. AWARD:
   The award of this bid is subject to cancellation upon the timely filing of a Bid Protest. The results of this bid will be posted on the F.I.U. Bid Bulletin Board for ten days after the opening.
4. CANCELLATION:
   For the protection of both parties, this contract may be cancelled in whole or in part by either party by giving thirty (30) days prior notice in writing to the other party.
5. DELIVERY:
   Vendors are requested to state earliest possible delivery in appropriate space on Page 1.
6. F.O.B. POINT:
   The F.O.B. Point will be the Owa Ehan Building-Room 148 (Food Lab) through Central Receiving, S.W. 107 Ave. & 8 Street (Tamiami Trail) Miami, Florida, 33199 (Tamiami Campus). See Item #1 of Special Conditions.
7. WARRANTY:
   The successful bidder shall fully warrant all items furnished hereunder against defect in materials and/or workmanship for a period of ____ from date of final payment by the University. Should any defect in materials or workmanship, excepting ordinary wear and tear, appear during the warranty period, the successful bidder shall repair or replace same at no cost to the University immediately upon written notice from the Director of Purchasing.
   "The successful bidder will not be liable under the above warranty for any defects or damages resulting from unforeseeable causes beyond the control and without the fault or negligence of the bidder, such as misuse or neglect by the University, Acts of God, fires, floods and hurricanes."

the start of the receiving procedure.

The temperature of highly perishable and chilled foods, such as milk and poultry, and of all frozen items should be taken with a dial-type "instant" reading thermometer. Frozen packages should be punctured with the thermometer shaft and readings taken after five minutes. Observe all frozen foods for signs of past thawing and refreezing, such as ice in the bottoms of containers, or signs of freezer burn (dehydration).

Although can cutting–opening a canned

food item and checking for drained weight, specific gravity, style, count, pack, and the like—is an accepted quality-control practice, it is not suggested as a part of the normal receiving and inspection procedure in the average food operation. Exterior labels should be sufficient to give the information needed for certifying receipts at this level. Can cutting is more useful as a management tool in determining which items will be purchased and how purchase specifications will be written.

Some purveyors who note that an adequate inspection procedure is not being carried out may well deliver items that do not meet the order specifications. Old bread has been taken from one restaurant and sent to another as fresh, ice has been added to chilled poultry shipments to increase the weight, and grades have been varied without detection.

Storage

Another important step in procuring quality food for use is storage. The primary purpose of this step is to have enough of the food item on hand to meet preparation plans. This should be accomplished with a minimum of loss through theft, spoilage, and waste.

No food item is ever improved by storage. (Even the aging of meats is only a form of controlled spoilage.) In fact, if the proper measures are not taken to prevent damage, most items will deteriorate in some way. It is often appropriate, therefore, to reduce the storage of foods by using more frequent deliveries or changing to a food form that requires less preliminary preparation. Elimination of all storage is an unrealistic goal, but storage may well be reduced. Then the food service operator must take measures to protect foods against improper storage.

The first considerations are the size and location of storage facilities. The size of the area depends on such factors as the geographical location of the enterprise, the frequency of deliveries, the amount of money that can be tied up in inventory, and management policy on the use of bulk purchasing to save money.

Of course, the extent of the menu and the volume of business affect the size of the storage facility needed. Operations serving certain government or health agencies may, in addition, be required to maintain certain minimum food stocks to be able to cope with emergencies.

Inventory turnover is used to express the ratio of the amount of inventory to the amount of food being used. It is found by the formula:

$$\text{cost of goods sold} \div [(\text{beginning inventory} + \text{ending inventory}) \div 2] = \text{inventory turnover}$$

It should fall between 25 and 40 per year for the average operation.

Extensive menus and improper usage and ordering records result in a sluggish inventory turnover and cause problems for the food service manager. Excessive amounts of money are tied up in inventories, foods have a greater chance of spoiling, and the inventory requires more administration time.

Types of Storage

In terms of storage, there are three basic forms of food items that each operation must plan for. *Dry stores* consist of packaged, canned, or other processed items that do not require any specific storage controls other than sufficient space and protection against extremes of temperature, insects, and rodents. *Perishables* or fresh provisions consist of fresh fruits, fresh meats, dairy products, fresh vegetables, and the like. These generally require some sort of refrigerated storage in order to maintain quality. *Frozen foods* may be either vegetable or animal and either raw or processed. They require maximum refrigeration in order to maintain their quality levels.

The food service operator must, of course, also provide for storage of nonfood items, such as dishes, paper goods, silver, cleaning supplies, and linens. These require only space, security, and proper issue procedures. They present no special problems, except for control of usage and reordering so that adequate stocks are kept on hand.

Storage areas should have locks, and each food item should be identified with a bin tag

Table 9-9. Refrigerator Storage Space by Commodity

Commodity	Storage Type	Container Size	Container Weight	Shelf Area (sq. ft.)
Meat (carcass)	Track, hooks	1 ft. of track for 1/4 carcass	150 lbs. (1/4 carcass)	2
Meat (cuts)	Tubs	2-ft. diam.x10-1/2 in.	40 lb.	3.5
Meat (cuts)	Trays	18x26x3 in.	40 lb.	3.3
Meat (cuts, beef)	Fibre box	28x18x6 in.	140 lb.	3.5
Meat (cuts, pork)	Wood box	28x10x10 in.	55 lb.	2.0
Milk	Can	13-1/2-in. diam.x25 in.	10 Gal.	1.2
	Case	13x19x7 in.	1/2 pt. (24)	1.7
	Case	14-1/8x17-1/2x7 in.	1/2 pt. (35)	1.7
Canned milk	Case	19x13x7-1/2 in.	(6) no. 10 Cans 38 lb.	1.7
Cheese, American	Daisy	13-1/2-in. diam.x7-1/2 in.	20-30 lb.	1.3
Ice cream	Cans	9-in. diam.x18-1/4 in.	5 gal.	
	Cartons	9x10 in.	2-1/2 gal.	
Butter (margarine)	Boxes	17-1/4x14x10 in.	60 lb.	1.6
Bacon	Slab	10x24x2 in.	15 lb.	1.6
Salt pork	Slab	12x30x2 in.	15 lb.	1.6
Shortening	Can	16-in. diam.x17 in.	50 lb.	1.8
Cooking oil	Can	9-1/2x9-1/2x13 in.	5 gal.	0.7
Grain	Sack	18x33x11 in.	98 lb.	4.0
Sugar	Sack	18x33x11 in.	100 lb.	4.0
Potatoes	Sack	18x33x11 in.	100 lb.	4.0
Onions	Sack	18x33x11 in.	100 lb.	4.0
Flour	Sack	18x33x11 in.	100 lb.	4.0
Eggs	Wood cases	26x12x13 in.	45 lb.	2.2
Eggs (frozen)	Cans	10x10x12-1/2 in.	30 lb.	1.0
Fruit	Lug	14x17x6 in.	30 lb.	1.7
Citrus	Crate	12x12x24 in.	75-80 lb.	2.0
	Carton	11-1/2x17x11 in.	75-80 lb.	1.4
Apples	Box	10-1/2x18x11-1/2 in.	44 lb.	1.3
	Carton	12-1/2x19x11 in.	44 lb.	1.6
Apricots	Box	12-1/2x16-1/8x5/8 in.	25 lb.	1.4
	Crate	16x16x5 in.	24 lb.	1.8
Berries	Crate	11x11x22 in.	36 lb.	1.7
Cherries	Lug	13-1/2x16x6 in.	25 lb.	1.5
Grapefruit	Box	11-1/2x11-1/2x24 in.	68 lb.	1
Grapes	Box	6x16x13-1/2 in.	30 lb.	1.4
Lemons	Box	10x25x13 in.	75 lb.	2.2
Limes	Box	10x19x10 in.	35 lb.	1.3
Melons	Carton	16x23-1/2x8-1/2 in.	variable	2.6
	Crate (flat)	13-1/2x16x5 in.	variable	1.4
	Crate	12x22x12 in.	variable	1.8
Peaches	Box	13-1/4x16x5 in.	variable	1.4
Pears	Box	13-1/2x21x8-1/2 in.	45 lb.	1.7
Pineapple	Crate	12x33x11 in.	70 lb.	2.7
Beets	Crate	18x22x13 in.	70 lb.	2.8
Brussels sprouts	Box	11x21x10 in.	25 lb.	1.7
Cabbage	Crate	18x22x13 in.	80 lb.	2.8
	Bag	16x32x11 in.	100 lb.	3.5
Carrots	Crate	18x22x13 in.	75 lb.	2.8
Cauliflower	Crate	18x22x9 in.	40 lb.	2.8
Celery	Crate	24x21x11 in.	variable	3.5
	Crate	22x16x21 in.	variable	2.5
Lettuce	Crate	19x20x14 in.	variable	2.6
	Carton	14x22x10 in.	variable	2.1
	Crate	13x21x10 in.	variable	1.9
	Paper box	13-1/2x21x10 in.	variable	2.0
Sweet potatoes	Crate	14x15x12 in.	50 lb.	1.5
Rhubarb	Box	11-1/2x18x6 in.	15-20 lb.	1.5
Tomatoes	Box	13-1/2x16x7 in.	30 lb.	1.4
FROZEN FOODS				
Turkey	Box	Hens 17x25x8-in.	variable	3.0
	Box	Toms 16x22x11 in.	variable	2.5

Commodity	Storage Type	Container		Shelf Area (sq. ft.)
		Size	Weight	
Chickens	Box (ice)	12-1/2x18x8-1/2 in.	16-32 lb.	1.6
Vegetables	Paper container	5-1/4x4x1-3/4 in.	10 oz.	*
	Paper container	5-1/4x4x1-3/4 in.	12 oz.	*
	Paper container	5-1/4x4x1-3/4 in.	16 oz.	*
	Paper container	10x5x2-1/2 in.	2-1/2 lb.	*
	Paper container	10-1/2x8x3 in.	5 lb.	.5
Fish	Paper container	9-1/2x7x1-1/2 in.	5 lb.	.5
Fruit	Paper container	12x8-1/4x3 in.	5 lb.	.7
Meat	Paper container	12-1/4x10x2-1/2 in.	10	.8
	Paper container	13-1/4x9-1/2x2-1/2 in.	10	1.0
	Paper container	14x10-1/4x2-1/4 in.	10	1.0
CANNED FRUIT, VEGETABLES				
Standard no. 2-1/2	Can	4x4-3/4 in.		
Coffee 1 lb.	Can	5-1/6x3-5/8 in.		
Standard no. 5	Can	5-1/8x5-7/8 in.		
Standard no. 10	Can	6-3/16x8-1/4 in.		
Standard gallon	Can	6-3/16x8-3/4 in.		
Dry milk	Can	6-5/8x7-1/2 in.		
STANDARD BOXES (CANNED FRUIT, VEGETABLES)				
6-oz. Cans	8 doz.	22-1/2x11-1/4x7-1/4 in.		1.7
8-oz. Cans	6 doz.	16-1/2x11x10 in.		1.2
No. 2 Tall	2 doz.	14x10-1/2x9-3/8 in.		1.0
No. 2-1/2	2 doz.	16-1/2x12-1/2x9-3/4 in.		1.4
No. 5	12/case	15-1/2x10-1/4x11-1/4 in.		1.2
No. 10	6/case	19x12-5/8x7 in.		1.5

*Area does not apply to very small containers.

that carries an item count record. A costing stock record card should also be kept in another location for pricing information, and to assist in making inventories and ordering materials.

Items may be stored in any form that meets the needs of the operation. The food may be arranged according to (a) type of food (canned fruits, canned vegetables, etc.); (b) stock number or other identifying symbol (used primarily by chain operations and government agencies); or (c) alphabetical order, within the major groups (dry, chilled, and frozen).

The alphabetical form of storage is recommended. It enables employees to take inventories more quickly, reduces the time needed to find an item, even by those unfamiliar with the storage spaces, and is efficient for purposes of issuing stocks.

With a preprinted issue form, listing foods in alphabetical order, a cook or ingredient man can request the necessary items from the storage area (based on the menu and forecasts) with little difficulty. The form requires no writing other than the number of units to be issued, and this enables workers to carry out the procedure with a minimum of delay.

Each type of food has certain basic storage requirements, if proper quality is to be maintained. These are discussed below.

Dry Stores. The storage area for dry provisions should be adequate in size to avoid overcrowding, provide for good air circulation, and permit efficient inventory and issue procedures.

A rule of thumb of ½ to 1 cubic foot per person to be served has been accepted by many as a reasonable estimate of the amount of space required by the average operation. The area should be easy to clean, well lighted, and constructed of materials that can hold heavy loads.

Both shelf and pallet storage should be available, and attempts should be made to eliminate conditions that contribute to excessive heat or the intrusion of insects or rodents. A temperature of 70 or 72 degrees Fahrenheit will generally promote a normal shelf life for dry stores, while higher temperatures will cause more rapid deterioration, particularly of canned goods that are acid. The

Date: Requested by:

Stock No.	Item	Unit	Expenditure Unit	Net Conversion	No. of Units	Total Expenditure
8950 127 8075	Allspice, ground	can	lb.	1		
8925	Almond paste	can	can			
8905	Anchovies	case	case			
8950	Antioxidant	jar	lb.	1		
8915	Apple cider	case	case			
8915 126 4060	Apples, no. 10	can	lb.	6.5		
8915 132 6348	Applesauce, no. 303	can	lb.	1		
8940	Applesauce, diet	can	case			
8940	Apricots, diet	can	case			
8915 286 5398	Apricots, no. 2-1/2	can	lb.	1.875		
8915 286 8696	Asparagus, no. 300	can	lb.	.906		
8940	Asparagus, diet	can	case			
8940	Baby food, assorted fruits and vegetables	jar	jar			
8940	Baby food, assorted meats and egg yolk	jar	jar			
8950 125 6333	Baking powder	can	lb.	1		
8950	Bay leaves	pkg.	lb.	1		
8915 127 9783	Beans, dry blackeye	bag	lb.	100		
8915	Bamboo shoots	can	case	1		

Figure 9d. A preprinted inventory and issue form, used to reduce time in requisitioning materials. The net conversion factor changes the unit container size into pounds for unit pricing. The stock numbers indicate by the first four digits the type of food (e.g., 8950 is spices; 8915 is fruits and vegetables; 8940 is used for nonstandard items that must be bought on the open market instead of through normal supply channels). (Courtesy of the United States Department of the Navy, Washington, D.C.)

humidity should be kept below 70 percent, if at all possible, for best results.

Perishables and Frozen Foods. Items that require frozen or refrigerated storage should be stored on pallets or on shelving in walk-in or cabinet-type refrigerators or freezers. Adequate lighting and air circulation must be provided. Frozen foods must be well wrapped or packaged to protect against dehydration (freezer burn). In all shelf storage (particularly when there are opened containers), items on lower shelves must be protected against contamination from items on the shelves above.

Approximately 20 cubic feet of refrigerated space will be needed for every 100 meals served per day. A walk-in refrigerator is desirable when the number of meals reaches the 300-to-400 level. If adequate space and funds are available, separate storage should be provided for vegetables, meat, and dairy items in the refrigerated area. This allows for better temperature control and prevents exchange of odors and tastes.

Frozen foods should be stored at temperatures from 0 to minus 20 degrees Fahrenheit. Other refrigerated foods should be held at the following temperatures: milk and eggs, 36 to 40 degrees Fahrenheit; meat, 32 to 36 degrees Fahrenheit; fruits and vegetables, 40 degrees Fahrenheit; and fresh fish, 23 to 30 degrees Fahrenheit.

The maximum storage times for foods are given in table 9-10. These may be compared with the guidelines for commercial storage of fresh fruits and vegetables that are given in table 9-11.

Table 9-10. Storage Times for Common Foods

Storage Method and Food	Maximum Time (Days)
Refrigerator (38-40° F.)	
Steaks, chops, and roasts	3
Freshly ground meats	2
Liver and other variety meats	2
Table-ready meats, frankfurters, etc.	7
Fish	2
Chicken	2
Turkey	3
Eggs	14
Milk	5
Cheese, cottage and cream	7
Cheese, cheddar and processed	until used
Butter	14
Margarine, lard, and oils	until used
Fresh fruits and vegetables	7
Freezer (0° F.)	
Frozen foods, meats, vegetables, juices, etc.	90
Unrefrigerated storage (70° F.)	
Potatoes, onions, and staples	7-14
Canned foods	180

Courtesy of the New York State College of Agriculture and Human Ecology, Cornell University, Ithaca, N.Y.

Issue Methods

The food ordered by a food service establishment goes either for end use (direct issue) or for storage and later issue. End use or direct issue items are those received on a frequent basis (usually daily) that go directly to the preparation areas for immediate use. Such materials as milk, bread, and fresh vegetables are often direct issues. More stable items should be received in the storeroom area and issued from storage by means of an issue voucher. This ensures maximum control and security. All items issued may then be traced to a particular department or recipe. The form of food control system used and the establishment's policy will determine whether this system should be followed.

An establishment that permits employees to enter storage areas and remove items at will and that uses the differences in food inventories to determine food costs must depend on adequate supervision to ensure that food items actually find their way into recipes and are not being diverted to other uses.

General Storage Area Guidelines

To provide a proper storage area and procedure, the following general storage considerations are suggested:

(1) Maintain temperature records of all refrigerated spaces, to control malfunction problems and prevent spoilage.

(2) Provide for gentle handling of all fruits and vegetables, to avoid bruising and damage that hasten decay.

(3) Make sure in stacking procedures that excessive weight is not placed on lower items.

(4) Watch for flippers, leakers, and springers in canned foods, which may indicate internal defects in the food.

(5) When containers are opened, cover items in cook's boxes to prevent contamination and eventual destruction of food materials.

(6) Clean cook's boxes daily, and remove

Table 9-11. Guidelines for Commercially Stored Fresh Fruits and Vegetables

Item	Storage	Handling
32° IDEAL		
Apples	Dry	Long shelf life, but will bruise easily. Emit ethylene gas.
Artichokes	Dry	Can mold if wet.
Asparagus	Moist	Stand upright in cold water.
Broccoli/Cauliflower	Moist	Store only briefly, 5 days maximum.
Cabbage	Moist	Don't trim outer leaves until ready to use.
Carrots/Celery	Moist	Wash & store in plastic bags.
Grapes	Dry	Wash just before use.
Kiwi fruit	Dry	Long shelf life if stored at 32°.
Lettuce	Dry	Keep away from cooler fans.
Mushrooms	Dry	Very short shelf life.
Onions (Green)	Dry	Very perishable.
Oranges (FL)	Dry	Proper rotation will maintain good fruit.
Peaches/Pears/Plums	Dry	To retard softening, refrigerate.
Radishes	Moist	Keep tops dry.
Spinach	Moist	Top ice to keep from wilting.
Strawberries	Dry	Highly perishable, wash just before use.
Item	**Storage**	**Handling**
40–55° IDEAL		
Avocados	Dry	Ripen at room temperature.
Cantaloupes	Dry	Very perishable. Ripen quickly at room temperature.
Cucumbers	Dry	Avoid chilling.
Grapefruit	Dry	Suffers chill damage below 40°.
Lemons/limes	Dry	Long shelf life. Will absorb odors.
Melons	Dry	Refrigeration retards ripening.
Oranges (CA)	Dry	Proper rotation will maintain good fruit.
Onions (dry)	Dry	Store well.
Peppers	Dry	Store briefly, never below 45°.
Pineapples	Dry	Will not ripen after harvesting.
Potatoes	Dry	Keep away from light.
Squash	Dry	Avoid bruising.
60–65° IDEAL		
Bananas	Dry	Storage below 58° will cause damage.
Tomatoes	Dry	Ripen at room temperature. Do not refrigerate unripe tomatoes.
Watermelon	Dry	Holding at room temperature can improve flavor.

From "Fresh Produce: More than 100 Marketing Ideas," pp. 20–21 1987 Foodservice Div., Produce Marketing Assoc. P.O. Box 6036, Newark, Delaware 19714.

any leftovers. Work them into later menus on a priority basis.

(7) When menus are constructed, check inventory for stored items that are not moving and for leftovers. Both should be worked into menus for quick disposition.

(8) Use a FIFO (first in, first out) issuing system so that newer food items are stored behind older ones, and older ones are issued and used first.

(9) Keep all storage areas locked and under the control of as few people as possible. Passing the keys to locked areas to anyone who calls for them is not a form of security storage.

(10) Take an inventory of all food items at least once a month. Make spot checks of some items, on a rotating basis, daily or weekly.

(11) Keep all storage spaces clean, particularly in refrigerated areas.

(12) Determine the frequency of use of items. Try to store items near where they are most often used.

(13) Avoid storing items together that will exchange strong flavors.

(14) Cross-stack bulk or bagged items for better air circulation, ease of stacking, and stability.

(15) Mark material to be stored with the date of receipt for better stores management.

One form of pricing also requires each item received to be priced individually for later issue control. The use of meat tags in this form of control is recommended.

(16) Defrost freezers regularly to prevent ice buildup on evaporators and loss of efficiency.

(17) Check inventory levels and ordering procedures regularly to make sure that excessive amounts are not being stored and that emergency orders are not being made routinely because certain stocks are undersupplied.

10 *Sanitation and Safety*

Objective: To consider the importance of sanitation in providing quality food service. The legal, moral, and economic reasons for sanitation as well as the specific problem agents and their effective control are discussed. The value of safety consciousness, common problems, and their prevention are explored.

What Is Sanitation?

"Sanitation is a way of life. It is a quality of living that is experienced in the clean home, the clean farm, the clean business and industry, the clean neighborhood, the clean community. Being a way of life it must come from within the people; it is nourished by knowledge and grows as an obligation and an ideal in human relations." With these words, the subject of sanitation is described by the National Sanitation Foundation.

Although sanitation is used in every aspect of life and requires specific actions from every member of the community, it assumes even greater proportions to the food service operator. In this business the level of sanitation maintained not only affects the individual and his immediate neighbor, but also has a profound effect on all who partake of food in the establishment.

The food service operator must maintain a high level of sanitation within his plant. He should apply principles of sanitary science in the removal or neutralization of any elements in his business that might be injurious to the health of his guests. This practice must be carried out through the action of all employees, and it thus is of prime concern to every manager in food service work.

The United States Public Health Service has identified sixty-two diseases that are communicable to man through man-to-man or animal-to-man channels. Of these, some forty can be transmitted by food.

Over 10,000 people annually in the United States have diagnosed incidents of food poisoning of various types. Many other incidents apparently take place, but go unreported. Food poisoning is, in the main, a direct result of sanitation problems and breaks. In 1985 alone, 56,000 people suffered the effects of salmonellosis—twice as many as in the previous ten years. A United States Department of Agriculture representative suggested that upwards of 40 percent of all chicken could be contaminated by the Salmonella bacterium. In 1987 the Food Safety and Inspection Division of the USDA (FSIS) instituted additional testing methods to uncover these problem cases, and producers tested organic acid processes to help reduce this disturbingly high percentage.

Federal, state, and local governments have recognized the potential danger to health in food service operations. They have produced many manuals and guides for the use of the food service operator, and have passed statutes and regulations to ensure compliance with sanitation standards.

Why Have a Sanitation Program?

Sanitation can be maintained only by operating personnel who are aware of the potential dangers and committed to carrying out acceptable sanitary procedures. It is the duty of the food service manager to train employees to meet sanitation goals and to ensure that proper practices are being followed.

A satisfactory sanitation program is needed for three kinds of reasons—legal, moral, and economic.

Legal Basis. Sanitation requirements are imposed on all operating establishments and enforced legally by such police powers as food operation permits, health cards, inspections of food establishments, construction regulations, and physical examinations of food handlers.

Most government agencies have constructed some form of health code as a part of their responsibility to protect members of the public who use the food service facilities. With increases in disposable income, more leisure time, and changes in life-style for many segments of the population, greater numbers of people will be partaking of meals away from home; they may require even more protection.

The food service manager is legally bound to carry out certain procedures and to avoid others. He follows these dictates under penalty of fine or imprisonment or both. If he is convicted of poor sanitary practices he may lose his occupational license or food serving permit. He is policed in carrying out these requirements by inspectors who visit his place of business to check on his compliance with current directives.

Sanitation is not only a question of the sanitary code; it is also a part of the common law. The food service operator assumes a certain moral liability when he invites an individual to partake of his menu offerings. This gives rise to a quasi-legal requirement to protect the individual from harm and to warn him of any possible danger.

Moral Basis. Compliance with good sanitary practices should not be just a matter of meeting the letter of the law. Compliance with the law is, of course, necessary and desirable, but a food service operator's moral commitment to his customers is of equal importance.

The host/guest relationship, as practiced for centuries, entails welcoming a person to an inn, hotel, or restaurant as one would to one's own home. Although the "economic man" philosophy is important to the food service operator attempting to realize a profit from an operation, this welcome should do more than result in repeat business.

A deeper moral obligation and relationship with the guest must be felt. Laws or not, moral standards dictate that the guest be given pleasurable and safe dining and protection from harm. The same practices that would be carried out in any home must be applied in larger food operations. Food must be dispensed with the same care that would be exercised if the guest visited the home of the operator.

Economic Basis. Finally, sanitation must be practiced for economic survival. An operation that presents unwholesome food in an unclean atmosphere will not long endure. Some operations appear to belie this statement, ignoring sanitary practices in the interest of expediency. But breaks in sanitary techniques will ultimately cause problems for an offending operator. An episode of food poisoning traced to his establishment might well result in enough bad publicity to cause financial failure for the company and litigation by an affected guest.

Sanitation can also have positive economic effects on an establishment. Sanitation principles that are properly practiced will result in less spoilage of food, greater yields for purchased foods, and, ultimately, a greater profit return to the establishment. Foods that are well wrapped, stored at the correct temperatures, and handled carefully will not spoil as rapidly as foods that are abused. Sanitation, then, is not an additional cost or chore, but rather a means by which greater profits may be realized.

Rarely do these three reasons act independently, nor should they. The food service operator must look at sanitation "as a way of life" and instill in himself and his employees the will and desire to follow acceptable sanitation practices.

Problem Areas

The major problem-causing agent within the control of the food service manager is, of course, the food served in his establishment. Although food may very well become the vehicle for health problems, it is the raison d'etre of the operation, and it cannot be eliminated.

Many factors have been identified as contributing to food-borne illness outbreaks. Ten special areas of concern have been identified in research conducted by the National Restaurant Association. These are of most importance to the food service operator attempting to prevent any incidence of illness related to the operation of his establishment. All ten are conditions that can be controlled within the food facility.

The actual problem agents that may be found in food service establishments are bacteria, natural food poisons, other poisons, parasites, and (in less harmful cases) yeasts and molds. To cause problems for man, these agents must be transmitted to an individual. Transmission may be accomplished in a variety of ways, but food is a common element in the transmission chain.

Bacteria

Bacteria are lower forms of life consisting of single-celled microorganisms, without chlorophyll. Many are only one micron (1/25,000 of an inch) in size. They may be classified as nonpathogenic (not able to cause disease in man), or pathogenic (able to cause disease). Many nonpathogenic types, such as those found in the intestinal tract, are necessary for the proper functioning of the human body, but the pathogenic types can cause very serious problems if they gain entrance to the body.

Dangerous bacteria may be already present in an establishment or introduced by food received from a purveyor. They are most often introduced into food within the establishment by the actions of employees, however.

Bacteria cannot move from place to place by their own power; they need some method of transmission. The most important carriers are (a) man, (b) insects, (c) equipment, and (d) rodents. Once transmitted to a food item, the bacteria may find their way into the body of a consumer.

The body's defense mechanisms, such as the mucous membranes of the nose and throat and the hydrochloric acid of the stomach, assist in overcoming many of the harmful bacteria that are introduced. But if bacteria are introduced in great numbers, or if certain bacterial by-products, such as toxins, are ingested, the body may not be able to overcome them, and distress will result.

The most important bacteria from the standpoint of the food service operation are the staphylococcus, streptococcus, salmonella, clostridium perfringens, clostridium botulinum, and vibro parahemolyticus.

Staphylococcus. Staphylococcus is a pathogenic bacterium identified under a microscope as a long chain of tiny circular "cocci." It may be found in great numbers in infected cuts, pimples, boils, and similar surface skin blemishes. It also appears in many nose and throat cultures taken from individuals suffering from upper respiratory infections.

Staphylococci can produce illness in man in their pure form (if enough of the bacteria are introduced into the host). They become an even greater problem when they are permitted to grow in a food. They then produce a toxin

DON'T SERVE ILLNESS TO OUR CUSTOMERS!

Important Factors Which Lead to Many Foodborne Illness Outbreaks

Prepared by the Public Health and Safety Committee NATIONAL RESTAURANT ASSOCIATION N R A *1530 North Lake Shore Drive, Chicago, Ill. 60610*

1. UNSAFE FOOD HOLDING TEMPERATURES	Examples: Holding prepared, potentially-hazardous foods at room temperature; unsafe refrigeration temperatures; unsafe hot holding temperatures.
2. POOR PERSONAL HYGIENE	Examples: Failure to wash hands before starting work, after using the toilet or after touching any soiled object; wearing soiled aprons and outer garments.
3. CROSS CONTAMINATION	Examples: Cutting raw foods and cooked or ready-to-serve foods on same cutting board without sanitizing between changed use; use of slicers, graters, choppers and grinders for more than one food product without cleaning between changed use; same for cook's knives.
4. UNSANITARY DISHWARE, UTENSILS AND EQUIPMENT	Examples: Improperly cleaned and sanitized tableware, utensils and cutting equipment; failure to protect sanitized ware from contamination.
5. INFECTED FOOD HANDLERS	Examples: Food handlers with infected cuts, burns or sores; boils or pimples; sore throat; nasal discharge or diarrhea.
6. IMPROPER FOOD HANDLING	Examples: Unnecessary use of hands during preparation and serving; thawing of frozen food at room temperature or in warm water.
7. UNSAFE COLD HOLDING AND REHEATING OF DELAYED-USE FOODS AND LEFTOVERS	Examples: Slow cooling and reheating of foods; large mass food storage in large-quantity containers; failure to reheat food to safe serving temperature; use of holding or warming units to reheat food.
8. IMPROPER FOOD STORAGE	Examples: Uncovered foods on refrigerator shelves; raw foods stored directly on shelves or against refrigerator walls; raw foods stored in direct contact with prepared foods.
9. INSECTS AND RODENTS	Examples: Failure to eliminate pest breeding or entry areas; failure to eliminate grime, spilled food and trash which become food, breeding and nesting attractions for pests; failure to report and take control action when pests or evidence of pests are noted.
10. CHEMICALS STORED NEAR FOOD	Examples: Storage of cleaning and sanitizing compounds, solvents, pesticides and other non-food chemicals near food; use of unlabeled containers in kitchen or serving areas.

Figure 10a. A poster listing ten factors important in the transmission of food-borne illness. (Courtesy of the National Restaurant Association, Chicago.)

by-product that is resistant to heat and may cause severe cases of food poisoning.

Streptococcus. Streptococcus is a pathogenic bacterium of the coccus family that appears under the microscope as a tiny chain-like organism. It has many forms, some of which cause such diseases as scarlet fever. Most of the problems it causes in the food area occur because the streptococcus is an airborne microorganism and may be found in nose and throat cultures obtained from both healthy and ill individuals. Streptococci do not produce a toxin, but, if permitted to grow in food, they will cause food poisoning in a person who later ingests the food.

Salmonella. Salmonella is a form of pathogenic bacterium that may be found in the intestinal tract of man. Large numbers are found in raw contaminated meat, poultry, and egg samples. There are many subforms of these bacteria, and, although they do not produce problem toxins, ingestion of the bacteria themselves in large numbers will cause gastro-intestinal illness in humans.

Research in genetic engineering has attempted to construct strains of Salmonella lacking the essential growth genes. Preliminary results in laboratory animals have produced Salmonella bacteria that make the animal immune to harboring other types and may eventually be developed into a vaccine, which could prevent food poisoning in humans. (See *St. Petersburg Times*, "Vaccine May Prevent Food Poisoning," June 28, 1987, p. 4a.)

Clostridium Perfringens. Clostridium perfringens is a soil- or dirt-related bacterium generally found in meats that have been contaminated with dirt. It produces a toxin that can cause food poisoning in a person eating the contaminated product.

Clostridium Botulinum. The least important form of bacterium in food poisoning episodes, but one of the most lethal when it does appear, is the clostridium botulinum, which causes botulism in man. It is also soil- or dirt-related and is spore-protected. It is usually harmless if eaten in its pure form, but, if permitted to develop a toxin in a food product without air (such as a canned food), it may cause vision or breathing problems and even death. The toxin is not heat resistant and may be destroyed by boiling the product for twenty minutes.

Vibro Parahemolyticus. A form of bacteria recently discovered in the United States, in California and New England, that has been prevalent in Japan is the vibro parahemolyticus. It appears that this organism will assume more importance as time goes on. It is found in raw fish and other seafood taken from polluted waters. When ingested, it produces symptoms similar to those of cholera. The bacteria appear to be destroyed by cooking, and thus they are of great concern only in raw products that have been taken from contaminated salt water sources.

Other. Some recently encountered food-borne psychrophilic (cold-loving) bacteria such as *Listeria monocytogenes* and *Yersinia* have been involved in serious outbreaks in milk, ice creams, and soft cheese made from unpasteurized milk. A few deaths have also occurred from *Vibrio vulnificus* bacteria found in raw contaminated oysters. Hepatitis A outbreaks have also happened and are traceable to food handlers who were carriers of the virus and who had served raw or uncooked foods such as salads.

The Mechanics of Bacterial Illness

Most bacteria produce health problems in the same way. Since they are living organisms, they require food, moisture, warmth, and usually air. Whether naturally present or introduced in a food, once there, they find a desirable environment and begin to multiply very rapidly. If they are permitted this process for a sufficient period of time, and if subsequent action is not taken to destroy them by processing the food, large numbers of bacteria will be taken into the body and may cause food poisoning. If the bacteria cause the problem, the illness is referred to as a food infection. If the bacteria are toxin producers, and the toxin causes the problem, the illness is referred to as a food intoxication.

Table 10-1. Food-borne Illness

Name of Illness	Causative Agent	Foods Usually Involved	How Introduced into Food	Preventive or Corrective Procedures
Illnesses of Frequent Occurrence				
Staphylococcus food poisoning	Staphylococcus entero-toxin—a poison developed by staphylococcus when it grows in food	Cooked ham or other meat, chopped or comminuted food, cream-filled or custard pastries, other dairy products, hollandaise sauce, bread pudding, potato salad, chicken salad, fish salad, meat salad, "warmed-over" food	Usually by food handlers through nasal discharges or purulent local skin infections (acne, pimples, boils, scratches, and cuts)	Refrigerate moist foods during storage periods; minimize use of hands in preparation. Exclude unhealthy food handlers (having pimples, boils, and other obvious infections)
Perfringens food poisoning	Clostridium perfringens	Meat that has been boiled, steamed, braised, or partially roasted, allowed to cool several hours, and subsequently served either cooled or reheated	Natural contaminate of meat	Rapidly refrigerate meat between cooking and use
Salmonellosis	Over 800 types of salmonella bacteria, capable of producing gastrointestinal illness	Meat and poultry, comminuted foods, egg products, custards, shellfish, soups, gravies, sauces, "warmed-over" food	By fecal contamination from food handlers, or by raw contaminated meat, poultry, liquid eggs, or unpasteurized milk	Insist on good personal habits by food handlers, and sufficient cooking and refrigeration of perishable foods; eliminate rodents and flies
Salmonellosis (a) typhoid fever (b) paratyphoid A	Salmonella typhosa S. paratyphi A	Moist foods, dairy products, shellfish, raw vegetables, water	By food handlers and other carriers	Prohibit carriers from handling food; require strict personal cleanliness of food preparation; eliminate flies
Illnesses of Less Frequent or Rare Occurrence				
Steptococcus food infection (beta-type scarlet fever and strep throat)	Beta hemolytic streptococci	Foods contaminated by nasal or oral discharges from case or carrier	By coughing, sneezing, or handling by food handlers	Exclude food handlers with known strep infections
Streptococcus infection (alpha-type, intestinal)	Enterococcus group; pyogenic group	Foods contaminated with excreta on unclean hands	By unsanitary food handling	Same as above; thoroughly cook food and refrigerate moist food during storage periods
Botulism	Toxins of Clostridium botulinum	Improperly processed or unrefrigerated foods of low acidity	From soil and dirt; from spores not killed in inadequately heated foods	Pressure-cook canned foods with pH over 4.0; boil home-canned foods for 20 minutes after removal from can or jar; cook foods thoroughly after removing before serving; discard all foods in swollen unopened cans
Bacillary dysentery (shigellosis)	Shigella bacteria	Foods contaminated with excreta on unclean hands	By unsanitary food handling	Enforce strict personal cleanliness in food preparation; refrigerate moist foods; exclude carriers
Amoebic dysentery	Endamoeba histolytica	Foods contaminated with excreta on unclean hands	By unsanitary food handling	Protect water supplies; enforce strict personal cleanliness by food handlers; exclude carriers

Name of Illness	Causative Agent	Foods Usually Involved	How Introduced into Food	Preventive or Corrective Procedures
Trichinosis	Larvae of Trichinella spiralis	Raw or insufficiently cooked pork or pork products	From hogs fed uncooked, infected garbage	Thoroughly cook pork and pork products over 150°, preferably to 160°
Fish tapeworm	Parasitic larvae	Raw or insufficiently cooked fish containing live larvae	Fish infested from contaminated water	Cook fish thoroughly; avoid serving raw fish
Arsenic, fluoride, lead poisoning	Insecticides, rodenticides	Any foods accidentally contaminated	Either during growing period or by accident in kitchen	Thoroughly wash all fresh fruits and vegetables when received; store insecticides and pesticides away from food; properly label containers; follow use instructions; use carefully; guard food from chemical contamination
Copper poisoning	Copper food—contact surfaces	Acid foods and carbonated liquids	By contact between metal and acid foods or carbonated beverages	Prevent acid foods or carbonated liquids from coming into contact with exposed copper
Cadmium and zinc poisoning	Metal plating on food containers	Fruit juices, fruit gelatin, and other acid foods stored in metal-plated containers	By the action of acid foods dissolving cadmium and zinc from containers in which stored	Discontinue use of cadmium-plated utensils as food containers. Prohibit use of zinc-coated utensils for preparation, storage, or serving of acid fruits and other foods or beverages
Cyanide poisoning	Silver polish		By failure to wash and rinse polished silverware thoroughly	Discontinue use of cyanide-based silver polish or wash and rinse silverware thoroughly

Courtesy of the National Restaurant Association, Chicago.

In order for bacteria to cause illness in man, they must be present, be carried through transmission channels, and find the necessary elements for continued existence and/or growth.

The food service manager or supervisor attempting to cope with the possibility of bacterial food poisoning, should approach the problem first from the preventive standpoint and then from the control aspect.

Preventive Actions

Prevention is action taken to keep bacteria from entering an establishment or from coming in contact with food. Although this cannot be accomplished completely, meaningful strides can be taken in this direction. The following specifics are suggested:

(a) Maintain proper housekeeping procedures. Keep areas and equipment in a high state of cleanliness. In addition to being unsightly, dirt collects bacteria. It is also abrasive to equipment and other surfaces. Make sure that proper cleaning procedures are used: (1) the dirt must be penetrated by the wetting action of a cleaning agent, (2) it must be suspended in solution, and (3) it must be rinsed from the item being cleaned. Give particular care to equipment and surfaces used in food preparation work, which may contain pieces of food, stains, or spillage.

Select the proper detergents and provide the proper cleaning tools so that dirt and soil are removed from an item, not just redistributed.

Plan for the accomplishment of housekeeping procedures so that employees know what is to be cleaned, when it is to be cleaned, and how it is to be cleaned. Without such a plan, housekeeping is accomplished only when other "more pressing" tasks are not waiting.

(b) "Build out" flies, roaches, mice, and rats. Search out the possible areas in which these pests gain entrance and multiply.

Flies grow in garbage and animal wastes. They live and breed in all forms of filth, and their presence usually is evidence of poor sanitary practices. Flies' legs have tiny sticky pads that enable them to hold onto smooth surfaces, even when suspended upside down (e.g., from a ceiling). These insects dissolve the food they wish to eat by expectorating internal body fluids on the item before drawing it into their bodies. They often defecate on the food item on which they are resting.

These actions transmit many types of bacteria from the flies' breeding places to the food or surfaces on which they land. Flies have been identified with the transmission of some thirty types of bacteria, notably those causing typhoid, dysentery, and diarrhea.

Although window screens, screen doors, and fan-created air drafts at door openings may prevent the entrance of flies, the best control is the elimination of their breeding areas. All garbage containers should be covered during use and cleaned well after use. Any areas around the establishment that contain filth and debris should be eliminated.

Roaches like to live in dark, damp, and dirty areas. They are found around water pipes, near sinks, and in cracks and crevices that give them protection. They come out for food and water when it is dark. Because of the areas in which they live and the oily condition of their bodies, roaches deposit bacteria on the foods, dishes, and utensils with which they may make contact. They are known to harbor many bacteria in their bodies, notably salmonella.

The best way to eliminate these pests is to fill all cracks and crevices that may harbor them. Food areas should be kept neat and orderly. Materials should be inspected for infestation when they are received. Since roaches need water and food to survive, these should be denied them by the use of good housekeeping procedures.

Mice and rats may also be a major problem in a food service operation. They destroy foods by gnawing, and they may transmit diseases by carrying bacteria on their bodies and in their droppings.

To control these pests, great attention must be paid to construction methods that will deny them access to the establishment and to the elimination of any openings that permit them entrance. Sources of food and nesting places must also be eliminated by proper storage of food and by good housekeeping methods.

Other pests, such as ants, weevils, and silver fish, also sometimes invade food service operations. Each creates special problems and may be combatted by special methods of control.

Although proper housekeeping and sanitary methods are the operator's best defense against all uninvited pests, when evidence of infestation is found, the use of a reputable pest control service is recommended to rid the establishment of them. In some areas of the country, periodic pest-control procedures should be utilized to prevent a pest problem from occurring. In any event, the operator can do much to make any problem that occurs a much less serious one.

(c) Purchase equipment that meets National Sanitation Foundation standards for ease of cleaning and freedom from harmful materials. Establish employee responsibility for specific areas to ensure that adequate cleaning is accomplished, and use follow-up inspections to check results.

The seal of approval of the National Sanitation Foundation on a piece of equipment means that the equipment has been approved for use in food service work, and that materials, construction procedures, and manufacturing methods have all met sanitation requirements. An operator can then be reasonably sure that the equipment is nontoxic, nonabsorbent, corrosion-resistant, and easy to clean. Areas that are difficult to clean and places that may harbor pests have been built out, and the equipment has been made as safe as possible from the sanitation viewpoint.

(d) Hire healthy food service workers and take measures to ensure that they remain that way while working in the establishment.

Require a preliminary health examination for all food handlers, but do not become complacent if employees simply meet blood test and chest X-ray requirements. (Syphilis has rarely been transmitted by a food handler through food.) Be more concerned with the acne sufferer, who may finger purulent blemishes and then introduce bacteria into the food.

It may be possible to search out carriers by routine nasal and anal cultures. (A carrier is an individual who harbors a disease but does not show evidence of its symptoms or effects.) Many cultures may show alpha or beta streptococci in nasal secretions, and occasionally an anal culture may uncover a salmonella carrier. However, this may be an extreme procedure to protect against food-borne infections, and each operator has to determine if the measure is warranted. In some establishments, such as hospitals, it may well be a requirement of the infections committee. In any event, it will be money well spent, if the procedure is feasible.

(e) Institute training programs to instruct workers in the methods of sanitary food handling, and enforce the rules designed to prevent outbreaks of food-borne illness.

Some workers come from socioeconomic backgrounds in which basic sanitary practices have not been followed. It might, therefore, be necessary to stress such factors as the need for frequent baths and the need to wash the hands after using toilet facilities. Habits are difficult to break. Without proper instruction and supervision, a worker will continue to do the things on the job that he routinely does at home. In all instruction, make sure that the workers know the "why" of each rule and procedure presented. They will then be more concerned with its accomplishment.

Provide and require clean uniforms, hair nets, and hats for workers. Provide disposable plastic gloves to be used when hand work on food items cannot be avoided by the use of equipment or tools. If hand washing and cleanliness are stressed (as they should be), make sure that facilities are available.

Arrange a liberal sick leave policy, so that workers will not come to work with head colds, coughs, or sore throats and thereby introduce bacteria into the establishment. A worker who loses a day's pay when he is ill will come to work with a sore throat. The establishment may not lose his day's work, but it loses something that is harder to replace or do without: safe food products.

(f) Use care in the selection of foods. Insofar as possible make sure that foods purchased are free from potentially dangerous organisms. Utilize the facilities of federal, state, and local inspection agencies to ensure receipt of quality food.

Check on the temperatures of foods received (where applicable), and packing and wrapping procedures. Be sure that potentially dangerous foods come from approved sources. (For example, oysters must come from approved beds, with no possibility of raw sewage contamination. A number of cases of hepatitis have been traced to oysters eaten raw that contained sewage contaminants.)

Buy only from reputable dealers, and learn the sanitary standards and philosophy practiced by these purveyors.

In addition to using government inspection systems, make sure that workers responsible for the selection and receipt of food stay alert to possible sanitation problems in the handling of food. There just are not enough government inspectors to catch every sanitation problem that can appear.

(g) Give adequate attention to storage procedures. Raw or processed foods held in storage awaiting service, reconstitution, or further processing must be adequately protected against possible contamination. Protect against flies, roaches, rodents, and possible contamination by sewage backup or overflow.

Provide the proper conditions for the storage of all fresh and processed foods, and inspect canned foods for "springers," "leakers," and "flippers," which may indicate internal bacterial contamination or decay.

Since we live in the real world, it is never possible to prevent the introduction of all problem bacteria into the food we purchase. Therefore, institute a program to ensure that the proper temperatures are being maintained to prevent bacterial growth in products that may have minimal contamination.

Sanitation Certification Programs

Prodded by governmental regulatory bodies and consumer-oriented groups and acting in a spirit of cooperation, a number of industry groups under the leadership of the National Institute for the Food Service Industry (NIFI) have developed a course in the essential principles and practices of safe food handling. The course meets the basic standards of the federal regulations on training managers in the food service industry, and it has also been certified as meeting the requirements of all states currently having mandatory sanitation training requirements.

As seen in Figure 10b, most states have shown some concern for the training of employees in sanitation. All supervisors should insure that these requirements are either met or exceeded.

Control Actions

Bacterial Growth. Even if all preventive measures have been enforced, minor amounts of pathogenic bacterial contaminants may still remain, since we do not operate in a sterile environment. Realizing this, the food service manager must then set up control procedures to ensure that potentially dangerous bacteria that are naturally present in the food or have been later introduced are either kept at a safe level or destroyed.

As fire needs fuel, heat, and air to exist, bacteria need food, moisture, heat, and often air to exist. To extinguish a fire we need only remove one part of the requirement triangle. If we remove the fuel it will go out; if we reduce the heat below the combustion temperature of the fuel by pouring water on it, it will stop; or if we keep oxygen out by smothering it with a layer of foam or dirt, it will expire.

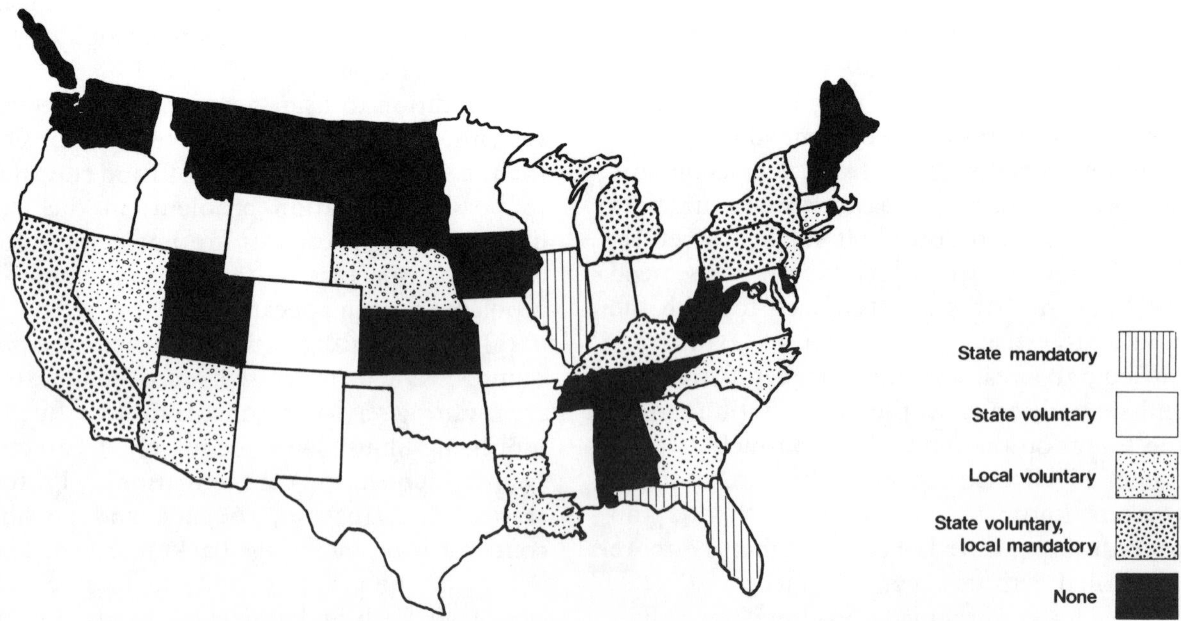

Figure 10b. Sanitation Training Today. (From Charles H. Sander, "Sanitation Training and Certification," *Cornell Hotel and Restaurant Administration Quarterly*, May 1978, p. 25; reprinted by permission.)

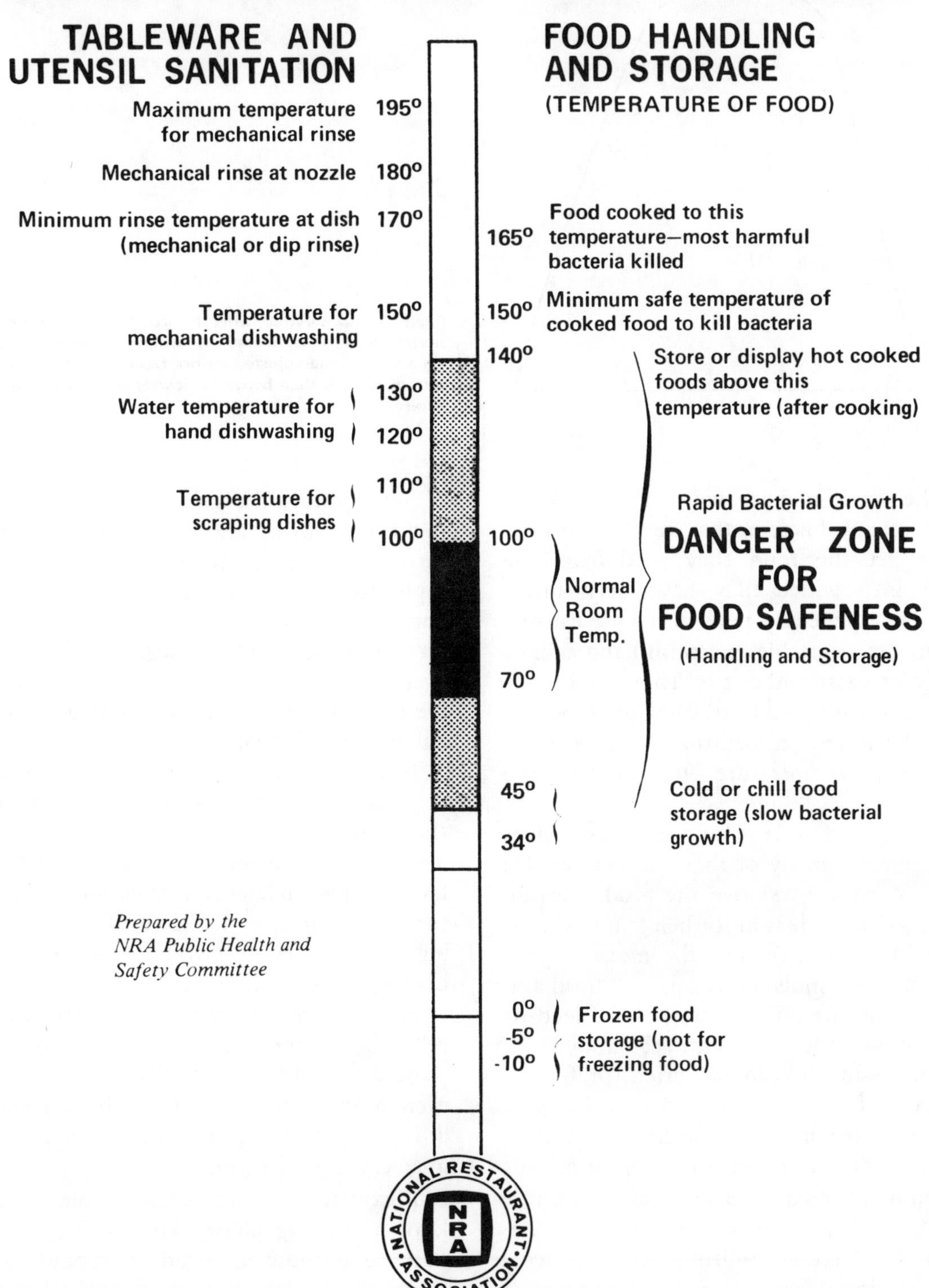

Figure 10c. A poster showing the important temperatures for sanitation (Courtesy of the National Restaurant Association, Chicago.)

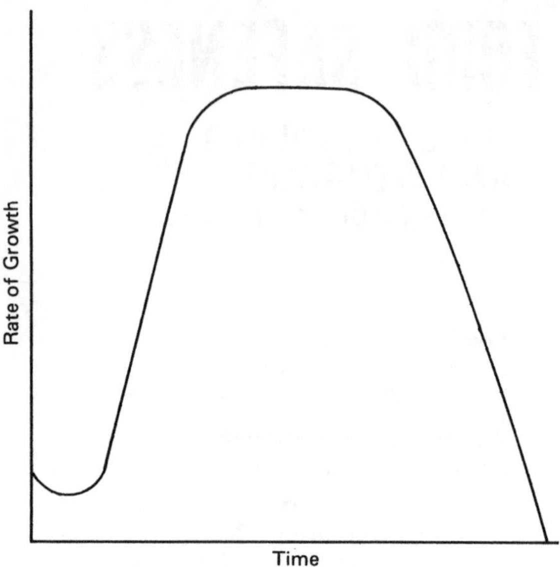

Figure 10d. A curve showing the growth rate of bacteria under normal conditions. Bacteria entering a new environment need time to become adjusted before rapid growth develops. The rate of growth then becomes slower, and finally the bacteria expire.

In the same manner we can control the activity of any bacteria that may be present. Bacteria get the food they need from the product into which they have been introduced. They generally need air (those causing botulism are a notable exception) and cannot multiply or exist without it. They need moisture in most cases and heat. They grow best in 50- to 140-degree temperatures (the closer to human body temperature—98.6 degrees—the better).

To control bacteria, a food service manager cannot remove many of these necessities. He cannot, of course, remove the food, because having food is his reason for being in business. He usually cannot remove the moisture and the air, because moisture is a part of food and air is part of the atmosphere people need to live. (However, these elements are removed by food processing in canned, dried, or freeze-dried products.)

The one area in which demonstrable control action may be taken is temperature. This has been mentioned in terms of storage, but it is even more important in the control of contaminants. Bacteria multiply in a process known as binary fission: each single organism splits in half, making two bacteria; each of these then further subdivides into two others. If temperatures, food types, humidity, pH (acidity), time, and other conditions are favorable, the bacteria multiply at a very rapid rate. For example, at 100 degrees Fahrenheit, bacteria double in number every fifteen minutes; at 50 degrees, they double every fifteen hours; at 36 degrees, they double every fifteen days; and at 0 degrees, most bacteria are dormant.

It is thus possible for a single bacterium, deposited in a favorable food item and under the correct conditions, to become many hundreds of bacteria in a relatively brief time. In fact a single bacterium, dividing itself every fifteen minutes, with the resulting cells dividing in a like manner, would produce 1 million bacteria within five hours.

Since bacteria rarely are deposited as single cells, but rather hundreds of them are deposited at a time, this multiplication becomes even more staggering. Under the correct conditions, bacteria can become a major problem in a very short period.

Fortunately, most bacteria have what is known as a lag phase. This is the time they take to become adjusted to a new environment, during which little growth takes place. The lag phase varies with the type of bacteria and the condition under which they were

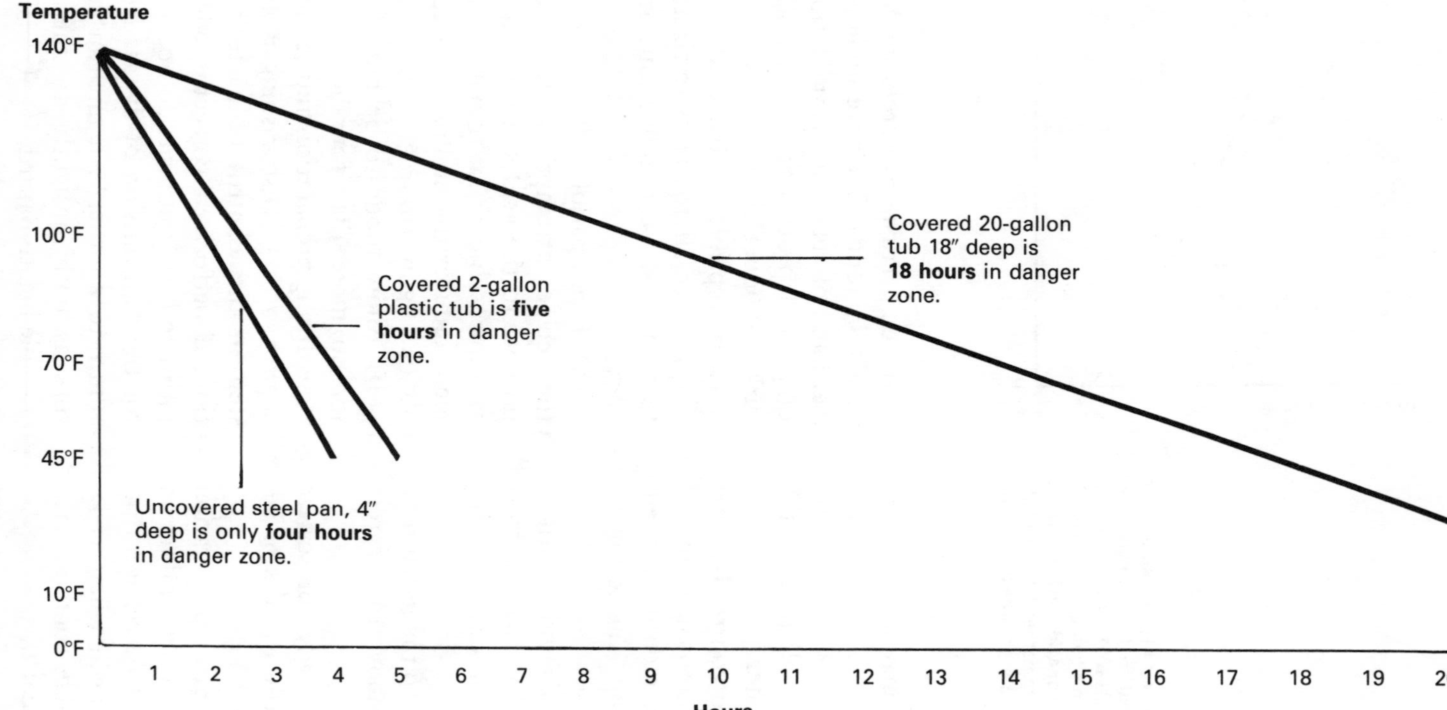

Figure 10e. Time needed to cool differing containers to safe temperatures. Blast freezer models can cool heavy loads of food down to 33 to 37 degrees in 90 minutes or less whereas a standard refrigerator may take 12 to 14 hours to reduce the volume of a high density of food to the same temperature range. (Source: *NRA News*, June/July 1986, p. 33.)

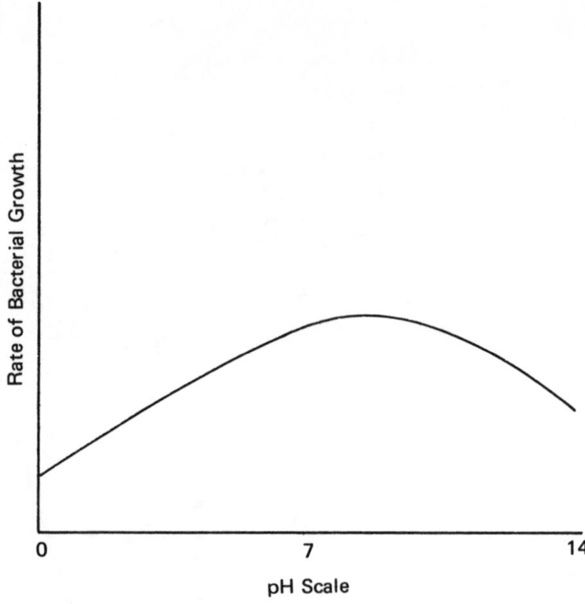

Figure 10f. **The pH scale indicates the acidity or alkalinity of a food, ranging from 0 (strongly acid) to 14 (strongly alkaline). Neutral foods (those having a pH of 7) or those on the alkaline side of the scale usually permit bacterial growth, as most pathogenic bacteria prefer nonacid environments. Limes, lemons, vinegar, peaches, and tomatoes fall in the pH range from 2.0 to 4.6; meat, fish, and eggs, which are good growth sources, range from 5.7 to 7.2.**

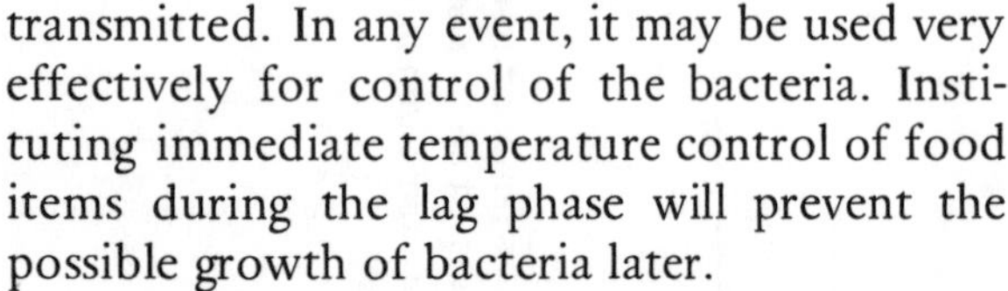

transmitted. In any event, it may be used very effectively for control of the bacteria. Instituting immediate temperature control of food items during the lag phase will prevent the possible growth of bacteria later.

The only effective way to control bacteria and their growth is to maintain a time and temperature relationship that destroys them or inhibits their reproduction. The following suggestions are made:

(a) If possible, defrost foods under refrigerated conditions. At the very least, defrost them quickly using a fan or in clean running water.

(b) If possible, heat foods to the lethal temperature for most bacteria (above 140 degrees Fahrenheit).

(c) Keep foods that are ready for service either hot or cold (above 140 degrees or below 45 degrees).

(d) Refrigerate all foods after preparation and during waiting or down times. It does no harm to put hot food in a cold refrigerator. Some cream soups tend to curdle when refrigerated; putting them in smaller containers for more rapid cooling will prevent this.

(e) Ensure that all masses of food are kept in containers that will effect maximum cooling in the shortest period of time.

(f) Be particularly careful with high-protein foods, or foods that have undergone substantial hand or machine manipulations. Chopped or ground protein foods, such as hamburger, turkey croquettes, and egg salads, are particularly susceptible to bacterial contamination.

(g) Cover all foods in refrigerators to protect against contamination from shelves above.

(h) If compatible with the food type and the recipe, attempt to bring the pH of a product to the acid side by adding such items as apples, vinegar, or tomatoes. This environment reduces the ability of bacteria to multiply (see figure 10f).

(i) Allow foods to be out of refrigeration for no more than four hours of cumulative time during preparation and service.

Dishwashing. Dishwashing is an important step in the control of bacteria. This function, if performed correctly, will ensure that intimate eating utensils do not become agents for the transmission of disease from one consumer to another. An unclean cup, glass, or fork is both unsightly to the guest and a possible health hazard.

Proper dishwashing requires equipment capable of carrying out the task, enough hot water, a layout of the facilities that protects dishes from reinfection after being washed, and trained operators who know what has to be done in the process.

Prescrapping the dishes, prerinsing them at 140 degrees Fahrenheit, and a final rinse at 180 degrees will ensure sanitary dishes, silver, and other utensils. The time relationship between the wash and the rinse cycles and the length of time dishes are exposed to each of these procedures are important to the effectiveness of the equipment and of the washing procedure.

Improperly washed dishes will, of course, result in customer dissatisfaction and give the impression that other sanitary methods are not being followed in the establishment. Good food preparation and excellent service may well be negated by exposing a consumer to unclean utensils. But more than this, disease may be transmitted through these intimate utensils.

Soiled dishes may usually be traced to one of the following causes: the amount of detergent is insufficient, the water temperatures are too low, the dishes are racked incorrectly, the wash and rinse times are inadequate, or the precleaning is not being done properly. Each of these causes must be traced if the sanitation break is to be corrected and dirty dishes prevented.

The amount of detergent may be insufficient if the wrong type of detergent is being used or if the facility has hard water, which uses up detergent in water softening. Food that is being passed into the wash tanks of the machine may be diluting the detergent. Too low a level of detergent in manually operated machines indicates that more is needed.

Low water temperatures are usually caused by insufficient heating capacities on booster heaters or hot water heaters to provide enough water at high temperatures for both dishwashing and other uses in the establishment.

Improper racking of dishes by poorly trained personnel prevents the spray from hitting the dishes in the designed manner so that the mechanical action of cleaning is lost. Some dishes are shielded from the spray and never receive adequate cleaning or rinsing.

Wash and rinse times, in terms of the amount of water that passes over a dish in the machine, are expressed in heat unit equivalents (HUEs). Stopped-up heads on spray arms or scrapping trays of the machine may prevent delivery of water in the correct amount for the correct period of time. Temperature capacities of heaters and pump performance may also be factors in this problem area.

Dishes may enter the machine improperly precleaned because of poor performance by workers or the lack of a satisfactory method or device for scrapping them to remove the bulk of the food soil. Excessive amounts of refuse may foul spray heads, cause detergent waste, and make the machine operate inefficiently.

Poisons

Poisons in foods may be natural or induced. The natural poisons are few in number and are usually well enough known to be avoided by the person responsible for purchasing. Examples of natural poisons are those found in water hemlock (which may be mistaken for horseradish) and toadstools (mistaken for mushrooms). Some mussels contain an alkaloidal poison, and rhubarb leaves have a high oxalic acid content, which is poisonous.

Induced poisons, however, are quite another matter. If care is not taken in the storage of cleaning materials, the marking of poisons, and the use of materials in equipment construction, poisonous substances may be introduced into previously safe foods. The following suggestions are made to ensure maximum safety:

(a) Keep only poisons that are absolutely necessary for sanitation purposes in the establishment.

(b) Label all poisons properly, and store them in a separate room away from the preparation, storage, and service areas for foods.

(c) After spraying, dusting, or other insect-

or rodent-control measures have been taken, wash all surfaces and equipment exposed to the procedure before using them.

(d) Label all bulk food containers properly to prevent errors in use. Seemingly innocuous salt was mistaken for sugar and used in formulas for infants in a hospital; it became an induced poison and caused the death of a number of infants.

A recent problem area has been the potential introduction of drug residues from animals to consumers who eat the contaminated meat. This could cause allergic reactions or anaphylactic shock in susceptible individuals.

Four out of every five food-type animals receive some sort of drug, either for growth or to prevent or cure disease. These drugs are usually some type of antibiotic. Many of these drugs remain as residues in the animal where they are passed on to the consumer, or else the drugs mutate bacteria in the animal that are then passed on to the new host—the consumer. This new bacteria form is then able to resist the actions of some antibiotics that previously were able to control the original form of the disease bacteria.

Penicillin and tetracycline are the antibiotics most widely used in animals, and they are known to result in allergic reactions in some individuals. In fact, in 1985 the FDA petitioned the Secretary of Health and Human Services to forbid the use of these drugs in animals, but the request was denied. Drugs such as DES (diethylstibestrol), a growth aid for animals that was also found to pass on to humans in the meat of animals, was banned by the federal government in 1979. As noted, sulfites in raw fruits and vegetables were banned by the FDA in August 1986, and labels were required on all prepared foods with concentrations over 10 parts per million as of January 1987.

Parasites and Other Minor Offending Agents

Parasites, such as Trichinella spiralis in contaminated pork products or the beef or fish tapeworms found in some food samples, may generally be controlled by proper purchasing and adequate cooking temperatures.

Many states require that all garbage fed to hogs be cooked. These regulations plus the practice of freezing many pork products for storage have reduced the trichinosis problem. Adequate cooking techniques for pork particularly, and the avoidance of raw forms of food, such as steak tartare and Oriental raw fish dishes, will prevent problems with these vectors. Of course the recently approved irradiation of pork products (1985) is also a control device to reduce the incidence of *Trichinella spiralis*.

Disposing of sewage in landfills has also begun to cause new parasite problems as this environment serves as a good media for the eggs of *Ascaris*. Later these could find their way, by the movement of groundwaters or later reclamation of the area, onto the leaves of fresh vegetables.

Yeasts and molds may cause minor problems in foods. Although they may invade particular forms and cause chemical changes that make the food unfit for use or unpalatable, they cannot be considered as causative agents of food poisoning.

No discussion of food poisoning would be complete without considering ptomaines. "Ptomaine poisoning" has become synonymous with food poisoning. Yet it is very unlikely that anyone has actually been poisoned by ptomaines. They are one of the final by-products of decayed organic matter. By the time these substances develop, the food has lost most of its original form and produces a pungent and disagreeable odor. A consumer would be very reluctant to approach the item, let alone eat it.

Metals such as cadmium, zinc, and copper may also be considered poisons. If attention is paid to equipment purchasing and use, few problems will arise with these metals. None of them should be used with acid foods. Galvanized equipment contains zinc and should therefore also be kept away from acids.

When aluminum was first introduced in food preparation work, some considered it a potentially dangerous metal to use with foods. Subsequent study has shown it to be safe in all food uses, however.

Many people assume that viral or other unrelated abdominal illnesses occur in association with particular forms of food. They may even accuse an operator of unsanitary procedures, particularly if the food they ate was one with a long history of illness associations (such as turkey and dressing). Liability insurance offers an important protection to the food operator in these situations. Some facilities take a sample portion of each item being served and keep it in a soufflé cup in the freezer for a period of three days, on a rotating basis, in case a food poisoning incident is alleged. If an establishment is accused of causing a health problem, the frozen sample of the suspect food can then be tested by a laboratory to determine whether it bears a cause-effect relationship to the illness. This system has been used for many years in institutions, particularly those under government control, that serve captive groups of consumers. When residents become ill, a particular food is often suspected of causing food poisoning.

The operator of a private establishment may not consider this safeguard merited in light of financial and logistical considerations. It is, however, a very effective protection against lawsuits based on alleged sanitation breaks, when the cause of an episode of vomiting or other abdominal distress might well have been a viral disease transmitted by air. It remains for the particular operator to determine if this procedure is warranted in his establishment.

Sanitation Instructions for Workers

Food workers should be instructed on a continuing basis in the following specific sanitation practices. The reasons for required actions should be given, so that better compliance will be realized.

1. Use food only from known sources and buy only from reputable dealers to ensure that food is safe and not grossly contaminated.

2. Wash hands before handling foods, after handling raw foods, and before handling ready-to-serve foods. Wash hands after using bathroom, or when hands are grossly soiled. This is done to prevent the transmission of bacteria to foods from the hands, from other substances, or from objects that have been touched by the hands.

3. Destroy all leaking, bulging, or corroded cans of food, because the food inside may be spoiled and cause illness in anyone who eats it.

4. Wash and sanitize all surfaces, equipment, and utensils that will come in contact with food or have been in contact with food, to prevent bacteria from being introduced into wholesome food.

5. Hold all foods at temperatures below 45 degrees or above 140 degrees except when actually preparing them. Bacteria will not multiply if food is held at these temperatures.

6. Cool all leftover hot food rapidly by placing it in refrigerators in shallow containers. Masses of hot food will take long periods to cool and may be at dangerous temperatures for too long a time if shallow containers are not used.

7. Keep all food service areas clean and neat. Dirt collects bacteria and may be a source of food contamination.

8. Do not intermix raw and ready-to-serve foods for storage or processing. Bacteria from raw foods may contaminate ready-to-serve foods that will not be heated again to kill bacteria.

9. Defrost at refrigerator temperatures. Defrosting at room temperatures, particularly for long periods of time, permits bacteria to multiply.

10. Handle dishes, glasses, and eating utensils by surfaces that will not be used for food or placed in the mouths of guests. Fingers may transmit bacteria to guests via tableware.

11. Cover all foods in refrigerators. Uncovered foods on lower shelves may be contaminated from above.

12. Do not smoke in food preparation areas or while handling foods. Fingers that touch the cigarette, pipe, or cigar, will probably

transmit saliva from the lips to the food being processed and thus introduce bacteria.

13. Use tools or utensils rather than hands for handling foods. If foods must be touched use disposable plastic gloves. This prevents the introduction of bacteria, since utensils and tools can be washed and sanitized more thoroughly than hands.

14. Dispose of all garbage and waste properly and keep it covered until pickup. This prevents the harboring of rodents and insects.

15. Do not taste foods with fingers or reintroduce the tasting spoon into a food after it has been tasted. This prevents the introduction of bacteria from either the hands or the mouth.

16. Store all foods at correct temperatures: dry, 50 to 70 degrees; frozen, zero or below; chilled, 45 or below. This prevents bacteria from multiplying and prevents foods from spoiling.

17. Treat dried or frozen eggs and dried milk as fresh after reconstitution, to prevent bacteria from multiplying. When water is added, these products are as dangerous a source for bacterial growth as fresh ones.

18. Be particularly careful of foods that are protein in nature or that contain eggs, or milk. These foods are more susceptible to contamination from any bacteria that may be present because bacteria thrive on them.

19. Inspect dishes, glasses, and other customer utensils for cracks and chips, and remove those that are defective. These areas not only are unsightly but also can harbor bacteria.

20. When in doubt, *throw it out.* Taking a chance with a suspect food that does not look, smell, or taste right is a dangerous practice. If proper procedures are followed, few foods will fall in this category, but when one does it is better not to take risks. After careful examination by a supervisor, if doubt still exists, the food should be destroyed.

Safety

Safety is related to sanitation and is also of great importance to the food service manager or supervisor. A program that will prevent injury to workers and guests must stress safety as a way of life. With passage of the Occupational Safety and Health Act, which covers every "workplace or environment where work is performed," the subject assumes even greater importance. The act requires the maintenance of safety records, the filing of safety reports, and strict adherence to good safety practices. Possible penalties for violations of the law range up to $10,000 fine and/or six months in jail. The act went into effect on April 28, 1971, and during its first six months, over 5,000 citations of safety violations were issued under its provisions, with penalties totaling more than $300,000. The regulating agency is attempting to branch out into jurisdiction over environmental conditions in workers' shower, locker, and dressing areas. It is thus imperative for managers and supervisors to keep up to date on the provisions of this law and to ensure that safety violations do not occur.

The posting of bulletins of advice for employees and the visitation of Occupational Safety and Health Act inspectors both are designed to help eliminate safety hazards and produce a safer work environment for employees.

Safety is of equal importance to management and workers. Both have an interest in preventing injuries and accidents, and both benefit from achieving this aim. The food service manager is responsible for instituting a program that will prevent these incidents and will train workers in good safety practices.

For many years the food service industry has had a poor safety record. The work uses many pieces of equipment and tools that can cause cuts and abrasions, and workers were in the past required to do much hand work. The steam, electricity, and gas used in food service facilities are potentially dangerous sources of burns, explosions, and accidental shocks to employees. Foods served at extremely high temperatures present a danger to both employees and guests. In addition, sanitation requirements dictated the use of building materials that were impervious to moisture, stain resistant, and easy to clean. Tiles and other materials that were often used are both tiring to stand on and slippery when wet.

An accidental injury to a guest may result in litigation against the food service operation and a monetary judgment against it. At the very least, it creates bad publicity for the facility and discomfort for the guest.

An accident to an employee or supervisor causes the loss of his services for a period of time. The employee may suffer a loss or reduction in wages in addition to his pain. The facility may be required to pay a higher workmen's compensation insurance premium because of an increase in the number of accidents.

Comprehensive liability and workmen's compensation insurance can, of course, shift the burdens of financial loss due to accidents or injuries. However, management must take positive steps to control safety in the food service and preparation areas.

Choking, Fainting, Heart Attacks, and So On. Although public facilities with the numbers and types of guests restaurants have are bound to experience some of these physical crises, the operation must be very careful to get expert legal advice before designing any plan or undertaking any type of training due to the potential legal ramifications. Of course, the Heimlich maneuver and CPR procedures (cardio-pulmonary resuscitation) are very effective in controlling two of these serious episodes. In fact, in certain localities someone in every licensed establishment must be trained in these procedures. But since there is the possibility of damage to the "patient" and the possibility of litigation even under conditions of offering humanitarian assistance, it is wise to seek legal advice. Where permission has been given, or is required, a professional should be used to train employees and/or supervisors.

General Safety Measures. The following safety suggestions relate to the prevention of all kinds of accidents:

(1) Hire workers who do not demonstrate a poor safety history. Some people appear to be accident-prone—they experience more than the average share of accidents.

(2) Provide safe work areas. This means constant inspection and attention to details that may cause safety problems.

(3) Furnish equipment and tools that are as safe as possible. Post all operating instructions to make sure that safety practices can be followed.

(4) Publish operational rules that incorporate safety features into the everyday procedures for preparing and serving products.

(5) Train workers in good safety procedures, and attempt to motivate them to work safely for the mutual benefit of themselves and the company.

(6) Investigate all accidents that do occur, and try to fix responsibility so that immediate corrective action may be taken.

(7) Conduct safety meetings and maintain safety records for periodic review. Conduct a safety award program for employees, if possible.

Falls. Falls are the number one problem in food service operations. They usually are related to either unsatisfactory lighting or a slippery, wet, or obstructed floor.

The following suggestions are designed to reduce these accidents:

(1) Use wooden duck boards or nonabrasive strips on hard-surfaced floors.

(2) Require employees to wear proper shoes, not those with leather heels or other slippery surfaces.

(3) Wipe up all spills of liquids, foods, grease, etc., immediately.

(4) Do not put items on the floor for storage even for a short period of time.

(5) Keep electric cords from crossing traffic aisles to remote outlets.

(6) Discourage employees from running, walking quickly, or engaging in horseplay.

(7) Provide handrails on stairways.

(8) Provide adequate lighting in all work areas and stairwells.

(9) Do not permit arm carrying of plates; require a tray or cart for service.

(10) Watch possible problem areas, such as the floor around the ice machine, where water may cause slipping.

Cuts and Bruises. Cuts and bruises are another common problem for the food service operator. They are usually related to equipment or utilities and may be prevented or reduced if proper precautions are taken:

(1) Post the operation regulations for all equipment, and require strict observance of them.

(2) Keep all knives sharp, and use the proper knife for the job. Dull knives require more pressure than sharp ones and cause more cuts.

(3) Use cutting board surfaces for cutting items. Hold materials to be cut in ways that avoid finger injury. Slice a portion from the bottom of an unstable item to enable a better hold during cutting.

(4) Keep side towels available so that workers can keep their hands and utensils free from grease. If a knife or implement falls, step back and allow it to hit floor. Attempts to catch a falling knife usually result in grabbing the sharp blade.

(5) When carrying knives from station to station, always keep the knife tip pointed at the floor.

(6) Cut away from the body when using cutting implements.

(7) Use tampers to push food into choppers and grinding machines.

(8) Do not place knives or cutting blades from equipment in pot sinks filled with water. Wash these items at once.

Burns. By the very nature of the work being done in a food service establishment, burns present a serious hazard. The following suggestions are made to prevent them:

(1) Require preparation employees to wear well-fitting uniforms with long sleeves.

(2) Keep dry potholders available for use.

(3) Position potentially dangerous equipment correctly. For example, trunnion kettles should pour laterally, not toward the worker.

(4) Keep handles of pots and pans turned in from the edge of the range so that they are not hit, causing spillage.

(5) Never overfill a container with hot food. Allow enough freeboard to accommodate splashing and prevent spillage.

(6) In case of a minor burn or scald, put the injured part under cold water or apply ice immediately to prevent blistering and pain.

Strains. The lifting of heavy or cumbersome objects can cause injury to employees. The following are good lifting practices:

(1) Lift with the heavy muscles of the legs so that strains are not taken on the back. Bend the knees, and push while lifting.

(2) Arrange equipment properly so that extremely heavy loads do not have to be lifted.

(3) Set weight limits, and require team lifting when necessary.

Explosions and Electric Shocks. Both the equipment and the products used in a facility may cause explosions or shocks. The following suggestions are made to prevent these problems:

(1) Be sure that all electrical equipment is grounded.

(2) Protect all gas equipment against explosion with gas cutoff devices that are activated at pilot light failure.

(3) Vent all gas equipment before lighting.

(4) Never work near electrical equipment with wet hands or while standing on wet floor surfaces.

(5) Use only equipment approved by the Underwriters Laboratory and the American Gas Association.

(6) Unplug all electric equipment before attempting to clean or adjust it.

(7) Keep covers near deep fat fryers.

Fires

Fires are a constant potential danger in food service operations. Employees must be familiar with possible sources and kinds of fire, the locations of fire extinguishers, and the actions to take if fire breaks out. A fire blanket should be kept near dangerous areas.

Fires are classified as follows: Class A, normal combustible materials; Class B, grease and oil; Class C, electrical; and Class D, burning metal (this last is unlikely in food service work). Class B and Class C fires are of most concern to the food service operator, because of the equipment and materials used and the work done in his facility. If proper housekeeping is practiced and materials such as boxes and paper are disposed of, Class A fires will be kept to a minimum.

In attacking a fire, the first few minutes are the most important, and the action taken then may well save the establishment. The goal is to remove either the fuel, the heat, or the oxygen. Class B and Class C fires generally require removal of the oxygen, while a Class A fire may also be combatted by removing the heat or the fuel.

Some newer forms of Halogenated noncorrosive, nontoxic extinguishers, which contain hydrocarbons in which one or more hydrogen atoms is replaced with Halogen atoms such as iodine, bromine, flourine, etc., are also excellent and might be considered for use in food service areas. Operating by removing the chemicals necessary for the flame chain reaction, they vaporize, are odorless, colorless, and nonconductive, and leave no residue.

Although various types of extinguishers are available, the best all-purpose model for a food preparation area is considered to be the CO_2 type, which can be used to fight all three types of fires. It emits a carbon dioxide gas that smothers fires, does not conduct electricity, is extremely cold, lowers the heat level, and does not damage food or equipment. Most other types of extinguishers, such as water, soda acid, and foam, can be used on only one type of fire, and some are dangerous when used near certain types of equipment or materials, such as grease.

Sizzle pans, broilers, deep fat fryers, and ranges appear to be the most common sources of fires. Fire protection of venting hoods with carbon dioxide or steam outlets, and periodic cleaning and fireproofing of these pieces of equipment might be well advised, to protect the establishment and to reduce fire insurance premiums. Keeping a container of baking soda relatively accessible to the cook will enable him to put out a minor grease fire on the range top or in the broiler. A container of salt is a second choice for attacking these fires.

The following procedure is suggested in fighting a kitchen fire:

(1) Turn off the equipment, and cover it, if possible. Remove the source of fuel if possible.

(2) Sound the alarm.

(3) Using the extinguisher, spray CO_2 directly on the fire.

11 *Beverage Management and Service*

Objective: To detail the history and classifications of wine, beer, distilled spirits and describe the manufacture of each. To acquaint the student with systems of beverage control and service, including purchasing, receiving, storage, and issuing as well as cash control and merchandising.

History of Alcoholic Beverages

Wine. Wine probably dates from prehistoric times when a cave dweller accidently left some crushed grapes behind. During his absence natural fermentation occurred, and fermented grape juice or wine was the result. Archaeologists maintain that grape wine was made 10,000 years ago, and it is possible that honey was fermented even earlier. Date and palm wine may have preceded grape wine. The Bible mentions wine frequently in both the Old Testament and the New Testament.

There are indications that the grapevine was cultivated about 6000 B.C. in Mesopotamia and Asia. By 3000 B.C. the vine was being cultivated in Egypt and Phoenicia, and there is some evidence of wine in China at about the same period. The art of making wine reached Greece by 2000 B.C., and the Greeks were probably the first to practice the aging of wines. They stored them in airtight clay cylinders called amphoras. Wine will age and improve under these conditions. The secret of aging wine was later lost, and some 1,500 years passed before the bottle and cork were used for the same purpose.

At about 1000 B.C. grapes were cultivated in Sicily and North Africa. During the next 500 years, the grapevine reached Spain, Portugal, the south of France, and probably southern Russia as well. Finally, with the advance of the Roman Empire, the vine spread into northern Europe and Britain. After the fall of the Roman Empire and through the early Middle Ages, the Church was the prime mover in viticulture due to its need for wine as both sacrament and sustenance. The Church led the way in both wine producing knowledge and methods. Meanwhile, in the Middle East, the Moslem religion predominated and wine consumption ceased. During this time in history wines were consumed very young and probably tasted acrid and crude by our standards, but they were made palatable by the addition of spices and honey.

When William of Orange came to power, England put high duties on French wines in order to punish France, but Portuguese wines were imported cheaply. About 1715 the Portuguese began fortifying their wines, and port dates from that time. The Portuguese were the first to ship corked bottles, a modern equivalent of the amphora. This allowed harsh wines to ripen and soften, thus ushering in the modern age of wines. By 1800 port was the most popular wine in England, and by the late 1800s, the vine had attained great economic importance in Europe. In fact, it was estimated that in Italy in 1880 about 80 percent of the population relied in part on the wine business for a living.

Distilled Spirits. The art of distillation was known in the ancient world, and it is recorded that the Chinese produced a distilled spirit from rice beer. Arak has been produced from sugarcane and rice in the East Indies since 800 B.C., and when Captain Cook took his voyages to the South Pacific, he found the natives there familiar with the distillation process.

The modern history of the distillation of alcohol dates from the Arabs (or Saracens) during the time of the early Middle Ages.

Table 11-1. Classification of Alcoholic Beverages

Fermented	Fermented and distilled	Compounded spirits
Grapes	Grain	Gin
Wines	Whiskey (also whisky)	
Appetizer	Rye	Liqueurs or cordials
Table	Bourbon	
Fortified	Blend	
Sparkling	Irish	
	Canadian	
Other fruits	Scotch	
Wines	Vodka	
Grain	Sugarcane and molasses	
Beer	Rum	
Ale		
Stout	Agave	
Porter	Tequila	
Sake		
	Fruit brandies	
Miscellaneous	Grape	
Pulque	Cognac	
Kava	Armagnac	
	California brandy	
	Spanish brandy	
	Greek brandy	
	German brandy	
	Apple	
	Calvados	
	Cherry	
	Kirsch	
	Plum	
	Mirabelle	
	Quetsch	
	Slivowitz	
	Apricot	
	Raspberry	
	Framboise	
	Strawberry	

Definitions

Beer—a liquor fermented from cereals and malt, flavored with hops.

Distilled spirits—potable alcoholic beverages obtained from the distillation of alcohol-containing liquids.

Wine—naturally fermented juice of ripe grapes or any fruit other than grapes. Wine not made from grapes must be clearly labeled, for example, apple wine, cherry wine. The term *wine* legally means grape wine.

From the Arabs we also gained the words *alcohol* and *still*. In 1800 rectification (or redistillation) was discovered. The importance of this technique is that it produced a much cleaner and more nearly pure spirit than had previously been possible. This new process produced a rather neutral spirit that could be enhanced by adding herbs and fruits, whereas previously these had been used to mask impurities. Some of the great liqueur formulas were developed in this way.

A grain spirit called whiskey was being produced during the Middle Ages in Scotland and Ireland. Cognac brandy appears to have been well established in England by 1688, which means of course that the distillation of wine into brandy had been going on for some time in France. Distillation was known in America from the time of the earliest settlers, and it was natural that the distinctive American spirit was a grain product—bourbon. In the early days, a distillery was always located near a suitable water supply. The best water came from soil with a limestone subsurface, like those in Kentucky and other areas with similar soil and water.

Beer. The origins of beer go back nearly as far as those of wine, and some form of beer has been made by almost all people at all levels of civilization. Beer was the forerunner of whiskey, and it has been made from whatever was available. In Africa, beer was made from millet; in Japan, from rice; and in Europe and North and South America, from barley.

Beer and winemaking are closely related, historically as well as from a processing standpoint; they both rely upon fermentation to produce alcohol. In beer making the carbon dioxide is retained, and the grain starch must be converted to simple sugars so the yeasts can act upon them. Beer and wine are both antecedents of distilled spirits.

Fermentation and Distillation

Fermentation. The chemical processes of fermentation do not need to be understood, but the result of fermentations does. Sugar is transformed into ethyl alcohol and CO_2. The CO_2 escapes and the alcohol remains. In spirits such as whiskey, this alcohol is distilled (or separated) from the liquid resulting from fermentation. Fermentation is caused by a living organism called yeast. Many yeasts are known and most will cause fermentation, but the nature of the finished product varies considerably according to the yeast used.

Specific yeasts are native to the great wine regions of the world and contribute significantly to the distinctiveness of the wines. In spirit and beer production, and increasingly in winemaking, the strains of yeast used are carefully controlled. Producers frequently culture their own yeast as evidenced by the fact that Anheuser-Busch, the nation's largest beer producer, is also the largest maker of yeast and produces yeast both for brewing and baking purposes.

Yeasts work by providing organic constituents called enzymes, which act as catalysts in chemical reactions. As catalysts, they are necessary for chemical reactions to occur, but they themselves are unaffected by these changes. In winemaking the other factor essential to fermentation—sugar—is naturally present in the fruit. In making distilled spirits such as whiskey, vodka, and gin, grain is used. The use of grains, which have starch instead of sugar, requires the distiller to add a step at the beginning of the process, for the yeasts only work on hexose, or simple sugars. Starch can be chemically converted to hexose sugars by the action of an enzyme called diastase that is found in malt. Malt is germinated barley specifically prepared for this purpose. Once the starches have been converted to sugar, the yeasts can act on them.

Distillation. Distillation refers to the separation and collection of the alcohol produced by the fermentation process. When a spirituous liquid is heated, it will vaporize, that is, change from a liquid state to a gaseous state. When this gas is cooled, it becomes liquid again and is mostly alcohol. Since the *wine* in brandy making and the *mash* in whiskey making are very complex products with a variety of components that have a variety of vaporizing temperatures, special techniques and equipment are required to produce the desired results, and the distillate will still not be pure alcohol. Anyone can distill alcohol with crude equipment, but obtaining a drinkable product is a matter of technique and skill.

The apparatus used in distillation is called a still. The original type of still, the pot still, is a kettle with a long spout that is curled at the end. As the kettle is heated, the vapors rise through the spout, and when they go through the coiled end, they cool (it is immersed in water) and are condensed into liquid again. The advantage of this apparatus is control: the more highly volatile elements, those even more volatile than alcohol, vaporize first and can be condensed and collected. These are known as foreshots in whiskey and headings in cognac. Next, the alcohol vaporizes, condenses, and can be collected separately. The least volatile elements are collected last. These are called feints for whiskey and tailings for cognac.

The disadvantage of this type of still is economic, for it is a batch process: the still is filled, the liquid distilled, then the still must be cleaned, and the process begun again with a fresh batch. The process is slow and demands great skill, but it is considered to produce a very fine product.

Most distilling today is continuous rather than batch and is done in patent stills (also called continuous or column or tower stills). Warm mash is fed into one end, and the finished spirit comes out the other end. The advantages of these stills are increased speed and lower cost of operation.

The higher the alcohol content, or proof, of a spirit, the lower its congeneric content will be. Congenerics are those flavoring elements that are attributable to the starting materials. Without congenerics, a spirit will have no distinctive taste or aroma or perhaps no taste or aroma at all. Since congenerics are essential to a product's individual distinctiveness and since spirits distilled at lower proofs retain more of them, one can see why proof of distillation is so critical an element in shaping the final character of a spirit. Full-flavored and full-bodied spirits such as Scotch malt whisky, Irish whiskey, cognac, and bourbon are distilled at relatively low proof. Any products distilled at 190 degrees proof spirits (95 percent alcohol) or over is, by definition, a neutral spirit.

Table 11-2. Beer Classification

Bottom fermentation

1. Lager: Lager beer accounts for about 90 percent of all malt beverage production in the United States. Lager beers are light bodied.
2. Bock: This is a dark-colored, heavy beer, sweeter and richer in flavor than lager. Traditionally prepared to herald the arrival of spring, true bock beer is only available for about six weeks.
3. Dark Beer: Made from malt that is toasted to a darker color. It is often confused with bock beer, but it does not have the sweetness of a true bock.
4. Pilsner: Beer in the style of Pilsen, Czechoslovakia. Pilsner has a pronounced "hoppy" character and is light bodied and light colored.
5. Bavarian: Also light in body and color. Bavarian-type hops are used, which give the beer its own distinctive character.

Top fermentation

1. Ale: Ale is characterized by its pronounced hop flavor, which makes it more bitter than lager beer. Ales are much favored by the English and Canadians.
2. Porter: Similar to ale but heavier and darker, with a rich and heavy foam. In flavor it is sweeter and less "hoppy" with a distinct malt character. Very dark malt is used in the brewing.
3. Stout: This brew is closest to porter, but it is even darker and heavier with more of a hop taste.

Classification and Production of Beers

Classification. Beers are classified according to the way in which the yeasts act. If the yeasts settle to the bottom and catalyze the fermentation from there, it is called a bottom-fermented product; if they more or less remain on the surface, it is classified as top-fermented.

Quality Criteria. The quality of a beer is largely determined by the quality of the ingredients used in making it. These include water, barley malt, hops, yeasts, sugar, and adjuncts. Finished beer is 85 percent (or more) water, and water is also used during the brewing process. The type of water used has a great deal to do with the quality of the finished beer. The water must be biologically pure and its mineral content must be known. If the available water is not suitable, it can be treated; in fact, not many beers are made today using natural, untreated water.

Malt is germinated barley, and it can either be purchased or produced by the brewery. By varying the treatment of the malt, the brewer can control the type of beer produced. These treatments include kilning (drying) and roasting. Hops are plants grown specifically for brewing. The best ones originally came from Bohemia, but today fine hops are also grown in the United States. Only the flower or cone of the female hop vine is used. The plant's virtue for brewing is the bitter flavor and distinctive aroma it imparts from its resins and oils. Additional ingredients are called adjuncts. Corn and rice are the most commonly used adjuncts in beer making.

Breweries are very particular about the strains of yeast they use in fermentation. A change in the yeast can change the character of a beer. Any yeast will cause fermentation to take place, but since consistency of the product is an absolute necessity, the yeasts must be carefully cultured to maintain purity. The sugars used in brewing are manufactured from specially treated cane sugar. The type of treatment chosen depends on what is desired for the flavor and character of the beer.

Production. The first step in the brewing process is called mashing. The malt and grains are crushed and mixed with water. If the grains are raw, the mixture is heated; otherwise it is not. This is done to obtain the maximum extraction of soluble materials. Then the liquid is strained, leaving the spent grains behind. This liquid is called "wort" (pronounced wurt). The next step is the addition of hops and, if desired, sugars to the wort, and the mixture is boiled for 2 to 2½ hours. This boiling sterilizes the wort, extracts the desired flavor from the hops, and darkens the liquid due to a small amount of caramelization.

The hops are then strained out, the wort cooled, and yeast is added. A critical factor during fermentation, which takes place now, is temperature control. Beers must be fermented at a lower temperature than ales are.

Aging and clarification are the next steps. The carbonic acid gas released during fermentation is saved and stored. Following fermentation the beer is separated from its yeasts and placed in storage tanks where it is kept at low temperatures. Sedimentation of the remaining yeasts and other solids will clarify the beer. This aging period results in a more mellow and stable product.

The carbonic acid gas earlier reserved from the fermentation is added to the beer at this point; some breweries obtain carbonation by a slow second fermentation (called Krausenating). Just before packaging, the beer is pressure filtered to assure sparkling brilliance.

Packaging is done in kegs, bottles, or cans. Since the kegs can withstand additional pressure that might be created by more fermentation, they do not have to be pasteurized, but bottles and cans do. This is the reason why bottles and cans do not have to be stored under refrigeration, while kegs must be stored at about 36 degrees F.

Spirit (Whiskey) Production

The grains used (which ones and the specific proportion are of great importance) are "mashed," that is, they are ground, mixed with water, and heated. The purpose of this is to put the grains into solution so various

Table 11-3. Quality Criteria in the Production of Spirits

Quality criteria
Quality of the grains used
Method of distillation used
Proof of distillation
Special postdistillation processes
Type of wood used for aging
Length of aging period
Blending procedures
Skill of blending

materials can be extracted. Following the mashing, barley malt is added. As pointed out earlier, this is germinated barley and contains an enzyme, diastase, that catalyzes the chemical transformation of grain starch to grain sugar. This step is called saccharification and must precede the addition of yeasts.

Fermentation begins when the yeasts are added and is an extremely important step. The distiller can exercise a great deal of control over the reactions. The temperature of fermentation, the fermentation environment, the exact strain of yeasts used, and the length of fermentation can all be controlled, and all can have profound effects upon the product. Additionally, the distiller can choose to ferment the mash in either of two ways: the sweet-mash method or the sour-mash method. Sweet mashing is simply the exclusive use of fresh yeast for fermentation, while sour mashing involves the use of screened residue from old yeasts. At least 25 percent of the total yeast used in the sour-mashing method must be obtained from a former fermentation, although it can be higher. The terms are actually misleading, since sour mashing results in a somewhat sweeter and more mellow product. Many products made by the sour-mashing technique are not labeled as such due to general consumer ignorance about what sour mashing is. The distillers feel, perhaps rightly, that the word *sour* has a negative connotation for the public.

The fermented liquid is then distilled, and since the proof of distillation is so important to the final character, it is closely regulated. Bourbon, for example, cannot be distilled at over 160 degrees proof spirits (80 percent alcohol); neutral spirits (used for gins, vodkas, and as cordial bases) must be distilled at 190 proof or over; cognac cannot be distilled at over 140 proof. Following distillation, the spirit is diluted with distilled water and put into wood for aging.

Wood aging involves a complex series of chemical reactions and results in evaporation, a darkening of the spirit, and a mellowing of the newly distilled whiskey or other product to soften its harshness. The specific wood used is critical and generally regulated by law. Bourbon and Canadian whiskies must be aged in new (unused) american white oak. In addition, the oak must be charred. This is done by setting the inside of the barrel on fire. The char aids in the mellowing of the spirit and has a clarifying action as well. Aging changes the bouquet as well as the taste. A spirit that is well matured in wood will be softer in taste, darker in color, and have a fuller and more complex smell compared to one with less aging time. Distilled spirits do not mature in the bottle as wines do: they only change while in wood.

The practices of maturation and blending are responsible for a great deal of the differences between products. The distiller can elect to age certain spirits longer than normal to obtain a superior product, and blends can be formulated to custom produce specific products for specific markets. A blend intended for the mass market will contain little really mature whiskey and is apt to be made from grain proportions that are less expensive. Premium blends, on the other hand, are made from the more expensive and higher quality grains and contain higher proportions of mature spirits.

The final step is adjustment to bottling proof with distilled water and then the bottling itself.

The main difference in the production of other distilled spirits is in the ingredients used. Brandies are distilled from wines. A product labeled simply "brandy" must, by law, be produced from grape wine; other brandies are labeled according to the fruit used. The most famous brandy, cognac, is a product that can only be made in a legally delimited area in France. It is distilled in traditionally shaped copper pot stills from grape wines made with grapes grown entirely within the Cognac region. Aging must be done in either the local oak, Limousin oak, or oak from the national forest of Troncais. After cognac, the next most famous brandy is probably armagnac which is produced in another specific area of France, the Basque region, near the Spanish border. In general, most wine producing areas make brandy as well. In Burgundy they distill a brandy referred to as marc, and in Italy a product called grappa is made. German, Spanish, and Greek brandies have their followers as well. In Alsace, France, the Black Forest region of Germany, and many eastern European countries, the local people are proud of their fruit brandies. These are quite different from grape-wine brandies in that they typically are not aged in wood and will be colorless and will not have the smoothness of a well-matured wood-aged spirit, although they may be very fragrant. This is especially true of products such as kirsch (cherry brandy) and framboise (raspberry brandy). These latter brandies should not be confused with fruit-flavored brandies, which are a staple inventory item on most bars and are actually cordials.

Rums are distilled from a spirituous liquid made by fermenting sugar cane or molasses. They are also wood aged but not for as long as whiskies or brandies. The popular rums are produced by distilling at high proofs and, as a consequence, are light in character. Vodka is a product made from neutral spirits and further processed to remove as many of the remaining congenerics as possible. The spirits are derived from grains, although they could be made from nearly anything since neutral spirits imply little if any flavor from the base product.

Gin is defined as neutral spirits distilled or redistilled with juniper berries and other aromatics and is, therefore, a manufactured product. The quality of the various herbs, seeds, berries, and roots used is very important to the flavoring process. Each firm has its own formulas, which account for the distinctiveness of the various products on the market. Gin is not aged, and flavoring agents are used to make the new spirit palatable; the quality is not improved by aging in wood.

Cordials or liqueurs are neutral spirits, brandy, gin, or other distilled spirits mixed or redistilled with or over fruits, flowers, plants, or other natural flavoring agents or extracts derived from such materials. United States law states that they must contain a minimum of 2.5 percent finished weight of sugar. There are three ways in which cordials can be made: percolation, maceration, and distillation. Percolation is similar to coffee making, while maceration can be compared to the brewing of tea. The third method, distillation, is actually one of two methods. In the first, a product made by one of the two previous techniques is distilled. This is done if the product is very highly flavored and a more delicate spirit is desired. The other method calls for mixing the flavoring ingredients with spirits and then distilling.

Types of Whiskies

Bourbon Whiskey. As an introduction, the spelling of the word *whiskey (whisky)* needs explaining. Scotch and Canadian products are spelled without the *e*—whisky—while American and Irish products are spelled with the *e* —whiskey.

Bourbon whiskey is defined by the United States government as "whiskey distilled at not exceeding 160 degrees proof from a fermented mash of not less than 51 percent corn grain and stored in charred new oak barrels."

Straight bourbon is the distilled product of one type of grain mixture and fermenting technique, and it is not blended with any other whiskey types. United States law states that straight bourbon must be a minimum of two years old, although most bourbons are at least four. Blended whiskey is a specific type and can command a premium price.

Another term used with whiskies is *bonding.* Bonding is simply government-controlled maturing, regulated by a federal law that dates back to 1887. In order to qualify for the bottled-in-bond labeling, the whiskey must be a straight whiskey, it must be produced in the same distillery by a single distiller, and it must be the product of a single season or year. The whiskey is aged for a minimum of four years in government-controlled warehouses, and taxes are paid upon withdrawal. Bottling must then be done at 100 degrees proof.

Blended Whiskey. There are two types of blended whiskey. One is called blended straight whiskey, which is a blend of two or more straight whiskies, and does not carry much weight in the market. The other is blended whiskey proper. By government regulation, this has to be at least 20 percent straight 100 proof whiskey blended with corn whiskey or grain neutral spirits and bottled at not less than 80 degrees proof.

Blended whiskey can be a high quality product (Scotch and Canadian whiskies are blended); and in the good blends, the straight whiskies are distilled and aged to play a special and definite role in the blend. The same is true of the grain neutral spirits. Some distillers also age their neutral spirits.

Grain neutral spirits result when a fermented grain mash is distilled at very high proof, 190 degrees proof or higher. You will remember that high-proof spirits have little individuality—hence they are called grain neutral spirits. The character of blended whiskies, therefore, depends primarily on the type, age, and quantity of straight whiskies used in the blend. Whiskies are blended for two very practical reasons: one is that there is a considerable market for products that are lighter in body and more delicate or less assertive in flavor; the other is to guarantee the consistency of the product.

A premium brand of blended whiskey may have as many as seventy-five different straight whiskies and grain neutral spirits. Fixed formulas are less important than the fixed product characteristics such as taste and bouquet. This puts a great responsibility on the master blenders, those persons who, operating mainly by nose and palate—not science—can unerringly produce consistent products year after year. The products from the still will vary slightly due to the conditions of the grain, even when the same grain proportions are used. There will even be differences between batches from the still that have come from the same mash. This is markedly so when pot stills are used—thus the importance of the master blender to control the final product.

Sometimes a small amount of sherry is added to the whiskies to aid the blending. This is legal up to 2½ percent. There is a period following the blending called "marrying." The purpose of this is, as the whiskey people so picturesquely put it, to allow the whiskies to get to know one another. Bottling is done after the marrying period, and after bottling, the product ceases to change and can be consumed anytime.

American blended whiskies must be closely labeled as such and are required by law to declare what percentage of the blend are straight whiskies and how old they are. Since Scotch and Canadian whiskies are also blended but are not required to divulge the proportions of their blends, the imported products have an advantage, which American manufacturers have long protested.

Rye Whiskey. All the preceding regulations about bourbon apply to rye as well with the notable exception that rye whiskey must be distilled from a fermented grain mash containing not less than 51 percent rye.

Tennessee Whiskey. There is a close relationship between bourbon and Tennessee whiskey, but they are not the same. Tennessee whiskey is defined as "a straight whiskey distilled in Tennessee from a fermented mash containing not less than 51 percent corn." There are actually a number of differences, and made in Tennessee is just one of them. Technically, bourbon could be made in Tennessee as bourbon is a process and style of spirit that could be and is made in a number of areas. Kentucky, Illinois, Virginia, Pennsylvania, and Maryland all produce bourbon. There is a limestone subsoil belt running through these areas, and the distilleries were originally located to take advantage of the excellent limestone waters.

Tennessee whiskey is also sour mash, but bourbon can be too. The primary difference is that Tennessee whiskey has an extra step in the processing called charcoal filtering. When the whiskey comes out of the still, it is slowly introduced into vats packed with charcoal. This charcoal comes from the Tennessee highlands hard maple trees, cut when the sap is down, and this filtering process takes longer than any other process except aging. The result is a very mellow whiskey. It is interesting to taste the whiskey as it comes from the still and again after filtering. It looks the same, completely colorless, but the taste of freshly distilled whiskey is fiery and raw, while the filtered product is amazingly soft and toned down. Following filtering, the aging process used is similar to that for bourbon and must be done in new, charred oak casks. There are two distilleries in Tennessee justly famous for their products, Jack Daniels and George Dickel.

Light Whiskey. Light whiskey was the American manufacturers' answer to the increasingly popular blended light products being imported into the United States. Specifically it was to compete best in the Canadian market. As the American manufacturers saw it, in addition to the labeling discrimination mentioned earlier, they faced another problem in competing with imports. They had to distill their component spirits at under 160 degrees or over 190 degrees proof, while the competition could distill at the proofs in between. The imported products would then be lighter than straight whiskies and more flavorful than neutral spirits.

Still another advantage was cooperage. If aging in charred new oak does in fact contribute so much to the finished character of a whiskey, it is obvious that a used barrel will have many of the acids and other wood agents removed, and there will be a lack of char too. The products would therefore be lighter.

In response to the imports and rapidly changing consumer tastes, the American manufacturers gained legislation in 1968 enabling them to produce "Light" whiskey. Light whiskey (with a capital *L*) is defined as whiskey distilled at over 160 degrees but less than 190 degrees proof and aged in used or uncharred oak barrels. Any statements of age do not have to mention the used barrels. Various designations were permitted for this product. "Light Whiskey" is straight Light whiskey while "Blended Light Whiskey" can have less than 20 percent by volume of 100 degrees proof straight whiskey added. Other than distillation proof and aging requirements, it is made the same as other American whiskies.

One final boon was that no blend statement had to appear on the back label as required with blended whiskey. On July 1, 1972, the first bottles of this new product were ready for sale amidst high expectations. The product was not, however, accepted by the consumer, and few people if any really know why. In cases such as this, where there are distilled products on hand that are not moving, they can be redistilled into neutral spirits and used as the spirit base in cordials or for vodkas and gins.

Scotch Whisky. The Scots, of course, claim to have been the first to distill whisky (as they spell it), but then, so do the Irish. Regardless of who was first, whisky has been made in the Scottish Highlands for centuries. The Scots may have also been the first to practice the two hallmarks of modern spirit making: aging and blending. In fact, it was the Scots' discovery and use of blended spirits that transformed Scotch whisky from a somewhat earthy and highly distinctive product to the light and far more gentle liquid known today as blended Scotch whisky, or just as Scotch.

Irish Whiskey. Whether the Irish or Scots were the first whiskey distillers can't be determined with any accuracy, but it is certain that both the Irish and Scots were doing freelance distilling of barley malt long before it became a commercial undertaking. In fact, due to the extremely high tax rates on Irish whiskey, there is still a great deal of freelance distilling going on. A secondary claim of the Irish is that missionaries carried the secret of distillation to France, thereby making them the forerunners of brandy.

Irish whiskey makers have a very difficult problem today. They produce an unblended pot-distilled spirit that has lost popularity over the years to the lighter, blended Canadian and Scotch whiskies. Nonetheless, Irish whiskey is one of the world's great spirits. Its production roughly follows that described for Scotch whisky with these exceptions. Only all-Irish grains are used (Scotland imports a great deal of the barley they use), primarily a mixture of malted and unmalted barley with some use of other grains such as rye, wheat, and oats. Drying over peat is not practiced, so there is no smoky taste. Distillation is different: pot stills are used exclusively, and they are far larger than those used for Scotch malt whisky, holding approximately 20,000 U.S. gallons. A second difference in distillation is the proof, which is 172 degrees.

Finally, Irish whiskey is triple distilled, the only spirit to be so handled. Only the middle product of the third distillation is Irish whiskey. It is calculated that only 10 percent of the wash becomes finished whiskey, and some of this will evaporate during aging.

Used oak casks are used for aging. Aging is usually for at least five years and often much more. Bottling proof is mostly at 80 degrees for the American market, and the aged whiskey is diluted with the proper amount of water to reach this proof. Irish whiskey is not a true blended whiskey in the accepted sense. Blending is done between casks for uniformity, but all whiskies so blended are made in exactly the same way. There is no blending of neutral grain spirits in Irish whiskey making. As explained earlier, there are always going to be differences between various batches and years. This is even more pronounced when pot stills are used.

Canadian Whisky. Canadian whisky (or whiskey) is one of the world's finest distilled spirits—a spirit whose most distinctive characteristic is its lightness of body. The quality of Canadian whisky is no accident. It is perhaps more rigidly controlled by both law and manufacturer than any other distillate. The Canadian distiller is subject to more government control than any other manufacturer of goods in that nation. In the final analysis, however, the individual manufacturer is responsible for quality and doesn't have to contend with any governmental interference as regards the specific distilling techniques. The reason for the fine quality of the spirits is in the ingredients.

In Canada, only cereal grains are used. Corn, rye, and barley malt must meet rigorous specifications. There are no differences in the basic method of manufacture from those already covered. The grain is milled, mixed with water, and heated, which causes saccharification, or conversion of starch to sugar. Specially cultured and very pure strains of yeasts are added; fermentation takes place, followed by distillation in column stills. The new spirits are aged in new, charred oak barrels, generally for periods of four to twelve years. United States' law requires a minimum of four years.

Besides the high quality of the ingredients, the other difference is the blending. Unlike American blends, they are not a mixture of straight whiskies and neutral grain spirits. The highest distillation proof of the spirits used is 185 degrees proof, which in the United States is legally whiskey, not neutral grain spirits. When the whiskies are sufficiently aged, the blending is done and the blends are allowed to marry for a time, then bottled. Proof at bottling follows the governmental requirements of the countries to which it will be exported. In the United States this is a minimum of 80 degrees proof. Whisky for Canadian consumption is bottled at 70 degrees proof under the British Sykes method of calculation. As a matter of fact, 70 degrees Sykes is equal to 39.9 percent alcohol or 79.8 degrees proof in the sense that we are used to it.

Corn Whiskey. This product is made from a mash containing at least 80 percent corn (bourbon, remember, must be 51 percent or more corn but not over 80 percent), and it may be aged in used or uncharred barrels. There are, however, no age requirements.

Classification of Wines

There are four general types of wine. Each type has a primary purpose, which only means that the wine is more generally consumed in that way. This general classification does not mean a wine cannot be properly used in other ways. These types and their primary uses are:

(1) *Appetizer.* These wines are used as an aperitif, to stimulate and prepare the palate for a meal. A dry Sherry is very nice before dinner.

(2) *Table.* The majority of wines will fall into this category. These wines are meant to be consumed with food, and since foods can cover a broad spectrum of tastes and flavors, so, too, can the wines. Included are both red and white wines, such as a Burgundy or Chablis (rosés are technically considered red wines)—dry wines (dry means lack of sugar or sweetness), sweet wines, and a variety of in-between tastes.

(3) *Fortified.* These are wines that have had alcohol added to supplement the alcohol naturally produced by fermentation. The fortification is generally done by adding brandy distilled from the same type of wine. They have many uses; the dry ones can be served as aperitif wines, and the sweet ones make excellent dessert wines. Port and Sherry are both fortified wines.

(4) *Sparkling.* The most famous example of this category is champagne, but there are many other sparkling products available. They are truly all-purpose wines, for they can be used as aperitifs, as table wines, dessert wines, and—most important of all—they are ideal as special-occasion wines.

Quality Criteria of Wine

There are four primary criteria that establish the quality of a wine. These are the grape, the general environmental conditions (such as climate and exposure), the soil, and the skill of the winemaker.

Grape. Of these four criteria, the grape is the most important, for if a winemaker picks a location with perfect soil characteristics that enjoys great weather during the year, and the winemaker is highly skilled and does everything right, all the winemaker can do is get the ultimate from the grape. If the grapes are classic varieties and if they have reached full ripeness, great wine could result. If the grape varieties are inferior, or if they do not attain maturity, great wine cannot result, regardless of the soil and skill involved. The grape is the limiting factor, and everything the winemaker does is calculated to bring out the very best the grape has to offer.

Wine made by different people will have individual characteristics, reflecting the various techniques used. Wine made from the same type of grapes grown on different soil will also be different. Grapes grown in cooler regions will produce a different wine than that same variety of grape grown in warmer areas. Yet all these differences, significant as they may be, are minor compared to the differences between the wines made from various grapes. A chardonnay from California will not taste exactly like a French Chablis or white Burgundy, although they are made from the same grape. If the wines are carefully and skillfully made, however, there will be a recognizable similarity between them, and this comes from the grape. This is the bond between wines.

Grapes belong to the overall botanical group called Ampelidaceae. In this family there are ten genera, but only one is important to the winemaker: *Vitis.* The great wines of the world come from the species of *Vitis* called *vinifera.* In America, we are likely to come into contact with another vine called *Vitis labrusca.* The widely planted concord grape is a member of this species. Two other native American vines are *Vitis riparia* and *Vitis rotundifolia.* These American vines produce a wine with a very distinctive taste and scent, yet it is quite different from those made from *vinifera* vines; and the first settlers in this country, accustomed as they were to the *vinifera* grape wine, found that the American grapes produced crude, objectionable-tasting wine. Unfortunately, the vines they brought with them could survive neither the northeastern climate nor the many pests and diseases they encountered, and it was not until California was discovered that the *vinifera* found a secure home in North America.

Two characteristics of the maturing grape

are of utmost importance to wine. These are the sugar content and the acid content. All the factors of rain, climate, warmth, and sun eventually come down to these two. Immature grapes will have insufficient sugar and excessive acid, while grapes that have become too ripe will have gained extra sugar at the expense of acid. Sugar is important because the alcohol results from the sugar being fermented by the yeasts. Grapes with low sugar will produce wines with low alcohol. Wines with insufficient alcohol taste weak and watery; they feel thin and do not have the stability of wines with normal levels of alcohol. They are also subject to undesirable reactions, will not last well over time, and probably will not travel well either. An additional problem is that if the grapes are low in sugar, they are unripe; and just as one could not expect to make a quality dish out of unripe fruit, neither can quality wine be made from unripe fruit. The winemaker can compensate for the alcohol problem by adding sugar to the fermenting grape juice, but the difficulty posed by lack of ripeness is not solved so easily.

The grape acids have a more-or-less fixed relationship to the sugar. When grapes are green or unripe, they will have insufficient sugar and excess acid. When they become overly mature, the sugar levels will be high, but the acid will be reduced. The acid level is important because the wine will have a flat taste without it. With proper acid, wine has a zip to it, a mouth-watering quality. The acids are also important for their preservation properties and for their ability to fix colors. If the grapes are picked early or if they do not mature fully, they are likely to have too much acid, and the wine will have a tart or sour taste.

Climate. This is the great variable factor, for while soil, grapes, and the winemaker's skill remain constant from year to year, the climate can be, and often is, dramatically different each year. Since the challenge is to bring the grapes to maturity, one can readily appreciate the effects of variances in temperature, rain, amount of sunshine, frost, hail, and other climatic factors.

Grapes do not, as a rule, attain classic quality unless they are somewhat challenged. Hot or even warm areas are usually not suitable, for the vine prefers a moderately cold winter. Without it, the vine will not mature over time properly and will not develop the gnarled, woody appearance so characteristic of old grapevines. Long summers are desirable, although the temperature should not be too hot. The ideal temperature for the photosynthetic efficiency of a grapevine is between 77 and 86 degrees F; at temperatures above 90 degrees F, photosynthesis becomes less efficient, and at 113 degrees F, it stops. Long falls with a lot of sunshine would be enjoyed by nearly all winemakers, and they are necessary for certain, late-ripening varieties. About 20 inches of rain is needed for proper growth, but this is a variable requirement as the vine can withstand conditions of drought and excessive rain better than most agricultural crops can.

Many vineyards are planted near rivers and lakes because these temper, or stabilize, the temperature. This is a critical factor in the most northern wine regions; the Finger Lakes of New York and the Rhein River of Germany, for example, soak up the heat from the sun during the day and retain it during the night. The result is that there are less temperature variations during a 24-hour period than would be true farther away from the water. It will tend not to get as cold during the evening, and the grapes can attain proper ripeness more rapidly.

Soil. The soil is a fixed factor as it requires thousands of years for its characteristics to change. Grapevines do not, surprisingly, require any particular degree of soil richness as most other crops do. Physical characteristics appear to be more important than chemical ones. The soil should be somewhat loose so that that the roots can grow deep and so there is adequate drainage. Gravelly soil meets these specifications, and some of the most favored wine regions in the world are on gravel. Clay soil does not meet these specifications, and clay is generally quit unsuitable for fine wine grapes. Gravelly and rocky soil has the additional virture of being able to retain heat much as water does, and this is an important characteristics in some areas.

Skill of Winemaker. This is a variable factor since winemakers change from time to time, especially with new vineyards and wineries. Winemaking is also becoming very much a scientific endeavor, and scientists and schools have done important and significant work in the areas of grape breeding, grape growing, site selection, harvesting, and control of fermentation and other chemical reactions that occur during winemaking. Science does not, however, have all the answers, and it appears that winemaking is still very much an art. Some individuals seem to have a skill that goes beyond science; they are able to draw more from the grapes than other people can. Great wine results from a combination of a skilled, experienced winemaker of integrity, taking full advantage of the scientific knowledge available, who has the proper grapes planted in the ideal locations, which, finally, enjoy suitable weather.

Production of Wines

Wine is the fermented juice of grapes. Fermentation is an extremely complex series of chain reactions but is generally illustrated by a simplified equation:

$$\underset{\text{Sugar}}{C_6H_{12}O_6} \rightarrow \underset{\substack{\text{Ethyl}\\\text{Alcohol}}}{2\,C_2H_5OH} + \underset{\substack{\text{Carbon}\\\text{Dioxide}}}{2\,CO_2}$$

When all the sugar is fermented into alcohol and carbon dioxide, the wine is said to be dry. It is not actually possible to ferment *all* the sugar, but the remaining sugars, called "reducing sugars," only total some .10 to .25 percent, and the typical human threshold for detecting sweetness is about .50 percent. These reducing sugars are, therefore, undetectable and the wine is very dry. Some wines are made with varying degrees of residual sugar, which is sugar remaining after the fermentation is complete. With most wines, it will amount to 1 to 3 percent, and the wine will taste from slightly sweet to sweet. A few wines will be made from grapes that have an extremely high sugar percentage, and the residual sugar content will be 10, 15, or even 20 percent (or higher). This occurs because the conversion of sugar to alcohol will eventually result in an alcohol content that prevents the yeasts from working any further—usually at about 14 percent. When the fermentation ceases, if any sugar has not been converted, it will remain as residual sugar. Examples of such wines are the famous French Sauternes, German beerenauslesen, and trockenbeerenauslesen. These naturally sweet wines are among the most difficult and expensive to make and are always scarce and costly. Another wine with high levels of residual sugar is porto from Portugal. This wine is made by stopping the fermentation with the addition of brandy prior to the completion of the sugar conversion. Such wines have high levels of alcohol (16 to 20 percent) and are sweet. A wine may also be sweetened by the addition of sugar following fermentation; these are generally among the least expensive wines.

Red wines are made by crushing the grapes and fermenting the juice with the skins. Red wines have a higher molecular weight, more flavor, and more aroma or bouquet than do white wines, and this is due to the contact of the grape skins during fermentation. The skins provide tannins, color compounds, and other chemical constituents to the wine. White wines are made by fermenting only the juice without the skins; they are therefore lightly colored (even white wines are not colorless) and lighter in body, flavor, and odor components. This is why white wines are chilled and reds (as a rule) are not. Red wines require higher temperatures to volatilize their flavor and odor compounds. Whites, having lesser amounts of such compounds, can be enjoyed at lower temperatures, although some white wines have considerable body and flavor, and these wines should not be served as cold as the others. Grapes, even red or black grapes, have clear juice, so white wines can be made from any grapes so long as only the juice is fermented. At least one famous white wine, champagne, is made from a mixture of black and white grapes. Red wines, on the other hand, can only be made from red or black grapes. Rosé wines are made from red or black grapes but are fermented only partially on the skins. After the desired color is attained, the skins are removed, and the fermentation continues with the juice only. Cheaper rosés can be made by mixing red and white wines, but the better ones are made naturally.

Sparkling wines can be made by a variety of methods. The classic one is the original champagne method. The term *champagne* can be used to describe a sparkling wine from the Champagne region of France, or it can be used to describe a *method* of producing a sparkling wine. There is only one true champagne wine (just as there is only one burgundy, or chablis or port or sherry), but the *method* can be used by any winemaker in any country. The essence of the champagne method is that a fermentation is induced *inside* the bottle. This is done by taking a low-alcohol, completely fermented wine and putting it into a bottle along with sugar and yeast. A fermentation will take place and the products of that reaction, carbon dioxide and ethyl alcohol, are retained in the bottle. By-products of fermentation, such as spent yeasts, are removed by a process the French call *degorgement*, and the wine will be perfectly clear, sparkling, and totally dry.

The varying degrees of sweetness found in sparkling wines are the result of an addition of small amounts of sugar to the wine at the time of *degorgement.* This is called the *dosage*. A wine with little or no *dosage* is termed a *brut*; they are normally the driest sparkling wines available. Other terms, such as extra dry, sec, and so forth, indicate additional sugaring of the finished wine. Sugar will mask a lack of balance and quality in the wine, so the best products will generally be the bruts. Wines made by this method in California can be labeled "fermented in *this* bottle."

Another technique is to use the *transfer method*. These wines get a second fermentation in a bottle, but following this, the contents of many bottles are blended together in pressurized tanks, filtered, and adjusted for sweetness or dryness. The wine is then put back into the bottles and corked. These wines can be labeled "fermented in *the* bottle."

A third way to produce these wines is the *Charmat process* (named for its inventor). This is a bulk fermentation process; the secondary fermentation takes place in tanks, and the finished wine is bottled under pressure. This is the least expensive of the three and requires the least amount of handwork. The champagne method requires considerable handwork and can therefore be very expensive. Wines made by the Charmat method are labeled "naturally fermented," and they may or may not have the phrases "bulk-fermented" or "Charmat Process."

Wines, unlike distilled spirits, age both in wood and in the bottle. Many wines get little or no wood aging prior to being bottled, but the better ones frequently do. Red wines are more likely to be wood aged than whites are, but some whites—particularly ones like California chardonnay and French white burgundy—will be aged in wood.

Aging of wines is often misunderstood and just as often overemphasized. Many red wines improve dramatically with a few years of age, while some reds require many years. The qualities of white wines that are most appreciated are their freshness and delicacy, and these qualities are often lost with age. A red wine intended to be aged will be very dark in color, have considerable tannin, which gives it a harsh taste, and an intense flavor. The odor will be characteristic of the grape and is called the *aroma*. Aging will result in a change of color whereby the red hue gradually changes to one of brown. Red wines therefore become lighter as they mature. The taste becomes less harsh and smoother due to the loss of tannins. The odor becomes fuller and more complex and is termed *bouquet.* These changes occur more rapidly in wood than in the bottle, but they continue after the wine is bottled. The same types of changes take place in white wines as well. The color, however, does not become lighter but rather, due to slow oxidation, the color darkens. (Over-oxidized or overmatured red and white wines alike have a brownish hue to them.) The aroma will gradually become more complex and bouquet will result, while the flavor becomes more fully developed, although the freshness and fruitiness will be reduced.

Management of Alcoholic Beverage Systems

Control. Control occurs when management has access to and uses information. There are two aspects to the informational nature of control. One is that control consists of information flowing upward to management. The other is that, based upon the meaning and interpretation of this information, management makes decisions, and then information is directed downwards through the operation. There are two types of upward-flowing information that management has access to: historical and analytical. Historical information informs management what has already happened; for example, the bar cost was 30 percent. Analytical information, on the other hand, tells management not only what has happened, but why and perhaps how. An example might be: The overall bar cost was 30 percent versus a desired standard cost of 26 percent; the beer cost was 32 percent versus a standard cost of 31 percent, and the wine cost was 45 percent, the same as the standard cost. The cost of distilled spirits however was 25 percent, well over the standard of 20 percent. Banquet and catering costs were in line with the standard. Analytical information such as this makes decision making easier. In this case management knows there is no problem with beer, wine, or banquets. The entire cost coverage is evidently in spirits and on the main bar. There are still a lot of brands, hours of operation, and bartenders and waitresses to examine in order to see where the problem is, and even more detailed information would be helpful. If management could isolate the variance to a particular bartender working a specific shift and under certain conditions or determine that most of the excessive cost is in one type of spirit, such as Scotch, problem solving and decision making obviously becomes even easier. The point here is not that decision making and problem solving are easy, for they are more complex today than ever before, but that the sophistication of information and control systems has advanced so that management can cope with today's complexity. To ignore what technology has made available is foolish because this technology enables management to keep pace with the rapidly escalating demands upon it.

Once the pertinent information has been collected, management must *act* upon it. Lack of *follow through* is probably as responsible for management failure as is lack of proper or adequate information. There are two ways in which information can be directed downwards through the operation: by taking either corrective or anticipatory action. Corrective action is the most common and occurs when management takes action and issues directives to correct mistakes or problems that have been identified. This is, of course, essential, but one can readily see that if all management does is correct existing or past problems, they can never plot a rational course through the future. The other type of action, anticipatory, implies that management issues directives based upon information which indicates that problems may or could or will occur. To summarize these points: If management obtains information that informs as to *what* happened but not why, how, where, when, they are not able to make decisions quickly or rationally. If management decision making is primarily based upon correcting problems, they are not managing efficiently—in fact, they may not be managing at all; they may be being managed (by the operation and by events).

Both types of information and decisions are necessary; we are talking here about a *primary* emphasis on the part of management to spend more time anticipating potential problems (and opportunities) and plotting rational strategies for coping than in looking back to see what went wrong. Managers who spend a majority of their time with past mistakes will always have mistakes and problems to solve because they never look ahead and make plans to eliminate or at least reduce them. This type of management style can be termed "management by crisis" or "fire fighting." They spend all their time putting out fires and not enough time figuring out how to prevent them from starting.

Beverage control, in one respect, is quite different from food control. While the manager of a food delivery system is primarily concerned with monitoring physical goods, an alcoholic beverage manager is primarily concerned with monitoring and controlling the activities of people. A food manager is obviously concerned with controlling people, but compared to the potential product problems, managing people is a secondary concern. A beverage manager is also just as obviously involved with product management, but it is not as critical as people management. The point can be summarized by this statement. If you allow a case of shrimp to sit on a recieving dock it *will* spoil; it *may* also be stolen but not necessarily. A case of liquor left on a dock, on the other hand, *will not* spoil, but it most certainly will be stolen!

The profit potential from the sale of alcoholic beverages is higher, from a percentage standpoint, than it is from food sales, so it is necessary to manage the beverage system at least as efficiently as the food system. This is not due solely to the product-cost factors, for it goes well beyond this. Food is sold at a markup of some 2.5 times (40 percent of sales), while the comparable beverage markup is about 4 times (25 percent cost of sales). These are general figures—many food service operations will have costs both above and below these—but they are an accurate representation of the industry as a whole. The cost of labor is the largest single cost in the food service industry today, and beverage systems are less labor intensive than food systems are. Less time and personnel are required to purchase, receive, store, inventory, produce, and serve alcoholic beverages than are needed for food.

General operating expenses are also less for a beverage system. These include heating, lighting, and cooling the facility, repairs and maintenance, advertising and promotion, administration, cleaning, and supplies. Investment has a more favorable ratio with sales and profits. Finally, a beverage system is easier to run and control than a food system is, partially due to the above factors but also because it is significantly less complex.

Standards. One of the more important responsibilities management has is to establish and enforce standards. This assumes that everything is done the same way, *at all times.* There is no point in having well-thought-out standards unless they are enforced. Virtually all chain organizations have operations manuals that carefully, and in some detail, set forth many of the organizational standards. Not all their individual units, however, are adequately or properly run, and one of the main reasons is failure to follow through, to adhere to and enforce the organization's standards.

The importance of standards is that they result in consistency, which in turn leads to predictability—of cost, quality, and control. This is the essence of management. What should be standardized? The answer is *everything*! Take glassware for instance. One of the best ways to control portions is to use a standard size and shape of serving glass. It is difficult, for example, to put 1.5 ounces of a cordial in a 1-ounce pony glass or 10 ounces of draught beer in an 8-ounce glass. Other areas in which standardization must be implemented are measuring devices, pouring procedures and techniques, garnishing, pricing, ordering and calling of drinks, check writing, drink formulas, station setup, cash handling, register procedures, requisitioning bar stock, ordering stock for the storeroom, and bottle arrangement in both the storage area(s) and the bar(s).

Beverage Purchasing

Objectives of Purchasing. The objectives of purchasing are to obtain the right quality and the *right* quantity at the *right* time and at the *right* price from the *right* supplier. *Quality* is defined by Webster with such terms as merit and excellence, but these terms are of limited use to a food service buyer. Value is the prime consideration, and value is quality in relation to price. Quality by itself has little meaning unless it is related to use (suitability) and ultimate cost. The highest quality (by definition) may not always be the *best* or *proper* quality for the establishment! The buyer must make two decisions. The first is a technical one of suitability: for example, what kind of product is best suited to the use? The second decision is to make the best match of the desired product to the other purchasing criteria—quantity, time, price, and supplier. The first decision is best made by a technical expert, for example, the bartender, or a knowledgeable food and beverage manager, while the second is best made by a purchasing professional or specialist.

The decision of *how much* to purchase must take into consideration a number of parameters. They are the: (1) storage space, (2) desired inventory turnover, (3) cost of storage, (4) cost of handling, (5) security of stock and storage areas, (6) risk of spoilage (none with distilled spirits but a factor to consider with beer and wine), and (7) operational flexibility.

The *time* parameter involves taking into consideration operational factors such as the movement of stock, availability of proper receiving personnel, availability of funds (very important in some locations where the goods must be paid for *prior* to delivery). Another consideration is physical proximity of supplier, and still another would be the necessity of balancing the need-to-cost factors.

The right *price* is actually an incorrect term, since *cost*—not price—is the critical factor. This is one of the major differences between food and beverage purchasing. With food, there can be dramatic variances between a product's price and its ultimate serving cost. This is due to the yield factors. With alcoholic beverages, yield factors are not as important since there are no peeling losses, cooking losses, trimming losses, carving losses, and so forth. The beverage purchaser must still consider, however, the ultimate *cost of serving* a product as opposed to the *cost of buying* it.

Discounting is a critical factor in establishing the cost of a product. Discount policies and procedures vary widely, depending mainly upon the location (control state versus open state) but also upon the purchasing power and volume of the organization. The buyer must strive to take maximum advantage of discounts consistent with the organization's financial policies and physical constraints.

The final element in purchasing is the supplier. Some of the decisions about suppliers that have to be made are: (1) How many are required. This decision must be made independently for each beverage category; wines, beers, and spirits. The spirits, in turn, can be broken down into call liquors and well (house or bar) liquors. (2) Reliability of supplier(s). (3) Service capability of supplier(s). (4) Product line. (5) Price structure and discount policies. (6) Nonproduct assistance. In many cases, there is little or no product differentiation, and in such cases, the supplier decision is largely based upon the nonproduct factors.

Purchasing Responsibility. This is a function that, in most food service operations, should not be delegated and *must* be performed by management. The reason is not that beverage purchasing is technically difficult (as it is with food) but is due to the basic difference between food and beverage control; beverage operations pose a *personnel control* problem, and line employees should not be allowed to make these decisions. Line employees (bartenders) can properly provide technical input into the product specification decision but should not have any control over the other decisions.

Purchase versus Order Decisions. It is useful to separate the decisions management must make into "purchase" decisions and "order" decisions. There are three types of actual purchase decisions that have to be made. They are: (1) what to buy, (2) how much to stock, and (3) who to purchase from.

These are basic management decisions and should not—cannot—be delegated. Management can and should get as much input from others into the decision-making process as possible, but ultimately management must make the decisions themselves. These decisions may be complicated to make because there is a lot that needs to be considered in making each one, and only management would normally have access to all the information and be able to consider the full range of decision parameters. The decision on how much to stock should not be delegated because management is ultimately responsible for inventory turnover and for using money and stock as profitably as possible. The decision of who to buy from should certainly not be delegated due to the potential for fraudulent activities.

Ordering decisions are those that result in the restocking of the inventory, and, if the basic purchase decisions are properly made, these decisions can be delegated. In fact, they should be, as the following example shows. The decision was made to buy Cutty Sark Scotch from the ABC distributing company and to carry two cases in storage. Once these decisions had been made, anyone can do the period-to-period ordering, as there is no more actual decision making to be done. If someone had access to a perpetual inventory (eliminating the need for access to the storage area), they would know that there was one case of Cutty Sark on hand, and the order would therefore be one case from the ABC company. This process certainly doesn't require management involvement, except for monitoring purposes.

If the basic purchase decisions are properly made, they should seldom have to be made again. One of the common management mistakes is to make these basic decisions each and every time an order is placed, which is an unproductive use of management time and an inefficient way to purchase.

Open versus Control States. Some states have an Alcoholic Beverage Control Board, which in essence means that a monopolistic state of competition exists; this is another way of saying there is no competition. The degree to which the states control the sale of alcoholic beverages varies. In some cases, they may allow many distribution locations but will wholesale all products themselves and control the retail selling price. In other cases, they will control all distribution themselves, and the only retail outlets for alcoholic beverages will be state-operated stores. In these states, there is a reduced range of decision options available to management. This has, however, the effect of making decisions simpler and less complex, so it could be said that management control is enhanced.

Some operating considerations in a control state are: (1) one price, (2) reduced brand selection, (3) no credit, (4) reduced delivery options, (5) problems with supplier "stock-outs," (6) reduced order options, and (7) reduced invoice and delivery adjustment options.

Some operating considerations in an open state are: (1) There is price competition but not on all products; (2) ordering and delivery are essentially the same as with other product lines; (3) although there are some credit restrictions, credit is generally available; (4) lower prices due to competition; (5) existence of special inducements; (6) discounting; and (7) increased demands upon management time.

Purchasing of Well versus Call Stock. There are two basic types of stock carried by a beverage operation. The brands guests normally request by name are referred to as *call* brands. Many guests, however, do not specify a particular brand but will order a "scotch and water," or "bourbon and soda," or "gin and tonic." In such cases, the bartender uses the standard product designated by management. This is referred to as the *well* brand (also called *house* or *bar* stock). There are several purchasing distinctions between the two that have to be taken into consideration. With call stock, there is limited price competition, limited management discretion in making brand decisions, and quality is not a decision factor as each brand has its own quality image. With well stock, there is the potential for a great deal of price competition; management has a wide range of discretion in brand decision making; and quality variances can be substantial.

Beverage Receiving

Management should be physically involved in receiving the alcoholic beverages. This has nothing to do with product complexity, as in the case of food. Alcoholic beverages are simple to receive from a technical standpoint since the product standards are consistent. (Cutty Sark is always Cutty Sark; it will not vary in quality from day to day and case to case as lettuce would.) Packaging is consistent, twelve bottles to a case, and all the bottles are the same size. There is no danger of spoilage if the product is not stored immediately.

The necessity for management supervision of the receiving process is due to the fact that the merchandise must be moved to storage areas immediately. Alcoholic beverages have a disconcerting tendency to disappear when unsecured. Whoever does the receiving should therefore have access to the storage area(s), and only management should be in this position. Control over liquor storage is not a responsibility that should be delegated, although it frequently is due to false assumptions about what a management person is. Anyone whose *primary* or *sole* responsibility consists of performing a task or job is not a member of management regardless of what his or her title may be. A manager is one whose primary or sole responsibility is to *direct the activities* of those who do perform line tasks, to make decisions, and often to develop policy and chart direction.

Management must obtain certain information from the receiving system. As a minimum, this information would include: (1) what was received, (2) who received it, (3) when it was received, (4) whether it was properly and quickly moved to the appropriate storage area(s), and (5) if the invoices were posted to the perpetual inventory.

Although the receiving of alcoholic beverages does not require a high degree of technical expertise, there are some specific things to check: (1) proof of spirits, (2) vintage date on wines, (3) beer date codes, (4) determining whether any bottles have broken, leaked, or been capped and sealed empty. This can be done by opening or weighing the cases, (5) visually inspecting cases for possible physical damage or leaking.

Beverage Storage

This is a holding phase, the objectives of which are: (1) to insure against theft, (2) to insure against unauthorized issuing, (3) proper rotation of stock, (4) constant knowledge of stock on hand, and (5) to maintain product quality.

The security of the product is the primary consideration, and this is achieved by having an adequate storeroom, which not only has one or two good locks on it but which is *kept locked.* The accessibility must be limited to as few people as possible. The more people who have access to liquor storage, the greater the possibility of keys being lost or getting into the hands of unauthorized people. There is also an increased possibility of mistakes being made in issuing or forgetting to lock the door and so forth. Aside from limiting key-holding authority, management should avoid the use of master keys. Regardless of the security measures imposed, keys will occasionally find their way to hourly employees, and the threat to security of having one key that opens all locks is obvious.

Another measure that could be considered is an emergency key system whereby keys to high security areas such as liquor storage are available for an emergency such as when liquor is needed, and no keys are generally available. In such cases, the key has to be signed out from the cashier (for example) and signed back in when returned. If this procedure were followed, management would have a record of who went into the liquor room, when they did so, and for what reason. There are few problems with fraudulent activities when there is full documentation of this sort. An additional security technique is to change locks with some frequency—but randomly, not according to a pattern, either of time or area.

The use of par stocks, or predetermined stock levels, is recommended. They serve a number of purposes. The most important of these are: (1) to provide stock information that can be used for ordering; (2) to control the size of inventory, which is necessary for good financial management. Stock levels have a habit of increasing over time unless they are carefully monitored by management.

The proper par stock is dependent on many factors, but a rough rule of thumb is 1.5 times the amount needed between orders. If, for example, an operation consistently moves (uses) two cases of the bar bourbon per week, a par stock of three cases would be established. This would insure the availability of the stock required under normal conditions and provide a surplus for those occasional periods when it moves faster. It also protects against temporary supplier stockouts and late deliveries. It is one of management's basic responsibilities to evaluate the use of all alcoholic beverage products and determine rational par stocks. This is not a responsibility that should be delegated.

Tags and/or stickers are often used in stock control. Bottles are tagged, or a sticker of some sort is affixed in the storeroom prior to being issued to the bar(s). The purpose of this is to prevent bar personnel from stocking the bar with their own merchandise. If this were done, the sales resulting from this stock could be kept, and the bar cost percentage would be unaffected. Under this system, if any unauthorized stock were to appear on the bar, it would not have a sticker and could readily be noted. The control concept is fine, but stickers and tags can often be easily obtained or duplicated. For the tag system to work, management has to check the bottles frequently and randomly. In spite of the obvious control loopholes, this can be effective if properly implemented.

Inventory

There are two kinds of inventories that can be used in a bar: perpetual and physical. The purpose of a perpetual inventory is to provide

Old Grand Dad Bourbon
Bottle size: 750 ml.
Bottle cost:
Par stock:

10/21	10/24	10/25	10/28	10/30	11/2	
12 / 2	10 / 3	7 / 1	6 / 2	4+12 / 1	15 /	

Interpretation: On 10/21 there were twelve bottles on hand, and two were issued to the bar. The next issue took place on 10/24 when three of the ten on hand were issued. There is no need for an entry every day, only when a transaction takes place. On 10/30, there were four bottles available; one case of twelve bottles was delivered and added to the inventory, while one bottle was issued to the bar. The current level of stock is always available when this record is kept up to date.

Figure 11a. Bin Card

a record of the stock on hand at all times *without* actually counting it. A physical inventory, on the other hand, is a record of the stock on hand by an actual count. The advantages of an accurate perpetual inventory should be obvious. Knowledge of stock level is necessary for many decisions, one of which is ordering. Ideally when an order is placed, the person ordering knows how much is on hand and how much is expected to be consumed (or the par stock). When both of these are known, ordering is easy, and a perpetual inventory can provide the current stock level without taking the time to physically count it. A perpetual inventory also provides control in that it eliminates access to stock as a condition for ordering. The inventory can be kept on "bin-cards," with each brand recorded on a separate card (see Figure 11a) or on an inventory sheet, with each brand on a separate line (see Figure 11b).

A perpetual inventory is an invaluable control tool, but it must be accurate. There are two conditions that must exist if the perpetual inventory is to be accurate. One is that all *additions* to the inventory level must be recorded immediately. This is easily done since a written record—the invoice—exists, and it should be a simple administrative task to insure prompt and regular postings. The second condition is that all *removals* of stock must be recorded and posted. This is the difficult part and is the reason many perpetual inventories are inaccurate and ineffective as control devices. Unless management can assure that *any* stock removed from storage is recorded, they might as well not keep a perpetual inventory. Another point is the necessity of spot-checking the inventory for accuracy since management cannot wait until a physical inventory is taken (often only once per month) to compare the perpetual to the actual.

A physical inventory is necessary because without it, an accurate cost accounting cannot be made. Costs are basically calculated as follows: goods available at beginning *plus* goods purchased or acquired during the period *less* goods remaining at end of the period. The results are the goods that were used and/or sold. Goods available at the beginning and remaining at the end are called opening and ending inventory, and the cost will not be accurate unless there is an accurate count of how much is on hand. The best procedure is to physically count the stock, and even though this may involve considerable estimation because of opened or partial bottles, it is the only truly accurate method for calculating the usage and hence the cost of products.

A physical inventory needs to be taken whenever totally accurate cost knowledge is

Brand	**Date**						
Scotch	3/1	3/2	3/3	3/4	3/5	3/6	3/7
Cutty Sark	6 / –	6 / 1	5 / 2	3 / 1	2+12 / 2	12 / 2	10
White Horse	4 / –	4 / –	4 / 1	3 / 1	2+6 / –	8 / 1	7
White Label	6 / 1	5 / 1	4 / 1	3 / –	3+12 / 2	13 / 2	11
Smugglers	4 / –	4 / –	4 / 1	3 / –	3+6 / 1	8 / –	8

Interpretation: Similar to the bin card (Figure 11a) except that a number of brands can be carried on each page and there is an entry each day, whether or not a transaction took place.

Figure 11b. Perpetual Inventory Sheet

necessary. They are generally taken monthly so operating statements can be developed but may be taken more frequently if management feels it necessary. All beverage inventory methods involve some degree of estimation due to the presence of partially filled, open bottles on the bar. The most accurate is probably weighing, although even this one uses estimating since bottle weights are not standard, content weights are not consistent due to proof differences (alcohol weighs less than water), and with cordials there are significant weight differences due to the sugar percentages.

Some inventories are taken by only counting the full bottles, the assumption being that there is a constant amount of liquor in the opened bottles. This may or may not be true, but over time–in a fairly high-volume operation–this could be accurate enough. Another technique is to use calibrated sticks or tapes to measure the amount of liquor left in the bottles. The problem with these devices is that liquors are packaged in many different bottle shapes, and you would need a specific tape for each one. Some bottles are themselves calibrated, and this makes estimating the remaining liquor easy and accurate, but not all bottles are made like this.

Due in part to all these problems, the most common method of taking a physical inventory is estimating the contents of the bottles, usually by tenths. This can be surprisingly accurate, especially if the person doing the calling is consistent. In fact, consistency is more important than total accuracy. If a caller always called a particular level the same, after two or three inventories it really would not matter if that call was exact. This technique is also fast, and management must try to get the needed information with the least expenditure of time and, hence, money. In other words, management should use the method that gives the best combination of high accuracy and low cost.

Management must maintain tight control over the size of inventories and the amount of money tied up. An important informational statistic is the inventory turnover. This is calculated by using this formula:

$$\text{Inventory turnover} = \frac{\text{cost of goods sold}}{\text{average inventory}}$$

The cost-of-goods calculation has been discussed. The average inventory is the total of opening and ending inventories divided by two. Table 11-4 gives an example of an inventory turnover calculation. The result, 2.44, means that the average inventory of $8,000 has been used or sold nearly 2.5 times during the period. If the turnover is too high, it indicates the inventory level is probably too low and there will be stock outs. If it is too low, there is too much stock being carried, and too much money being tied up unnecessarily. An inventory control program will be based on a turnover standard. Management should carefully consider all the decision factors and decide upon the most rational stock level. Once this is established, the turnover figure

Table 11-4. Inventory Turnover Calculation

1. Required data:	
Opening inventory = $10,000.00	
Purchases = 20,000.00	
Closing inventory = 8,000.00	
2. Cost-of-goods-sold calculation:	
Opening inventory	$10,000.00
Plus: purchases	20,000.00
Equals: total goods available for sales	$30,000.00
Less: ending inventory	8,000.00
Equals: cost of goods sold	$22,000.00
3. Average inventory calculation:	
A. Opening inventory	$10,000.00
Plus: ending inventory	8,000.00
TOTAL	$18,000.00
B. $18,000 ÷ 2 = $9,000.00	
Average inventory = $9,000.00	
4. Inventory turnover calculation:	
Cost of goods sold / Average inventory	$22,000.00 / $9,000.00
Inventory turnover = 2.44	

should be calculated monthly and compared with the standard. Whenever there is a variance, management must investigate to determine whether it can be justified or if there is a problem and what is wrong. It is important that the standard be specific for each operation. While industry and organizational standards are useful as a frame of reference, every operation is unique, and the standard should reflect that uniqueness.

Issuing

Issuing is an important aspect of a beverage control program. It is not necessarily critical to food control, and this is another difference between food and beverage control. Valuable information can be generated from the issuing function: what left the storage area, the value of the issued stock, when the goods were removed, who took them, what department they went to, who authorized the removal. It is difficult to control the issuing of food since there is such a broad range of products. They are stored in many areas; many employees have access to the stock; and the need for the products is more or less constant throughout the day. With alcoholic beverages, the situation is very different. They are stored in very few locations, often a single storeroom; very few individuals have access to the storage area(s); and the need for the products is such that they can be issued on a limited schedule, frequently only once daily.

The key to an effective issuing system is establishment of a par stock on the bar. A par should be set up for every brand poured, and a rule of thumb is to calculate it as about 1.5 times the daily usage. The par should not be set up so that the bar never runs out, for that would result in an overstocked bar. It should instead handle normal business with a reasonable safety margin. There will be periods when the par is known to be inadequate, and management can readily adjust it according to the situation. It should be returned to the normal level immediately, however. Examples are: A regular pattern of widely disparate sales over the week such as when Saturday night is significantly busier than any other day or else on special occasions such as New Year's Eve.

Issues to the bar should be made on a daily basis by building up to the par stock for each brand. This is done by replacing each empty bottle with a full one. The only authorization for removal of stock from the storeroom should be a written requisition. One of the advantages of the bottle-for-bottle system is that literally anyone can prepare the requisition. If the closing bartender puts all the empties aside, the requisition is simply a listing of the empties, and no one is really making a stocking decision. These requisitions become the source of posting stock depletions to the perpetual inventory.

Issuing patterns should be observed and documented. Deviations from normal levels of activity must be questioned, investigated, and justified. Variances will occur, but management must assure they are legitimate when they do occur.

Another use for issuing information is that issues can be costed and used as a rough guide to running costs. This does not eliminate the need for physical inventories, but it can often yield sufficiently accurate cost estimates between physical inventories.

Cash Control

One of the primary objectives in beverage control is to safeguard cash and assure that all transactions result in cash being collected for the operation. Since beverage control is mainly a personnel problem, there must be a great deal of management vigilance over the service function. If beverage operations could sell all the liquor in a bottle, there would be few control problems, but the fact is that all the liquor is not sold. Some is wasted, some is stolen, some is given away, much is sold, but the proceeds do not all go to the house; they are sold by and for the employees. Among the basic register controls are: (1) Bunching of checks cannot be allowed—all checks should be rung up as separate transactions. (2) Guest checks must be consecutively numbered and *audited.* (3) There should be separate cash drawers for individual cashiers or bartenders. (4) Cash drawers should be periodically pulled for spot cash checks. (5) Accumulated cash should be regularly removed from the bar and dropped in an inaccessable drop box or safe. (6) Each shift should be started with a fresh bank. (7) Overages and shortages should be reviewed regularly with the cashiers and bartenders. (8) Register tapes should be checked constantly for continuity of transaction numbers, blank spots, and number of no-sale transactions. (9) Any additions not performed by a register should be done on a machine with a tape and the tape should be attached. (10) The cash drawer should be closed between transactions. (11) Registers should not be reset to zero at the end of a shift or day. (12) Insist that all guests get a check or register receipt to avoid unregistered sales. (13) Only management or the accounting office should have the authority to take register readings. (14) Register readings are best taken the next day, prior to opening.

Bar Production Control

In addition to cash control, there are many other things that management must pay close attention to. Bartenders may substitute bar brands when call brands are requested. Since the call brands are generally priced higher, the difference can be kept without affecting the bar cost.

Overpouring and free pouring. The problem here, from a conceptual standpoint, is that if such practices are permitted, then management is delegating the responsibility for making one of the basic management decisions—that of determining the portion sizes. Letting bartenders free pour is essentially the same as letting them make basic portion decisions and doing so perhaps hundreds of times daily.

Watering the bottles is a practice that is quite easy to do and difficult to detect if the bar personnel do not get too greedy and go overboard. Collusion is always a potential control problem, but it presents a greater hazard in the beverage operation than with other departments. Many managers make the mistake of thinking that if the spirits are under control there is little potential for theft, but it is possible to lose a lot of money on beer, wine, and soft drinks. When draught beer is used, the number of potential glasses or mugs in a barrel can be increased substantially by putting an excessive head on the glass. Some bars and lounges will sell a lot of soft drinks, and the usage of these products must be monitored along with everything else.

Glassware has to be standardized, and management must constantly check to assure that the proper sizes and shapes are being used. One of the most effective ways to control portion sizes is through carefully selected glassware, and this technique should be employed to its maximum.

Beverage Control Systems

Inventory System. This is also called the *ounce control system*; it is an accurate but time-consuming and complicated method. The basic idea is that management determines the standard usage of products and compares it to the actual usage. It is similar to most food control systems in that it is product and cost oriented. The system is set up as follows: (1) Obtain a daily count of every drink sold; (2) calculate the liquor usage by multiplying the drinks sold by the amount of liquor in each drink; and (3) compare this calculated usage to the actual liquor used as determined by a physical inventory.

Although this will yield very useful information and can really help the operator zero in on problem areas, unless there is some type of electronic point-of-service (POS) equipment available so that the drink sales information can be readily, quickly, and accurately obtained, this system is not of practical use. A point of departure from traditional control theory is the relative unimportance of percentages. Most operators live and die by their cost percentages, but they are not a necessary part of this cost system. For example: If the gin-drink sales were all carefully tabulated and a calculation made that indicated that 15.4 bottles of gin *should* have been used for all purposes and physical inventories showed an actual usage of 15.5 bottles, there would be no problem. It is not necessary to make a percentage calculation. If the physical inventory showed a usage of 18.9 bottles, the percentage knowledge is still unnecessary. In the latter case, management would know that nearly 3.5 bottles of gin were used but not sold. As the discussion on beverage control brought out, the 3.5 bottles could have been stolen, wasted, spilled, given away, used for overportioning, sold but the money not collected, and so forth. Knowledge of the percentage is of very limited usefulness to management in so far as identifying and solving these problems are concerned.

Standard Sales Value. This system is based on the establishment of a standard or potential sales value for each brand of liquor on the bar as well as for beers (both bottle and draught) and wines. Management then makes a determination as to what the sales *should have been* and compares them to actual sales. In concept, this is very different from the inventory system and from most food control systems. Since food control is *primarily* a product challenge, the control system primarily concentrates on products and product costs. Since beverage control is *primarily* a personnel problem, it follows that the control systems concentrate on the illegal activities of people and the results of these. These results are generally in the form of lost sales and/or missing cash. Beverage control systems should therefore focus on identifying what *sales* should be, not what *costs* should be.

The first step in setting up the standard sales value system is to determine what each bottle would yield in sales if everything were done perfectly. For example, call Scotches are sold for $1.75 per drink; the portion size is 1 ounce and 750 ml. bottles (25.4 oz.) are used. The standard sales value would be $44.45 ($1.75 × 25.4 oz.), and there should be $44.45 in *recorded sales* for each bottle of call Scotch *used*. Well (or bar) Scotch, on the other hand, is sold for $1.25 per 1-oz. drink, and its standard sales value would be $31.75. These figures make the potential loss from fraudulent activities clearer. If a bartender pours an entire bottle of well Scotch when call brands are asked for, the difference in the bottle sales value, $12.70 ($44.45 - $31.75), could be kept. It would be even more profitable for the bartender to bring in a bottle, costing perhaps $9.00, and sell it for $44.45, making a personal profit of $35.45. In both these cases, the cost percentage will not be affected, emphasizing the drawback of total reliance upon percentage control systems.

All products cannot be calculated in this manner, for some will be used in a variety of drink types, and multiple portion sizes and prices could be used. In such cases, if there were accurate drink sales information available, it would be easy to calculate the standard sales value. To use a very simple example, suppose gin were used for only two drinks, a martini and a gin and tonic, and that of every one hundred gin drinks sold, martinis accounted for sixty-five. The martini gin-portion size is 2.5 ounces, while the gin and tonic is

Table 11-5. Standard sales value calculation

Drink	Drinks Sold	Portion Size	Total Liquor Used	Percent of Total Liquor Used	Ounce Share of Each Quart	Drinks per Quart	Price per Drink	Sales	Standard Bottle Sales Value
Martini	65	2.5 oz.	162.5 oz.	82.3%	26.3 oz.	10.5	$2.25	$23.63	
Other	35	1.0 oz.	35.0 oz.	17.7%	5.7 oz.	5.7	$1.10	$ 6.27	$29.90
	100.0		197.5 oz.	100.0%	32.0 oz.	16.2		$29.90	

1 ounce. The martini sells for $2.25, and gin and tonic for $1.10. The standard sales value of $29.90 would be calculated as shown in Table 11-5. It is very important that the sales mix of products such as gin be checked periodically to determine whether the sales patterns have changed.

At the end of a cost period, a physical inventory will yield the numbers of bottles used for each brand. These are multiplied by the standard sales value of that brand. The total dollar amount represents the sales which could, and should, have been realized (see Table 11-6). Variances between the standard sales and actual sales must be investigated, and management must be willing to follow-up and take whatever action necessary to bring the two into an acceptable ratio. Perfection is obviously not a rational goal, but there must be a standard that is considered attainable, and management must insist it be met. Management may, for example, accept 98 percent or 96 percent (or whatever) of the calculated sales as a reasonable figure, realizing that human error is a factor—that there will be some waste, some mistakes, and some customer rejection or walk outs and so forth. The acceptable variance should be as small as possible, and it should be justifiable. In other words, management should be able to document the expected variance with some precision.

This type of control system also ignores cost percentages. It does take into consideration any variances in the sales mix from period to period and is therefore more accurate than a percentage system.

Electronic Computerized Systems. The rationale for these increasingly popular systems is simple. Most operators do not get the maximum available from each bottle. The primary reason is that all the liquor is not sold. As stated, it may be stolen, given away, drunk, spilled, lost through breakage and/or evaporation, or wasted through overportioning. Or it may also be sold, but the sales transactions won't necessarily be recorded and turned in. Companies that manufacture these equipment systems claim these losses can

Table 11-6. Calculation for Sales Realized

Product Category	Opening Inventory	Total Weekly Issues to Bar	Total Available for Sale	Ending Inventory	Usage	Standard Sales per Bottle ($)	Total Standard Sales ($)	Actual Sales ($)	Plus or Minus
Scotches									
Call	6.4	10.0	16.4	3.7	12.7	48.00	609.60		
Well	4.5	8.0	12.5	4.2	8.3	35.20	292.16		
Total	10.9	18.0	28.9	7.9	21.0	83.20	901.76		
Bourbons									
Call	2.5	6.0	8.5	2.2	6.3	48.00	302.40		
Well	4.6	5.0	9.6	3.8	5.8	35.20	204.16		
Total	7.1	11.0	18.1	6.0	12.1	83.20	506.56		
Gins									
Call	3.5	7.0	10.5	4.4	6.1	33.38	203.01		
Well	2.7	4.0	6.7	3.1	3.6	29.90	107.64		
Total	6.2	11.0	17.2	7.5	9.7	63.28	310.65		
Vodkas									
Call	2.4	5.0	7.4	1.4	6.0	33.38	200.28		
Well	5.1	7.0	12.1	4.9	7.2	29.90	215.28		
Total	7.5	12.0	19.5	6.3	13.2	63.28	415.56		
TOTAL	31.7	52.0	83.7	27.7	56.0	292.96	2134.53	2001.56	(132.9) (6.2%)

total as many as seven drinks per bottle. These systems are therefore *primarily* designed to assure that all the liquor in each bottle is *sold.*

Some of the capabilities and advantages of these systems are: (1) measurement of standard portions, (2) recording the fact that a drink has been prepared, (3) keeping sales records by specific drinks, (4) calculating current inventory levels, (5) storage of pouring stock in remote locations, (6) cocktail mixing, (7) reduction or elimination of spillage and overpouring, (8) increased pouring speed resulting in greater potential for number of drinks served, (9) bottle can be drained more completely relative to a hand-pouring system, (10) makes possible the use of half-gallon bottles that result in a lower purchase cost per ounce, (11) centralization of pouring stock for multiple bars, (12) proper and adequate training of bar personnel should be easier, and (13) reduction or elimination of pricing errors.

None of the systems available will offer all these potential advantages, nor is it necessary for most beverage operations to have them all. An operator should evaluate their own specific system and decide which of these benefits are most needed and look into equipment that meets those particular needs best.

There are also some potential disadvantages with these kinds of equipment. Among the major ones are: (1) These equipment systems are quite complex, especially those that rely upon mechanical components, and there is always the possibility of a breakdown and loss of the system for a meal period or even days. (2) Much of this equipment is costly, and the capital investment may not be justified. (3) Routine maintenance and post warranty repairs can be expensive and must be considered on a cost-for-value basis. (4) One of the more common arguments against such types of systems is the potential for loss of customer goodwill, perhaps even resulting in customer distrust. Although this attitude is undoubtedly overemphasized, it is certainly a potential problem. (5) Manual mixing is seldom completely eliminated, which seriously compromises the control aspects.

Because these systems are new to many employees, and because they have a bad reputation with bar personnel (who hardly constitute an unbiased opinion source), and because they are complex, management must put a high priority upon training and implementation of the system. A formal training program is absolutely necessary; it is not possible to merely hire people and point them towards a work station as is often done. These training costs should be predetermined and included in the system cost analysis. As a result of employee mistrust and feelings of being threatened, sabotage is a distinct possibility, and management must be aware of how such techniques could be implemented and how the system could be protected against them. Management should also investigate the possibility of maintaining a spare-parts kit that would allow unit employees to trouble shoot the system, perform some repairs or even do partial replacement.

Before a rational decision can be arrived at regarding purchase of such a system, a number of determinations must be made. One of the most important is what the current cost structure is and what, if any, savings are likely. These savings must be compared to the total system cost, and a pay-back calculation must be made. Total cost includes not only the purchase price but handling and maintenance costs and the opportunity value of the cash tied up.

Some of the operational factors to be considered are: (1) How much liquor is mixed and sold directly to the customers? (2) What will be the impact upon the physical facilities? (3) Will there be an increase in employee productivity? (4) Will management become more productive? (5) Is the sales pattern such that a large majority of the drinks sold can be served through the system?

Marketing, Promoting, and Merchandising of Alcoholic Beverages

These three terms are often used interchangeably by food service operators yet they have very different meanings. *Marketing* is the management philosophy of doing business from the perspective of the customer. This is an important point, for the food service industry has traditionally taken a production sales philosophy and has conducted its business from the perspective of the producer or seller.

Promoting involves promotions, which are scheduled events that provide clients with an incentive to use the facility, its products, and services. Promotions should bring certain benefits to the operation, including increased demand for the products and services at non-peak sales periods, thereby increasing revenue during those periods. They should reinforce top-of-mind awareness, that is, customer's strong awareness of the establishment so that when they make a decision to go out, this establishment is always considered. Promotions should also break monotony and provide novelty.

Promotional activities are frequently planned independently of each other with no overall promotional strategy, and this limits their effectiveness and leads to results that are greatly inconsistent. Promotions should be planned annually as part of a total marketing strategy, and they must have *measurable objectives* and *budgets.*

Merchandising is trying to influence the consumers' purchase decision once they are inside the establishment.

Understanding the 1980s Consumer in Order to Plan for Better Profits

The consumers the food service industry is serving today are quite different in some respects from those of just a few years ago. There is a great deal of ongoing social research attempting to identify current trends in the American life style, and many food service concepts reflect the current trends in consumer tastes. One of the phrases used to describe the new consumer is "new value people." Their concentration is on themselves —or *me*; they tend to reject the Protestant ethic that has dominated American values since the beginning. In general, they accept dining out (and drinking) as a need, not a want—a critical difference—and they regard pleasure as natural rather than sinful. Not all people, however, reflect the "new values" concept, and trends must be evaluated on that basis. The food service operator must still know their market, as always. The point here is that the market may well be very different and is changing rapidly also. Market study is thus a much higher priority for management than it has been in the past. The following discussion reflects some of the lifestyle trends as identified by the social research firm of Yankolovich, Skelley, and White as well as some of the conceptual responses food and beverage operators have made to these trends.

Focus on Physical Self. This is manifested by a greater awareness of physical fitness, a move towards looking and feeling good. The great interest in activities such as jogging and the proliferation of retail sporting goods stores are two examples of this strong trend and how it has spread throughout American culture. In response, some operators promote and merchandise lighter beverages, such as light beers, white wines, and wine cocktails. Many operators are disturbed by such trends since a switch from predinner cocktails to white wine can have far-reaching effects upon the profitability of an establishment. There are some operators, though, who take a more positive approach; they assume that if the consumer wants wines and other light beverages before dinner, there must be a way to make money on them. It does not take a sophisticated marketing analyst to conclude that it is far easier to sell patrons something they want then to create a desire for something they do not want or have no interest in.

Naturalism. The "new-value" consumer favors the natural over the artifical. One result of this is that function is replacing gimmickry. This trend is demonstrated by the increasing popularity of wine, which in addition to being perceived as lighter is also viewed as a "natural" beverage. One very successful approach to meet this trend is the promotion of fruit-based alcoholic drinks, a concept that has been profitable for many operators, especially when done with flair and imagination.

Acceptance of Alcoholic Beverages. Alcoholic beverages in general have reflected a variety of social trends in this country over the years. One need only consider the Eighteenth Amendment to the Constitution—Prohibition—to realize this. It certainly did not stop people from drinking, but quite obviously it must have had wide support in order to be ratified as a constitutional amendment. But today there is increasing acceptance of alcoholic beverages, and this offers big opportunities to the food and beverage operator. Here are some of the things operators are doing: broadening the beer brand base, often specializing in a variety of imported and premium beers; appealing to the increased female market with sweeter, less potent drinks, many of which can be frozen; developing a specialty coffee program, offering such items as Irish coffee, Mexican and Italian coffees, and so on.

Search for Novelty and Fun. The trend of the late 1960s was to create novelty through design features of a concept. Novelty, however, by definition, is fleeting, and establishments that depended on atmosphere as their primary unique selling point found this a confining and expensive way to operate. As a result, more and more operators are attempting to create novelty in other, more long-term and less expensive ways. In some cases, the service people themselves are part of the atmosphere and fun and are promoted as such. Promotions and entertainment can be changed frequently to create the desired image. The trend for novelty and fun is resulting in the development of creative and interesting foods and drinks as well as unique ways of presenting them. Glassware is especially important to the perception of alcoholic beverages as interesting and different, and there are a lot of innovative designs available today. Some establishments have also had success using such nontraditional pieces as Mason jars, oil cans, jelly jars, and graduated cylinders such as those used in laboratories.

Search for Elitism and Quality. This shows in status-conspicuous consumption, and the operator must not deny the customer the opportunity to "trade-up." Quality is fundamental to the *me* purchase, and the attitude is that "nothing is too good for me." There are many ways to cash in on this attitude. One would be to use name brands in the well; another might be to have special premium brands available. Examples of the latter are the increasing popularity of unblended malt Scotches, imported beers, and premium champagnes. (Moet and Chandon cannot make enough Dom Perignon to satisfy the apparent demand.)

Increased Value of Time and Movement Away from Systems and Order. This trend indicates that consumers will respond favorably to quick service and are receptive to self-service concepts. One potential danger of self-service is the creation of forced patterns of behavior, and this should be avoided, for people do not want to be locked into overly structured environments.

The attitude seems to be "let's do our own thing," and it is reflected by casual dress—strict dress codes are out—people ordering white wine with steaks, odd food combinations—a good example would be Hyatt's Ginsberg and Wong concept, a combination of Jewish deli and Chinese foods. These trends are not mutually exclusive; they are all interrelated, and today's operators need to know that they exist and must determine the extent to which their own market reflects them.

The Primary Factors Influencing a Consumer's Purchase Decision

There are four factors that management must concentrate on:

1. Personal selling
2. Packaging of products
3. Point of sale (POS) merchandising
4. Menu, wine list, drink list

Personal Selling. Food service operations have a big advantage over many other forms of retailing in that all purchases can be influenced both by direct sales personnel (waiters, waitresses, bartenders) and indirect salespeople (hostesses, management, maître d'). In order to influence the decision effectively, however, these personnel must know the guests as individuals, what their specific likes and dislikes are; they must know the product line thoroughly, develop credibility, be enthusiastic, and develop strong and open communication. The reason few operations do an effective job of personal selling is that some or all of these key points are ignored. Service personnel do not, as a rule, really know their customers; they do not intelligently *anticipate* customer needs and wants and, as a result, spend most of their time *reacting* to them. Product line knowledge on the part of the sales people is of overwhelming importance; yet how often do they really have in-depth knowledge? If a cocktail waitress or waiter were asked the difference between the three brands of cognac stocked, would she or he know? What is the difference between the various imported beers? What proof is the vodka? What wine goes with the veal special tonight and why? Providing extensive product knowledge should be a major goal of any training program and is essential to a productive personal selling effort.

Developing credibility is obviously important; otherwise the selling effort is likely to have a negative rather than positive effect. One way to develop credibility is to know both the guest and the product line. Any salesperson who demonstrates that he or she knows what they are talking about and knows which products will best satisfy *your* specific desires as a customer, will be trusted.

Enthusiasm is another way to develop credibility. If a salesperson is genuinely excited about a new wine or a particular wine for the food ordered or a special drink the house makes, the guest is likely to go along with the suggestion; even better, the guest may get excited and enthusiastic too. Enthusiasm can backfire, however, if the basic requisites of patron and product knowledge are not fulfilled. That aside, there is really no acceptable type of service person other than one who is alive and enthusiastic. These are personal traits so easy to spot during hiring that one wonders how so many of the people who end up bartending, waiting on tables, and hosting ever get there in the first place.

Product Packaging. Packaging is an important attribute of all products, and foods and beverages are no exception. Products that are properly packaged and presented can almost sell themselves. I have already mentioned the use of specialized and interesting glassware; garnishes can also be quite effective. One objective of management should be to exceed the consumer's expectation through innovative packaging. Whenever a situation is created so that the guests feel the product delivers more than they expected, the establishment wins. The reverse is true as well. When a guest's expectations have been raised by a skillful salesperson, decor, menu, or some combination of these, there had better be a payoff at least equal to that expectation or the operation loses. This may explain why many ill-conceived promotions do not work; management puts great effort into creating interest but little into assuring that the interest will be sustained.

Point of Sale Merchandising. The usual techniques of POS merchandising are to have displays like a visible wine cellar or display carts for wines, cordials, coffee specialties, and other beverages; put a bottle on the table; set tables with wine glasses; use table tents, and have other displays in various places. All these have been tried and will work if properly executed. The objective is to influence the consumer's purchase decision at the point of sale. Food service operations have another great advantage here over most retail businesses: when the consumer enters a restaurant, he or she has already made a general purchase decision. Restaurants do not get browsers or shoppers. What the operator should do is direct the sale, and this is the value of POS merchandising, to direct the sales to certain items as well as to build the overall check averages through selling items the guests may *not* have already decided to purchase. These

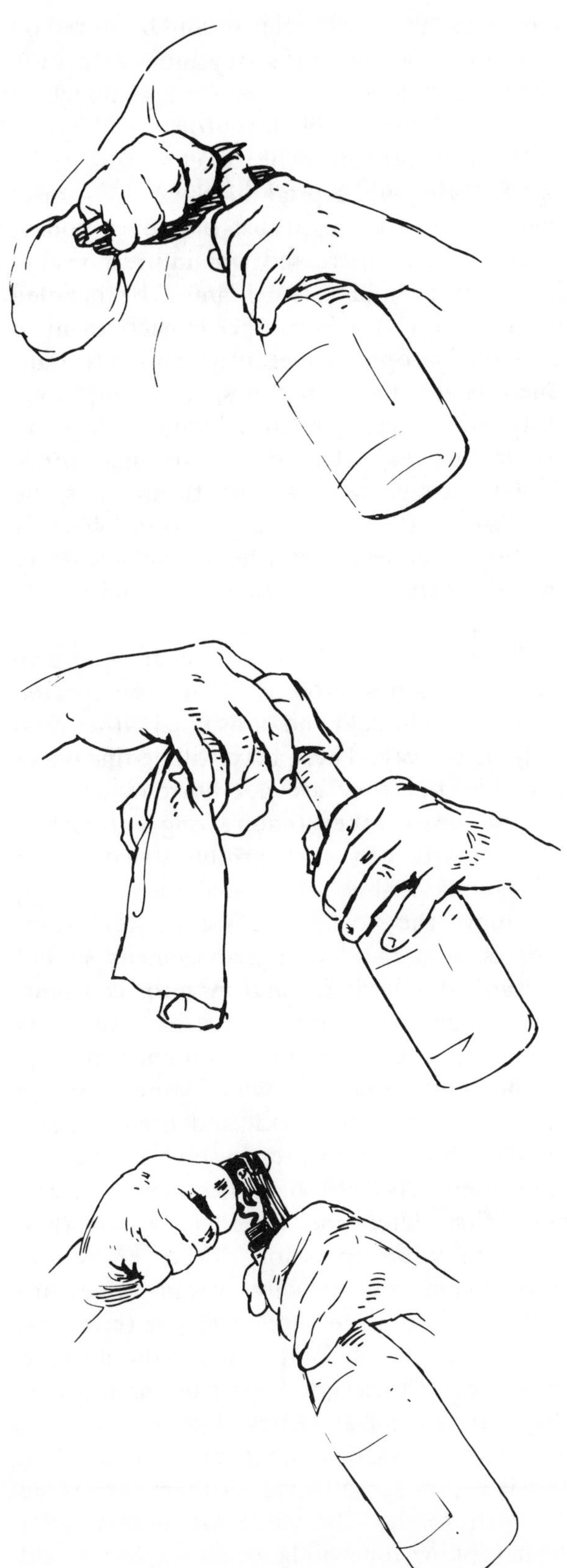

Figure 11c. Opening a bottle of wine. The metal or plastic capsule is cut about one half inch below the neck of the bottle and removed; (2) the neck is wiped with a clean cloth; (3) the bouchon, or cork, is pierced completely through with the corkscrew, removed, checked by smelling for a "corked odor" and placed on the table near the host or hostess; (4) the neck of the bottle is wiped, and a small amount of wine poured in the glass of the host or hostess for tasting. The wine should be poured gently along the edge of the glass without resting the bottle on the glass, then rotated slightly as it is lifted away to prevent dripping. A tasting cup, which hangs on a chain around the neck of the *sommelier* (wine steward) is used by him to taste the wine. After the wine is accepted, it is poured for other guests, with the host or hostess last.

would include cocktails, wines, side orders, desserts, after-dinner drinks, and so forth.

Menus, Wine List, and Drink List. These are the other primary factors that influence the consumer's purchase decision. A wine list can be a powerful marketing tool, but it seldom is. There are two aspects to the list: the content and the design. The content should reflect the type of establishment and match the foods. Many operators will turn over the development of their wine list to their supplier although they would never think of letting their food supplier make up their food menu. The technical consideration of what to put on the wine list should be made by management, who should consider the establishment image, the consumer profile, the types of food they serve, and what is available. Suppliers can obviously be very helpful in providing information for this decision, as could the bar personnel, especially if they have a lot of experience within that particular market. The second consideration—the one of design—could be farmed out to a design consultant or a printing company if management does not feel they have the requisite talent or background.

Wines, Their Sales and Service

There are two ways to approach a wine program. In some hotels, clubs, and restaurants, expensive and extensive wine lists will be used. The wines will often be purchased long before they are ready to be consumed, particularly some red wines. In such cases, management must assume the responsibility for holding the products over many years. This requires very specific storage conditions. Wine should be held in an area that is cool (55 degrees F is ideal), and where the temperature does not fluctuate. Variable temperatures are actually more harmful to wine than temperatures that are higher than 55 degrees F. The storage area should be dark since light, especially sunlight, is harmful. The wines should also be protected from vibration and movement. Overly dry conditions should be avoided because of the possibility of drying the corks, and the bottles should be stored on their sides (so the corks stay moist). In addition, the storage area must be big enough to accommodate a sizable inventory.

Management must be able to financially justify tying up capital in these inventories due to the very high cost of money today. There are also increased training responsibilities, for premium wines must be handled carefully, and the consumer expects them to be served properly, elegantly, and with flair. There is also the factor of speculation; this is truly what management is doing. They are committing capital to goods that may prove to be very valuable in the future, but the possibility also exists that the wines will not develop as expected and hence will not repay the considerable *total* expense of holding and handling.

The other, more usual, type of wine program is to stock products that are expected to move, to be sold and consumed rather than to be laid away. There may still be fine wines available, but they are not horrendously expensive, nor do they require long maturation. The operator can stock products that can be sold at reasonable prices, make a fair profit, and move the stock. In this case, stock turnover is a statistic that management should establish standards for and monitor constantly. Storage conditions do not have to be as stringent due to the reduced holding time.

The most common use of wine is at the table to accompany food, and there are lots of rules about what wines to serve and how to serve them. As with any rules, however, you must first determine whether or not they apply to your operation. There are sound gastronomic reasons why certain wines are well suited to some foods and not to others, and anyone in the food business should have some idea of these good companions and why they are so good. Wines, like foods, have different flavors, colors, textures, and aromas; and it makes sense to match them just as we do with foods. Chocolate sauce may be a great topping for vanilla ice cream, but would probably not be appreciated with lime sher-

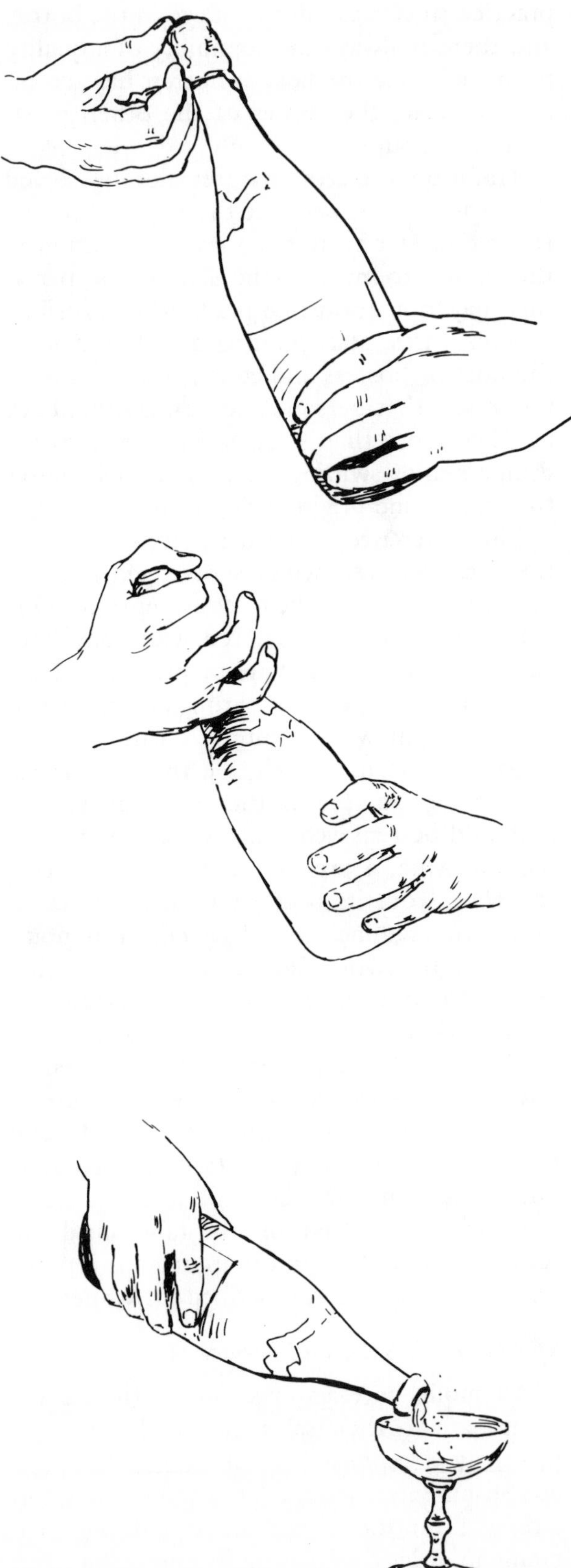

Figure IId. Serving champagne. Champagne should be uncorked by holding the bottle poised away at a 45-degree angle, after the wire holding the cork has been removed. By holding the cork steady with one hand, twist the bottle gently back and forth. In this way, the cork will be expelled by the gas and not cause the champagne itself to bubble or overflow. The neck should then be wiped, and the pouring done as with still wines. To prevent injury to guests, the bottle should always be pointed away from them when opening.

bet, and if you tried to serve it with broccoli, there would be real problems. The food service operator should understand which wines compliment which foods.

There is another theory that has current popularity: any wine is all right with any food; it all depends upon what you like. The truth of the matter lies somewhere between the two extremes of only certain wines with particular foods or any wine with any food. If a guest asks advice or requests guidance, stick to the traditional combinations; they are sound. If, however, a guest orders a sweet white wine with a strip steak, you would of course serve it, just as you would accede to a request for chocolate sauce with broccoli, although you would never suggest it. Rather you would suggest something that is acceptable from a sensory viewpoint, such as hollandaise sauce or mornay sauce.

The wine order should be taken when the food is ordered, and the wine should be brought to the table as soon as possible. This only applies to corked bottles; wines served by the glass or in carafes should be brought to the table whenever the guest is ready for it. Once the bottle arrives, it should be shown to the person who ordered the wine so he or she can check the bottle, label, and vintage year (if it is a vintage wine). From this point on, red and white wines are handled differently.

White wines are generally appreciated best when chilled, and fifteen to twenty minutes in an ice bucket is sufficient. After a white wine is approved, it should be left on or beside the table in an ice bucket. The best time to open the wine is just prior to serving the food, although this is not always possible. The top portion of the lead-foil cap should be cut away and the cork removed with a corkscrew. There are a variety of corkscrews available, and the service person can use any one that feels comfortable. Once the cork is out, the bottle lip should be wiped and the cork given to the host or hostess (the person ordering the wine) for inspection. The next step is to pour a small portion of wine for tasting purposes. This is traditional and is a sound practice since wine does change in the bottle, and there is always the possibility of a quality problem. Once the host or hostess has accepted the wine, the glasses of the other guests should be poured.

Tradition dictates that females be served first, then males, and last the host or hostess. Depending upon the table layout, location in the dining room, and the size of the party, this may not always be practical or possible. In such cases, start pouring on either side of the host or hostess and continue around until you reach that person. The glasses should not be filled more than ½ or ¾ full as many wine drinkers enjoy swirling the wine in their glasses to aerate it and brighten the smell and taste.

The difference in red wine service is due to the fact that red wines should generally be opened *prior* to their consumption. One reason is that a mature red wine may have sediment, particles that are by-products of the changes the wine goes through while aging. This sediment will not interfere with the taste or smell, but it will change the appearance and perhaps the feel in the mouth as well, so it should be removed. This is done by decanting the wine, a process of carefully pouring the wine from its bottle into another vessel. When the sediment is observed, stop pouring, and the wine should be clear. Another reason for opening reds before consumption is that they often benefit from a "breathing" period or exposure to the air, which has the same effect as swirling the wine in the glass. After the wine is opened (and decanted if necessary), a tasting portion is poured as with whites, and if the wine is satisfactory it is left on the table until the food is served. The procedure from this point on is identical to that described for whites.

Spirits, Their Sales and Service

Alcoholic beverages provide profits disproportionate to their sales level, and spirits are primarily responsible for this. Beverage establishments should, therefore, develop strong promotions and merchandising programs in order to sell as much as possible. The

Figure 11e. Typical shapes and sizes of wine and beer glasses. Wine glasses should never be filled to the brim and should have rounded sides and be narrower at the top to bring out the aroma or bouquet. The stems are for holding so that the hand will not unduly influence the temperature of the wine. Beer glasses should be clean, be free from all lint, fat, or soap to permit foam development, and be filled to brim with one-half inch of head.

objective should be to create an image of constant activity and innovative, clever ideas. Follow the four rules for influencing the consumer's purchase decision and keep in mind the life-style trends. A few examples of activities that could be promoted are:

1. Use a different or nontypical liquor in drinks; for example, try a tequila collins or an applejack lemonade.
2. Keep the glass program. These are good PR. and they can spread the establishment's logo as well. For example, how many people go to New Orleans determined to have an Irish coffee at Pat O'Brien's simply because they have seen a Pat O'Brien Irish coffee mug on someone's mantle?
3. Develop special drinks named after regular customers, either groups or individuals.
4. Do something creative and unusual for bar snacks.
5. Try flaming beverages.
6. Introduce table-side preparation of specialty drinks.
7. Install a soft-serve ice cream machine on the bar and develop a line of ice cream drinks and alcoholic desserts.
8. Develop a menu featuring coffee cordial specialties.
9. Use the "signature" item concept; the operator offers products unique to that establishment. It could be Irish coffee, ice cream specialties, flaming drinks, and so forth. The key point is that no one else around has anything quite like it.

Alcoholic beverages should be served with as much flair as possible, for the service could become part of the merchandising program. Flaming or other special touches while preparing beverages at the table is certainly effective merchandising if done properly. Bringing the bottle to the table and pouring the drink poses some control problems, but none that could not be handled satisfactorily, especially if it were done with only a few products; for example, cognac or Grand Marnier with after-dinner coffee.

A nice service touch that actually enhances control is achieved when the server brings an iced glass to the table, with the mixer and the liquor in a shot glass both on the side. The liquor and mixer either are poured in front of the guests or can be left for the guests to mix themselves. This is an elegant way to serve drinks, and management can observe whether or not the correct portions are being dispensed (providing, of course, the correct shot glasses are being used). This service cannot be instituted in all types of units, but where feasible it is strongly recommended.

Beers, Their Sales and Service

There are two ways in which beer can be handled and sold: in bottles (or cans) or in kegs. Keg beer, or draught beer (pronounced draft), is significantly more profitable, though many operators have difficulty controlling draught beers. Bottled or canned beers are pasteurized and are stable at room temperatures, so they do not require refrigeration. Kegs, on the other hand, are not heat treated and must be kept at 40 degrees F or less, preferably between 36 and 38 degrees F. If it warms to above 45 degrees F, the beer may change in taste and odor and could become sour and cloudy. All beers, even pasteurized cans and bottles, are perishable and must be rotated to insure constant stock turnover. In storage, beer must be protected from light (especially sunlight), and although bottled and canned beer need not be refrigerated, they should not be stored in warm or hot storage areas. A recommended storage temperature would be about 70 degrees F.

A key to beer quality and, hence, to sales, is cleanliness. With draught beer this is of extreme importance, and the establishment must take the necessary time and effort to flush the lines on a daily basis (or perhaps even whenever a keg is changed) and clean the lines biweekly. Both kinds of beer must be served in sparkling clean glassware. If there is any dirt, grease, or detergent residue on the glass, the beer will not hold a head. Instead of the head being thick and foamy and composed of small bubbles, it will have large coarse bubbles that will break up quickly.

The person pouring the beer, whether it is from a tap or bottle, should always attempt to put a full, creamy head on top. The beer will not only have a better appearance but will drink better as well. Try this test sometime. Take two clean glasses and one bottle or can of beer. Pour one glass very carefully down the side and avoid putting any head on it. Pour the second straight down the middle of the glass, encouraging the development of a full head. Then taste both glasses carefully. Most people would prefer the beer with the head. A further disadvantage if there is no head is that the carbonic acid gas stays dissolved in the beer and is consumed, filling the patron up faster and resulting in less repeat sales. Beer manufacturers work very hard to make a product that will produce a full, thick head, and they do not recommend pouring the beer in any way that discourages that.

There is one control problem specifically associated with the head on a glass of beer. If a bartender uses a tapered glass (one with a wider top than bottom) and creates an excessive head, he or she would get many more glasses from the barrel than could normally be expected. This is because the upper part of the glass (being wider) contains the major portion of the potential volume, and if a 1 ½-inch rather than a 1-inch head were consistently poured, it would make a significant difference in the amount of beer poured.

Establishments today should concentrate their sales efforts on products that fit the modern life styles. Light beers are consistent with the physical fitness trends and desire for lighter, lower calorie products. Imported and premium beers appeal to the elitists and quality-conscious consumers. With the increasing acceptance of alcoholic beverages and the adventurous spirit of patrons today, a specialty beer program and beer promotions offer some great opportunities. Beer tastings can be staged for customers, and beer can be promoted as a food accompaniment because beer goes well with nearly all foods and may be the beverage of choice with certain foods. Foods with high acidity (some German dishes and vinegar-based salad dressings, and so on) clash with wine but go fine with beer. Pizza and hamburgers are also foods that match up very well with beer. Beer could be the best beverage to promote in many types of ethnic restaurants and can offer a big potential for many fast food concepts as well.

Part II

Preparation and Service

12 *Pantry Items and Salads*

Objective: To expose the student to the unique operations carried out in the pantry area and the factors that are important to successful operation there. Emphasis is on preparation procedures used in making salads, sandwiches, garnishes, appetizers, cold desserts, and beverages.

Whether it is called the cold meat section, the garde-manger, the pantry, or the salad section, this department of the food operation handles a variety of tasks, from making coffee to plating ice cream. Many items that go unused in other departments are here put to efficient use in salads, hors d'oeuvres, canapés, gelatin molds, and the like. Here are practiced the artistic skills for which the food service industry has become well known. The judicious use of the pastry tube, the construction of a multilayered gelatin salad, or the use of an ice carving for a buffet table may well make good food outstanding.

In the pantry are prepared seafood cocktails, cold sauces, salad dressings, plate garnishes, appetizers, sandwiches, uncooked desserts, and beverages. The food cost is usually quite low on these items, and the profit realized on each is higher than in most other departments in the kitchen. However, because of the complexity and repetitious nature of the hand work required to prepare them, labor costs in this area are usually higher than they are in many of the other sections of the kitchen.

The space devoted to this part of the kitchen must be adequate for the preparation and plating work to be performed. Sufficient refrigerated and frozen food holding space are needed as well. The tools used are many and varied, mostly those used in the hand. Where mixers, steam-jacketed kettles, or ovens are provided, they are usually much smaller than those in other sections of the kitchen. Deep sink areas and self-leveling and other forms of dish storage should be provided. Pass-through refrigerators, a cold bain-marie section, and a waitress tray rest and assembly area are also needed.

Sight, speed, and *specialty* might well be the key descriptive words for this important part of the kitchen, and the food service manager or supervisor should ensure that all are provided for in the production from this area.

Many operations have experimented quite successfully with exposing this department to the view of customers, locating sandwich and salad preparation stations in consumer areas. Others permit consumers to assemble their own salads and relishes or to select items from displays on traveling carts.

Sandwiches

One of the most important products prepared in the pantry is the sandwich. It traces its origin to the Earl of Sandwich, who had his servant deliver a meal of bread and meat to him so that he could remain at the gaming table while he ate. The variations of sandwiches available in food operations today differ considerably from this original concept. Many cannot be eaten without the use of a knife and fork.

Sandwiches may be served hot or cold, with or without gravy or sauce. They may be open faced, closed, grilled, rolled, deep fried, multilayered, or produced in the Earl's way: with more function than form. Sandwiches are made of regular or specialty breads and may be filled, spread, or covered with a variety of items from meats and cheeses to jams, jellies, and specialty spreads.

Sandwiches challenge the preparation worker, stimulate the diner, and usually contribute a major share of the profit.

In all sandwiches there are four basic considerations: (1) the filling spread or substance, (2) the vehicle (for example the bread type), (3) the method of preparation, and (4) the garnish or esthetic form of presentation.

Sandwiches that are to become mobile, of course, require wrapping, holding, or storage. In food service work these are a minimal number, and only apply in certain types of operations and serving outlets.

Fillings and Spreads. All kinds of fillings and spreads for sandwiches have been tried. Sliced sirloin of beef, turkey, chicken salad, cream cheese, tongue, cheese spreads, jelly, apple butter, and hundreds of other foods have all found their way into sandwiches. Although certain combinations have gained greater consumer acceptance than others (e.g., bacon, lettuce, and tomato or peanut butter and jelly), opportunity still remains for the sandwich maker to be creative. A sandwich original, merchandised in an unusual way and at an attractive price, may become one of those that later hits the best seller list.

A few general suggestions about fillings are offered here:

(1) A sandwich is not an appetizer unless it is designed for that purpose (such as a tea sandwich). Sandwich fillings should, therefore, fill the consumer's needs and be suited to the pricing structure and menu pattern. From 1½ to 2 ounces of filling material or 2 ounces of solid meat will be sufficient for the average sandwich.

(2) Although paper-thin slices of the heavier meats (such as roast beef) will create an apparently fuller sandwich and one that chews better (even using the lower grades of meat), be careful to avoid making "sawdust" by cutting the meat too thin.

(3) Protect the bread vehicle from all absorbable fillings by spreading it with whipped butter. One pound of butter or margarine whipped with ½ cup of milk makes a highly satisfactory protective spread.

(4) Avoid the use of leftovers in sandwiches unless it is certain that they have been protected from bacterial growth and that proper temperatures have been maintained. Be particularly careful of chopped or heavily packed items, which tend to encourage bacterial growth if they become infected.

(5) Do not use mayonnaise, lettuce, or tomatoes on sandwiches that must be held for long periods of time, since these contribute to sogginess and create sanitation problems.

(6) Make sure that all fillings are reasonably easy to eat.

(7) Portion fillings by weight for solid products and with adequate measuring devices, such as food scoops, for mixtures.

Breads. Bread is the vehicle most often used to present the sandwich filling to the guest. A sandwich may be made from almost any type of bread—white, whole wheat, rye, hard rolls, etc. Sweet or specialty breads, such as date nut, banana, and orange, are used particularly for the more dainty sandwiches.

There are no standard combinations of fillings vis-à-vis bread forms; this is left to the imagination of the operator and the choice of the consumer. Types of breads may be varied

Table 12-1. Sandwich Supplies and Quantities for Average Portions

Supply	Quantity
Bread	2 slices per serving. 1-1/4 pound loaf white bread cuts 19 (5/8") slices, without end crust. 1-1/2 pound loaf white bread cuts 24 (5/8") slices, without end crust. 2 pound sandwich loaf white bread cuts 28 (1/2") slices, or 36 (3/8") slices, without end crust. 3 pound sandwich loaf white bread cuts 44 (1/2") slices, or 56 (3/8") slices, without end crust. 1 pound loaf whole wheat bread cuts 16 (5/8") slices, without end crust. 2 pound loaf whole wheat bread cuts 28 (1/2") slices, without end crust. 3 pound loaf whole wheat bread cuts 44 (1/2") slices, or 56 (3/8") slices, without end crust. 1 pound loaf rye bread cuts 23 (3/4") slices, without end crust. 2 pound loaf rye bread cuts 33 (3/4") slices, without end crust. *Note:* The thickness and number of slices will vary in different localities. Slices from a 3 pound loaf are larger in surface area than those from a 2 pound loaf.
Buns	1 sandwich bun per serving.
Butter	softened—1 pound will spread 96 bread slices if 1 teaspoonful is used per slice.
Bacon	1 pound averages 25 medium strips, or 1-1/2 cups cooked and chopped.
Cheese	
Sliced	1 pound averages 16 slices (1 ounce each).
Cottage	1 pound averages 1 pint.
Cream	1 pound averages 1 pint.
Processed, grated	1 pound averages 1 quart.
Celery	1 pound averages 1 quart chopped.
Chicken	
Diced	5 pound fowl averages 1 quart cooked and diced.
Sliced	1 pound averages 12 slices (1-1/2 ounces each) or 16 slices (1 ounce each).
Eggs	hard cooked—1 dozen averages 3-1/2 cups chopped.
Jelly or preserves	1 pint will spread 16 sandwiches.
Lettuce	1 medium head averages 16 leaves.
Margarine	softened—1 pound will spread 96 bread slices if 1 teaspoonful is used per slice.
Mayonnaise	1 pint will spread 50 bread slices, if 1 teaspoonful is used per slice.
Meat	
Sliced	1 pound averages 8 slices (2 ounces each).
Ground raw	1 pound averages 1 pint.
Ground cooked	1 pound averages 3 cups.
Nut meats	1 pound averages 3-3/4 cups chopped.
Onions	1 pound averages 1 pint chopped.
Olives	drained—1 quart averages 3 cups chopped.
Pickles	drained—1 quart averages 3 cups chopped.
Peanut butter	1 pound averages 1-3/4 cups.
Sandwich filling	3 quarts will spread 60 sandwiches if one no. 20 scoop is used per sandwich.

Supply	Quantity
Salmon	1 pound averages 1 pint flaked.
Tuna fish	1 pound averages 1 pint flaked.
Tomatoes	1 pound averages 3-4 medium tomatoes.

From *Modern Sandwich Methods,* p. 8; copyright 1964, American Institute of Baking, Chicago; reprinted by permission.

in color to give variety to sandwiches, and crusts may be removed for ease of eating. Day-old bread is preferable to strictly fresh bread. Its lack of extreme softness makes sandwiches hold up much better.

Methods of Preparation. Sandwiches may be made to order in a la carte fashion or made en masse for serving to a large number of guests. The following general suggestions are offered:

(1) Prepare sandwiches in an area that has adequate work space, ready access to refrigeration, and cutting and assembly areas.

(2) If at all possible, make sandwiches to order. If sandwiches must be stored, wrap each sandwich individually in a polyethylene wrapper and refrigerate it. Freezing may be used for longer periods of storage; most breads and fillings handle the process very well. When sandwiches are wrapped for cafeteria or vending service, be sure that the filling is exposed to the customer's view.

(3) Handle sandwiches and fillings only when necessary. Use a tool if it will do the job. Use plastic throwaway gloves when hand work is necessary.

(4) When preparing a large number of like sandwiches, prestack slices of bread and carry out the same procedures for two stacks at each step. Sandwiches can be made one on top of the other up to four in a stack before cutting and removing them to a tray.

(5) When using moist fillings, coat each slice of bread with whipped butter.

(6) Keep fillings under refrigeration until used, not on a slicing machine or an unrefrigerated cutting board.

(7) Although club sandwiches (multiple breads and fillings) may be used for variety, keep them realistic in terms of the consumer's ability to eat them.

(8) Avoid the use of toothpicks to hold sandwiches together for service. When a device is necessary, use a skewer that the guest can see or a toothpick with a plastic end indicator.

(9) Try rolled, unusually cut, and new color combination sandwiches for variety and better customer acceptance.

(10) Brush sandwiches that are to be grilled with butter or margarine. To vary this, use egg dip, for a French-toast-style sandwich.

(11) Use the broiler for open-faced sandwiches that require heating or melting. Choose the type of cheese to be used carefully to ensure adequate melting and prevent stringiness. Emulsified varieties melt more smoothly and quickly; hard cheeses will achieve better spread if reduced to small pieces.

(12) Deep fry sandwiches with regular egg wash coating at 370 degrees.

(13) Toast breads before filling, unless using a rotary-type toaster or a grill.

Garnishes. A garnish should be added to a sandwich, as to any food, when it is ready to be served. The garnish may take the form of a relish, a spread, or a visual accompaniment only. Garnishes in general should be edible. In choosing the garnish an attempt should be made to vary it in taste, texture, color, and form with the sandwich.

Salads

Salads are an important product of the pantry area. They may be very simple or very

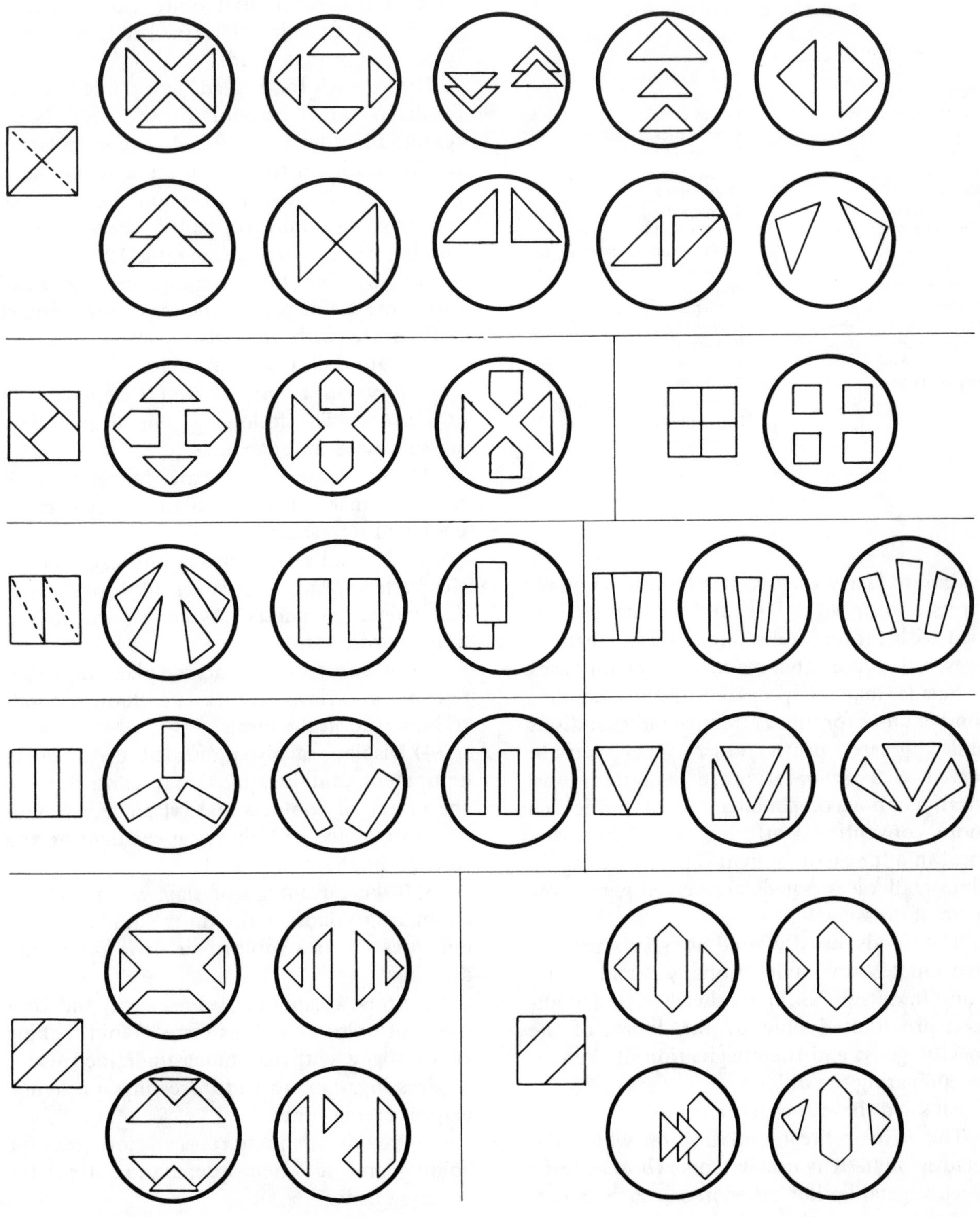

Figure 12a. Ways of arranging sandwiches for variety, visual acceptability, and combination with other items, such as soups. (From *Modern Sandwich Methods*, p. 9; copyright 1964, American Institute of Baking, Chicago; reprinted by permission.)

Table 12-2. Common Garnishes

For Sandwiches	For Salads
Radish roses	Radish roses
Celery curls	Celery curls
Carrot curls	Carrot curls
Apple slices	Cheese slices or strips
Olives	Croutons
Pickles	Pepper rings
Parsley	Onion rings
Potato chips	Tomato slices or wedges
Condiments or sauces	Hard-boiled eggs
Pimientos	Fruits (peaches, cherries, etc.)
Tomato slices	Coconut
Lemon slices	Nuts
Watercress	Pimientos
Deviled eggs	Olives
Bacon slices	Pickles
Mushroom caps	Anchovies
Pepper rings	Cucumber rings
	Red or green pepper rings
	Pickled beets
	Asparagus tips
	Chives

elaborate. They may contain combinations of fruits and/or vegetables, and be further fortified with protein items such as fish, meats, or eggs. Salads are often made with gelatin bases.

Salads may be prepared and served at a diner's table for more effective merchandising and a greater profit return. They may be served as a separate course in a traditional meal, as an accompaniment to an entrée in a more conventional offering, or as the entire meal in a luncheon or light dinner offering. In almost all cases, salads are served with some form of dressing.

The foods usually used in salads provide rich sources of vitamins, notably A and C, and iron. In salads, as in sandwiches, the items used are limited only by the desires of the specific guest and the imagination of the person preparing the dish.

All salads have four basic parts:

The *base* is the foundation on which the salad is built. It is usually some form of leafy green vegetable, but other items, such as cottage cheese, may also serve in this capacity.

The *body* of the salad consists of the main ingredients used. These should relate to the purpose of the salad. Accompanying salads contain less substantial body elements than salads used as main offerings. The latter usually contain protein foods.

The *garnish* for a salad, like that for other foods, is the decoration of the dish. It attempts to provide visual and taste stimulation to the salad and to make it more attractive in these areas. It may be an onion ring, a tomato, strips of pimiento, radish rosettes, or a number of other items (see table 12-2).

The *dressing* that accompanies the salad forms the major part of the seasoning. It must both agree with the salad components and accentuate their taste and texture.

Preparation Principles and Characteristics of Quality. The following general guidelines are suggested for all salads:

(1) No matter what the foundation or makeup, make sure the salad is clean, crisp, cool, and refreshing.

(2) Have all salad items in bite-sized pieces. Keep the forms and types of foods easily discernible to guests. Avoid all mashed or mushy products.

(3) In constructing salads, plan for color, texture, and flavor contrasts with other foods to be served in the meal.

(4) Display salads and salad dressings in equipment and locations that contribute to the effect of coolness and crispness. Copious amounts of ice and blue or green lighting and surroundings are suggested.

(5) Take advantage of flair when possible by mixing salads at the diner's table, or permit guests to assemble their own salads and dressings.

(6) Stress cleanliness, appearance, and contrasts of color as well as taste. Avoid making salads soggy with too much undrained water or dressing. Do not add dressings until just before serving time.

(7) Provide adequate refrigeration areas for holding and sufficient preparation areas for making salads.

Salad Greens

Although in the strict sense of the word, salad greens are simply vegetables, by long

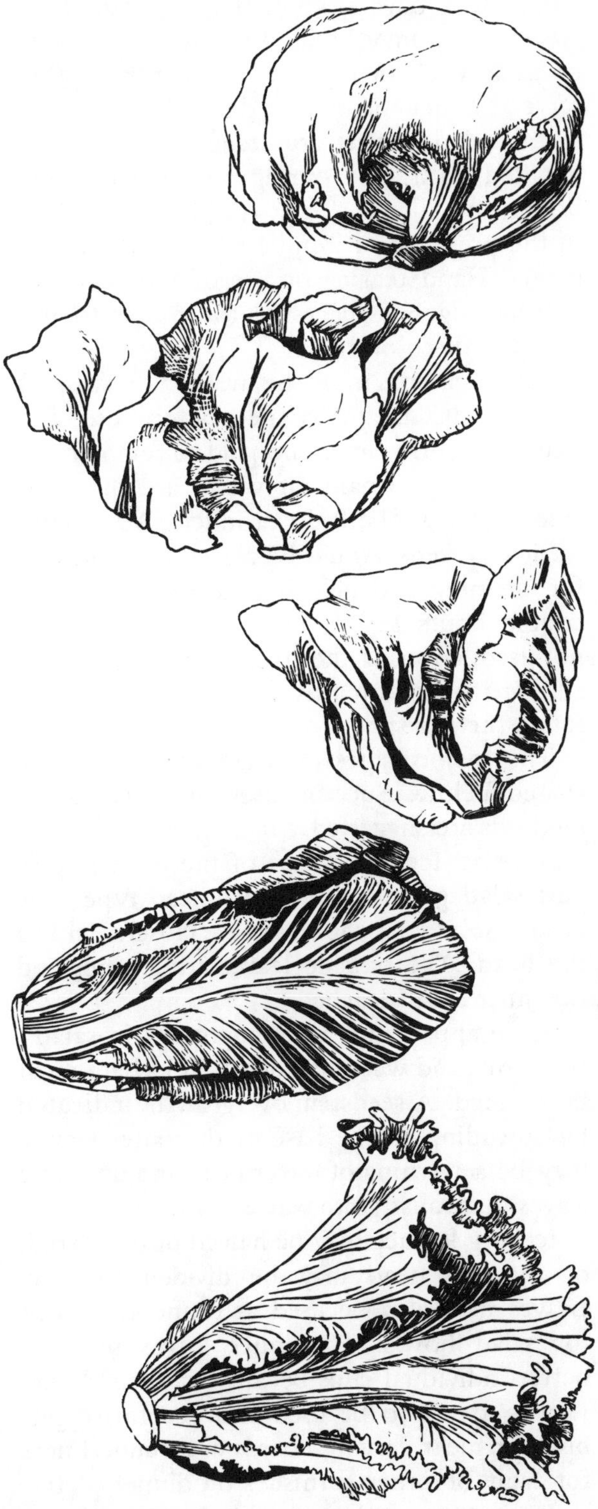

Iceberg or crisp head lettuce, a tight firm head with medium green outer leaves and bleached inner ones.

Butterhead, a softer, less firm, and less brittle head than iceberg.

Bibb, a variety of butterhead that is smaller and more tender than the big Boston butterheads.

Cos or romaine, a coarse and sweet variety with dark green leaves.

Leaf lettuce, a smoother and crisper textured variety than cos, with leaves that are very tender.

Figure 12b. The major kinds of salad greens found on the market. Two other varieties, not depicted, are curly endive (chicory) and escarole. Both are dark green with crisp outer leaves and bitter flavor. Endive has a narrow, tightly curled leaf while escarole has a broader and less curly leaf. On the average 100 portions will require 10 heads for garnish and 20 heads for salad.

usage they have become a class unto themselves. They may be used in any kind of salad or as any element of it, but generally they serve as either the base or the body.

All salad greens are fragile and must be handled with care during preparation. They bruise and discolor very readily, particularly in the presence of iron-based knives or implements. Hand tearing or use of stainless steel cutting edges is suggested for greens to prevent this discoloration.

Salad greens must be washed, rewashed, drained, dried, and crisped before use. Particular attention must be paid to removing all dirt and bugs (many of which are the same green color as the leafy product). After being washed, greens should be placed in a colander for draining and held in a refrigerator for a couple hours before use. If a refrigerator is not used, covering the greens with a towel and adding ice on top may help to improve and retain their crispness.

The major types of salad greens are discussed below. Specific uses and preparation methods are suggested.

Iceberg. Iceberg is one of the most important salad greens of the crisp head type. The head is solid, and the leaves are closely held to the head. The outside leaves are greener and the inner ones bleached.

Since appearance is so important in salads, rusty tips and wet slime decay in iceberg must be avoided. A seedstem overgrowth, indicated by spreading at the base of the outer leaves, may be a warning of bitter taste and unusable leaves that must go to waste.

Iceberg lettuce may be halved or quartered, or the full head may be divided for use. Leaves may also be used as foundation cups for salad bowls. The inner leaves serve as better individual cups because of their shape. Leaves may also be used as a decorative garnish for meat carving boards or as underliners for fruit or other garnishes on dinner plates.

To prepare iceberg, hold the top of the head and strike the stem end sharply on a flat solid surface. This will loosen the solid core and permit it to be twisted out of the head easily. Then place the head in cold running water in a vegetable sink or in a colander to separate and wash the leaves. Finally, drain the lettuce and crisp it in a refrigerator or under ice.

Butterhead. The butterhead varieties—big Boston, white Boston, and bibb—are smaller, less crisp, and more tender heads. They should be clean and have few, if any, wilted or discolored leaves, although the big Boston variety may have some minor brown tinting of the edges of the leaves.

The texture of the leaves of butterhead is more tender than of crisp head. The leaves may be used whole on salad plates or mixed with other greens.

To prepare butterhead, the stem end is trimmed, wilted leaves are removed, and water is run through the center of the head to ensure complete washing. The head is then drained and the leaves wiped or patted with a towel to dry.

Bibb. Bibb lettuce, often incorrectly referred to as big Boston, is a form of butterhead. It has a looser head formation and much larger, smoother, and less firm leaves than the iceberg varieties. There is a more standardized deep green color throughout the head, with fewer differences between inner and outer leaves. It is smaller and more tender than the big Boston variety of butterhead.

Because of the texture and relative size of the leaf, bibb serves well as a base for salads, a decoration, or a garnish. It may, of course, also be used as the body of the salad.

Bibb lettuce is prepared in the same fashion as iceberg lettuce, although the stem core is much smaller and easier to remove. It should be cleaned, crisped, and stored.

Other Lettuces. Leaf lettuce varieties, cos lettuce (also known as romaine), chicory (curly endive), and escarole are often used in salads. These are all similar in that they do not form rounded heads, and usually have more elongated leaves than the types considered above. They usually have more twisting and curling to the leaves and a much more pronounced flavor.

All these forms of greens may be used in salads to give variety in taste and texture. The flavors of chicory and escarole are somewhat more bitter than the taste of romaine.

In preparing all these greens, cleanliness and crispness are the major goals. The removal of sand, grit, and dirt is of prime concern.

Leafy Vegetables. Other leafy vegetables that may be used in salads are turnip and mustard greens, regular or red cabbage, and Chinese cabbage. All these leafy vegetables when young and tender are used in the body of salads. Regular cabbage, because of its strong flavor, is usually used in cole slaw where sugar and sauce accompaniments make it more acceptable.

Cleanliness and removal of defective leaves are as important with these forms of greens as with those previously considered. Insects and worms are often a major problem in tight cabbage heads, and a saltwater soaking solution is often used to remove these pests before the product is prepared.

Salad Vegetables

Vegetables of many types may be used in salads in either raw or cooked form. Attempts should be made to ensure that they preserve their taste and texture and that they are free from defects. Canned vegetables (and fruits) should be well drained before they are added to a salad to avoid excessive moisture and discoloration of the other salad ingredients.

Some of the more common varieties of vegetables used in salads are cucumbers, beets, radishes, tomatoes, peppers, celery, kidney and lima beans, onions, cauliflower, and peas. All should be of high quality, flavor, and texture and free from decay or damage. Although some use may be made here of leftover vegetables, salads must not end up as substitutes for the garbage can.

All inedible parts of vegetables should be removed, and the sizes of pieces should be varied to create interest. All foods should be compatible in taste, but the textures should be varied. Bite-sized pieces should be provided, and stems, seeds, and fibrous portions removed for both visual acceptance and ease of eating.

Salad Fruits

Fresh, raw, canned, or dried fruits are also used effectively in salads. Fruit salads are generally considered more delicate and lighter in substance than vegetable salads. They may be used to accompany an entrée of more substantial form or served as a light and refreshing main item.

Some fruits, such as bananas and apples, darken from oxidation when exposed to air. If these fruits are to be used in salads, an antioxidant dip or a coating of citrus juice should be applied to prevent this browning. The Cortland apple resists browning and is a very acceptable salad fruit.

Fruits lend themselves very readily to inclusion in gelatin salads and assist in making some of the more attractive of these.

In preparing the fruit, seeds, inedible skins, stems, and the like must be removed to make the salad much less difficult to eat.

Protein Foods for Salads

Protein foods such as chicken, turkey, ham, crab, lobster, shrimp, salmon, cheese, and eggs have long been used in some of the more substantial salads. This use enables the operator to dispose of leftovers from other departments in many cases. Caution must, of course, be exercised to make sure that the protein item being used is in a sanitary condition.

Protein foods used in salads are often marinated to change their flavor. Variations in slicing methods are also used to stimulate diner interest. Combinations of flavors and textures must be considered. Some meats require cubing, stripping, or dicing to make them easier for consumers to manage.

Dressings

Dressings are an important product of the pantry section. They add a specific taste to salads and accentuate the flavors of the basic salad ingredients. They should suit the salad to which they are applied, but most often

Table 12-3. Variations Made from Base Dressings

From	To Make	Add
Mayonnaise	Thousand island	Chopped hard-cooked eggs, chili sauce, pickles, and pimiento
	Sour cream	Lemon juice, sour cream, and onion
	Russian	Chili sauce, Worcestershire sauce, and onion
French dressing	Garlic	Garlic powder
	Chiffonade	Hard-cooked eggs, beets, and green pepper
	Vinaigrette	Parsley, chives, hard-cooked eggs, and capers

they are selected by the consumer from the establishment's choice of offerings.

There are three major types of dressings: mayonnaise, French, and cooked. However, many variations can be made from these by adding combinations of ingredients (see table 12-3).

In addition to salad dressings, the pantry often prepares various cold sauces, which are used in appetizers, canapés, or entrées.

French Dressing. French dressing is the basic form of salad dressing. It is a combination of salad oil and vinegar (sometimes lemon juice) in a ratio of approximately three to one, with seasoning of salt, pepper, and paprika. A small amount of sugar is sometimes added to mellow the taste of the strong acid. French dressing can be used in its pure form, or it may be changed by the addition of catsup, garlic, mustard, or other such ingredients.

In its true form, French dressing is a pure, temporary emulsion in which the oil and the acid are combined only by rapid shaking or other agitation. This separates the oil into small drops and prevents them from joining as they remain dispersed throughout the acid. Upon settling, the oil droplets once again cling together and separate from the acid.

Mayonnaise. Mayonnaise is the same form of dressing as French but with one major difference—the addition of an emulsifying agent that keeps the fat dispersed throughout the acid. In mayonnaise this agent is usually egg yolk. Like French dressing, mayonnaise may be used as a base for the addition of other ingredients or seasonings to give a variety of dressings.

In the past, most quantity food operations prepared their own dressings in-house. Although some still do, these are now the minority. Most food operations find it cheaper to buy the ready-made product or to buy the base dressings and vary them to meet individual needs.

Cooked Salad Dressing. Another form of basic dressing is a substitute for mayonnaise. It is a cheaper product that is built up with fat and egg content to give it many of the characteristics of mayonnaise. It differs from mayonnaise mainly in the amount of fat and egg included and the use of a starch thickener. As a practical consideration, many quantity food operations use better grades of cooked salad dressing and find them a desirable, and a much less expensive, alternative to mayonnaise.

In the event that a particular operation desires to produce its own dressings, the following suggestions are offered. A detailed comparison of cost and quality of purchased dressings should be made before attempting to produce salad dressings in-house in volume, however.

Mayonnaise

(1) Use only fresh eggs and salad oil of the highest quality. A winterized form of salad oil, able to stand refrigerated storage, is desirable.

(2) Have egg yolks and oil at room temperature to get the best mixture.

(3) Add oil in small amounts and beat very rapidly for proper emulsification.

(4) In case of a broken emulsion, start the process again with new materials, and add the

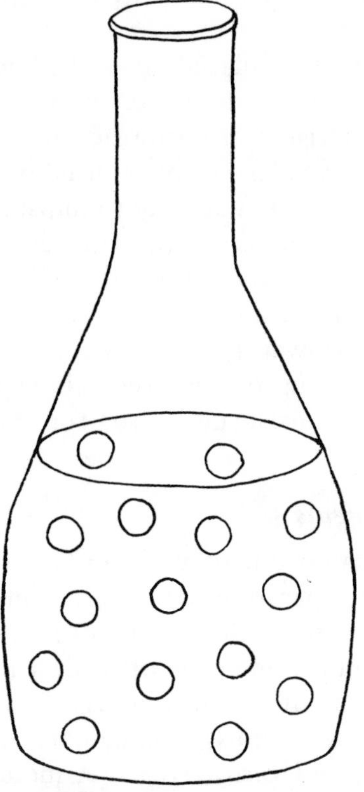

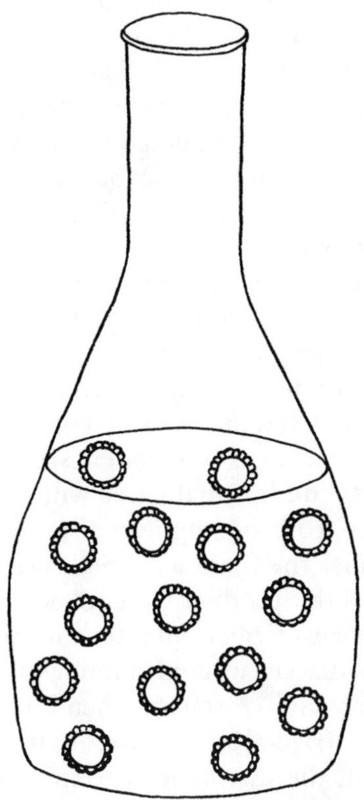

Figure 12c. The bottle on the left shows a temporary oil in water emulsion, such as an oil and vinegar French dressing, which may be obtained by rapid agitation of the container. With the passage of time, however, the water squeezes out the fat. The fat globules then mass together and separate from the water. The size of the droplets of oil and the degree of shaking or whipping affect the endurance of a temporary emulsion: smaller droplets and longer agitation result in longer-lasting emulsions. The bottle on the right shows a more permanent emulsion, such as a mayonnaise. An emulsifying or stabilizing agent has been added, which surrounds each fat globule and prevents it from clumping or settling out of the remainder of the product. Eggs, gelatin, flour, and paprika are most often used to stabilize dressings. Eggs are considered the most efficient agent. In the less expensive salad dressings, starch is the agent of choice.

broken emulsion in small amounts to the fresh mixture.

(5) Protect finished mayonnaise from extreme cold or from freezing to prevent a separation.

Cooked Salad Dressing

(1) Separate the starch to prevent lumping.

(2) Use only low heat in cooking to prevent scorching or overcooking of the dressing.

Pastas

Sometimes referred to as alimentary pastes or farinaceous foods, pastas are products made from the hard durum wheats. They are very high in starch or carbohydrate content and are used in many parts of the meal from soup to main dishes and salads.

All pastas are generally made the same way, although the choice of flour and the addition or exclusion of eggs make minor variations. In salads, the main pasta that is used is macaroni. This either takes the place of other salad vegetables or is combined with protein items, such as fish and meats, particularly for more substantial salad offerings.

In preparing pasta products, it is important to bear in mind that the uncooked item will increase approximately three times in volume in cooking.

A trunnion steam-jacketed kettle is one of

the most satisfactory utensils for preparing pasta products. The water should be boiling rapidly. The kettle should have three parts of water for one part of the product to be cooked. One tablespoon of salt should be added to each gallon of water for flavoring. Two tablespoons of salad oil added to the water will reduce the tendency of the water to boil over and will prevent the pieces of pasta from sticking together.

The product should be added all at once to the rapidly boiling water and stirred during the first few minutes of cooking to help prevent sticking. A wooden spoon then placed across the lip of the pot will also prevent the water from boiling over as cooking continues, because the foam will break against the spoon. When the product has cooked (approximately twelve to fifteen minutes), it should be rinsed immediately in cold running water to remove excess surface starch. Then it can be stored in the refrigerator for use. If it is to be marinated, the marinade is often added before the pasta cools in order to achieve maximum flavor transfer.

Pastas may also be cooked in a low-pressure steamer (five pounds of pressure) using the same three-to-one water-to-solid ratio. Although the cooking time is not reduced appreciably, this does give a very satisfactory product and provides some flexibility in the use of equipment.

The smaller varieties of pastas should be used in salads in order to keep the pieces bite-sized. All pasta products should be cooked to the *al dente* stage.

Marinades

In its strict sense a marinade is a combination of a food product and French dressing; the food is soaked in the dressing so that it picks up the dressing's delicate flavor. The process is used in salads and other dishes, and dressings other than French are also used.

Of course, most greens will not permit the extended application of a dressing—the tender product wilts. However, the more substantial ingredients, such as meat, fish, pasta, and vegetables are often marinated in order to vary their tastes.

The product is placed in a shallow pan, coated with the marinade, covered, and placed in a refrigerator until ready to be used. Acid-type marinades are often used with less tender cuts of meat not only to impart flavor but also to tenderize them. The tenderizing effect does not apply to salad ingredients; the basic reason for using a marinade here is to give flavor. However, there is one salad in which the wilting of the greens is expressly desired, and a marinade is used for that purpose.

Accompaniments

Although a salad may well stand by itself in a particular operation or application, long usage in the United States has often dictated that an accompaniment be offered. This may take the form of a relish or vegetable tray containing such items as cucumber wheels, radish roses, and carrot sticks. A more common salad accompaniment is a serving of bread sticks, melba toast, rye crisp, or the like.

A consumer's choice of accompaniments can be permitted, but where circumstances dictate selection by the operator, taste and texture differences should be the main considerations in choosing the accompanying item. An attempt should be made to vary both from those of the salad being served.

Measures to Increase Acceptability and Sales

Salads are generally a very profitable item for the food service operator, and all possible methods should be used to increase their selection by customers.

The following merchandising suggestions are offered:

(1) Cleanliness, crispness, and color sell salads. Make these items paramount in preparing them.

(2) Use colors such as blue and green in dishes, lighting, and surroundings, and use plenty of ice to give the desired effect of coolness.

(3) Prechill salad plates before putting on the salad. A plate hot from the dishwashing machine will ruin a good salad.

(4) Use showmanship at every turn in preparing salads.

(5) In buffets and cafeterias, display salads at the beginning of serving lines in as many attractive varieties as possible. People "eat" with their eyes and appetites before they actually consume the food. If salads are put at the end of the line, the diner might be psychologically "full" after selecting an entrée, vegetables, and bread, and may then pass up the salad. In buffets, putting the salad in a leading position reduces the consumption of more expensive meat or entrée items.

(6) In table service facilities, toss and mix salads at the diner's table if at all possible.

(7) Provide only quality dressings to flavor quality salads.

(8) Display salads attractively. Make sure that salad plates are not overfilled and that salads do not hang over the rims of plates.

(9) If possible, permit the customer to construct his own salad at a salad bar.

(10) Dress salads just before serving.

(11) If onions are used in salads, have portions available without onions, to meet the desires of those who do not like onions.

(12) If wooden salad bowls and mixing bowls are used, be sure they are kept in sanitary condition and are not excessively scarred by previous use.

(13) Pay particular attention to sanitation in the preparation of all salads, and check the work habits of the personnel preparing them. These items are not cooked before service.

Garnishes

Garnishes are used to make a dish of food more attractive visually and more pleasant gastronomically. They may be a separate dish, such as a relish tray offered with a salad course, but usually they are included on the plate or other container as part of a food offering. Garnishes are used with all parts of the meal. They can do much to give interest to a food item and make it more appealing to a guest. Garnishing can also be overdone. The amount or type used may be inappropriate or repetition may make a garnish appear trite and tired, so that it detracts from the food item.

Many pantry stations prepare garnishes not only for the foods handled in this section but also for the range, grill, and broiler stations of the kitchen.

The following suggestions are offered:

(1) Use garnishes that are edible. If possible, remove the inedible parts.

(2) Choose a garnish that augments and enhances the item with which it is served; it should not overpower it.

(3) Maintain the proper color, size, texture, and taste relationships to the item being garnished. Try the garnish out to see how it looks on the plate and how it tastes with the item, before using it.

(4) Keep the traditional garnish where it is expected and necessary. Otherwise, avoid the trite and try the unusual. Parsley is the most overused garnish.

(5) Keep the quality of garnishes high. Do not make the garnish a substitute for the garbage container.

(6) Garnish below as well as above foods, with green leaf underliners, sauces, salad variations, and the like.

(7) Garnish around the food item with table arrangements, ice carvings, tray selection arrangements, and lighting.

(8) Keep a close control on garnish costs. Many garnishes may contribute excessive costs to an inexpensive offering.

(9) Purchase economically and appropriately for garnishing. For example, fruits that have to be drained before use waste syrups; a large item that must be subdivided before being used as a garnish adds preparation costs.

(10) Plan how the garnished plate will look, and show the worker a finished item or a picture to ensure that the product will be arranged as planned.

(11) Avoid toothpicks in garnishes unless they can be clearly seen by the consumer.

(12) Consider the labor costs necessary to

The French knife is designed to chop, cut, or mince items without being lifted off the cutting board. The shape of the blade permits a rocking motion to be used.

To get ready cubes or minced sections of vegetables such as onions, make cuts on the horizontal and vertical planes before cutting them crosswise.

To make radish roses, clean the radishes thoroughly by washing, and cut off any roots. Then make cuts down the sides, close to the skin, in three or four areas going all around the radish. Place the roses in a bowl of ice water to assist in opening the petals.

Radish fans are made from longer varieties of radishes. After the radish has been washed and the roots removed, thin crosswise cuts are made into the radish. It is then placed in ice water to assist it in opening like a fan.

Figure 12d. A few of the special procedures that are part of the preparation work of the pantry.

prepare a particular garnish. Many require excessive hand work and should be avoided or purchased in prepared forms for better labor utilization.

(13) Prepare garnishes in individual servings, prearrange them on sheet pans, and store them in refrigerators for later use, so that when the main food item is ready it need not sit around getting cold while the garnish is arranged.

Finger Foods

Finger foods are foods that are to be eaten with the hands rather than utensils. Such forms as sandwiches, cookies, and fruits may be served at the table. Others, such as hors d'oeuvres, are served as an introduction to the meal before guests come to the table.

Finger foods are usually intended to stimulate and tempt the appetite, but at a social function offering alcoholic beverages with no plans for a group dinner, they may take a more nutritious and substantial form, such as tiny tea sandwiches, dips, chips, and nut dishes.

Finger foods are technically appetizers, but by long usage they have also assumed other functions, even substituting for meal periods when served at cocktail parties and similar social functions.

Hors d'Oeuvres. An hors d'oeuvre is a food item that is small enough to be eaten in one or two bites. It is eaten with the fingers, generally before the guests are seated at a table.

Hors d'oeuvres may be served hot or cold. They may be eaten as prepared or dipped in a sauce by the consumer. A toothpick or cocktail fork may be used with some items because of their temperature or because their surface texture makes them undesirable to eat with the fingers.

Hors d'oeuvres are available in a wide variety of forms: protein foods such as spiced meat chunks, cheese cubes, Swedish meatballs, stuffed and rolled meat stacks, shrimp, tiny sausages, and bacon-wrapped chestnuts; and vegetable items, such as celery sticks, olives, and radishes.

Canapés. Canapés are also food items that may be eaten with the fingers in one or two bites at the introduction of a meal. Canapés, however, are carried on or in a bread, cracker, or pastry shell or base.

Use of Finger Foods. Hors d'oeuvres, canapés, and othe finger foods have become an important part of the pantry section production, and form one of the main profit-producing offerings of the operation. Using a minimum amount of food materials, many of which are leftovers or odd lots unsatisfactory to meet meal demands, these items are put together in appealing ways by workers with artistic ability.

It has been considered inappropriate to use recipes for these foods. Rather, operations have basked in the ability of their workers to produce items of many and varied designs and forms. As labor costs have escalated, however, and productivity in relation to cost has become a prime concern, many food service operators have found it necessary to reevaluate the use of introductory foods.

It is true that these items yield a high profit and provide satisfactory outlets for many foods that cannot otherwise be used. But, unless labor costs are closely controlled, the meticulous hand work required to produce these attractive items can easily swallow up the raw food cost profit. In such a situation, use of the many frozen and ready-made products now available may be advantageous to the food operator. These convenience items require only final preparation by oven or microwave heating, and in-house labor costs are conserved. A management decision must be made on this question, based on labor cost, productivity, and raw item purchase cost considerations.

If items are prepared within the establishment, the following suggestions are offered:

(1) Be sure that the temperature and appearance of these food items are strictly controlled.

(2) Make all items easy for the customer to handle with one hand. For some food forms, plates and cocktail forks should be provided.

(3) Plan for duplicate or multiple serving stations to increase consumer satisfaction. Arrange to have a waiter or waitress pass trays of items to guests around the room, if appropriate. Use guest labor where possible, and position tables for access from both sides to facilitate both speed of service and replenishment.

(4) Make maximum use of leftovers, makeovers, and odd lot items, but be particularly careful of sanitation.

(5) Arrange all tables and trays for visual variety in color combination, shape, and height. Offer an adequate range of tastes and textures.

(6) Use bases and containers that contribute to the attractiveness of the items being presented, such as an ice carving for cold shrimp, a grapefruit for skewered items, or a hollowed melon bowl for other items.

(7) Use the unproductive time of employees for pre-preparation of items that can be held in refrigerators for later use.

(8) Use a variety of biscuits, breads, and pastries as bases, but prepare these items at the last minute to avoid sogginess.

(9) Make extensive use of a pastry tube for piping, and make unusual shapes of cut items, such as strips, spots, and wheels, for attractive displays.

(10) Trim crusts from breads and reserve them for use in meat products as extenders, in puddings, or as a source of crumbs.

(11) Soggy bases are the major problem of many canapés. To avoid them, use a butter spread, toast the bread, and do not prepare canapés too far in advance.

(12) Use day-old bread for canapés. After slicing, roll the slices with a rolling pin to flatten, spread, and concentrate them and give a better yield. Cut the slices into a variety of shapes after chilling.

(13) Vary bread colors and types for a checkerboard effect. Roll pullman slices with a rolling pin before filling and cutting. If bread is baked on the premises, have food coloring added to some loaves for variety.

Appetizers

Appetizers are defined as small amounts of food or drink served either early in a meal at the table, or before coming to the table, like hors d'oeuvres and canapés. They are designed to introduce the diner to the meal he is about to experience. They stimulate the visual, olfactory, and oral senses and tempt the appetite.

Appetizers take many forms and are composed of a variety of foods. In addition to those previously noted, the following classes are considered important: protein foods, juices, cheeses, eggs, fruits, and vegetables.

Cocktails. Although appetizers may be served in a variety of ways—salads, relish trays, canapés, or hors d'oeuvres, for example—the major presentation is often the cocktail.

The term *cocktail* includes both alcoholic and nonalcoholic varieties and combinations of the two. A cocktail may be made of a fish, a vegetable or fruit or their derivatives, or a mixture of juice and sherbet known as a *shrub.*

In recent years the use of nonalcoholic cocktail appetizers has been declining in many establishments (except those under a table d'hote pricing system), as alcoholic cocktails replace them. Many operators have drastically reduced their offerings of appetizers to two or three items, reflecting this change in consumer dining habits. Sufficient interest remains, however, for the prospective food service manager or supervisor to consider some basic principles of appetizer use and preparation procedures.

Use and Preparation. Seafood such as shrimp, crabmeat, scallops, lobster, and oysters lend themselves very readily to use as cocktail appetizers because of their delicate and bland flavors. They are usually served with a tangy cocktail sauce and a lemon wedge to overcome any sweetness they might have.

Other cocktail appetizers may be mixtures of fruits, fruit juices, or vegetable juices. Fruits should be as fresh as possible and devoid of seeds, inedible pulp, and membranes. The items used should be neither sweet nor sour but mildly tart to help stimulate the appetite. Unless a facility is operating on a most austere budget, canned fruit cocktail should not be considered a satisfactory appetizer. Fresh fruits sectioned in the kitchen or containers of presectioned fresh fruits are the items of choice. Some suggestions for appetizers are given in table 12-4.

In preparing appetizers, the following suggestions are offered:

(1) Keep all items visually attractive.

(2) Make the item as easy to eat as possible, using bite-sized pieces.

(3) Make extensive use of underliners, garnishes, and sauces.

(4) Dare to be different in the choice of

Table 12-4. Common Appetizers, Hors d'Oeuvres, and Canapés

Anchovy canapés	Ham wheels
Apple and cheese wedges	Honeydew melon stuffed with fruits
Apple juice	Lobster cocktail
Avocado and grapefruit sections	Meat balls
Avocado and shrimp canapes	Melon balls
Bacon-wrapped frankfurters	Orange fruit cup
Bismarck herring	Orange juice
Blended fruit juices	Oyster cocktail
Broiled grapefruit	Pineapple fruit cup
Carrot curls and sticks	Pineapple juice
Celery sticks and fans	Pizza puffs
Cheese cubes	Salami wheels
Chestnuts wrapped in bacon	Salmon
Cocktail wieners	Sardines
Codfish balls	Shrimp cocktail
Crab and grapefruit cocktail	Smoked oysters
Cranberry juice	Stuffed celery or olives
Deviled eggs	Sweet-and-sour meatballs or pork bits
Deviled ham	Tuna bits or dips
Dips of various types	Vegetable flowerets
Frosted fruit cups	Vienna sausage
Frosted shrubs (fruit juice and sherbet)	

foods and containers. Tall-footed supreme dishes, frosted glasses, and the like contribute to appeal.

(5) Unless the pricing structure dictates otherwise, avoid canned fruits, beverage bases, and similar items.

(6) Keep appetizers on the tangy side. Use juices and sauces to maintain the tart aspect, if necessary. Avoid sweet-tasting foods in appetizers.

Ice Creams, Toppings, and Ices

Ice creams, sherbets, ices, and related toppings are another product group of the pantry section. They are used in a limited way in appetizers, and more commonly as dessert items.

It used to be standard procedure for ice cream to be made in the bakery section of a food operation, at first using raw base ingredients and later prepared mixes. However, as a result of increased labor costs, more specialization of production, and the elimination of baking by many establishments, most now purchase these products ready-made.

Controlled by both federal and state regulations almost everywhere in the country, ice cream is defined as a product composed of at least 10 percent milk or butterfat with a minimum weight allowance. Other ingredients such as emulsifiers and stabilizers are also usually controlled, but the fat content and minimum weight standard usually prevail. French ice cream and frozen custard are mixtures similar to ice cream, but with egg yolks added to make a richer product. Ice milk, on the other hand, contains less of the milk solids and butterfat than ice cream.

Sherbet is a fruit-flavored product that contains milk and milk solids but is low in these ingredients. Ices are products composed mostly of water, containing no dairy products, and very high in sugar content. A frozen product similar to ice cream that is available in some states is called *mellorine.* It contains vegetable fat, notably soybean, cottonseed, or corn oil, in place of butterfat.

Ice cream and similar products are prepared by combining butterfat (or a substitute), milk solids, sweeteners, stabilizers, emulsifiers, in some cases egg yolks, and flavoring agents. After undergoing pasteurization to kill patho-

Table 12-5. Usual Content and Ingredients of Ice Cream and Similar Products

	Milk Fat	Total Milk Solids	Sweetener	Stabilizer	Emulsifier	Acid Ingredients	Egg Yolk Solids	Vegetable and Animal Fat	Overrun
Plain ice cream	10-14%	20%	15-16%	0-0.5%	0-0.2%	–	–	–	70-80%
Bulky flavored ice cream	8%	16%	15-16%	0-0.5%	0-0.2%	–	–	–	60-70%
Frozen custard, French ice cream, French custard ice cream	10-16%	20%	15-16%	0-0.5%	0-0.2%	–	1.4%	–	70-80%
Ice milk	2-7%	11-15%	17-19%	0-0.5%	0-0.2%	–	–	–	50-80%
Fruit sherbet	1-2%	2-5%	25-35%	0-0.5%	0-0.2%	0.35-0.5%	–	–	30-40%
Water ices	–	–	25-35%	0-0.5%	–	0.35-0.5%	–	–	25-30%
Mellorine	–	20%	15-16%	.5-1%	0-0.2%	–	–	8-10%	70-80%

Courtesy of the National Dairy Council, Chicago.

genic bacteria and homogenization to prevent lumping, the mix is frozen by a method that permits both rapid freezing and incorporation of air (known as overrun). After the product is hardened or aged to prevent crystal formation, it is ready for service. The common ingredients of each type are listed in table 12-5.

Uses. Ice cream products should be purchased for specific uses in accordance with customer preferences, menu plans, and profit margins desired. Overrun measures, which indicate the respective amounts of air and solid matter in the product, are good indicators of quality. The overrun may be easily measured by a weight determination: one gallon of ice cream weighs on the average 4.5 pounds.

Ice cream may be served by itself in a dessert dish or be used in such products as baked Alaska—ice cream, cake and/or fruit, covered with meringue and browned in a very hot oven (450 to 500 degrees). It may also be served in individual meringue shells or be used in ice cream cakes or pies. A popular ice cream dessert is the parfait, in which ice cream is covered with a liqueur or a variety of sauces.

Pseudo-ice-cream-type products, such as mousses (whipped cream combined with gelatin and a sweetener and then frozen without stirring) or bombes (two flavors or kinds of ice cream products frozen together in a mold) are also used.

Ice cream products must be kept at temperatures close to 0 degrees Fahrenheit for storage, and they then should last up to two months. Individually wrapped two-ounce blocks of ice cream may be purchased for use in schools or cafeterias. Bulk containers range in size from one to five gallons.

When bulk containers are purchased, ice cream scoops are used for portioning. The temperature at dipping time should be between 8 and 10 degrees. If ice cream is too cold it is difficult to scoop and has little taste. If it is too warm it tastes too sweet and melts. Ice cream should not be permitted to melt and refreeze. When it does, it forms large rough crystals that detract from the smooth texture desired. This characteristic may be used to indicate when adequate temperatures have not been maintained.

Ice cream scoops come in notched nonmechanical spoon form and the more common mechanical forms, which have a rotating dasher to remove the contents. Size numbers (indicated in the dasher mechanism) run from 30 to 6. Those most often used for ice cream products are number 30 (58 to 62 scoops per gallon), number 24 (47 to 51 scoops per gallon), number 20 (38 to 42 scoops per gallon), and number 12 (22 to 26 scoops per gallon). The number 30 scoop is preferred for parfaits, the number 20 for a la mode servings, and the number 12 for ice cream dishes and sundaes.

For best dipping results, ice cream scoops should be kept in running water tanks. Before dipping, excess water should be tapped out of the scoop to prevent crystalization in the ice cream. The dipper is started at the outside edge of the container at a depth of not more than a half inch. Scooping should be done in layers with care taken not to crush out the overrun and thereby reduce the expected yield. Scoop edges should be kept sharp. For quantity service, such as in banquets, scoops may be preportioned onto sheet pans and kept in freezers for later service. Parfaits may also be made in advance and held in freezers.

Cleanliness is extremely important in the ice cream serving area. Overhead lids must be kept closed when dipping is not being done to prevent contamination of the product from above and to avoid excessive changes in temperature.

Toppings

Sauces of various types may be served over ice creams. There are hard sauces of butter, sugar, and water, and fruit sauces of cornstarch-thickened fruit juice or syrup. Purchased toppings and ready-made syrups may also be used.

Frozen Desserts

Ice cream, sherbets, and the like can be made on the premises into parfaits, mousses, and bombes. These contribute to extending the menu and do not require labor during the freezing process. They command relatively high menu prices in comparison to their labor and raw material costs.

The following suggestions are offered in preparing these desserts:

(1) Chill all molds before they are used, to hasten the cooling of the product and to prevent sticking on removal.

(2) When cream is used, whip it only to the stage where it stands alone. Overwhipping will cause loss of volume and drying.

(3) Use adequate portions of whipped cream or toppings to garnish the dessert, and pipe them from a pastry tube.

(4) Use gelatin in mousses to ensure that they maintain their frozen condition.

(5) To remove a frozen product from a mold, dip the mold in warm water for a few seconds and then invert it on a cold dish. Wipe the bottom of the mold dry before inverting it. A warm cloth wrung out dry and placed on the outside of the mold may sometimes be used to unmold the contents.

(6) If possible, line a mold with waxed paper before putting in the product, to assist in later removal.

(7) To enrich an ice recipe, add milk where water is called for.

(8) Remember that very sweet recipes freeze more slowly than less sweet ones.

(9) Use lemon juice (2 teaspoons to 1 pint of cream) to increase the ability of cream to whip. Cool the cream, the bowls, and the implements to be used in whipping, to reduce the time required.

(10) Use cream as a stabilizer in frozen desserts and to improve the texture of the product. Evaporated milk may be substituted in many recipes, however, to reduce costs.

Beverages

A beverage is any liquid used as a drink in a food establishment. Beverages may come from animals (milks are the prime example) or be extracted from fruits or vegetables. They may also be reconstituted from purchased fruit-flavored beverage bases.

Beverages may serve as appetizers in a meal, as stimulating drinks between meals, as accompaniments to a course, or as the final course of a meal. The following beverages are considered below: coffee, tea, cocoa, milk, soft drinks, and fruit nectars, concentrates, and juices.

Coffee

Coffee is obtained from the tropical or semitropical countries of Africa, Asia, Central America, and South America. It is the bean of an evergreen, roasted and ground for use. Coffee is roasted on a scale from light to dark and ground in varying sizes for percolator, urn, or vacuum use. That used in quantity food operations is generally of a medium roast and urn grind.

There are three main components of coffee: caffeine, flavor substances, and tannins. Caffeine is a stimulant to the central nervous system. It is liberated from the coffee grounds by water at a temperature of from 190 to 203 degrees Fahrenheit. (In some types of coffee, the caffeine is removed during processing.)

Flavor substances, which give taste to the brew, are liberated from the coffee grounds by water at temperatures ranging from 185 to 203 degrees Fahrenheit. These substances are very volatile; high temperatures and prolonged heating drive them off and result in coffee with little taste.

Tannins are bitter flavor substances that are found in coffee and in other foods. They are liberated from the coffee grounds into suspension by high temperatures and prolonged periods of heating.

Once roasted, coffee beans are subject to rapid deterioration, losing flavor and aroma. When coffee is ground, the rate of deterioration increases. Storage at high temperatures, with high moisture levels, or with excessive exposure to air will also increase the rate of flavor loss.

Coffee is usually purchased by food operators in vacuum-packed tins, in kraft paper bags, or in premeasured urn bags. As freshness is a determinant of the quality of the brew, steps should be taken to ensure that a quick turnover of ground coffee is maintained, so that large amounts are not permitted to accumulate. Those amounts that are on hand must be adequately protected against excessive exposure to moisture, heat, and air.

Making Coffee. In making coffee there are five basic factors that must be controlled. The first is the quality and freshness of the coffee to be used. (This has been discussed above.)

The second is the cleanliness and condition of the equipment used to make the coffee. Although many forms of coffee makers are available (see chapter 7), only the automatic and urn types are considered important in quantity food work. The equipment must be functioning properly and be well cleaned after each use. Equipment that is not working properly may provide incorrect amounts of water or water at temperatures that liberate tannins. Improperly cleaned equipment may contain residue coffee oils that have become rancid and give an off taste to the brew.

The third factor is the recipe used in making the coffee, the type of water used, and the ratio of water to coffee. Hard water contains undissolved ions such as calcium and iron solids that can react with coffee-making equipment and foul the heat-producing components with boiler scale deposits. Hard water may also cause a bitter taste in the brew. Sodium-type water softeners may also result in bitter-tasting coffee. The use of a polyphosphate filter on the line is better.

The amount of water used in relation to the amount of coffee determines the strength and taste of the brew. A ratio of 2.5 gallons of water to 1 pound of coffee is considered an acceptable formula.

The fourth consideration is the temperature of the water and the time the coffee remains in contact with the water. The water should be just below the boiling point at temperatures ranging from 195 to 205 degrees Fahrenheit. Water that is too hot or that remains in contact with the coffee too long will liberate tannins into the brew and give it a bitter taste. One of the advantages of an urn is that the water remains in contact with the coffee only until draining takes place.

The fifth consideration is the time that elapses between preparation of the coffee and service. Coffee brew deteriorates very rapidly while being held at serving temperatures. It gives off its volatile flavor substances and becomes a highly unsatisfactory product if it sits for long periods. The use of smaller equipment and more frequent preparation of batches will add much to successful coffee.

In making coffee, the following suggestions are offered:

(1) Use soft water, if possible. Do not use sodium-type softeners.

Table 12-6. The Chemistry of Softening Water for Coffee Making

Synthetic Zeolite Water Softener (Ion Exchange Method)

Calcium ions (and often magnesium and iron salts) cause hard water. Passing the water through a bed of sodium zeolite beads converts it as follows:

$$\underset{\text{sodium zeolite}}{Na_2Ze} + \underset{\text{calcium ions}}{Ca} \longrightarrow \underset{\text{calcium zeolite}}{CaZe} + \underset{\text{sodium}}{2\,Na}$$

The calcium ions join with the zeolite part of the molecule and replace the sodium part of the molecule, making calcium zeolite and releasing sodium into the water.

The water softener may then be regenerated by flushing it with a rock salt solution (NaCl), which reverses the original reaction, reconstitutes the sodium zeolite, and flushes away troublesome calcium chloride ($CaCl_2$) into the sewer pipes, as follows:

$$CaZe + 2\,NaCl \longrightarrow Na_2Ze + CaCl_2$$

Polyphosphate Filter

The above water-softening procedure is very effective for most food service needs, such as conserving soap in dishwashers and general cooking use. Free sodium in the water causes problems in the brewing time and taste of coffee, however. To eliminate the sodium, a polyphosphate filter on the incoming water line to the coffee brewing equipment is the method of choice. The mineral salts or calcium ions are kept in suspension so that they do not cause scale on the equipment as they are heated, and no sodium is released into the coffee water to cause taste problems.

Boiler Scale

Rainwater containing dissolved carbon dioxide releases calcium salts from the soil and makes water hard. When water containing calcium ions and dissolved hydrogen carbonates is heated in equipment, it causes a boiler scale ($CaCO_3$) to be deposited on the equipment, according to the following reactions:

$$H_2O + CO_2 \longrightarrow H_2CO_3$$
$$H_2CO_3 + CaCO_3 \longrightarrow Ca + 2\,HCO_3$$
$$Ca + 2\,HCO_3 + \text{heat} \longrightarrow CaCO_3\downarrow + H_2O + CO_2\uparrow$$

(2) Use paper disposable filters in the leacher if possible.

(3) If a muslin filter is used, keep it in water between uses to reduce the oxidation of oils.

(4) Keep the coffee temperature below boiling. Hold it at 185 to 190 degrees Fahrenheit.

(5) Make fresh coffee frequently, and reduce the period between preparation and service.

(6) Keep all equipment clean.

(7) In manual urns that require a worker to pour water over the grounds, after the coffee has been made, remove the grounds, drain off one measure of the brew, and remix it with the remaining urn contents, to agitate the coffee so that the strength of the brew will be the same throughout.

(8) Remove the muslin bag after the coffee is made to make sure that it does not rest in brewed coffee.

Instant or soluble coffee is also available in dehydrated or freeze-dried form and may be used when only a small amount is to be prepared. Iced coffee is also offered in many food service establishments. To prepare it, the brew should be made twice as strong, in order to compensate for the melting ice that is added when the product is served. A ratio of 1.5 gallons of water to 1 pound of coffee is recommended. It should be stored in a nonmetallic, covered container at room temperature to prevent cloudiness in the brew. A serving of six ounces is appropriate in a twelve-ounce glass, to allow room for the necessary ice.

Tea

Tea is a plant that grows in Indochina and Southeast Asian countries. The leaves are used both green and after various stages of fermentation, which result in less bitter brews. The three main types available are *green teas* (unfermented leaves that give bitter, astringent

Table 12-7. Coffee Problems and Possible Causes

Problem	Causes
Rancid taste or odor	Equipment not cleaned properly. Dirty filter. Serving pots or cups need additional cleaning. Paper filter picked up an off odor.
Bitter taste	Overextracted brew—coffee in contact with water too long. Held too long or at too high a temperature after brewing. Brewed coffee poured through grounds for mixing. Artificial water-softening equipment is extending brewing time.
Weak and watery brew	Wrong brewing formula. Brew not mixed thoroughly. Brewing time too short. Wrong type of grind for equipment being used.
Sediment in brew	Defective filter. Wrong grind for filter and equipment used. Wrong type of cloth filter made of too loose a material.

Courtesy of the Coffee Brewing Center of the Pan-American Coffee Bureau, New York.

brews), *oolongs* (semifermented leaves), and *black teas* (fully fermented leaves).

The maturity of the leaves and their resultant desirability are described by such terms as souchong and pekoe.

Tea, like coffee, contains flavor substances, tannins, and a stimulant form of caffeine sometimes known as theine. It comes in bulk form, in individual- or multiple-portion bags, or in instant, soluble varieties for use in iced-tea dispensers or to mix with hot water in either a cup or a pot.

In making tea, four basic factors should be considered:

(1) Use soft water, if at all possible, to get best results.

(2) Use water that has been freshly heated. Overboiled water loses excessive amounts of air and has a flat taste that is carried over in the brew.

(3) Use the correct ratio of tea to water. A ratio of 6 ounces of tea to 6-1/2 gallons of water is recommended.

(4) Permit a steeping period. Tea must remain in contact with water longer than coffee in order to extract the brew. Use either an urn or a steam-jacketed kettle, and keep the bag of tea in contact with the water. This produces a better brew than use of a filter and water flowing over the leaves.

For iced tea, the brew must be stronger to compensate for the melting ice that is added at the time of service. Iced tea brews should be made in small batches, so that the time between preparation and service is reduced. The tea must be kept at room temperature because cloudiness develops in tea that is refrigerated, either from the cold or from hardness in the water, which precipitates tannins. This clouding may be reversed by adding either hot water or an acid such as lemon juice to the product. Individual tea dispensers usually result in better iced tea production.

Tea should be made for immediate use. It may be held at a temperature of 185 degrees Fahrenheit for a brief period of time. Left-over tea can be used for iced tea if it is chilled so that it may be served with a minimum amount of ice.

It is best to use only stainless steel, glass, crockery, or earthenware equipment to make tea. This will prevent unfavorable taste reactions in the brew. Stainless steel is the material of choice in quantity food situations.

1

ACCURATE MEASUREMENT

4 oz. NEVER LESS THAN 3⅓ TO EACH 64 oz. WATER. FINE GRIND COFFEE ONLY SHOULD BE USED. IF 3 oz. PACKAGE IS USED, BEVERAGE YIELD SHOULD BE NO MORE THAN 54 oz.

2

IF PAPER FILTER IS USED, PLACE IN CARTRIDGE AND ADD COFFEE - A LEVEL BED IS IMPORTANT.

3

IF CLOTH FILTER IS USED, RINSE IN HOT WATER AND PLACE ON FRAME - ADD COFFEE TO CARTRIDGE, PLACE FRAME IN POSITION - A LEVEL BED IS IMPORTANT.

4

FOR FILTER PACKS IT IS EXTREMELY IMPORTANT TO FOLLOW THE MANUFACTURER'S INSTRUCTIONS WHEN INSERTING THE PACK.

5

PLACE CARTRIDGE IN POSITION ON COFFEEMAKER GENTLY, DO NOT TILT OR SLAM. PLACE EMPTY BOWL IN POSITION, PRESS START BUTTON.

6

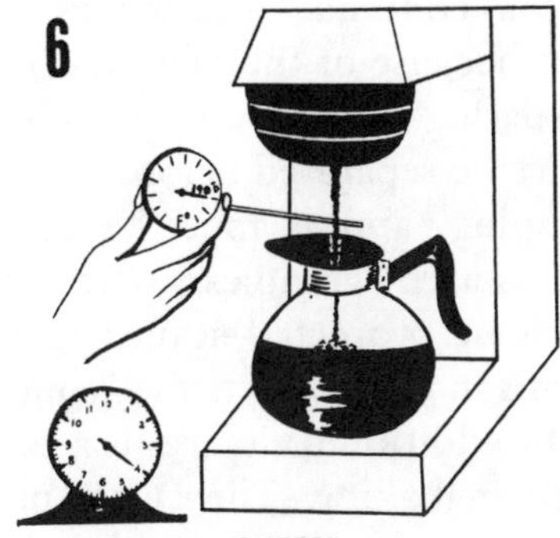

CHECK:

TEMPERATURE - THE COFFEE COMING FROM THE CARTRIDGE SHOULD BE AT LEAST 190° F.

TIME - ALL HALF-GALLON BREWERS SHOULD DELIVER A BOWL IN FROM 3' 20" to 4' 20".

7

REMOVE SPENT GROUNDS IMMEDIATELY AFTER BREW IS COMPLETE, COFFEE IS NOW READY TO SERVE. RINSE EMPTY CARTRIDGE IN HOT WATER.

8

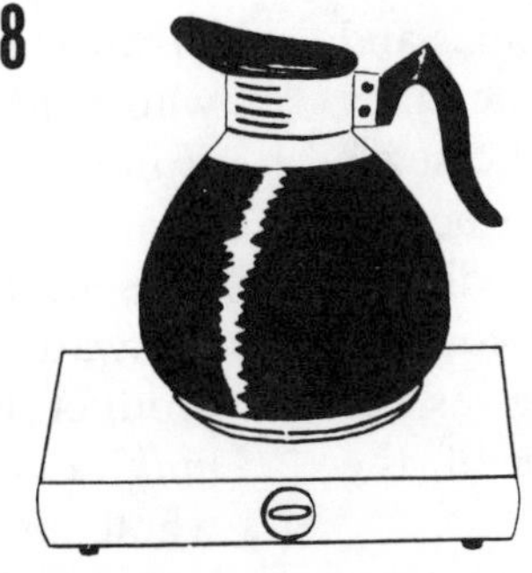

HOLD BREWED COFFEE AT 185 to 190°F FOR NO LONGER THAN ONE HOUR.

NEVER REHEAT OR BOIL BREWED COFFEE AND NEVER MIX A FRESH BATCH OF COFFEE WITH OLDER COFFEE.

9

SANITATION:

RINSE CARTRIDGES AND BOWLS AFTER EACH BREW. WIPE UNDERSIDE OF BREWING HEAD ON COFFEEMAKER DAILY WITH A CLEAN DAMP CLOTH. USE A STRONG URN CLEANING SOLUTION AT SEMI-WEEKLY INTERVALS TO CLEAN ALL PARTS THAT COME INTO CONTACT WITH COFFEE OR COFFEE AROMA.

☆ ☆ ☆

Published by the Coffee Brewing Center of the Pan-American Coffee Bureau to promote consistent brewing procedures in making Good Coffee.

Figure 12e. Detailed instructions for half-gallon automatic coffee makers. (Courtesy of the Coffee Brewing Center of the Pan American Coffee Bureau, New York.)

Cocoa

Cocoa, like coffee and tea, contains both flavor substances and a stimulant (theobromine). Unlike the others, it also has a starch and fat content of from 6 to 25 percent, which gives it food value in the form of calories.

Cocoa is a product obtained from the seeds of the cacao tree of Central and South America. The seeds are roasted and may be in their natural state or treated with an alkali that darkens them, improves their flavor, and changes their acid nature. Cocoa treated this way is known as *Dutch-processed cocoa.*

In addition to the carbohydrates and fat cocoa contains, it provides nutrients to the diet because of the milk that is usually used in preparing it. Because of its starch content it must be separated before it is used, to prevent lumping, and it must be cooked to prepare the starch granules. After cooking, cocoa must be protected against surface skin, which forms in all products that contain starch.

In addition to its use as a beverage, cocoa is used in baking. The Dutch-processed variety cannot be used as an acid with a soda, such as in a chocolate cake, because the alkali treatment gives it a neutral reaction rather than an acid one.

In beverages, a ratio of 1 pound of cocoa to 5 gallons of liquid is used. There are two methods for making cocoa, both of which allow for separation of the starch granules and prevention of lumping. A syrup may be made by mixing the dry cocoa first with the sugar and then with a small amount of water before adding milk, salt, and any other ingredients. Or a paste may be made of the dry cocoa and cold milk or water, which also separates the starch, before adding the remainder of the ingredients.

Cocoa products are usually whipped after preparation to prevent a surface skin from developing. Addition of a fat type of garnish, such as whipped cream or a marshmallow, serves this same purpose.

Processed products akin to cocoa are also available. Because of their ease of use and lower cost, these prepared cocoa items are used in many operations in place of regular cocoa. These products vary in fat content and in the addition of sugars etc., so most are not called cocoa but some like term.

Milk

Milk is the most nearly perfect of foods: like all foods for the young of a species, it contains all the necessary nutrients for the preservation and growth of the creature.

Although milk from various types of animals (sheep, goats, camels, etc.) is used, cow's milk in the United States is by far of most importance.

Milk contains protein (in the form of casein), fat, carbohydrates, minerals, and vitamins. It is usually provided to quantity food service establishments in a form fortified with 400 units of vitamin D. Since most of the fat and the fat-soluble vitamin A are contained in the cream portion—the lightest part of the milk—most milk is also homogenized. In this process, the fat globule is broken up and dispersed throughout the entire product.

Although milk may still be purchased raw or certified in some states, all milk used in quantity food establishments should be pasteurized before use to prevent the transmission of such diseases as tuberculosis, diphtheria, and brucellosis.

Milk is used in many areas of food preparation. Various forms of milk lend themselves to different uses, often at lower prices than whole milk. Three important varieties are: *evaporated milk,* in which half the water is removed, and the milk is sterilized and canned; *condensed milk,* in which a third of the water is removed, sugar is added, and the product is sterilized and canned; and *dried milk,* a completely dehydrated form of either whole or skimmed milk. Condensed, evaporated, and dried milk find their greatest applications in baking and other food preparation processes. Specific caveats as to the use of milk in creamed soups, sauces, and baking are considered in chapters 13 and 17.

For beverage use, however, whole milk is of most importance, while low-fat and nonfat milk are also used. In milk for drinking, the prime concerns are proper processing by the purveyor and strict sanitary and temperature control at the user establishment.

Milk may be purchased in individual half- or full-pint containers, in bulk milk cans, or in plastic and cardboard containers of up to five gallons. Milk from bulk containers should be portioned from refrigerated dispensers by means of gravity feed through a tube. The use of containers that require dipping through the top opening should be avoided.

Cream

Cream is a component of milk that may be kept and used by the pantry section. The butterfat content determines the form of the cream. Whipping cream has 30 percent butterfat and light or coffee cream approximately 18 percent butterfat. Half-and-half (mixtures of milk and cream) and nondairy vegetable substitutes are also used. If a dairy product is used, it must be strictly controlled from a sanitary standpoint as to temperature and storage.

If cream is to be whipped, the use of chilled cream, bowls, and beaters will result in greater volume, and the addition of confectionery sugar will give a more pleasant taste. The use of a nondairy substitute made from vegetable substances may result in a price saving without reducing the consumer's acceptance.

Soft Drinks

Many carbonated drinks are usually available in quantity food operations. Although most carry a generic designation, such as ginger ale, orange soda, or lemon and lime, others have gained greater popularity under a brand name.

The major uses of soft drinks in the quantity food operation are to accompany food and to mix with liquor. They are available in individual-portion bottles or cans, in quart sizes, or in syrups that are dispensed from centralized bulk units.

No special problems arise except with opened quart-sized units, which tend to lose their carbon dioxide. Refrigeration aids in the retention of the carbonation, and for this reason opened containers of soft drinks should be kept cold.

Fruit Juices, Nectars, and Concentrates

The last major class of beverages is fruit juices, nectars, and concentrates. Fruit nectars and juices, which have been discussed as appetizers, may also be used as meal accompaniments, particularly at breakfast. A very acceptable substitute for these, and a desirable alternative to more expensive beverages such as milk, may be beverage base concentrates. These are available in gallon and quart sizes and are mixed with water in ratios ranging from 1-to-2 to 1-to-4. They provide very economical and acceptable beverages, particularly for low-budget feeding operations such as schools, institutions, and colleges. In operations that charge a base price per meal, these drinks usually hold up well against higher priced beverages such as milk in selection by consumers given a free choice.

Fruit juice concentrates of orange, lemon, and similar flavors are also available in frozen form. Usually mixed with water on a 1-to-3 ratio, they provide a very desirable alternative to squeezing fresh fruits for juice. In some areas, fresh juice in a pasteurized form is also available in quarts or gallons.

Gelatin

Gelatin is an incomplete protein obtained from the horns, hoofs, and other connective tissues of animals. It swells to a jellylike mass in cold water, and dissolves in hot water. It finds extensive use in the pantry section in salads, desserts, and decorative work for buffets.

Gelatin may be used in plain form or flavored with the addition of sugar. It is mixed with such foods as egg whites and whipped cream in many recipes.

Gelatin must generally be dispersed and softened in a cold liquid (either water, fruit juice, or some like substance) before it is used. It is then mixed with hot liquid to dissolve it. Flavored gelatin that is already mixed with sugar, however, may be dissolved in hot liquid immediately.

Gelatin requires a cold surrounding to "set up." This jelling may be hastened by the use of ice as part of the liquid in a particular recipe. Rapid stirring or placing the container in a cold bain-marie will also reduce the firming time. If the mold is chilled or lightly oiled before the gelatin is poured in it, removal of the molded gelatin when firm will be easier.

Layering different colored gelatins and designs made with foods of various colors give pleasing visual effects. Gelatin should set to a syrupy consistency before any ingredients are added, to prevent them from floating to the top. Raw pineapple and figs cannot be used with gelatin because certain enzymes in these products will not permit the gelatin to set properly.

If foods are added that contain great amounts of acid (such as fruits), a greater proportion of gelatin must be added to the recipe to ensure proper set. More plain gelatin should also be added if a product is to be held for later serving on a cafeteria line or buffet table.

To unmold gelatin, the mold is dipped briefly in warm water, removed from the water, wiped dry on the bottom, and inverted on a plate. A warm wet cloth may be used, if additional heat is necessary.

The use of gelatin should be considered in a sauce aspic or sauce chaudfroid on a display buffet or salad table. Meats such as turkey, chicken, and ham may thus be decorated with a minimum amount of labor or talent and still make a very impressive display. Designs with gelatin aspic may also be used for fish molds, mousse recipes, and the like. For designs, foods with striking color contrasts, such as black olives, red pimiento, yellow lemon rind, orange peels, and carrots, should be selected.

A ratio of 6 cups of consommé to 3½ tablespoons of gelatin will furnish a highly acceptable aspic. A chaudfroid sauce consisting of 4 tablespoons of flour, 4 tablespoons of fat, 4 tablespoons of gelatin, and 4 cups of milk will make a satisfactory covering for a display item.

An item to be decorated should be covered with two or three pourings of a chaudfroid sauce. After it is cooled, one covering of the aspic is poured over it. The decorations are set in, and three or four more layers of aspic are poured over for a very effective display. Aspic may also be used alone to cover a display item.

Ice Carvings

Another relatively easy and impressive display that the pantry section can prepare is an ice carving. Whether the maximum 300-pound block is used or a 150- or 50-pound block, the carving will make a very attractive display for a buffet table or other such offering.

Employees with some basic decorating or artistic talent may try simple forms, using a plan, a wood chisel, a hammer, and an ice shaver. The following suggestions are offered:

(1) Plan what is to be attempted. Avoid the difficult and do not attempt to cut the pattern too deeply at the start. A more complex display can be produced with practice.

(2) Cut out a design for guidance from a piece of heavy paper, in the exact size the finished item is to be.

(3) Carve at room temperature or in a chill box. Work slowly, cutting only small sections at a time. As the ice begins to melt, return it to the freezer for firming.

(4) Illuminate the finished carving with lighting from below. Eliminate melted water from the buffet table by wrapping the container with a sheet or tablecloth.

Convenience or Ready Items

In every type of food discussed above, convenience or ready food items are available for use by the food service supervisor.

Preportioned sandwich meats and fish are supplied. Turkey may be bought in cooked rolls for easy use. Premixed sandwich fillings are also sold in such varieties as ham and chicken salad. Ready-made frozen sandwiches that require only microwave or steam-injection heating are available.

Salad greens may be purchased already prepared and mixed in plastic bags, ready for the addition of the desired dressing. Potato, macaroni, and gelatin salads, in all forms, are packaged in individual ready portions.

Salad dressings in gallon containers or individual portion units are available in a range of types wide enough to suit most menus. Peeled and sectioned citrus fruits may be purchased for use in salads.

Prepared appetizers, hors d'oeuvres, and canapés are available in many varieties, usually frozen. They need only be heated for service. Instant coffee, tea, and chocolate drink mixes are also provided by purveyors.

It remains for the food service operator to determine whether the quality and cost considerations of these convenience items warrant their use in a particular establishment. Labor costs, time, and quality must be judged to decide which items will be prepared in-house and which will be purchased in a form that requires little or no additional preparation before service.

13 *Soups and Sauces*

Objective: To describe the basic principles of stock, soup, and sauce making, using either traditional or convenience techniques. The characteristics of each are given, and the many varieties are discussed as are thickening agents and their uses.

Soups and sauces, and the stocks from which they are made, can be considered together, because the methods used to produce them are closely related, they require similar handling during and after preparation, and (except for the choice of thickening agent and seasonings) many possess the same basic characteristics.

Stock

The most important item in this class, and the precursor to the other two forms, is stock. It is the base element from which good soups and sauces are made. How it is produced and used may cause the resulting soup or sauce to receive accolades or maledictions. The French, who always place great emphasis on their sauces, have long given credit to their stocks for the successes achieved in this area.

Most quantity food operations have, for years, made their own stocks. Many still do. Some pay proper attention to what should be used in each stock pot and how it should be handled, while others use the stock pot as a garbage disposer in which all forms of bones, cuttings, carcasses, trimmings, and peelings are deposited.

With the advent of an extensive supply of prepared bases, bouillon cubes, and browning agents, many operators have come to use these convenience items to produce their basic stocks, in lieu of manufacturing the bases themselves. The reduction in time and labor makes use of these convenience items expedient. In addition, drastic changes in purchasing procedures have reduced the availability of suitable bones and other necessary raw materials used in stocks. Some facilities, of course, continue to produce their own stocks with no difficulty. These traditionalists often refuse to use prepared bases, branding them inferior.

Despite the change in attitude that appears to be taking place in many segments of the industry toward more convenient stock production, the food service manager or supervisor should know the traditional method of stock preparation. He can then make his own choice as to what source to use. At the very least, the convenience item should be made to conform as closely as possible to the traditionally manufactured product.

Preparation. Stock may be defined as a liquid flavored by extractives from such food items as meats, poultry, fish, and vegetables. A satisfactory stock usually requires about five pounds of solid base item to each gallon of water. Better results are obtained if the less tender and older cuts of meat are used in addition to the structural bones of the cut. For example, beef shins and beef necks or old fowl give better results than younger animals or more tender cuts.

The bones of the animals are the main source of stock derivatives, and the more surfaces exposed to the water the better the results. Bones are therefore cut in relatively small pieces (three to four inches), and heavier ones are cracked to ensure complete extraction of the marrow. Meats included in stock should also be cut in small pieces to give adequate exposure to as many surfaces as possible. Grinding the meat achieves this result and also contributes to later clarification of the stock.

Vegetables, spices, and seasonings may be added to a stock during processing to give it the desired flavor. Heavy-bodied items such as peppercorns should also be cracked to ensure adequate dispersal of their flavor. Where vegetables, herbs, and heavy seasonings are used, a bouquet garni is usually made so that these can be easily removed from the stock before straining. (A bouquet garni or sachet bag is a cheesecloth tied around flavoring items, attached to a string, and suspended in the stock pot, so that it is easy to remove.)

Salt is rarely used in stocks, since later reduction of the product would then make it too salty for general use. Seasonings and flavorings are usually avoided when a vegetable stock is produced.

All stocks should be started in cold water: this helps to keep the stock clear. The stock pot should be held at simmering temperature and remain uncovered during the cooking process. This permits the maximum extraction of nutrients and flavors and produces a much clearer stock.

Stocks are cooked for periods ranging from one hour for some fish stocks to as much as eighteen hours for heavier beef varieties. During cooking they must be periodically skimmed to remove the floating flocculate and fats that rise to the surface.

Clear stock is usually prepared in a range-top stock pot or steam-jacketed kettle with a bottom spigot for each removal. Clearness is also achieved by the use of clarifying agents: ground meat and egg whites. These protein substances coagulate in cooking and trap minute particles in the stock that would otherwise contribute to cloudiness. The clarifying agents may be added at the beginning of the cooking period with the remainder of the ingredients or after the stock has been allowed to cool, in which case the stock temperature must be brought back to boiling after these items have been added. In either event, after the mass rises to the top of the pot with the trapped minute food particles, the clear stock is decanted and strained through cheesecloth into a storage container.

Because of its protein nature, stock is a highly perishable item. Each stock must reach boiling temperature to ensure the destruction of any bacteria. It must be held under refrigeration if made for later use, and measures must be taken to cool it rapidly. A five-gallon container of hot stock may take up to twelve hours to reach a temperature in the innermost portion of the product that will prevent bacterial growth. The operator should reduce the size of the containers to two gallons at the most, and use a cold bain-marie to quicken cooling before the stock is placed under refrigeration. After the stock has cooled, fats not removed during skimming will rise and harden on the top surface and may be removed.

Types of Stocks. Stocks may be classified by color (brown or white) or by the type of food used to produce them (chicken, beef, game, fish, or vegetable). The most common classification is into four basic types from both systems:

(1) *Brown stocks* are usually made with the less tender cuts of beef and bones that have been browned in an oven first to gain the desired color. Vegetables and seasonings are usually added for flavor.

(2) *White stocks* are more delicate in flavor and lighter in color. They are generally made of unbrowned beef bones, although the younger form of the species—veal—gives a more desirable white stock.

(3) *Chicken stocks* are made from chicken or other poultry. They are light in color and have the characteristic poultry taste, which is required in many products using stocks.

(4) *Fish stocks* are obtained by simmering the bones and other unused portions of one or several kinds of fish, with additional seasonings.

Soups

Many forms of food are products of only one geographic location, but soups are a cosmopolitan food found in almost all countries of the world. Many have special preparation methods and ingredients that make them indigenous to a specific country such as Italian minestrone or Russian borsch. Whatever particular characteristics may apply, the basic food form appears to cut across most national boundaries.

Soup is a one-dish item that may serve as a complete meal or, in less substantial form, as a prelude to a more complete menu offering. Soups are tasty, nutritious, popular with consumers, and highly profitable for most food operations.

Soups offer a very desirable vehicle in which to use leftover foods. They thus contribute to profit by allowing an operator to recoup from forecasting errors and the like. However, they should not become the dumping ground for food items that do not measure up to standard quality.

Soup should fulfill a specific primary purpose, whether it is introduction to the meal or a meal in itself. It should have a flavor characteristic of its type. Any food items that are included must be easily identifiable (cut in bite-sized pieces), and the soup should have a minimum amount of surface fat.

Since the basic requirement for a good soup is a good stock, preliminary attention should be given to providing this ingredient.

Types of Soups. There are various methods of classifying soups. One of the best is by the following four classes:

(1) *Clear soups* are made from basic stocks by combining two or more stocks or essences. They may be served plain, with a distinctive garnish, or with other ingredients added.

(2) *Creamed soups* are made from a basic stock that has been thickened by a milk or cream sauce, or more heavily thickened by a starch item such as rice or macaroni.

(3) *Pureed soups* are those that have been thickened by a puree of their ingredients, usu-

Table 13-1. Classifications of Soups

Clear	Creamed	Pureed	Miscellaneous
Beef broth	Cream of asparagus	Bean	Borsch
Chicken broth	Cream of celery	Kidney bean	Clam chowder
Chicken gumbo	Cream of chicken	Lentil	Corn and tomato
Chicken noodle	Cream of mushroom	Pea	Fish chowder
Clam	Cream of potato	Potato	Ham chowder
Clear turtle	Cream of spinach	Rice and tomato	Minestrone
Consommé	Cream of tomato		Mulligatawny
French onion			Oxtail
Onion			Oyster stew
Scotch broth			Vichyssoise

ally foods that are heavy in starch. The soup is forced through a food mill or china cap to gain the desired thickening effect.

(4) *Miscellaneous soups* are those that do not fit the other three classifications. This category includes chowders, cold soups, and other forms.

Preparation. In the preparation of soups in quantity, the following suggestions are offered:

(1) Use an acceptable stock for the type of soup to be prepared. If the stock is unclarified, clear it when cold, using egg white or a combination of egg white and ground beef, if appropriate (1½ pounds of ground beef and 2 egg whites will clarify 1 gallon; 1 egg white will clarify 1 quart).

(2) Prepare the soup that is actually being featured on the menu. If bouillon is offered, be sure to prepare the one-stock variety; a combination of stocks is really consommé.

(3) Plan the soups to be offered on the menu based on the leftover items that may have to be used from the previous day's operation.

(4) Make sure that all fat is skimmed from cold stock before soup is made from it.

(5) Add spices toward the end of the cooking period to get maximum flavor.

(6) Be particularly careful in preparing creamed soups. Excessive amounts of heat, salt, or acid may cause curdling of the milk or cream that is added to the soup for richness. Dairy items must be protected by preparing them in a white sauce before combining them with other soup ingredients. The heat level and amount of salt must be strictly controlled. Small amounts of baking soda are often added to acid forms of cream-thickened soups, such as cream of tomato, in order to change the pH to the alkaline side and thus prevent curdling.

(7) Combine or adjust leftover soups where necessary to get maximum use from them. Pureed soups may be changed to creamed soups by the addition of a white sauce; clear chicken soups may be changed to chicken noodle by adding uncooked noodles, which also have the effect of thickening the soup as they cook.

Table 13-2. Garnishes for Soups

Asparagus tips	Macaroni
Bacon strips, cooked	Noodles
Breadsticks	Parmesan cheese
Cauliflower flowerets	Parsley
Chives	Sausage slices
Crackers	String beans
Croutons	Tapioca
Cucumber pickles	Vegetables, diced
Dumplings	Watercress
Lemon slices	

(8) Vary the garnishes used with soups to increase the number of possible presentations. Use garnishes that are appropriate. If possible, combine them with the soup just before service, to prevent sogginess and deterioration.

(9) If possible keep canned soups on hand as backup items to supplement the soups being offered in case the forecasts are in error.

(10) If attention cannot be given to producing high quality soups, use the canned condensed varieties, many of which are very good.

Sauces

Sauces and gravies are the second major form of food that depends on good stocks for its quality. Unlike soups, they are not complete food items that can stand alone; rather they contribute to the use of another food and assist in presenting it in its best light.

Although sauces and gravies are considered in the same general framework, gravies are a unique class. They differ from sauces in that they are made from the drippings of roasted meats, which they use as their base stock.

Some of the earliest sauces were made when the blood drippings and other extractives of game and fowl slain on the hunt were thickened with bread and eaten by the hunters. Sauces were later used to cover the strong tastes of foods that had "matured" beyond the point of desirable flavor. They were also used to cover up the strong game flavors of the wild animals that were hunted. Enshrined by the French, they are used today as an important supplement to food items in every part of the meal, enhancing the foods and making them much more acceptable and exciting.

Sauces may be used as a background for a food item (for example, a tomato sauce served with a veal cutlet); as a binding agent to hold foods together (as in a chicken croquette); or as an accompaniment or topping to another food form (for example, hard sauce served with steamed pudding). They are served hot or cold and may act to subdue or to accentuate a particular flavor. They are used in a wide range of recipes from desserts to entrées and in forms ranging from butters to gravies.

Whatever the form or type, the sauce used should complement the food with which it is presented. It generally should accentuate the original taste of the item, not overcome it so that the consumer tastes the sauce alone.

The sauce should be smooth, be free of lumps, and have some spreading consistency. It should not be so loose and uncontrolled as to flood the plate and all the other foods on it, nor so thick and firm that it holds the shape in which it was portioned onto the plate.

The cold sauces, such as mayonnaise and its variations, and the dessert sauces and toppings have been discussed in chapter 12 on pantry production. The others, which are the concern of the range station, are included here.

Table 13-3. Major Classes of Sauces by Color

Class	Sauce	Description
White	Béchamel	White roux with milk and/or cream
	Cheese	Cream sauce with grated cheese added to desired thickness
	A la king	Cream sauce with mushrooms, green peppers, and pimientos
	Egg sauce	Cream sauce with hard-cooked eggs, parsley, and/or pimientos
	White wine	Cream sauce and wine in which fish has been cooked
	Mornay	Cream sauce with eggs and cheese
Blond	Velouté	Blond roux with butter and/or margarine and chicken stock
	Poulette	Velouté with shallots, mushrooms, and parsley
	Supreme	Velouté with eggs and cream
	Newburg	Velouté with sherry and paprika
Brown	Espagnole	Beef stock and brown roux
	Brown sauce	Espagnole with carrots, celery, and onions
	Mushroom	Espagnole with mushrooms
	Bordelaise	Brown sauce with shallots and red wine
	Bercy	Brown sauce with shallots and white wine
Red	Tomato	Minimally thickened and highly seasoned tomato sauce
	Creole	Tomato sauce with celery, onions, green peppers, and mushrooms
	Pizza	Tomato sauce with oregano, basil, and garlic, reduced to moderate thickness
	Barbecue	Tomato sauce with Worcestershire, catsup, mustard, sugar, and chili powder
Yellow	Hollandaise	Egg yolks, butter, and lemon juice
	Béarnaise	Hollandaise with tarragon vinegar or cider vinegar substituted for lemon juice
	Mousseline	Hollandaise with whipped cream

Types of Sauces. Although sauces number in the hundreds, varying with the desires of the person preparing them and the ingredients used, most may be classified into five main categories or mother types:

(1) *Béchamel* is prepared from a white stock of veal or unbrowned beef. It is often made from a white roux, with milk or cream added, and is thus referred to as a cream sauce.

(2) *Velouté* is also made from a white stock but gets its characteristic color from the addition of a blond roux. Chicken is the stock of choice because of its color and taste, although some fish stock is used.

(3) *Espagnole* is the classic brown sauce made from beef stock and a brown roux.

(4) *Tomato sauce* is made from almost any stock and tomatoes, which give it a red coloring, with high seasoning and minimal roux thickening.

(5) *Hollandaise* is a yellow sauce made basically from butter and eggs. It is highly perishable and one of the most difficult sauces to prepare.

Components of Sauces. In constructing a satisfactory sauce there are four major categories of ingredients. The specific ingredients are varied in amount and kind according to the particular sauce desired.

The first is the stock or vehicle. It must contain the particular color and taste required. The second component consists of the seasonings and additives that furnish the major taste of the sauce or vary the taste given by the other basic ingredients. The third factor is the color agent. This may come from the stock, the ingredients added, or the thickening agent. The final ingredient is the thickening agent, which binds the sauce together.

It is possible to produce the same result from different components in a sauce. For example, brown color can be achieved by using a brown stock in the sauce or by browning the roux.

Thickening Agents. The thickening agents most often used for sauces are roux and eggs. A roux is a mixture of fat and flour in a one-to-one ratio (one pound of fat to one pound of flour). Roux may be used with varying amounts of liquid depending on the degree of thickening desired. They may be exposed to varying degrees of heat to gain the different colors that are characteristic in particular sauces.

Flour is a major ingredient of roux. Wheat flour of the bread type is most often used in quantity food work, although other starch products, such as corn, tapioca, rice, potato, and arrowroot starches, have been used. Cornstarch is the thickening agent of choice in Chinese cooking and is used extensively in sweet sauces. A whitewash of cornstarch and flour in equal amounts mixed with a water dilutant is often used to thicken liquid products such as soups and stews. Tapioca forms of converted starches are used in many frozen convenience food products because they withstand freezing and reconstitution better than other forms of starches. Some of the other starches are used in the dessert area.

The choice of thickening agent depends on the agent's thickening power. This, in turn, depends on the size of the starch molecule, the concentration of the agent in the liquid to be thickened, and the temperature to which the mixture is heated.

Most starches are composed of amylose and amylopectin molecules. Some starches have only one type. The amylose molecule is partly soluble in hot water and opaque, while the amylopectin molecule forms a viscous, translucent paste when mixed with water.

Starch molecules thicken a product by absorbing water and swelling or gelatinizing. They form larger cells, giving the product more solid material per unit of liquid. Although starches will absorb some moisture while cold, heating is necessary to get complete gelatinization and lose the starch taste.

Most starches reach maximum thickness at approximately 194 degrees Fahrenheit (90 degrees centigrade). Exposure to higher temperatures for long periods of time or excessive stirring may rupture the starch molecules and cause them to lose their maximum thickening

Table 13-4. Relative Thickening Power of Starches

The length of the chain and the size of the starch molecule determine the thickening power of the agent, from stiff, firm gel to viscous, fluid gel. The order of common starches is:

Most Stiff					Least Stiff
Cornstarch	Wheat flour	Rice starch	Potato starch	Arrowroot	Tapioca

One tablespoon of cornstarch, potato starch, rice starch, or arrowroot or four teaspoons of granule form tapioca equal two tablespoons of wheat flour in thickening power.

Thickening Proportions

Consistency	Liquid	Fat	Thickening Agent
Thin	1 qt.	¼ cup	¼ cup flour
Medium		½ cup	½ cup flour
Thick		1 cup	1 cup flour
Thin	1 gal.	6 oz.	6 oz. flour
Medium		8 oz.	8 oz. flour
Thick		12 oz.	12 oz. flour

Thin consistency is used for soups, medium for vegetable sauces and gravies, and thick for croquettes, for example.

power. This occurs particularly in roux that are browned to give color to a sauce.

Because of its propensity to absorb hot liquid, starch that is not separated into granules will absorb liquid on the outside of the mass and form lumps, with unmixed starch (molecules not exposed to the heated liquid) on the inside. This may be avoided by first separating the starch granules, using either fat or a cold liquid. Sugar is also used to separate starch in some recipes, such as for cocoa, but it is not usually appropriate in making sauces.

The fat in a roux may be vegetable shortening, butter, margarine, or the drippings from roasted meats. It will, of course, contribute a color to the final product, so the eventual use of the roux must be planned before the fat is selected.

Egg yolks are also often used as thickening agents. They contribute a characteristic color and flavor to the sauce, as well as the desired consistency. The only problems they present are those of overcooking the egg and of curdling the sauce. Both are related to heat, and they occur particularly in hollandaise and related sauces.

Preparation. The specific ingredients for each type of sauce are listed in recipes. As noted above, the type, quality, and clarity of the stock used is an important element in the preparation of any sauce. After this has been provided, most other ingredients and procedures give the preparation worker little difficulty. The one major exception is the thickening agent, as discussed above.

First the fat is melted, then the flour is stirred into it for separation, and finally the mixture is cooked to remove the starch taste. The roux may then be used to thicken other products by either mixing liquid into it or mixing it into liquid. In either case, rapid agitation with a whip is suggested during the mixing, to achieve a smooth texture. A final cooking period for proper thickening is then required.

In some items, such as gravies or soups, the starch used as the thickening agent is first mixed with a cold liquid (water) and then added to the product while the mixture is agitated rapidly with a wire whip. This is the *whitewash* that is called for in many recipes.

Mixtures of equal parts of butter and flour

may also be kneaded together in a dry state, stored in the kitchen, and pinched off as needed to add to a hot product for thickening.

Eggs used to thicken sauces must be protected from overcooking by use of a double boiler or by rapid agitation and pinpoint control of the heat source. Before adding eggs to a hot mixture, some of the hot product must first be added to the egg yolk while the two are rapidly mixed together. This process is called *tempering.* It raises the eggs to a temperature that will be compatible with the bulk of the hot mixture, so that the eggs will not solidify when added to the sauce. If eggs are added to a hot mixture without tempering, they may rapidly cook on the outside and produce fleck "scrambles" throughout the final product.

In making hollandaise sauce, the heat level must be properly maintained or eggs will cause additional problems. High heat levels may curdle the sauce. The nature of the product and its warm temperature may cause bacterial problems if the sauce is not used rapidly. It should therefore be made in very small quantities.

If curdling occurs, additional hot water may be added to the mixture using rapid agitation. This process will often reconstitute the separated sauce.

Other cautions to observe in making sauces are:

(1) If pan drippings are insufficient for making gravy, add water and scrape down the pan while heating it to gain the necessary amount. Bouillon cubes or au jus base may be used as an acceptable substitute.

(2) Cook most flour-thickened products over direct heat or flame. Stir egg-thickened items constantly while thickening takes place, or heat them over water in a double boiler.

(3) Acid will break starches very quickly. In items containing acid, increase the starch level.

(4) Do not store sauces that contain milk, cream, or eggs. To ensure adequate cooling, never store sauces of any kind in containers of more than two gallons. Sauces with acid pH levels present less of a problem in terms of bacterial growth.

(5) Keep flour-thickened sauces tightly covered during storage or paint on a layer of fat or butter to prevent a surface skin from forming.

(6) Do not cook roux too quickly. Allow enough time for complete gelatinization of the flour to take place.

Convenience Items

Soups, sauces, and gravies are available in convenience forms in a variety of package sizes. Made from flours, hydrolyzed vegetable proteins, flavorings, spices, colorings, and fats according to type, they provide an acceptable alternative to the long preparation process.

A la king, barbecue, creole, hollandaise, mushroom, and béarnaise are all available in convenience forms. Starch thickening packets and instant chicken and beef bases for sauces are also sold. Beef, chicken and turkey gravy bases are available. Many require only removal from a container, while others must be reconstituted with water or other liquids before they are ready for use.

Versatility may be achieved by starting with a basic mix, such as brown sauce, and adding other ingredients to get the desired results. In this manner a more complete and personal offering may be obtained from the basic convenience item.

Soup bases may also be used. Here again, further ingredients may be added to make the offering more elaborate.

Butters and Glacés

Demiglacé and glacé de viande are types of pseudosauces that are used in certain types of food preparation. A demiglacé is a reduction of a brown sauce and stock mixture, while a glacé de viande is a reduction of the stock alone. Both are utilized to coat certain meat dishes for better appearance or flavor.

Butters may be melted and clarified or whipped at various stages of darkening and then mixed with various flavorings or additives to use with entrées of fish or poultry or in other courses of the meal.

Table 13-5. Convenience Sauces and Gravies

Product	How Used	How Packed	Processor
Sauces			
A la king sauce	Poultry and egg dishes	50-oz. cans	Campbell
A la king sauce	Poultry and egg dishes	6 1-lb. tins 25-lb. drum	Durkee
Barbecue sauce	Meat loaf; creole cookery for ribs, chicken, and fish	50-oz. cans	Campbell
Barbecue sauce	Meat loaf; creole cookery for ribs, chicken, and fish	6 14.5 oz.-tins 25-lb. drum	Durkee
Barbecue sauce	Meat loaf; creole cookery for ribs, chicken, and fish	4 1-gal. containers	General Mills
Brown sauce	Base for onion, mushroom, or pepper sauce	6 no. 10 cans	General Mills
Catsup	Sandwiches, French fried potatoes, and meat loaf	14-oz. bottle no. 10 tin 0.5-oz. single-serving pouch	Heinz
Catsup (hot)	Sandwiches, French fried potatoes, and meat loaf	12-oz. bottle	Heinz
Catsup (with onions)	Sandwiches, French fried potatoes, and meat loaf	14-oz. bottle	Heinz
Catsup (with relish)	Sandwiches, French fried potatoes, and meat loaf	14-oz. bottle	Heinz
Cheese sauce	Macaroni, casseroles, vegetables, and sandwiches	6 1-lb. tins 25-lb. drum	Durkee
Cheese sauce	Macaroni, casseroles, vegetables, and sandwiches	6 no. 10 cans	General Mills
Cheese sauce	Vegetables and sandwiches	6 1-lb., 4-oz. cans	McCormick
Cheese sauce	Macaroni, casseroles, vegetables, and sandwiches	12 16-oz. tins 6 no. 10 cans	Milani
Cheese sauce (cheddar)	Macaroni, casseroles, vegetables, and sandwiches	....	Nestlé/Maggi
Cheese sauce (mild/sharp)	Casseroles, macaroni, rarebit, hamburgers, and Mexican food	12 5-lb. cans 6 no. 10 cans	Nodaway Valley Foods
Cheese sauce	Macaroni, casseroles, vegetables, and sandwiches	6 no. 10 cans	Swift
Chili sauce	Sloppy Joes, casseroles, tacos, tamales, and enchiladas	6 15-oz. tins 25-lb. drum	Durkee
Chili sauce (without tomato)	Spaghetti, macaroni, pizza, lasagna, and meat loaf	12 22-oz. bags	Durkee
Chili sauce	Meat loaf, fried fish, and casseroles	12-oz. bottle no. 10 tin	Heinz
Creole sauce	Meat loaf slices, pork chops, and baked chicken	3 no. 10 cans	Carnation/Chef-mate
Creole sauce	Meat loaf, pork chops, and baked chicken	12 3-lb., 3-oz. cans	Le Gout

Product	How Used	How Packed	Processor
Fermiere sauce	Veal and poultry	50-oz. can	Campbell
57 sauce	Steaks, chops, fish, and cheese	5.25-oz. jar 8-oz. jar 1-gal. jar	Heinz
Grenadine syrup	Add to dessert, vegetable, and entrée sauces	1-pt. bottle 1-qt. bottle	Giroux
Hollandaise sauce	Seafood, vegetables, and eggs	6 11.5-oz. tins 25-lb. drum	Durkee
Hollandaise sauce	Seafood, vegetables, and eggs	12 3-lb., 2-oz. cans	Le Gout
Hollandaise sauce	Seafood, vegetables, and eggs	6 2-lb. cans	McCormick
Hot dog sauce	Hot dogs, burgers, and corn bread	no. 10 can	Chef Boy-ar-dee (American Home Foods)
Italian sauce	Meatballs, fish portions, and veal steaks	3 no. 10 cans	Carnation/Chef-mate
Italian sauce (Italienne)	Meatballs, fish portions, and veal steaks	12 3-lb., 3-oz. cans	Le Gout
Marchand de vin sauce	Roasts and steaks	50-oz. can	Campbell
Marinara sauce	Seafood	12 3-lb., 2-oz. cans	Le Gout
Monosodium glutamate	Flavor-enhancer for sauces	6 2-lb. shakers 10-lb. can 25-lb. drum 100-lb. drum	Accent International
Mushroom sauce	Meat and poultry	50-oz. can	Campbell
Mushroom sauce	Meat and poultry	12 3-lb. cans	Le Gout
Mustard	Sandwiches and hot dogs	6-oz. jar 9-oz. jar 1-gal. jar 0.25-oz. single-serving pouch	Heinz
Mustard (brown)	Corned beef, hot dogs, and roast beef	6-oz. jar 9-oz. jar 1-gal jar	Heinz
Newburg sauce	Seafood	50-oz. can	Campbell
Newburg sauce	Seafood	12 3-lb., 2-oz. cans	Le Gout
Onion sauce	Meat	12 3-lb., 2-oz. cans	Le Gout
Pepper sauce	Liquid pepper seasoning for a variety of menu items	2-oz. bottle 12-oz. bottle	Tobasco
Pizza sauce	Pizza and hamburgers	no. 10 can	Chef Boy-ar-dee (American Home Foods)
Sauce-quik	Base for over 30 different sauces	4-lb. tin	Accent International
Savory sauce	Steaks, roasts, fish, and poultry	7.25-oz. jar	Heinz
Sloppy Joe sauce (without tomato)	Sandwiches	12 20-oz. bags	Durkee
Spaghetti sauce	Spaghetti, macaroni, pizza, lasagna, and meat loaf	50-oz. can	Campbell

Product	How Used	How Packed	Processor
Spaghetti sauce (meatless)	Spaghetti and meat loaf	no. 10 can	Chef Boy-ar-dee (American Home Foods)
Spaghetti sauce (with meat)	Spaghetti and meat loaf	no. 10 can	Chef Boy-ar-dee (American Home Foods)
Spaghetti sauce (with mushrooms)	Spaghetti, meat loaf, or as Spanish sauce	no. 10 can	Chef Boy-ar-dee (American Home Foods)
Spaghetti sauce	Spaghetti, macaroni, pizza, lasagna, and meat loaf	6 15.5-oz. tins 25-lb. drum	Durkee
Spaghetti sauce (without tomato)	Spaghetti, macaroni, pizza, lasagna, and meat loaf	12 15-oz. bags	Durkee
Spaghetti sauce	Spaghetti, macaroni, pizza, lasagna, and meat loaf	6 no. 10 cans	General Mills
Spaghetti sauce	Spaghetti and meat loaf	12 1-lb. cans	McCormick
Spaghetti sauce	Spaghetti, macaroni, pizza, lasagna, and meat loaf	6 no. 10 cans	Swift
Stroganoff sauce	Beef and veal	50-oz. can	Campbell
Stroganoff sauce	Beef and veal	12 3-lb., 2-oz. cans	Le Gout
Supreme sauce	Poultry and vegetables	50-oz. can	Campbell
Supreme sauce	Poultry and vegetables	12 3-lb., 2-oz. cans	Le Gout
Sweet n' sour sauce	Meat slices, meat patties, or over shrimp or ham	3 no. 10 cans	Carnation/Chef-mate
White cream sauce (béchamel)	Variety of uses	50-oz. can	Campbell
White sauce	Creamed vegetables and entrées; base for other sauces	6 no. 10 cans	General Mills
White sauce	Creamed vegetables and entrées; base for other sauces	12 1-lb., 2-oz. cans	Le Gout
White sauce	Creamed vegetables and entrées; base for other sauces	12 14-oz. cans	McCormick
Worcestershire sauce	Meats and cheese fondue	5-oz. bottle 1-gal. jar	Heinz
Gravies			
Beef gravy base		12 1-lb. cans	Accent International
Beef gravy base		6 1-lb. tins 25-lb. drum	Durkee
Beef gravy base		6 no. 10 cans	General Mills
Beef gravy mix		6 1-gal. bags	Carnation/Trio
Beef gravy mix		....	Nestlé/Maggi
Beef gravy mix		6 5-lb. plastic tubs	Swift
Beef au jus gravy		12 3-lb., 2-oz. cans	Swift
Chicken gravy base		12 0.75-lb. cans	Accent International

Product	How Used	How Packed	Processor
Chicken gravy base		6 20-oz. tins	Durkee
Chicken gravy mix		6 1-gal. bags	Carnation/Trio
Chicken gravy mix		....	Nestlé/Maggi
Gravy coloring		12 1-qt. bottles 4 1-gal. bottles	Grocery Store Products/ Kitchen Bouquet
Mushroom gravy base		6 1-lb. tins 25-lb. drum	Durkee
Onion gravy mix		6 1-lb. tins 25-lb. drum	Durkee
Smoky ham gravy base		12 1-lb. cans	Accent International
Swiss steak gravy		....	Le Gout
Turkey gravy mix		6 1-gal. bags	Carnation/Trio

From *Food Service Magazine,* March 1971, pp. 50-52; reprinted by permission.

14 *Meat, Poultry, and Fish*

Objective: To introduce the wide variety of meat, poultry, and fish used in quantity food service, the history of their use, grading systems, composition, and forms available, as well as purchasing and cooking procedures. Quality control and convenience items are discussed.

Meat

The history of the use of meat is as old as man himself. It was an important dietary factor in America before the coming of the white man, as the Indians hunted bear, deer, and buffalo. They were forced many times to move their campsites in order to follow the animals on which they depended. When threatened by colonists, the Indians fought to retain access to these meat animals.

Cortez's introduction of Spanish Andalusian cattle (thought to be the progenitors of the Texas longhorn breed) and de Soto's importation of cattle into Florida are noteworthy in the history of meat use in the United States. The introduction of cattle and sheep into the Virginia colonies also contributed to the use of meat. In all cases, the varieties brought in were the breeds of animals indigenous to the colonists' native areas and the types of animals whose meat the people of that geographic and ethnic background preferred. These preferences still remain, despite the cosmopolitan nature of today's population.

Meat was procured first from wild animals by hunting and later from animals raised by an agrarian society. With the division of labor and its mobility and specialization of workers, raising and processing of meat became an industry unto itself.

In the early days, the meat-packing industry operated without any public control, and its labor exploitation and sanitary violations were beyond belief. Novelist Upton Sinclair, in an attempt to awaken the social responsibility of the country to the labor problems in the meat-packing industry, wrote *The Jungle.* Although the book was intended for other purposes, it effectively exposed the unsanitary conditions prevalent in the industry. As a direct result of this book, the Federal Meat Inspection Act of 1906 was enacted. This act, with amendments, is the main control on the industry to this day.

Composition of Meat

Meat is generally the main item of a meal. It is the most accepted and satiating food on the menu and generally the most expensive as well.

Meat, like fish, poultry, milk, eggs, and cheese, is a complete protein. It is approximately 75 percent water and 25 percent solids, and it contains all the essential amino acids that enable the body to rebuild and repair tissue. Since meat comes from animals, its proportion of amino acids is almost exactly the same as that of human protein. Meat also supplies iron, phosphorus, potassium, sodium, and magnesium in varying amounts, and is a liberal source of such vitamins as the B complex group, A, and D.

The muscle fibers of meat are the most desirable parts for consumption by man. These are enclosed in connective tissue, and attached to bones. Other parts of the animal are also used for food and contribute variety in taste to the diet. These are certain organs and glands of the animal and are called *variety meats.*

Whatever its form or the animal from which it comes, meat is almost completely digestible. Some cuts are more tender than others, due to the animal's age, its degree of activity, its type of feed, or the type of connective tissue in the cut. All cuts provide the same basic benefits, however, regardless of their tenderness or their price (which is determined by the desirability of the cut).

Availability of Meat

The supply of meat available on the market, like that of all other animal and vegetable products controlled by the laws of nature, experiences peaks and valleys. Although artificial insemination of animals, new processing techniques, and better animal husbandry methods have reduced the extremes of availability, natural law still dictates a rise and fall of the supply.

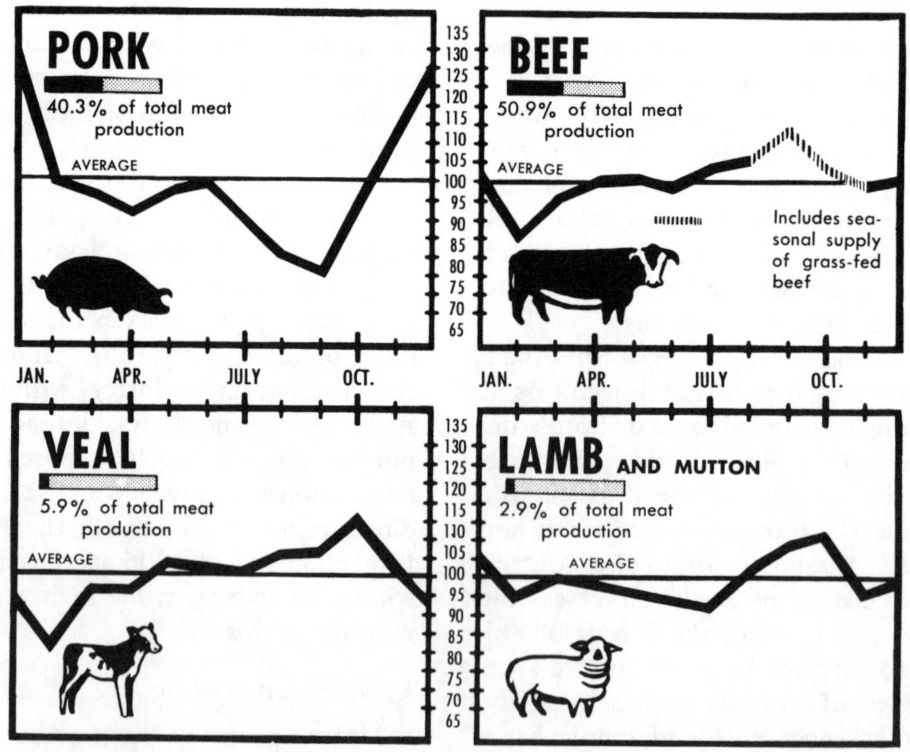

Figure 14a. The monthly variations in production of the four main types of meat, shown as percentage variations from an average 100 percent supply. The graphs are based on data collected over a twenty-year period. (Courtesy of the United States Department of Agriculture, Washington, D.C.)

Most animals are born in the spring and achieve the ability to withstand the rigors of winter weather by the time it arrives. Ranch-grown animals, which cannot change grazing locations because of confinement, are slaughtered in winter. When snow covers the pastures and grazing lands normally available for feeding these animals, many ranchers ship them to market rather than feeding them barn fodder at a much higher price. This results in an increase in supply, and a general lowering of the market price, which is based on almost pure competition.

Animals are also subject to diseases. Although many have been largely controlled, some still contribute to the death or disability of large numbers of animals, and affect market supplies.

These supply factors interact with demand features of the market place to provide either incentives or deterrents to buyers and sellers. The interaction establishes the amount of meat available at a given price and time.

The Meat-Processing Procedure

Operating from a main meat-packing plant or from a branch house in a location that facilitates the processing and distribution of the animals, packers purchase meat animals from ranchers and farmers. Cattle, hogs, and sheep are the main animals processed.

Since meat products are animal in nature, they have the ability to transmit diseases to man. They are therefore subject to rigid inspection by either federal, state, or local government agencies. The animals are given both a premortal and a postmortal inspection to determine their fitness as food. In addition, the physical condition of the plant, the slaughtering procedures used, and the processing procedure are closely controlled.

If a piece of meat is to move in interstate commerce, be graded as to quality, be shipped outside the United States, or be sold to an agency of the United States government, it must receive federal inspection. In all other situations, it is inspected by local government agencies whose standards closely approximate those of the federal government.

After inspection, the meat may be graded. In this process it is assigned a grade that indicates its eating quality. In the case of beef, a yield grade also indicates the amount of salable meat the animal carcass will yield.

Although a sanitary inspection is required to establish the origin of every animal product and its fitness as food, the determinations of quality and yield are a matter of choice. Many packers do not agree with the need for quality inspection and have assigned their own grades or brands, called *packer grades,* to substitute for the federally administered system. If the ultimate user does not have the expertise to determine the quality of a meat product himself, it is strongly recommended that he buy federally graded meat. Only then will he be assured of receiving the quality he desires, at the price he is willing to pay. Packer grades, although closely approximating the federal ones, do not in all cases reflect the objectivity and impartiality that have made the federal grades so dependable.

Figure 14b. This type of stamp is used by federal inspectors to mark meat carcasses and products that have passed tests for wholesomeness. The number indicates the establishment in which the product was prepared. (Courtesy of the United States Department of Agriculture, Washington, D.C.)

Table 14-1. Packer Grades for Beef

Beef Packing Company	Brand Names in Descending Order of Quality
Armour and Company	Armour Star Deluxe, Armour Star, Quality, Banquet, Dexter
Cudahy Packing Company	Puritan, Fancy, Rex, Rival, Thrift
Geo. A. Hormel and Company	Best, Merit, Value, Hormel
Hygrade Food Products Corporation	Peerless, Honey Brand, Favorite
E. Kahn's Sons and Company	American Beauty, Bouquet, Quality, Poplar
Oscar Mayer and Company	Yellow Band, Capital, Special
John Morrell and Company	Morrell Pride, Morrell Xtrafine, Morrell Famous, Morrell Special, Morrell, Allrite
Rath Packing Company	Black Hawk Deluxe, Black Hawk, Kornland, Racorn, Sunvale, Budget
Wm. Schluderberg-T. J. Kurdle Company	Esskay Quality, Esskay Grade
Swift and Company	Premium, Select, Arrow
Tobin Packing Company	Arpeako Prize, Arpeako Delux, Arpeako Select, Arpeako Standard
Wilson and Company	Certified, Special, Ideal, Leader, Wilsco

From *Food Marketing Handbook,* pp. 2-5; Extension Service, New York, New Jersey, and Connecticut State Colleges of Agriculture and Home Economics, New York, 1960; reprinted by permission.

Beef

Beef is the most important meat used in the United States. It is defined as the meat from bovine cattle that are one year of age or older.

Beef may come from a dairy animal such as the Jersey or Holstein; from a beef animal such as the Angus or Hereford; or from a combination breed such as the Milking Shorthorn. Because the prime purpose of the animal affects both breeding and feed management procedures the beef animals will normally give higher quality and yields of meat than dairy animals.

In order to meet more recent demands for animals with less fat and, of course, to produce more efficient profits, livestock operators have introduced some exotic breeds into the United States: Blond d'Aquitaine from the Southwestern Pyrenees region of France and Pinzgauer from Austria. Breeders have tried new cross breeding for the same purposes, resulting in the Beefmaster (half Brahmanand half Hereford-shorthorn, the Brae (a Black Angus with a differing feed regimen), and the Beefalo (a bison-cattle cross that results in less fat content). The

Table 14-2. Breeds of United States Beef Cattle

Breed	Description
Shorthorn	An all red, all white, or combination red and white animal; first introduced into the United States from England in the 1700s
Hereford	A red animal with white face, head, and breast; very hardy and managed very well on range feeding; introduced into the United States from England
Angus	An all black animal; introduced into the United States from Scotland in the 1800s
Brahman	An American-bred gray animal with a "hump" above its shoulders; a result of crossing (Asian) Indian cattle with the best of United States breeds
Santa Gertrudis	An American-bred animal developed to withstand high range temperatures; a cross between a Brahman bull and a Shorthorn cow

Courtesy of the American Meat Institute, Chicago.

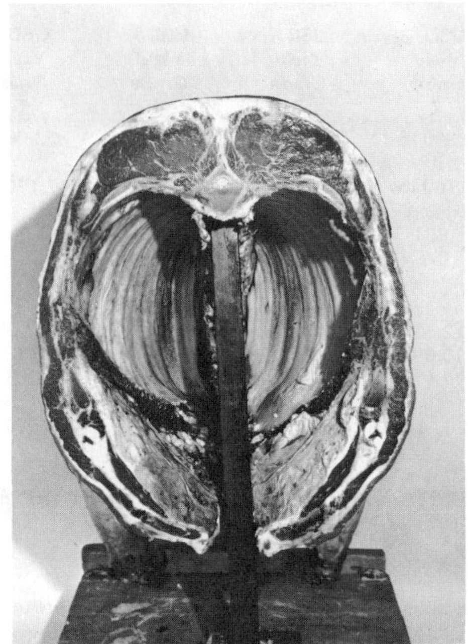
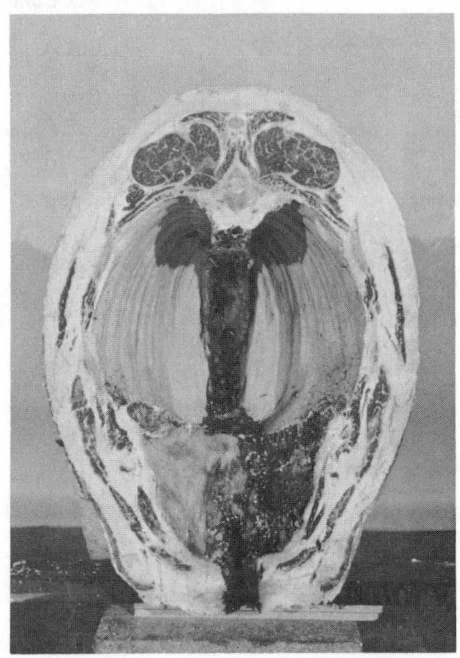

Figure 14c. Two steer carcasses, crosscut at the twelfth rib, show the significance of yield grades in beef. The carcass at the left is yield grade 2, while that on the right is yield grade 5. (Courtesy of Iowa State University.)

Brae, for example, has 84 percent less fat and 43 percent fewer calories than traditional beef cattle while the Beefalo has 80 percent less fat and 55 percent fewer calories than regular beef animals.

Grades and Yields

The quality of beef is graded on a composite evaluation of three factors: *conformation,* or the shape of the animal; *finish,* or the relationship of fat to lean to bone; and *quality,* or the grain structure of the meat. The overall quality grade, expressed as a standard, then reflects the degrees of tenderness, juiciness, and flavor to be expected from a particular animal or cut of meat. There is also a series of yield grades, which indicate the weights of retail cuts of various quality grades that may be expected from a particular animal.

Beef is quality graded in eight general classifications: *prime, choice, good, standard, commercial, utility, cutter,* and *canner.* Cows (the mature females of the breed) are not eligible for designation as prime. Bulls (mature males) and stags (males castrated after reaching sexual maturity) have a separate set of quality range designations: *choice, good, commercial, utility, cutter,* and *canner.*

Beef may also be graded for yields of retail cuts on a scale of U.S. Department of Agriculture grades numbered 1 through 5. Yiela grade 1 is the highest and grade 5 the lowest. Each yield grade of beef will give approximately 4.6 percent more eatable retail cuts than the grade below.

Value differences between yield grades, calculated by the Economic Research Service of the Department of Agriculture, have indicated an average differential of $3.61 per hundredweight between each yield grade. Thus, if the price differential between adjacent yield grades is more than $3.61 per hundredweight of carcass, it may well be advantageous to buy the lower yield grade, since the greater yield will not overcome the increase in price.

Quality grade determinations must also be closely studied. Although only the gross grades are provided, there remains a near-common area between the top of one grade and the bottom of the next higher grade. For

Table 14-3. Comparison of Yield Grades

	USDA Yield Grade 1	USDA Yield Grade 2	USDA Yield Grade 3	USDA Yield Grade 4	USDA Yield Grade 5
Required yield of retail cuts	30,000 lbs.	30,000 lbs.	30,000 lbs.	30,000 lbs.	30,000 lbs.
Amount of carcass beef needed	36,585 lbs.	38,760 lbs.	41,210 lbs.	43,990 lbs.	47,170 lbs.
Number of 600-lb carcasses needed	61	65	69	73	78
Yields after preparing and trimming retail cuts:					
Fat trim	7.5%	12.6%	17.7%	22.8%	27.9%
Bone and shrink	10.5%	10.0%	9.5%	9.0%	8.5%
Trimmed cuts	82.0%	77.4%	72.8%	68.2%	63.6%
Sales value per cwt. of carcass, at 1968 retail prices*	$72.77	$69.16	$65.55	$61.94	$58.33
Gross margin as a percentage of sales, assuming quality grade is USDA choice and purchase price was $43.00 per cwt.*	40.91%	37.83%	34.40%	30.58%	26.28%

Adapted from Marketing Bulletin no. 45, Consumer Marketing Service, United States Department of Agriculture, Washington, D.C.

*Cutting and trimming costs increase for fatter carcasses. If these are included, differences in sales values and margins between yield grades will also increase.

example, a top choice grade cut may, for all practical purposes, be so close to a low prime grade cut that the difference in price may be used to dictate purchase of the choice meat.

Classification of Beef Animals

Since sex, age, and management procedures have an important effect on the meat provided by an animal, consideration of these factors is important for the prospective food service manager or supervisor. The classifications of beef are made on the basis of the animal's sex and sexual development.

Steers. Steers are male animals, almost always from a beef breed, that have been castrated before reaching sexual maturity. This procedure permits the animal to develop a blocklike, heavy flesh covering that the mature unaltered male animal cannot attain.

Heifers. Heifers are female animals, almost always from a beef breed, that have never calved and are not pregnant. Although it is possible to differentiate between a steer and a heifer by means of bone configuration in the pelvic area, the differentiation is not important because the quality of meat from heifers and steers of the same breed is comparable.

Cows. Cows are mature female animals that have borne young. Those from the beef breeds may grade out at acceptable quality levels, even though they are excluded from the prime grade, as previously noted. Dairy cows, usually receive very low grades, however, since they generally are slaughtered only when they are no longer able to fulfill their milk-giving function.

Stags. Stags are mature male animals that have been castrated after reaching sexual maturity. Although some altering of their flesh is possible, many of the undesirable characteristics of the adult male have been formed, and they are therefore graded in the bull category.

Bulls. Bulls are uncastrated males. With no attempt made to alter the action of the male hormones, they exhibit the characteristic broad shoulders, heavy neck, and trim hindquarters. They therefore yield less desirable meat cuts and meat of lower quality.

Quality Determinants

In addition to the sex, the age of the animal, the degree of activity, the breed, and the feeding management that has been used all contribute to the quality and yield to be realized from a particular animal.

Age. Although beef is defined as meat from an animal one year or older, the age above that year plays an important part in the acceptability of the product. The flesh of younger animals is bright, clear, and red. It has a good distribution of fat, and the fat is solid and creamy in color. The bones are moist and bloody with heavy amounts of cartilage. Animals that are too young (and should properly be classified as veal) have not had an adequate time to develop the desirable characteristics of flesh and fat distribution, while older animals generally develop undesirable texture and taste characteristics.

Sex. As noted, the sex hormones play an important part in determining the texture and taste of meat. In addition, they cause flesh formation in one area at the expense of another, often producing less flesh in the more desirable meat areas, particularly in male animals. This is the most important reason for castration.

Activity. In general, as an animal gets older and its degree of activity increases, its flesh develops more taste and less tenderness. It is generally accepted that the degree of activity of a muscle is inversely proportional to tenderness and directly proportional to taste. Premortem injections of enzymes and postmortem aging of meats are often used to improve their taste and tenderness.

Breed. Animals are bred and managed to perform their prime economic function. The dairy herds keep females to produce milk, often using an artificial insemination procedure, while male calves are sold as vealers at a tender age. Dairy cooperative associations maintain prize bulls for breeding purposes and ship frozen semen to technicians in dairy areas. The mature cow is not geared to provide great amounts of flesh, but rather great quantities of milk. Conversely, beef animals are selectively bred for meat, so that they develop the block configuration that produces the greatest yield from an animal.

Feeding Management. Silage, grass, and grain feeding are all used in the production of beef. In areas where ranges and pastures are used even for feeding beef animals, the result will generally be less flesh and of a lower grade. The addition of grains to the diet produces the finish (the marbling of fat) that gives the flesh a higher quality.

Identification and Purchase of Beef

Beef is not all steaks and roasts. Only about 17 percent of the animal is the loin area, which provides the club, T-bone, and porterhouse steaks. But menus need not offer only these choice cuts; other parts of the animal also have important uses. The manager or supervisor must be able to identify specific cuts and must know the desirable uses of each.

Beef may be purchased by the side (this is a rare form of purchase owing to labor, transportation, and merchandising limitations); by the quarter; by the primal cut; by the retail cut; or in portion-controlled cuts. It may be purchased in chilled or frozen form.

If a butcher is employed and/or available to the facility, the operator may do comparative pricing of the different forms available and then purchase by the quarter or by the primal cut, whichever is more advantageous. The butcher breaks the meat down into usable retail portions, while good use may often be made of secondary parts of the animal that are by-products of the process. However, although the price on a quarter or primal cut usually looks more attractive, labor costs and actual yields may give an entirely different picture.

The menu form and pricing structure also influence the form in which the meat is purchased. Some menus readily lend themselves to use of the less desirable parts of the animal that are collected when in-house butchering is practiced, while other menus do not.

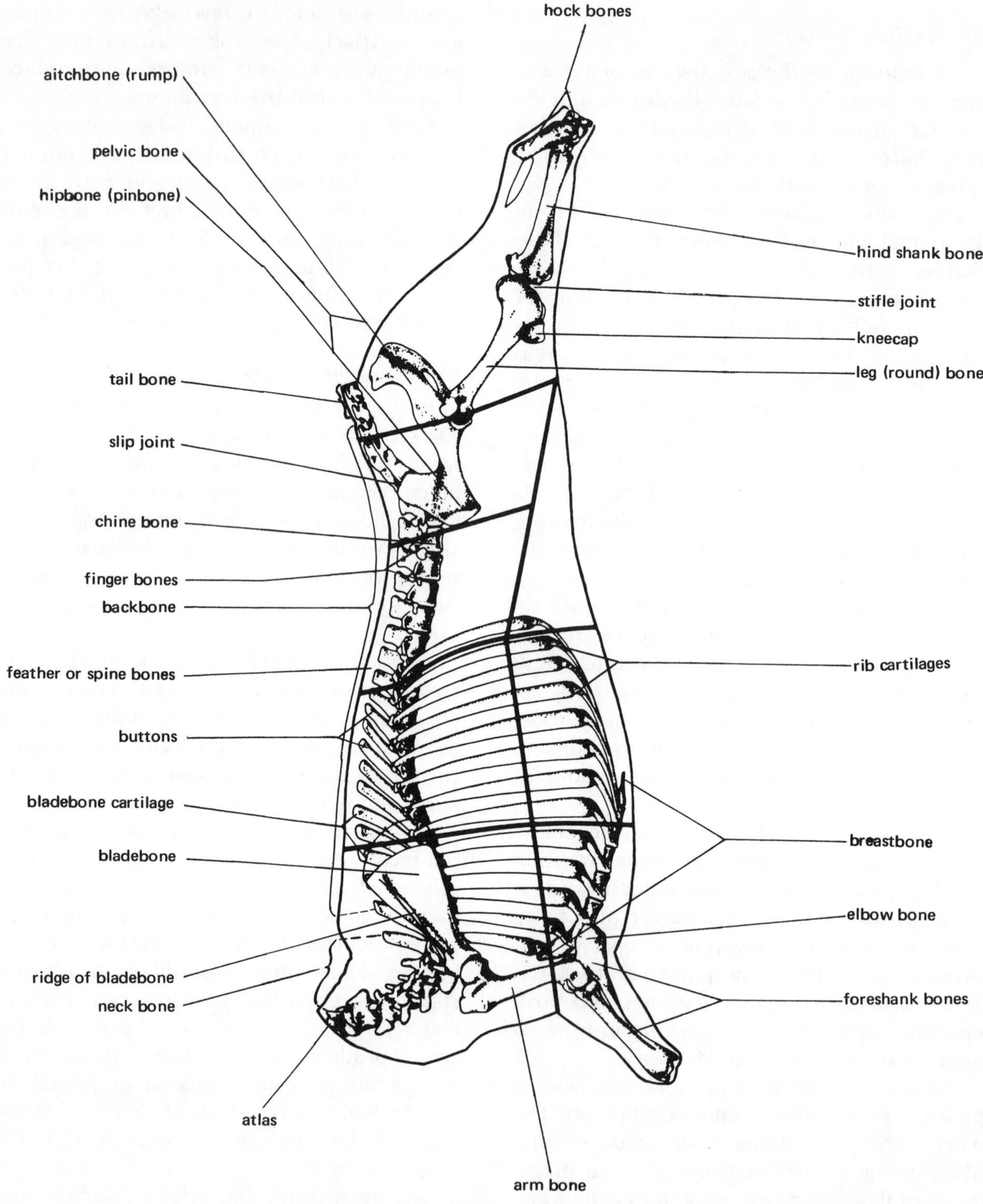

Figure 14-d. The bone structure of a beef animal. Knowledge of the skeleton is helpful in identifying the particular cut of beef. Beef animals have redder flesh, larger cuts of meat, and larger bones than other meat animals. (Courtesy of the National Live Stock and Meat Board, Chicago.)

Whatever the gross form of purchased meat, the food service manager or supervisor should recognize the type of animal, know the primal and retail cuts, and be aware of the correct preparation methods for each. To do this, he uses a combination of external and internal standards. Institutional Meat Purchase Specifications (IMPS) established by the United States Department of Agriculture and specifications of the National Association of Meat Purveyors are helpful guides. As noted in chapter 7, the USDA Meat Acceptance Service is available for those who choose to transfer the purchasing responsibility to this organization.

All beef animals have the same general anatomical structure, with thirteen ribs. Although there are some minor differences between male and female pelvic bone formations, these are not considered important, and identical cuts of meat can be carved from animals of either sex.

In identifying a particular cut of meat, the use that should be made of it, and the preparation method of choice, most attention should be given to the bone configuration and muscle formation. These two factors, plus the color of the flesh, the size of the cut, and the finish of the meat, identify the particular cut.

Beef animals are divided into different usable meat cuts according to systems that originated in different geographic locations: Chicago, New York, Boston, and Philadelphia. The major dividing systems are the Chicago and the New York methods. This book reflects the Chicago system with notice of New York differences when they are considered important.

In the Chicago method the beef carcass is divided into the eight primal cuts listed in table 14-4. The carcass may also be divided into the forequarter and the hindquarter without subdividing it into the primal cuts. In such a case, one rib is left on the hindquarter in order to maintain its shape and to ensure that the full hindquarter is provided. The remaining twelve ribs are included in the forequarter.

Although sizes of cattle vary, a 1,000-pound steer will yield approximately 580 to 590 pounds of meat, with a side weighing approximately 280 to 290 pounds. The forequarter will weigh about 150 pounds and the hindquarter about 140 pounds. The left side of the animal weighs slightly more than the right side because it contains the additional size of the kidney knob and the hanging tenderloin.

Forequarter Primal Cuts

The *chuck* is the major cut of the forequarter and the largest primal cut of the animal. It accounts for approximately 26 percent of the carcass, and contains about two-thirds of the less expensive cuts.

The chuck is divided from the rib primal cut between the fifth and sixth rib leaving five ribs with the chuck and seven with the rib. It is fairly square in shape. Three bone structures help to identify it: its rib endings, which are cut to separate the plate from the chuck; the arm bone, which is cut to remove the foreshank; and the scapula or bladebone. The chuck may also be purchased boneless. In that case, the shoulder clod muscle, which covers the scapula, may be either intact or removed.

Because of its location the chuck contains many muscles that have been used extensively by the mobile animal. The meat is replete with connective tissue, and most cuts will have outstanding flavor, but they will be less tender than other cuts. In higher grade animals, however, the shoulder clod can sometimes give a desirable dry roast.

Table 14-4. Primal Cuts of Beef (Chicago Method)

Cut	Percent of Carcass
Hindquarter	
Round	24
Loin end	9
Short loin	8
Flank and suet	8
Forequarter	
Rib	9
Plate	12
Chuck	26
Shank	4

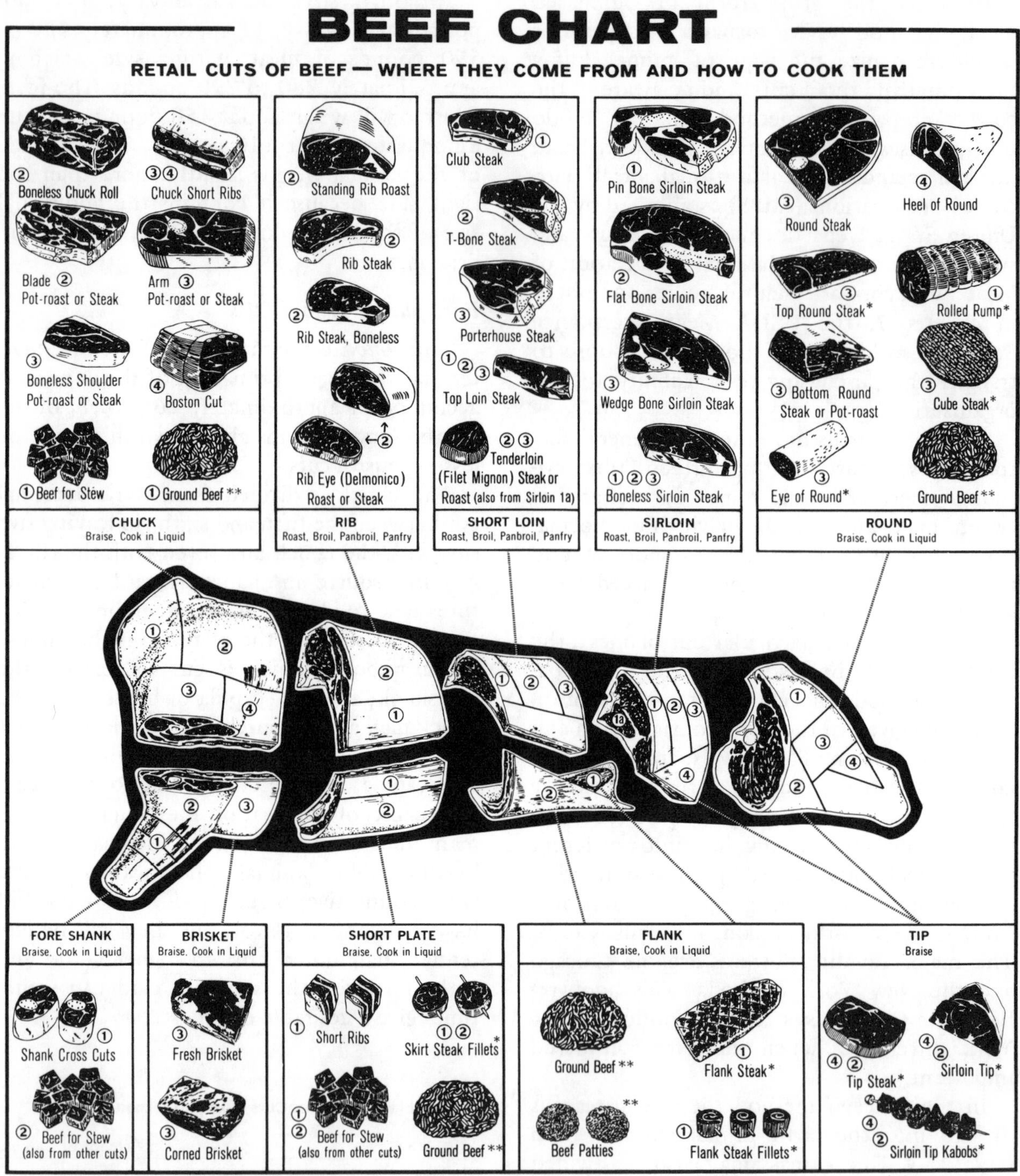

Figure 14e. Chart of the primal and retail cuts from beef animals, indicating the acceptable preparation methods. (Courtesy of the National Live Stock and Meat Board, Chicago.)

The chuck may be subdivided into or purchased in the following retail cuts: blade steaks or blade roasts; cross-arm roasts or arm steaks; Boston, English, or bottom chuck roasts; stew beef; and ground chuck. The blade steaks or blade roasts may be identified by the backbone and the bladebone. The blade in some cases may take the shape of the number seven. The cross-arm cuts will usually have some rib bone and the round arm bone that has been cut through.

The *rib* is the most important primal cut of the forequarter from the standpoint of usability and price. It may be subdivided into rib steaks, be boned and trimmed for a rolled rib roast, or be trimmed for a standing rib roast. It is, of course, identified by the backbone, the rib bones, and the rib eye muscle. The rib may be cut from the plate either seven or ten inches from the backbone along the ribs. It may also be purchased oven-ready—boned and tied.

The *plate, brisket,* and *shank* primal cuts may be included in one heading. They rarely are purchased separately but rather are by-products that remain when a forequarter is purchased and the chuck is broken (cut) from it. The plate, below the ribs, is best known for short ribs of beef. It contains the rib ends left after the seven- or ten-inch rib primal cut has been taken. Some rolled beef, boiling beef, or beef "bacon" may also be derived from this cut. The shank is generally used only for soup stock or as stew beef. The brisket is the most desirable cut of the three. It may be processed into a highly popular corned beef, or, cut as one muscle from brisket to shank, it may be made into pastrami.

Hindquarter Primal Cuts

The largest cut of the hindquarter is the *round.* It provides about 24 percent of the entire usable carcass to the food service operator. It may be subdivided into rump, sirloin tip, round (retail), heel of the round, and hind shank cuts.

The rump may be boneless and rolled or include the aitchbone (the pelvic bone of the animal). It is generally triangular in shape and makes a very satisfactory roast. It may also be cut into cube, minute, or country fried steaks, particularly if it is from a higher grade animal.

The sirloin tip, or knuckle, also has a triangular shape and often contains the kneecap of the animal. If unboned, it may be used as a roast or divided into steaks.

The retail round may be used as a "steamship roast" (a large roast—about fifty pounds—sliced with showmanship at a buffet table) with the knuckle and both top and bottom round included. It may also be subdivided into the top, or inside, round and the bottom, or outside, round; then the two are used as roasts or cut into steaks. The full round, in roast or steak form, contains the leg bone of the animal. The top round is one large muscle, and the bottom round two separate muscles, one of which is the eye of the round. The top of the round is the most tender part of the cut. The round may also be divided into cube, minute, or Swiss steaks.

The diamond or heel of the round is the least tender cut of the primal round and is best used for pot roast, stew meat, or ground beef.

The hind shank, like the forequarter shank, is used as stew meat, as ground beef, or for stock.

The *loin end* (also called the *sirloin, butt,* or *hip*) of the animal is a most important hindquarter primal cut. Separated from the short loin, it provides steaks of a very similar bone configuration to those taken from the short loin in some cuts and a very different appearance in others. The backbone and hipbone are the most important identifying features. The appearance of the bone identifies the particular part of the sirloin: pinbone sirloin, which is the first end of the hipbone, is the first two or three steaks from the sirloin; flatbone or double bone sirloin, which is best used for family steaks or sirloins for two, consists of the next four or five steaks; and wedgebone sirloin finishes out the cut. The loin end is primarily adaptable for use as steaks.

PORTERHOUSE, T-BONES, LOIN CHOPS

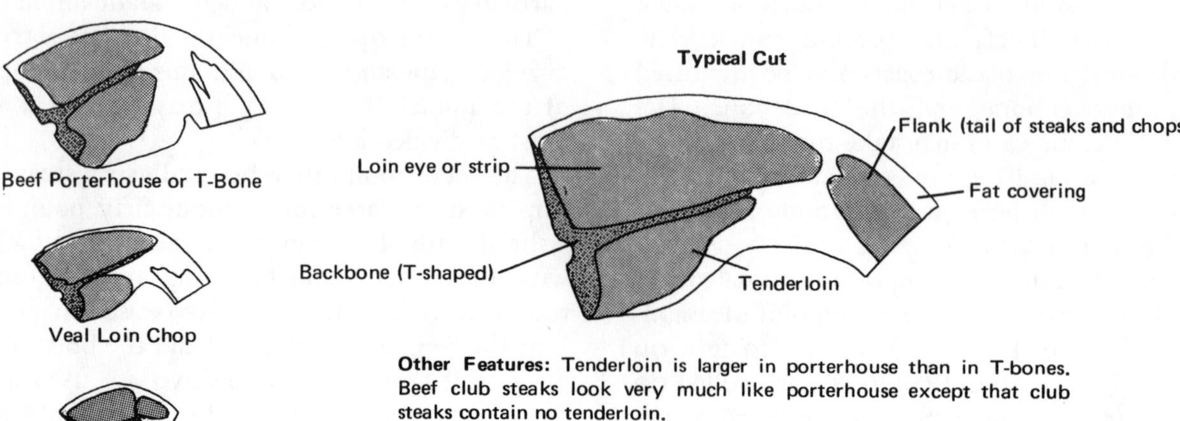

Other Features: Tenderloin is larger in porterhouse than in T-bones. Beef club steaks look very much like porterhouse except that club steaks contain no tenderloin.

BLADE STEAKS

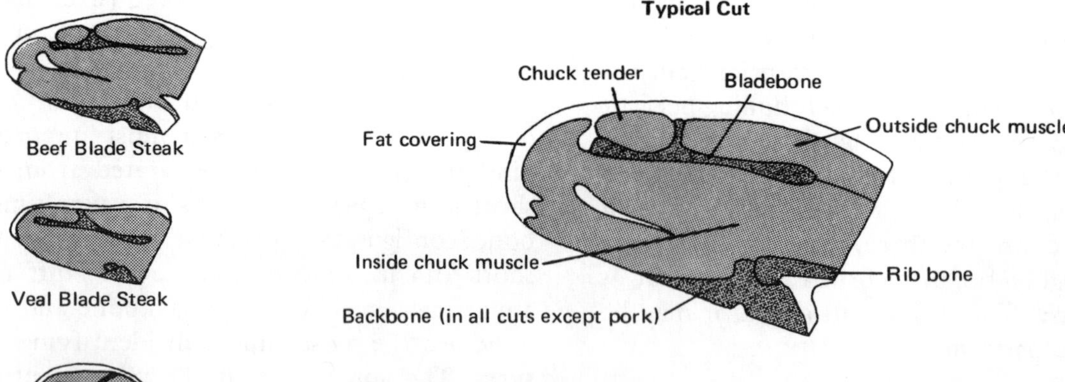

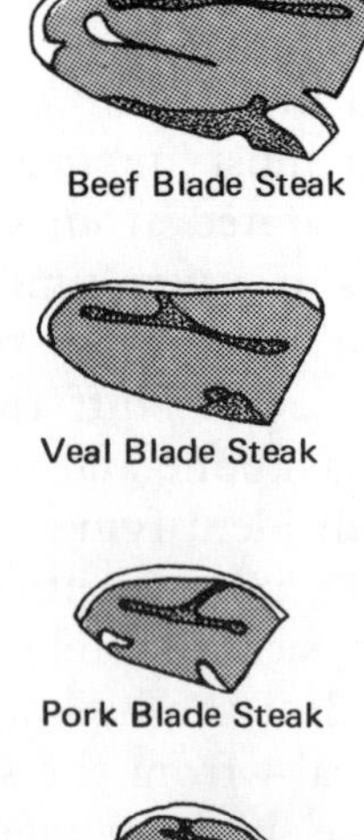

Other Features: Inside chuck muscles run in different directions. Backbone is in all cuts except pork. Rib bone is in all cuts except pork unless the cut is made between the ribs.

Figure 14f. Use of bone configurations and muscles to identify cuts of meat from specific parts of the animal. (Courtesy of the National Live Stock and Meat Board, Chicago.)

ROUND STEAKS, HAM, LEG STEAKS

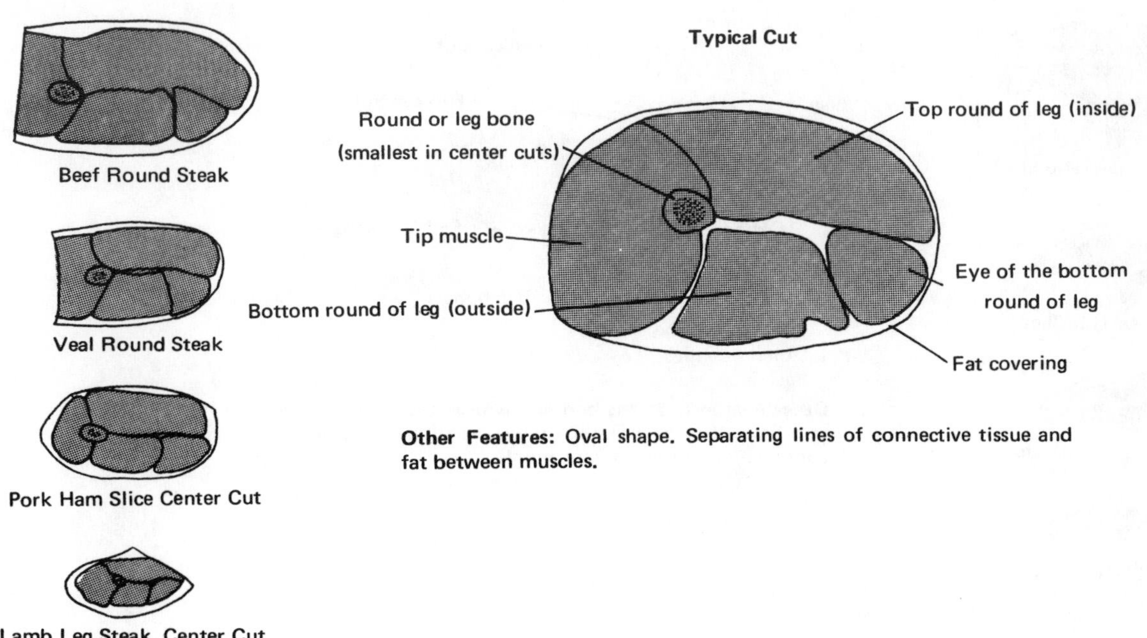

Other Features: Oval shape. Separating lines of connective tissue and fat between muscles.

SIRLOIN STEAKS, CHOPS

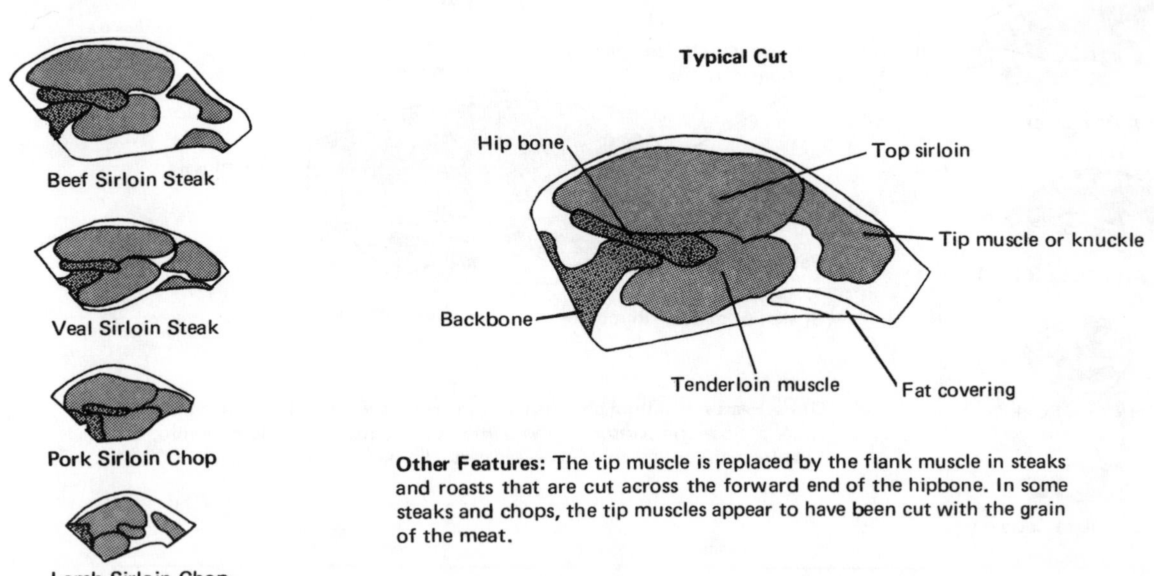

Other Features: The tip muscle is replaced by the flank muscle in steaks and roasts that are cut across the forward end of the hipbone. In some steaks and chops, the tip muscles appear to have been cut with the grain of the meat.

Figure 14f (continued).

RIB STEAKS, CHOPS

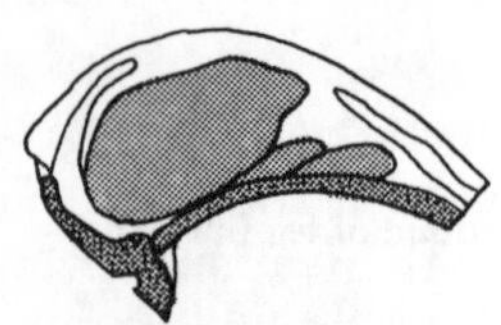
Beef Rib Steak

Veal Rib Chop

Pork Rib (Loin) Chop

Lamb Rib Chop

Typical Cut

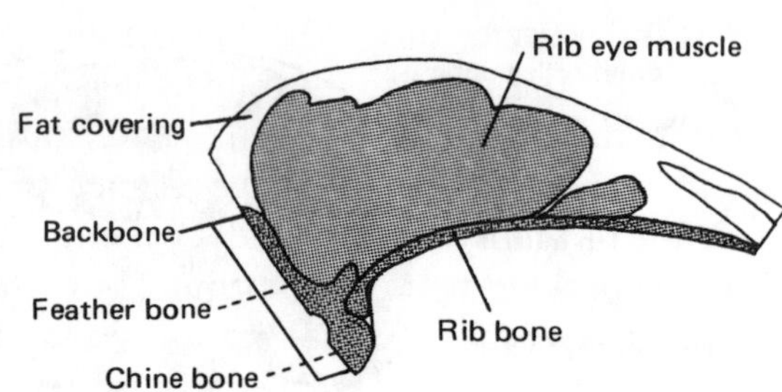

Other Features: Steaks and chops near the chuck or shoulder have a thin layer of meat over the rib eye called the rib cover. The rib eye is a continuation of the loin eye muscle.

ARM STEAKS, CHOPS

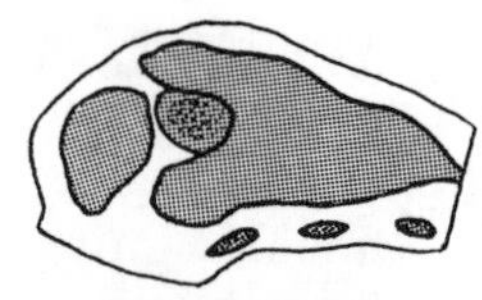
Beef Arm Steak

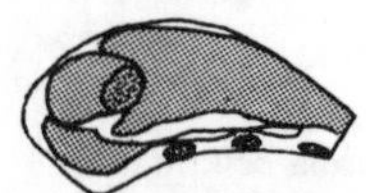
Veal Arm Steak (Chop)

Pork Arm Steak

Lamb Arm Chop

Typical Cut

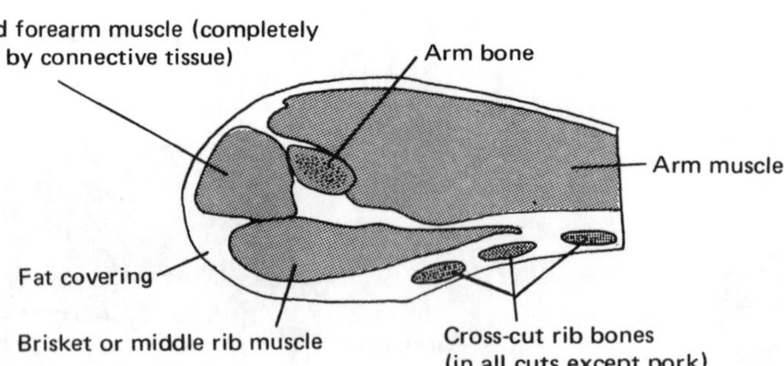

Other Features: Although cuts from the round and arm look somewhat alike, a close comparison shows a wide difference in muscle structure. Cuts from the round contain no cross-cut rib bones.

Figure 14f (continued).

The *short loin* is the most desirable part of the hindquarter for steaks. The backbone is its major identifying feature, and it has varying amounts of the tenderloin muscle, according to the type of steak. The first cuts from the loin are called club or Delmonico steaks and have little or no tenderloin muscle; the T-bone steaks are next, with a fair amount of tenderloin in addition to the main muscle of the loin; and finally come the porterhouse steaks with the greatest amount of tenderloin muscle. An average animal will provide from twenty to twenty-four loin steaks approximately one inch thick from each side of the carcass.

The tenderloin muscle may be removed from the short loin to be used separately. This is normally done with lower grade beef, since the tenders of almost every animal will be desirable, even though the other parts of the animal may not be. When the tender is removed from the loin end, the loin steaks may then be called sirloin strips; they may be either with bone or boneless. The less desirable end of the tenderloin may then be used as tenderloin tips, while the choicer end may become filet mignon or be cooked in one piece as a chateaubriand and sliced in roast fashion.

The *flank* and *suet* complete the hindquarter. The flank is best used for flank steak, or London broil, with the remainder of the cut going for ground beef or stew beef. The suet is the beef fat, predominately that surrounding the kidney. It may be used in mincemeat, used for larding less tender cuts, or included in the fat-rendering bucket.

Coloring

The coloring of beef flesh is important in identifying the species of the animal and determining its age, grade, and sex. Although the use of governmental inspection and grading procedures will obviate the need for many of these determinations, a few general principles should still be known by the manager or supervisor of a quantity facility.

All beef is more red in color than other meat animals. The deepness of the color comes from the hemoglobin properties of the blood and the glycogen and myoglobin properties of the muscles.

The age of the animal, the type of feed used, and the amount a particular muscle has been used greatly influence the richness of color within a species. In beef, more mature animals have darker meat than younger animals, and muscles that receive greater use have deeper colors. The fat of older animals and of animals that have received a diet of nothing but grass normally is yellower than that of younger animals or those that have been finish-fed with grain. The bones of older animals are usually much whiter, while those of less mature animals are more moist and reddish in color.

Variety Meats

Livers, hearts, tongues, kidneys, sweetbreads, brains, and tripe are variety meats that are found in beef animals and many other meat animals as well. They provide excellent sources of protein and generous amounts of the A, B complex, and D vitamins, depending on the particular part used.

Although these products do not enjoy general popularity, they should be considered for inclusion on a particular menu because of their excellent yield and the price specials they offer when the supply, which is quite constant, exceeds the limited demand. In a gourmet or ethnically oriented establishment, these foods often find greater acceptance than in more cosmopolitan facilities.

Moistness, firmness, and freshness of appearance are important indicators of high quality in these items. The size of the particular organ is an important indicator in identification, since it is related to the size of the animal.

Processed, Convenience, and Ready Forms of Beef

As noted above, beef like many other meats may be purchased either chilled or frozen. It may also be purchased in such diverse forms as ground beef, bologna, or portion-controlled individual retail cuts.

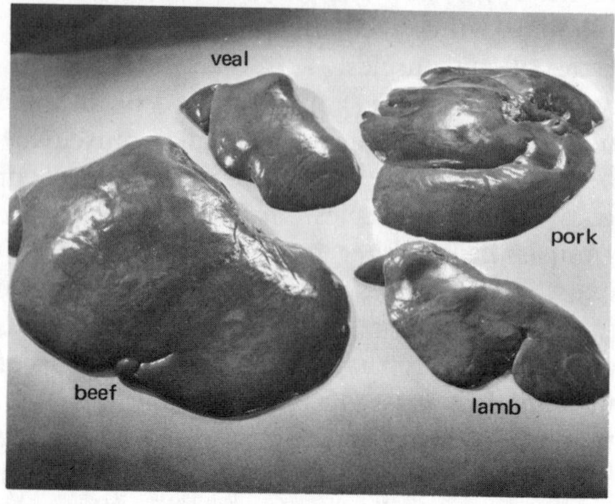

Livers: beef and pork—roast, braise, fry; veal and lamb—broil, panbroil, fry

Hearts: braise, simmer

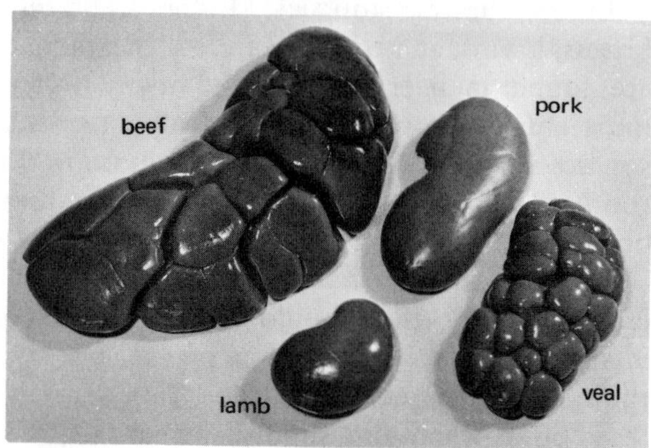

Kidneys: beef and pork—simmer, braise; veal and lamb—broil, panbroil, braise, simmer

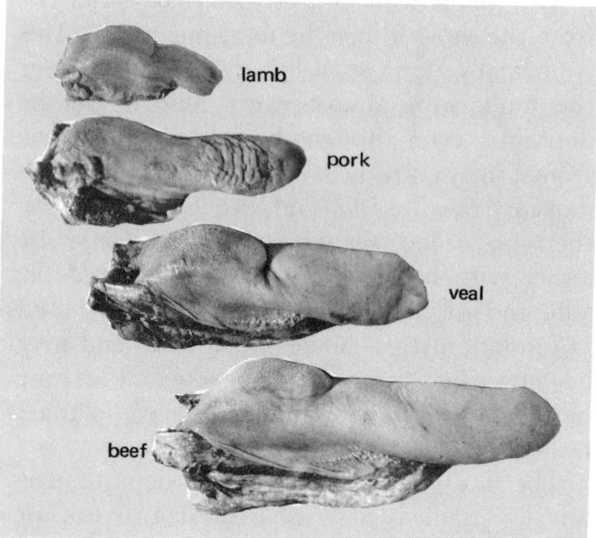

Tongues: simmer

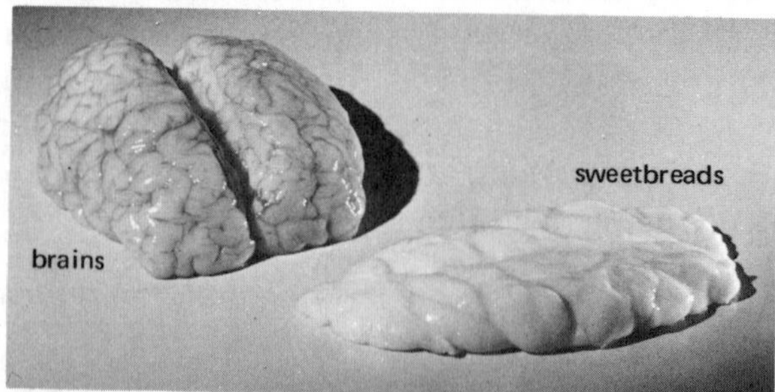

Brains and Sweetbreads: broil, fry, braise, simmer

Figure 14g. Variety meats and methods of cooking them. (Courtesy of the National Live Stock and Meat Board, Chicago.)

Ground beef, ground chuck, and ground round are all available. Their lean-to-fat ratios vary from 75 percent/25 percent to 80 percent/20 percent. The specific use and cooking procedure must be determined and related to the fat content. Ground round usually has the lowest fat content of the three.

Bologna and other prepared sausage products are usually cooked, cured, and sold ready for eating, requiring only reheating in some cases. Varying amounts of lean and fat may be provided in a particular product, and meat from several different animals may be used for some. The food service manager or supervisor has to determine what to purchase in accordance with his specific needs.

Portion-controlled meats, generally in patty or steak form, are also available to the operator. Like other products, these should be considered from the standpoint of menu requirements, labor considerations, quality of the product, and consumer desires.

Frozen, preportioned cube steaks, Swiss steaks, strip steaks, tenderloin steaks, butt steaks, and rib eye steaks are available in uncooked form. Ground beef patties, meatballs, and rolled, tied, oven-ready rib roasts are also sold. Ready meat foods and combinations of meat and other foods are also provided in frozen or canned form. The frozen varieties, in either individual or multiple unit packages, appear to give the best quality. An operator may find such items as cooked roast beef, ground beef patties, Salisbury steaks, boneless short ribs, and beef stroganoff.

The canned meat items are generally a mixture of beef (or other meats) with other types of foods such as chili beans and sauce, ingredients to make meat balls, and stew vegetables. Like all other canned foods, canned meats are completely cooked to sterilization temperatures and require only additional heating prior to service.

Cooking Beef

Beef, like all other meats, is cooked in order to make it more palatable, tender, and digestible, to destroy bacteria, and to improve its appearance. Beef may be eaten raw (in such dishes as steak tartare), but this generally creates an unnecessary health risk; most recipes and most consumers still call for beef to undergo some form of cooking.

Table 14-5. Meats Used in Common Sausages

Type	Major Meat Ingredients
Bologna	Beef; beef and pork; or beef, veal, and pork
Cervelat	Beef and pork
Frankfurters	Beef; beef and pork; or beef, veal, and pork
Lebanon bologna	Beef
Liver sausage	Pork livers, or pork, veal, and beef livers
Salami	Beef and pork

Well-prepared beef should retain as much juiciness and taste as possible. Two basic forms of cooking are used: (1) dry heat cooking such as in an oven or on a broiler, and (2) moist heat cooking in a liquid such as stock or water. The type of cooking selected depends on the natural tenderness of the meat and the amount of collagen or elastin that is found in the particular cut.

A third method of preparation, although not strictly a cooking procedure, is reconstitution, which may be carried out in a microwave oven, a convection oven, or a water bath. This method is applied to a beef item that has already been fully prepared, usually a ready food item.

All beef cuts may be identified as either tender or less tender, according to the criteria previously noted (age, sex, and degree of activity are most important). Those classified as tender are generally cooked by dry heat, while those classified as less tender are cooked by moist heat.

Some variations may be made, allowing less tender meats to be roasted or broiled with the use of a tenderizing agent such as an acid type of marinade, an enzyme such as that found in meat tenderizer, or knife scoring or mechanical tenderizing methods. Use of low-temperature and long-cooking-period procedures may enable some less tender (or tough) cuts to be cooked by dry methods with acceptable results. Selected cuts of higher grade animals may also be cooked by dry methods (e.g., the shoulder clod of the chuck may be roasted), although a lower quality cut would require moist cooking. These are all exceptions, though, rather than the rule. The basic premise is still dry heat with tender meat and moist heat with tough.

The application of heat to the meat protein first causes a solidification and firming of the beef, as coagulation takes place within the tissue. This basic principle has been used by chefs for many years: they learn to test for the internal condition (doneness) of a roast or steak by the touch of their fingers. During the firming of the tissue some shrinkage occurs, as moisture is driven from the product. The firming process takes place within a temperature range of 140 to 160 degrees Fahrenheit. From 160 to 170 degrees, a reverse tenderizing effect takes place: the collagen is gelatinized, and fat in the tissue is melted. Continual and prolonged heating above this point results in a loss of additional moisture accompanied by toughening and drying of the meat. The fat continues to melt in an attempt to overcome the drying and toughening process. Thus, higher quality cuts, which possess more fat and collagen marbling of the tissue, are better able to stand prolonged heat application than products of lower quality grades. However, excessive application of heat is discouraged for all cuts.

As the meat cooks and these changes take place, there is a noticeable shrinkage, which is a direct result of moisture and fat evaporation. A change of color also takes place, varying with the form of cooking employed, as the oxymyoglobin of the meat is changed by the heat into hematin. With high enough external temperatures, the surface of the meat also becomes crisp and takes on accompanying flavor changes. Additional applications of heat may result in surface burning and flavor loss, as flavor substances are driven out with the drippings. Important nutrients may also be lost in this manner.

In cooking beef, or any other meat, the major concern of the food service operator is to achieve the degree of taste, color, and tenderness desired by the consumer. It is equally important that he achieve the highest yield possible, with a minimal loss of moisture, so that profit requirements are satisfied. In this process, the factors of time and tem-

Table 14-6. Methods of Cooking Beef

Cut	Dry Heat	Moist Heat*
Brisket		Simmer
Chuck roast	Roast (if high grade)	Braise
Club steak	Broil or panbroil	
Flank steak	Broil (if marinated and scored)	Braise
Ground beef	Roast, broil, panfry, or panbroil	
Plate beef		Simmer
Porterhouse steak	Broil or panbroil	
Rib roast	Roast	
Rib steak	Broil	
Round roast	Roast	Braise
Round steak (minute)	Panbroil or panfry	
Rump roast	Roast (if high grade)	Braise
Short ribs		Braise
Sirloin roast	Roast	
Sirloin steak	Broil or panbroil	
Stew meat		Stew or simmer
T-bone steak	Broil or panbroil	
Tenderloin	Roast or broil	

*Items to be cooked by moist heat methods should first be browned in fat for maximum surface color.

perature are of most importance, although the quality of the meat, the degree of aging, the location of the cut, and the size of the particular piece are also important.

Temperature and Time. The temperature applied, the time exposed, and the internal temperature reached are the most important factors in achieving both maximum yield and retention of flavor and nutrients. Temperatures must always be considered in relation to the time required for the cooking process, because one is generally inversely proportional to the other. As the applied temperature is raised, the time required to reach a desired internal temperature is reduced.

Use of higher external temperatures conserves greater amounts of vitamins and nutrients, because the meat is cooked for a shorter time. These higher temperatures, however, may cause greater shrinkage of the product and loss of moisture, as fat, water, and collagen deposits are squeezed out. Higher temperatures will also cause more surface coloration and crispness. Conversely, lower temperatures require longer cooking periods, but will result in greater yields. Losses of some nutrients will also be higher, since the heat destroys important vitamins, such as thiamine and niacin. But better flavor and more uniform tenderness of the product should result from the application of heat at lower levels. Less fuel will be used, and fewer cleaning procedures will be necessary to remove carbonized deposits on equipment.

The internal temperature of the meat, however, has a more dramatic effect on yield, cooking losses, and tenderness than these factors, and, within reasonable ranges, less concern may be paid to the external heat application. A study conducted at Ohio State University found that variations of oven temperatures from 200 to 375 degrees Fahrenheit had little effect on yields and total losses; but raising internal temperatures from 140 to 158 and 176 degrees Fahrenheit significantly increased these losses and reduced yields. (See Hunt, Seidler, and Wood, "Cooking Choice Grade, Top Round Beef Roasts," *Journal of the American Dietetic Association* 43 [October 1963] : 353.)

Quality of Meat. The higher quality meats have less shrinkage and give higher yields and greater palatability than the lower quality ones. Fat coverings produce faster transmission of applied heat, and, although losses do develop, more fat is available to maintain the tenderness and taste than in lower grade cuts.

Degree of Aging. The degree of aging also appears to affect the yield of beef, although this may be a reflection of the fact that only higher quality meats are aged for any significant period of time. Moreover, some moisture loss takes place during the aging process, and this leaves less for later loss. In any event, yields are usually greater for aged products.

Location and Size of Cut. The part of the animal used, with its particular fat, bone, and lean configuration, and the size of the cut also appear to affect the yield. Both bone and fat conduct heat from circumambient areas more rapidly than lean. Thus, the less fatty and boneless cuts cook more slowly. The amount of heat penetration required by the mass of the cut and the total surface area available for heat penetration also influence the time required for cooking. Generally, the larger cuts of meat require less cooking time *per pound,* although the total cooking time is more than for smaller cuts.

Degree of Doneness. As the degree of cooking increases, shrinkage also increases and yield decreases. This happens because either the externally applied temperature or the cooking time has been increased.

Some chefs still suggest the application of searing temperatures (well above the regular roasting ranges) to achieve maximum surface color, before the heat is reduced to a more reasonable level. Most studies have shown this to be a poor practice. They indicate that more uniform, lower temperatures applied throughout the cooking period will produce the desired coloring with a dramatic reduction of moisture loss.

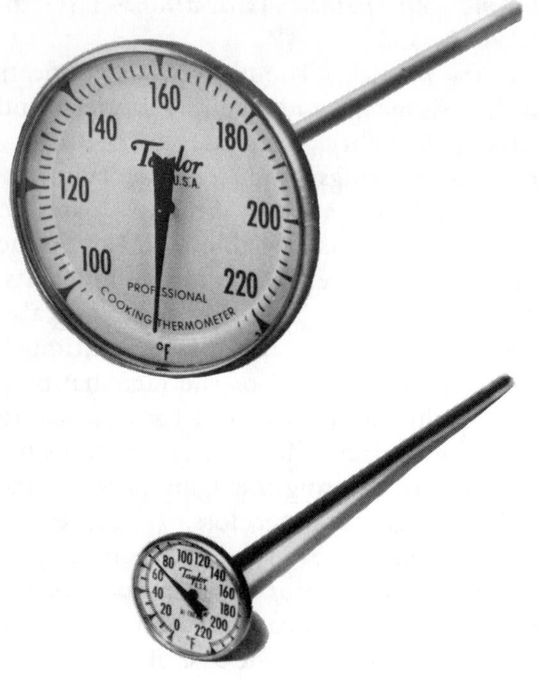

(Courtesy of Thermometer Corporation of America)

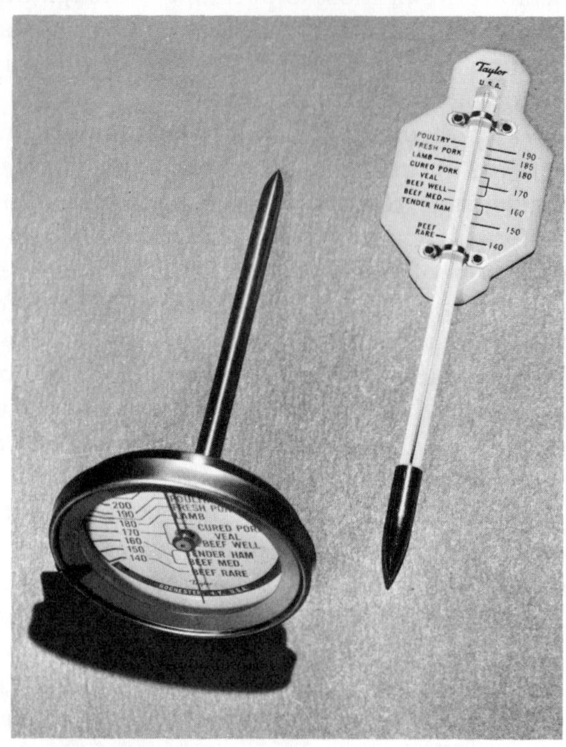

(Courtesy of the National Live Stock and Meat Board, Chicago)

Figure 14h. Meat thermometers that may be used with roasts.

Control Devices

Many experienced chefs are able to use their index fingers or thumbs and index fingers together to ascertain the "set" of the protein and determine the internal temperature of the meat. Less experienced persons will only get burned fingers for their efforts. An oven thermometer, correctly operating oven controls, an interval timer or clock, and a meat thermometer are the only methods that ensure correct cooking times and temperatures have been maintained. It is best to use them; they pay off.

Dry Heat Cooking

Roasting. Only the most tender cuts should be selected for roasting (see table 14-6). Less tender cuts of higher grade animals may also be used, particularly if low temperatures (200 to 250 degrees Fahrenheit) and longer cooking times are used.

The oven is preheated and tested with an oven thermometer (usually set between 250 and 350 degrees, depending on the size and type of the cut). After the meat is salted and seasoned, it is placed fat side *up,* and a meat thermometer is inserted in it. (Some cooks have questioned the use of salt because it retards browning, but roasted items are cooked long enough so that this is not considered a problem.)

If possible, cuts to be roasted together should be uniform in size. If cuts of different sizes must be used, the thermometer should be inserted in the smallest of the lot. It must be in solid tissue and not touching bone. The operator should realize that the yields of items of varying sizes will differ.

Workers must not cover, add water, or baste roasts. Covering the meat will capture the steam, which will speed cooking but may cause surface coloring problems. Basting should be unnecessary, as the fat covering of the meat performs this function.

An oven roasting plastic film for wrapping

meats is available from a number of sources. It has been used in homes and is finding some quantity food applications. It reduces cooking times, increases yields, and assists in tenderizing the products. Workers must follow the manufacturer's time and temperature directions if this wrap is used.

The roast is removed when it reaches the desired degree of doneness. Time must be allowed for a postoven rise (fifteen to twenty minutes) to ensure completion of the cooking, and to allow the heat to dissipate, so that carving is easier. The internal temperature may continue to rise another ten degrees after the roast is removed from the oven, and this must be planned for.

To recapture the drippings, either au jus or to make gravy, a small amount of water is added to the pan, and the mixture is heated while the worker stirs and scrapes the pan to remove the maximum amount of drippings.

Frozen Meats. Meats received in a frozen state may be roasted by dry heat without first being thawed. The time required for cooking varies with the cut, but studies conducted by the University of Illinois in cooperation with the National Association of Meat Purveyors and the National Live Stock and Meat Board indicate that a frozen cut requires from 1.30 to 1.45 times as long to cook than the same cut chilled (see table 14-16).

More uniform results may be achieved by defrosting the frozen meat under refrigeration and handling it as a chilled product during roasting. If adequate lead times are provided, and refrigerator space is available, this is the method of choice.

Broiling. The most tender cuts of beef may be broiled. Cuts such as flank steak may also be broiled in a very satisfactory manner after being marinated in an acid mixture (such as a vinegar-base marinade) and scored in a diamond pattern to cut striated tissue.

The broiler is preheated to the highest setting. Generally no cut less than one inch thick should be broiled, or excessive internal temperatures may be reached before the outside is cooked.

A coating of oil on both sides of the item to be broiled will help prevent surface drying. Seasoning should not be used at this point. The fat cover must be slashed to prevent a curling of the meat, because fat shrinks in cooking faster than meat does.

One side is broiled until the meat is half done; then seasoning is added and the meat is turned. The fork should be inserted in the fat cover or a steak turner should be used, because puncturing the meat will increase the loss of juices. Meat is not turned more than once, unless the operator wishes to make double grid marks in an "XX" pattern on each side for the sake of attractiveness.

The meat should be broiled two to three inches from the heat source, if it is one inch thick. The color of the meat close to the bone and the reading from a meat thermometer will supplement time guides to indicate completion of cooking.

Panbroiling or Grill Broiling. An aluminum or Teflon-coated pan or a grill may be used for broiling. The surface of the pan is rubbed very lightly with fat. A grill need not be greased, because enough fat will cook out of the meat to prevent sticking.

Panbroiling may be used for the tender cuts or less tender ones that have been tenderized and cut into thin slices (such as minute steaks). After one side is cooked, the meat is turned with tongs or a steak turner, being careful not to pierce any fat covering at the outside edge of the meat, which would then release melted fat into the pan. Excess fat is periodically removed from the pan or grill surface during cooking.

The item may be tested for doneness by making a cut near bone (if appropriate), or a thermometer may be used to indicate completion of cooking. Use of timetables and experience with standard cuts will give workers better indications of the correct cooking times. Items are seasoned just before serving.

Panfrying, Sautéing, and Grilling. Panfrying and similar methods of cooking do utilize moisture, but because the liquid is a fat they are considered forms of dry heat cookery.

Tender and slightly less tender cuts of meat are prepared by these methods.

A grill or heavy-duty frying pan is used. The item to be cooked is first dredged in flour and browned on both sides in hot fat. Then it is cooked at a moderate temperature until done.

Panfrying differs from panbroiling in that the fat is not removed from the cooking surface. Panfrying gives a deeper color and crisper surface to the product than panbroiling does.

Deep Frying. Although deep frying is considered a form of dry heat cookery, it is rarely used for beef products, except for some variety meat items. It is discussed in connection with the meats for which it is used more often (such as veal).

Moist Cooking Methods

Braising. Braising is the cooking of less tender cuts of meat in a small amount of liquid such as water or stock. The cooking pot is covered, and the moisture inside generates steam, which tenderizes the tougher cuts of meat. A preliminary browning of the meat surface is usually required to give an adequate surface color. Braising may be done in an oven, but it is usually carried out on a range top. The cooking process may be accelerated by tenderizing the meat—pounding it by machine or by hand to break the connective tissue.

The procedure for braising is to dredge the meat in flour and brown all sides in a small amount of fat. A small quantity of liquid is

Table 14-7. General Beef Cookery Timetable

Cooking Method	Minutes			Comments
	Rare	Medium	Well Done	
Roasting (oven temp. 300°-325°)	11-25 per lb. (140° internal temp.)	12-28 per lb. (160° internal temp.)	13-30 per lb. (170° internal temp.)	*Larger roasts* (20-25 lbs.): use the smaller number of minutes per lb.; remove from oven when about 15° below desired internal temp. *Smaller roasts* (5-6 lbs.): use the larger number of minutes per lb.; remove from oven 5°-10° below internal temp. Bone-in cuts take fewer minutes per lb. than solid meat cuts
Broiling (1-2 inches thick)	15-40 (total)	20-50 (total)	25-60 (total)	Use thermometer to test for doneness, or make a cut in the meat (close to a bone, if possible); color will be bright pink for rare, pinkish for medium, and greyish brown for well done
Panbroiling and panfrying (½-1½ inches thick)	4-12 (total)	8-20 (total)	12-25 (total)	
Braising			20-60 per lb.	Larger cuts take 20-30 minutes per lb.; cuts under 5 lbs. take about 60 minutes per lb.; thinly cut items, such as Swiss steak, take 1-2 hrs. total
Simmering			40-50 per lb.	
Stewing (cubes)			120 (total)	

Note: Times given are general ranges; specific experience with oven loads, sizes of cuts, types of cuts, and oven efficiency is necessary to determine correct times and to control the variables.

then added, the pot is covered, and the food is permitted to cook at a low temperature until done. The liquid may be water, wine, stock, or similar fluid. A meat thermometer may be used to determine completion of the cooking or a cook's fork may be inserted to test for doneness. The meat is removed when done, and a gravy is then usually made from the cooking medium.

Stewing or Simmering. The less tender cuts of meat are generally stewed or simmered. In the former procedure the meat is cut into small pieces, covered with liquid, usually water, and seasoned. The container is then covered and the meat is cooked at a temperature just below boiling. Close to the end of the cooking period, the vegetables are added—timed so that they will be done at the same time as the meat and not overcooked. If carrots are used with other vegetables, they may have to be put in a little sooner than the others because they require more time for cooking.

The simmering process is quite similar, except that the meat is usually not cut into small pieces. Such cuts as corned beef, tongue, and beef shanks are often simmered.

In both stewing and simmering the meat must be completely covered with moisture to ensure uniform cooking throughout the product. The temperature must be kept below boiling, because boiling temperatures will cause the meat to become tough and stringy. Surface browning is usually carried out before the liquid is added.

Reconstitution

When prepared convenience beef (or other meat) products or ready items are used, they may require reconstitution, by boiling, steaming (atmospheric or under pressure), convection or conventional oven heating, microwave oven cooking, or infrared oven cooking. The form of reconstitution is based on the food type and the packing method employed.

In most cases, only reheating or defrosting is required, since the item has already been prepared and is in ready form. For true convenience items, the cooking procedures are the same as for the chilled or frozen product, since the item may simply be preportioned (for example a strip sirloin steak). For ready foods, the type of equipment, reconstituting time, and temperature required are often specified by the producer of the particular item.

Convenience food items in portion-controlled sizes that require cooking from the frozen, raw state may be brought to serving temperatures in any of the conventional dry or moist methods discussed above. Cuts of meat under a half inch in thickness should be cooked from frozen state, without thawing, to prevent excessive drying; cuts over a half inch thick should generally be defrosted before cooking.

Individual- or bulk-portion polyethylene pouches of cooked, ready beef items, in all-meat or combined forms, may be reconstituted in a pot of boiling water, a steamer,

Table 14-8. Typical Reconstitution Methods and Times for Beef

Equipment or Method	Food Item	Operating Temp.	Time
Atmospheric steam	Precooked frozen roast beef slices	220°	2-4 minutes
Conventional oven	Precooked frozen meatballs	350°	20 minutes
Convection oven	Precooked frozen meatballs	350°	10 minutes
Microwave oven	Precooked chilled beef stew casserole	2,000 watts	75 seconds
Microwave oven	Precooked chilled meat loaf	2,000 watts	75 seconds
Boiling water	Precooked frozen roast beef slices	212°	8 minutes
Infrared reconstituting oven with refrigerated cycle	Frozen uncooked hamburger patties	1,000°	4 minutes

microwave equipment, or special reconstituting equipment. Foil packages may also be completely reconstituted in all types of equipment except boiling water and microwave ovens: the water seeps into the package and dilutes the contents; the foil reflects microwaves, causing uneven heating and possible damage to the equipment. Models of microwave equipment are now being developed, however, that *can* be used with foil and other metal containers.

Cooked beef ready portions that would suffer from changes in color during reconstitution (such as rare roast beef) appear to reconstitute best using either a radiant heat source alternating with a refrigerated air flow over the product or a series of pulsating microwave applications alternating with rest periods between bursts. Both methods generally prevent surface scorching and additional drying of the product, and use heat to bring the product to serving temperature (120 degrees) without causing additional cooking.

In ready items where color change or additional cooking is not a major consideration, the other methods of reconstitution appear to give equal results. (For a more complete consideration of the reconstitution of portion-controlled, frozen, cooked beef cuts, see Clinton Rappole, "Serving Frozen Ribeye," *Cornell Hotel and Restaurant Administration Quarterly,* August 1972, pp. 29-32, and L. E. Bond, "Frozen Roast Beef to Order," *Cornell Hotel and Restaurant Administration Quarterly,* August 1968, pp. 42-46.)

Veal

Veal is a term used to describe the meat of immature bovine animals of either sex. Most of the supply is a spinoff of the dairy industry, and most of the animals are male. With the advent of artificial insemination, and the centralization of top quality bulls for breeding purposes, there is little need for most male dairy cattle. The male beef cattle are altered to provide steers later, and they command better prices as beef than they would as vealers.

Most vealers are under three months of age, and the majority are only three to six weeks old. They have little time to develop fat under the feeding regime used, and their flesh contains much connective tissue. The flesh of veal is quite homogeneous and extremely high in moisture. It is much lighter in color than the meat from mature beef, and, although extremely tender, it lacks flavor.

Meat from an animal between three months and one year old exhibits more of the characteristics of mature beef than true veal and is graded as calf. It will carry this designation in the grading roll on the cuts. A form of beef called baby beef, which is specially managed, fed, fattened, and slaughtered at approximately 16 months to give smaller and more tender cuts, has no relation to either veal or calf, but is considered to be in the beef category.

Veal and calf are graded as *prime, choice, good, standard, utility,* and *cull.* They may be purchased by either the foresaddle or the hindsaddle, or in retail cuts or convenience forms. The configuration of a specific cut is identified in the same way as those of beef, since it is the same type of animal at a less mature age. Only the color of the flesh, the size of the cut, and certain parts of the bone structure differ. Some bone fusion has not yet taken place, but this is not an important consideration in selection and use of the animal.

A dressed carcass of veal may weigh from 50 to 150 pounds. The most desirable meats have a fine-textured appearance, with soft flesh. The bones are also soft and very red in color. There is little fat in the flesh.

Except for the veal cutlet, veal is not a very popular item with most consumers in the United States, although some ethnic groups find it highly desirable.

Foresaddle Primal Cuts

The animal may be divided into the foresaddle and the hindsaddle by cutting completely across the carcass between the twelfth and thirteenth ribs. Or it may be divided into sides, like those of mature beef, and then into quarters or retail cuts.

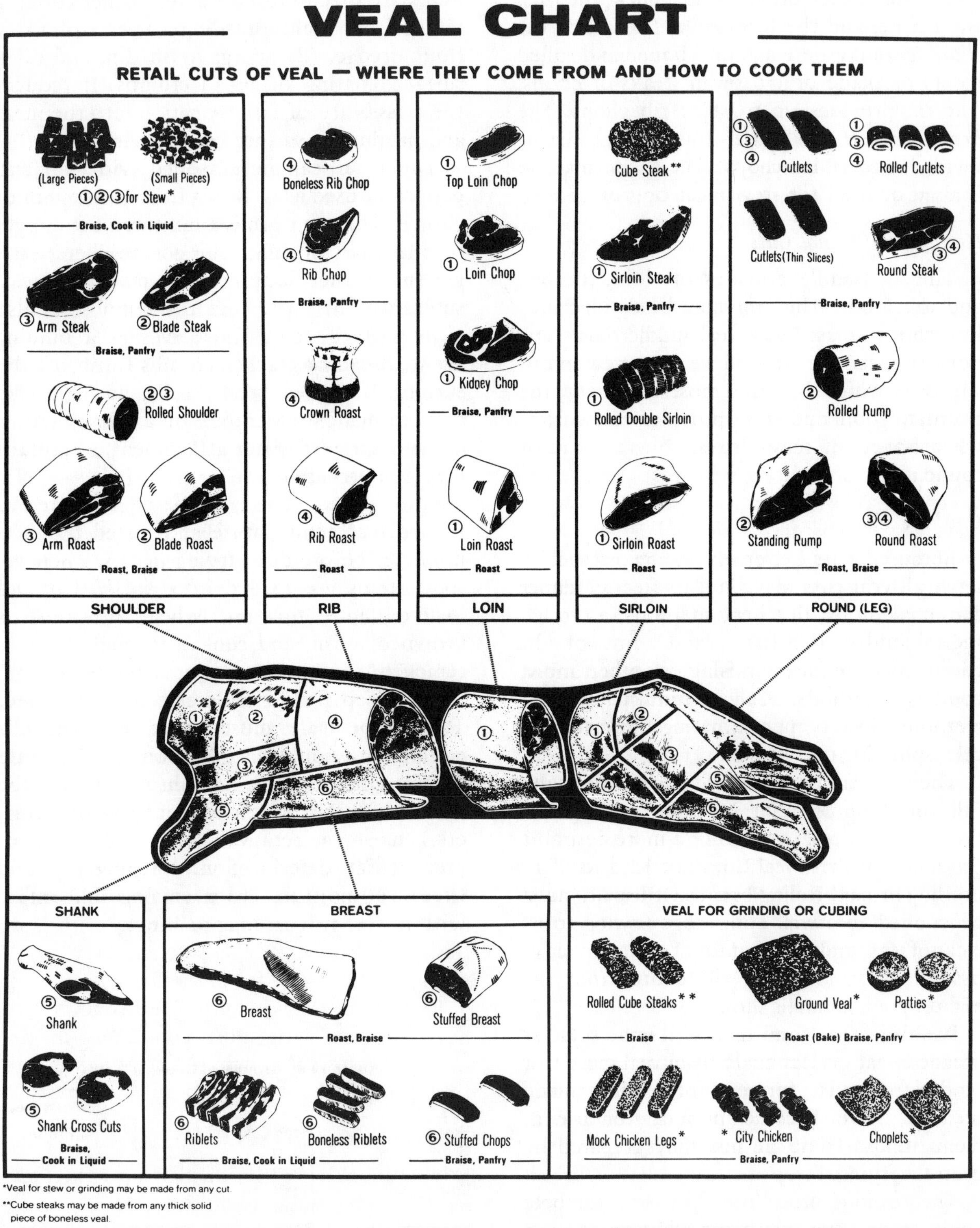

VEAL CHART

RETAIL CUTS OF VEAL — WHERE THEY COME FROM AND HOW TO COOK THEM

SHOULDER

(Large Pieces) (Small Pieces)
①②③for Stew*
Braise, Cook in Liquid

③ Arm Steak ② Blade Steak
Braise, Panfry

②③ Rolled Shoulder

③ Arm Roast ② Blade Roast
Roast, Braise

RIB

④ Boneless Rib Chop

④ Rib Chop
Braise, Panfry

④ Crown Roast

④ Rib Roast
Roast

LOIN

① Top Loin Chop

① Loin Chop

① Kidney Chop
Braise, Panfry

① Loin Roast
Roast

SIRLOIN

Cube Steak**

① Sirloin Steak
Braise, Panfry

① Rolled Double Sirloin

① Sirloin Roast
Roast

ROUND (LEG)

①③④ Cutlets ①③④ Rolled Cutlets

Cutlets(Thin Slices) ③④ Round Steak
Braise, Panfry

② Rolled Rump

② Standing Rump ③④ Round Roast
Roast, Braise

①②③④⑤⑥

SHANK

⑤ Shank

⑤ Shank Cross Cuts
Braise, Cook in Liquid

BREAST

⑥ Breast ⑥ Stuffed Breast
Roast, Braise

⑥ Riblets ⑥ Boneless Riblets
Braise, Cook in Liquid

⑥ Stuffed Chops
Braise, Panfry

VEAL FOR GRINDING OR CUBING

Rolled Cube Steaks**
Braise

Ground Veal* Patties*
Roast (Bake) Braise, Panfry

Mock Chicken Legs* * City Chicken Choplets*
Braise, Panfry

*Veal for stew or grinding may be made from any cut.

**Cube steaks may be made from any thick solid piece of boneless veal.

Figure 14i. Chart of the wholesale and retail cuts of veal. Since the vealer is a young beef animal, the bone configuration and cuts are the same as those of beef, although flesh color, taste, fat covering, and use of the meat differ. (Courtesy of the National Live Stock and Meat Board, Chicago.)

The foresaddle provides the chuck, the ribs, the breast, and the foreshank. The *chuck* (or *shoulder*) may be made into boned and rolled roasts or blade or cross-arm steaks or chops. The *rib* provides rib roast or rib chops. The *breast* may be stuffed and used as a roast or divided into riblet chops. The *shank* may be braised or used for stew meat or ground veal.

Hindsaddle Primal Cuts

The hindsaddle provides the loin, the leg, and the flank. The *loin* may be divided into loin chops or used as a veal saddle roast. The *flank* is used for ground veal or stew meat. The *leg*, which has the most value for the quantity food operator, provides veal cutlets when boned. It may also serve as a rump or round roast.

Cooking Veal

Because of its extremely tender nature, almost all veal cuts may be classified as tender and cooked by dry heat methods, although the shoulder, the flank, and some of the chops may require braising or other moist cooking methods. Calves require cooking methods closely approximating those for the corresponding cuts of beef.

The taste and texture of veal meat usually call for some breading or other coating and the use of sauces, to produce a more desirable product. Further, veal does not lend itself to broiling or panbroiling because it usually must be cooked to a well done stage (owing to its lack of fat and large amount of connective tissue). Only loin and rib chops from the highest grade animals should be broiled.

Prefabricated convenience items, such as breaded veal cutlets made from veal pieces, or tenderized cuts formed into patties and breaded, have become popular for use as menu items. These are normally prepared by deep fat frying.

The cooking procedures discussed for beef apply to veal cuts, with the addition of deep fat frying.

Breading. The veal, or other items, to be deep fried should first be breaded, and veal items are often breaded before other cooking methods as well. Breading consists of (1) a flour dredge, (2) an egg wash dip, and (3) a surface coating of bread crumbs. It reduces the possibility of fat absorption into the meat and produces a surface coating with color.

The flour can be seasoned with salt and pepper or used as is. Bread flour is the item of choice. The egg wash is a mixture of four eggs to one quart of milk. This acts to liberate the gluten in the flour and to make a sticky substance that will hold the crumbs. It also gives surface color and serves as a binding agent. Bread or cracker crumbs finish off the surface. Leftover bread, rolls, and the like may be made into crumbs on a Schnell cutter or with a mixer grater attachment, or crumbs may be purchased.

Deep Frying. The fat must be preheated to the correct temperature and tested by thermometer before deep frying begins. Then the food items are loaded into the basket and lowered into the fat. When the meat is browned, crisp, and cooked throughout, it is removed from the fat, drained, and served.

The deep fryer should not be overloaded. The temperature must be correct, and the equipment should have a good recovery rate to prevent excessive fat absorption by the product. Foreign particles (excessive breading, etc.) must be removed with a skimmer to prevent fat deterioration. Keeping salt and excessive moisture from coming in contact with the fat will prolong its life.

Table 14-9. Methods of Cooking Veal

Cut	Dry Heat	Moist Heat
Breast	Roast	Braise
Ground veal	Roast	
Leg	Roast	
Loin	Roast	
Rib	Roast	
Shoulder	Roast	Braise
Stew meat		Simmer
Veal chops	Panfry or grill broil	
Veal cutlet	Panfry or deep fat fry	Braise
Veal steaks		Braise

Table 14-10. General Veal Cookery Timetable

Cooking Method	Minutes	Comments
Roasting (oven temp. 300°)	25-45 per lb. (170° internal temp.)	All cuts are cooked to well done; minutes per lb. vary according to size of cut, amount of bone, and density of cut
Broiling		Not generally used for veal cuts because of their texture and lack of fat
Panbroiling or panfrying (½-1½ inches thick)	15-30 (total)	Very few cuts lend themselves to these cooking methods
Braising	up to 60 per lb.	A ½-inch veal cutlet takes about 1 hr. total; a stuffed veal breast takes about 60 minutes per lb.
Simmering		Not generally used for large veal cuts
Stewing (cubes)	120 (total)	
Deep frying (fat temp. 350°)	4-5 (total)	Used for breaded cutlets

Note: Times given are general ranges; they vary according to the type of cut, thickness, and mass of the meat.

Pork

Pork is the meat of swine. It is the second most popular meat in the United States despite the taboos against its use by some religious groups. It is one of the most versatile types of meat, and much of the supply sold is in cured forms.

Although there are weight and sex classifications of pork animals, most are not considered to be of great importance, since pork from almost any classification may be used effectively. There is a saying that packers use all of the hog except the squeal—and they're working on that!

Pork is usually less expensive than other types of meat. All the cuts are considered tender, and the weight ranges available make for good portion control.

The major classifications of swine are *barrows*—the same as beef steers; *gilts*—the same as heifers; *sows*—the same as cows; *stags*—the same as beef stags; and *boars*—the same as bulls. Subclassifications according to weight and body type, such as *suckling or roasting pig* (ten to thirty pounds) and *fat pork* (one hundred fifty to two hundred fifty pounds) are also made.

The grade of pork is based on the animal's sexual condition at time of slaughter, the quality of the meat, and the ratio of lean to fat in the carcass. Sow carcasses are graded under different criteria than barrows or gilts, but all are graded in the following United States Department of Agriculture classifications: 1, 2, 3, 4, and utility.

Retail Cuts

Pork is generally sold not in carcass form, but in the wholesale or retail cuts in which it will be used. Although the animal has fourteen ribs, its general bone structure and muscle structure are similar to the beef animals previously considered. The flesh is a light pink or rose color, with a fine grain and an extensive marbling of fat. Lower grade animals have a darker and softer flesh.

Since the primal cuts are practically the same as the retail cuts, only the latter are considered here.

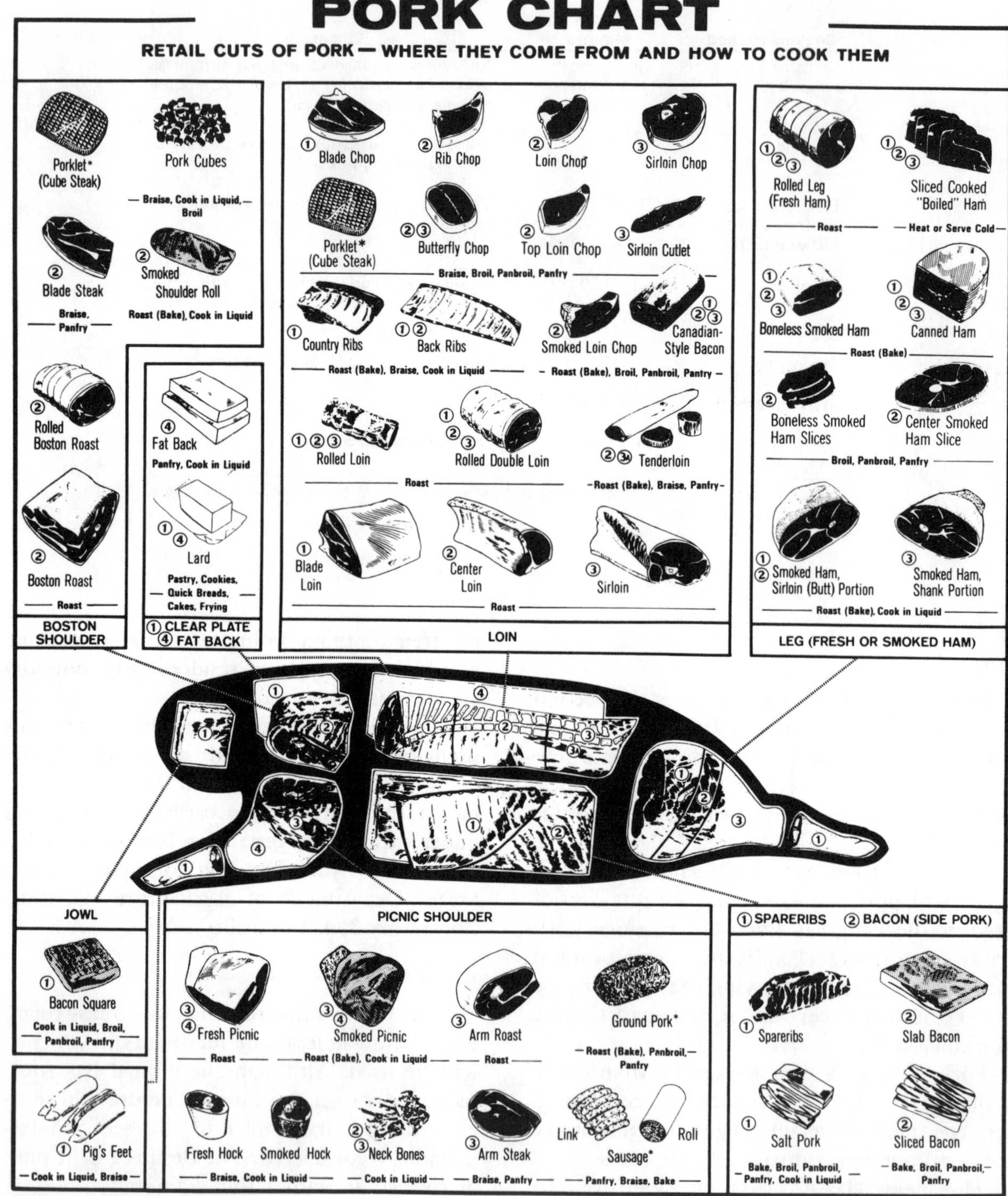

Figure 14j. Chart of the retail cuts from pork animals and their preparation methods. (Courtesy of the National Live Stock and Meat Board, Chicago.)

The *jowl*—the face meat of the animal—may be sold as fresh pork for food seasoning. It is more often flattened, squared, cured, and sold as jowl bacon.

The *fat back* and the *clear plate* may be used to make lard or salt pork. They have little use in quantity food work, except as seasoning.

The *Boston butt* is the shoulder of the animal. It may be used as a roast, cut into shoulder pork steaks, or smoke cured for smoked butt or daisy ham. It is identified by the shoulder blade and is similar in structure to the beef chuck roast. It may be combined with the picnic to form a full fresh shoulder roast.

The *picnic* is the lower half of the shoulder cut. It is identifiable by the arm and fore-shank bones and may have the hock on or off. It is available fresh, pickled (or corned), and smoked.

The *loin* corresponds to the rib and full loin of beef. It extends from shoulder to ham (hind leg). It is identifiable by its bone structure, the eye of the loin, and the tenderloin. It is available as a full loin, or it may be separated into blade, center cut, and loin end chops, named for the position in the loin from which they come. It is also available boned and smoked. The eye of the loin may be cured and smoked to make Canadian bacon. This is frequently done with lower grade animals. The tenderloin may also be removed from the loin and used as a separate roast.

The *side* provides spareribs (corresponding to short ribs of beef), bacon, and salt pork. All are available in smoked, salted, or fresh form. The entire area corresponds to the flank, short plate, and brisket of beef.

The *ham* is one of the most important cuts of pork animals. It is available in full, shank, or butt end cuts. Most hams are cured, fully cooked, or canned. The ham is identified by the leg and hip bones of the animal.

The *hocks* and *feet* are also sold for consumption but have little use in quantity food service work.

Cooking Pork

Because of the meat's fat and resulting tenderness, almost all pork cuts may be prepared by dry heat methods as well as other methods. The butterflying of pork chops or tenderloin gives better use of the cut. Double pork chops may also be stuffed with good results.

Whatever form of cooking is used a moderate temperature must be maintained (275 to 350 degrees Fahrenheit), and the meat must be cooked to a well done stage. Excessively high temperatures will toughen it, while insufficient internal temperatures may cause sanitation problems. To ensure complete safety and to avoid excessive toughness and dryness, an internal temperature of 165 to 170 degrees is recommended. Although 185 degrees was the recommended internal temperature for many years, the present practices of cooking all garbage fed to hogs and freezing much of the fresh pork (at 0 degrees for ten days or more) have reduced the possibility of trichinosis, and the 165- to 170-degree range is considered sufficient to ensure that an internal temperature of 137 degrees (the lethal temperature for trichinae) has been reached. With irradiated pork, cooks can use lower temperatures since the trichinae have been destroyed. However, to ensure uniformity and to make sure that all pork is cooked correctly (irradiated or nonirradiated), it is best to use the 165- to 170-degree range.

Table 14-11. Methods of Cooking Pork

Cut	Dry Heat	Moist Heat
Bacon	Fry, panfry, panbroil, or bake	
Boston butt	Roast	Simmer (if smoked)
Chops	Broil, panfry, or panbroil	Braise
Ham	Roast	Simmer
Loin	Roast or broil	
Picnic	Roast	Simmer
Sausage	Broil, panfry, or panbroil	Braise
Spareribs	Roast, broil, panfry, or panbroil	Braise or simmer
Steaks	Broil, panfry, or panbroil	Braise

A butterfly chop may be made from a thick chop cut from a boneless loin. The chop is cut almost in two through the thickness, so that the halves can be opened out to lie flat while still attached at the center. In cutting the chops the butterfly slice is made first and then the chop is severed from the loin.

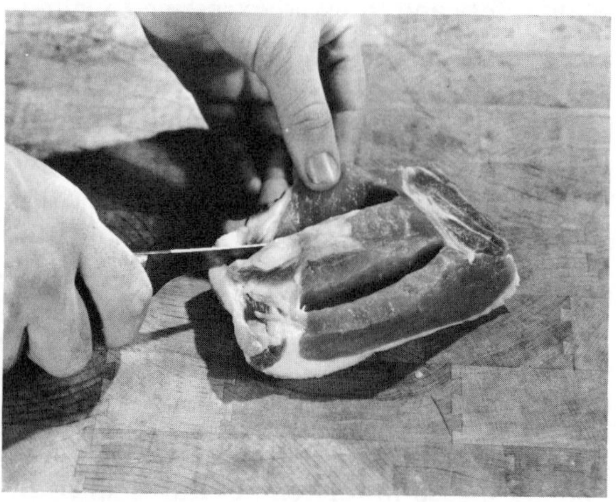

Pockets for dressing may be made in a chop that has been butterflied. The chop is closed at the butterfly cut and two slits made (on either side of the butterfly cut) in the other edge of the chop. After dressing is inserted, the chop is folded open again and the dressing is held in place.

Chops with bones may be stuffed by piping dressing in through a cut alongside the bone. During cooking the cut will close and hold the dressing inside the meat.

Figure 14k.. Methods of varying the pork chop by butterflying and stuffing it. (Courtesy of the National Live Stock and Meat Board, Chicago.)

Table 14-12. General Pork Cookery Timetable

Cooking Method	Minutes	Comments
Roasting		
Fresh cuts (oven temp. 300°-325°)	35-50 per lb. (165°-170° internal temp.)	An internal temp. of 131°-137° is required to ensure safety from trichinosis; although 185° used to be recommended for this purpose, under modern hog feeding and pork freezing methods, a 165°-170° internal temp. is considered adequate and will avoid drying out or toughening the meat.
Cured, cook-before-eating cuts (oven temp. 300°-325°)	30 per lb. (160° internal temp.)	
Cured, fully cooked cuts (oven temp. 300°-325°)	15 per lb. (130° internal temp.)	
Bacon and similar items (oven temp. 400°)	15 (total)	
Broiling (oven temp. 350°)		
Fresh chops (1 inch thick)	20-25 (total) (165°-170° internal temp.)	Almost any fresh chop may be broiled.
Cured chops (1 inch thick)	20-25 (total) (160° internal temp.)	Almost any cured chop may be broiled.
Bacon	4-5 (total)	
Panfrying, panbroiling, or braising (oven temp. 325° or low heat on range top)	30-120 (total)	Most cuts will cook in 30-50 minutes; some, such as spareribs, take up to 2 hrs.
Simmering	15-50 per lb.	Cooking times vary depending on the degree of the cure and the size of the cut

Prepared, Convenience, and Ready Pork Items

Only about 30 percent of the pork supply is used in fresh form; most of the meat is processed or cured in a variety of products: sausage, composed of approximately 75 percent lean and 25 percent fat, in fresh, smoked, or ready-to-use form; liverwurst; salami; bacon; canned ham; and a variety of ready-made pork dishes. In addition, variety meats, such as livers, brains, and kidneys, are available to the quantity food facility.

The same cooking procedures apply to these pork products as to processed and ready beef items, except that a satisfactory internal temperature must be reached. Supervisors

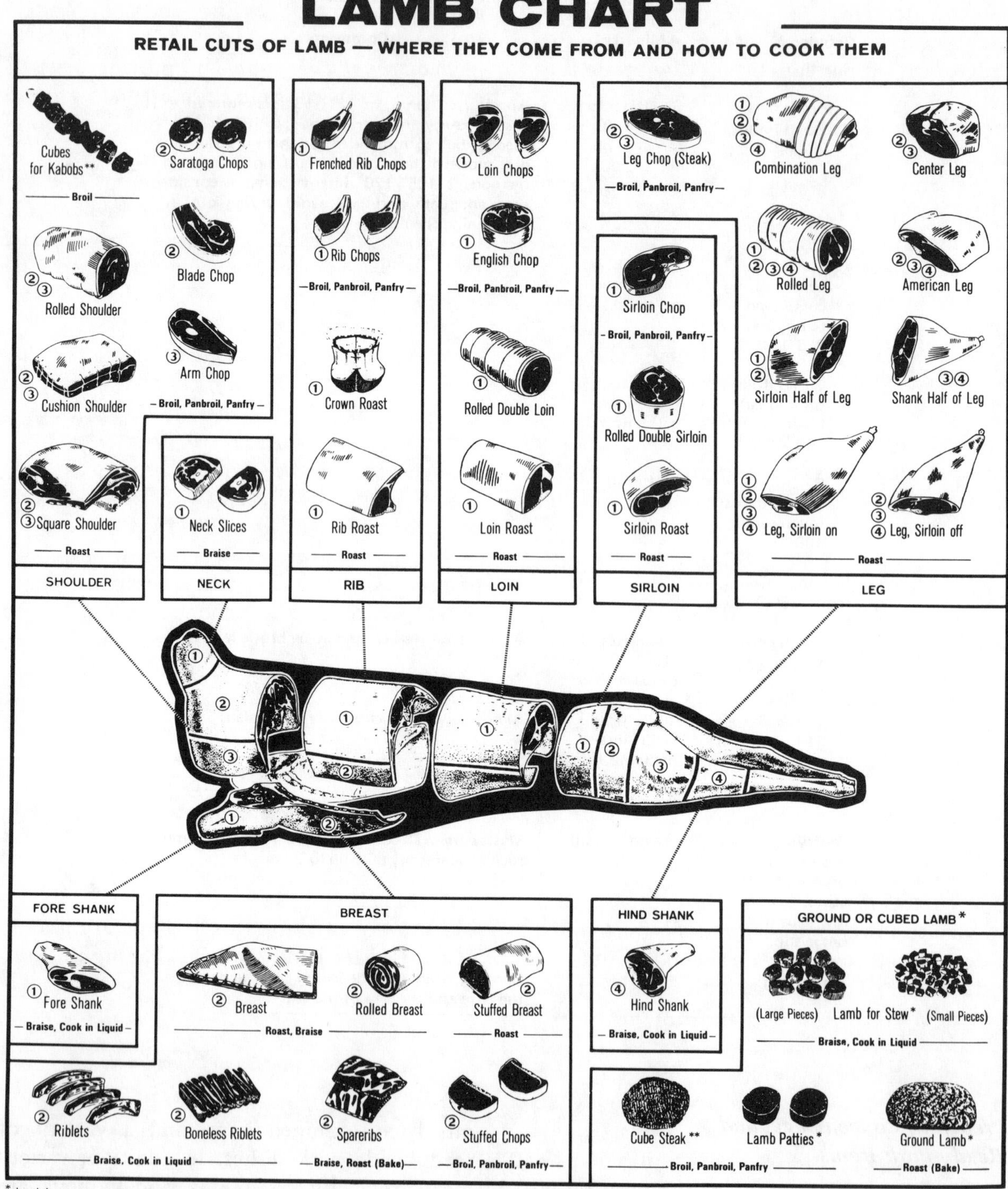

Figure 14/. Chart of the wholesale and retail cuts of lamb and their preparation methods. (Courtesy of the National Live Stock and Meat Board, Chicago.)

must determine the exact degree of cure, so that the item may be categorized as either ready-to-eat, tenderized, or smoked. Only the ready-to-eat items can be used without further cooking; the others must be cooked to an internal temperature of 165 to 170 degrees in order to be considered safe.

The nature of the cure gives a salty taste to many cured products because smoke evaporates moisture in the meat and brine cures soak salt into the meat. Cooking the cured cut in water or presoaking it in several changes of water may be necessary to reduce the saltiness before the cooking process is begun. The temperatures required for processing canned products make them safe to eat without further cooking, and most dry, smoked, sausage-type products, such as frankfurters and salami, are ready-to-eat, requiring only heating, in some cases, before use.

Lamb and Mutton

Although trailing behind pork, beef, and veal in popularity, lamb and mutton command attention in quantity food work. Clientele of southern European and British backgrounds are particularly fond of these meats. Lamb is the more important type, and the chops and legs are the choicest cuts.

Lamb is the meat from young sheep up to one year of age. The average lamb carcass dresses out at about thirty-five pounds. Spring lamb is meat from a much lighter animal (twenty to thirty pounds) under eight months of age. Mutton comes from sheep beyond two years of age. There is a middle classification, yearling mutton, for animals from one to two years old.

Lamb is easily identifiable by size and color. It is light to dark pink in color, while mutton is dark red. The lamb carcass has a spool or ankle break joint (an unfused ankle joint) in both the front and the hind legs. Mutton, coming from older animals, does not have this.

Lamb Primal Cuts

Lamb is sold by the foresaddle or hindsaddle (cut across the entire carcass), in wholesale cuts, or in retail cuts. It is graded *prime, choice, good, utility,* and *cull.* Mutton is not eligible for the prime grade.

The *chuck* or *shoulder* provides roasts, shoulder lamb chops, stew meat, and ground patties. Its rib, blade, and arm bones are good points of reference.

The *rack* or *rib*, which contains the rib bones and the rib eye muscle, can be made into chops or be used as a whole crown roast. For a roast, the rib bones are Frenched (the meat is removed from the rib ends) and then shaped and tied into a crown for roasting. Rib chops should be at least one rib thick.

The *breast* may be used for stew meat or ground meat. It may also be boned, rolled, and stuffed as a roast.

The *loin* may be used as a roast, cut into chops, or cut full across with the backbone removed and rolled into English chops.

The *leg* may be divided into sirloin chops or used as a full roast with a Frenched shank bone or with the shank bone removed (called an American leg). The bone and muscle configurations are similar to those of beef animals.

Cooking Lamb

Most lamb cuts are tender because they come from such young animals. They should be cooked at low temperatures for maximum retention of juice and usually are cooked to a well done stage. Broiling, roasting, braising, and stewing are the forms of preparation most often used for lamb products. Panbroiling and

Table 14-13. Methods of Cooking Lamb

Cut	Dry Heat	Moist Heat
Breast		Braise or stew
Ground lamb	Broil	
Leg	Roast	
Loin	Roast, broil, panbroil, or panfry	
Rack	Roast, broil, panbroil, or panfry	
Shoulder	Roast, broil, panbroil, or panfry	
Sirloin	Roast, broil, panbroil, or panfry	
Stew meat		Simmer or stew

Table 14-14. General Lamb Cookery Timetable

Cooking Method	Minutes: Rare	Minutes: Medium	Minutes: Well Done	Comments
Roasting (oven temp. 300°)	25-30 per lb. (150° internal temp.)	25-30 per lb. (160° internal temp.)	30-35 per lb. (175° internal temp.)	Although most recipes call for lamb to be cooked well done, and many consumers appear to prefer it this way, it may also be prepared medium or rare, if desired, without sanitation problems
Broiling			15 (total)	Time will vary depending on the thickness of the cut
Panfrying or panbroiling			10 (total)	Time will vary depending on the thickness of the cut
Braising or simmering (stew meat)			60-120 (total)	

panfrying are also used. Cuts from the leg, loin, and rack are most often roasted, broiled, panbroiled, or panfried. The less tender cuts, from the shoulder, breast, and shank, are most often braised or stewed, although they sometimes are cooked by dry methods. For example, blade chops may be broiled, or shoulder cuts roasted.

Lamb fat hardens more readily than other animal fats, and this may create some problems if the meat is not served at very hot or very cold temperatures. The fell, or skin membrane, that covers the lamb flesh may be left on during cooking, as it helps to speed the cooking process, but it should be removed from roast meats before they are sliced.

Table 14-15. Summary of Cooking Methods for Meats

Method	Beef	Veal	Pork	Lamb	Poultry
Tender cuts Dry cook: roast or broil	Ribs Loin Ground beef Liver Sweetbreads Brains	Ribs Loin Leg Ground veal Liver Kidneys Brains	Ribs Loin Ham Ground pork Liver Kidneys Brains	Ribs Loin Leg Ground lamb Liver Kidneys Brains	All poultry cooked to 190 degree internal temperature
Semitender cuts Cook with some moisture: braise or panfry	Round Rump Chuck Kidneys	Shoulder Breast	Shoulder Spareribs Heart	Shoulder Heart	
Tough cuts Cook with moisture: simmer or stew	Brisket Plate Neck Heart Tongue	Neck Shank	Feet Jowl	Neck Breast	

Table 14-16. Summary of Roasting Times, Temperatures, and Yields

Roast Name	N.A.M.P. Number	Weight Range (lbs.)	Oven Temp.	Internal Temp. Removed from Oven	Internal Temp. After 20 Min.	Minutes per lb. Chilled	Minutes per lb. Frozen	Average Cooked Yield*	Servable Slices†
Beef									
Inside round	1168R	11-13	300° F.	150° F.	161° F.	19-22	30-32	73%	59%
Gooseneck	1170R	10½-12½	300° F.	150° F.	158° F.	15-18	22-26	78%	65%
Knuckle	1167R	7-9	300° F.	150° F.	160° F.	29-32	40-42	70%	52%
Top sirloin	1184R	6½-9	300° F.	150° F.	161° F.	25-27	38-42	74%	58%
Ribs, boneless	1110R	9½-11½	300° F.	150° F.	161° F.	20-23	29-30	80%	43%
Chuck roll	1116R	10-12½	300° F.	150° F.	157° F.	19-22	29-30	78%	64%
Shoulder clod	1114R	9-12	300° F.	150° F.	161° F.	22-25	32-34	76%	57%
Ham									
Fresh, boneless	1402R	10¼-12	325° F.	170° F.	179° F.	24-27	34-35	67%	49%
Lamb									
Leg, boneless	1234AR	3½-5	325° F.	165° F.	168° F.	32-34	48-51	71%	59%
Shoulder, boneless	1208R	3-4½	325° F.	155° F.	163° F.	29-34	55-58	76%	61%
Veal									
Leg, boneless	1335R	7½-10½	325° F.	160° F.	168° F.	27-31	38-43	71%	58%
Chuck, boneless	1309R	8½-15	325° F.	160° F.	169° F.	22-26	33-38	71%	58%

From *Roasting Frozen Meat,* a report prepared by the National Live Stock and Meat Board, Chicago; reprinted by permission.

*Fresh weight minus thawing losses (where applicable), cooking drip, and evaporation losses.

†Final yield after losses from shrinkage during cooling (1 hr.), fat trim before slicing, and slicing scraps.

Note: Based on a study of different handling methods for 860 frozen roasts in institutional food service. Roasts done in electric stack ovens, 3 roasts (6 for lamb) per aluminum roasting pan, 2 pans per oven.

Meat Extenders and Substitutes

Vegetable protein type products are available on the market to be used as replacements for meat or as substitutes in various meat dishes. They are usually soybean-based and may be made to conform very closely to the taste and texture of true meat products. They find their best application in meat loaf, salads, patties and the like. The United States Department of Agriculture, in Bulletin no. 19, authorizes a maximum of 30 percent hydrated textured protein substitution for meat in Type A school lunches. An operator should consider use of these substitutes, guiding his decision by tests conducted within his establishment.

Poultry

Whether it is chicken, turkey, duck, or goose, poultry is an important protein item for the quantity food service operator. From the development of the broiler industry in the 1930s, poultry has experienced a meteoric rise in popularity. Broilers now reach marketable weight in only eight to ten weeks; as a result, they sell at a price well suited to almost any quantity food operation and any customer. In most sections of the country, Americans eat more chicken than they do either lamb or veal. Although ducks, geese, and turkeys are popular mainly as traditional holiday fare, turkey has made significant inroads into everyday food service consumption.

Most poultry is purchased dressed and drawn or in a ready-to-cook state. It may be chilled, iced, or frozen. Chicken is quite perishable and will not last longer than one or two days at normal refrigerated storage temperatures. Therefore the method of purchasing must be closely related to the time and type of use. Chicken may also be purchased canned, in individual pieces or diced.

The age and classification of the bird indicate how tender it will be and the most appropriate method of preparation. Age and sex have a pronounced effect on the use that may be made of poultry, as they do on other animals.

Types and Classes of Poultry

Chickens are classified as broilers, fryers, roasters, Cornish game hens, capons, and stewing chickens. Broilers are of either sex, are from nine to twelve weeks old, and weigh

Table 14-17. Summary of Broiling Times and Temperatures

			Minutes Approx. Cooking Time (at 350° F.)			
Cut	Thickness	Weight	Rare	Medium	Well Done	Internal Temp.
Beef						
Chuck steak	1 in.	1½-2½ lbs.	24	30		140-170° F.
	1½ in.	2-4 lbs.	40	45		140-170° F.
Rib steak	1 in.	1-1½ lbs.	15	20		140-170° F.
	1½ in.	1½-2 lbs.	25	30		
	2 in.	2-2½ lbs.	35	45		140-170° F.
Rib eye steak	1 in.	8-10 oz.	15	20		140-170° F.
	1½ in.	12-14 oz.	25	30		140-170° F.
	2 in.	16-20 oz.	35	45		140-170° F.
Club steak	1 in.	1-1½ lbs.	15	20		140-170° F.
	1½ in.	1½-2 lbs.	25	30		140-170° F.
	2 in.	2-2½ lbs.	35	45		140-170° F.
Sirloin steak	1 in.	1½-3 lbs.	20	25		140-170° F.
	1½ in.	2¼-4 lbs.	30	35		140-170° F.
	2 in.	3-5 lbs.	40	45		140-170° F.
Porterhouse steak	1 in.	1¼-2 lbs.	20	25		140-170° F.
	1½ in.	2-3 lbs.	30	35		140-170° F.
	2 in.	2½-3½ lbs.	40	45		140-170° F.
Filet mignon	1 in.	4-6 oz.	15	20		140-170° F.
	1½ in.	6-8 oz.	18	22		140-170° F.
Ground beef patties	1 in.	4 oz.	15	25		
Pork, smoked						
Ham slice, tendered	½ in.	3/4-1 lb.			10-12	160° F.
	1 in.	1½-2 lbs.			16-20	160° F.
Loin chops	3/4-1 in.				15-20	160° F.
Bacon				4-5		
Canadian bacon slices	¼ in.			6-8		160° F.
	½ in.			8-10		160° F.
Pork, fresh						
Rib or loin chops	3/4-1 in.				20-25	165-170° F.
Shoulder steaks	1/2-3/4 in.				20-22	165-170° F.
Lamb						
Shoulder chops	1 in.	5-8 oz.		12		170-175° F.
	1½ in.	8-10 oz.		18		170-175° F.
	2 in.	10-16 oz.		22		170-175° F.
Rib chops	1 in.	3-5 oz.		12		170-175° F.
	1½ in.	4-7 oz.		18		170-175° F.
	2 in.	6-10 oz.		22		170-175° F.
Loin chops	1 in.	4-7 oz.		12		170-175° F.
	1½ in.	6-10 oz.		18		170-175° F.
	2 in.	8-14 oz.		22		170-175° F.
Ground lamb patties	1 in.	4 oz.		18		

Courtesy of the National Live Stock and Meat Board, Chicago.

Note: Rare beef steaks are cooked to an internal temperature of 140° F.; medium to 160° F.; and well done to 170° F.

Poultry inspection mark (left) and grade mark (right).

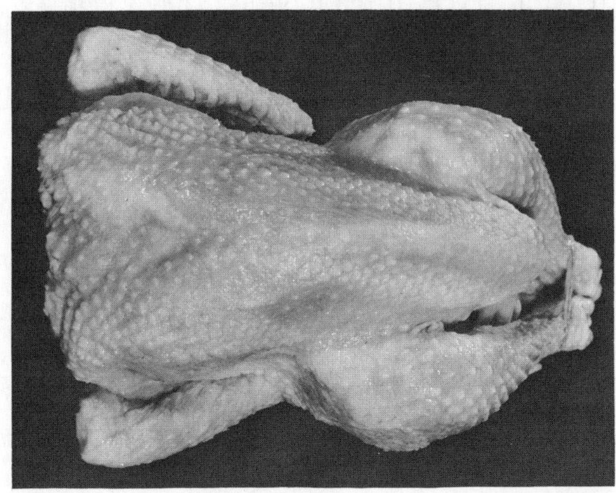

U.S. Grade A: full fleshed and meaty, well finished, attractive appearance.

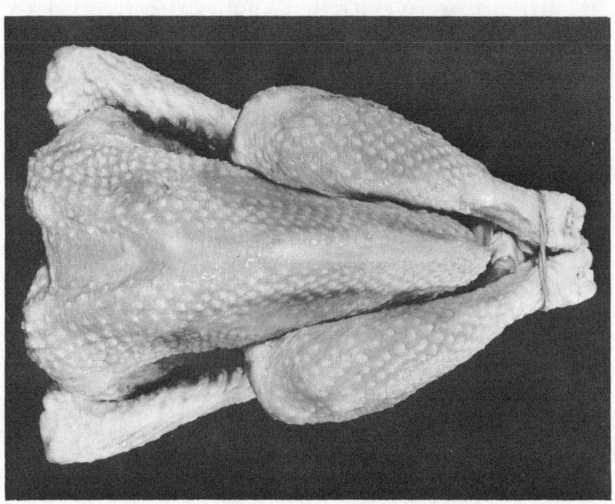

U.S. Grade B: slightly lacking in fleshing, meatiness, and finish, or some dressing defects.

Figure 14m. The official poultry inspection marks of the U.S. Department of Agriculture are put on containers or affixed to the birds. The differences between a grade A and a grade B chicken may be noted in the pictures. (Courtesy of the United States Department of Agriculture, Washington, D.C.)

from 1 to 2½ pounds. Fryers are slightly older, from twelve to sixteen weeks, and weigh from 2½ to 3½ pounds. Roasters are much older birds, about seven or eight months, and weigh from 2½ to 5 pounds. Cornish game hens are young chickens, from five to seven weeks, who weigh from 1 to 2 pounds. A specially bred rock Cornish game hen with all white meat in the same weight range is also sold. Capons are male birds castrated at about eight weeks of age, and slaughtered at seven to ten months. They weigh 4½ to 7½ pounds. Stewing chickens or fowl are older females, over ten months, and weigh from 2½ to 5½ pounds.

Turkeys are classified as fryer-roasters, young toms, and hens. Fryer-roasters are younger birds, up to sixteen weeks of age, and weigh from 4 to 8 pounds, while young toms and hens are from five to seven months old and weigh from 6 to 24 pounds, with hens weighing the lesser of the two.

Ducks are marketed as broilers (or fryers) and roasters. The broiler or fryer is under eight weeks of age, and the roaster over. Weights of ducks run from 3 to 7 pounds.

Geese are classified as young or mature. A young goose is under six months of age, and a mature goose over that. Weights run from 4 to 20 pounds in the two classes.

Poultry have varying amounts of connective tissue, according to their age. Younger birds have more pliable breastbones, beaks, etc. All poultry should be plump, have a good fat cover, have a straight breastbone, and be free of pinfeathers, cuts, bruises, and the like on their skin. Poultry is inspected by the United States Department of Agriculture and assigned grades of A, B, or C, depending on quality characteristics.

Chickens and turkeys have both white and dark meat, while Cornish game hens have all white meat, and ducks have all dark meat. The white meat is usually more tender and drier because it has less fat, while the darker meat is a better source of riboflavin and thiamin.

Cooking Poultry

Both dry and moist cooking methods are used for poultry. Dry heat is most suited to the young and tender birds. Older birds may be cooked best by moist heat methods.

All poultry must be cooked to well done, but overcooking and excessively high temperatures may make it tough and dry. An internal temperature of 190 degrees Fahrenheit is recommended. The yield on poultry varies from 50 to 55 percent, with larger birds giving increased yields.

Turkeys, ducks, geese, and chickens may be roasted, either whole or divided into parts. The poultry should be well washed, salted, and rubbed with fat prior to roasting. It is

Table 14-18. General Poultry Cookery Timetable

Cooking Method	Minutes	Comments
Roasting (oven temp. 300°-350°)	20-50 per lb.	Large birds, such as turkeys, will take fewer minutes per lb.; cut up pieces will take less total cooking time (about 50 minutes total for cut-up chicken).
Broiling	15-20 per side	Used only for very young and tender birds
Deep frying (fat temp. 325°)	25 (total)	If poultry is precooked, deep frying time may be reduced to the time required to reach desired browning
Panfrying	60 (total)	Not usually used in quantity food operations
Braising or fricasseeing	60-90 (total)	Used for older, tougher birds and for gizzards and hearts
Stewing	180-240 (total)	

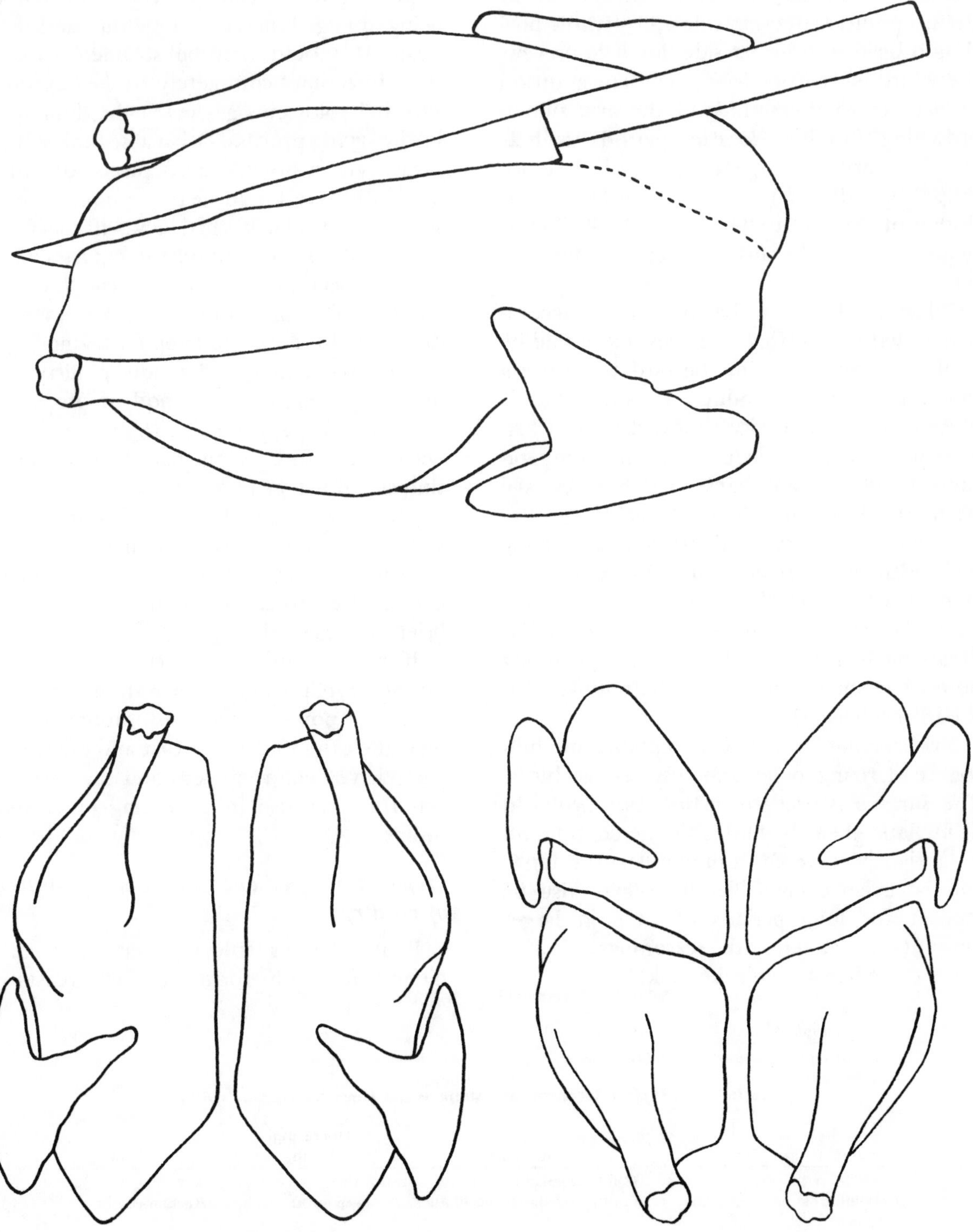

Figure 14n. A chicken may be cut into two, four, eight, or twelve pieces prior to cooking, depending on the menu and the pricing system. Frozen poultry should be thawed under refrigerated conditions before sectioning and preparation. Broiler chickens take about twenty-four hours to thaw, while a twenty-pound turkey may take up to four days.

baked with the fat side up or, in the case of cut up poultry, the skin side up. A whole bird should be placed breast side down to prevent the white meat from drying out. The addition of paprika to the surface of the bird aids in browning. For long roasting periods, such as those required for large turkeys, a cheesecloth drape dipped in fat will do much to prevent drying of the surface. Geese and ducks do not require greasing because of their high fat content.

When poultry is to be roasted and accompanied with a stuffing, the dressing should be cooked separately from the bird to ensure a safe and sanitary product. Dressing that is placed inside the cavity of a turkey or a hen may not reach an adequate internal temperature to destroy any bacteria that may have been introduced into the mixture.

Poaching poultry products before roasting will result in better yields under most circumstances. Geese and ducks are better steamed before roasting to reduce the amount of fat. Steaming is also a quick method of cooking poultry when the meat is to be removed for use in another dish.

Fricasseeing is a very acceptable method for tenderizing older and less tender birds. The surface is dredged in flour and browned in fat, and then the bird is simmered in liquid in a tightly covered container on the range top or in an oven. Older birds may also be stewed for long periods of time in larger amounts of water with seasonings. This is often done in a steam-jacketed kettle.

Much poultry can be deep fat fried, after being dredged in flour or flour and an egg wash. It should first be steamed, to ensure that it becomes completely cooked before the external color changes reach the desired level in the frying process. Otherwise, unless a pressure fryer is used, many pieces of chicken may still have blood near the bone when the surface is well browned, and, if the flesh is permitted to cook fully, the exterior browning will become excessive. Oven "frying" of chicken after precooking it in a steamer produces an alternative to deep fat frying.

For very young and tender poultry, broiling is an acceptable method of preparation. The pieces are sprinkled with salt and brushed with fat, before being placed in the broiler, skin side down at first.

The gizzard and heart of poultry may be cooked by any moist heat method, such as braising. The liver is very tender and may be cooked by either dry or moist methods for brief periods of time.

If proper sanitary principles are followed during preliminary preparation and after cooking, poultry such as turkey may be picked clean (after the breast and other usable parts have been removed) and the scraps frozen for later use in a la king or croquette dishes.

Prepared, Convenience, and Ready Forms of Poultry

Poultry is available in a variety of convenience and ready forms. Turkey breasts may

Table 14-19. Typical Reconstitution Methods and Times for Frozen Poultry

Equipment or Method	Food Item	Operating Temp.	Time
	Ready Items		
Conventional or convection oven	Poultry meal with vegetables	475°-500°	20-30 minutes
Deep fat fryer; finish in oven	Cornish game hen breast a la Kiev	375°—fryer; 350°—oven	until brown—fryer; 18 minutes—oven
	Convenience Items		
Conventional or convection oven	Turkey breast, boneless	400°	1-3/4 hours
Deep fat fryer	Chicken legs	330°	20 minutes

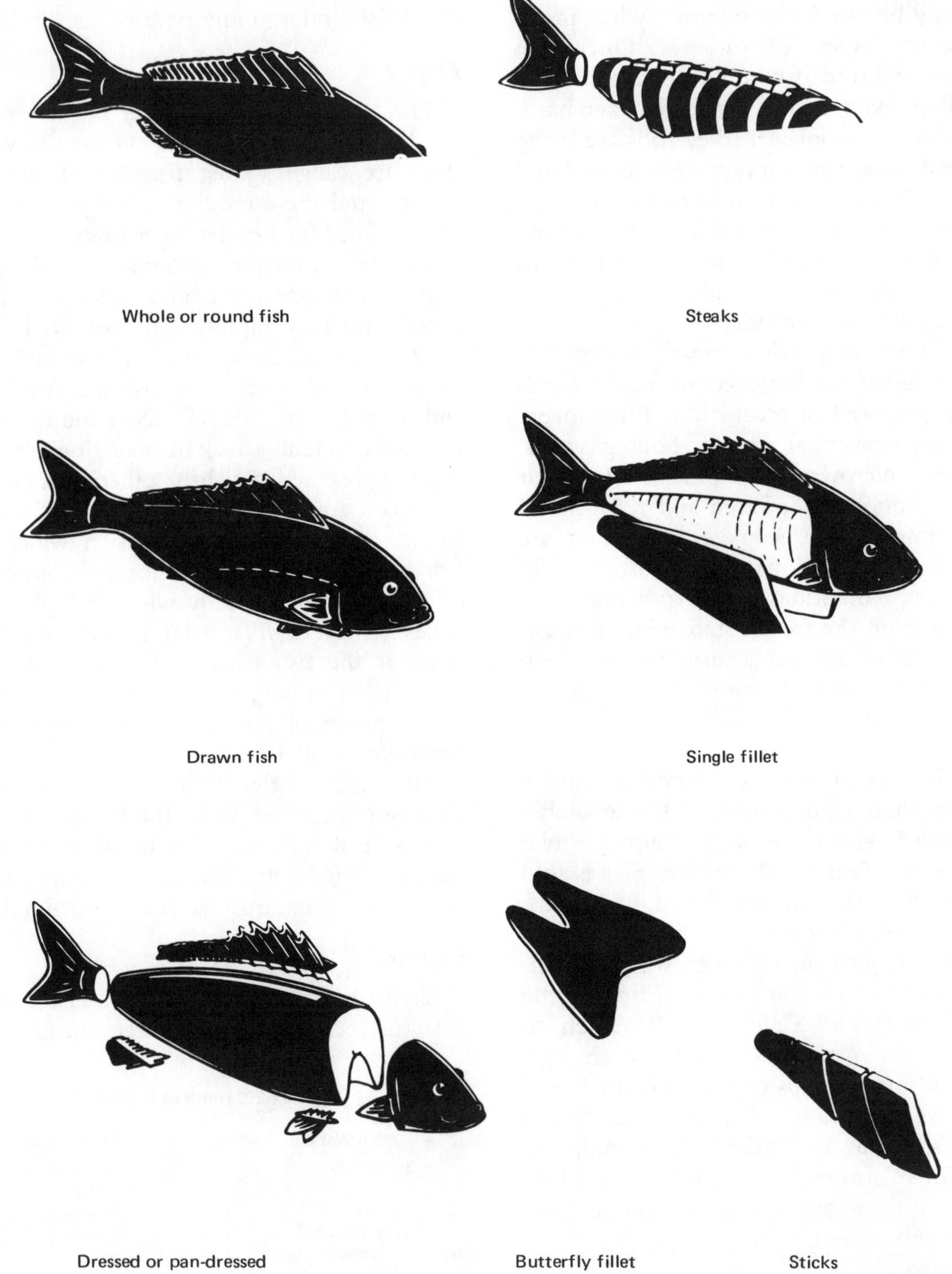

Figure 14o. The major forms in which finfish are marketed. (Courtesy of the United States Department of the Interior, Washington, D.C.)

be purchased separately, and diced turkey meat may be purchased in either white meat, dark meat, or mixed varieties. Chicken is available in breaded or unbreaded pieces, as smoked chicken, and in canned chicken hash. Cooked and uncooked turkey rolls are being produced. There are various preportioned and ready poultry dishes, such as turkey tetrazzini, chicken a la king, and chicken cacciatore. Once again, the operator must determine his own particular needs and adopt the purchasing policy that best fits them.

Like beef and other meat convenience items, poultry convenience or ready foods may be prepared or reconstituted in conventional or convection ovens, boiling water, steamers, microwave equipment, deep fat fryers, or pulsating infrared and refrigerated cycle equipment. Uncooked items that are not to be deep fried may be defrosted under refrigerated conditions prior to cooking or prepared from the frozen state without thawing. The latter method is suggested. All deep fried items are cooked without defrosting.

Fish

Fish is a complete protein food that usually costs less than meat or poultry. It is available from both fresh and salt water sources in two major forms: finfish and shellfish. Fish is sold fresh, frozen, canned, dehydrated, and freeze dried. Some research is now being done on fish farming, particularly on growing a northern lobster in a shorter period of time in the warmer waters of California. Research to duplicate the taste and texture of shrimp, tuna, and other forms of fish with soy-based protein substances is also being done. White bland fish forms are washed, denatured, and made into "shrimp," "crabmeat," or "lobster," with chemically compounded taste components added.

Approximately forty-four types of fish or seafood items are used, with forms of sale ranging (in addition to the fresh) from block-frozen shrimp, scallops, or crabmeat to cello-wrapped fish fillets and the IQF (individually quick frozen) item or the larger pack. Sixty percent of the fish used in the United States is imported, and less than 20 percent of all fish undergo any type of inspection.

Finfish

Fish are classified as either fat or lean depending on the species and the area in which they are caught. Most fish are of the lean variety, and these require cooking procedures that will not further dry their flesh.

Fish live in waters that range from 40 to 50 degrees in temperature, and they are prone to deteriorate very rapidly once removed. They must be protected against rapid decay. Indicators of high quality in fish are firm flesh and a very faint "fishy" odor. Indicators of freshness include a lack of objectionable odor and the presence of tightly adhering scales.

Finfish are available in a number of market forms: *rounds*—the condition in which the fish are caught; *drawn*—evicerated; *dressed*—evicerated and pan-ready with head, fins, and scales removed; *fillets*—lateral cuts from the sides of the fish with no bones; *steaks* cuts across the fish perpendicular to the spine; and *sticks*—pieces of fish cut in block style from nonuniform fillets.

Although continual inspection for wholesomeness is carried on by the Bureau of Commercial Fisheries for finfish and the United States Public Health Service for shellfish beds, no grading standards for fish are maintained.

Shellfish

Shellfish are divided into two main forms (1) crustaceans, such as lobsters, shrimp, and

Table 14-20. Kinds of Fat Fish

Salt Water	Fresh Water
Butterfish	Brook trout
Eel	Chub
Herring	Lake trout
King mackerel	Whitefish
Pompano	
Sablefish	
Salmon	
Shad	
Smelt	
Spanish mackerel	
Tuna	

From *Fresh and Frozen Fish Buying,* pp. 16-21, Circular no. 20, United States Department of the Interior, Washington, D.C., 1961.

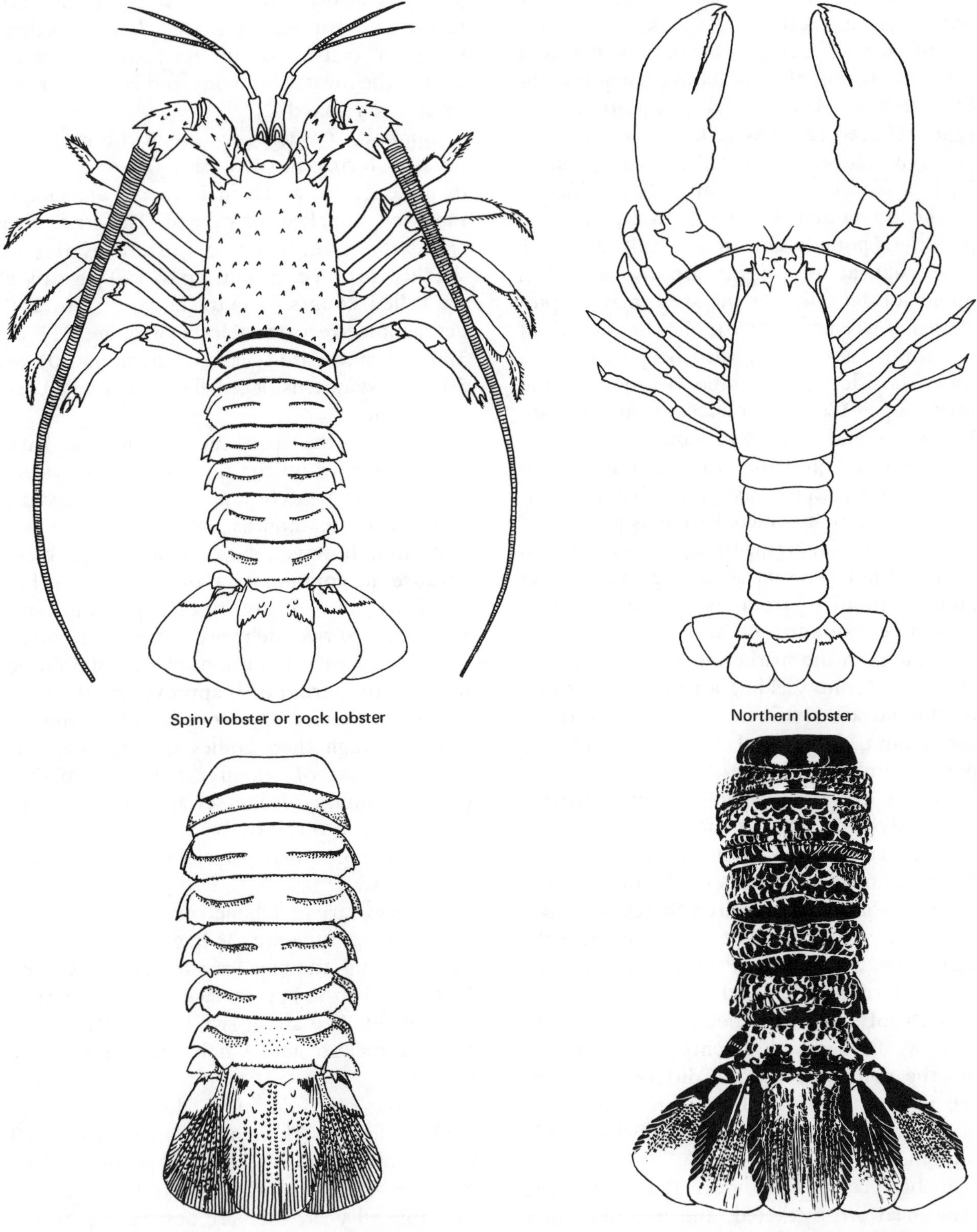

Figure 14p. The major forms of lobsters marketed in the United States. (Courtesy of the United States Department of the Interior, Washington, D.C.)

crabs, and (2) bivalve mollusks, such as oysters, clams, mussels, and scallops.

Crustaceans. Lobsters are one of the most desirable forms of crustaceans. They may be the classical Maine or claw variety or the types referred to as spiny lobster or crayfish. The tail section is also sold separately, either fresh or frozen. Maine lobsters are classified as chicken—1 pound; select—1¼ to 3 pounds; or jumbo—3 pounds and over. Weaks and one-claw culls at all weights are also available. Spiny lobsters, live in the shell, may be purchased at weights from 1 to 4 pounds. Tails of the spiny variety may also be purchased in four classifications: jumbo—16 ounces and over; large—12 to 16 ounces; medium—9 to 12 ounces; and small—6 to 9 ounces.

Shrimp are probably the most important part of the crustacean supply. They are marketed as green and uncooked or as peeled and deveined, and in fresh, frozen, or dehydrated form. Shrimp are sold according to count per pound, running from under 10 headless shrimp per pound to 68 and over per pound, depending on the marketing area. For general purposes shrimp yielding a count of 30 to 42 per pound are considered medium; 26 to 30 per pound, large; and fewer than 25 per pound, jumbo.

Shrimp are also available breaded, frozen, and ready for cooking or in canned varieties.

Crabs run in size from the king crab of Alaska at 6 to 20 pounds to the blue crab of the east coast of the United States at ¼ to 1 pound. Two other varieties are important: the dungeness crab of the Pacific coast and the rock crab of New England.

Both soft- and hard-shell crabs are featured in many food establishments. These are simply the same blue crabs at different times of the year; the soft-shell type are taken after molting and before the new shells have fully formed.

In blue crabs, lump meat, flake meat, and claw meat are marketed, and it is important to know the differences. Lump meat is solid white meat from the body, and should be used when appearance is important; flake meat is also from the body but in smaller pieces; clawmeat has a brownish color and comes, of course, from the claw. In other types of crabs, no differentiation is made among the meats, and body and claw meat are most often mixed.

Mollusks. Oysters are one of the most important forms of mollusks. They come in diameters from a half inch up and are sold in the shell, shucked, or canned. The grade size is based on the count of eastern oysters in shucked form per gallon: up to 160 per gallon are called counts or extra large; 161 to 210 per gallon are extra selects or large; 211 to 300 per gallon are selects or medium; 301 to 500 are standards or small; and over 500 are very small.

Although the spawning season does have some influence on the taste of oyster, oysters may be eaten safely any month of the year, even in those months without an *r*. Water pollution, however, poses a special problem because it contaminates oysters (and other shellfish). Since many oysters spawn in estuaries close to river delta areas, which are often sources of heavy pollution, oysters should be received only from beds approved by the Public Health Service. Oysters eat by drawing sea water through their bodies and straining out minute forms of sea life. Thus, any pathogenic pollutants from sewage effluents are also drawn into the oyster and may be passed on to the consumer, particularly if the oyster is eaten raw.

Scallops are available in two sizes: the ocean or sea type are the larger form, and the bay or cape the smaller size. In the United States, only the eye or shell-controlling muscle is eaten. It is about two inches diameter in the sea scallop and a half inch in the bay scallop.

Scallops are sold in shucked form, either fresh or frozen. There are approximately 110 to 170 per gallon of the sea type and 500 to 850 per gallon of the bay type. Although available all year, they are best tasting during the winter months because of the reduction of activity and the eating habits of the fish.

Clams may be purchased either in the shell, shucked, or canned. There are soft- and hard-

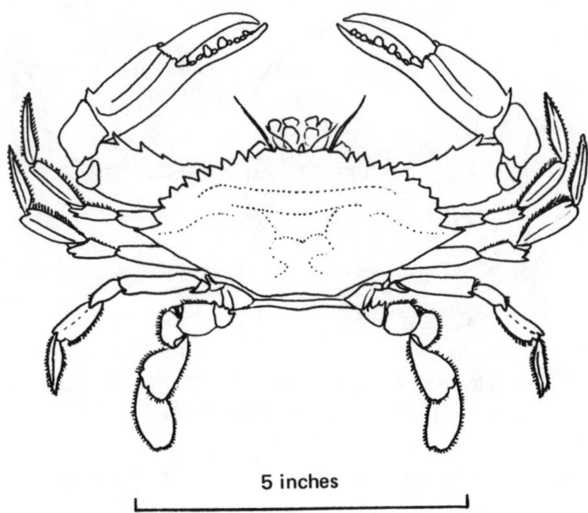

Blue Crab: from Atlantic and Gulf coasts; weighs 1/4 to 1 lb.; at different seasons, is the hard-shell crab and the soft-shell crab. *Market forms:* Hard-shell—live; cooked in shell; fresh cooked meat; frozen cooked meat; canned meat. Soft-shell—live; frozen uncooked.

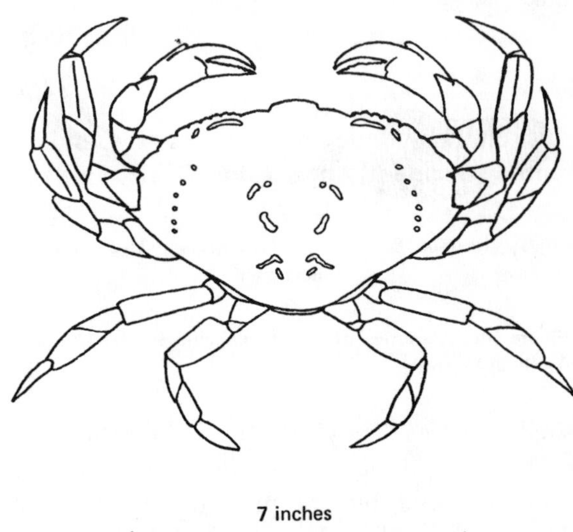

Dungeness Crab: from Pacific coast; weighs 1-3/4 to 3-1/2 lbs. *Market forms:* live; cooked in shell; fresh cooked meat; frozen cooked meat; canned meat.

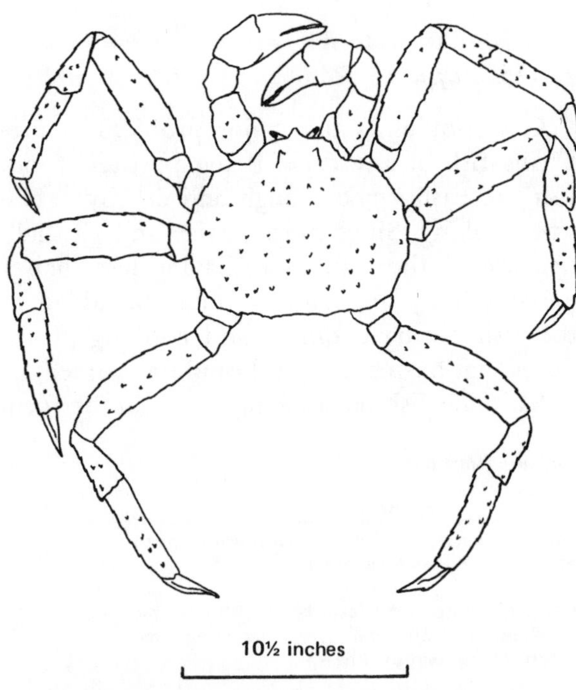

King Crab: from Pacific Ocean off Alaska; weighs 6 to 20 lbs.; big ones measure 6 ft. from tip of one leg to tip of opposite leg. *Market forms:* frozen cooked in shell; frozen cooked meat; canned meat.

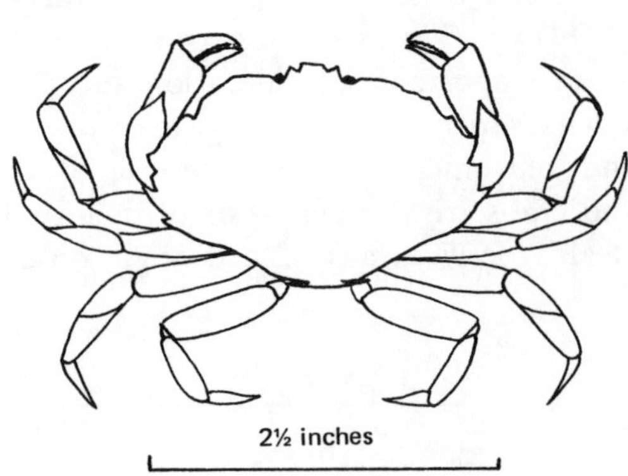

Rock Crab: from New England and California coasts; weighs 1/3 to 1/2 lb. *Market forms:* live; fresh cooked meat; canned meat.

Figure 14q. The major varieties of crabs used in quantity food service operations. (Courtesy of the United States Department of the Interior, Washington, D.C.)

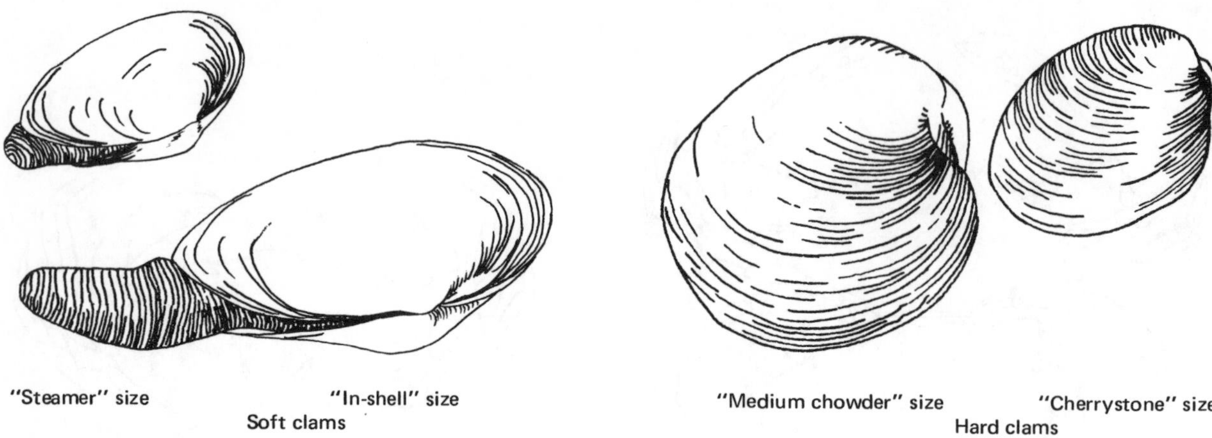

Figure 14r. Varieties of clams available in the United States. (Courtesy of the United States Department of the Interior, Washington, D.C.)

shell varieties. They may be sold by the dozen or by the pound in the shell; when shucked they are sold by the pint, quart, or gallon. They may also be purchased frozen in shucked form.

East coast clams are classified as littlenecks, cherrystones, chowders, or steamers; the west coast varieties are butter, littleneck, and razor clams. The eastern littlenecks and cherrystones are the smaller hard-shell clams that are often served on the half shell, while the larger varieties are used in soups and chowders.

Quality Considerations. Quality of shellfish is an important consideration for the food service supervisor. Odor, tightness of the shell, and movement of the antennae of lobsters and crabs are the best tests of quality. Public Health Service tags of bed origin on oysters, clams, and mussels are the best indicators of their quality and fitness for use as food. Clams, oysters, and other mollusks that have gaping shells and lobsters that have drooping tails and no movement of body members may be dangerous products.

Cooking Fish

Overcooking is the major problem in preparing fish of any type. Being a protein food, fish are easily made tough and dry by excessive cooking. Since most finfish and all shellfish are of the lean type, having less than 5 percent body oil, some fat must be added to the fish during cooking, and cooking procedures that hasten drying should be avoided.

Sautéing fish or brushing on fat in the form

Table 14-21. General Fish Cookery Timetable

Cooking Method	Minutes	Comments
Baking (oven temp. 350°)	up to 60 (total)	Lean fish must be basted occasionally with drippings to ensure that they do not become overdry
Broiling	8-10 per side	Fat varieties broil better than lean; brush fish with fat and cook 2-4 inches from heat source; cooking time varies with type of fish and thickness
Deep frying (fat temp. 350°-375°)	5-7 (total)	Coat with egg wash and breading first; take care not to overload basket or break fish during handling
Poaching	10 (total)	Use a court bouillon or water and salt solution, and keep at a simmering temperature
Oven frying (oven temp. 450°-500°)	12-15 (total)	An alternative to deep frying; fish should first be breaded

Cutting the lobster

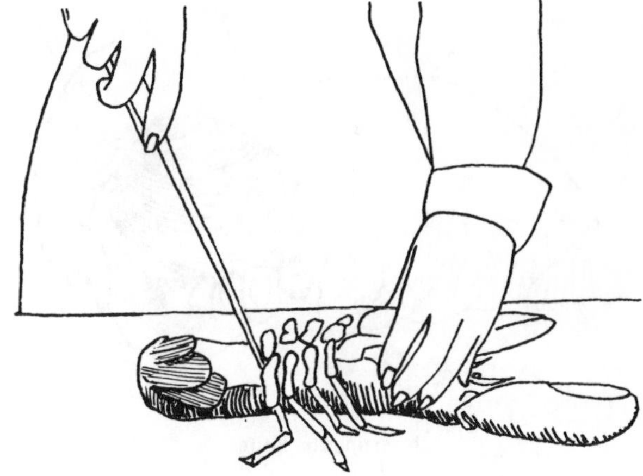

Removing the stomach and intestinal vein

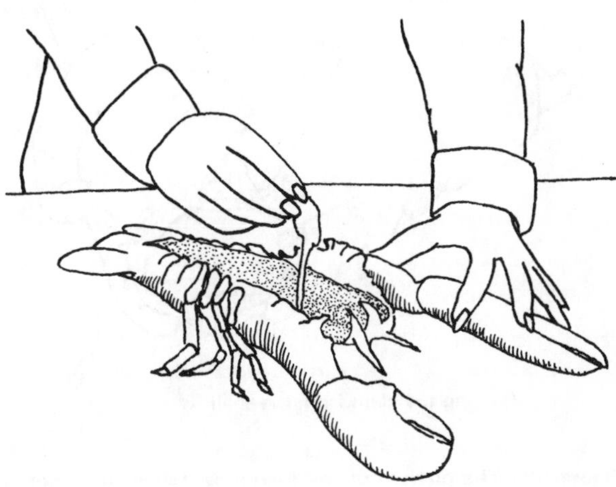

Brushing with butter

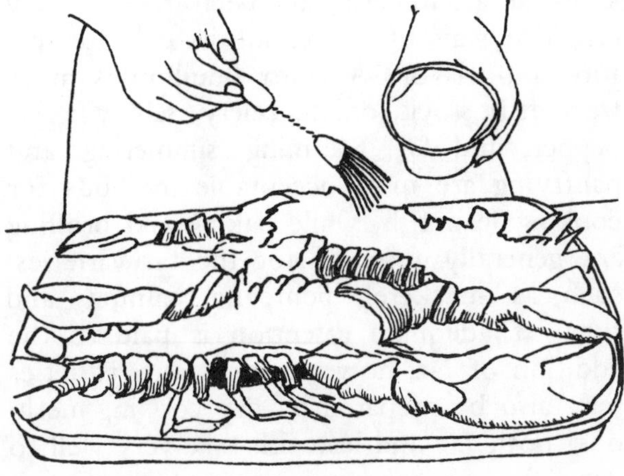

Figure 14s. To prepare a lobster for broiling, a cut is made between the body shell and the tail to sever the spinal cord. The stomach, just back of the head, and the intestinal vein from stomach to tail are removed. The green liver and coral roe are retained and used. The lobster may then be broiled for fifteen minutes, stuffed or unstuffed. (Courtesy of the United States Department of the Interior, Washington, D.C.)

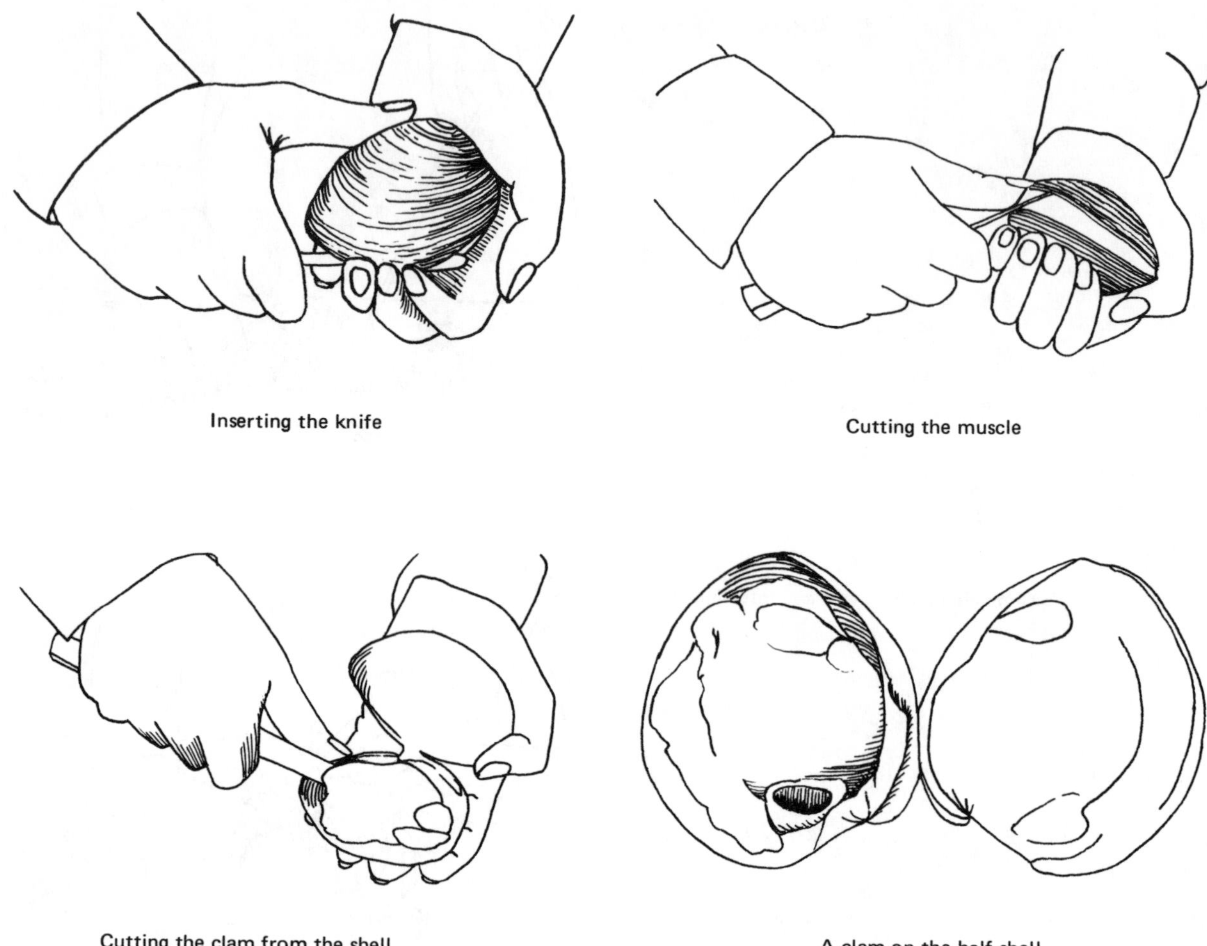

Figure 14t. The method of shucking a hard-shell clam. Soft-shell clams are easier to open. Preboiling the clams for five minutes will facilitate opening. (Courtesy of the United States Department of the Interior, Washington, D.C.)

of oil, butter, or margarine is an acceptable procedure. Poaching—a method of cooking the fish in a court bouillon, salted water, or stock at a simmering temperature—is a very effective way of conserving its delicate texture and flavor. A court bouillon is made from fish stock, onion, celery, salt, vinegar, pepper, and fat. Steaming, simmering, and panfrying are more acceptable methods for cooking lean fish, while baking and broiling are generally reserved for the fat varieties, such as mackerel, pompano, salmon, and tuna. If adequate attention is paid to the addition of fat, however, the leaner varieties may also be prepared by dry cooking methods. Both fat and lean fish take very well to deep frying. To avoid overcooking, finfish should be cooked just to the stage where flakiness develops in the flesh. Shellfish are done when their flesh firms at 140 degrees Fahrenheit (full flake stage).

Frozen fish (unless ready portioned) should be defrosted before cooking. They may be thawed in clean running water, under an electric fan, or under refrigeration. In any event, the defrosting period should be as brief as possible, and the fish must never be refrozen. Shellfish generally require some preliminary preparation before general cooking is begun.

Lobsters may be boiled, baked, or broiled. They may be served in the shell, or the meat may be removed and used in other dishes. To boil lobsters, they are plunged head first into boiling salted water (enough to cover), and cooked for twenty minutes at simmering tem-

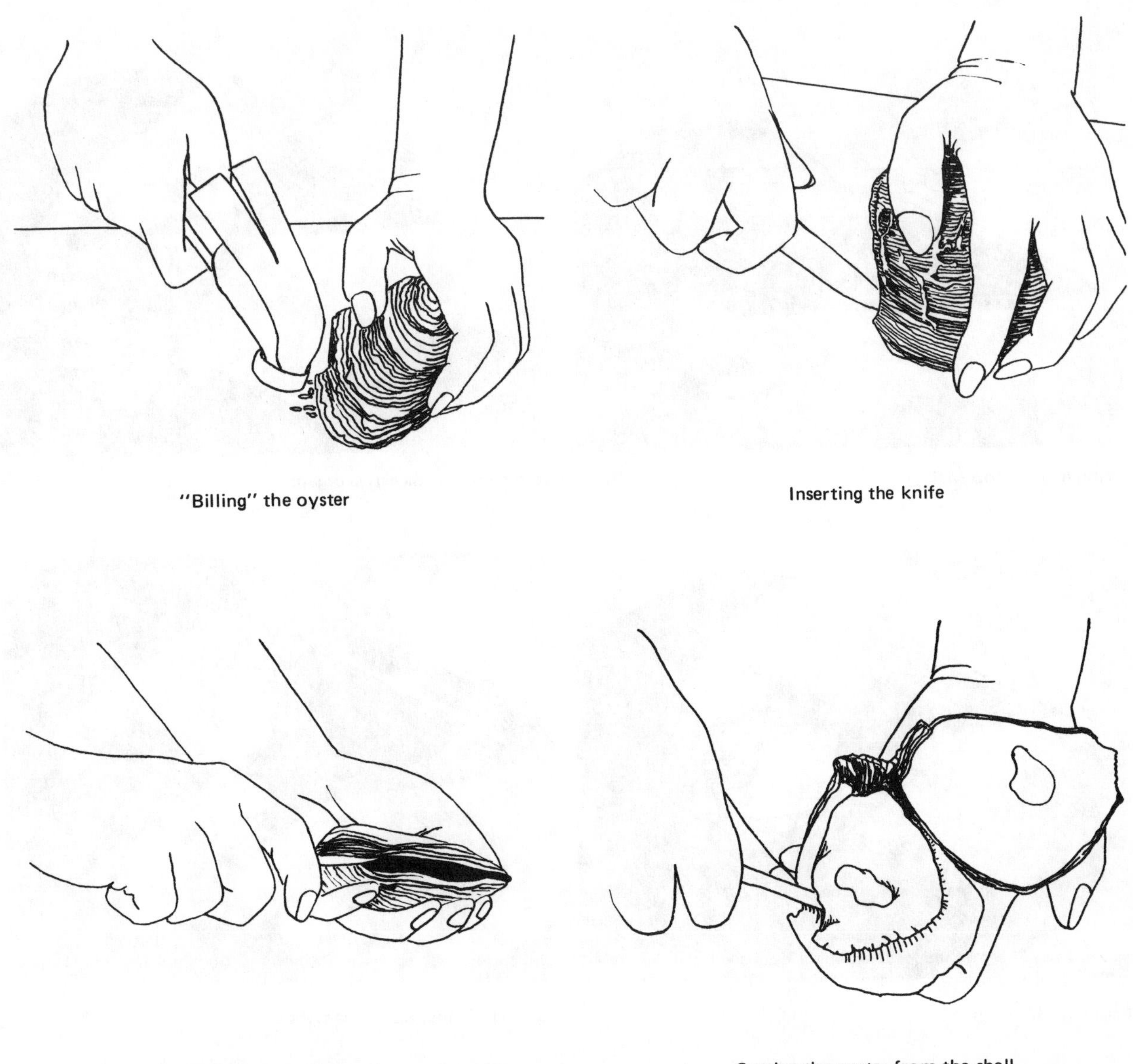

"Billing" the oyster

Inserting the knife

Cutting the muscle

Cutting the oyster from the shell

Figure 14u. After the oyster has been washed and rinsed, it is shucked by breaking off the bill, inserting the knife, and cutting the muscle that is close to the flat upper shell. The oyster may be cut completely from the shell and removed, or it may merely be loosened and left in the shell for service. (Courtesy of the United States Department of the Interior, Washington, D.C.)

peratures. If the lobster is to be baked or broiled, it may first be boiled in this manner. The spinal cord is cut and the lobster is split to remove the stomach and intestines. Then it is brushed with butter and baked or broiled.

Clams purchased shucked or canned need no preliminary preparation. Sanitary precautions must be maintained, however, on shucked clams prior to preparation and service. Clams in the shell should first be washed and cleaned by allowing them to sit in a mixture of 1/3 cup of salt to 1 gallon of water. This removes the sand from inside the shell. The shell may then be opened by inserting a knife between the halves and prying it open. The clam may be put in a small amount

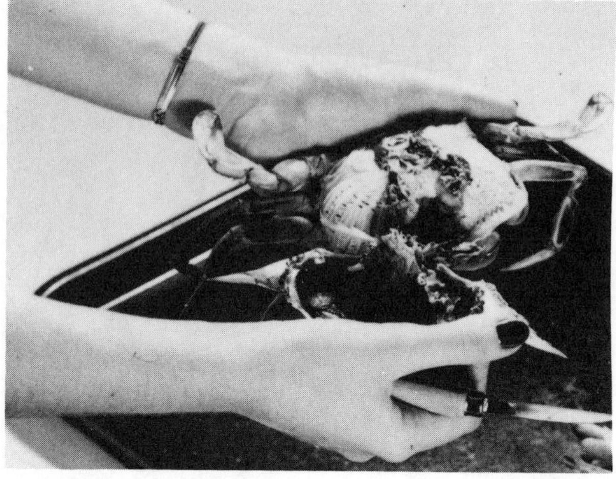

Removing the top shell

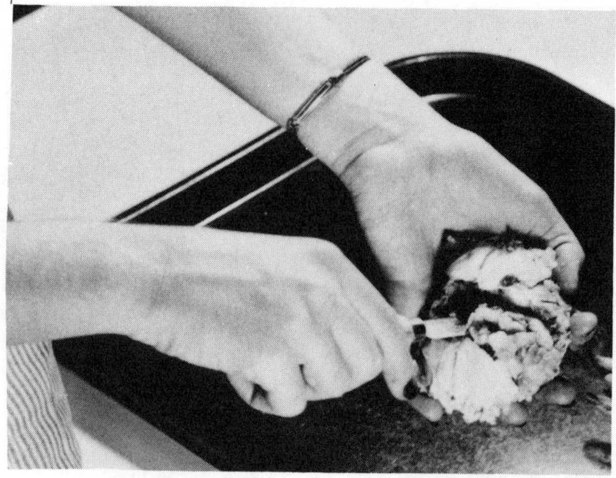

Removing the digestive organs

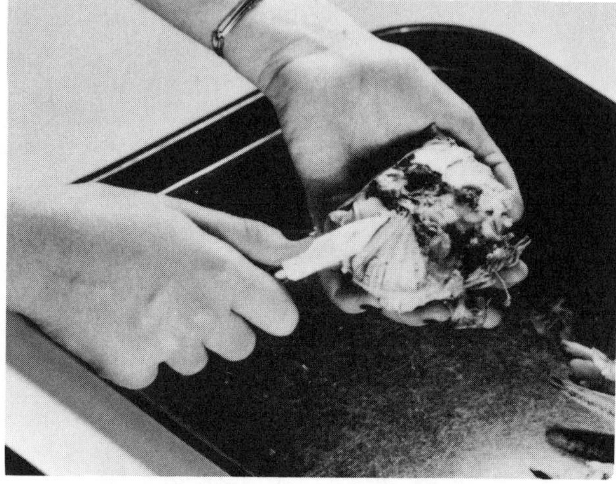

Scraping off the gills

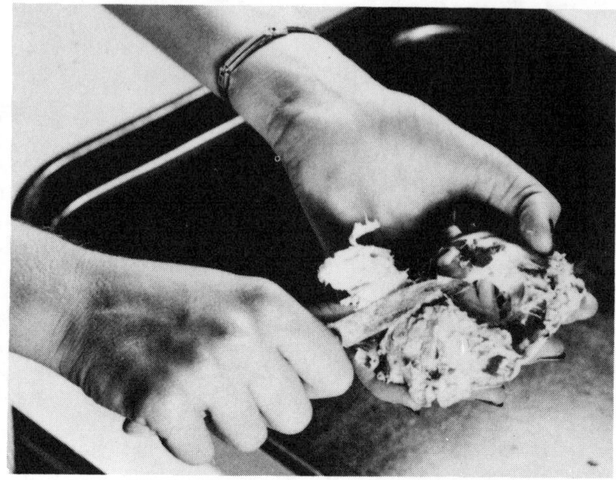

Slicing off the top of the right side

Figure 14v. Removal of the meat from a blue crab. After the shell and legs have been cut or broken off, the gills and other organs in the center of the body are scraped off. The meat is pried out of the shell from both sides of animal. Claws must be cracked to remove the meat. (Courtesy of the United States Department of the Interior, Washington, D.C.)

of boiling water for five or ten minutes to help to open the shell. Clams may then be served raw, broiled, steamed, roasted, or deep fried, or they may be made into chowders.

Oysters that are purchased shucked need no special preliminary preparation. Those purchased in the shell, however, require some preparation before they are baked, broiled, fried, or served raw. The oyster should be washed and rinsed in water. The shell is opened by placing a knife between the halves at the thin end. Breaking the "bill" of the oyster will make it easier to open. The meat is then cut from its shell and made ready for cooking or service.

Crabs are generally boiled in salted water for fifteen to twenty minutes before removing the meat from the shell. The cooked meat is

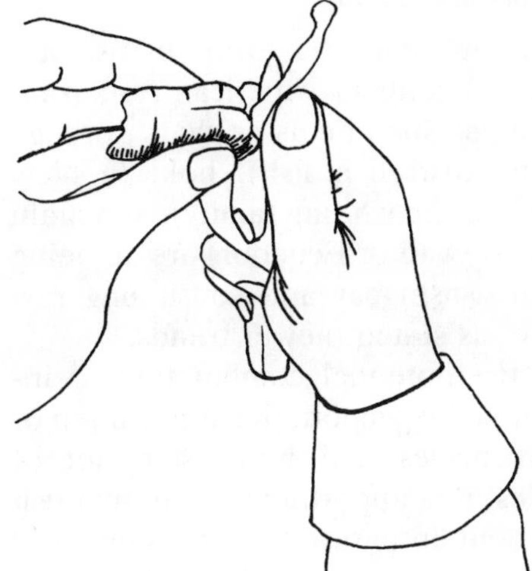

Figure 14w. The sand vein of a shrimp is removed after the shrimp has been cooked and shelled. A slit is made along the back of the shrimp and the vein is found just under the surface. (Courtesy of the United States Department of the Interior, Washington, D.C.)

then taken from the claws, the legs, and under the shell and used in a specific recipe.

Shrimp that are purchased raw are usually boiled in salted water for five to eight minutes before being used in a recipe. The shrimp may be peeled either before or after cooking. If the shells are left on until after cooking, a deeper red color remains on the meat. The sand vein (the intestinal track) is removed, and the shrimp are then ready for use in any recipe.

Prepared, Convenience, and Ready Forms of Fish

Preportioned forms of convenience and ready fish such as breaded shrimp, deviled crab, stuffed flounder, or seafood packs of oysters, scallops, and fish sticks are available. They may be prepared or reconstituted in conventional or convection ovens, microwave ovens, infrared and refrigerated cycle equipment, deep fryers, or broilers.

Table 14-22. Typical Reconstitution Methods and Times for Fish

Equipment or Method	Food Item	Operating Temp.	Time
Deep fat fryer	Frozen raw fish	360°-365°	3-5 minutes
Conventional or convection oven	Frozen raw fish	375°-400°	20-40 minutes
Microwave equipment	Frozen raw fish	2,000 watts	30 seconds to defrost; 90 seconds to cook
Infrared and refrigerated cycle equipment	Frozen raw fillets	1,000°	3-4 minutes
Conventional or convection oven	Precooked fish sticks; fried clams	425°	15 minutes
Broiler	Precooked fish sticks; fried clams	350°	6 minutes

Newer Forms and Trends

Newer or more exotic forms of fish are seen today in mainland American restaurant establishments. Such items as shark, orange roughy (an Australian fish), hoki (a New Zealand fish of the whiting family), and mahi mahi (from Hawaii or Ecuador) are all being offered. The sushi bar and consuming raw seafood are, as stated, newer trends.

Due to the potential combination of incomplete or no inspection, the importation of foreign fish species, and the consumption of raw varieties, it is important to note that fish could well contain parasites such as the eggs of the roundworm anisakid or decipiens. These eggs and worms, a natural part of the food chain found in the sea, are mostly deposited in shellfish from the body droppings of larger sea animals such as seals and sea lions. As the fish feed on these smaller crustaceans, they in turn consume the eggs of the parasite and could pass them on to the human consumer.

As a precaution, cooking to an internal full flake state with no trace of translucency (140 degrees Fahrenheit) is the best defense against this potential problem. If the flesh must be eaten raw or undercooked, a prefreezing period of minus 4 degrees Fahrenheit for seven days is the next-best procedure.

15 *Vegetables and Fruits*

Objective: To consider the classification and composition of vegetables and fruits, including their nutritional value, structure, coloring, and flavors. The student is introduced to principles of availability and quality control. All phases of preparation are covered in detail.

Classification

Although fruits and vegetables are botanically related plants that manufacture essential nutrients from soil, water, and sunlight, they are different in their use and preparation as foods. Fruits are used primarily as appetizers, desserts, and garnishes, while vegetables are used as main meal accompaniments. There are, of course, exceptions to both these broad rules, but custom has dictated these basic differences.

Fruits are parts of plants that contain seeds. They differ from vegetables not only in their use but also in their acid content, sweetness, texture, and amount of preliminary preparation and cooking required.

With these differences in mind, both fruits and vegetables are considered in this chapter, although both are also discussed in chapter 8 (pantry) and fruits appear again in chapter 14 (baking).

Vegetables

Vegetables are classified according to either the botanical families to which they belong or the part of the plant used as food. The family relationship is of little concern to the food service manager or supervisor, although some references to family groups will be made when appropriate. The part of the plant used for food is a much more important classification system in food preparation work, because vegetables of the same group present common characteristics that dictate similar preparation methods. The main categories of vegetables by parts of the plant eaten are listed in Table 15-1.

Composition

Like all living things, vegetables are composed mainly of water; it ranges from 70 to

Table 15-1. Classes of Vegetables

Part Eaten	Representative Vegetables
Roots	Beets, carrots, radishes
Tubers	Potatoes
Bulbs	Garlic, onions
Leaves	Cabbage, greens, lettuce
Stems	Asparagus, celery
Flowers	Broccoli, cauliflower
Fruit	Cucumber, squash
Seeds	Beans, peas

95 percent in different vegetables. Most also have liberal amounts of carbohydrates, varying with the type of vegetable and the part that is used. Vegetables have been classified according to the percentages of carbohydrate they contain. The carbohydrate may be in the form of sugars or more complex starches. Preparation and storage procedures for particular vegetables should relate to the type of carbohydrate they contain.

Vegetables also provide mineral salts to the diet and usually have generous amounts of vitamins A and C. The green and yellow vegetables provide more vitamin A than other vegetables. Vitamin C is available in most green vegetables. The basic minerals provided are calcium and iron salts. Some vegetables also provide protein and fats, but generally in negligible amounts.

Plant pigments, which give the vegetables their characteristic colors, and some flavoring substances are also present. Specific preparation methods may be required in order for the plant pigment to retain its attractiveness and clarity of color in cooking. Both desirable and undesirable flavoring substances in vegetables dictate particular food preparation practices.

Physically vegetables are made up of a substance called cellulose. The physical characteristics and tenderness of this substance depend on the age of the plant, the degree of ripeness, the plant family, and the part of the plant being used for food. Cellulose fiber is generally indigestible and provides a bulk necessary to the diet for elimination functions. The plant structure is made of walls of cellulose held together with pectins, which act as cementing substances.

Depending on the final use to be made of a vegetable, procedures may be undertaken either to change the pectin and cellulose in a vegetable to tenderize it and to liberate the flavoring substances and nutrients it contains or to strengthen the pectin and cellulose in order to conserve the vegetable's physical structure (for example, during a canning procedure).

Purposes of Preparation

The major consideration in preparing vegetables is to provide a product that is more digestible and has a more desirable flavor. An attempt is made to conserve the maximum amount of the available nutrients in the vegetable while neither overcooking nor undercooking it.

Many vegetables, because of their age, ripeness, and cell structure, can be eaten raw. A consumer eating them in this manner receives the maximum benefit from their nutrients and reaps the added benefit of having to use his face and jaw muscles, which contributes to good dental health. Raw vegetables are often used as components of relish trays, garnishes, and appetizers.

Some vegetables, however, do not lend themselves to raw consumption and must undergo cooking procedures before they become acceptable to the consumer.

Availability

Vegetables are available fresh or processed in canned, frozen, or dried form. They are sold in convenience forms (diced, for example) for use in other recipes or in ready food dishes that need only reheating prior to service.

In selecting vegetables, the order of preference among available forms is fresh, frozen, freeze dried, dried, and canned. Fresh, of course, are most desirable, but frozen vegetables are a very acceptable alternative, and give more flexibility in storage. They are blanched before being frozen, in order to inactivate their enzymes, and the cooking process needs only finishing before service and consumption.

Freeze dried or dried vegetables may or may not be blanched, but the moisture removal reduces storage space needs and prevents spoilage. Many vegetables do not handle dehydration well and are not processed this way.

Canned vegetables are completely cooked at temperatures that will protect them against anaerobic bacteria. This makes additional cooking detrimental, and only heating should be done. Canned vegetables are good standby items, but should be used only as a last resort if fresh or frozen are not available at reasonable prices.

Quality Standards

Although federal standards and grades for vegetables are available at both the wholesale and the consumer levels, their use is generally voluntary and not enforced in many areas. Some states with major agricultural crops apply more stringent controls than the federal government does. In addition, grades or standards vary with different forms of vegetables. Experience and sight have often superseded the grades that exist.

As a general rule, a U.S. no. 1 grade represents an acceptable product of good quality. A grade of U.S. Fancy or U.S. Extra no. 1 is assigned to a product outstanding for its type. A U.S. no. 2 vegetable should be viewed with some suspicion, since this is usually the lowest packable grade.

Preliminary Preparation

Although processed vegetables require no preliminary preparation, all fresh vegetables do. It is extremely important that preparation be carried out carefully to preserve the maximum usable portion of the product. Laxity in this process might well result in the loss of valuable nutrients or the waste of usable portions, causing low yields and creating profit problems. Attention to this step may also pay big dividends in producing a more acceptable product and a more satisfied guest.

All vegetables should be washed with a stiff brush in copious amounts of water to ensure the complete removal of dirt, insect sprays, grit, and the like. A deep vegetable sink that is used for food preparation alone will facilitate this process. A saline soak may be required in certain circumstances to remove insects embedded in leafy vegetables, such as cabbage. Particular care must be taken in cleaning vegetables that will not be cooked before eating.

Damaged leaves, skins, fibrous stems, and the like should be removed, but this process must be kept to the minimum necessary, in order to conserve nutrients that may be located just under the skin or other discarded part of a vegetable.

Cutting should be done with kitchen equipment or a sharp knife that will prevent excessive bruising of the tissue. If possible a nonferric blade should be used, to prevent discoloration of vegetables that contain certain flavor tannins.

Although cooking vegetables in their skins will conserve the maximum amount of available nutrients and generally give a more desirable product, it is not usually feasible in quantity food situations, unless the vegetable is to be served this way.

Vegetables to be peeled in mechanical vegetable peelers should be sorted or cut into equal-sized units to ensure uniformity of peeling in the batch. This prevents the smaller diameter vegetables from being destroyed while larger ones continue to require peeling. Vegetables should also be cut into pieces of uniform size to ensure equal cooking throughout the batch.

If a vegetable is subject to discoloration due to oxidation after skin removal, it should be protected against this undesirable condition by the use of an antioxidant or by keeping it in water until used. Procedures must be scheduled to prevent the holding of vegetables for long periods of time, and vegetables should be kept refrigerated from the time of preliminary preparation to the time of cooking, in order to delay enzyme action and conserve nutrients.

Cooking Fresh Vegetables

The cooking of vegetables softens the cellulose and makes them easier to digest. It also gelatinizes the starch and makes it easier for the body to use. The cooking method selected for a particular vegetable should be the one that can be completed in the shortest period of time with a minimum loss of color, taste, and nutrients.

The desired flavor, the type and age of the vegetable, and its color and flavor components all influence the method of cooking that should be used. The cooking time and degree of doneness are influenced by the type of equipment used, the size of the batch being prepared, and the end use to be made of the product.

Most of the basic cooking methods may be used for vegetables: baking, boiling, steaming, sautéing, broiling, or deep frying.

Baking. Potatoes, both Irish and sweet, winter squash, pea beans, navy beans, and eggplant all bake very satisfactorily. Uniformity of size, meticulous attention to cleanliness and trimming, and the addition of some sort of oil (such as salad oil or butter) will do much to keep the items soft and tender despite the moisture loss experienced in the baking process. Aluminum foil may be used to speed cooking, prevent excessive surface drying, and make serving easier. The skin of baked potatoes must be punctured after removal from the oven to prevent steam build-up from causing sogginess in the potato.

Other vegetables are often baked in scalloped form (combined with a white sauce), as containers for other foods (e.g., stuffed green peppers or stuffed baked tomatoes), in casserole dishes, or in soufflés (combined with beaten egg whites).

Baked vegetables may be candied with brown sugar, butter, and salt or mixed with cheese, eggs, or other food items (such as in duchesse potatoes) to give them variety.

Steaming. Almost any type of vegetable in either fresh or frozen form may be steamed. Either high or low pressure may be used, although high pressure steam is more desirable, particularly for frozen items. When steaming frozen vegetables, the blocks of food must be broken apart to ensure uniform cooking. Uniform-sized pieces should be provided in each batch. Two 2½-pound packages of frozen vegetables, or an equal amount of the fresh variety, is a desirable size for the cooking batch, to allow uniformity of preparation and provide freshly prepared items for service. Larger batches create heat transmission problems due to their mass; the weight of the batch may damage vegetables on the bottom, particularly if they are tender varieties; and on the average there is too long a wait between preparation and service in most operations.

If different vegetables are to be combined, cooking temperatures and times must be consistent with the requirements of each or the vegetables must be prepared separately before being combined.

All vegetables should be cooked until tender. After cooking, seasoning is added according to the recipe. Butter or margarine is easier to add when melted. Approximately four ounces is usually added to each five pounds of vegetables.

Boiling. Although almost any vegetable may be boiled, this method is not generally used unless a particular menu or recipe calls for it. Steaming is a very acceptable substitute for boiling most forms of vegetables and requires less time. If boiling is used, it should be done in as little water as possible in a covered pot for all but the very strong vegetables. After cooking, the vegetables should be drained immediately to prevent excessive absorption of moisture. The hardier vegetables with more cellulose structure, the strong-flavored ones (e.g., onions, turnips, and carrots), and some of the greens (such as spinach) appear to endure boiling much better than more tender items.

Sautéing. Vegetables such as potatoes, eggplant, and zucchini are often sautéed in a little fat. Because of the amount of hand work and watching required, an acceptable alternative for this process is oven cooking in fat. Using the proper oven temperature, a very similar product may be obtained.

There are several vegetable recipes that combine green peppers and onions with blander vegetables, such as potatoes, to get a dish with maximum flavor. Surface breading is also applied to many vegetables in order to achieve a high level of surface browning.

Deep Fat Frying. A very acceptable manner of preparing many forms of vegetables is deep frying. A surface coating on the item forms a crust in the hot fat that seals the outside of the vegetable and prevents fat from entering, while maximum flavor is maintained. The temperature of the fat is important: too low a temperature or an overloaded batch will permit fat to be absorbed into the product before the crust is formed. After cooking, excessive fat is removed from the surface of the vegetables, and they are salted at this time. Since salt is an enemy of fat and will hasten its decay, it should not be applied until the products are out of the deep fat fryer. Vegetables that are to be deep fried should also be relatively free from surface moisture, since this will cause foaming and hasten the breakdown of the fat used for frying.

Broiling. Although broiling may be used to cook some vegetables, it is most often used to brown a vegetable or vegetable dish that has been prepared in another manner or to melt a surface garnish, such as cheese. Tomatoes and onions are two of the most important vegetables that are broiled not only as a method of preparation but for garnishing purposes.

Combinations and Additives

Almonds, pimientos, mushrooms, cheeses, bread crumbs, onions, and green peppers are among the items most commonly combined with vegetables. Parsley, of course, is used to excess in many of the garnishes offered with vegetables. Like other trite ones it should be avoided, if possible, and more novel garnishes found.

Cream, hollandaise, creole, Polonaise, and cheese sauces are often used with vegetables in particular recipes.

Choice of a Cooking Method

The following general factors should be considered in selecting the preparation method for a particular vegetable:

(a) Bake vegetables in their skins, if the menu plan and serving procedure allow this. Baking drives moisture out of the product, but keeping skins on conserves more nutrients. No water needs to be added and no vitamins or minerals are leached out in the cooking medium. In addition, no paring is done that would dispose of subsurface nutrients. If a vegetable cannot be baked without peeling, peel the skin as minimally as possible to ensure adequate nutrient retention and maximum serving yield.

(b) Steam items unpeeled, if possible, or with a minimal amount of paring. Steam puts very little additional moisture in contact with the vegetable, and permits a rapid cooking period, to conserve color, texture, and nutrients, because of the high temperatures that are possible in steam equipment.

(c) Sauté vegetables with a small amount of fat if they lend themselves to this method of preparation, as it is a highly acceptable way of conserving food values.

(d) Cook vegetables in water only as a last resort, and then use a minimum amount of water. Vegetables may be cooked in their skins in boiling water, but this process is generally not used in quantity food work. Cover the cooking container when boiling mild vegetables, and leave it uncovered when cooking stronger ones in order to volatilize their strong and undesirable flavors.

Cooking Different Types of Vegetables

Colors, textures, and flavor substances are the important factors to consider in cooking vegetables.

Color Considerations. Vegetables are classified by color according to four basic groups, and each has particular cooking requirements.

Green vegetables receive their color from chlorophyll substances. This group includes such vegetables as spinach, broccoli, and asparagus.

Red-yellow-orange group vegetables are colored by carotenoid and xanthophylls. Such vegetables as carrots, sweet potatoes, and squash are in this group.

White vegetables, such as potatoes and parsnips, gain their color (or lack of it) from flavones and anthoxanthins.

Table 15-2. Effects of Cooking Media on Vegetable Colors

Vegetable Pigment	Effect of Acid Medium	Effect of Alkaline Medium	Effect of Heat
Yellow-orange	No effect	No effect	No effect
Red	Maintains red	Turns blue*	Reduces color intensity
White†	Maintains white	Turns yellow-brown	Turns brownish
Green	Turns brownish	Intensifies green	Turns olive brown

*This reaction is reversible by changing the pH back to acid.

†Discoloration of some white vegetables (e.g., potatoes) due to oxidation may be controlled with the use of an antioxidant, such as sodium bisulfite.

Red vegetables, such as beets and red cabbage, owe their red color pigment to anthocyanins.

To conserve the true color of vegetables, an operator must maintain control over time and temperature relationships, the acidity or alkalinity of the cooking medium, and the degree of volatilization of vegetable acids. Excessively high temperatures, extended cooking periods, hard water, or covering the cooking utensil at the wrong time may ruin a naturally attractive vegetable color. Specific suggestions are offered below.

Green vegetables may be affected by an acid cooking medium or excessive heat. Either of these can change the chlorophyll substances to brownish or olive green pheophytins, giving the vegetable a color more representative of canned products.

Cooking green vegetables as quickly as possible and using a cut form of the vegetable that will cook faster will both contribute to maximum retention of the natural green coloring. Steam cooking is the method of choice for both fresh and frozen varieties of green vegetables. Keeping the cooking medium in the alkaline pH range also assists in maintaining this green color. Hard water and the addition of baking soda have both been used to achieve this. Neither is suggested, however, as each may also break down and seriously alter the texture of the vegetables. In addition, soda may destroy vitamin C in the product.

White vegetables are most affected by an alkaline environment, which is often found in hard water areas. This causes the white to change to a yellowish tint. The surface darkening of potatoes is also a color problem. It is basically due to oxidation. Both problems may be prevented by shifting the cooking medium slightly to the acid side. Softening the water used in cooking will also help prevent discoloration of white vegetables.

Red vegetables are most often affected by the environment in which they are cooked. They retain their original color in an acid medium, turn to purple in a neutral one, and change to bluish tints in an alkaline medium. Attempts to maintain an acid cooking environment by the addition of vinegar, apples, lemon juice, and similar items have been successfully used to keep red vegetables red.

Red-yellow-orange vegetables are the least affected in terms of color changes. All may be safely processed with maximum color retention in any convenient manner and medium.

Flavor Considerations. Flavor in vegetables is usually associated with sugars or acid substances, many of which are volatile. Although some flavor change from raw to cooked state is desirable in most products, in addition to the changes in texture that are a goal of cooking, the goal is generally to retain the maximum flavor. The major problems evolve around the differences between the vegetables with mild and strong flavors. Vegetables of the cabbage family, cauliflower, turnips, and onions are considered strong in flavor. All the rest are generally considered mild. Strong vegetables should be cooked in a manner that will neutralize or reduce their flavors.

Most objectionable flavors are the result of

acids or sulfur compounds in the vegetable. The cooking procedures should attempt to dissipate these offending agents, for example by cooking the vegetable in a large amount of water, uncovered, so that the acids volatilize. Or the cooking procedures may try to neutralize the strong flavor by using agents such as milk with cabbage, for example. Cooking at high temperatures for prolonged periods of time will liberate more of the offending flavor substances and increase their taste in the vegetable, so maximum reduction of the cooking time should be a prime objective. An acid cooking medium often causes additional problems with vegetables containing an offensive sulfur agent, and pH control must be maintained to prevent this.

Mild vegetables create no special flavor problems for the food service operator. Cooking times and temperatures should be accommodated to the preparation procedure that has been selected for them.

Texture Considerations. The texture of a vegetable is related to the type and amount of cellulose present in it. Age also plays an important part: more mature items are usually firmer and less yielding. Proper purchasing may do much to provide raw vegetables to the cook that will ultimately be highly acceptable to the guest. Even when good vegetables are bought, however, certain procedures must be followed to ensure the production of high quality vegetable dishes.

Although cooking is designed to help tenderize the vegetable, soften the cellulose, and gelatinize the starch content, it must be done only to a predetermined minimum stage. Vegetables should never be overcooked, particularly if they are to be further processed in another cooking procedure, held in steam tables, or kept in other heated areas where additional procedures will take place.

In addition, vegetables must be batched in such a way that the weight of the mass from above or the temperature of the mass or of the container does not reduce the vegetable texture to an unrecognizable pulp.

An acid medium tends to strengthen the cellulose, while an alkaline one appears to assist in softening it. From a practical standpoint, however, pH control should be related to the control of tender colors rather than attempting to manage texture changes with it.

Special Problems with Tannins. Tannins are flavor substances found in many vegetables that may cause both color and cooking problems if not properly controlled. In combination with ferric salts, found in iron knives, utensils, or pots, tannins may change a white vegetable to a greenish-grey that will later oxidize to brown. In scalloped and casserole dishes that contain vegetables high in tannins, such as asparagus and potatoes, they may also cause a curdling of milk ingredients. Use of a white sauce may be required to protect the milk from the tannins, just as a white sauce is required in cream of tomato soup, to prevent the acid of the tomato from causing the same reaction.

Preparation of Frozen Vegetables

Almost all vegetables are available in a frozen processed form. Partially cooked by blanching, which stops their enzyme action and gives them maximum color set, they retain their flavor, texture, and natural color. The blanching permits the final cooking period to be reduced, resulting in a highly acceptable product.

Steaming in a high pressure steamer is the method of choice for preparing frozen vegetables, using a perforated pan. Although some steam equipment has both a defrosting and a cooking cycle, it is strongly suggested that the frozen blocks of vegetables be separated to ensure uniform cooking. Otherwise the outside of the pack may receive excessive heat exposure, while the inside fails to reach the al dente stage. Measures must also be taken to ensure that the steamer is not overloaded during a run.

Preparation of Canned Vegetables

Although canning is a very effective way to process vegetables, it requires heating the product to temperatures that will make it safe. Canned vegetables have experienced the maximum color and texture changes they can withstand and are not usually able to handle additional cooking. The method of choice for preparing canned products is to drain the liquor, heat it in a steam-jacketed kettle, and add the vegetables to it again. This permits the vegetables to receive heat from the liquor without additional cooking. Placing an opened can in a bain-marie may work well for the hardier vegetables, such as carrots, but is unsatisfactory for most canned vegetables.

Preparation of Dehydrated and Freeze Dried Vegetables

Many vegetables are processed in dehydrated or freeze dried form and require reconstitution before use. Most require the addition of a specified amount of warm water before cooking. Then they should be cooked at very low temperatures.

Cooking Specific Common Vegetables

Asparagus. Asparagus is available fresh, frozen, and canned. Fresh asparagus should have firm and closed tips with a minimum amount of wilting. The green stalk should be brittle and tender. Canned and frozen forms are labeled stalks, tips, or cuts, to indicate a decreasing length of the shaft. The white butts of the stalk are generally unproductive.

Wash fresh asparagus well. While holding the stalk in both hands, break it with a bending motion. The snap will separate the tender from the less tender pieces. Discard the lower fibrous part, which breaks from the stalk at the natural weak point. If the lower portion of the remaining stalk has an extra large diameter, it may be split lengthwise for easier cooking. It is preferable to leave the stalk whole, however.

Cook fresh asparagus in five-pound batches in a steamer under low pressure (five to seven pounds) for approximately ten minutes or under high pressure (fifteen pounds) for approximately three minutes. Asparagus may also be cooked standing upright in enough water to cover half the stalk. When the stalks are about cooked, the container is covered and the tips are permitted to finish cooking. Total cooking time, depending on the size, is twelve to eighteen minutes. Frozen asparagus may be cooked in five-pound batches in a low pressure steamer for approximately nine minutes or in a high pressure steamer for two minutes. Canned asparagus is separated from the liquor, the fluid is heated, and the solid is recombined for heating before serving.

Margarine or butter may then be added (four ounces to each five pounds), and the vegetable is served. Asparagus may also be served in a salad, in combination with an entrée such as ham or turkey, or with a sauce such as supreme or hollandaise.

Beans (Green or Wax). Green and wax beans are available fresh, frozen, or canned. Fresh beans should be firm and tender. They should snap crisply when broken. Beans that have separated will be stringy. Seeds should be small and immature for best tenderness.

Wash fresh beans and break or cut them into small pieces or cut them lengthwise on the diagonal (French style). Steam them in five-pound batches at low pressure for fifteen to twenty minutes or at high pressure for six minutes. If beans are cut French style so that more of the lateral area of the bean is exposed, the cooking time will be reduced. Beans may also be cooked in a small amount of water in a steam-jacketed kettle or on the range, covered, for approximately fifteen to twenty minutes.

Frozen beans may be cooked in five-pound batches in low pressure steamers for approximately twelve minutes or at high pressure for five to eight minutes. Canned beans are labeled according to the style of cut: whole, French style, cuts, etc. They are prepared in the same way as other canned vegetables, with the liquor heated and the beans added to it.

After cooking, beans should be drained and butter, margarine, salt, and pepper added. Slivered almonds, bacon bits, pearl onions, or mushrooms may be added to vary the serving method, or the beans may be served in casseroles or other dishes. Leftovers may be incorporated into soups, be used in salads, or be reheated for use as a vegetable again.

Beans (Dry). Beans, in varieties including California pea, great northern, lima, pinto, and many others, may be purchased dry or, in processed forms, canned and even frozen in some instances. Lima beans, Mexican beans, and black-eyed peas are also sold in fresh form.

Dry beans are rich sources of protein and the B complex vitamins. They must be sorted and washed to remove stones and the like. Boil the beans in water (three times the volume of the beans) for two minutes, remove them from the heat, and permit them to soak for one hour. After adding meat seasoning and/or salt, return the beans to a slow boil. Most varieties will cook within two hours. Beans may also be cooked in a low pressure steamer (after soaking) for approximately one hour.

Shelled fresh lima beans may be cooked in salted water for approximately twenty minutes or at five pounds of pressure for approximately ten minutes. Frozen limas in five-pound batches will cook at low pressure in eight to ten minutes and at high steam pressure in approximately five minutes.

Canned beans are usually seasoned or combined with other items after reheating for use. Ham or other pork seasoning, green peppers, corn, or onions may be added for variety.

Broccoli. Broccoli is available fresh or frozen. The fresh variety is best when dark green in color with closed, compact buds and tender but firm stalks. Broccoli should be thoroughly washed and a small amount of the stalk cut off. If the stalks are very mature they should be split lengthwise for more uniform cooking with the buds. Fresh broccoli may be cooked in a low pressure steamer in five-pound batches for approximately fifteen minutes, or in a high pressure steamer for three to five minutes. It may also be cooked in a small amount of water in a steam-jacketed kettle or in a range-top container, kept uncovered during the first few minutes of cooking and later covered, for a total cooking time of about twenty minutes. Frozen broccoli may be cooked in low pressure steam for approximately twelve minutes or in high pressure steam for about three minutes.

Cabbage. Because it is available the year round and has storage qualities, cabbage is usually available only in fresh form. Some is processed into canned sauerkraut. A variety of cabbages are available—the most important being domestic, Danish, Savoy, and red. All cabbage heads should be solid, firm, and heavy for their size. Worms, head decay, and wilting should be avoided where possible. Cabbage may be cooked shredded or in wedges in low pressure steam for ten minutes or in high pressure steam for four to five minutes. It may also be cooked in a large amount of water, uncovered, to volatilize the acids that affect its color and taste. It will take about twelve to fifteen minutes, depending on the size of the cut. An acid substance, such as vinegar or lemon juice, should be added to the cooking medium to help it retain its color. Cabbage may also be cooked in a water and milk combination, which will reduce its strong flavor and lessen the required cooking time.

Carrots. Carrots are available fresh, frozen, or canned. Fresh carrots should be firm, smooth, and free from surface injuries or decay. Most are shipped with the tops removed. To cook fresh carrots, remove the tops, if they are still on, and scrape or peel the vegetable by machine or by hand. Carrots may be diced, sectioned, or kept whole for cooking. The larger carrots are best used in moist cooking recipes such as stews. Carrots may also be shredded or grated for use in salads or cut into sticks for relish trays. Cook fresh carrots in low pressure steam for fifteen to twenty minutes or in high pressure steam for about five to eight minutes. They may also be boiled for twenty to twenty-five minutes. Frozen carrots will cook at low pressure in about eight minutes and at high pressures in about five. Canned carrots come in whole, sliced, or cut forms and are handled like any other canned vegetable. No color or texture problems should arise with carrots, as they are a very hardy vegetable.

Cauliflower. Cauliflower is available both fresh and frozen. Fresh varieties should have compact, white or creamy flowerets, and fresh green outer leaves. To prepare cauliflower the leaves are removed, and the stem growth is cut off. The head is washed and may be soaked in saltwater for ten to fifteen minutes to remove any embedded insects. Flowers are divided into flowerets and cooked in low pressure steam for about ten minutes or in high pressure steam for three to five minutes. Cauliflower may also be cooked in a large amount of boiling water, uncovered, for ten to fifteen minutes. Frozen cauliflower may be cooked in five-pound batches in low pressure steam for five to eight minutes or in high pressure steam for three to five minutes. Tender raw flowerets may be washed, chilled in ice water, and used on relish trays. Cooked cauliflower is often served with a cream or cheese sauce.

Corn. Corn is available fresh, frozen, or canned. Fresh corn may be sold in the husks or without them. In selecting corn, the time between harvest and use is important, since the product readily gives up sugar and tenderness. Choose corn with husks that are bright and that fit the corn firmly, with dark brown silks. Corn should have full ears and be tender and juicy. Large, dry, hard kernels indicate overmaturity. Remove the husks, and cook the ears in a small amount of salted water for about five minutes. Corn may also be steamed under low pressure for about eight minutes or baked for about thirty minutes. Frozen whole kernel corn may be steamed under low pressure for about five minutes or under high pressure for about three minutes. Canned corn, in whole kernel or creamed style, may be heated directly in the juices of the can. Corn may be added to lima beans to make succotash, mixed with other vegetables, served buttered, or used in other dishes.

Eggplant. Eggplant is available most of the year and is therefore used mainly in fresh form. An acceptable eggplant should be firm, and heavy for its size, with a dark purple color to the skin. It should be peeled, washed, and cut into half-inch slices. During the period of preparation it should be kept in salted water to prevent oxidation. Eggplant may be breaded and deep fat fried at 375 degrees for five minutes or baked in a 375 degree oven for thirty minutes and served with a tomato or cheese sauce.

Mushrooms. Mushrooms are available all year in fresh, frozen, canned, or dehydrated form. Quality mushrooms are clean, white or creamy in color, and smooth. Size is not a good indicator of maturity or tenderness as it is with most other vegetables. Fresh mushrooms should be washed, cut or sliced, and cooked in a small amount of water for about three minutes. They may also be broiled for ten minutes, deep fat fried at about 390 degrees for three minutes, or sautéed in a small amount of fat for five minutes. Canned mushrooms are, of course, already cooked and need only reheating for use, while frozen varieties may be handled in the same manner as fresh, except for a slight reduction in the cooking time.

Onions. Dry onions are available in Bermuda, Spanish, or globe varieties, in fresh, frozen, or dehydrated form. Green leeks or shallots are also available, fresh, canned, or processed into convenient forms as flakes, powders, or salts. Fresh dry onions should be firm and clean, with dry skins, while green onions, leeks, shallots, and the like should have green tops, blanched shafts, and crisp and tender texture. Both forms should be washed and have the skin removed. Green onions may be served raw or cooked in a small amount of boiling water for about ten minutes. Dry onions may be boiled uncovered for ten to twenty minutes, sautéed for ten minutes, French fried in rings at 375 degrees for five minutes, or steamed at five pounds of pressure for five to ten minutes. Dry onions may also be used in sandwiches or in other recipes. Bermuda and Spanish onions are mild varieties of the dry type and thus lend themselves to raw use better. Frozen onions may be treated like fresh ones after defrosting. Dehydrated onions may be added to other cooked products containing liquid or rehydrated and then added to uncooked dishes.

Peas. Peas are available all year in fresh, frozen, or canned form. Fresh peas, like corn, lose sugar and flavor very rapidly after picking, and care must be taken to use them soon after purchase. Fresh peas should have well-filled, fresh pods and not be too flat or have surface markings. Peas should be removed from the pods, washed, and cooked in a small amount of water for about eight minutes. Some sugar may be added to the cooking water to increase their sweetness. Peas may also be cooked in low pressure steam for about five minutes or in high pressure steam for about two minutes. Frozen peas will cook in low pressure steam in about four minutes and in high pressure in one to two minutes. Canned peas must be removed from their liquor and the liquor heated before the peas are put back in to heat. They are very tender and will be reduced to pulp in a very short period of extra heating. Dried peas are also available and may be used in soups, meat loaves, and the like.

Peppers. Both sweet and hot peppers are available fresh, canned, or freeze dried. The sweet or bell variety is usually green, and should be firm, well-shaped, and bright. After maturing, these peppers turn bronze or bright red in color. Hot peppers are usually red and generally smaller than the sweet kind. Fresh peppers should be washed and the stems and seeds removed. They may be used as containers for a stuffing or be sautéed, baked, or broiled. If they are to be stuffed they should be parboiled for five minutes or steamed at low pressure for about three minutes before stuffing. The stuffing is also cooked, and then the product is baked at 350 degrees for fifteen minutes. Strips of pepper may be sautéed or added to other dishes. Freeze dried varieties may be rehydrated and used as fresh.

Canned pimientos are already cooked and may be used as a garnish or in recipes.

Potatoes. Potatoes are available fresh, frozen, and dehydrated in a variety of forms. Fresh potatoes are sold in new and mature stages and in boiling and baking varieties. New or immature potatoes are more subject to injury and decay. Look for potatoes that are firm, reasonably well-shaped, and free from surface injuries or decay. Medium-sized potatoes are best for overall use. The russet or Idaho varieties are best for baking because of their higher specific gravity, while potatoes with a lower specific gravity are best for salads, boiling, or hashed browns.

Fresh potatoes should be peeled and washed. They may be cooked by almost any

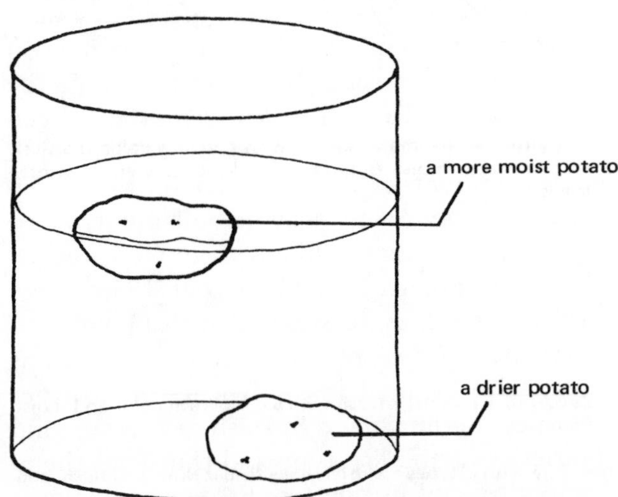

Figure 15a. A salt solution made with one pound of table salt to one gallon of water may be used in a simple test to separate potatoes for various uses, according to their specific gravity. The solution has a specific gravity of 1.08. Potatoes with a specific gravity of more than 1.08 (those with a drier body) will sink. Such potatoes are best used for baking, French frying, and other dry cooking processes. Potatoes with a lower specific gravity (moister ones) will float and are best boiled, for use in potato salad and other dishes.

Butternut, a winter squash with a smooth, light-brown skin and minimal seed area.

Acorn, a winter squash that is dark green in color and quite small.

Hubbard, a winter squash that is very large and may be green, blue, or orange-yellow in color.

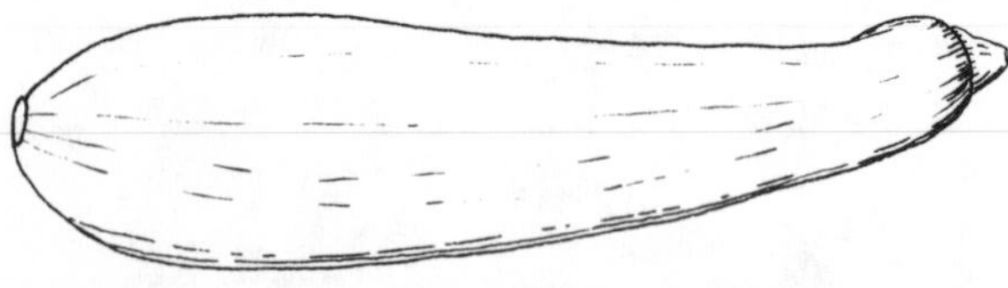

Straightneck, a summer squash with a yellow color and flesh that is more moist but does not keep as well as winter squashes.

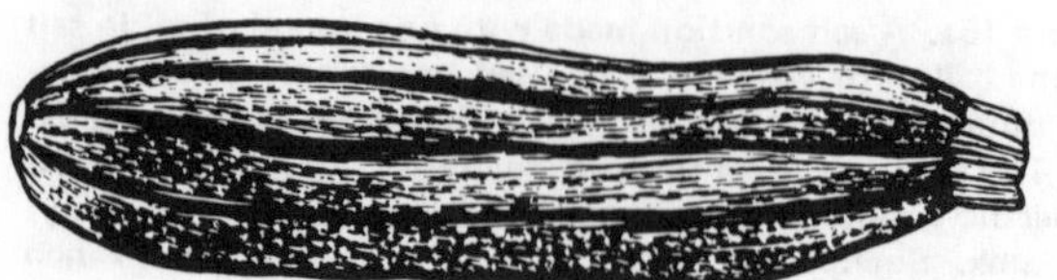

Zucchini, a summer squash with a dark green color and moist flesh.

Figure 15b. Some common varieties of summer and winter squashes. The winter types are drier, have firmer skins and flesh, and keep better than the summer ones.

method. For baking, potatoes should be washed and oiled without peeling. Once peeled, potatoes must be protected against oxidation by the use of an antioxidant agent or a water bath. Temperatures below 50 degrees Fahrenheit may change the starch to sugar, which can cause excessive browning if the potato is deep fried. The change is reversible, however. Potatoes may be baked at 400 degrees for about one hour. They may be deep fried in fat at 375 degrees in about seven minutes. Boiling takes ten to twenty minutes, panfrying ten minutes, and steaming at five pounds of pressure about twelve minutes. Instant potatoes may be mixed with hot milk to produce whipped potatoes. Dehydrated forms may be reconstituted with moisture and used as fresh. Frozen varieties may be French fried, oven-browned, or panfried.

Sweet Potatoes and Yams. Sweet potatoes and yams come fresh or canned. The moister and deeper orange varieties with heavy middles and tapered ends are erroneously referred to as yams, but are actually sweet potatoes. Higher quality fresh potatoes of both types are smooth, firm, and bright in surface appearance. They may be boiled, baked, fried, candied, or glazed. They are cooked peeled or in the jacket. They may be first cooked in the jacket and then the inside may be removed, mixed with other ingredients, and piped back into the jacket. Yams and sweet potatoes boil in about thirty minutes or bake at 250 to 300 degrees in about fifty minutes. They will steam under low pressure in approximately twenty minutes. The canned varieties come whole, mashed, or in pieces. They are completely cooked and need only to be reheated for use.

Spinach and Other Greens. Spinach, beet greens, turnip greens, kale, and the like are available fresh, frozen, or canned. Fresh greens should have good color, be fresh, and be tender. Wash greens well a number of times in different water changes, and remove wilted leaves and damaged stems. Greens cook in low pressure steam in about fifteen minutes. In boiling water in a covered container they take ten to fifteen minutes. Frozen greens will cook in low pressure steam in about five minutes. Canned varieties may be heated directly in their liquor.

Squash. Both summer and winter squashes are available fresh and frozen. Many forms are also sold canned. Most winter squashes are large and have thick skins that are green, bluish-green, or orange in color. Summer squashes are usually smaller, with thinner skins and moister flesh. Summer squashes in fresh form should be heavy in relation to their size, tender, and free from surface damage or decay. Winter squashes should have hard skins and be free of surface decay. Summer squash is usually cooked unpeeled after it has been washed and the stem has been removed, while winter varieties are cut into pieces for cooking with the skin either on or off. Summer squash may be cooked in a small amount of water for twelve to eighteen minutes or steamed at low pressures for about twelve minutes. Winter squash may be cooked in a small amount of water for twenty minutes or in low pressure steam for fifteen minutes. It may also be baked in the oven at 400 degrees for about thirty minutes.

Tomatoes. Tomatoes are available fresh or canned at all seasons of the year. Cherry tomatoes are best for salads, garnishes, and broiling, while larger tomatoes may be selected for specific uses and more general applications. Choose tomatoes that are free from surface bruises, firm, and plump. Tomatoes need no cooking, but they may be cooked in a variety of ways. They are commonly broiled, baked, fried, and stewed. The skin may be easily removed after blanching the tomato in hot water.

Canned tomatoes in whole, paste, or puree form are also available and in many cases are far more advantageous to use than fresh ones. The ultimate use of the product is an important factor in selecting the processed item, since the more concentrated products with higher specific gravities and greater densities command higher prices. The lower grades of whole canned tomatoes, which have fewer whole pieces and lower prices, may be selected if the tomatoes will later be subdivided in the particular recipe.

Fruits

Fruits are the seed-bearing parts of plants. They contain 80 to 90 percent moisture in the form of water. They are rich in carbohydrates (starches and sugars) and are similar in structure to vegetables—cellulose and pectin substances form their framework. Fruits are much higher in sugars, and resulting sweetness, than vegetables are and have liberal amounts of vitamins and minerals, notably vitamins A and C, calcium, copper, and iron. The cooking of fruits is limited to baking, broiling, sautéing, blanching, or using them in baked goods recipes. Most, however, are eaten raw because of their sweet taste and delicate texture.

The basic preparation problems with fruits are ensuring adequate washing procedures and protecting particular fruits from oxidation and discoloration. Although surface characteristics are important in the grading and selection of fruits, these may have little relation to use and defects often do not impair the eating quality of the product.

Fresh fruits are most often used in salads, in fruit bowls, in fruit cups, on cereals, as appetizers, as garnishes, and in some baked products. Most baking, however, and many other recipes use processed fruits that have been frozen or canned after being specifically selected for the use to which they will best relate.

Preparation of Specific Fruits

Apples. Apples are one of the most widely used fruits in the United States. Hardness, firmness, and good surface coloring are important characteristics to look for in selection. Highly acid varieties are best used for baking, while the sweeter, less tart varieties lend themselves better to raw uses. A few apples may be used successfully for either purpose. Varieties such as Gravensteins, greenings, and McIntoshes are very good for baking and general cooking, while delicious, Rome beauties, and northern spies are very good dessert apples. Cortlands are the best for salads because of their ability to resist surface darkening or discoloration after cutting. Apples may be baked, made into salads, used in sauces, or used in desserts. Most facilities use a canned spiced apple for a garnish and a frozen solid pack for pie and other bakery products.

Avocados. Avocados are desirable fruits for fruit cups and salads. Medium-sized avocados that are firm but starting to soften are the most desirable to buy. The fruit is cut lengthwise all around the outside and extending in to the seed. Then the two halves are twisted in opposite directions to loosen them from the seed. The skin is peeled off and the flesh dipped in lemon juice to prevent discoloration. The avocado half may be filled with a shrimp or other salad or the flesh may be divided into strips or balls for use in a salad or garnish.

Bananas. Bananas are one of the few fruits that develop ripeness and better flavor after harvesting. They are available fresh or canned and are used in salads, cereals, fruit cups, and a variety of desserts, both baked and unbaked. Choose fresh bananas that are plump and have green tips and good yellow coloring. Cakes, pies, and puddings can use the canned variety as well as the fresh with little loss of quality.

Berries. Blueberries, blackberries, loganberries, raspberries, and strawberries are seasonal fruits. In fresh form, they have shorter lives than many other forms of fruit. Many are also available in frozen or canned processed form, and for general cooking or baking purposes these give the food operator more flexibility. Select berries that are bright, clean, and fresh in appearance, and check the packing boxes for stains that indicate crushing. Berries must be washed and inspected before use in a particular recipe. All should be used in a relatively short time because of their rapid spoilage rate. The frozen and canned varieties are good for general use when fresh berries are out of season.

Cherries. Cherries come in sweet and sour varieties. They may be used fresh as a dessert fruit. In canned or frozen form, they find much greater use in garnishes or for baking. The sour cherry, of course, is used more in baking than the sweet varieties, such as bing or lambert. Pitted cherries packed in water are available canned for most baking recipe use.

Grapefruit. Grapefruit is a classic breakfast fruit, an appetizer, or a dessert item. It is available from either California or Florida and may be served halved, cut into segments, or as juice. It is also sold in segments in fresh form or canned, and as juice canned. Grapefruits are available in seedless and pink varieties. These may be selected for specific purposes. Quality is determined by firmness, thin skins, and heavy weight for the size of the fruit. In preparing grapefruit for use the flesh must be separated from the membranes to make eating easier. The entire pulp may be removed and the skin refilled with a mixture of fruits or other food items.

Lemons and Limes. Lemons and limes are most often used in beverages and for garnishes in food preparation. Firmness, brightness, and good weight for the size are indicators of quality. It is important to select fruit of an appropriate size for the use to which it will be put. Little use is generally made of these products in baking because mixes are more readily available.

Melons. Honeydew, Persian, Cranshaw, casaba, and cantaloupe are available fresh. Since many factors determine quality, such as flavor, time of picking, and surface condition, the only reasonable test is a cut into the flesh. Most melons are used as appetizers or desserts, simply cut into balls or wedges. Some, such as the cantaloupe, may also be filled with other fruits or ices.

Oranges. Oranges may be purchased for juice or for general table use. With such a variety of concentrates available, it is not considered worthwhile in most instances to buy juice oranges. Firmness, heaviness, and skin texture give indications of quality. Oranges may also be purchased fresh in sectioned form. The navel orange is easier to section than other varieties and is best for table consumption.

Peaches, Pears, and Plums. Peaches, pears, and plums are used mostly as dessert items, as garnishes, or in general cooking. The average food service operation will probably use only a small number of these fruits in fresh form, and most will be purchased in canned or frozen form. Style, count, syrup density, and processing (such as spicing) are the major considerations in purchasing and using these fruits. No preliminary preparation is needed, and no unusual processing problems should be encountered.

Pineapples. Pineapples may provide an unusual merchandising item in a particular menu pattern. Used on a buffet table at a reception or halved and scooped out as the container for a salad, a pineapple may make a most effective display piece. In most circumstances, however, processed pineapple in precounted slices, crushed, or in tidbits and in a specific type of syrup is a much more desirable item for quantity food work. If fresh pineapple is purchased, the outside covering should be used. Select pineapples that are firm, bright, and clean, and inspect the bases for softness and decay. A pineapple may be cut with a meat saw and the flesh may be scooped out to provide a very attractive salad bowl. The whole fruit uncut may be used for table appointments.

16 *Eggs, Cheese, Milk, and Cereals*

Objective: To introduce the student to the composition, grading systems, and uses of eggs, cheese, milk, and cereal products. Products derived from these foods, special forms, and convenience items are all discussed. Cooking methods for each category are given, including problem areas.

Eggs

Although some societies use the eggs of many birds as food, in the United States chicken eggs are of most importance to food operations. Some eggs from ducks and geese are also used, but in small amounts compared to the number of chicken eggs.

Structure and Composition

Eggs are a complete protein food, providing the proteins that sustain life and that replace and repair body tissue. They are very versatile and may be used in almost any aspect of food service work. Eggs provide liberal amounts of vitamin A, vitamin B_2 (riboflavin), phosphorus, iron, and fat, in addition to the amino acids that make them a complete protein.

Eggs are provided with a protective but porous shell. They have two distinct internal ingredients, the yolk and the white.

The Shell. The shell protects the egg. It is basically composed of calcium substances. The shell is porous, but it has a covering substance called the *bloom* that limits the passage of substances in either direction through it. As an egg ages, the bloom disappears, and this permits more rapid deterioration of the egg: internal materials then evaporate through the unprotected shell, resulting in shrinkage of the contents.

Shell color has no relationship to the quality, grade, or desirable use of the egg; it relates only to the breed of hen that laid the egg. Any color of egg may be used in any method of food preparation. Some consideration must be given, however, to the desires of the customers. If a facility's consumers do believe the color of the shell is important, provisions should be made to ensure that the preferred color is used. New Englanders, for example, prefer the brown egg to the white for most uses.

The egg shell is pliable when it is laid by the hen; it solidifies as the egg enters the atmosphere. The substances within the shell also shrink, because of the change in temperature, and this causes an air cell to form between the shell and the contents. The candling process (projecting a strong, concentrated light through the translucent shell to determine the inside condition of the egg) will

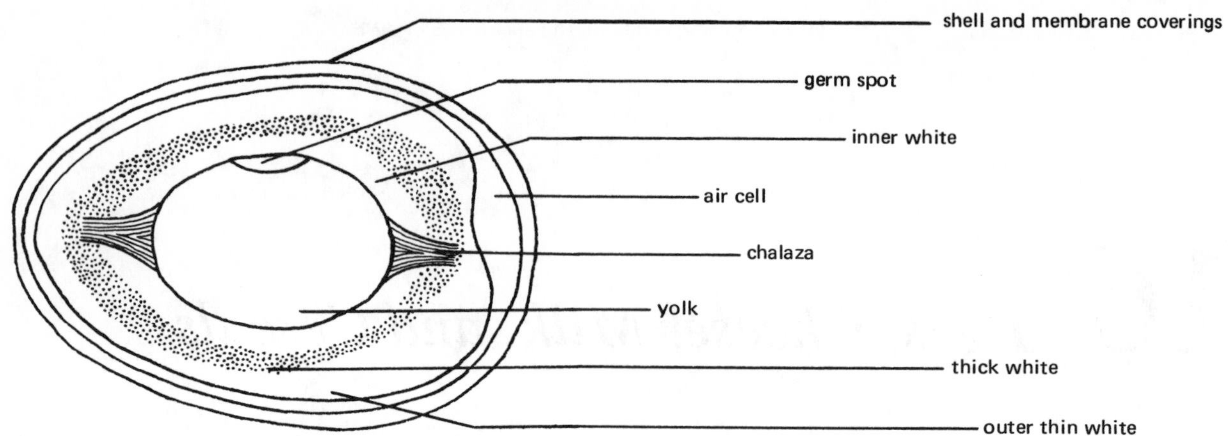

Figure 16a. A cross section of a hen's egg showing the major parts that are important in preparation. As the egg ages, the yolk shifts from its central position, and the air cell becomes larger owing to the loss of matter through evaporation.

usually show the air cell located at the large end of the egg.

Internal Contents. Given the proper time and temperature, a fertile egg would, of course, become a young chick. Everything in the egg is designed for this purpose. Of course, most eggs that are eaten are not fertilized and provide nutrients in their original form. Some health food faddists, however, pay premium prices for eggs that are developing chick embryos.

The *white* of the egg is basically composed of protein and albumin. It is of varying viscousness and contains three different layers, although only two are discernible when the egg is broken from the shell—an outside layer of thin white and an inside layer of thicker and more viscous white. A thick, white, cordlike material called a chalaza is part of the inner layer of white not discernible once outside the shell. Two chalazae hold the yolk in suspension within the shell. As the egg becomes older the egg white becomes more watery, and, when broken out of the shell, the egg becomes less able to hold a concentrated shape on a plate, pan, or grill. This may be used as an indicator of the quality and/or age of an egg.

The *yolk* provides the fat and minerals in the egg. As noted, it is held in a central position within the white by anchoring chalazae. In lower quality eggs, the yolk loses its central position as the white becomes more watery and its holding power weakens. This shift is a noticeable indication of quality in eggs that are broken out of the shell. The yolk, too, may become more liquid and less firm with age, owing to a transfer of fluid from the surrounding white. This may cause the yolk of an older egg to rupture more easily when broken from the shell or at least to spread more, producing a less concentrated and upstanding appearance.

The color of the yolk may vary in intensity from light yellow to deep orange-yellow. The color has no relation to the age or food value of the egg. It varies with the type of feed eaten by the hen and the breed of the bird. The yolk contains the fat-soluble vitamin A and most of the other nutrients in the egg, except the protein and a portion of the riboflavin (which are both found in the white).

Grades and Sizes

Eggs are classified by grade and by size. The grade indicates the internal quality of the egg and the appearance and condition of its outside shell. The size indicates the minimum

U.S. CONSUMER GRADES
Interior quality; condition and appearance of shell

top views

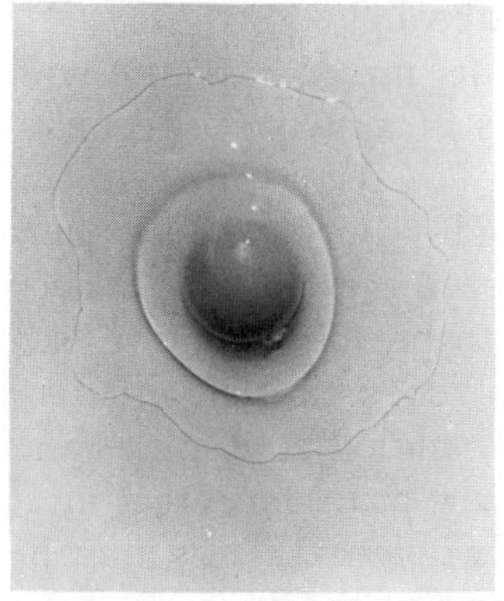
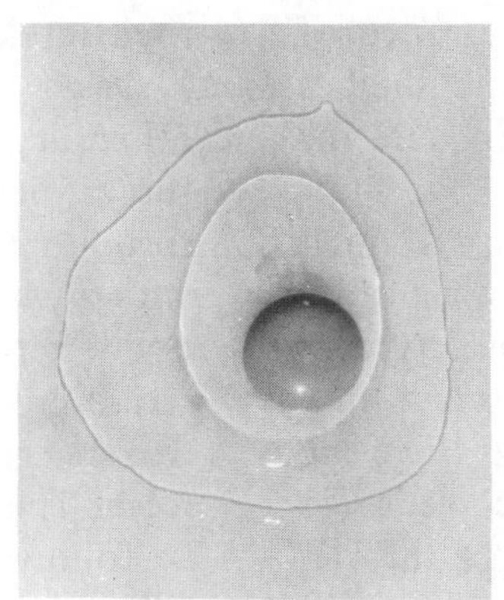
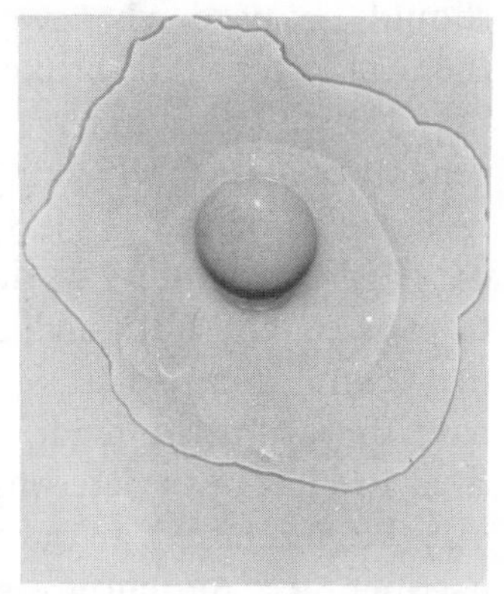

side views

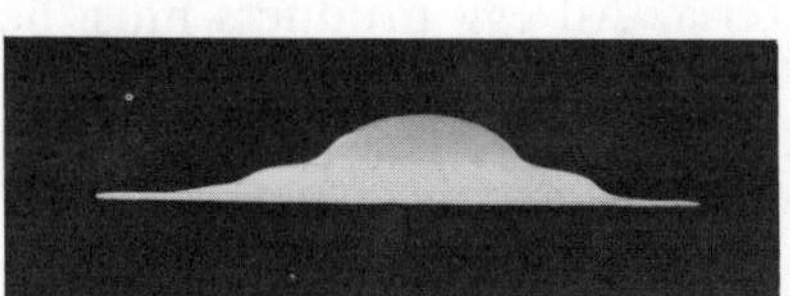
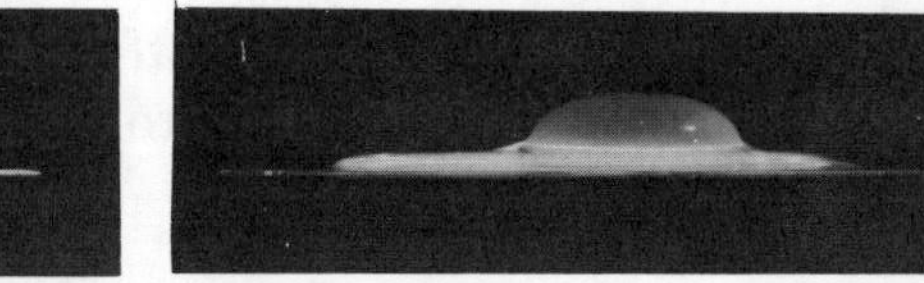
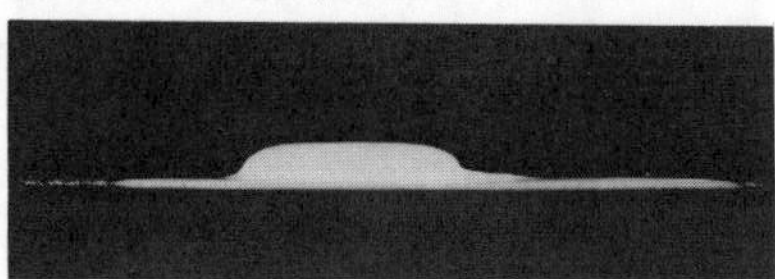

Grade AA (or Fresh Fancy): egg covers a small area; white is thick, stands high; yolk is firm and high

Grade A: egg covers a moderate area; white is reasonably thick, stands fairly high; yolk is firm and high

Grade B: egg covers a wide area; has a small amount of thick white; yolk is somewhat flattened and enlarged

U.S. WEIGHT CLASSES
Minimum weight per dozen

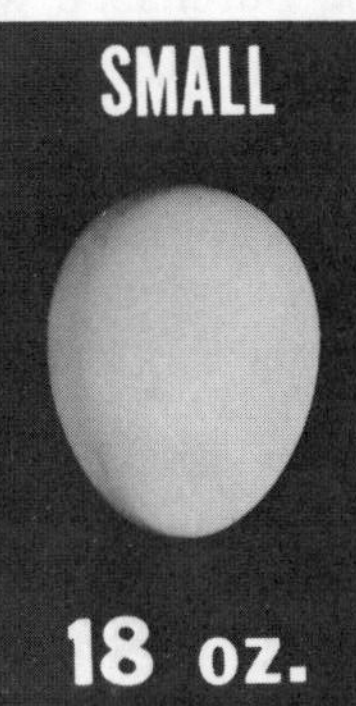

Minimum weight per thirty-dozen case: jumbo, 56 lbs.; extra large, 50½ lbs.; large, 45 lbs.; medium 39½ lbs.; small, 34 lbs.; peewee, 28 lbs.

Figure 16b. Grade and size classifications for eggs. (Courtesy of the United States Department of Agriculture, Washington, D.C.)

weight per dozen. Eggs of the highest quality carry the United States Department of Agriculture grade AA (or Fresh Fancy), while lower quality eggs, in descending order, are graded A, B, or C. The higher grade eggs should be used whenever the appearance of the egg after it is broken from the shell is important. The lower grades are adequate for general cooking and baking.

The size of the egg has no relation to quality. Eggs are graded in six sizes, from jumbo to peewee, and both high and low quality eggs may come in any size. Size should accommodate the use to be made of the egg. Once the final use has been determined, the correct size may be purchased. In purchasing eggs, the Department of Agriculture suggests as a general rule of thumb that when the price per dozen of a larger size is less than seven cents more than the price of the next smaller size within the same grade, the larger size should be purchased for the best value.

Convenience Egg Products

Eggs may also be purchased in forms suited to specific purposes of a quantity food operation. Hard-cooked eggs are sold in tubes, ready for cutting and sectioning. Raw eggs are available dried or frozen. Dried and frozen eggs are available whole, or yolks and whites may be bought separately. Convenience forms of eggs should be purchased when they offer the maximum benefit from the product for the eventual use that will be made of it.

A convenience egg product that is made of egg whites plus a substitute for the yolks is available for use by those desiring to restrict their intake of cholesterol.

Dried eggs may be mixed directly with other dry ingredients of a recipe or reconstituted before use. To reconstitute them, sprinkle them in cold water and mix them with a wire whip. Frozen eggs must be thawed under refrigeration, to prevent excessive bacterial growth. Once reconstituted, dried or frozen eggs may be handled as if they were fresh. The strict sanitary procedures that must be followed in using whole fresh eggs must be adhered to in using one of convenience forms as well, because either form may contain salmonella bacteria. All egg products must be heated to sufficiently high temperatures during cooking to destroy any bacteria they may harbor.

Uses of Eggs

Eggs are a most versatile food, with numerous uses in food preparation work. They may serve in their natural form as a breakfast food or as a salad ingredient. They may act as a leavening agent in such foods as cakes and soufflés. They are used to thicken such products as custards and sauces, and they bind ingredients together in dishes such as meat loaf

Table 16-1. Equivalent Amounts of Eggs in Different Forms

Form	Amount	Equivalent Weight, Measure, or Number
Fresh eggs		
whole	10 eggs	2 cups (1 pint) or 1 lb.
	1 dozen	1.5 lbs.
	1 lb.	1 lb. frozen eggs or 5 oz. dried eggs + 1 cup water
yolks	2 dozen	2 cups (1 pint) or 1 lb.
whites	16 egg whites	2 cups (1 pint) or 1 lb.
Dried eggs		
whole	1 lb. + 5 cups water	36 fresh eggs whole
yolks	1 lb. + 1-3/4 cups water	54 fresh egg yolks
whites	1 lb. + 10-1/2 cups water	100 fresh egg whites
Frozen eggs		
whole	1 lb.	10-1/2 fresh eggs whole
yolks	1 lb.	29 fresh egg yolks
whites	1 lb.	16 fresh egg whites

or in procedures such as breading for deep fat frying. They may be used to clarify a soup stock, to glaze a baked product, to emulsify a salad dressing, or to garnish a menu item. Eggs also color, flavor, and contribute food value to the dishes in which they are used.

The following general suggestions are made concerning the use of eggs:

(a) It is most important that the quality of the egg relate to its intended use. Where appearance and flavor are less important, such as in baking, thickening, or binding applications, lower grade eggs may be used with equal effectiveness and with better expenditure of funds than higher grade eggs.

(b) The coagulation of the egg protein is one of the main results desired in the use of eggs. This may be accomplished either by applying heat or by violent agitation such as whipping or beating. The following considerations are important:

(1) Egg protein coagulates at 140 to 158 degrees Fahrenheit, depending on whether the white is used alone or in combination with the yolk. The white alone coagulates at lower temperatures than a combination of the two. Other ingredients combined with the egg may act to raise or lower the coagulation temperature. Sugar, for example, raises the temperature, while acids tend to lower it. Too high a temperature or exposure of the egg to heat for too long a period of time will toughen the egg and squeeze fluid out of it. This process, known as syneresis, is demonstrated in many a pan of scrambled eggs that has been held on a steam table awaiting service. Salt is another important element in hastening the coagulation of egg protein. The addition of salt to a recipe will enable eggs to cook at lower temperatures.

(2) The coagulation of an egg by beating is best reserved for the white alone. If fat from the yolk or from some exterior source is included, it may prevent or seriously hinder the coagulation. Eggs are easier to separate for beating when they have been warmed to room temperature. Beating then produces a greater volume as well. Supervisors must make sure that excessive beating is not carried out, for it will result in a dry product and less volume. Firm peaks are all that are required in most recipes. The addition of an agent such as sugar, lemon juice, or cream of tartar will stabilize the egg white and enable it to hold more air, thus increasing its volume during coagulation. These products should be added late in the whipping period to ensure maximum volume without unduly extending the processing time.

(3) Keep the temperature ranges low and the cooking processes slow for eggs. Prepare eggs as close to serving times as possible, by batch cooking or cooking to order for a la carte menu systems. If eggs *must* be held or transported while hot, undercook them slightly to compensate for the further heating that they will experience.

(4) In poaching eggs ensure that the water is kept at simmering temperature. The addition of two teaspoons of vinegar to each pint of water will help keep the egg white from spreading in the water. Break the egg into a bowl or dish and slip it into a shallow, simmering water bath. After coagulation has taken place, remove the egg with a slotted spoon.

(5) Use simmering temperatures to cook soft- or hard-boiled eggs. After removal from the cooking container, the egg should be placed immediately in cold water to stop the cooking process. This will also make removal of the shells easier if that is required. Hard- or soft-cooked eggs may also be prepared in a steamer. Hard-cooked eggs that are to be mixed with other foods later may be steamed after being broken into a pan. Overcooking hard-boiled eggs (particularly lower grade eggs) will produce a black or greenish ring around the yolk, because iron substances in the yolk join with sulfur compounds in the white and form ferrous sulfide.

(6) For fried eggs, omelets, and scrambled eggs, use a grill or an omelet pan. Un-

salted butter or a vegetable-based grill frying agent will help to prevent sticking. Omelets and scrambled eggs are both beaten until the yolks and whites are mixed. A ladle is used to measure portions onto the cooking surface. Fried eggs should be broken into individual dishes before cooking. For scrambled eggs, add half an eggshellful (or one tablespoon) of water or milk for each egg used. Agitation of the pan, gentle stirring, or raising the coagulated portion to let the uncoagulated portion run underneath will keep omelets or scrambled eggs more tender. Baking powder may be added to omelet recipes for greater fluffiness. Fried eggs must always be made with high grade eggs to ensure that the yolk does not break. When breaking a quantity of eggs for cooking, break each egg first into a small dish, and then add it to the larger container with the others. This ensures that one bad quality egg will not contaminate the batch, since it will be discovered before it is added to the others.

(c) Only whole eggs are used as binding or coating agents. The egg is beaten just enough to mix the white with the yolk completely. Then it is ready to be used for the purpose intended. When used as a binding agent (in meat loaf, for example), the egg is mixed directly with the other food items. For breading, eggs are mixed with milk in a ratio of four or five eggs to each quart of milk. The product to be breaded is dredged with flour and immersed in this egg-milk mixture, which furnishes the sticky gluten substance that holds the bread crumbs on the surface when they are applied in the last step of the procedure. Egg wash mixtures of five or six eggs to each quart of milk are painted on bread or pastry products to give them an attractive surface glaze and browning. The mixture is brushed on the tops of pies, yeast rolls, and similar items before they are baked.

(d) Eggs to be used for thickening should be beaten just enough to combine the yolks and whites. They are used in such products as custards and fondues. The proportion of egg to liquid and the amounts of other ingredients that either hinder or aid coagulation of egg protein will determine the degree of thickening produced. In mixing eggs with hot products, it is important to temper the egg mixture to prevent the egg yolk from overcooking. Tempering is accomplished by adding a small amount of the hot mixture to the egg while rapidly stirring the two. The egg mixture may then be added to the rest of the hot mixture. It is also possible to temper the eggs by adding the whole hot mixture to them if rapid agitation of the combination is carried out during the adding process. Egg mixtures should be protected against long exposure to high temperatures. This may be accomplished by using a double boiler on the range top or a water bath for oven-baked products such as custards. All egg-thickened products should be tested for completion of cooking and thickening. The product should have the ability to cling to and coat a utensil, such as a spoon, or a baked egg-thickened product should show no evidence of coating when an implement such as a knife is inserted in the middle of it.

Preventing Problems in Preparing Eggs

Fried Eggs. The most common faults in fried eggs are yolks that break too easily and hard, rubbery texture. Fragile yolks are most often found in low quality eggs. Tough consistency results from cooking at too high a temperature. Covering the egg while it cooks or basting it with fat will prevent excessive hardness from developing. Fried eggs may be prepared in a fry pan, on a grill, or in a roast pan. They cook within five minutes. If at all possible, eggs should be prepared to order. If the eggs are broken ahead of time and sufficient work surface is provided, this can be handled by any type of quantity food service.

Scrambled Eggs. Tough, rubbery, or weeping eggs are the most common problems of scrambled eggs. These conditions are usually caused by excessive heat, holding, or the addition of too much moisture to the eggs. When large masses of scrambled eggs are cooked care must be taken to allow for postpreparation heating, and eggs should therefore be removed from the heat while still slightly undercooked.

Hard-cooked Eggs. Excessively high temperatures will cause hard-cooked eggs to toughen and may cause a greenish black ring to develop around the yolk. Eggs should be cooked at below-boiling temperatures for twenty to thirty minutes. Quickly cooling the egg in cold water will prevent further cooking and make shell removal easier.

Putting cold eggs into hot water, or dropping eggs into the pot with little care will cause shells to break. A few drops of vinegar or lemon juice in the cooking water helps prevent shell breakage and keeps leakage to a minimum.

Poached Eggs. Unattractive appearance and excessive spreading of the egg white are two of the main problems that arise in poaching eggs. They may be prevented by not permitting the water to boil, which diffuses the egg white, and by adding a little vinegar to the water to assist coagulation.

Soufflés. The major problems in soufflés are insufficient volume, falling after removal from the oven, and toughness. Beating the egg foam too little or too much, mixing it too vigorously with the other ingredients, or exposure of the soufflé to extreme temperature changes may cause loss of volume. Excessively high oven temperatures will usually cause toughening unless the soufflé is baked in a water bath protection. Reduced temperatures are more often used to eliminate the need for a water bath. Baking at a moderate temperature, not permitting the soufflé to experience dramatic changes in temperature (e.g., from an extremely hot oven to a drafty room), and immediate service after completion of baking will help to prevent collapses.

Custards. Common problems with custards are curdling, failure to thicken properly, and toughness. Curdling usually occurs because excessive heat is applied. Insufficient thickening of a baked custard is generally a result of undercooking. Toughening occurs from exposure of the custard to long periods of heat. A water bath will prevent this.

Omelets. The major problems with omelets relate to ensuring attractiveness of appearance and avoiding toughness in the underside while the upper portion cooks. Excessive cooking can also cause overdryness. Using a seasoned pan of the correct size and running the uncooked upper portion under the coagulated portion will reduce toughening. Practice in preparing omelets will bring improvements in their appearance. Modified omelet pans that produce the fold are available and may be used if desired.

Darkening of Eggs. Color changes may appear in any egg product that is cooked in an aluminum pan, particularly if it is stirred with a metal spoon. This may be prevented by using a wooden spoon for stirring eggs or by cooking them only in pans made of other metals.

Distinguishing Cooked and Uncooked Eggs. If hard-cooked and raw eggs are both put in the same refrigerator and get mixed, they may be identified by spinning them. The hard-cooked egg will spin, while the uncooked egg will make only one or two turns because its uncooked contents are less stable.

Cheese

Cheese is a dairy food made from whole milk, skimmed milk, or a mixture of the two. Milk from cows, goats, mares, and ewes is used in different cheeses. The names of many cheeses are derived from their places of origin. Cheese is a complete protein food and furnishes generous amounts of fat, calcium, phosphorus, and vitamin A. It is available in many forms to meet many tastes, and it may be used in all courses of a meal from appetizer through dessert.

Cheeses are classified according to their method of manufacture, the percentage of moisture they contain, and whether they are ripened. All cheese is manufactured by coagulation of the milk proteins casein and lactalbumin, using either the enzyme rennet or increased acidity. Most cheeses are processed

Table 16-2. Types, Uses, and Storage of Cheeses

Type of Cheese	Color, Texture, Flavor	Shape	Use	Storage
Blue	Blue-veined; crumbly; semisoft to hard; sharp, salty flavor	Wedge; 6-in-. round	Appetizers; salads; salad dressings; cooked foods; desserts	Refrigerated, wrapped to retain moisture; keeps three weeks or more
Brick	Creamy yellow; semisoft; small holes; mild to sharp flavor	Loaf; brick	Appetizers; sandwiches; salads; desserts	Refrigerated, wrapped to retain moisture; keeps two weeks
Camembert	Creamy, with edible white crust; soft; surface-ripened	Wedge; round cake	On crackers or with fruit, for appetizers or desserts	Refrigerated; keeps up to one week
Cheddar	White to orange; hard; mild to sharp in flavor depending on aging	Circular; wedge; slice	Appetizers; sandwiches; salads; cooked foods; desserts. Most popular cheese in the United States	Refrigerated, wrapped to retain moisture; keeps three weeks or more
Cream	White; nonripened; soft and smooth; mild, delicate flavor	Package; loaf	Appetizers, sandwiches; salads; cooked foods; desserts	Refrigerated, wrapped to retain moisture; keeps up to one week
Edam	Red wax outer surface, yellow interior; semisoft to hard; nutlike flavor	Loaf; cannon ball	Appetizers; salads; cooked foods; desserts	Refrigerated, wrapped to retain moisture; keeps three weeks or more
Gouda	Red wax outer surface, creamy yellow interior; semisoft; nutlike flavor	Spherical with flat end	Appetizers; salads; cooked foods; desserts	Refrigerated, wrapped to retain moisture; keeps three weeks or more
Mozzarella (pizza)	White; stretchy; nonripened; soft; when served hot becomes chewy	Irregularly spherical	Appetizers; cooked foods	Refrigerated, covered; keeps up to one week
Muenster	Creamy white; semisoft; tiny holes; pungent flavor	Cylindrical and flat; loaf shape	Appetizers; sandwiches	Refrigerated, wrapped; keeps about two weeks
Parmesan	Yellow-white; hard; sharp flavor	Wedge; grated	Grated on soups, breads, spaghetti; used in cooked foods	Cured; keeps indefinitely
Provolone	Light yellow; semihard; smooth and somewhat plastic; mellow, smoky flavor	Pear-shaped; sausage-shaped	Appetizers; sandwiches; cooked foods; desserts	Refrigerated, wrapped to retain moisture; keeps three weeks or more
Ricotta	White; nonripened; soft, cottage-type cheese; sweet	Similar to cottage cheese	Appetizers; salads; cooked foods; desserts	Refrigerated, wrapped to retain freshness; keeps up to one week
Romano	Yellow-white; hard; granular; piquant flavor	Wedge; grated	Grated for seasoning	Refrigerated if whole; dry grated keeps indefinitely
Swiss	Light yellow; large holes; hard; nutlike, sweet flavor	Slice; circular or loaf block	Appetizers; sandwiches; salads; cooked foods	Refrigerated, wrapped to retain moisture; keeps two weeks

from the curd, which then separates, although a few are made from the whey portion. Cheeses are classified as hard, semihard, semisoft, and soft, depending on their percentage of moisture. The harder varieties contain 30 to 40 percent moisture. They store and resist spoilage better. The softer varieties, with higher percentages of moisture, are much more perishable. All four types of cheese may be further classified on the basis of the extent and type of ripening or aging they undergo. Most cheeses (except a few of the soft varieties) are ripened. Bacteria and molds are the main ripening agents. Aging reduces the percentage of moisture in a cheese, contributes a more distinctive flavor, and reduces the toughness that newly manufactured cheeses have.

Cheese may also be purchased in processed and "cheese food" forms, classified according to the amount of moisture, the percentage of solid or fat, and the emulsifiers or other ingredients that have been added. These have many general food applications, because their unique mixtures and processing enable them to endure some food preparation techniques better than unprocessed cheeses.

Cheese Cookery

All cheeses, like other dairy products, must be cooked as short a time as possible and at moderate temperatures. Attempts must be made to protect the cheese against exposure to direct heat or extreme temperatures. The use of measures such as breading or positioning the cheese carefully in a prepared dish may protect it against excessive broiler or oven temperatures. A double boiler may be used to protect cheese against range temperatures that are too high. Excessive temperatures may make cheese tough and stringy, as the fat is melted and separated from the remainder of the cheese. Naturally the amount of fat in the cheese will determine its ability to withstand high temperatures. Cheeses with higher percentages of fat will still have more left at the end of cooking although some has been lost in the process.

Grating or dividing cheese before cooking will also aid in producing a more acceptable dish, because the cooking process may be accelerated without excessive exposure to heat. In most recipes, when the cheese has melted it is ready for service.

If the cheese used in a sauce curdles because too much fat has separated from the protein, it may sometimes be recombined into an acceptable sauce by rapid beating, provided the heating process has not been carried too far. The main protection against failure, however, is use of moderate temperatures and short cooking times.

Processed cheeses and cheese foods generally have greater spreading ability and have fewer cooking hazards than most natural cheeses. The uncured, soft cheeses, such as mozzarella, demonstrate a characteristic stringiness and elasticity when exposed to heat. Although this may be a desirable and expected result in some products, such as pizza, in others, such as sauces, sandwiches, and casseroles, the aged or emulsified cheeses or cheese foods will give much better results.

Purchasing and Storage of Cheese

Cheeses and cheese foods may be purchased in almost as many forms as there are varieties of cheeses. Common forms include loaves, blocks, wedges, cylindrical wheels, packages, balls, slices, and bricks. Cheese is also sold grated or mixed with other ingredients, such as croutons and green peppers for use in salads.

To maintain maximum quality, cheeses should be kept refrigerated and well wrapped to prevent loss of moisture. The harder cheeses store well, and the softer and uncured varieties have a very short shelf life. Pasteurized and processed packaged cheeses and cheese foods need no special storage conditions until they are opened. After that they should also be refrigerated to keep well for maximum periods. The hard cheeses may be frozen, if longer storage is desired, and will maintain their moisture and flavor for longer periods in this condition.

Milk

Defined as the most nearly perfect food for man, milk has been used for centuries. The milk of animals, a by-product of animal gestation, provides man with protein, fat, carbohydrate, calcium, and riboflavin. It is also usually supplemented with liberal amounts of vitamin D.

The basic types available and the uses of milk as a beverage and in desserts have been covered in chapter 12. This chapter discusses the use of milk in general food preparation procedures and the major processes it undergoes.

Milk is marketed in many forms, including whole fresh, skimmed, buttermilk, and cream. It may be processed into condensed, evaporated, or dried milk. It is the basic ingredient of ice cream, butter, cheese, yogurt, and sour cream.

Milk Cookery

When milk is used in recipes it must be protected against direct heat applications, excessively high temperatures, and lengthy exposure to heat. The acids and tannins contained in some foods also cause problems when combined with milk in recipes.

The protein of milk, casein, may be precipitated by salt, acids, tannins, and excessive heat. The lactalbumin of milk is the main constituent of the scum that may form when milk is heated. Lactose, or milk sugar, causes browning when overheated. These are the main problems that arise when milk is used in cooking.

Heating. Milk must always be heated at moderate temperatures or over a water bath. Stirring the product will prevent scorching on the surface of the pan or container. Covering the container and adding a fat to the surface of the milk will assist in preventing formation of a surface skin.

Acid. When milk is to be mixed with a food that is high in acid or with vegetables containing large amounts of tannins, both of which may curdle the milk, the use of a white sauce is recommended. This helps to neutralize the acid and protect the milk protein. Because milk has a pH of about 6.6, introducing it into a highly acid environment generally causes it to curdle. Some recipes call for the addition of small amounts of baking soda to act as a buffering agent in the mixture and keep the pH of the recipe higher (less acid).

Butter

Although butter is a form of fat, it is considered in this chapter because its dairy nature imposes requirements on its use that are similar to those of other dairy products. Made from sweet or sour cream, and graded by the U.S. Department of Agriculture on a scale ranging from Grade AA or 93 score through cooking grade or no-grade butter, it is available in one-pound packages (in quarters or solid) and in five- and twelve-pound packages of patties, with 72 or 90 to the pound. Butter contains some 80 percent milk fat by weight and has similar characteristics to the cream from which it is made, requiring most of the same cooking precautions. It may be used as a spread, in baking, as a seasoning and coating for vegetables, and in frying. Like milk, it browns very readily under high temperatures, and, because of its fat content and milk basis, it will burn rapidly when used as a frying medium if the heat is not adequately controlled.

Margarine, a vegetable-based substitute, has replaced butter in many cooking applications because of its lower cost. With fortification of nutrients and improved processing methods, it closely approximates butter. The identification of cholesterol as a possible factor in causing heart disease has given margarine an advantage over butter that helps to overcome some of its less desirable features. As dairy-producing states have relaxed their restrictions on the coloring and mixing procedures used for margarine, it has received more and more widespread use. Margarine may also contain hydrogenated animal fats, however. If cholesterol content is a dietary concern, the specific ingredients of the margarine must be determined.

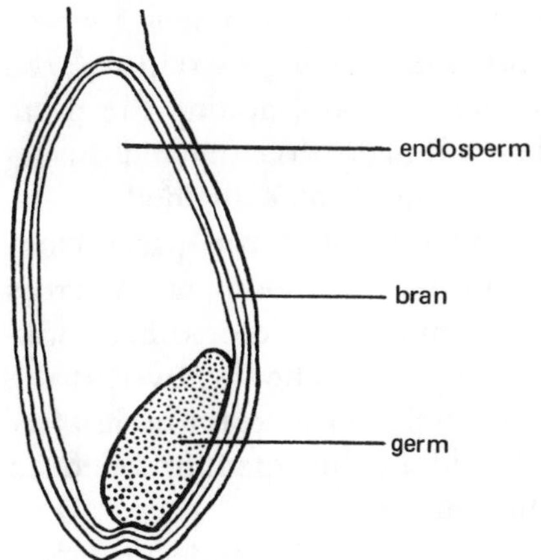

Figure 16c. A cross section of a wheat kernel, showing the major parts. Although grains differ slightly in makeup, all have the same major components. Bran layers contain cellulose, with some protein and minerals. The germ is rich in minerals, vitamins, fat, and protein. The endosperm contains the major part of the food supply and is composed mostly of starch.

Cereals and Grains

Cereals and grains are made from wheat, oats, corn, rice, and barley. Classed as carbohydrate foods, they are the edible seeds of these grasses. Cereals may be used as breakfast foods, be processed into pasta products, or be made into flours. All are good sources of protein. Depending on the particular part of the grain kernel that is used, they may also provide liberal amounts of iron, phosphorus, and thiamine.

All grains used for food have the same basic structural components: outer bran, endosperm, and germ. The bran contains the greatest amount of cellulose plus some protein, the endosperm is the carbohydrate component, and the germ is richest in protein, fats, and vitamins.

For use as breakfast foods, cereal grains may be processed unbroken, cracked, flaked, rolled, puffed, or produced in granular form. They may be enriched, made ready to eat, or partially cooked. As flours, grains are ground and may be bleached or enriched. (The various forms and uses of flours are considered in chapter 17 on baking.) For pasta, the flours of grains are made into doughs and shaped or cut into such products as macaroni, spaghetti, and noodles.

Grain Cookery

Whatever the particular form of grain, the basic considerations in cooking are to reduce the cellulose to a more chewable mass, to gelatinize the starch, and to process the protein. Particular cooking procedures must be varied to meet the demonstrated needs of the specific cereal used and the form in which it was purchased.

Breakfast Cereals. Lumping is a major problem in cooked breakfast cereals (and many other starch products as well). To avoid it, breakfast cereals should be poured into rapidly boiling, salted water for cooking. Although some stirring is suggested, too much agitation may result in a gluelike product. Finely ground, granular cereals may be separated first in cold water and stirred into a paste before being added to the boiling water. Generally, a four-to-one ratio of water to cereal should be maintained during cooking.

Pasta. Pasta products should also be cooked in salted water with a four-to-one ratio of water to cereal. They may be prepared very readily in a steam-jacketed trunnion kettle. Pastas will approximately triple in volume with cooking. Cooking times range from ten minutes for some noodles to twenty minutes for some forms of macaroni. All should be rinsed with cold water after cooking to remove excess surface starch. They may then be reheated in hot water. Placing a strainer in the cooking container first and adding the pasta product in that will make draining and rinsing easier. A small amount of oil added to the cooking water will prevent the pasta from sticking or boiling over. A spoon placed across the lips of the trunnion kettle or other cooking container also prevents boiling over. If the product is to be held on a steam table after cooking, it should be buttered or oiled to keep it from lumping.

Rice. Rice is grown in long- and short-grain varieties and is sold in brown, regular, and converted forms (parboiled or precooked). It differs somewhat from the other cereals considered, in that it retains its form and it requires less water for cooking. The long grains are less likely to stick together during cooking than the short. Parboiled rice requires more cooking than regular rice, while precooked rice requires less.

In cooking rice, one measure of regular rice requires about two measures of liquid. The parboiled variety requires slightly more liquid and the precooked somewhat less. For example 2½ quarts of boiling liquid are used to cook 2 pounds 10 ounces of regular rice; about 2¾ quarts are needed for the same amount of parboiled rice and 2¼ quarts are needed for the precooked forms.

Rice, like most other cereals, will increase about three times in volume during cooking, because the grains rupture and absorb moisture.

Brown rice is rice that has undergone less processing than white and is similar in texture to wild rice. It requires longer cooking than the other varieties. Wild rice is not a form of rice at all, but rather the seed of a wild grass. It is often mixed with less expensive regular or parboiled rice for better economy.

Rice may be cooked in a range-top container, an oven, a steamer, or a steam-jacketed kettle. Range-top preparation in a covered container or steam-jacketed kettle will take fifteen minutes for regular rice, twenty minutes for parboiled, and forty-five minutes for brown. In a 350-degree oven parboiled rice takes thirty minutes, regular rice twenty-five minutes, and brown rice one hour. A low-pressure steamer prepares regular rice in about ten minutes and parboiled in fifteen to twenty minutes.

Rice being held for service should be kept in shallow pans to prevent packing. Leftover rice may be refrigerated or frozen. A half cup of water is then added for each quart of rice and the product is reheated for service.

17 *Bakery Products*

Objective: To present the terminology, tools, and procedures of baking with emphasis on the problems that may be encountered with baked goods. The ingredients and their qualities and functions are described, and the various types, including convenience items, are detailed.

Modern Trends

Traditionally, the baker in a quantity food facility has carried out his specialized duties within his own work space, usually completely divorced from the other food preparation functions. Assisted by helpers, pastry cooks, ice cream makers, and others, he produced desserts, pastries, puddings, baked fruits, and specialty items for both general and banquet menus. The baker was largely autonomous in his location, hours of work, and supervision of subordinates. In many operations, he started work at a very early hour in order to meet breakfast and luncheon requirements for freshly baked items. His equipment was considered to belong to the baking area alone. This highly specialized journeyman has always been a very definite asset to a successful food service organization.

In recent years, however, a shortage of these technical practitioners has developed. In addition, many operations have not been able to afford the equipment needed for the bake shop or to devote the physical space required. As a result, establishments have looked elsewhere to procure bakery items. In many locations, local commercial bakeries have met the needs of food service operators who were unwilling or unable to produce their own baked goods. More recently, national chain companies have begun to produce frozen baked products that challenge the products of locally operated bake shops.

Cost and quality comparisons between self-produced and commercially produced convenience bakery items suggest, in many cases, that use of the outside baking facility is preferable. Centralized commissaries have also been used by government and chain food operations to increase efficiency and lower costs.

Of course, many decry the disappearance of the in-house baker and suggest that nothing can replace homemade Danish, cheesecake, or apple pie. Some establishments will be able to maintain the capability to produce their own bakery items at a reasonable cost. Others will attempt to do this but fail, because they cannot attract the necessary talent. Most will eventually join the mass movement to commercial and convenience bakery products, while making only a few items on the premises.

Although this trend is apparent, each quantity food operator must make an individual decision about his source for bakery products. Whatever course he chooses, it is important that the manager or supervisor know the rudiments of bakery work and be able to evaluate the baked products produced or purchased. He must be knowledgeable about the specialized equipment, the major ingredients of baked goods, the procedures used to produce them, and the indicators of quality in them.

Equipment

The major pieces of equipment used in a bake shop are generally similar to those used in general food preparation work.

Ovens. Ovens, of course, are essential in all baking areas. Many shops use the conventional decked ovens, but larger operations may well use rotary ovens to give maximum capacity within the available space. Steam inserts are usually provided in bake shops, to produce the desired crust color and degree of hardness in certain baked products.

Ranges. A range-top heat source or at the very least a hot plate must be provided for the baking area.

Mixers. The standard vertical mixers usually do very nicely in baking operations, provided the size is adequate for the amounts of materials processed. Larger operations may find the horizontal models to be more effi-

Figure 17a. A revolving-tray, rotary oven gives more flexibility of space, ease of tray handling, and maximum efficiency in larger operations. (Courtesy of the Middleby-Marshall Oven Company, Chicago.)

cient for the control of dough temperatures and mixing times.

Proof Boxes. The production of quality yeast-leavened items requires satisfactory temperature and humidity conditions. Therefore, some form of proofing equipment must be provided. For most establishments except the very large ones, a satisfactory proofing atmosphere may be maintained with a manually controlled electric heating coil and a water reservoir to generate steam in an enclosed cabinet. A steam line to control the humidity is a desirable addition.

Bread-making Devices. A dough divider—a device for dividing dough into predetermined volumes—is a desirable addition for any establishment operating its own baking facilities. Loaf rounders and bread slicers are also necessary for a large-scope operation.

Surface and Storage Areas. Wood-covered working tables that are larger in surface area than conventional work tables must be provided in the average bake shop to facilitate the cutting, rolling, and panning of bakery products. In some states, however, wooden tables of any type are forbidden in food preparation areas, and another surface material must be used. Sufficient bin storage and refrigeration must also be available to maintain the perishable items that are used or produced in the bakery.

Small Tools and Utensils

The hand tools and utensils required in the baking area differ very little from those used in general food preparation. Special utensils worthy of note are discussed below. Additional specialized hand tools and utensils are shown in figure 17b.

Pans. Bread, roll, cake, and pie pans of aluminum or aluminum steel are desirable. Aluminum steel is preferred in that it does not require burning or prebaking to condition the pan properly. The pans must be provided in sizes consistent with the requirements of and portion sizes used by the operation.

Roll Divider. A manually operated divider that is used to section two pounds of dough into individual rolls should be available in almost every bake shop. It is operated by raising the fin area and placing a pan of proofed dough under it. The handle is then depressed and the dough is cut into thirty-six pieces. They may be baked in this form, or arranged on sheet pans, or hand-rolled to fashion them into other shapes.

Baker's Scale. A scale is required in the baking area to weigh recipe ingredients.

Baking Ingredients

In bakery products the ingredients that are used most are flour, sugar, leavening agents, moisture, fats, and additives such as salt and flavoring agents.

Flour

Flour is the most important ingredient in baked products. It forms the structure of the item and influences its texture, taste, and nutritional value. The most important flour used in baking is wheat flour.

A very complicated milling process is used to crush the wheat kernel and separate its various layers. The process results in several break lots, middlings, streams, and refined flours. Each requires specific milling procedures to achieve the desired flour. Consumers still seem to prefer white bleached flour to the darker natural varieties used by their peasant ancestors. Many of the refining and bleaching procedures reduce the nutritive quality of the flour, however. The loss of natural nutrients necessitates later addition of nutrients to make the product approximate the nutritive value it had before it was milled.

Wheat flour is composed of protein, starch, enzymes, fat, sugar, minerals (ash), and moisture. The percentages of these ingredients vary with the type of wheat and the milling process.

Protein is one of the most important elements in wheat flour. The specific proteins in wheat flour are glutenin and gliadin. They can be mixed with water to form a substance known as gluten. This is an elastic, sticky material that eventually forms the basis of a

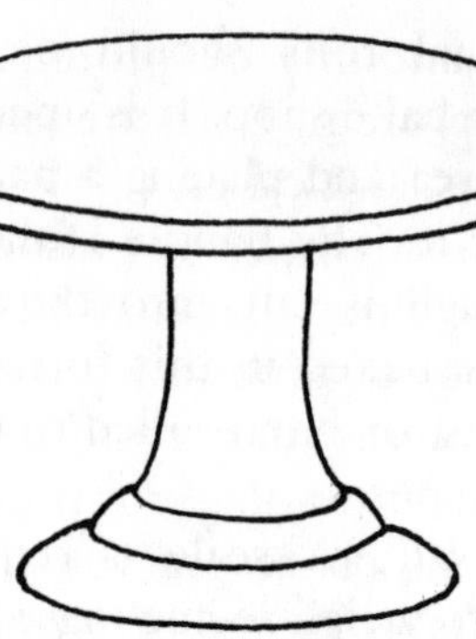

A turntable for cake decorating.

A peel for removing items from ovens.

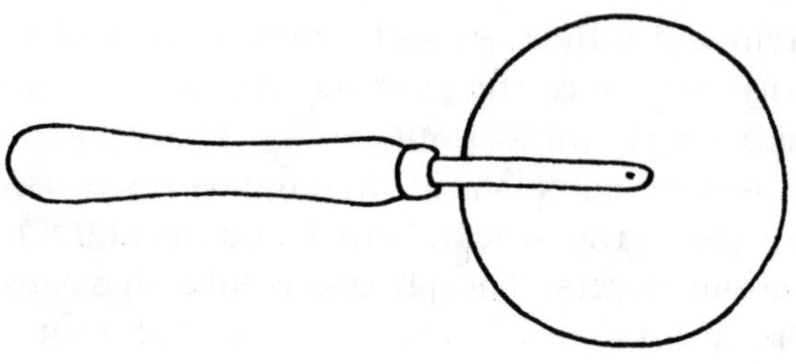

A pastry wheel for cutting dough.

A pie pin or one-handed rolling pin.

A rolling pin.

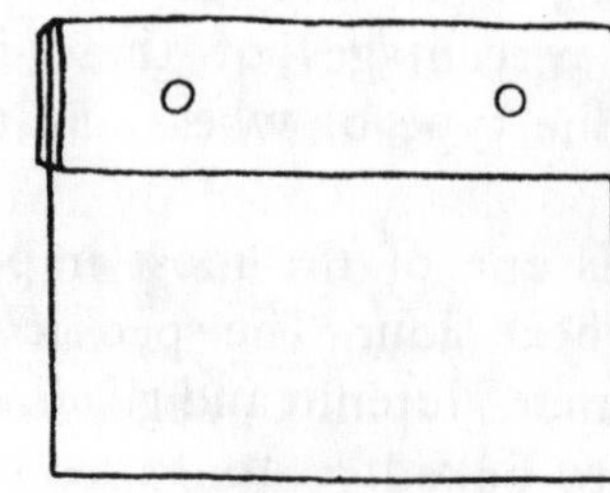

A dough scraper for bench work.

Figure 17b. Some of the more common hand tools and utensils used in baking.

baked product. The amount of gluten formed depends on the kind and percentage of protein available in a particular flour.

Starch is the second most important part of the flour. In yeast-leavened products, the starch is changed to sugar by the yeast during the fermentation process. In other products, the starch is gelatinized by heat and moisture to form a structure during baking. It is also dextrinized during cooking to give baked goods some of their characteristic color. The enzyme diastase in flour breaks the starch down into sugar, when the flour is mixed with moisture and then heated. This contributes to fermentation and to the action of the yeast. The enzyme reaction also contributes to caramelization of the sugar, which gives a brown color to the baked product.

Kinds of Flour. Wheat is classified according to the type of seed and the location and time in which it is grown. There are durum, hard spring, hard red winter, and soft winter wheats. The durum and hard wheats produce flours that have more protein, while the soft wheats produce flours less rich in protein. The amount and type of protein found in a flour determine the specific use to which it should be put.

Hard wheat flours with strong proteins in amounts close to 12 percent are best used for breads and rolls, while the softer flours with lower percentages and weaker proteins are best used for baked goods requiring less structure and tensile strength. Depending on the type of wheat, the parts of the kernel used, and the milling process, the flours that are used for making breads and rolls are classified as bread flour, hard wheat flour, 100 percent hard wheat straight flour, or patent hard wheat flour. Straight flours contain all the streams from a milling process, while patent flours come from portions of the endosperm.

Whole wheat flour (graham flour) contains all the milling streams and may be used in making whole wheat products. It is, of course, dark in color and is very strong in protein and gluten.

Pastry flour, made from the softer wheats, has smaller amounts of protein. Cake flour has still less protein. Both are suitable for pie crusts, pastries, and cakes.

Hard and soft wheats are also blended into an all-purpose flour that may be used to produce a number of products. Like other products or procedures that try to be all things to all people, this flour does not produce as good an item in all classes as the more specific types of flours. It should be avoided in preference to a flour suited to the particular use.

Flours that are milled to prevent packing and that therefore require no sifting before measuring are also available. Since quantity recipe ingredients are usually measured by weight, the benefit of this flour is lost, and its additional cost makes it of little use to the quantity food service operator.

Rye flour is the only other grain of importance that is milled into flour for baking. It is classified as light, medium, or dark, depending on the type of milling and the color of the finished flour. Rye flour does not have the ability to make gluten from its protein content, and some wheat flour is usually added to prevent the final product from being too compact and heavy.

With the present concern about ecology and interest in a return to natural foods by many members of the society, more unrefined, purer wheat flours will apparently be used in the future.

Sugar

Sugar may be used in granulated, brown, or confectionery form in baked products. Honey, molasses, and glucose are also used, or simple sugars may be fermented from the starch of flour in the product.

Sugar contributes to the sweetness of a baked product and serves as food for the yeast in products leavened by that method. Sugar added to a yeast-leavened recipe provides a starter amount and permits the product to rise more rapidly. It also gives smoother texture to baked products, contributes to their brownish color, and helps to tenderize them.

Certain items require particular forms of sugar, although granulated is used in most recipes. Brown sugar, a less refined sugar that comes in light and dark varieties, is used in some recipes for its color and taste. The more refined and pulverized powdered (confectionery) sugars are used in such products as icings. The degree of fineness is signified by the number of *X*s, ranging from 4X to 10X. The 10X sugar is the finest grain available.

Leavening Agents

Leavening—the incorporation of air into a product—may be accomplished in a variety of ways. Air may be whipped in; steam generated by heating moisture may put air into the item; or carbon dioxide may be generated by yeast, soda and acid, or baking powder in the product. Leavening agents increase the volume of a product and improve its texture. They have the effect of making the item lighter.

Whipping. Air may be incorporated either manually or by machine. Such processes as creaming fat and sugar together or beating or whipping a batter or eggs incorporate air. If such a process is used, later mixing procedures must be carried out in such a way as to maintain the maximum incorporation of air. This is why folding or the lowest mixer speeds are used to incorporate or combine other items with an air-leavened product.

Steam. Steam may also be used as a leavening agent. Water within the product is heated very quickly and vaporizes into steam, which acts to raise the product. This action is demonstrated, for example, in cream puffs. Most baked products, however, do not depend on steam alone for leavening action, but rather use it in addition to another method.

Yeast. Certain products use yeast as the leavening agent. Yeasts are single-celled plants that are naturally present in the atmosphere. Selected strains of them are cultured to produce a very effective leavening agent for baked goods. Yeast is a strong leavening agent and must be supported by stronger dough structures. To develop this structure, the dough is usually kneaded in yeast-leavened products and a proofing (rising) period is specified in the recipe to permit the yeast to act.

Yeast is available in compressed or active dry form with most of the moisture removed for better storage. Compressed yeast must be stored under refrigeration at 30 to 35 degrees

Table 17-1. Hydrolysis of Starch and Fermentation by Yeast

Three distinct functions are carried out in yeast-leavened products.

1. The diastase enzyme, which is present in wheat, reacts in the presence of moisture and increased temperature to break starch down into maltose.

$$\underset{\text{starch}}{(C_6H_{10}O_5)_x} + \underset{\text{water}}{H_2O} \xrightarrow[\text{(amylase)}]{\text{diastase}} \underset{\text{maltose}}{C_{12}H_{22}O_{11}}$$

2. The enzyme maltase, from yeast, breaks the maltose down into usable glucose.

$$\underset{\text{maltose}}{C_{12}H_{22}O_{11}} + \underset{\text{water}}{H_2O} \xrightarrow[\text{(yeast)}]{\text{maltase}} \underset{\text{glucose}}{2C_6H_{12}O_6}$$

3. The glucose is then fermented into ethyl alcohol and carbon dioxide by the yeast enzyme zymase.

$$\underset{\text{glucose}}{2C_6H_{12}O_6} \xrightarrow[\text{(yeast)}]{\text{zymase}} \underset{\text{ethyl alcohol}}{2C_2H_5OH} + \underset{\text{carbon dioxide}}{2CO_2\uparrow}$$

After the maximum amount of carbon dioxide has been generated and entrapped by the dough, the product is baked. The heat evaporates the alcohol and destroys the yeast.

Fahrenheit, while dry yeast may be stored in any area protected from excessively high temperatures and humidity. Because of its lack of moisture, dry yeast is about twice as effective as compressed yeast and only half as much is required. Most yeast-leavened products require from 1 to 5 percent of the weight of the flour in compressed yeast.

The yeast, in combination with its enzymes maltase and zymase, acts on the simple sugars derived from the flour to produce carbon dioxide and alcohol. The carbon dioxide causes the leavening, while the alcohol is driven off in the heating process. Yeast depends very heavily on the surrounding temperature for its life and rate of action. Controls must be maintained to ensure that the yeast is not killed and that the temperature range favorable for maximum action is maintained.

Soda and Acid. Another leavener used in certain baked products is sodium bicarbonate (baking soda), which is combined with an acid food, such as chocolate or cocoa (except the Dutch-processed kind, which has a more neutral pH), molasses, or buttermilk, to produce a reaction that generates carbon dioxide and thus leavens the product. Because of possible variance in the strength of the acid, however, many recipes call for the addition of a baking powder as well, to give better leavening control.

Baking Powders. Single- and double-action baking powders are used to leaven baked products. The single-action types require only addition of moisture to start carbon dioxide generation, while the double-acting powders produce gas through two procedures, one in the presence of moisture and the other when the product is heated.

Moisture is a very severe enemy of baking

Table 17-2. Baking Soda and Baking Powder Carbon Dioxide Generation

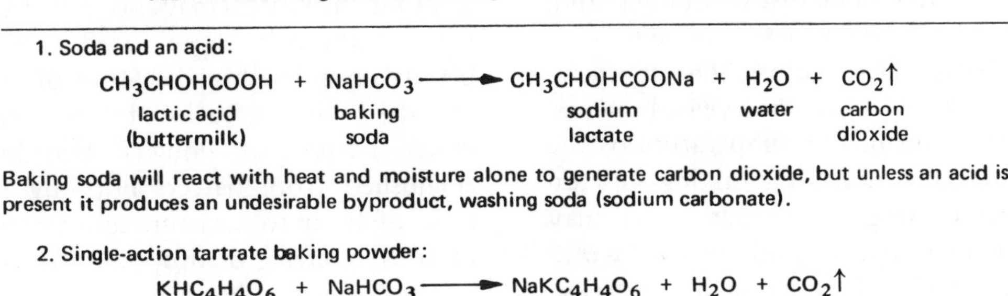

1. Soda and an acid:

$$CH_3CHOHCOOH + NaHCO_3 \longrightarrow CH_3CHOHCOONa + H_2O + CO_2\uparrow$$

lactic acid (buttermilk) + baking soda → sodium lactate + water + carbon dioxide

Baking soda will react with heat and moisture alone to generate carbon dioxide, but unless an acid is present it produces an undesirable byproduct, washing soda (sodium carbonate).

2. Single-action tartrate baking powder:

$$KHC_4H_4O_6 + NaHCO_3 \longrightarrow NaKC_4H_4O_6 + H_2O + CO_2\uparrow$$

cream of tartar + baking soda → sodium potassium tartrate + water + carbon dioxide

$$H_2C_4H_4O_6 + 2NaHCO_3 \longrightarrow Na_2C_4H_4O_6 + 2H_2O + 2CO_2\uparrow$$

tartaric acid + baking soda → disodium tartrate + water + carbon dioxide

3. Single-action phosphate baking powder:

$$Ca(H_2PO_4)_2 + 2NaHCO_3 \longrightarrow CaHPO_4 + Na_2HPO_4 + 2H_2O + 2CO_2\uparrow$$

calcium dihydrogen phosphate + baking soda → calcium hydrogen phosphate + disodium hydrogen phosphate + water + carbon dioxide

4. Double-action sodium aluminum sulfate (SAS) baking powder:

$$Al_2(SO_4)_3 + 6NaHCO_3 \longrightarrow 2Al(OH)_3 + 3Na_2SO_4 + 6CO_2\uparrow$$

aluminum sulfate + baking soda → aluminum hydroxide + sodium sulfate + carbon dioxide

Single-action baking powders react to produce carbon dioxide immediately on the addition of moisture, while the double-acting varieties produce some carbon dioxide when moisture is added and the remainder only when the product is heated. Because of this, greater quantities of single-acting baking powders are required in recipes, where lesser quantities of double-acting varieties can be used.

powders, and provisions must be made to protect containers against the accidental introduction of moisture. A wet spoon or a container left uncovered will do much to reduce the effectiveness of the baking powder.

Ammonia. Ammonium bicarbonate, a form of ammonia, is sometimes used to leaven cookies, which require fast rising action and are thin enough to permit the ammonia gas to escape during baking. Double-action baking powder is most often used as the leavening agent, however.

Moisture

Moisture is usually provided in baked products in the form of water or milk and in lesser amounts by eggs. It contributes to formation of the gluten in flour, acts as an agent to dissolve dry ingredients, and permits the enzyme actions to take place between yeast and flour. When milk and/or eggs are part of the liquid they help to improve the texture and flavor, add to the nutritive value of the product, and, because of their sugar and fat content, contribute to better crust colors. The temperature of the water used in some yeast-leavened products may control the temperature of the dough for fermentation after mixing. Certain types of water (e.g., extremely soft) may cause problems in baked goods, as they weaken the gluten and make the dough too sticky. Some products use moisture for steam generation, which is their major form of leavening.

Fats

Fats and shortenings are used in baked products to improve their tenderness, taste, and texture. They are not dissolved in the moisture, but rather melt and are absorbed on the surface of other materials to separate cell particles or lubricate the strands of gluten in the dough. They give a shortness to the crumb and crust and prevent overdevelopment of the gluten strands.

Fats that are creamed in the process of making cakes contribute to the incorporation of the air cells, which give the cake better texture and lightness.

Many types of fats are available for use in baked products. Such factors as color, flavor, and degree of plasticity are important in selecting a particular one. Lard, butter, vegetable oil, and hydrogenated shortening are the ones most often used in baked goods.

Additives

Additives such as salt, extracts, nuts, fruits, chocolate, raisins and the like are all used in baked products. Each produces a desired taste or color effect, but some, such as salt or cocoa, also have other important functions. Salt may act to toughen the gluten and permit it to hold more air, while cocoa may serve as the acid that reacts in combination with baking soda to produce carbon dioxide. Specific applications of these additives will be covered in the discussion below of the products to which they best relate.

Types of Flour Products

Flour mixtures may be classified by the type of leavening agent used as either yeast breads or quick breads. More often they are classified by the ratio of liquid to flour as either batters or doughs. Doughs are distinguished from batters both by the higher ratio of flour to moisture and by their ability to resist pouring or dropping. Doughs are, of course, easier to handle and are often rolled, folded, or otherwise manipulated in making specific products.

Yeast Breads

Yeast breads are soft doughs that are leavened with yeast. They are made with a high protein, hard, wheat flour or with specialty flours such as whole wheat or rye.

Ingredients. Flour is the major ingredient of yeast breads. It acts as the framework and joins with the moisture to produce the all-important gluten.

Water or other moisture in a yeast-leavened product mixes with the flour, as noted, and dissolves the sugar and salt. The amount and type of water will determine the stiffness of the dough, and its temperature will delay or

Table 17-3. Types of Batters and Doughs

Name of Mixture	Typical Item	Proportions	
		Liquid	Flour
Pour batter	Griddle cake	1 part	1 part
Drop batter	Muffin	1 part	2 parts
Soft dough	Biscuit	1 part	3 parts
Stiff dough	Pastry	1 part	4 parts

speed the fermentation process. Hard water retards fermentation, while water that is too soft produces a softened gluten and a sticky dough.

The salt in yeast breads contributes flavor and aids in firming the gluten strands. Too much salt in the recipe will reduce the action of the yeast during fermentation.

Yeast is, of course, the leavening agent. It grows best at 70 to 90 degrees Fahrenheit and at a pH range of 5.0 to 5.5. If higher temperatures are used, the yeast will grow more rapidly than the dough can accommodate, and volume will be lost. If temperatures are too low, fermentation will be retarded or nonexistent. Yeast is destroyed at temperatures above 140 degrees Fahrenheit. When dissolving compressed yeast in water, precautions must be taken to ensure that the thermal death point is not reached.

Sugar is not generally used in yeast products; rather the yeast activity is produced from the flour alone. If sugar is used, it may be in the form of malt, which helps convert the starch of the flour to maltose for better yeast action, or granulated sugar may be used as a yeast starter. Sweet doughs, although yeast-leavened, do contain more sugar.

Fat is used in small amounts in some yeast-leavened products. It acts as a lubricant for the dough, making it more pliable and helping to reduce and tenderize the gluten.

Milk is used in some breads and other yeast-leavened products to increase their nutritive value, contribute to crust color, and aid in fermentation. If fresh milk is used, it must be scalded first to reduce enzyme activity that would otherwise be harmful to the fermentation process. For this reason, and for its ease of use, dry milk is more often called for in basic yeast recipes.

Mixing. Yeast breads may be mixed in one of two basic ways—the straight dough method or the sponge dough method. The straight dough method permits all the ingredients to be mixed at one time, while the sponge dough method, which is used more often in commercial bread operations, consists of two mixing and two fermentation processes. Part of the flour, water, yeast, sugar, and shortening are mixed and allowed to ferment. Then the mixture is combined with the remainder of the ingredients, they are mixed again, and a second fermentation period is allowed.

Whichever method is used, the mixing must permit proper development of the gluten structure and proper distribution of the yeast cells and other ingredients throughout, so that a quality bread will result.

Fermentation. Fermentation of the dough is always required in yeast-leavened products to allow the manufacture of carbon dioxide, and the development of the dough structure to support it. During this process, humidity must be controlled. Crusting of the dough will develop from dehydration, and this will cause gas to be trapped in certain areas, with a resulting loss of uniform texture. Temperature must also be controlled to ensure adequate yeast growth and proper development of carbon dioxide. A temperature of approximately 80 degrees Fahrenheit and a relative humidity of 78 percent are recommended.

The fermentation period continues until the dough has reached nearly maximum growth. This varies according to the recipe, temperature, and humidity, but it is indicated when punching the dough leaves a slight depression. Then the dough is punched down, and the back, front, and sides are folded up over the top. It is permitted to finish fermentation before being cut into units appropriate to the particular product. The edges of each unit are rounded off and turned under to give an attractive top surface, and the dough is permitted to rest in the pan for a period of

Table 17-4. Common Yeast Bread Problems and Causes

Problems	Possible Causes
Heavy	Too little fermentation; problems with yeast; too much flour
Cracked crust	Dough too stiff
Crumbly	Insufficient fermentation; no salt
Coarse texture	Poor yeast function; fermentation problems

ten to fifteen minutes for a final stretching of the gluten and the development of some surface crusting, which gives better carbon dioxide retention. The product then receives a second proof for about one hour at approximately 95 degrees and a humidity of 88 percent. After that, it is ready for baking.

Baking. Yeast products may be painted with an egg wash or melted butter before baking. They are baked at temperatures from 400 to 450 degrees Fahrenheit. Lower temperatures will permit more carbon dioxide development before the yeast is destroyed but the grain of the product will be seriously affected. Higher temperatures will cause premature browning of the outside of the product and less volume because the yeast is destroyed sooner. Products that are higher in sugar or milk content should be baked at lower temperatures to prevent overbrowning. Steam may be used to form a hard crust on items.

Bread is completely baked when it has gained the characteristic color, has shrunk from the sides of the pan, and has an oven spring resistance to finger pressure.

Quality Indications. Yeast breads should be moist, soft, and tender in texture. They should be light, the color should be good, and the crust should have good texture. The grain of the product should be relatively fine, and there should be no large gas holes.

Specialty Breads and Flours

Rye bread may be made following the same general procedures as for wheat bread, using the straight dough method but taking into consideration the following special factors:

(a) Wheat flour must be added to rye flour, whether light, medium, or dark (pumpernickel) rye is used, in order to manufacture gluten. The darker the rye, the smaller the loaf volume will be.

(b) Sours may be used as wild yeast sources in rye bread for their distinctive taste. If they are used, however, the volume will be further reduced.

(c) Rye bread should be baked with steam in the baking compartment for best crust results. Whenever low pressure steam is used in baking, it should be turned on while the oven is reaching operating temperature.

(d) The fermentation periods for rye doughs are usually shorter than those required for wheat doughs.

Whole wheat doughs require shorter fermentation periods than other wheat flours. The temperature of the dough is more important than it is for other wheat doughs in that too warm a temperature will cause the bread to be crumbly. Whole wheat products must be baked at lower temperatures and for longer periods of time than white breads.

Sweet doughs are yeast-leavened doughs that are richer in sugar, shortening, eggs, and milk than other yeast breads and rolls. They provide such items as coffee cakes, cinnamon rolls, and Danish pastries. More yeast is usually used, since the excess sugar retards the action of the yeast. Regular sweet dough differs from rolled sweet dough. Both require a fermentation period, like other yeast products, but two to four ounces of shortening are rolled into rolled sweet dough after proofing. The dough is then folded, refrigerated, folded again, and rolled a second time to create layers of fat and dough that give it flakiness. Butter is usually the fat of choice, although some shortenings may be used. The dough is refrigerated to make rolling easier. A variety of fillings or coatings and a multitude of shapes may be used to give the product interest.

No final proofing of rolled sweet dough is

necessary, but, if it is proofed, the temperature must be kept below the melting temperature of the fat to prevent the product from becoming soggy. The dough should be baked at temperatures that will achieve fast cooking, to avoid melting the fat from the layers.

Quick Breads

Quick breads are flour mixtures that are leavened by baking powder, baking soda, or steam. Typical items are popovers, griddle cakes, muffins, and biscuits. Quick breads are easily made and offer variety in taste and texture of flour mixtures.

Containing the same basic ingredients as yeast-leavened flour mixtures, quick bread batters or doughs are classified in three basic types: a pour batter, which consists of a one-to-one liquid-to-flour ratio, such as that for a popover; a drop batter, with a one-to-two ratio, such as that for a muffin; and a soft dough, with a one-to-three ratio, such as that from which a biscuit is made.

Mixing. There are two basic methods for mixing quick breads—the muffin method and the biscuit method. In the muffin method, the dry ingredients are mixed together, and the fat and liquid are then added all at once and mixed only enough to combine the ingredients. This prevents both loss of leavening power and overdevelopment of gluten, which can produce toughness in the product or a tunneling effect: the overdeveloped gluten framework channels the carbon dioxide upward, creating a tunnel within and a peak at the top of the product.

The biscuit method is used for soft dough products. A solid fat is cut into the dry ingredients, the liquid is added and mixed just until the ingredients are combined, and the dough is rolled out on a floured board and cut into the desired shapes.

Leavening. Quick breads are leavened by the generation of carbon dioxide from a combination of baking soda and an acid, such as sour milk, or from baking powders. A pour batter that generates instant steam is leavened by that agent.

In all quick breads, the leavening agent acts rather quickly, and these products should be baked soon after mixing. The role of the gluten is not as important as it is in yeast breads, since the leavening agent's action does not stretch the gluten strands as much. In fact, mixing and development of gluten should be kept to a minimum and the softer flours should be used if possible. Cake flour may well be used in biscuits, waffles, muffins, and griddle cakes to keep the gluten strength down. Popovers, however, should be made with a heavier bread flour because they need to have a strong exterior to contain the steam that develops so quickly in them.

Quality Indications. Biscuits should have even sides and level tops. The tops should be golden brown. Their texture should be layered, flaky, and light, with no bitter taste.

Muffins should have good shape and color. The tops should be slightly rounded with no peaks, and the texture should be smooth and light.

Cakes

Cakes are flour mixtures that have proportionately more fat, sugar, and eggs than the

Table 17-5. Common Biscuit and Muffin Problems and Causes

Problems	Possible Causes
Biscuits	
Tough	Too much mixing; not enough fat; too much liquid
Dry	Too little liquid; overcooking
Crumbly	Too much fat
Hard crust	Overcooking; too high a temperature
Uneven tops	Pin rolled over sides of dough, making uneven thickness
Heavy	Error in measurement of ingredients; too much mixing
Muffins	
Tunnels and peaks	Too much mixing
Heavy	Not enough leavening; not enough fat
Tough	Too much mixing; not enough fat

mixtures previously considered. They are sweeter to the taste and have a more delicate texture. The production of a successful cake is predicated on strict adherence to the measurements of the recipe and use of the proper ingredients, method of mixing, size of pan, and baking temperature.

Cakes are classified as butter cakes—those that contain fat—and foam cakes—those with no fat. Butter cakes usually depend on a baking powder or baking soda and acid leavening. Foam cakes depend on beaten eggs for their leavening.

Ingredients. All cakes must be made with soft wheat flours that have a low profile of gluten. A short patent flour gives a better texture and grain.

Shortening is used for both leavening and tenderizing cakes. Shortenings with emulsifiers achieve better results in these functions and give a finer grain to the cake.

Sugar gives sweetness to cake, contributes to its coloring, and prevents the gluten from becoming too strong when the batter is mixed. Too much sugar will prevent the cake from forming an adequate frame and will cause it to fall.

Eggs contribute flavor and color to a cake and help to develop the framework. In a foam cake, the beaten egg whites serve as the main leavening agent.

Water and milk are the main liquids used in cakes. Dry milk is most often used for purposes of economy. The liquid contributes to gluten development, and when milk is used it also contributes flavor and color. Both substances provide some leavening action from their production of steam.

Cakes are leavened by air incorporated during the mixing and/or creaming processes, by beaten egg whites, by chemical agents that make carbon dioxide, or by steam generated from the liquid ingredients.

Flavoring agents are added to cakes according to the specifications in a particular recipe.

Mixing. There are two basic methods for mixing cakes—the conventional and the quick methods. The conventional method uses a creaming action to mix the fat and the sugar while incorporating air. The eggs are then added and the remainder of the wet and dry ingredients are added alternately. In the quick or dump method, all dry ingredients are placed in the mixing bowl, the fat and part of the liquid are added and mixed, the beaten eggs and remaining liquid are then added, and the mixing is completed.

Foam (nonfat) cakes are mixed by whipping the egg whites and sugar until stiff and then either blending or folding in the remaining ingredients.

In mixing cakes, all ingredients should be at room temperature to ensure maximum volume. The bowl should be scraped down periodically to make sure that all ingredients are completely mixed. Low mixer speeds should be used for cake mixing except when whipping egg whites. Nonfat cakes may easily be overbeaten to a dry stage. They then lose volume, as the protein of the egg is unable to hold the incorporated air, and the walls collapse. Cream of tartar may be used to help stabilize the egg foam.

Baking. Butter cakes should be baked in greased pans, while ungreased tube pans are used for air-leavened cakes. Parchment or waxed paper may be placed in the bottoms of the pans to make cake removal easier. Pans may also be lightly floured after greasing. Silicone-treated pans ease cake removal also.

Pans should not be filled more than half or two-thirds full, and the amount of batter in each pan should be weighed or a counterbalance process should be used to ensure equal amounts in each container. Tapping or spinning the pan will distribute the batter to all its corners so that no air bubbles remain.

Oven temperatures of 350 to 375 degrees for butter cakes and 250 to 350 degrees for foam cakes are recommended. The cake will increase in volume during baking. When done it will shrink from the sides of the pan, turn a darker color, and resist finger pressure with oven spring. A toothpick or other narrow implement inserted into the center will come out clean of batter.

Table 17-6. Common Cake Problems and Causes

Problems	Possible Causes
Butter cakes	
Too dark a crust	Oven too hot; too much sugar or milk in recipe
Too light a crust	Oven too cool
Peak in center	Too much mixing; batter too stiff; not enough fat
Fallen in center	Too much fat, sugar, or leavening; cake underbaked; oven too cool
Sticky crust	Too much sugar; not enough mixing
Heavy	Error in recipe; too much fat, sugar, or liquid; not enough leavening
Soggy crust	Cooled in pan too long; too much liquid
Crumbly	Too much leavening or shortening
Large holes in cake	Leavening not mixed properly; air trapped in batter
Uneven height	Batter not spread evenly; oven not level.
Foam cakes	
Too dark a crust	Oven too hot; too much sugar
Too light a crust	Oven too cool
Sticky crust	Too much sugar
Heavy	Eggs over- or underbeaten; loss of air in combining ingredients
Tough or thick crust	Oven too hot; cake overbaked; too much sugar
Tough texture	Overmixing; too high a temperature
Dry texture	Eggs overbeaten; too much baking

The cake should not be moved after it has started to rise, and it should be removed from the oven as soon as it has finished baking. All cakes should be allowed to stand for five minutes after baking; then the sides are loosened from the pan and the cake is inverted on a cooling rack or sugar-coated pan bottom of the same or the next larger size. Fat-free cakes are hung inverted to cool before they are removed from the pan so that they retain their maximum volume.

The cake is ready for icing when it has completely cooled. Some experts suggest icing cakes as soon as possible to improve their keeping quality, while others wait until the next day to ice them.

Quality Indications. A butter cake should have a slightly rounded top that is free from cracks. The texture should be fine-grained, moist, and tender. The color of the crumb should be consistent with the type of cake being prepared.

A foam cake should be very light in relation to its size. It should have a very fine texture, be tender, and have a spongy resistance to pressure, although it should be easy to break into pieces.

Pies

Ingredients. Pies are made from plain pastry, which is a stiff dough made from flour, salt, fat, and water. The flour most often used in quantity food work is a pastry flour that permits a sufficient layering without overproduction of gluten. The salt contributes to the flavor and has a firming effect on the dough mixture. The shortening, which may be lard or a plastic type of vegetable or animal fat, gives tenderness and flakiness to the pastry by melting between the strands of gluten. It is cut into the flour mixture and forms flakes when the pastry is rolled. The water produces the gluten structure of the pastry when combined with the flour.

A general pastry may be satisfactorily made with three pounds of flour and one ounce of salt to two pounds of shortening, with one pound of water. Scaling should be approximately 8½ ounces for a bottom crust, and 7 ounces for a top crust.

Mixing. Pastry dough is mixed by cutting the fat into the flour and salt mixture until small lumps of fat, about the size of small peas, are formed. Cold water is added, and the mixture is combined to the point at which it masses together in the bowl.

For best results, the fat should be at room temperature, but the water should be cold to prevent the fat from becoming too soft and fluid. If the fat softens, it will coat the flour too completely and prevent the formation of a sufficient amount of gluten to give the pie structure.

Shaping and Baking. When the mixing has been completed, the dough should be permitted to rest in the refrigerator for fifteen to thirty minutes to allow hydration of the flour to take place. The dough will then roll with better results. A longer refrigerated rest period will usually result in even easier handling, and one or one-and-a-half hours is not uncommon. The dough may then be rolled by hand or by machine, to create a pastry that has bits of fat and pockets of air trapped between the lateral layers. The dough is fitted snugly in a pie pan and baked. A flaky crust will develop as the fat melts and the air cells expand.

Types of Pies. Pastry may be baked as a double crusted pie with a filling, such as an apple pie; as a single crusted pie with a filling, such as custard or squash pie; or as a single crust that will later be filled. Single crusts may also be made from such items as graham cracker crumbs mixed with butter for binding.

Pie-making Cautions. Measures should be taken to avoid overstretching pastry dough, as it will then shrink when it is baked. Single pastry shells must be docked with holes to prevent excessive blistering of the crust and to release the trapped air, since there is no filling to hold the shell to the pan. The edges of the top and bottom crusts of fruit pies should be moistened, sealed together, and folded under before being fluted in order to prevent leakage. Care should also be taken that pastry trimmed from the edges of one pie is not used as part of other crusts, because the dough becomes tough with excessive manipulations.

Cuts must be made in the top of the pie crust to permit steam to escape and to prevent the pie from peaking when it bakes. When a variety of pies are being produced at once, the type of cut in the top can be varied with each, to enable identification before the pies are portioned.

A higher initial oven temperature or a coating of melted butter will prevent the bottom crust of a filled fruit pie from becoming soaked. The tops of two-crust pies should be painted with an egg wash or milk for better browning. Pies with cooked fillings should be baked at 425 degrees for ten minutes and finished at 400 degrees. Pies with uncooked fillings should be baked at 400 degrees for 10 minutes and finished at 375 degrees. Single-crust pies may be baked at 450 degrees.

Fruit fillings should be made by removing the prepared fruit from its liquid and thickening the juice with cornstarch, an instant-setting gel, or other thickeners called for by a particular recipe. Custard, pumpkin, and squash fillings are made before being poured

Table 17-7. Common Pie Problems and Causes

Problems	Possible Causes
Too much shrinkage	Dough manipulated too much; too much water
Crust not flaky	Shortening too warm
Crust tough	Dough overmixed; too much water; not enough fat
Bottom crust soggy	Filling not thickened properly; bottom not baked enough
Single crust blisters	Air trapped between crust and pan; improper mixing of fat
Top crust peaks	Insufficient escape for steam; oven too hot
Meringue bleeds or slips	Pie too cool when meringue added; no stabilizer in egg white

into single shells. Gelatin pie fillings are placed in baked pie shells and chilled for further setting.

Meringues. Meringues made from egg whites and sugar are used for covering and decorating pies. They may also be made into meringue shells that are baked and then filled with ice cream or fruit for dessert items.

There are three stages in whipping egg whites to make meringues, described in terms of their ability to hold peaks and resist pouring. As the beating starts, a froth forms. At stage I, the egg white has been broken, and protein has formed a seal on the air bubbles, but the foam is unable to hold peaks. At stage II, the cells are fine, and all but the very peak of the foam is able to hold its shape. At stage III, the mixture has become very white, dry, and stiff. If it is permitted to stand, fluid will drain.

Achieving stability and preventing slippage or weeping are the major factors to consider in making meringues. Adding a stabilizer and/or an acid to lower the pH will give better stability. Adding the sugar as a hot syrup when the egg whites are at stage I will generally give a better product. Dry sugar may be added to the egg whites before they reach stage I and will give finer texture and more volume, after longer beating, but the mixture will usually weep, if the syrup method is not used. If possible, the meringue should be put on a pie while the filling is still hot.

Quality Indications. Pastry should be flaky, crisp, tender, and golden brown in color. It should have a rough blistery surface, and it should not crumble.

Puff Pastry

Puff pastry is a specialized pastry product, composed of flour, water, special puff pastry shortening, and salt. It is used to make many specialty desserts, such as napoleons and cream rolls, and for patty shells to be used in canapés. Puff pastry achieves its leavening and flakiness from a process of folding the dough and the shortening. Bread flour or all-purpose flour is usually used, and, although butter is a very acceptable fat, specially made puff paste shortenings give excellent results.

The basic principle of manufacture is to cut in a quarter to a third of the shortening, as is done for plain pastry, and then to add the remainder to the rolled out dough. The dough is folded over and rerolled four or five times, with refrigerated rest periods between rollings.

The dough and shortening must be of the

same consistency for proper mixing to take place, and if butter is used as the fat it should be the unsalted variety so that it can be handled more easily.

Cookies

Cookies are a highly profitable dessert item. Most are made from a soft dough, but rolled cookies are made from a stiffer dough. A sponge or foam cookie is also produced, made with a higher egg content.

Ingredients. Made from sugar, flour, shortening, eggs, milk, and leavening agents, cookies closely approximate cakes, and their ingredients perform similar functions.

Butter is the fat of choice. A fast-acting, ammonia-producing leavener is most often used. The type of sugar used affects the spread of the cookie on the baking sheet; the finer sugars produce less spread.

Pastry flour is the flour of choice in making cookies, and, although all cookie sheets are greased and floured before baking, it is important not to use excessive flouring during the rolling procedure.

Mixing. Cookies may be mixed by the creaming method or the one-stage dump method, in which all ingredients are combined at the same time. The creaming method will result in less spread of the cookie batter on the baking sheet. Overmixing of the batter will also result in less spread, as more gluten is developed.

After mixing, the batter is rolled, chilled, and cut into the desired shapes with a cutter. It may also be rolled on waxed paper, chilled, and cut into strips. The softer doughs may be dropped on baking sheets for cooking. In sponge or foam batters, the eggs are whipped to give more structure, and the cookies are dropped from a pastry bag or a spoon onto a baking sheet and then flattened.

Table 17-8. Common Cookie Problems and Causes

Problems	Possible Causes
Too much spread	Too much sugar; batter too soft; too much grease on baking sheet
Not enough spread	Sugar grind too fine; too much mixing
Tough	Too much mixing; flour too strong in gluten; not enough fat
Hard and dry	Too much flour; overcooking

Baking. Cookies are baked at temperatures from 375 to 400 degrees. They must be protected against drafts after removal from the oven. When several batches are being done in sequence, it is important that cool sheets be used for each batch. Otherwise the hot baking sheet may melt the fat in the batter before the baking process begins in the oven.

Cookies should be removed from the sheet immediately after they come out of the oven, to prevent overbaking. If they are to be left on the sheet, they should be removed from the oven before completion of the baking process and finished by heat from the sheet.

Quality Indications. All cookies—dropped, rolled or icebox—should have good shape, color, and texture. They should be neither too hard nor too soft and crumbly.

Choux Paste

Choux paste is a type of pastry used to make items such as cream puffs and éclairs. Shells made from choux paste may be used for hors d'oeuvres, as the base for creamed type entrées, or in dessert items, their most common application.

Ingredients and Mixing. Flour, water, fat, and eggs are the major ingredients of choux paste. The water and fat are heated to boiling temperatures, the flour is added, and the mixture is stirred vigorously until it masses together in the pan. It is then removed from the heat source and the eggs are added while the batter is vigorously beaten. Excessive beating at this stage, however, may make the product too thin. It will then require cooling in order to gain the desired drop consistency. Care must be taken that the water does not boil away during heating, thereby reducing the available liquid in the recipe, and that flour, when added, is completely stirred into the product.

Shaping and Baking. The paste may be dropped on a greased baking sheet or piped from a pastry tube to make éclairs or other special shapes. It is baked at a high initial temperature (425 degrees) in order to generate a sufficient amount of steam and cause the structural framework to set. After the first twenty minutes, the temperature is reduced to a more moderate level (350 degrees) for completion of the baking process, during which the product dries as its moisture is evaporated. After the pastries cool, the filling of choice may be inserted in them.

Jelly Rolls

A sponge type of cake that is filled with jelly or lemon filling and rolled into a layered log is a jelly roll. The cake is made of cake flour, eggs, sugar, salt, and baking powder. It gets its leavening from both the baking powder and the whipping of the eggs (which should be warm to develop better volume). After the ingredients have been combined, the mixture is baked on sheet pans, lined with parchment or greased brown paper, at 375 to 400 degrees for approximately fifteen minutes. When baking is completed, the cake is turned out onto a pastry cloth. The cloth should fit the size of the pan and be sprinkled with granulated or confectionery sugar, to prevent the cake from sticking. The filling is then added, and the cake is rolled tightly and cooled, still wrapped in the cloth. After cooling, the cloth may be removed, and the cake will hold its log shape for portioning into slices.

Petits Fours

A petit four is a small, dainty tea cake, iced and decorated, in one of a variety of shapes. Any kind of cake may be used, but butter cakes are easier to handle and cut. Petits fours gain most of their value from the eye appeal of their shapes, surface coverings, and decorative schemes. Cakes baked the day before are more easily cut into small shapes and decorated; freshly baked cakes tend to crumble and flake off their crumbs. Chilling the cake before it is iced makes frosting easier. After the cake has been sectioned, the shapes are placed on an elevated cooling rack and a fondant icing is poured over to coat them. The icing that runs off can be scraped from the undersurface and reheated for use again. After the icing has cooled, set, and hardened, the petit four may be decorated with an attractive design using a cooked or buttercream frosting. Petits fours are usually served in individual paper containers.

Icings

An icing or frosting contributes to the taste of a baked product, makes it more attractive to the consumer, and helps prevent loss of moisture. The ingredients normally used in icings are sugar, liquid, fat, salt, and, in most, some form of stabilizer. Icings should have a smooth texture, which may be controlled by the type of sugar or the cooking procedure used. Corn syrup, cream of tartar, and the creaming of uncooked icings tend to do most to keep the texture smooth and velvety by preventing the development of unusually large crystals. Icings should be easy to spread, a factor dependent on the liquid and type of fat used. A good icing should not be sticky. It may be soft or hard after preparation, depending on the method used.

The major types of icings are cooked and uncooked. Fondant and boiled icings are the most important in the cooked class, and royal and buttercream are the most important uncooked varieties.

Fondant icing is a mixture of granulated sugar, corn syrup, water, and salt, cooked to the medium ball range (approximately 240 degrees Fahrenheit) and then quickly cooled to about 115 degrees while being worked with a spatula on a wet marble slab until it becomes stiff. The working and the cooling keep the crystal formation smaller. The fondant icing may then be heated over water to spreading consistency. It is applied by pouring, as noted in the discussion of petits fours above.

Boiled or cooked icings are made by heating sugar syrup and mixing it with beaten egg whites or by adding the egg whites to the sugar syrup mixture and beating both over heat. It is beaten to the proper thickness and spreading consistency and will harden after it is spread on a cake.

Royal and *buttercream* frostings both have bases of egg whites, confectionery sugar, and flavoring. The major differences between the two are that royal frosting does not contain fat, and it hardens when it has set, while buttercream contains butter and/or egg yolks and remains soft after spreading.

Applying Icings. All cakes that are to be iced should be cool and free from excessive surface crumbs. Sheet cakes may be frosted on one side only or made into layers. The top of the bottom layer is frosted, the top layer is fitted on, and the top and sides of the combined cake are frosted. Round layer cakes are handled in the same manner. A spatula works well to achieve the maximum spreading of icings. A wooden turntable makes it easier to ice the sides of round layer cakes and decorate the surfaces. The spatula may be held against the side of a turning cake to accomplish the process more efficiently.

Puddings, Cobblers, and Similar Desserts

Such diverse products as the classic blanc mange (cornstarch pudding), bread pudding, apple cobbler, and meringue ring are part of the bake shop production.

Puddings may be boiled, steamed, or baked. They make up the largest class and provide much opportunity to use leftover or odd lot items in very attractive, delicious, and profitable dishes. Stale bread, leftover rice, and unused fruits may easily be made into these desirable products. Lemon, vanilla, hard, or other sauces may also be prepared to increase the appeal of a pudding.

Most puddings are thickened by eggs, cornstarch, tapioca, or the base item, such as bread or rice. Baked puddings are drier than the other varieties because the baking drives off most of the moisture. Fruits are used extensively in puddings, and liberal amounts of sugar and flavoring agents are used, giving most puddings their sweet taste.

Doughnuts

Regular doughnuts are made from a dough that closely approximates cookie dough, but because of their lack of shortening and their novel preparation method, they are considered separately here. In addition, other types of doughnuts are made from yeast doughs, raised and filled with jelly or cream.

Most doughnuts are cooked in deep fat at temperatures from 360 to 375 degrees. The major factors to be considered in their preparation are the temperature of the fat and the frying time. A lowering of fat temperature or too large a load in the fryer at one time will cause the doughnuts to absorb too much fat. Excessive time in the fryer will make them too dark in color.

Many operations use a mix to prepare doughnuts instead of making batter. Others buy their doughnuts from commercial outlets.

Convenience Bakery Products

Although convenience and ready foods are used in many segments of the food industry, nowhere have they received more attention than in the baked goods market. More work has been done in preparing highly acceptable baked products than any other kind of food.

Because of the size of the market, the major thrust of the food processor has always been toward the home consumer. Much effort was expended in providing convenience baked goods long before food processors attacked entrée items. The housewife with less skill in baking and less desire to prepare foods in this area welcomed ready baked products. The processors have spent a longer time perfecting these products than later offerings. Many of them produce excellent bakery goods that would be difficult to duplicate in an in-house baking facility. In view of the shortage of bakers and the reasonable cost and high quality of many of these items, serious consideration should be given to use of convenience and ready items.

Table 17-9. Convenience Baked Goods

Item	Preparation Method
Cakes, frozen	Thaw for 30 minutes and use
Cake mix	Add water and eggs; pour into pans; bake at 350° for 30 minutes
Canapés, frozen	Thaw for 30 minutes and use
Danish pastry, frozen	Defrost and use
Dinner rolls, frozen, uncooked	Defrost and permit to rise for approximately 20 minutes; bake at 400° for 10 minutes
Muffin mix	Combine mix and water; add baking soda; pour into greased and floured tins; bake at 400° for 20 minutes
Pies, frozen, uncooked	Bake at 400° for 1 hour
Pie filling, canned	Open can and use
Pie shells, unbaked	Fill and bake

Mixes are available for many items, such as pancakes, cakes, cookies, doughnuts, and icings. Completely ready items are available for cakes, pies, cheesecakes, Danish pastries, and breads. Puff pastry is available ready for baking. Fruits are prepared and frozen. Eggs are sold already separated. There are even apples that are made to taste like blueberries. Puddings and icings come canned and ready for use. Frozen bagels, petits fours, and canapés just require defrosting.

Bread, rolls, and doughnuts have long been purchased from commercial sources. It is now time for other baked ready items to receive like attention. The variety and quality of many of these products are outstanding, and, if convenience and ready foods are ever to find favor and extended use, surely this will be the area. With talent so short and manufactured quality so high, it is an unusual operation that will be able to justify maintaining its own baking facility because of the results.

18 *Spices, Condiments, and Fats*

Objective: To expose the student to spices and condiments and outline desirable procedures for their purchase, storage, and use. To describe the types and uses of fats and oils, discussing the specialized functions of deep-fat frying, baking, grilling, and use in salads.

Spices and Herbs

Although generally considered a single class, spices and herbs differ somewhat botanically, if not in their use. Spices may come from any part of a plant, while herbs are always the leaves.

Spices are available in whole or ground form. Herbs are available both fresh and dried.

Most spices and herbs are aromatic in nature and are used to enhance foods by contributing to their flavor, aroma, and color.

Purchase and Use. Color, aroma, and strength of flavor are important considerations in the selection and purchase of spice products. Brand name purchasing and attention to the type of container will do much to ensure that the items purchased are of acceptable quality. Spices and herbs should be stored in cool, dry areas, because excessive heat and moisture will cause them to lose their flavor. Whole spices keep much longer than finely ground ones. Dehydrated herbs will last almost indefinitely, if they are adequately protected from moisture.

Spices are intended to add to the flavor of food, not to overcome it. Whole spices are best added at the start of the cooking period, while ground ones are best added during the last few minutes, since their flavors and aromas are more easily dissipated. Whole spices should be tied into a bouquet garni so that they may be easily removed from the container at the end of the cooking.

It is not possible to specify the types or amounts of spices to use, since tastes differ markedly. Certain spices have traditionally been used with particular foods, however, and these are suggested in table 18-1. The amounts used vary according to recipe or taste. When experimenting with spices in a recipe, it is recommended that no more than a quarter teaspoon of spice to each pound of meat or pint of soup or sauce be used at first. Smaller amounts of the stronger spices, such as cayenne pepper, are suggested. More may be added later according to the taste desired.

Fresh herbs must be used in larger amounts than the dried or instant varieties. All fresh herbs should be finely divided and crushed for maximum release of flavor.

Table 18-1. Common Spices and Uses

Spice	Origins	Available Forms	Flavor	Uses
Allspice	Jamaica, Mexico, Central and South America	Whole and ground	Reminiscent of several spices—cinnamon, nutmeg, and cloves	Whole: pickling meats, gravies, boiling fish. Ground: baking, puddings, relishes, fruit preserves, tomato sauce.
Anise	Spain and Mexico	Seed	Used in flavoring licorice	Cookies, candies, sweet pickles, beverages. Sprinkled on coffee cakes and sweet rolls.
Bay leaves	Turkey, Greece, Yugoslavia, and Portugal	Leaves	Sweet and herbaceous with delicate floral spice note	Pickling, stews, sauces, and soups. Good with variety of meats such as fricassees, kidneys, hearts, and oxtail. Add leaf with whole peppercorns to tomato sauce for boiled cod.
Caraway seed	Netherlands	Seed	Combination of dill and anise	Rye bread, sauerkraut, new cabbage, noodles, and soft cheese spreads. Sprinkle over French fries, pork, liver, and kidneys before cooking.
Cardamom seed	Guatemala, India, Ceylon	Whole and ground seed	Sweet and spicy	Whole: used in mixed pickling spice. Seed: (removed from pod) flavors demitasse. Ground: flavors Danish pastry, bun breads, coffee cakes. Sprinkle on iced melon.
Celery seed	India and France	Seed and salt	Parsley and nutmeg flavor	Pickling, salads, fish, salad dressings, and vegetables.
Chervil	France and U.S.	Leaves	Resembles parsley, but is milder	Meats, vegetables, sauces, and salads. Makes delicious herb butter when blended into softened butter.
Cinnamon	Indonesia and Indochina	Stick and ground	Pungently sweet aroma and flavor	Whole: pickling, preserving, puddings, stewed fruits, hot wines, and teas. Ground: baked goods, often in combination with allspice, nutmeg, and cloves. Use with toast is widespread.
Cloves	Zanzibar and Madagascar	Whole and ground	Sweet and pungent	Whole: pork and ham roasts, pickled fruits, spiced sweet syrups. Ground: baked goods, chocolate puddings, stews, and vegetables.
Coriander	Morocco and Yugoslavia	Whole and ground seed	Sweet, dry, musty spice character, tending toward lavender	Whole: mixed pickles, gingerbread, cookies, cakes, biscuits, poultry stuffings, mixed green salads. Ground: in sausage making, bun flavoring. Rub on pork before roasting.
Cumin	Morocco and Spain	Seed and ground powder	Penetrating	Good in soups, cheese pies, and stuffed eggs.

Spice	Origins	Available Form	Flavor	Uses
Dill	Iran, Morocco, and Spain	Seed and weed	Clean and aromatic, with a green weedy note	Pickling, sauerkraut, salads, soups, fish, and meat sauces, gravies, spiced vinegars, green apple pie. Sprinkle on potato salad or cooked macaroni.
Fennel	India and Rumania	Seed	Aromatic sweet taste somewhat like anise	Sweet pickles, Italian sausage, boiled fish, pastries, and candies. Add a dash to apple pie.
Garlic (dehydrated)	U.S.	Powder, salt, and instant minced	Extremely pungent	Can be used to add garlic flavor to any food.
Ginger	Jamaica, India, and West Africa	Whole and ground	Warm and fragrant, with pungent spiciness	Whole: chutney, conserves, pickling, stewed dried fruits, and applesauce. Ground: gingerbread, cakes, pumpkin pie, Indian pudding, canned fruits, pot roasts, and other meats. Rub chicken with ginger and butter mix before roasting.
Mace	East and West Indies	Ground	Resembles nutmeg	Fish sauces, pickling, and preserving. Good in stewed cherries. Essential in fine pound cakes and many chocolate dishes.
Marjoram	France, Chile, and Peru	Leaves	Peculiar sweet and minty herbaceous flavor	Delicious when combined with other herbs in soups, stews, and poultry seasonings. Good in fish and sauce recipes. Sprinkle over lamb.
Mint flakes	U.S. and Europe	Flakes	Strong and sweet	Stews, soups, beverages, jellies, sauces, and fish.
Mixed vegetable flakes	U.S.	Flakes		Soups, stews, sauces, stuffings.
Mustard	U.S., Canada, Denmark, U.K., and Netherlands	Seed and powder	Yellow variety is milder; brown is more pungent	Whole: salads, pickled meats, fish, and hamburgers. Powdered: meats, sauces, and gravies.
Nutmeg	East and West Indies	Whole and ground	Sweet and spicy	Whole: grated as needed. Ground: baked goods, sauces, and puddings. Topping for custards, whipped cream. Good on cauliflower and spinach.
Onion (dehydrated)	U.S.	Instant chopped, powder, granulated, salt, and flakes		Soups, chowders, stews, salads, dressings, sauces, steaks, and hamburgers.
Oregano	Greece, Italy, and Mexico	Leaves and ground		Used on fish, shellfish, salad dressings, vegetables, meats, gravies, and canapés.
Paprika	Spain, Central Europe, and U.S.	Powder	Slightly aromatic	Can be used as a red garnish for any pale food. Important in chicken paprika and Hungarian goulash. Used on fish, shellfish, salad dressings, vegetables, meats, gravies, and canapés.

Spice	Origins	Available Form	Flavor	Uses
Parsley	U.S.	Flakes		Soups, salads, fish sauces, and vegetable dishes.
Pepper, black and white	India, Borneo, and Indonesia	Whole, ground, and coarse ground black pepper, whole and ground white pepper	Warm, pungent, and aromatic	Adds tang to any food. Whole: pickling, soups, and meats. Ground: meats, sauces, gravies, many vegetables, soups, salads, and eggs.
Poppy	Netherlands	Seed	Nutlike	Topping for breads, rolls, cookies. Excellent in salads and eggs.
Red pepper	U.S., Africa, Japan, Turkey, and Mexico	Whole, crushed, and ground (cayenne)		Whole: pickles, relishes, hot sauces. Crushed: sauces, pickles, highly spiced meats, a prime ingredient for many Italian dishes, including certain sausages. Ground: used with discretion in some salads, meats, sauces, and fish.
Rosemary	France, Spain, and Portugal	Leaves	Sweet and fresh	Lamb dishes, soups, and stews. Sprinkle on beef before roasting. Flavors fish and meat stocks. Add a dash to boiled potatoes in early stages of cooking.
Saffron	Spain	Flower parts	Distinctive and agreeable	Baked goods. Adds golden color to rice. Excellent for some chicken recipes.
Sage	Yugoslavia and Greece	Leaves, rubbed, and ground	Camphoraceous with minty spiciness	Particularly good with pork and pork products. Used in sausages, meat stuffings, baked fish, and poultry.
Savory	France and Spain	Leaves and ground	Sweet and herbaceous, resembling thyme	Combined with other herbs, makes an excellent flavoring for meats, meat dressings, chicken, and fish sauces.
Sesame	U.S., Central America, and Egypt	Seeds	Nutlike	Baked on rolls, breads, and buns. Add to lightly cooked, cold spinach blended with soy sauce.
Sweet pepper	U.S.	Flakes	Red is sweet, not hot	Sauces, salads, vegetables, casseroles.
Tarragon	France and Spain	Leaves	Minty, herbaceous, like anise	Sauces, salads, chicken, meat, eggs, and tomato dishes.
Thyme	France and Spain	Leaves and ground	Strong and distinctive	Stews, soups, and poultry stuffings. Excellent in clam and fish chowders, sauces, croquettes, chipped beef, and fricassees.
Turmeric	India, Haiti, Jamaica, and Peru	Ground	Mild, like ginger and pepper	Flavoring and coloring in prepared mustard. In combination with mustard, for meats, dressings, and salads.

Spices and herbs are sometimes added to products before they are cooked or are used in uncooked items, such as dressings. They must then stand for a period of time in order to allow extraction of flavor to take place.

Imitation flavor spices and herbs are also available. While they are cheaper, they do not give equal results. An essence of the real flavor is simply sprayed on a base grain to produce these products. They do not last as long as true spices and will not give as satisfactory a flavor.

Condiments

Combinations of spices, herbs, seasonings, and base products that are used in cooking or serving foods are referred to as condiments. They season the items and stimulate the appetite by increasing the appeal of the offering. They are available in portion-controlled packages and larger, more economical units. The units purchased should be related to the use to which they will be put. In quantity food work, the use of a dispensing device for a bulk unit or packaging of the condiment into smaller units during slow periods may be well advised, when cost comparisons are made between portion packs and quantity units.

Table 18-2. Ethnic Spices

Italian	Chinese	Mexican
Garlic	Ginger	Chili powder
Basil	Anise seed	Cumin seed
Oregano	Garlic	Oregano
Sage	Red pepper	Garlic
Fennel seed		Coriander seed
Greek	**Hungarian**	**Spanish**
Oregano	Paprika	Saffron
Mint	Poppy seed	Paprika
Cinnamon	Caraway seed	Garlic
Fennel	Garlic	Cumin
Coriander	Cinnamon	Sweet pepper
Indian	**French**	**German**
Curry	Tarragon	Carraway seed
Cumin seed	Shallots	Dill
Coriander	Chives	Poppy seed
Turmeric	Thyme	White pepper
Ginger	Rosemary	
Cardamon seed		

(Source: *Restaurant Hospitality*, June 1987, p. 61.)

Table 18-3. Common Generic Condiments

Name	Description and Use
Barbecue sauce	A hot, spicy sauce with a tomato and vinegar base. Used in barbecued dishes or added at the table.
Catsup	A tomato-base sauce that is widely used in dishes or at the table.
Curry powder	A mixed condiment that is highly seasoned and used in East Indian dishes. May contain ginger and cayenne pepper.
Horseradish	A very hot root product mixed with vinegar. May be used in hot sauces, such as fish cocktail sauce, or with bland dishes for taste stimulation.
Mustard	Mustard seed mixed with vinegar. Comes in mild and strong varieties. Used in food preparation or at the table.
Soy sauce	A thick Oriental sauce made from soy beans. Used in many Chinese dishes or at the table.
Tabasco sauce	A hot and tangy sauce made from red peppers mixed with vinegar. Used in many Creole dishes.
Vinegar	A dilute form of acetic acid procured from apples or grapes. May be further flavored with such items as tarragon leaves. Used in prepared dishes and salad dressings.
Worcestershire sauce	A combination of vinegar, soy sauce, spices, and seasonings used in prepared dishes or at the table.

Table 18-4. Types and Properties of Shortenings

Shortening Made From	Smoke Point (°F.)	Melting Point (°F.)	Congeal Point (°F.)	Creaming Range (°F.)	Iodine Number	Free Fatty Acid Content	A.O.M. Stability Test	Processing Treatment	Taste	Color	Pack Sizes	Principal Use	Outstanding Properties
Pure vegetable oils	450	104	88-91		65	.04	200+	Extra hydrogenated with methyl silicone	bland	white	50-lb. tin or cube, 110-lb. tin, 5-lb. prints	Deep frying	Low absorption ratio; withstands flavor transfer; for heavy duty frying
Pure vegetable oils	425	114	88-96	65-95	75-80	.04	70+	Hydrogenated	bland	white	50-lb. tin or cube, 110-lb. tin	All-purpose: deep frying and baking	Withstands prolonged high temperature; has wide plastic range; excellent for pie crusts, sweet doughs, cakes, and rolls
Blend of veg. oils and animal fats	425	119	104-107	65-95	56-62	.04	90+		bland	white	50-lb. tin or cube, 110-lb. tin	Deep frying and baking	Economical; for all-purpose use
(as above)	450	113-115	99-103		51-56	.04	120+	Methyl silicone	bland	white	50-lb. tin or cube, 110-lb. tin, 5-lb. prints	Economy deep frying	Withstands heat well; nongreasy; good for potatoes, chicken, seafoods
Vegetable oils	350	116-118	95-99	60-95	80-85	.04		Hardened	bland	white	50-lb. tin or cube, 110-lb. tin, 5-lb. prints	Dual purpose: pan frying and baking	All-around standard shortening with good creaming qualities; makes smooth icings, fine-textured cakes, flaky pastry and biscuits, excellent pie crusts
Pure vegetable	340	114S	90-95	65-95	72-77	.08		Fully hydrogenated plus emulsifiers	bland	white	50-lb. tin or cube, 110-lb. tin, 5-lb. prints	Baking specifically	High emulsifying; absorbs more sugar, eggs, and liquid; superior creaming and dispersion; makes flaky pastry, rich icings

Hydrogenated vegetable oil with silicone added	450	104	89-92		65-70	.04	200+	Extra hydrogenated, with methyl silicone	bland	white	50-lb. cube	Deep frying	For heavy duty frying
Pure vegetable	450					.05	90	Methyl silicone		golden	6 1-gal. tins/case 5-gal. tin	Deep frying	Unsurpassed lifespan for a liquid frying medium
Pure vegetable oil	450	(liquid, 17 hrs. cold test)			108-111	.04	15	Refined, bleached, deodorized	bland	clear golden yellow	2 and 5 gal. tins	Salad dressings, cakes, waffles	Gives fried foods a glossy sheen; light bodied; blends quickly
Cottonseed	450	(liquid, 15 hrs. cold test)			108-112	.05	15	Refined, bleached, deodorized	bland	clear golden yellow	1 and 5 gal. tins	Salad dressings, cakes, waffles	Gives fried foods a glossy sheen; light bodied; blends quickly
Imported and domestic vegetable oils	340	80						Lecithin added	pleasing flavor (butter)	deep golden	no. 10 tin (6 lbs.) 5-gal. tin (38 lbs.)	Pan and grill fry-seasoning and basting	Semiliquid, no salt or moisture; fries with minimum of spattering; lecithin helps keep foods from sticking; brings out good color and true food flavors
Imported and domestic oils	450	Liquid (opaque)			98-102	.10	40	Refined, bleached, deodorized, votated	bland	deep golden	5 qt. tin	Pan and grill frying	Provides a delightful flavor, aroma, and color to fried foods
Margarine: veg. oils, nonfat milk, salt, vitamins									rich	yellow	30-lb. tin, 5-lb. chips, 1-lb. prints	For cream-in functions	Use where flavor and ingredients are creamed or blended
All-purpose margarine (Similar to above)									richer	yellow	30-lb. tin	For roll-in functions in baking	Makes flavorful, flaky, tender pastry

Courtesy of Kraft Foods, Chicago.

Most condiments keep very well and require no particular storage precautions. They resist bacterial multiplication and decay because of their acid pH. Some attention must be paid to quality, however, in purchasing condiments, since they vary considerably in specific gravity, form, ingredients, and consequent price. Satisfactory comparisons of the offerings available may be made only on taste, use, and price bases. Using these criteria, the best condiment available for a particular need may be selected.

Fats and Oils

Fats are the glycerol esters of fatty acids. Available in liquid and solid forms, they are used in almost every area of food preparation.

Liquid fats have a higher percentage of unsaturated fatty acids, while the naturally solid fats are made up of more saturated fatty acids. By the process of hydrogenation, liquid fats may be made solid as the unsaturated acids are converted to saturated ones.

Purchase and Use. Fats are used in deep frying, baking, grilling, and salad dressings. Fats in the form of butter and margarine are also used as spreads and additives to foods.

There are single-purpose and multiple-purpose fats. Most manufacturers provide a wide range to meet the various needs of the food service operator. Information about specific kinds of fats that the supervisor or manager of any food service operation must know is given below.

Deep frying fat is an important element in any food service operation. If it is not selected properly or is abused in use excessive costs will be incurred.

Look for the deep frying fat that has the longest frying life. A high smoke temperature and additives to extend frying life and protect against oxidation are desirable features.

Keeping the fat temperatures at reasonable levels for frying and at low levels when not in use will do much to keep the fat operational. Make sure that foods are dry when placed in fryers and that salt and foreign particles are not introduced.

Table 18-5. Smoke Points of Fats

Type	Initial Smoke Pt.	After-Use Smoke Pt.
Lard	361–401 F.	331–349 F.
Veg. oil	441–450 F.	367–369 F.
Emulsified Veg. shortening	356–370 F.	336–349 F.
Animal/veg. shortening		
Emulsified	351–363 F.	329–334 F.
Nonemulsified	448 F.	367 F.

(Source: Lowe, Pradhan, and Kasteliz, *Journal of Home Economics* 50 (1958): 778–779. Restaurants USA, June/July 1987, p. 33.)

Fat should be filtered daily, and new fat should be added to replace that absorbed in foods. Off flavors and excessive darkening of foods are indications that the entire batch should be replaced. A subjective decision must be made about when fat is no longer usable. It is based on such factors as the fried product's color, appearance, and eating quality, and the fat breakdown, foam, and smoke emission. Some objective measures of fat color and free fatty acids are available, but a more objective method is still needed for determining when fat should be discarded. Use of a high quality fat and attention to proper care of it remain the operator's best defenses against dissatisfied customers and excessive fat costs.

Baking fats are used in cakes, pies, cookies, and icings. Such factors as creaming ranges, emulsifier content, taste, and keeping quality are important considerations in choosing these fats.

Shortening with a creaming range between 60 and 95 degrees Fahrenheit gives the baker more flexibility in such products as cakes. Emulsifiers provide better absorption of the fat, disperse it more thoroughly throughout the product, and allow it to absorb more moisture. A bland taste is required for fats in some uses, such as for pastry.

Grilling or frying fats should have low melting points and should contain additives to give them nonsticking properties. Bland taste is important, unless a specific taste, such as that of bacon grease or butter, is desirable.

Salad oils must have the ability to remain

clear at low temperatures (the oil is then referred to as winterized) and be free of foreign materials, odors, or unpleasant tastes. Some oils are used in frying and in baked products, and these have different smoking temperature and flavor requirements.

19 *Service and Merchandising*

Objective: To consider the basic principles of food service and merchandising so that presentation of food enhances its acceptability. Emphasis is on the particulars of product flow, effective display, and various service styles. Special situations and smoking areas are also discussed.

The merchandising and service of food to the guest are both of extreme importance to the quantity food service supervisor. The closest attention to detail in the purchasing and preparation of items may be completely negated by a lax method of service and delivery of the food to the guest. In fact, service is really an integral part of the preparation process.

Flow of the Product

Of primary concern in attaining proper service is the flow of the food items. The manager or supervisor who has spent a good deal of time developing the proper functional flow relationship between his purchasing, storage, and preparation areas must not assume that the flow requirements stop at the dining room door. Cohesiveness between service and preparation personnel must be maintained so that well-prepared food reaches the consumer in a well-prepared state. Status and role problems between front-of-the-house staff members and food preparation personnel or a lack of quality controls at critical points in the flow of the food must not be permitted to reduce the excellence of the items offered.

Attention should be given to the layout of service and preparation areas in relation to each other. A hot item may quickly become cold if it has to wait for an item being produced for a fellow diner. If holding units are not available to avoid heat loss in foods awaiting pickup, or if service personnel cannot be signaled promptly to pick up foods that are ready for service, the quality of the food is sure to suffer.

A well-prepared platter or plate may arrive at a diner's cover in less-than-acceptable condition if service personnel are forced to travel great distances or to carry stacked plates on their outstretched arms so that one entrée sits on the entrée below.

The lack of a sauce, condiment, or spice that should accompany an item may make the food unacceptable to the diner. He impatiently awaits the sour cream for his baked potato, the sauce for his steak, or the cream for his coffee before consuming the meal that was hot when it arrived.

All these omissions reflect an improper flow of menu items from the kitchen preparation stations to the ultimate consumer, be he a banquet diner, a dining room guest, or a patient in a remote ward of a general hospital. The service and preparation functions do not operate as separate entities completely divorced from one another. They are dependent on each other to bring ultimate satisfaction to the guest.

Employee motivation to achieve this goal comes from within, after external conditions have been designed to contribute to employee job satisfaction. This desire to satisfy the consumers must be developed, so that all employees work in an effective relationship with one another. Too often the service workers consider themselves to be either a cut above or a cut below those who prepare the food (depending upon the type of establishment). They dismiss complaints or problems of guests as solely preparation problems. Preparation personnel, on the other hand, cannot bring themselves to empathize with the service worker, who must present the food to the guest face to face.

Some indoctrination and training should be given to both groups in an attempt to mold them into a united team that will achieve the organization's goals. These goals should also be congruent with the goals of each worker.

Speed and Ease of Work

The use of an expeditor, especially during the peaks of meal periods, should be considered by a manager or supervisor responsible for food production. This person should increase efficiency and enable waiters and waitresses to devote more time to the guests. The expeditor is often warranted in a table service restaurant whether a limited or an extensive menu is offered. He may also work to advantage calling out diets on an automated-belt serving line of a hospital serving special fare.

The type of dinnerware used, the serving stations developed, and the travel required of serving personnel are also important considerations. Service workers belong in the dining room as much as possible. They should be only lightly burdened with purely preparation tasks.

The operator must plan for lead times for various menu items, landing areas, and tray slides to ease the handling of dishes. Waiter replenishment stations in the dining room, heat lamps at serving centers, and self-leveling, heated dish dispensers may do as much to provide good quantity food offerings as the proper purchasing and preparation of raw food items.

Showmanship

Another extremely important factor that the food service manager or supervisor should consider is showmanship in service. Plate makeup, color combination, and garnishing have been previously considered; many other factors contribute to making food more acceptable and esthetically pleasing to the guest.

It may be possible, for example, to improve both showmanship and flow by having a rolling roast cart in the dining room on which meats are sliced at the diner's table. Placing food preparation stations in the dining room at a combination production and serving location may also help service and provide a form of entertainment to the guests. Here a broiler cook may perform his many duties as guests make up their own salad and raw bar servings. The arrangement thus contributes to both flow and show.

The dessert cart, the flaming entrée, and the salad cart for combining and tossing salads at the diner's table generally increase sales and diner satisfaction. But even if it is not feasible to use these particular techniques, others may be attempted with equally good results.

Sizzle platters, on which butter is placed just before service of a steak, increase the guest's olfactory, aural, and visual delight. The pastry bag and tubes may be put into play to pipe a vegetable, garnish, or accompaniment in a new, attractive display. A plank may be used to set off an entrée to advantage.

Cafeteria displays and arrangements may provide better showmanship and higher check averages if thought is given to the color grouping of vegetables, the positioning of gravies and sauces to prevent dripping, and the use of ice, color, and light to increase the appeal of food.

Trays carried by service personnel at ear lobe height do little to show the offerings of the kitchen to other diners, while a mobile cart carrying either entrées or desserts presents the food for all to see. The finishing flame applied at a gueridon may not actually cook the entrée in the traditional way, but it does call attention to the presentation method and cultivates guest satisfaction. Brandy of 80 proof (40 percent alcohol) or higher heated over the flame unit of a chafing dish, poured over the chafing dish ingredients, and ignited with a long match provides showmanship. The deep blue flames set against a gleaming silver tray in a dimly lighted room will do much more to sell a menu item than a secretly held recipe. (The operator should be sure that a wet towel and chafing dish cover are available to snuff out an overactive flame quickly.)

Service Appropriate to the Menu

In attempts to better the flow of food and to offer more showmanship, the menu and the form of the food remain important considerations. It is difficult to offer skewered, broiled items such as kabobs if hand labor is not available to spear the items or if the size and texture of the items purchased do not lend themselves to holding on skewers. It is equally difficult to maintain a ham in an attractive condition when it must be held on a steam table for any length of time, regardless of the showmanship employed, because of the very nature of the meat.

A strict portion-control procedure and the use of food scoops may do much to maintain the food cost percentage but the uniform,

Figure 19a. A typical French cover. Water goblet is at point of the knife with red wine to its right and white wine below. Usually only two wine glasses are placed on the table at one time.

mounded shapes can detract greatly from showmanship requirements.

The particular characteristics of a food or the menu's requirements as to extent and type of service (e.g., the number of side dishes required) impose certain restrictions on the scope of showmanship and the cohesiveness of flow that can be maintained. It is important, therefore, to consider the foods and the menu when deciding which show and flow applications are appropriate. Here, too, the menu reigns supreme.

Types of Table Service

There are basically four ways of offering prepared food to guests in a table service establishment: French, English, Russian, and American. Each has been used in quantity food situations and has certain desirable characteristics that a specific operation should consider.

French service is the traditional, classic form of service, in which the *chef de rang* and the *commis de rang* join in finishing the cooking procedures started in the kitchen. From a gueridon cart, the final touches are given to foods with a flair of showmanship that is long remembered. However, few establishments are still able to command a sufficient check average to support the labor and time required for French service. In those facilities that do retain it, it is present in spirit more than in form. The waiting team is reduced to one, and the flaming, portioning, and serving of an item is done *after* preparation rather than as an integral part of it. Nevertheless, with a little advance planning to relate the service to preparation, much of the flair can be retained.

Soups may be brought into the dining room in tureens and ladled into the guest's soup plate from a rechaud where they are kept warm. In like manner, meat items may be carved and the mixing of sauces or salads may be finished in the dining room at the guest's table for maximum effectiveness. A sommelier (wine steward) with a tasting cup and a wine basket can do much to bring back the flair of wine service and increase the check average.

In typical French service, after the food has been finished on the *rechaud* and plated from the *gueridon* onto the dinner plate, it is served from the right to the guest, centering the entree or meat item directly in front of the guest. If working as a team, the *commis de rang* holds the plate while the food is transferred from the *rechaud* to the plate by the *chef de rang*. If only one person is working the station, the food may be transferred directly onto the plate, which sits on the *gueridon* by the chef.

Russian service may be best used in banquet operations, clubs, fraternities, sororities, and the like. The food is plated on large, showy, silver trays in the kitchen and individually served to each guest by the waiter, providing a showmanship that makes it more appealing to the guest. Food can be kept at high quality, and most of the individual service and arrangement duties that normally fall to the cooks are transferred to the service personnel. Unlike French service, the food items, except for beverages, are delivered from the show platters to the guests from the left side and usually by the service personnel using a serving spoon and combination in the right hand (see Figure 19b). In some dishes, it is possible for the server to present the platter, tray, or container and allow the guest to serve him or herself, but this is usually an exception.

English table service, although appropriate to the home, has some application in certain restaurants. It is a family style of service, with meats and vegetables brought to the table in large containers and portioned by the host or hostess. This method has the effect of making portions seem larger while passing some of the serving tasks on to the guest, which many seem to enjoy. Placing the salad and relish table in the dining room for guest use is a form of English service.

American service, like most other systems developed in the United States, is designed to give an operator the greatest control and the most efficiency. It detracts from most types of showmanship, however, save in the garnishing and appearance of the food itself.

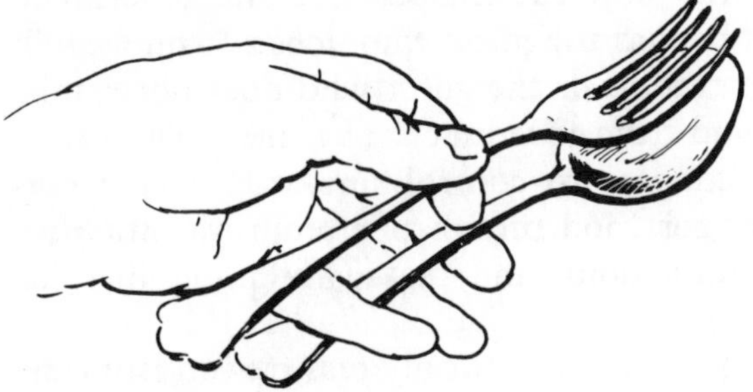

Figure 19b. The use of the fork and serving spoon to transfer food items from trays or other containers to the plates of guests. This lends an atmosphere of luxury to the serving procedure in the Russian style. It, of course, may be used in the plating procedure in the French style, although both hands are generally used here if two-person teams are available.

Food preparation personnel do all of the plate arranging, and service personnel only deliver the item to the guest and provide the required accessory items. As with the Russian service, all food items are delivered from the left side of the guest with the entire plate previously arranged as to amount of food, placement, garnish, and so on.

Each service style should be considered by a food operation from the viewpoint of such variables as check average, skill of preparation and service personnel, turnover, equipment available, and menu form. Menu construction and preparation methods may then be related to the type of service that has been selected so that maximum dining pleasure may be offered. In many cases it will be possible to achieve optimum use of personnel in both the front and the back of the house if menu, preparation, and serving procedures are integrated.

Smoking in Food Service Facilities

Among the leading consumer-oriented issues of the 1970s, and one that will apparently be with us well into the next century is the issue of smoking. Motivated by governmental research and action which indicated that cigarette smoking is injurious to health, consumer groups have had legislation enacted which makes smoking illegal in a number of locations.

Smoking of any kind has been forbidden in many public buildings and in stores and elevators in some states. The federal government has forbidden pipe and cigar smoking in aircraft engaged in transporting the public and has relegated cigarette smoking to specific areas of the aircraft.

Encouraged by these changes, many nonsmokers and reformed smokers have initiated actions either to have smoking banned completely or highly controlled in food service establishments. Many states either have considered or have passed legislation to control smoking in public dining rooms.

The issue of smoking in public dining rooms is one the food service operator must resolve for the general benefit of both present and potential consumers. Only in this manner can the manager meet the needs of her or his market. Like alcohol, politics, and religion, this issue has become a very emotional one, and the major function of the restaurant or food service manager is to insure a detached but fair consideration of all factors.

Many states that have passed legislation restricting smoking have limited the law to restaurants over a certain number of seats and have excluded bars from the legislation. (In one state with this form of legislation, many restaurants have changed their names to bars to escape the law, according to one expert.) Other states have required that a certain percentage of the seats in restaurants with a certain number of seats or more be reserved for nonsmokers. The major concern is to protect the nonsmoker from the smoke coming from a tobacco-using guest.

As of December 1986, sixteen states have restricted smoking in restaurants, and thirty-nine have restrictions on smoking elsewhere. One large city in California has banned all smoking in all restaurants. The state of Minnesota requires a 30 percent allocation in all restaurants for nonsmokers, and New York has proposed that a 50 percent allocation of seats for nonsmokers means that the no-smoking provisions have been met. In New York, employees can refuse to work in smoking areas.

A recent survey conducted by the Gallup organization for the National Restaurant Association showed that 61 percent of those polled preferred to sit in no-smoking areas, and 90 percent agreed that no-smoking areas should be provided (*Florida Restaurateur*, May 1987, p. 29).

Whether the manager feels the policy is right or wrong or is in agreement or not, he or she must try to satisfy the needs of all guests. If a guest asks for a table by the window or to be seated in a booth and it is possible—we oblige. Why then not make it possible for a guest to be at a table without being bothered by the smoke of another guest if that is requested? The alternative to this—since most of the population does not smoke—will be either that the guest who does not smoke will not return, or the guest who does not smoke will ask the government to make a law against smoking or to control smoking. It is important for food service operators to anticipate these actions and to make provisions for guests.

In the bar or lounge areas, fewer problems should result for research has shown that nonsmokers also tend to be nondrinkers. (Where separate tables have been reserved for nonsmokers in dining rooms, many operations have found that the average bill of fare at these tables is lower due to less use of alcohol.) No special areas at the bar or at lounge tables need be reserved for the nonsmoker.

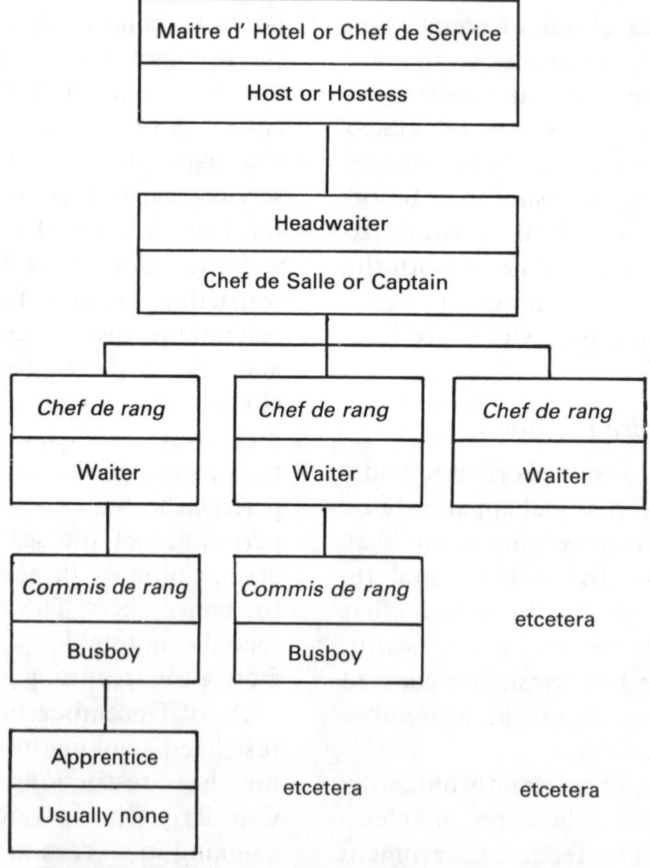

Figure 19c. Typical service team in the front of the house operation. The continental name given to each server is compared with its American counterpart. This chart shows the normal "chain of command" arrangement for front of the house operations.

Banquet Service

Both American and Russian service lend themselves very well to banquet service. The choice of one or the other depends on the check average and the number of guests to be served. To ensure that an accurate forecast will be made and that top quality food will be provided, some form of guarantee policy should be established. Provisions to ensure that those planning banquets make the necessary information available to the food facility will do much to make the event less of a problem for both the diners and the preparation staff. No-shows and unexpected guests cause waste or rush preparation problems when no guarantee has been required.

An effective policy is to require that a definite number to be served be submitted to preparation personnel twenty-four hours in advance of the event. Plans are then made to serve that number plus an additional 10 percent. If the established number of guests plus 10 percent appear, no preparation problems are experienced. The additional place settings may be supplied and a premium price collected. If fewer guests than the established number appear, the facility will charge full price for at least 90 percent of the forecasted number and half price for the remainder. This encourages banquet planners to make their forecasts closer to their actual preliminary estimates. Otherwise they tend to make arrangements for the highest possible number of guests, since they too do not want to run short. But realistic estimates will give both preparation and service personnel fewer problems.

Fast Food Facilities

Fast food operations offer convenience and ready food items to a highly mobile guest. Location of the facility and speed of service are the primary concerns in the merchandising scheme. It is as important to have good site selection in terms of the traffic count as it is to have an easily prepared and desirable food item. The customer is asked to provide much of the labor in the delivery system, and showmanship is relegated to a secondary position. Waxed paper wrappings, disposable plates, paper bags, and disposable cups with lids are used to advantage by these types of operations.

General Service Considerations

As noted, excellent food served poorly can result in the failure of a restaurant, while average food served in an outstanding manner often results in success. The service, or front of the house, aspect of food service facilities, long considered important, has recently become even more important to the consumer. Of course, at times, the fast food or self-service method will do, but many people still look forward to a night out or the big event when a meal is more than sustenance. Eating a meal becomes a happening, an event, an occasion.

Each restaurant or food service outlet, depending on its menu, decor, style, check average, market, and so on, must design its own program to provide the service—be it French, modified French, American, Russian, and so forth. There are, though, some commonalities applicable to all operations that the management needs to consider.

Service Team. The servers, whether called waiters, servers, captains, busboys, or maitre d's, are the major representatives of the management to the guest. The guest is greeted by these individuals, seated and served by them, and through them the guest expresses her or his pleasures, requests, frustrations, and problems.

Many food service operations foolishly hire as front of the house staff anyone who is available and to whom they can pay the smallest amount of wages. They expect, and sometimes encourage, turnover of employees to save on costs related to longevity and assume that "most anyone" can do the job. This philosophy is fallacious. Management should give great attention to the hiring of service personnel, both in its outward signals and inward concerns. The person hired should represent the establishment, to be sure, but smiles are often not enough. (Some companies hire young, smiling service workers, assuming that this covers all aspects. But a smile doesn't mean competence, and a forced smile can do much to discourage some guests.) Attitudes, motivation, competence, and desire to serve are important aspects of service. A service person who feels that he is doing someone a favor when he waits on them or who looks at the duties as only a source of tips, does a disservice to guests and becomes a problem for management.

Given the correct prerequisites, the service team is headed by a maitre d' hotel, host, or hostess (whatever they are called in a particular establishment), who is in charge of the service aspect of the business. This person should be in complete charge to ensure proper coordination between the kitchen, dining rooms, and bars as well as coordination between individuals and teams in the dining rooms.

This job involves greeting and seating guests, not merely meeting the needs of the establishment with the assignment of stations and so on, but to meet the needs of the guests upon whom the organization depends for its survival. The guest should not be made to wait while the host or hostess does other things, nor should the guest be refused a specific table because "that section is closed" or the stations are trying to "be evened up." Guests should be made to feel that they are really welcome, be presented with menus, and, if appropriate to the establishment, have drink or aperitif orders taken before the server's appearance.

The service personnel, be they captains, waiters, or *chefs de rang*, should be molded into a team to provide quick, efficient, and competent service to the guest while meeting the guest's specific needs as well as the needs of a properly functioning organization. Of course some fast food operations design chairs to be uncomfortable so they are not conducive to long-term comfort, and they also play lively music to ensure fast rates of guest turnover (since turnover is inversely proportional to check average, low checks–high turnover). But, generally, if someone wants to linger over a drink or wait before ordering, this request should be honored just as the house can honor the needs of a guest who has a theater date and has requested faster service to meet the curtain time.

Without making this text a specific manual on service, the following major points are important for service personnel, and managers should ensure that they are followed:

1. Service is one-third of the total food service package—the food and back of the house, the ambience, and the service. Service is a team effort and as noted is probably the most important of the three.
2. The service personnel must know the tools of service, their capabilities, and their limitations. They must know how to do what they do, what they should not do, and what they should do if they can't do what they are supposed to do.
3. Most guests are rational, reasonable people who will make "normal" requests and meet the service personnel half way. But some will not. Certain guests will argue, have extra and special problems, and demand excessive attention. We can't please everyone, but we can try. Within limitations, make an attempt or refer to higher authority for resolutions of problems.
4. Waiters belong in the dining room, not in the kitchen or in the rest room. That is why in the continental system, the *chef de rang* remains in the dining room while the *commis* delivers food from the kitchen to each service station. A similar program should be followed with each serving team, or there should be cooperative efforts with service personnel from differing stations. It is frustrating for a guest to wait for the service person to return from the kitchen so that a condition may be resolved, a condiment asked for, or another item ordered.

Removing nicks in a cleaver with the coarse stone, stroking in long figure eights, first one side of edge, then the other.

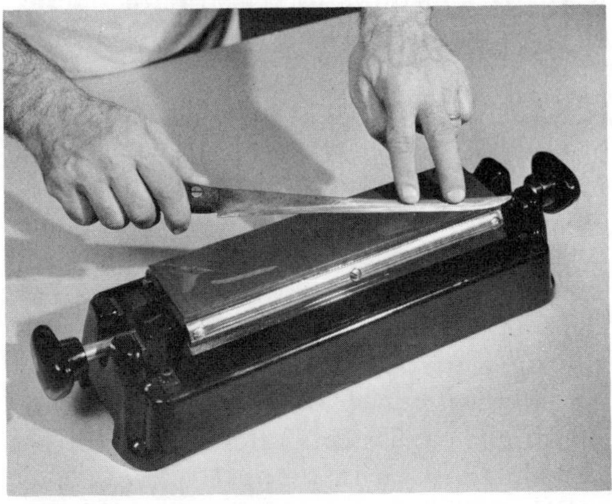

Restoring the edge on a butcher knife with the medium stone, stroking in long figure eights, holding an even angle for both sides.

Honing a keen edge on a boning knife with the fine stone, stroking in long figure eights, finishing gently on both sides.

Figure 19d. The method used to sharpen blades and renew the efficiency of knives. (Courtesy of the Norton Company, Troy, New York.)

5. The service person should know what is being served, how it has been prepared, and what its basic ingredients are—not so that she or he has the talents of a chef, but rather to answer the guests' questions. Does it come in a bowl, on a skewer, is it sauced, and so on. These are important to know.
6. There are no strangers in a good food service facility. Regular customers should, of course, be addressed by name, but newer customers should be addressed with the same degree of cordiality, even if their names are unknown.
7. Service persons should sell, suggest, offer. Even if there is no tip program where they will receive a percentage of the check, the increase in check average will mean an increase of sales for the restaurant, and this can only be good.

Carving and Slicing Meats

Carving and portioning meats (the most expensive menu items) may be completed in the kitchen (in American, English, and Russian service), at the diner's table (in French service), or at the serving station (in buffet or cafeteria service). Personnel responsible for this function should be well trained in the proper procedure to use, because inattention to details during this important step can overcome all the purchasing and yield standards that have previously been attained.

The equipment used should be in top condition for efficiency, and the correct knife should always be used for the particular task. Knives should be sharp, and a magnetized steel should be available at the carving station to straighten the edge as required during the carving process.

A varying-grit sharpening stone (coarse, medium, and fine) is suggested for maintaining knives in top condition. The coarse stone sharpens and removes knicks in blades, while the medium renews the cutting edge. The fine surface hones the sharpened edge.

Sharpening is done by holding the blade of the knife to be sharpened at a 45-degree point angle to the stone to be used. The cutting surface of the blade is also rotated to a 45-degree attitude angle to the stone. The blade is then drawn across the oiled stone surface in a figure-eight pattern, first on one side of the blade and then on the other.

Meats should not be carved until the post-oven rise period is over, so that cooking has been completed and excess internal heat dissipated. Meats that are too hot will flake during carving and result in a reduced yield.

If carving is done in the kitchen, many cuts of meat, such as a boneless rib, may be portioned quite readily on a meat slicer. In addition, a portion scale should be used to check periodically on the portion size. Eyeballing the cut is sometimes used instead of a scale, but those performing it should be well trained and experienced.

All meat except steaks should be cut across the grain in order to avoid stringiness and flaking. The angle and direction of the blade should be kept constant although some change can be made when using beef and ham slicers, which are more pliable. Most meat should be sliced in a number of pieces to make up a portion rather than in one large piece. (Exceptions to this rule are made for beef rib and similar cuts.) Better control can be maintained with several pieces, and psychologically the portion appears more satisfying. Slicing at an angle on such cuts as corned beef and flank steak is desirable for maximum tenderness and better display of the cut. Thin slices are also advantageous with these less tender pieces.

Plates or utensils to receive the slices should be well heated so that the meat retains the maximum warmth. Heating devices should also be used above meats that are being sliced so that they do not cool too rapidly.

If cutting boards are used in view of the customers, they should be well garnished and contribute to a pleasant dining experience.

Attention must be given to preliminary preparation methods to enable the carving and serving procedures to produce the most desirable result. Foods that are well prepared deserve to be well served. Some planning will ensure that this goal is realized.

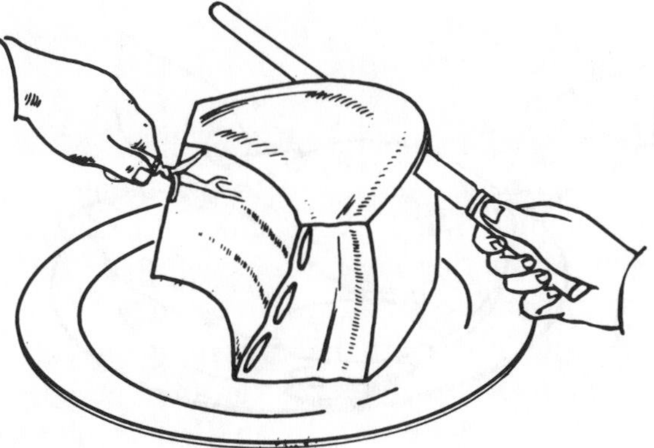

Before roasting, remove the short ribs and separate the backbone from the ribs. The backbone can then be removed in the kitchen after roasting. This makes the carving much easier, as only the rib bones remain. The roast is placed on the platter with the small cut surface up and the rib side to the carver's left.

Either the standard carving set or the roast meat slicer and carver's helper can be used on this roast.

With the guard up, insert the fork firmly between the two top ribs. From the far outside edge, slice across the grain toward the ribs (top illustration). Make the slices 1/8 to 3/8 inch thick.

Release each slice by cutting close along the rib with the knife tip (middle illustration).

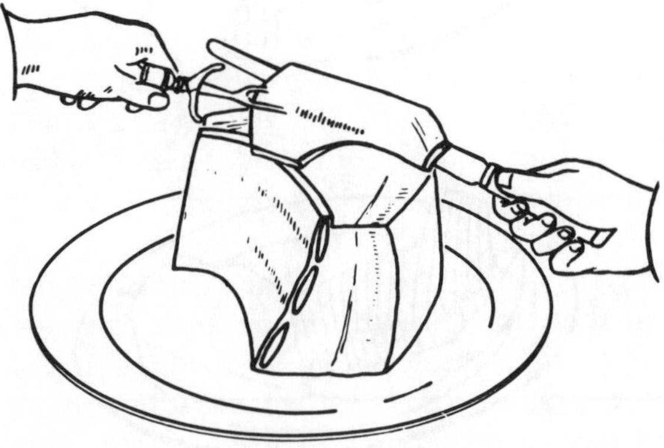

After each cut, lift the slice on the blade of the knife to the side of the platter (bottom illustration). If the platter is not large enough, have another hot platter near, to receive the slices.

Make enough slices to serve all guests before transferring the servings to individual plates.

Figure 19e. Carving technique for a standing rib roast. (Courtesy of the National Live Stock and Meat Board, Chicago.)

Place the ham on the platter with the fat or decorated side up. The shank end should always be to the carver's right. The thin side of the ham, from which the first slices are made, will be nearest or farthest from the carver, depending on whether the ham is from the right or the left side of the pork. The illustrations show a left ham with the first slices cut nearest the carver.

Use a standard carving set or the slicer and carver's helper on baked ham.

Insert the fork and cut several slices parallel to the length of the ham on the nearest side (top illustration).

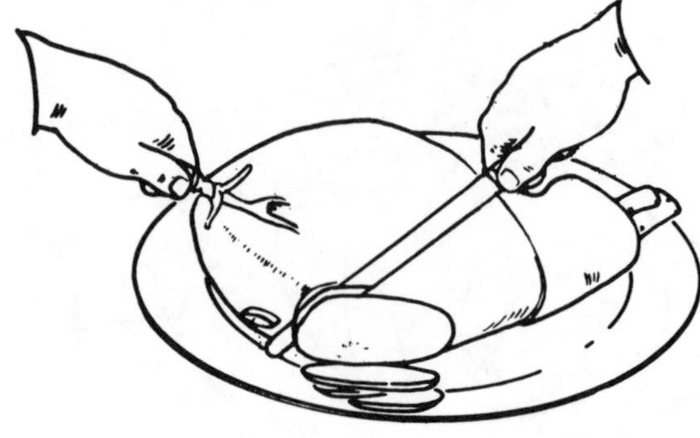

Turn the ham so that it rests on the surface just cut. Hold the ham firmly with the fork and cut a small wedge from the shank end (second illustration). Removing this wedge makes the succeeding slices easier to cut and to release from the bone.

Keep the fork in place to steady the ham, and cut thin slices down to the leg bone (second illustration).

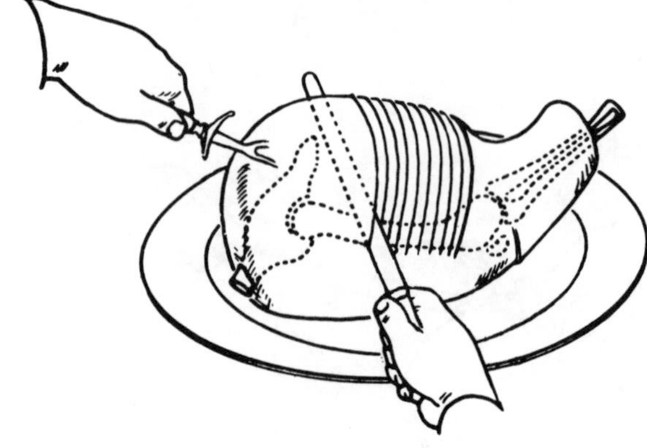

Release the slices by cutting along the bone at right angles to slices (third illustration).

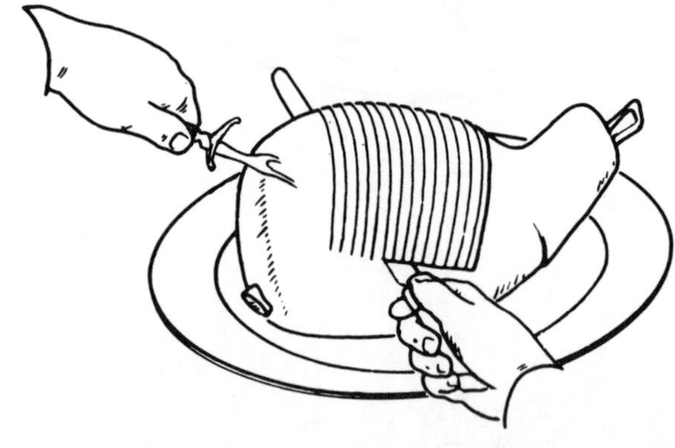

For more servings, turn the ham back to its original position and slice at right angles to the bone (bottom illustration).

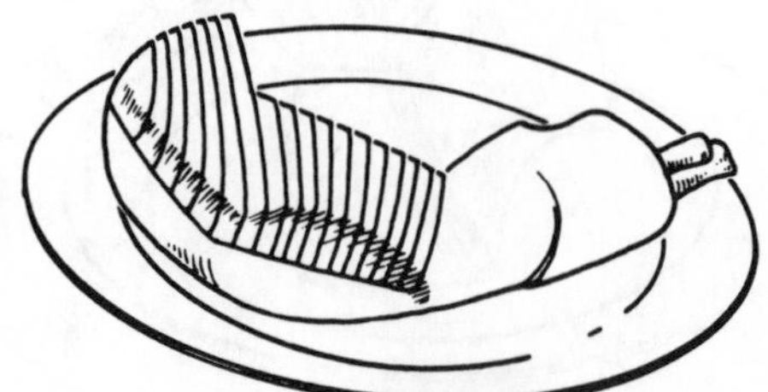

Figure 19f. Carving technique for a baked whole ham. (Courtesy of the National Live Stock and Meat Board, Chicago.)

Center-Cut Ham Slice: Divide into thirds and turn one of the sections on its side as shown. Make slices the desired thickness across the grain. Carve other sections in the same way. Remove the bone from the end section before slicing.

Cushion Lamb Shoulder: This cut is boneless and easy to carve. Cut slices about 3/8 inch thick through the meat and dressing.

Picnic Shoulder: The carving procedure is almost identical to that for baked ham. Take slices from the smaller meaty side, and turn the shoulder to stand on this surface. Slice to the bone, starting at the shank end. Release the slices by cutting along the bone.

Beef Tongue: Slice off excess tissue and cartilage from the large end of the tongue. Continue making thin, even, and parallel slices. This gives lengthwise slices from the small end of the tongue, as shown.

Half Ham (Shank End): Remove the cushion section, turn it on the cut side (as shown), and make slices beginning at the large end. For further servings from the remaining section, separate it from the shank by cutting through the joint. Remove the bone, turn the section, and slice it.

Beef Brisket: Place the cut on the platter with the round side away from the carver. Trim off excess fat. Make slices in rotation from three sides, as shown. The slices should be thin and at a slight angle. Carving in this way makes all cuts across the grain.

Figure 19g. Carving techniques for various meat cuts. (Courtesy of the National Live Stock and Meat Board, Chicago.)

20 *Legal Liability*

Objective: To consider the current conditions in the hospitality industry as they relate to the liabilities of the restaurant and food service operator.

Tort Law

Although the food service business is primarily concerned with the purchasing, preparing, and serving of food products, a new element has become extremely important to the entrepreneur concerned with serving food to the public. The "age of litigation" has arrived, and consumers are suing all segments of the business community, from physicians to restaurant operators, for wrongs (real or imagined) imposed on the consumer during the business relationship.

According to Richard K. Willard, assistant attorney general of the United States, speaking to a restaurant association meeting, a jury in 1985 awarded $1.5 million in damages to the estate of a woman who was killed when a horse fell through the roof of her 1980 Ford Pinto. Wolves had frightened the horse, who had been confined in a field surrounded by a barbed wire fence. The horse broke through the fence, ran out on the road, and was hit by the passing car. Knocked into the air, he fell through the roof of the car, killing the woman. And the Ford Motor Company was made to pay the award. Many strange events characterize modern liability. Emergency rooms at hospitals close due to the premium rates for malpractice insurance on doctors. Liability insurance costs for restaurants average 110 percent increases in one year. Lawyers advertise on television or travel to Puerto Rico to sign up those who are injured in a hotel fire. Maybe Lloyds of London was correct when it said that the American civil justice system is "rotten to the core."

The food service operation does business in a hostile environment, promising an intimate service to its guests while relying on its employees to follow the laws, regulations, and common practices related to the guest-host relationship. It is not only in the business of serving food and drink to guests, but it is also in the business of protecting the guests while they are in the establishment, providing the actual items listed on the menu, enforcing the no-smoking and other laws of the community, and properly and legally dispensing alcoholic beverages to guests. In addition, it is charged with treating its employees in a manner that is consistent with federal and local regulations, in regards to minors, women, minorities, the handicapped, and so on.

To protect themselves against many of these problems, most restaurants, of course, carry some form of insurance package. Property insurance, liability for actions against others, workmen's compensation, auto insurance, robbery and theft insurance are all needed. But in most insurance areas, there have been excessive increases in premiums, some loss of availability, and many headaches for operators.

A guest falls on a wet floor; another finds a bone in a food item that he says caused him injury; an employee delivering a pizza has an automobile accident with the company car; or a patron who ate and drank at the establishment hits another vehicle on the way home and is arrested for drunken driving. A waitress is assigned to duties and asked to wear a uniform that she believes is indecent, or an employee is discovered to have AIDS and is discharged from his duties because of his possible ability to infect others. These are all potential liability situations.

The largest concerns for food service establishments are slips and falls, poorly lit areas, the security of customers, and liquor liability as a result of guests' actions after they have been served alcoholic beverages. What can be done? What must be done?

Just as with sanitation, the operation has a legal, moral, and economic obligation to its guests. The legal one has been well documented by trial lawyers who will seek and often win awards based on what they will receive in fees. Of course, the economic implications can be staggering—witness the horse coming through the roof in the opening paragraph. The moral obligation should apply in any case because of the guest-host relationship.

It is not the intent of this chapter to make the reader a "do it yourself attorney," for of course, each establishment must have access to a professional for legal purposes. The intent is to educate about the many potential legal problems and hazards that exist in the typical food service establishment. The proper purchase, preparation, and arrangement of an entree on a plate are not the only (or in some cases not the major) problems that face the food service manager. There are many more.

Although the typical freestanding restaurant (because it does not furnish lodging) is distinguished from the inn and the laws relating to innkeepers, the owner is still required under common law to protect his or her guests. The term "to take reasonable care" so that the guest will not be injured in a manner that "the prudent person" would prevent or exercise serves as the basis for any claim of negligence on the part of a hotel operator or a restaurant or food service operator that might result in a liability judgment. The failure of the operator or of an employee to do something such as wipe up spilled water or to post a sign indicating a wet floor or to replace a burned-out bulb in a darkened area might result in a judgment according to the laws of torts.

A tort is any wrongful conduct that does harm. Tort law provides punishment for those who do wrong and compensates those who are harmed (sometimes, it appears, excessively). At times this tort award, despite the degree of negligence (if in fact two or more people or organizations are considered to be jointly liable but in different degrees), goes to what is known as the "deep pockets" principle and attacks the one who has the most money and the ability to pay the full judgment. (This is illustrated with the award noted in the opening paragraph, when the auto manufacturer was made to pay the judgment since it was the most solvent party.)

There are, of course, hundreds of potential actions, activities, and conditions within food service operations that could cause potential problems in relationships with guests and visitors. Of these, the two most important are the dispensing of alcoholic beverages and the serving of food.

At common law, the seller of alcoholic

Table 20-1. Liquor Liability Laws of Each State as of 1985

State	Dram Shop	Common Law Negligence	No Law	State	Dram Shop	Common Law Negligence	No Law
Connecticut	x			Illinois	x		
Delaware			x	Indiana		x	
District of				Iowa	x		
Columbia		x		Kansas			x
Maine	x			Michigan	x		
Maryland			x	Minnesota	x		
Massachusetts		x		Missouri		x	
New Hampshire			x	Nebraska			x
New Jersey		x		North Dakota	x		
New York	x			Ohio	x		
Pennsylvania	x			Oklahoma			x
Rhode Island	x			South Dakota		x	
Vermont	x			Texas		x	
Alaska	x			Wisconsin		x	
Arizona		x		Alabama	x		
California	x			Arkansas			x
Colorado	x	x		Florida	x		
Hawaii		x		Georgia	x		
Idaho		x		Kentucky		x	
Montana			x	Louisiana		x	
Nevada			x	Mississippi		x	
New Mexico	x	x		North Carolina	x	x	
Oregon	x	x		South Carolina			x
Utah	x			Tennessee		x	
Washington		x		Virginia		x	
Wyoming	x	x		West Virginia			x

From National Restaurant Association, *Restaurant Business*, Sept 20, 1985, p. 124. Address: 633 Third Ave., NY, 10017.

beverages was not usually held liable for the actions of a drunken guest since the drinker was considered to be responsible for his or her own actions. However, many states passed "dram-shop" laws, which placed third-party liability on the part of the seller or server of alcoholic beverages for illegal or irresponsible activities.

The present actions of many states in regards to drunk or impaired drivers, the interest being shown by the general public, and the awards being made by many courts to plaintiffs against restaurants and bars as third party negligent participants warrant attention. Thirty-four states have passed some sort of driving while impaired (DWI) legislation since 1981. The basis of the driving under the influence (DIU) or driving while impaired statutes generally applies to the body blood alcohol content (BAC). In most states a level of .10 percent is considered tantamount to a drunken driver (although some states accept concentrations of from .05 to .09 percent). In general terms (and only for discussion, since each individual differs according to body metabolism, weight, height, amount of food eaten, and so on), a 150-pound man consuming four drinks in one hour would have a BAC of .10 percent.

Some states have outlawed the happy hour or two-for-one drink promotions, and many private groups have put pressure on legislators for more effective drunk-driving laws. Judges have become more strident, and many courts and juries have awarded large sums to plaintiffs against establishments that served alcoholic beverages to patrons who were later convicted of DWI.

Some establishments have put "breathalizer" equipment in to help determine when and if a patron is impaired. Many attorneys, however, have suggested that this should not be done and that the only rational approach that should be used is to monitor speech patterns, behavior, and the demeanor of patrons to determine when and if service should be discontinued.

Of course someone must check to determine if a person is of the proper age to be served, and management should use a taxi to send home a guest who seems too impaired to drive. The practice of giving free nonalcoholic beverages to "designated drivers" who transport other drinking members of the dining party should be encouraged. Any action that tends to indicate the establishment is exercising reasonable care in this matter will help to dispel unwarranted litigation attacks. Management should also undertake training of all employees, pointing out the danger signals and indicating to bartenders and servers how to handle problem cases and situations. Some states have taken actions to remedy the apparent inequities by limiting awards or reducing liabilities, but vigilance still remains important for operating establishments.

With food, as well, a contractural relationship exists with each guest. Here there is an implied obligation to serve food, as advertised and fit for consumption, under similar arrangements of tort law. Finding a pearl in an oyster that causes damage to a person's teeth is not the same as finding a piece of glass in a chocolate eclair. It remains important for each establishment to show that wholesome food has been purchased, stored, prepared, and served, and that diligence and reasonable care have been applied in each aspect of the process.

Proper screening of potential employees to check for past records of violence known by former employers and personal reference checks should also be done to ensure that your agents, that is, the employees, are well intentioned and worthy of trust. Risk situations must be identified and outlined to employees. Safety concerns should be uncovered and procedures undertaken to record and investigate all incidents that happen during accidents or events. Quality-assurance committees (see Chapter 21) can do much to uncover unsafe conditions and events.

Relationship with Employees

Dealings with guests are not the only potential legal problems for establishments, and this is not the only area that should concern management. In not dealing properly with the operation's staff, a manager can experience many potential problems and conditions that may lead to legal problems, lawsuits, excessive monetary awards, or simply unpleasant working relationships.

Uniforms for women employees may be interpreted as a form of sexual harassment and result in jury awards under Title VII of the Civil Rights Act. The rules of the Equal Employment Opportunity Commission can be violated due to improper work scheduling. Unsafe internal working conditions with potential danger to employees can result in excessive workers' compensation insurance premiums or actions by the Occupational Safety and Health Administration (OSHA) on behalf of employees.

With increases in insurance premiums in all facets of the industry (some as high as 300 percent) and some insurance companies refusing to write any insurance at all on certain types of facilities or risks, and with higher amounts of deductibles being required by many organizations, it is time that torts and legal liability become of greater concern to food service management.

Increased liabilities have cut across all fields from medicine to transportation to the restaurant. It is time for the typical food service operation to maintain an internal risk-management program and thus, by proper vigilance, training, and attention to detail, be able to make the operation a better insurance risk. Keep in mind that fires, slips, falls, the security of customers, and liquor liability are the most important potential causes of problems in this "age of litigation" where the duties of the food service management are more than preparing and serving food.

21 *Quality Assurance*

Objective: To introduce the reader to the importance of high standards of quality as a basis for success in the competitive, fast-changing food service business.

The Importance of Quality

Many factors have been identified as being important to the successful operation of a food service establishment—menu, pricing structure, management style, location, and so on. Location (as previously noted) has long been considered by many hotel planners as having particular importance to a specific hotel. In other words, if the hotel (or by extrapolation the restaurant) were located in the right place, it would probably succeed. Conversely, if it were not in close proximity and in the correct attitude to its market, it would fail. There is some validity to this concept, though it is extremely important to remember that this is by far not the only important element. In fact, if location is considered the one, the only, and the most important element, this approach creates great problems for the operation. Quality, for example, is more important than quantity or location almost every time.

The history of quality control can be traced to the beginning of the Industrial Revolution, in general, and to the World War II period, in particular. Prior to the Industrial Revolution, almost all work was undertaken and completed by artisan practitioners who operated on a "bespoken" or individual-order basis. These craftsmen made a suit or a house or a pair of shoes for a particular client and were sought out by the client because they were thought to possess the necessary skills and abilities that would result in excellent products or services.

Such capable craftsmen were the products of long apprenticeships, under master craftsmen of their own particular trade. After a long and tedious period of training, they were certified (many times as a result of the production and acceptance of their "masterpiece") as being independent journeymen in their own right. They knew that in working on their own, the product or the service they produced was theirs—it might carry their name, logo, trademark, but in any case it was something that could be attributed to them, something that would follow them and help create their reputations.

This same practice applied to chefs who devised individual recipes, concocted them, closely supervised their preparation and service, and assisted in presenting them to the guests just as it applied to the glassblower, coppersmith, or farrier. It also applied to the maitre d' (host), who personally greeted, seated, and served his guests throughout a meal period and who became known for his table.

With the development of the Industrial Revolution, though, and the resulting dependence on factories, machines, assembly lines, and other systems to produce the many products required for an inventory that would often be unassignable or untraceable to one particular worker, a less stringent personal relationship began to exist between the producer and the user. This same impersonal relationship became echoed in many hotels and restaurants as the guest-host relationship became one of necessity, expediency, and convenience rather than one of affinity created because of a longstanding personal relationship. For example, as society became more mobile and people moved from place to place, the need became: "I am hungry, I need a meal." If a particular operation was available, it was used. The guest assumed he might never see the host again, and the host, chef, or server felt the same. Likewise a shoe machine worker would make a pair of shoes for a mass of faceless people whom he would never meet or who would never trace the shoes to him. They were for a size 8 or 8½, and he knew nothing more.

Beginning with this impersonal relationship, enterprises developed that were eager to produce more, sell more, ship more, and meet ever-expanding demand without much concern for quality. This culminated in the World War II period, when the needs of a greatly expanding economy, taxed by the demands of war, moved the country into full employment and full utilization of resources. This expanding production required thousands of units from butter to bullets as well as the facilities to move troops, defense-related workers, and others nationwide on short notice. Quantities needed were sometimes superimposed on quality in the areas of products, transportation, food service, and others. These conditions and their results are well illustrated by considering a time early in the war when torpedoes made by some American plants for use in American submarines to sink enemy ships were found to have faulty gyroscopic functions. Many either went off course when fired or in some extreme cases would turn around and return toward the firing submarine.

In many fields of endeavor, due to the total employment conditions and the need to recruit workers quickly to achieve the desired results, workers were hired without adequate experience, training, or backgrounds. This also resulted in lowering quality standards.

Within the government, however, some attempt was made to address the question of quality, particularly as it related to the war weapons, for no military force could defeat its enemies if its weapons would not fire correctly. Utilizing statistical sampling techniques and controls, a quality-assurance program was developed by the government and transferred to defense plants. This program resulted in the improvement of major problems (particularly in the weapons area) and resulted in helping achieve a successful conclusion to the American war effort.

After World War II the United States was the only major industrialized nation whose capacity to produce had not been damaged or destroyed by the war. With other countries throughout the world needing products and materials, American manufacturers had an almost complete monopoly, which often led to sacrificing quality for quantity. Workers, who were often paid on a piecework basis, attempted to keep up with speeded-up assembly lines, and quality suffered even more as mistakes and errors were permitted to happen.

At about the same time, General Douglas MacArthur, in charge of the occupation of Japan, saw the need to help the Japanese develop the capabilities to once again assume a rightful place in society. With most of their production destroyed, new facilities were built, and plans were made to restart production. As part of this plan, he asked W. Edwards Deming, an advocate of quality control and a pioneer in the effort produced during World War II, to go to Japan and offer information in this area. The rest, of course, is history.

The Japanese embraced quality-control principles, integrated them into their operational plans, and eventually began delivering automobiles and other products superior in quality to much being produced by the United States. The original American principle of quality control, which was discarded in the name of quantity and expediency, was accepted by the Japanese and resulted in their return to full and effective production methods. No longer did "Made in the U.S.A." necessarily mean a product was good.

So effective has the quality-control movement been that it has been embraced by most other countries in the industrialized West and by American companies, hotels, and restaurants as well. In the food service industry, the system has come full circle; the guest is no longer willing to accept any meal under any conditions (although there are still situations where this does happen). Rather, the guest is eager to experience a healthful, pleasant, entertaining dining experience that is indicative of quality. It is important that the food service manager or supervisor ensure that the guest receives this experience.

Plan

With many establishments traditionally hiring workers with little or no training or background who have personal goals of working in the industry only until something more lucrative comes along, it would appear that the need for quality control certainly exists. Such is the case in many operations. High turnover, absenteeism, and discipline rates are all attributed to problems in the hiring and staffing procedures and, of course, resulting problems with quality. This means quality cannot be adequately controlled, offered, or achieved unless attention is paid to adequately hiring, training, and placing the worker (see Chapter 3 on personnel). Assuming that these measures have been followed, the next step is to institute an adequate control program for quality.

Program

As suggested, the quality level management strives for is predicated on the needs and desires of the particular market being served and the standards management decides on. But true quality goes beyond this, for given these parameters (unless the owner, manager, or supervisor is able to carry out all facets of the operation), the employees must grasp the benefits that come from providing quality service both to themselves and to the operation's guests.

The first step, therefore, in starting a quality-assurance program is a general policy statement that considers the goals desired and the benefits to be derived from such a plan. The benefits listed are not only to the guest and the operation, but also to the management and the employees in general. With this policy statement determined and communicated, it is possible to approach the next step of getting the involvement and commitment of the employees in order to carry out the training programs necessary to gain the desired results.

Participants

Management should attempt to gain complete participation by all employees in the establishment's quality program. Although a personal commitment should be required from all levels of the operating organization in meeting the standards of quality decided upon, the creation of the standards—and the overall administration of the program—should be controlled by management personnel and, if possible, be well supported by volunteers from the general operating levels.

Volunteers from the rank and file levels

who have helped to create standards have a personal involvement in having them met. As a result, they are more likely to exercise the necessary measures to ensure that the standards have been achieved. The more employees involved and the more levels represented, the more likely it is that the program will reach its goals.

Standards

Each job must be broken down into tasks and eventually into the individual procedures needed to accomplish each task. For each of these, a standard should be developed. These standards should be based on the two major concerns of procedure and attitude. Standards should be clearly expressed in terms of measurable, observable, and determinable factors. For example, the greeting of a guest who enters the dining room needs to be expressed in terms of manner, timing, attitude, anticipation, and so on, including and detailing all the elements involved. These standards must be expressed in specific measurable terms that can be used later to measure performance. The standards need to be communicated to all involved. The amount of time in which a guest should be met at the entrance door, presented with a menu, and have a drink order taken are examples of elements in writing precise standards.

For each position and for all tasks attributable to that position, a set of these standards should be available for indoctrination, training, and supervision of workers. Some of the important standards deal with items such as:

1. Customers—concerns or accommodations such as making separate checks if asked, permitting substitutes on menus, serving sandwiches or smaller snacks during the period when full meals are normally served.
2. Anticipating customers' needs—for example, being ready before the customer asks with napkins when chicken or ribs are served or having catsup ready and available when French fries are ordered or offering a second cocktail when the first is almost empty.
3. Customers' concerns—attempting to be aware of customers' moods and needs during the meal and before they leave.
4. Attitude—determining the attitude the server displays in appearance, voice, tone of voice, or body language, indicating that the guest is welcome and the server is ready to serve.
5. Selling techniques—ways in which servers suggest sales to increase check averages and benefit both establishment and server.

Errors

Measures must be taken to identify errors and to evaluate their implications and costs. All individuals in the operation, from management to supervisors, employees, and even guests, should have the means and motivation available to uncover errors and report them to those concerned. Of course, guests should be the last ones to uncover and report a breach of quality control because measures should be available and operational to permit the error to be uncovered much sooner at a much higher level. With an adequate training and indoctrination program, quality concerns should be addressed by the person who carries out the function so that lapses in quality do not occur, there are no errors involved, and the guest receives the level of quality and service and product planned for. This is ideal. If permitted to occur, problems in not achieving quality standards can result in guest dissatisfaction and a guest who will not return, or breakage of an item, waste, and poor publicity or public relations.

Finally, it is necessary to have committees at the organizational, departmental, and operating levels. An executive committee is needed to determine objectives and policy; a company quality-assurance committee, to administer the general program; a department head and staff committee, to create standards and correct discrepancies; and of course the quality circles at all operating levels and departments. The guest comment program (in whatever form) is, in most cases, a last resort to indicate a lapse in an internal program or standards that should have been addressed.

Location may still be important, but for most operations—even for fast foods, where the standards of speed, convenience, and communication might be even more important to the operation and ultimately to the product and service delivered to the consumer—quality still counts more. It is, therefore, important for each supervisor to help develop a set of standards for each position and methods by which everyone involved can tell whether these standards are being met.

Appendix 1. Standard Weights, Measures, and Conversion Charts

Appendix Table 1. Abbreviations of Standard Measures

t.	teaspoon	gal.	gallon
T.	tablespoon	oz.	ounce
C.	cup	lb.	pound
pt.	pint	pk.	peck
qt.	quart	bu.	bushel

Appendix Table 2. Equivalent Measures

Liquid	Dry
3 t. = 1 T.	16 oz. = 1 lb.
16 T. = 1 C. = 8 oz.	2 gals. = 1 pk.
2 C. = 1 pt. = 16 oz.	4 pks. = 1 bu.
2 pts. = 1 qt. = 32 oz.	
4 qts. = 1 gal. = 128 oz.	

Note: Solid ingredients are weighed where possible. If flour is measured by volume, it must be sifted first because of its tendency to pack during transit. Other difficult-to-measure items, such as brown sugar and solid fat, must be packed solidly into the volume measure to get the correct amount. Liquid ingredients are measured by volume. In measuring by volume, be sure that the amount goes to the measuring mark called for in the recipe, not above or below.

Appendix Table 3. Measures of Oven Temperatures

250° to 350° F.	low or slow
350° to 400° F.	moderate
400° to 450° F.	hot or quick
450° to 500° F.	very hot

Appendix Table 4. Weights and Approximate Measures of Foods

Food	1 Ounce Equals	1 Cup Equals	1 Pound Equals
Allspice	4-1/2 T.		
Almonds, shelled		5-1/3 oz.	3 C.
Apples, medium			3
Apples, diced			3 C.
Applesauce			1-1/2 C.
Apricots, dried		5-1/3 oz.	3 C.
Asparagus, fresh			16 to 18 stalks
Bacon, raw		11 slices	20 to 25 slices
Bacon fat		8 oz.	2 C.
Baking powder	2-2/3 T.	6 oz.	2-2/3 C.
Bananas, medium			3
Bananas, diced		6-1/2 oz.	2-1/2 C.
Beans, green, fresh			1 qt.
Beans, kidney		6 oz.	2-2/3 C.
Beans, lima		6-1/2 oz.	2-1/2 C.
Beans, navy		7 oz.	2-1/4 C.
Beef, cooked, diced		5-1/3 oz.	3 C.
Beef, ground		8 oz.	2 C.
Beets, fresh			2-3
Beets, cooked		12 oz.	1-1/4 C.
Bran		2 oz.	2 qts.
Bread crumbs, dry		3 oz.	5-1/3 C.
Bread crumbs, soft		2 oz.	2 qts.
Brussels sprouts			1 qt.
Butter	2 T.	8 oz.	2 C.
Cabbage, shredded		3 oz.	5-1/3 C.
Carrots, small			5-6
Carrots, grated, raw		4 oz.	1 qt.
Cauliflower, medium			1 head
Celery		4 oz.	1 qt.
Cheese, American, grated		4 oz.	1 qt.
Cheese, cottage		7 oz.	2-1/4 C.
Cheese, cream		4 oz.	1 qt.
Cherries, pie		5-1/3 oz.	3 C.
Cherries, pie, pitted		8 oz.	2 C.
Cherries, glacéed		6-1/2 oz.	2-1/2 C.
Chicken, cooked, diced		5-1/3 oz.	3 C.
Chocolate	1 square		16 squares
Cinnamon	4 T.	4 oz.	1 qt.
Citron		6-1/2 oz.	2-1/2 C.
Cloves, ground	3-1/2 T.	4-1/4 oz.	3-3/4 C.
Cloves, whole		3 oz.	5-1/3 C.
Cocoa	4 T.	4 oz.	1 qt.
Coconut, shredded		2 oz.	2 qts.
Coffee, ground, medium		3-1/4 oz.	5 C.
Corn, no. 2 can		8 oz.	2 C.
Cornflakes		1 oz.	1 gal.
Cornmeal		5 oz.	3-1/4 C.
Cornstarch	3-1/2 T.	5 oz.	3-1/4 C.
Crab meat		3 oz.	5-1/3 C.
Cracker crumbs		2-1/2 oz.	6-1/3 C.
Crackers, graham, 1½" x 2½"		18	96
Crackers, graham, crushed		18	
Crackers, white soda, 2" x 2"		20	176
Cranberries		4 oz.	1 qt.
Cream of wheat		5-1/3 oz.	3 qts.
Cucumbers			3 C. 3 medium
Currants, dried		5-1/4 oz.	3 C.
Dates, pitted		6-3/4 oz.	2 C.
Eggs, hard-cooked		4	
Eggs, whites		8 oz. 7 to 9	14 to 16

Food	1 Ounce Equals	1 Cup Equals	1 Pound Equals
Eggs, whole		8 oz. 4 to 5	8 to 10
Eggs, yolks		8 oz. 12 to 14	24 to 26
Farina, uncooked		5-1/3 oz.	3 C.
Figs, dry		5-1/3 oz.	3 C.
Flour, cake, sifted		3-1/2 oz.	4-1/2 C.
Flour, graham		4-1/2 oz.	3-1/2 C.
Flour, rye		3-1/3 oz.	5 C.
Flour, white, sifted		4 oz.	1 qt.
Flour, whole wheat		5-1/3 oz.	3 C.
Gelatin, flavored		4-1/2 oz.	3-1/2 C.
Gelatin, unflavored	4 T.	4 oz.	1 qt.
Ginger, crystallized, cut fine	1 T.		
Ginger, dry	5 T.		
Grapes, seeded, cut			2-3/4 C.
Grapefruit			2 C.
Ham, ground		8 oz.	2 C.
Hominy, pearl		5-1/3 oz.	3 C.
Horseradish, prepared		4 oz.	1 qt.
Lemons, medium			3 to 4
Lemon juice		8 oz.	2 C. 8 lemons
Lemon peel	4 T.		
Loganberries, no. 2 can			2-1/4 C.
Lettuce, average head		8 to 9 oz.	
Macaroni, dry		3-1/2 oz.	4-1/2 C.
Marshmallows			60
Mayonnaise		7-1/4 oz.	
Milk		8 oz.	2 C.
Molasses			1-1/3 C.
Mushrooms, fresh			1-3/4 qts.
Mushrooms, sautéed			1-1/2 C.
Mustard, dry	5 T.	3-1/4 oz.	5 C.
Noodles, dry			3 qts.
Nutmeg, ground	3-1/2 T.	4-1/2 oz.	3-1/2 C.
Oats, rolled		3 oz.	5-1/3 C.
Oil, corn		7 oz.	2-1/4 C.
Olives, green, diced		20 olives	
Olives, ripe, diced		44	
Olives, stuffed		56	
Onions, chopped		8 oz.	2 C. 4 to 5 medium
Orange juice		4 oranges	
Orange peel	3 T.		
Oysters			1 qt. large 40 to 45
Paprika	4 T.	4 oz.	1 qt.
Peaches, fresh, medium			3 to 4
Peanut butter		9 oz.	1-3/4 C.
Pears, medium			3 to 4
Pecans		3-1/2 oz.	4-1/2 C.
Pepper, white	4 T.	4 oz.	1 qt.
Peppers, green, chopped		2 to 3 medium	
Pickles, chopped		12 small	
Pimientos		4 diced 7 oz.	
Pineapple, sliced, canned		3 slices, diced	8 to 12 slices
Pineapple juice		8 oz.	2 C.
Pork, ground			2 C.
Potatoes, white, raw, medium			3 to 4
Potatoes, white, cooked, diced			2 C.
Prunes, cooked			3 C. (no juice)
Prunes, dried			2-1/2 C.
Pumpkin, canned		8 oz.	2 C.

Food	1 Ounce Equals	1 Cup Equals	1 Pound Equals
Raisins, seedless		5-1/3 oz.	3 C.
Rice, raw		8 oz.	2 C.
Rice, cooked			2 qts.
Rhubarb, 1/2" pieces		4 oz.	1 qt.
Salad dressing, French		8 oz.	2 C.
Salmon, canned			2 C.
Salt	2 T.	8 oz.	2 C.
Shortening		6-1/2 oz.	2-1/2 C.
Shrimps		5 oz.	3-1/3 C.
Soda	2-1/3 T.		
Spaghetti, dry		4 oz.	1 qt.
Spinach, cooked			2-1/2 C.
Squash, Hubbard, cooked			2-1/4 C.
Strawberries, crushed			2 C.
Strawberries, fresh, whole			3 C.
Sugar, brown		6 oz.	2-3/4 C.
Sugar, confectioner's		5-1/3 oz.	3 C.
Sugar, cubes			120 cubes
Sugar, granulated		8 oz.	2 C.
Tapioca, instant		6-3/4 oz.	2-1/2 C.
Tapioca, pearl		5-1/3 oz.	3 C.
Tea		2 oz.	
Tomatoes, canned		8 oz.	2 C.
Tomatoes, fresh, medium			3 to 4
Tomato juice		8 oz.	2 C.
Tomato puree		8-1/2 oz.	
Tuna fish		8 oz.	2 C.
Vanilla wafers, crushed			5 C.
Veal, ground		8 oz.	2 C.
Vinegar		8 oz.	2 C.
Walnuts		4 oz.	1 qt.
Water			2 C.
Yeast, compressed	2 cakes		

Appendix Table 5. Portions and Yields of Foods

Food	Portion Size	Portions per Unit Purchased
Vegetables		
Fresh	2½ to 4 oz.	3 to 5 per lb. AP
Frozen	2½ to 4 oz.	5 per lb. AP
Canned	2½ to 4 oz.	20 to 25 per no. 10 can
Meats		
Bacon	2 strips	11 per lb. AP
Ground beef	4 oz. AP	4 per lb. AP
Chops	4 oz. AP	4 per lb. AP
Roasts	3 to 4 oz. EP	2 to 3 per lb. AP
Chicken	¼ bird	4 per 3-lb. fryer
Turkey	3 to 4 oz. EP	2 per lb.
Variety meats	3 to 4 oz. EP	4 to 5 per lb.
Sausage patties	2 oz.	4 per lb.
Sausage links	2 links	6 to 8 per lb.
Fish		
Fillets	3 to 4 oz. EP	4 per lb.
Steaks	5 oz. AP	1 per steak AP
Frozen	2 to 3 oz. EP	5 to 8 per lb.
Canned	3 to 4 oz. EP	4 to 5 per lb.
Juices		
Canned	4 oz.	12 per 46-oz. can
Frozen concentrate	4 oz.	32 per can

Note: AP means as purchased; EP means edible portion.

Appendix Table 6. Amounts of Foods for 50 Servings

Food and Purchase Unit	Amount per Unit	Approximate Serving Size	Servings per Pound (AP)	Amount to Buy for 50 Servings	Comments
MEATS					
Beef					
Rib roast, rolled, boned, 7-rib	12 to 15 lbs.	2-1/2 to 3 oz. cooked (3-1/2 to 4-1/2 inch slice)	2-1/2 to 3	17 to 20 lbs.	May use sirloin butt, boned
Rib roast, standing, 7-rib	16 to 25 lbs	3 to 3-1/2 oz. cooked	2 to 2-1/2	20 to 25 lbs.	
		4 to 5 oz. cooked	1-1/3 to 1-2/3	27 to 36 lbs.	
Chuck pot roast, bone-in, top	9 to 12 lbs.	3 to 3-1/2 oz. cooked	2 to 2-1/2	20 to 25 lbs.	
Chuck pot roast, bone-in, cross-arm	6 to 9 lbs.	3 to 3-1/2 oz. cooked	2 to 2-1/2	20 to 25 lbs.	Top chuck is more tender
Round steak		4 to 4-1/2 oz. clear meat, uncooked	2-1/2 to 3	17 to 20 lbs.	Bottom round requires longer cooking than top round
Stew, chuck and plate, clear meat		5 oz. stew	3 to 5	10 to 17 lbs.	Yield per lb. of raw meat depends on amount of vegetables added to stew
Lamb					
Leg roast	6 to 8 lbs.	2-1/2 to 3 oz. cooked (3-1/2 to 4-1/2 inch slice)	1-1/2 to 2-1/2	20 to 35 lbs.	Great variation is due to difficulty in carving
Shoulder roast, boneless	4 to 6 lbs.	2-1/2 to 3 oz. cooked (3-1/2 to 4-1/2 inch slice)	2-1/2 to 3	15 to 20 lbs.	
Stew, shoulder and brisket, clear meat		5 oz. stew	2-1/2 to 3	17 to 20 lbs.	Yield per lb. of raw meat depends on amount of vegetables added to stew
Pork					
Loin roast, trimmed	10 to 12 lbs.	2-1/2 to 3 oz. cooked (3-1/2 to 4-1/2 inch slice)	2 to 2-1/2	20 to 25 lbs.	
Ham					
Fresh, bone-in	12 to 15 lbs.	3 to 3-1/2 oz. cooked	2 to 2-1/2	20 to 25 lbs.	
Smoked, tenderized, bone-in	12 to 15 lbs.	3 to 3-1/2 oz. cooked	2-1/2 to 3	17 to 20 lbs.	Smoked shoulder may be substituted for ground or cubed ham in recipes
Canned, boneless, ready-to-eat	2 to 9 lbs.	3 oz. cooked	4 to 5	10 to 12 lbs.	

Food and Purchase Unit	Amount per Unit	Approximate Serving Size	Servings per Pound (AP)	Amount to Buy for 50 Servings	Comments
Veal					
Leg roast	15 to 20 lbs.	3 to 3-1/2 oz. cooked	1-1/2 to 2-1/2	20 to 35 lbs.	Great variation is due to difficulty in carving
Shoulder roast, boneless	8 to 14 lbs.	3 to 3-1/2 oz. cooked	2-1/2 to 3	17 to 20 lbs.	
Cutlet		4 to 5 oz. uncooked	3 to 4	12 to 17 lbs.	May use frozen cutlets
Ground meat					
Patties	1 lb. raw meat measures 2 C. packed	4 to 5 oz. uncooked (1 or 2 patties)	2-1/2 to 3	17 to 20 lbs.	May use one kind of meat only or combinations, such as 10 lbs. beef and 5 lbs. veal or pork, or 10 lbs. fresh pork and 5 lbs. smoked ham
Loaf or extended patties	1 lb. raw meat measures 2 C. packed	4 to 4-1/2 oz. cooked	3-1/2 to 4	12 to 15 lbs.	May use one kind of meat or a combination
Bacon					
Sliced	30 to 36 medium or 15 to 20 wide strips per lb.	3 strips	10 to 12	5 to 6 lbs.	1 lb. cooked and diced measures 1-1/2 C.
		2 strips	7 to 10	5 to 7 lbs.	
Canadian, sliced	12 to 16 slices per lb.	2 or 3 slices	5 to 8	7 to 10 lbs.	
Liver		4 oz. cooked	3 to 4	13 to 17 lbs.	
Sausage					
Links	8 to 9 large per lb.	3 links	3	17 to 20 lbs.	Yield varies with proportion of fat that fries out in cooking
Cakes		6 to 8 oz. raw (2 cakes)	2 to 2-1/2	20 to 25 lbs.	
Wieners	8 to 10 per lb.	2 wieners	4 to 5	10 to 11-1/2 lbs.	
FISH					
Fresh or frozen fillets		4 to 5 oz.	3 to 4	14 to 17 lbs.	
Oysters					
For frying	24 to 40 large per qt.	4 to 6 oysters		7 to 8 qts.	
For scalloping	60 to 100 small per qt.			4 to 5 qts.	
For stew	60 to 100 small per qt.	4 to 6 oysters		3 qts.	

Food and Purchase Unit	Amount per Unit	Approximate Serving Size	Servings per Pound (AP)	Amount to Buy for 50 Servings	Comments
POULTRY					
Chicken					
Fryers, dressed	2½ to 3½ lbs.	¼ fryer		35 to 40 lbs.	Dressed means bled and with feathers removed
Fryers, eviscerated	1¾ to 2½ lbs.	¼ fryer		25 to 30 lbs.	Eviscerated means ready to cook
Fowl					
For fricassee, dressed	3½ to 6 lbs.	4 to 6 oz. bone-in	1 to 1½	35 to 50 lbs.	
For fricassee, eviscerated	2½ to 4½ lbs.	4 to 6 oz. bone-in	1¼ to 2	25 to 35 lbs.	
For dishes containing cut-up cooked meat, dressed		1 to 2 oz. clear meat	2½ to 3	17 to 20 lbs.	4 lbs. raw yield about 1 lb. cooked boned meat
For dishes containing cut-up cooked meat, eviscerated		1 to 2 oz. clear meat	3 to 4	13 to 17 lbs.	3 lbs. raw yield about 1 lb. cooked boned meat
Turkey					
Young tom, dressed	12 to 23 lbs.	2 to 2½ oz. clear meat	1 to 1½	35 to 50 lbs.	1 lb. raw yields 4 to 5 oz. sliced clear meat or 5 to 6 oz. cooked boned meat
Young tom, eviscerated	10 to 18 lbs.	2 to 2½ oz. clear meat	1½ to 2	25 to 35 lbs.	Yields of all turkeys depend on type and size of bird: broad-breast and larger birds yield more than standard type and smaller birds
Old tom, dressed	20 to 30 lbs.	2 to 2½ oz. clear meat	1 to 1½	35 to 50 lbs.	
Old tom, eviscerated	16 to 25 lbs.	2 to 2½ oz. clear meat	1½ to 2	25 to 35 lbs.	
VEGETABLES					
Asparagus, by lb. or in bunches	2 to 2-1/2 lbs. per bunch; 32 to 40 stalks per bunch	3 oz. or 4 to 5 stalks	3 to 4	12 to 16 lbs.	Yield may be increased if tough part of stalk is peeled
Beans, green or wax, by lb.	1 lb. measures 1 qt. whole or 3 C. cut up	2-1/2 to 3 oz. or 1/2 C.	4 to 5	10 to 12 lbs.	
Beets					
By lb.	4 medium per lb. (1-1/2 to 2 C. cooked and diced)	2-1/2 to 3 oz. or 1/2 C.	4 to 4-1/2	12 to 14 lbs.	
By bunch	4 to 6 medium per bunch	2-1/2 to 3 oz. or 1/2 C.	4 to 4-1/2	12 to 14 lbs.	
Broccoli, by lb. or in bunches	1-1/2 to 2-1/2 lbs. per bunch	2-1/2 to 3 oz.	2-1/2 to 3	17 to 20 lbs.	Yield may be increased if tough part of stalk is peeled

Food and Purchase Unit	Amount per Unit	Approximate Serving Size	Servings per Pound (AP)	Amount to Buy for 50 Servings	Comments
Brussels sprouts, by qt. berry basket	1 to 1-1/4 lbs. per basket	2-1/2 to 3 oz.	4 to 6	10 baskets or 12 lbs.	
Cabbage, by lb.					
Raw	4 to 6 C. shredded per lb.	1 to 2 oz.	8	8 to 10 lbs.	
Cooked	2 qts. raw shredded per lb.	2-1/2 to 3 oz. or 1/2 C.	4	12 to 15 lbs.	
Carrots, by lb.					
Cooked	6 medium per lb.	2-1/2 to 3 oz. or 1/2 C.	3 to 4	14 to 16 lbs.	1 lb. raw yields 2 C. cooked and diced; after cooking, 3-1/4 C. diced weigh 1 lb.
Raw		strips, 2 to 3 inches long		2 to 2-1/2 lbs.	3-1/2 C. diced raw weigh 1 lb.
Cauliflower, by head, trimmed	1 to 3 lbs. per head	3 oz. or 1/2 C.	2	28 to 32 lbs.	A 3-lb. head yields 3 qts. raw flowerets
Celery, pascal, by bunch					
Cooked	1 medium bunch weighs 2 lbs.	2-1/2 to 3 oz. or 1/2 C.	3 to 4	7 to 10 bunches	1 medium bunch yields 1-1/2 qts. raw diced
Raw	1 medium bunch weighs 2 lbs.		8 to 10	3 to 4 bunches	1 qt. raw diced weighs 1 lb.
Cucumbers, single	1 cucumber weighs 10 to 14 oz.	5 to 7 slices (1/4 C.)		8 to 9 cucumbers	1 medium yields 1-3/4 to 2 C. of peeled slices
Eggplant, single or by dozen	1 small eggplant weighs 1 lb.	2-1/2 oz. (1-1/2 slices)	4	10 to 12	A 1-lb. eggplant yields 8 to 9 slices
Lettuce, by head	1 medium head weighs 1-1/2 to 2-1/2 lbs. before trimming	1/6 to 1/8 head		4 to 5 heads for garnish; 6 to 8 heads for salad	10 to 12 salad leaves per head; 1 head untrimmed yields 1-1/2 to 2 qts. shredded; 2 qts. shredded weigh 1 lb.
Mushrooms, by lb. or basket	1 basket weighs 3 lbs.				1 lb. raw sliced tops and stems measures 7 C.; 2-1/2 C. sautéed weigh 1 lb.
Onions, by lb.	4 to 6 medium per lb.	3 to 3-1/2 oz. or 1/2 C.	3 to 4	14 to 16 lbs.	1 lb. yields 2-1/2 to 3 C. chopped; 1 C. chopped weighs 5 oz.; 1 C. sliced weighs 4 oz.
Parsley, by bunch	1 bunch weighs 1 oz.				1 medium bunch yields 1/4 C. finely chopped; 1 C. chopped weighs 3 oz.
Parsnips, by lb.	3 to 4 medium per lb.	2-1/2 to 3 oz.	3 to 4	15 lbs.	

Food and Purchase Unit	Amount per Unit	Approximate Serving Size	Servings per Pound (AP)	Amount to Buy for 50 Servings	Comments
Peppers, single or by lb.	5 to 7 per lb.				1 lb. yields 2 C. finely diced; 1 C. chopped weighs 5 oz.
Potatoes, sweet, by lb.	3 medium per lb.	3-1/2 to 4 oz.	2-1/2 to 3	17 to 20 lbs.	
Potatoes, white					
By lb.	3 medium per lb.	4 to 4-1/2 oz. or 1/2 C. mashed or creamed	2 to 3	15 to 20 lbs.	1 lb. yields 2-1/4 C. diced
By bushel	1 bu. weighs 60 lbs.	4 to 4-1/2 oz. or 1/2 C.	2 to 3		
By bag	1 bag weighs 50 lbs.	4 to 4-1/2 oz. or 1/2 C.	2 to 3		
Rutabagas, by lb.	1 to 2 per lb.	3 to 3-1/2 oz. or 1/2 C.	2 to 2-1/2	20 to 25 lbs.	1 lb. yields 1-1/2 C. mashed or 2-1/2 C. diced
Spinach, by bag or bushel	10 or 20 oz. per bag	3 to 3-1/2 oz. or 1/2 C.	2-1/2 to 3	17 to 20 lbs. home-grown or 12 to 15 10-oz. bags cleaned	A 10-oz. bag yields 2 qts. raw, coarsely chopped for salad
Squash					
Summer, by lb.		2-1/2 to 3 oz. or 1/2 C.	3 to 4	13 to 16 lbs.	
Winter, by lb.		3 oz. or 1/2 C. mashed	2	25 to 30 lbs.	
Tomatoes, by lb., 8 lb. basket, or 10-lb. carton	3 to 4 medium per lb.	3 slices raw	5 (sliced)	10 lbs. for slicing	1 lb. yields 2 C. diced or cut in wedges
Turnips, white, by lb.		3 oz. or 1/2 C.	3 to 4	15 to 20 lbs.	
FRUITS					
Apples					
By lb.	2 to 3 medium per lb.	1/2 C. sauce		15 to 20 lbs. for sauce or pie	1 lb. before peeling yields 3 C. diced or sliced; 4-1/2 to 5 C. pared, diced, or sliced weigh 1 lb.
By pk.	1 pk. weighs 12 lbs.	1/2 C. sauce		15 to 20 lbs.	1 pk. (12 lbs.) makes 4 to 5 pies, 4 to 5 qts. of sauce, 7 to 8 qts. of raw cubes
By bu.	1 bu. weighs 48 lbs.	1/2 C. sauce		15 to 20 lbs.	
By box	1 box contains 80 to 100 large or 113 to 138 medium	1/2 C. sauce		15 to 20 lbs.	
Bananas, by lb. or dozen	3 to 4 medium per lb.	1 small	3 to 4	15 lbs.	1 lb. yields 2 to 2-1/2 C. sliced thin or 1-1/4 C. mashed; for 1 C. sliced or diced, use 1-1/3 medium; for 1 C. mashed, use 2-1/4 medium
Cranberries, by lb.	1 lb. measures 1 to 1-1/4 qts.	1/4 C. sauce	12 to 14 for sauce	4 lbs. for sauce	1 lb. makes 3 to 3-1/2 C. sauce or 2-3/4 C. jelly

Food and Purchase Unit	Amount per Unit	Approximate Serving Size	Servings per Pound (AP)	Amount to Buy for 50 Servings	Comments
Grapefruit, by dozen, box, or half-box	54 to 70 medium per box; 80 to 126 small per box				1 medium-small yields 10 to 12 sections or 1-3/4 C. broken sections
Lemons, by dozen, box, or half-box	210 to 250 large per box; 300 to 360 medium per box; 392 to 432 small per box			25 to 30 lemons (1-1/4 qts. juice) for 50 glasses of lemonade	1 medium yields 1/4 C. juice and 1 t. grated rind; 4 to 5 medium yield 1 C. juice
Oranges, by dozen, box, or half-box	80 to 126 large per box; 150 to 200 medium per box; 216 to 288 small per box	1/2 C. sections		40 to 50 oranges	Use medium oranges for table and salad; 1 medium yields 12 sections and 1/2 to 2/3 C. diced
Peaches					
By lb.	3 to 5 per lb.	3 oz. or 1/2 C.	4	10 to 12 lbs. for slicing	1 lb. yields 2 C. peeled and diced
By pk.	1 pk. weighs 12-1/2 lbs.	3 oz. or 1/2 C.	4		
By 1/2 bu.	1/2 bu. weighs 25 lbs.	3 oz. or 1/2 C.	4		
Pineapple, single	1 medium weighs 2 lbs.	1/2 C. cubed		5 medium	1 medium yields 3 to 3-1/2 C. peeled and cubed
Rhubarb, fresh, by lb.		1/2 C. sauce	5	10 lbs.	10 lbs. yield 6 qts. sauce
Strawberries, by qt.	1 qt. yields 3 C. hulled	1/2 C.		10 to 13 qts.	1 qt. yields 4 to 5 servings of fruit
	1 qt. yields 1 pt. hulled and crushed	1/3 C. for shortcake		8 to 10 qts.	1 qt. yields 6 servings of sauce for shortcake
STAPLES					
Cocoa	1 lb. measures 4 C.; 1 C. weighs 4 oz.			2 C. (1/2 lb.) for 50 C. beverage (2-1/2 gals.)	
Rice	1 lb. raw measures 2-1/8 C.	1 no. 16 or no. 12 scoop	15 to 20	2-1/2 to 3 lbs.	1 lb. cooked measures 1-3/4 qts.
Sugar					
Cubes	50 to 60 large or 100 to 120 small cubes per lb.	1 large or 2 small	50 to 60	3/4 to 1 lb.	
Granulated	1 lb. measures 2-1/8 C.; 1 C. weighs 7 oz.	1-1/2 t. to sweeten coffee	50 to 60	3/4 to 1 lb.	
Bread, by loaf					
White and whole wheat	1-lb. loaf yields 18 slices	1-1/2 slices to accompany meal	12	4 loaves	
	2-lb. club loaf yields 24 slices	1-1/2 slices	8	3 loaves	
	2-lb. Pullman (sandwich) loaf yields 36 slices	1-1/2 slices	12	2 loaves	

Food and Purchase Unit	Amount per Unit	Approximate Serving Size	Servings per Pound (AP)	Amount to Buy for 50 Servings	Comments
Bread (cont.)					
Rye	1-lb. loaf yields 17 slices	1-1/2 slices	11	4-1/2 loaves	
	2-lb. short loaf yields 29 slices	1-1/2 slices	10	5 loaves	
	2-lb. long loaf yields 36 slices	1-1/2 slices	12	2 loaves	
Butter	1 lb. measures 2 C.; 1 oz. measures 2 T.		48 to 60	1 to 1-1/2 lbs.	Available in wholesale units cut into 48 to 90 pieces per lb.; 60 count gives average size cut
Cheese					
Brick	1 brick weighs 5 lbs.	1-oz. thin slices for sandwiches	16	3-1/4 lbs. for sandwiches	
		4/5-oz. cubes for pie	20	2-1/2 lbs. for pie	
Cottage	1 lb. measures 2 C.	no. 10 scoop (approximately 1/2 C.)	8 to 9	6 lbs.	1 lb. yields 12 to 13 of the no. 16 scoops and 25 of the no. 30 scoops
Coffee					
Ground	1 lb. drip grind measures 5 C.			1 lb.	Makes 50 C. when added to 2-1/2 gals. of water
Instant				2-1/2 C.	Add to 2-1/2 gals. of water
Cream					
Heavy (40 percent) to whip		1 rounded T.		1 pt. (yields 1 qt. whipped)	Doubles its volume in whipping
Light (20 percent) or top milk for coffee	1 qt. yields 64 T.	1-1/2 T.		1-1/4 qts.	
Fruit or vegetable juice	1 46-oz. can measures approximately 1-1/2 qts.	4-oz. glass or 1/2 C.		4-1/3 46-oz. cans (6-1/2 qts.)	
	1 no. 10 can measures 13 C. or 3-1/4 qts.	4-oz. glass or 1/2 C.		2 no. 10 cans (6-1/2 qts.)	
Fruits, dried					
Prunes	1 lb. contains 40 to 50 medium	4 to 5 for stewed fruit		5 to 6 lbs.	
Honey	1 lb. measures 1-1/3 C.	2 T.		5 lbs.	
Ice cream					
Brick	1-qt. brick cuts 6 to 8 slices	1 slice		7 to 9 bricks	Available in slices individually wrapped
Bulk, by gals.		no. 10 scoop		2 gals.	1 gal. yields 25 to 30 servings
Lemonade		8-oz. glass (3/4 C.)		2-1/2 gals. (25 to 30 lemons for 1-1/4 qts. of juice)	
Peanut butter	1 lb. measures 1-3/4 C.			4 lbs. for sandwiches	
Potato chips	1 lb. measures 5 qts.	3/4 to 1 oz.		2 lbs.	

Food and Purchase Unit	Amount per Unit	Approximate Serving Size	Servings per Pound (AP)	Amount to Buy for 50 Servings	Comments
Salad dressings					
Mayonnaise, by qt.		1 T. for salad		1 to 1-1/2 qts. for mixed salads; 3 to 4 C. for garnish	
French				3/4 to 1 qt.	
Sandwiches					
Bread	2-lb. (14-in.) loaf cut 30 to 35 medium or 35 to 40 very thin slices	2 slices	7 to 8 medium; 9 to 10 very thin	3 loaves	
Butter, by lb.		spread on 1 slice		3/4 lb.	
		spread on 2 slices		1-1/2 lbs.	
Fillings		2 T. or no. 30 scoop		1-3/4 to 2 qts.	
		3 T. or no. 24 scoop		2-1/2 to 3 qts.	
Tea, iced	1 lb. measures 6 C.			3 oz.	Makes 50 glasses when added to 2-1/2 gals. water and chipped ice
Vegetables, dried					
Beans, navy	1 lb. measures 2-1/2 C.			5 to 6 lbs.	

From Marion Wood Crosby and Katharine W. Harris, *Purchasing Food for 50 Servings,* rev. ed., Cornell Extension Bulletin no. 803; New York State College of Home Economics, Ithaca, N.Y., 1963; reprinted by permission.

Appendix Table 7. Fractional Equivalents of Measures for Use in Converting Recipes

Fraction	1 Tablespoon	1 Cup	1 Pint	1 Quart	1 Gallon	1 Pound
1	3 t.	16 T.	2 C.	2 pts. (4 C.)	4 qts.	16 oz.
7/8	2-1/2 t.	1 C. less 2 T.	1-3/4 C.	3-1/2 C.	3 qts. plus 1 pt.	14 oz.
3/4	2-1/4 t.	12 T.	1-1/2 C.	3 C.	3 qts.	12 oz.
2/3	2 t.	10 T. plus 2 t.	1-1/3 C.	2-2/3 C.	2 qts. plus 2-2/3 C.	10-2/3 oz.
5/8	2 t. (scant)	10 T.	1-1/4 C.	2-1/2 C.	2 qts. plus 1 pt.	10 oz.
1/2	1-1/2 t.	8T.	1 C.	2 C.	2 qts.	8 oz.
3/8	1-1/8 t.	6 T.	3/4 C.	1-1/2 C.	1 qt. plus 1 pt.	6 oz.
1/3	1 t.	5 T. plus 1 t.	2/3 C.	1-1/3 C.	1 qt. plus 1-1/3 C.	5-1/3 oz.
1/4	3/4 t.	4 T.	1/2 C.	1 C.	1 qt.	4 oz.
1/8	1/2 t. (scant)	2 T.	1/4 C.	1/2 C.	1 pt.	2 oz.
1/16	1/4 t. (scant)	1 T.	2 T.	1/4 C. (4 T.)	1 C.	1 oz.

Courtesy of the Hobart Manufacturing Company, Troy, Ohio.

Appendix Table 8. Conversion Chart of Weight Measures for Recipes in 25-Portion Increments

Instructions

1. Locate the column that corresponds to the original yield of the recipe you wish to adjust. For example, let us assume your original recipe for meat loaf yields 100 portions. Locate the 100 column.

2. Run your finger down this column until you come to the amount of the ingredient required (or closest to this figure) in the recipe you wish to adjust. Say that your original recipe for 100 portions of meat loaf requires 21 lbs. of ground beef. Run your finger down the column headed 100 until you come to 21 lbs.

3. Next, run your finger across the page, in line with that amount, until you come to the column that is headed to correspond with the yield you desire. Suppose you want to make 75 portions of meat loaf. Starting with your finger at 21 lbs. (in the 100 column), slide it across to the column headed 75 and read the figure. You will need 15 lbs. 12 oz. of ground beef to make 75 portions with your recipe.

4. Record this figure as the amount of the ingredient required for the new yield of your recipe. Repeat steps 1, 2, and 3 for each ingredient in your original recipe to obtain the adjusted ingredient weight needed of each for your new yield. You can increase or decrease yield in this manner.

5. If you need to combine two columns to obtain your desired yield, follow the above procedure and add together the amounts given in the two columns to get the amount required for your adjusted yield. For example, to find the amount of ground beef for 225 portions of meat loaf (using the same basic recipe for 100 we used above) locate the figures in columns headed 200 and 25 and add them. In this case they would be 42 lbs. plus 5 lbs. 4 oz., and the required total would be 47 lbs. 4 oz.

6. The figures in Appendix Table 8 are given in exact weights, including fractional ounces. After you have made yield adjustments for every ingredient, you may round off fractional amounts that are not of sufficient proportion to change product quality. No rounding off was required in the examples we have used here.

Portions												
25	50	75	100	200	300	400	500	600	700	800	900	1000
*	*	*	1/4 oz.	1/2 oz.	3/4 oz.	1 oz.	1-1/4 oz.	1-1/2 oz.	1-3/4 oz.	2 oz.	2-1/4 oz.	2-1/2 oz.
*	*	*	1/2 oz.	1 oz.	1-1/2 oz.	2 oz.	2-1/2 oz.	3 oz.	3-1/2 oz.	4 oz.	4-1/2 oz.	5 oz.
*	*	*	3/4 oz.	1-1/2 oz.	2-1/4 oz.	3 oz.	3-3/4 oz.	4-1/2 oz.	5-1/4 oz.	6 oz.	6-3/4 oz.	7-1/2 oz.
1/4 oz.	1/2 oz.	3/4 oz.	1 oz.	2 oz.	3 oz.	4 oz.	5 oz.	6 oz.	7 oz.	8 oz.	9 oz.	10 oz.
*	*	*	1-1/4 oz.	2-1/2 oz.	3-3/4 oz.	5 oz.	6-1/4 oz.	7-1/2 oz.	8-3/4 oz.	10 oz.	11-1/4 oz.	12-1/2 oz.
*	3/4 oz.	*	1-1/2 oz.	3 oz.	4-1/2 oz.	6 oz.	7-1/2 oz.	9 oz.	10-1/2 oz.	12 oz.	13-1/2 oz.	15 oz.
*	*	*	1-3/4 oz.	3-1/2 oz.	5-1/4 oz.	7 oz.	8-3/4 oz.	10-1/2 oz.	12-1/4 oz.	14 oz.	15-3/4 oz.	1 lb. 1-1/2 oz.
1/2 oz.	1 oz.	1-1/2 oz.	2 oz.	4 oz.	6 oz.	8 oz.	10 oz.	12 oz.	14 oz.	1 lb.	1 lb. 2 oz.	1 lb. 4 oz.
*	*	1-3/4 oz.	2-1/4 oz.	4-1/2 oz.	6-3/4 oz.	9 oz.	11-1/4 oz.	13-1/2 oz.	15-3/4 oz.	1 lb. 2 oz.	1 lb. 4-1/4 oz.	1 lb. 6-1/2 oz.
*	1-1/4 oz.	2 oz.	2-1/2 oz.	5 oz.	7-1/2 oz.	10 oz.	12-1/2 oz.	15 oz.	1 lb. 1-1/2 oz.	1 lb. 4 oz.	1 lb. 6-1/2 oz.	1 lb. 9 oz.
*	*	2 oz.	2-3/4 oz.	5-1/2 oz.	8-1/4 oz.	11 oz.	13-3/4 oz.	1 lb. 1/2 oz.	1 lb. 3-1/4 oz.	1 lb. 6 oz.	1 lb. 8-3/4 oz.	1 lb. 11-1/2 oz.
3/4 oz.	1-1/2 oz.	2-1/4 oz.	3 oz.	6 oz.	9 oz.	12 oz.	15 oz.	1 lb. 2 oz.	1 lb. 5 oz.	1 lb. 8 oz.	1 lb. 11 oz.	1 lb. 14 oz.
*	*	2-1/2 oz.	3-1/4 oz.	6-1/2 oz.	9-3/4 oz.	13 oz.	1 lb. 1/4 oz.	1 lb. 3-1/2 oz.	1 lb. 6-3/4 oz.	1 lb. 10 oz.	1 lb. 13-1/4 oz.	2 lbs. 1/2 oz.
*	1-3/4 oz.	2-3/4 oz.	3-1/2 oz.	7 oz.	10-1/2 oz.	14 oz.	1 lb. 1-1/2 oz.	1 lb. 5 oz.	1 lb. 8-1/2 oz.	1 lb. 12 oz.	1 lb. 15-1/2 oz.	2 lbs. 3 oz.
1 oz.	2 oz.	2-3/4 oz.	3-3/4 oz.	7-1/2 oz.	11-1/4 oz.	15 oz.	1 lb. 2-3/4 oz.	1 lb. 6-1/2 oz.	1 lb. 10-1/4 oz.	1 lb. 14 oz.	2 lbs. 1-3/4 oz.	2 lbs. 5-1/2 oz.

*The amount cannot be weighed accurately without introducing errors.

Portions												
25	50	75	100	200	300	400	500	600	700	800	900	1000
1 oz.	2 oz.	3 oz.	4 oz.	8 oz.	12 oz.	1 lb.	1 lb. 4 oz.	1 lb. 8 oz.	1 lb. 12 oz.	2 lbs.	2 lbs. 4 oz.	2 lbs. 8 oz.
1 oz.	2-1/4 oz.	3-1/4 oz.	4-1/4 oz.	8-1/2 oz.	12-3/4 oz.	1 lb. 1 oz.	1 lb. 5-1/4 oz.	1 lb. 9-1/2 oz.	1 lb. 13-3/4 oz.	2 lbs. 2 oz.	2 lbs. 6-1/4 oz.	2 lbs. 10-1/2 oz.
*	2-1/2 oz.	3-1/2 oz.	4-1/2 oz.	9 oz.	13-1/2 oz.	1 lb. 2 oz.	1 lb. 6-1/2 oz.	1 lb. 11 oz.	1 lb. 15-1/2 oz.	2 lbs. 4 oz.	2 lbs. 8-1/2 oz.	2 lbs. 13 oz.
*	2-1/2 oz.	3-1/2 oz.	4-3/4 oz.	9-1/2 oz.	14-1/4 oz.	1 lb. 3 oz.	1 lb. 7-3/4 oz.	1 lb. 12-1/2 oz.	2 lbs. 1-1/4 oz.	2 lbs. 6 oz.	2 lbs. 10-3/4 oz.	2 lbs. 15-1/2 oz.
1-1/4 oz.	2-1/2 oz.	3-3/4 oz.	5 oz.	10 oz.	15 oz.	1 lb. 4 oz.	1 lb. 9 oz.	1 lb. 14 oz.	2 lbs. 3 oz.	2 lbs. 8 oz.	2 lbs. 13 oz.	3 lbs. 2 oz.
*	2-3/4 oz.	4-1/4 oz.	5-1/2 oz.	11 oz.	1 lb. 1/2 oz.	1 lb. 6 oz.	1 lb. 11-1/2 oz.	2 lbs. 1 oz.	2 lbs. 6-1/2 oz.	2 lbs. 12 oz.	3 lbs. 1-1/2 oz.	3 lbs. 7 oz.
1-1/2 oz.	3 oz.	4-1/2 oz.	6 oz.	12 oz.	1 lb. 2 oz.	1 lb. 8 oz.	1 lb. 14 oz.	2 lbs. 4 oz.	2 lbs. 10 oz.	3 lbs.	3 lbs. 6 oz.	3 lbs. 12 oz.
*	3-1/4 oz.	4-3/4 oz.	6-1/2 oz.	13 oz.	1 lb. 3-1/2 oz.	1 lb. 10 oz.	2 lbs. 1/2 oz.	2 lbs. 7 oz.	2 lbs. 13-1/2 oz.	3 lbs. 4 oz.	3 lbs. 10-1/2 oz.	4 lbs. 1 oz.
1-3/4 oz.	3-1/2 oz.	5-1/4 oz.	7 oz.	14 oz.	1 lb. 5 oz.	1 lb. 12 oz.	2 lbs. 3 oz.	2 lbs. 10 oz.	3 lbs. 1 oz.	3 lbs. 8 oz.	3 lbs. 15 oz.	4 lbs. 6 oz.
2 oz.	3-3/4 oz.	5-3/4 oz.	7-1/2 oz.	15 oz.	1 lb. 6-1/2 oz.	1 lb. 14 oz.	2 lbs. 5-1/2 oz.	2 lbs. 13 oz.	3 lbs. 4-1/2 oz.	3 lbs. 12 oz.	4 lbs. 3-1/2 oz.	4 lbs. 11 oz.
2 oz.	4 oz.	6 oz.	8 oz.	1 lb.	1 lb. 8 oz.	2 lbs.	2 lbs. 8 oz.	3 lbs.	3 lbs. 8 oz.	4 lbs.	4 lbs. 8 oz.	5 lbs.
2-1/4 oz.	4-1/4 oz.	6-1/2 oz.	8-1/2 oz.	1 lb. 1 oz.	1 lb. 9-1/2 oz.	2 lbs. 2 oz.	2 lbs. 10-1/2 oz.	3 lbs. 3 oz.	3 lbs. 11-1/2 oz.	4 lbs. 4 oz.	4 lbs. 12-1/2 oz.	5 lbs. 5 oz.
2-1/4 oz.	4-1/2 oz.	6-3/4 oz.	9 oz.	1 lb. 2 oz.	1 lb. 11 oz.	2 lbs. 4 oz.	2 lbs. 13 oz.	3 lbs. 6 oz.	3 lbs. 15 oz.	4 lbs. 8 oz.	5 lbs. 1 oz.	5 lbs. 10 oz.
2-1/2 oz.	4-3/4 oz.	7-1/4 oz.	9-1/2 oz.	1 lb. 3 oz.	1 lb. 12-1/2 oz.	2 lbs. 6 oz.	2 lbs. 15-1/2 oz.	3 lbs. 9 oz.	4 lbs. 2-1/2 oz.	4 lbs. 12 oz.	5 lbs. 5-1/2 oz.	5 lbs. 15 oz.
2-1/2 oz.	5 oz.	7-1/2 oz.	10 oz.	1 lb. 4 oz.	1 lb. 14 oz.	2 lbs. 8 oz.	3 lbs. 2 oz.	3 lbs. 12 oz.	4 lbs. 6 oz.	5 lbs.	5 lbs. 10 oz.	6 lbs. 4 oz.
2-3/4 oz.	5-1/2 oz.	8-1/4 oz.	11 oz.	1 lb. 6 oz.	2 lbs. 1 oz.	2 lbs. 12 oz.	3 lbs. 7 oz.	4 lbs. 2 oz.	4 lbs. 13 oz.	5 lbs. 8 oz.	6 lbs. 3 oz.	6 lbs. 14 oz.
3 oz.	6 oz.	9 oz.	12 oz.	1 lb. 8 oz.	2 lbs. 4 oz.	3 lbs.	3 lbs. 12 oz.	4 lbs. 8 oz.	5 lbs. 4 oz.	6 lbs.	6 lbs. 12 oz.	7 lbs. 8 oz.
3-1/4 oz.	6-1/2 oz.	9-3/4 oz.	13 oz.	1 lb. 10 oz.	2 lbs. 7 oz.	3 lbs. 4 oz.	4 lbs. 1 oz.	4 lbs. 14 oz.	5 lbs. 11 oz.	6 lbs. 8 oz.	7 lbs. 5 oz.	8 lbs. 2 oz.
3-1/2 oz.	7 oz.	10-1/2 oz.	14 oz.	1 lb. 12 oz.	2 lbs. 10 oz.	3 lbs. 8 oz.	4 lbs. 6 oz.	5 lbs. 4 oz.	6 lbs. 2 oz.	7 lbs.	7 lbs. 14 oz.	8 lbs. 12 oz.
3-3/4 oz.	7-1/2 oz.	11-1/4 oz.	15 oz.	1 lb. 14 oz.	2 lbs. 13 oz.	3 lbs. 12 oz.	4 lbs. 11 oz.	5 lbs. 10 oz.	6 lbs. 9 oz.	7 lbs. 8 oz.	8 lbs. 7 oz.	9 lbs. 6 oz.
4 oz.	8 oz.	12 oz.	1 lb.	2 lbs.	3 lbs.	4 lbs.	5 lbs.	6 lbs.	7 lbs.	8 lbs.	9 lbs.	10 lbs.
4-1/2 oz.	9 oz.	13-1/2 oz.	1 lb. 2 oz.	2 lbs. 4 oz.	3 lbs. 6 oz.	4 lbs. 8 oz.	5 lbs. 10 oz.	6 lbs. 12 oz.	7 lbs. 14 oz.	9 lbs.	10 lbs. 2 oz.	11 lbs. 4 oz.

5 oz.	10 oz.	15 oz.	1 lb. 4 oz.	2 lbs. 8 oz.	3 lbs. 12 oz.	5 lbs.	6 lbs. 4 oz.	7 lbs. 8 oz.	8 lbs. 12 oz.	10 lbs.	11 lbs. 4 oz.	12 lbs. 8 oz.
5-1/2 oz.	11 oz.	1 lb. 1/2 oz.	1 lb. 6 oz.	2 lbs. 12 oz.	4 lbs. 2 oz.	5 lbs. 8 oz.	6 lbs. 14 oz.	8 lbs. 4 oz.	9 lbs. 10 oz.	11 lbs.	12 lbs. 6 oz.	13 lbs. 12 oz.
6 oz.	12 oz.	1 lb. 2 oz.	1 lb. 8 oz.	3 lbs.	4 lbs. 8 oz.	6 lbs.	7 lbs. 8 oz.	9 lbs.	10 lbs. 8 oz.	12 lbs.	13 lbs. 8 oz.	15 lbs.
6-1/2 oz.	13 oz.	1 lb. 3-1/2 oz.	1 lb. 10 oz.	3 lbs. 4 oz.	4 lbs. 14 oz.	6 lbs. 8 oz.	8 lbs. 2 oz.	9 lbs. 12 oz.	11 lbs. 6 oz.	13 lbs.	14 lbs. 6 oz.	15 lbs. 12 oz.
7 oz.	14 oz.	1 lb. 5 oz.	1 lb. 12 oz.	3 lbs. 8 oz.	5 lbs. 4 oz.	7 lbs.	8 lbs. 12 oz.	10 lbs. 8 oz.	12 lbs. 4 oz.	14 lbs.	15 lbs. 12 oz.	17 lbs. 8 oz.
7-1/2 oz.	15 oz.	1 lb. 6-1/2 oz.	1 lb. 14 oz.	3 lbs. 12 oz.	5 lbs. 10 oz.	7 lbs. 8 oz.	9 lbs. 6 oz.	11 lbs. 4 oz.	13 lbs. 2 oz.	15 lbs.	16 lbs. 14 oz.	18 lbs. 12 oz.
8 oz.	1 lb.	1 lb. 8 oz.	2 lbs.	4 lbs.	6 lbs.	8 lbs.	10 lbs.	12 lbs.	14 lbs.	16 lbs.	18 lbs.	20 lbs.
8-1/2 oz.	1 lb. 1 oz.	1 lb. 9-1/2 oz.	2 lbs. 2 oz.	4 lbs. 4 oz.	6 lbs. 6 oz.	8 lbs. 8 oz.	10 lbs. 10 oz.	12 lbs. 12 oz.	14 lbs. 14 oz.	17 lbs.	19 lbs. 2 oz.	21 lbs. 4 oz.
9 oz.	1 lb. 2 oz.	1 lb. 11 oz.	2 lbs. 4 oz.	4 lbs. 8 oz.	6 lbs. 12 oz.	9 lbs.	11 lbs. 4 oz.	13 lbs. 8 oz.	15 lbs. 12 oz.	18 lbs.	20 lbs. 4 oz.	22 lbs. 8 oz.
9-1/2 oz.	1 lb. 3 oz.	1 lb. 12-1/2 oz.	2 lbs. 6 oz.	4 lbs. 12 oz.	7 lbs. 2 oz.	9 lbs. 8 oz.	11 lbs. 14 oz.	14 lbs. 4 oz.	16 lbs. 10 oz.	19 lbs.	21 lbs. 6 oz.	23 lbs. 12 oz.
10 oz.	1 lb. 4 oz.	1 lb. 14 oz.	2 lbs. 8 oz.	5 lbs.	7 lbs. 8 oz.	10 lbs.	12 lbs. 8 oz.	15 lbs.	17 lbs. 8 oz.	20 lbs.	22 lbs. 8 oz.	25 lbs.
11 oz.	1 lb. 6 oz.	2 lbs. 1 oz.	2 lbs. 12 oz.	5 lbs. 8 oz.	8 lbs. 4 oz.	11 lbs.	13 lbs. 12 oz.	16 lbs. 8 oz.	19 lbs. 4 oz.	22 lbs.	24 lbs. 12 oz.	27 lbs. 8 oz.
12 oz.	1 lb. 8 oz.	2 lbs. 4 oz.	3 lbs.	6 lbs.	9 lbs.	12 lbs.	15 lbs.	18 lbs.	21 lbs.	24 lbs.	27 lbs.	30 lbs.
13 oz.	1 lb. 10 oz.	2 lbs. 7 oz.	3 lbs. 4 oz.	6 lbs. 8 oz.	9 lbs. 12 oz.	13 lbs.	16 lbs. 4 oz.	19 lbs. 8 oz.	22 lbs. 12 oz.	26 lbs.	29 lbs. 4 oz.	32 lbs. 8 oz.
14 oz.	1 lb. 12 oz.	2 lbs. 10 oz.	3 lbs. 8 oz.	7 lbs.	10 lbs. 8 oz.	14 lbs.	17 lbs. 8 oz.	21 lbs.	24 lbs. 8 oz.	28 lbs.	31 lbs. 8 oz.	35 lbs.
15 oz.	1 lb. 14 oz.	2 lbs. 13 oz.	3 lbs. 12 oz.	7 lbs. 8 oz.	11 lbs. 4 oz.	15 lbs.	18 lbs. 12 oz.	22 lbs. 8 oz.	26 lbs. 4 oz.	30 lbs.	33 lbs. 12 oz.	37 lbs. 8 oz.
1 lb.	2 lbs.	3 lbs.	4 lbs.	8 lbs.	12 lbs.	16 lbs.	20 lbs.	24 lbs.	28 lbs.	32 lbs.	36 lbs.	40 lbs.
1 lb. 1 oz.	2 lbs. 2 oz.	3 lbs. 3 oz.	4 lbs. 4 oz.	8 lbs. 8 oz.	12 lbs. 12 oz.	17 lbs.	21 lbs. 4 oz.	25 lbs. 8 oz.	29 lbs. 12 oz.	34 lbs.	38 lbs. 4 oz.	42 lbs. 8 oz.
1 lb. 2 oz.	2 lbs. 4 oz.	3 lbs. 6 oz.	4 lbs. 8 oz.	9 lbs.	13 lbs. 8 oz.	18 lbs.	22 lbs. 8 oz.	27 lbs.	31 lbs. 8 oz.	36 lbs.	40 lbs. 8 oz.	45 lbs.
1 lb. 3 oz.	2 lbs. 6 oz.	3 lbs. 9 oz.	4 lbs. 12 oz.	9 lbs. 8 oz.	14 lbs. 4 oz.	19 lbs.	23 lbs. 12 oz.	28 lbs. 8 oz.	33 lbs. 4 oz.	38 lbs.	42 lbs. 12 oz.	47 lbs. 8 oz.
1 lb. 4 oz.	2 lbs. 8 oz.	3 lbs. 12 oz.	5 lbs.	10 lbs.	15 lbs.	20 lbs.	25 lbs.	30 lbs.	35 lbs.	40 lbs.	45 lbs.	50 lbs.
1 lb. 5 oz.	2 lbs. 10 oz.	3 lbs. 15 oz.	5 lbs. 4 oz.	10 lbs. 8 oz.	15 lbs. 12 oz.	21 lbs.	26 lbs. 4 oz.	31 lbs. 8 oz.	36 lbs. 12 oz.	42 lbs.	47 lbs. 4 oz.	52 lbs. 8 oz.

*The amount cannot be weighed accurately without introducing errors.

Portions												
25	50	75	100	200	300	400	500	600	700	800	900	1000
1 lb. 6 oz.	2 lbs. 12 oz.	4 lbs. 2 oz.	5 lbs. 8 oz.	11 lbs.	16 lbs. 8 oz.	22 lbs.	27 lbs. 8 oz.	33 lbs.	38 lbs. 8 oz.	44 lbs.	49 lbs. 8 oz.	55 lbs.
1 lb. 7 oz.	2 lbs. 14 oz.	4 lbs. 5 oz.	5 lbs. 12 oz.	11 lbs. 8 oz.	17 lbs. 4 oz.	23 lbs.	28 lbs. 12 oz.	34 lbs. 8 oz.	40 lbs. 4 oz.	46 lbs.	51 lbs. 12 oz.	57 lbs. 8 oz.
1 lb. 8 oz.	3 lbs.	4 lbs. 8 oz.	6 lbs.	12 lbs.	18 lbs.	24 lbs.	30 lbs.	36 lbs.	42 lbs.	48 lbs.	54 lbs.	60 lbs.
1 lb. 10 oz.	3 lbs. 4 oz.	4 lbs. 14 oz.	6 lbs. 8 oz.	13 lbs.	19 lbs. 8 oz.	26 lbs.	32 lbs. 8 oz.	39 lbs.	45 lbs. 8 oz.	52 lbs.	58 lbs. 8 oz.	65 lbs.
1 lb. 12 oz.	3 lbs. 8 oz.	5 lbs. 4 oz.	7 lbs.	14 lbs.	21 lbs.	28 lbs.	35 lbs.	42 lbs.	49 lbs.	56 lbs.	63 lbs.	70 lbs.
1 lb. 14 oz.	3 lbs. 12 oz.	5 lbs. 10 oz.	7 lbs. 8 oz.	15 lbs.	22 lbs. 8 oz.	30 lbs.	37 lbs. 8 oz.	45 lbs.	52 lbs. 8 oz.	60 lbs.	67 lbs. 8 oz.	75 lbs.
2 lbs.	4 lbs.	6 lbs.	8 lbs.	16 lbs.	24 lbs.	32 lbs.	40 lbs.	48 lbs.	56 lbs.	64 lbs.	72 lbs.	80 lbs.
2 lbs. 2 oz.	4 lbs. 4 oz.	6 lbs. 6 oz.	8 lbs. 8 oz.	17 lbs.	25 lbs. 8 oz.	34 lbs.	42 lbs. 8 oz.	51 lbs.	59 lbs. 8 oz.	68 lbs.	76 lbs. 8 oz.	85 lbs.
2 lbs. 4 oz.	4 lbs. 8 oz.	6 lbs. 12 oz.	9 lbs.	18 lbs.	27 lbs.	36 lbs.	45 lbs.	54 lbs.	63 lbs.	72 lbs.	81 lbs.	90 lbs.
2 lbs. 6 oz.	4 lbs. 12 oz.	7 lbs. 2 oz.	9 lbs. 8 oz.	19 lbs.	28 lbs. 8 oz.	38 lbs.	47 lbs. 8 oz.	57 lbs.	66 lbs. 8 oz.	76 lbs.	85 lbs. 8 oz.	95 lbs.
2 lbs. 8 oz.	5 lbs.	7 lbs. 8 oz.	10 lbs.	20 lbs.	30 lbs.	40 lbs.	50 lbs.	60 lbs.	70 lbs.	80 lbs.	90 lbs.	100 lbs.
2 lbs. 12 oz.	5 lbs. 8 oz.	8 lbs. 4 oz.	11 lbs.	22 lbs.	33 lbs.	44 lbs.	55 lbs.	66 lbs.	77 lbs.	88 lbs.	99 lbs.	110 lbs.
3 lbs.	6 lbs.	9 lbs.	12 lbs.	24 lbs.	36 lbs.	48 lbs.	60 lbs.	72 lbs.	84 lbs.	96 lbs.	108 lbs.	120 lbs.
3 lbs. 4 oz.	6 lbs. 8 oz.	9 lbs. 12 oz.	13 lbs.	26 lbs.	39 lbs.	52 lbs.	65 lbs.	78 lbs.	91 lbs.	104 lbs.	117 lbs.	130 lbs.
3 lbs. 8 oz.	7 lbs.	10 lbs. 8 oz.	14 lbs.	28 lbs.	42 lbs.	56 lbs.	70 lbs.	84 lbs.	98 lbs.	112 lbs.	126 lbs.	140 lbs.
3 lbs. 12 oz.	7 lbs. 8 oz.	11 lbs. 4 oz.	15 lbs.	30 lbs.	45 lbs.	60 lbs.	75 lbs.	90 lbs.	105 lbs.	120 lbs.	135 lbs.	150 lbs.
4 lbs.	8 lbs.	12 lbs.	16 lbs.	32 lbs.	48 lbs.	64 lbs.	80 lbs.	96 lbs.	112 lbs.	128 lbs.	144 lbs.	160 lbs.
4 lbs. 4 oz.	8 lbs. 8 oz.	12 lbs. 12 oz.	17 lbs.	34 lbs.	51 lbs.	68 lbs.	85 lbs.	102 lbs.	119 lbs.	136 lbs.	153 lbs.	170 lbs.
4 lbs. 8 oz.	9 lbs.	13 lbs. 8 oz.	18 lbs.	36 lbs.	54 lbs.	72 lbs.	90 lbs.	108 lbs.	126 lbs.	144 lbs.	162 lbs.	180 lbs.
4 lbs. 12 oz.	9 lbs. 8 oz.	14 lbs. 2 oz.	19 lbs.	38 lbs.	57 lbs.	76 lbs.	95 lbs.	114 lbs.	133 lbs.	152 lbs.	171 lbs.	190 lbs.
5 lbs.	10 lbs.	15 lbs.	20 lbs.	40 lbs.	60 lbs.	80 lbs.	100 lbs.	120 lbs.	140 lbs.	160 lbs.	180 lbs.	200 lbs.
5 lbs. 4 oz.	10 lbs. 8 oz.	15 lbs. 12 oz.	21 lbs.	42 lbs.	63 lbs.	84 lbs.	105 lbs.	126 lbs.	147 lbs.	168 lbs.	189 lbs.	210 lbs.
5 lbs. 8 oz.	11 lbs.	16 lbs. 8 oz.	22 lbs.	44 lbs.	66 lbs.	88 lbs.	110 lbs.	132 lbs.	154 lbs.	176 lbs.	198 lbs.	220 lbs.

5 lbs. 12 oz.	11 lbs. 8 oz.	17 lbs. 4 oz.	23 lbs.	46 lbs.	69 lbs.	92 lbs.	115 lbs.	138 lbs.	161 lbs.	184 lbs.	207 lbs.	230 lbs.
6 lbs.	12 lbs.	18 lbs.	24 lbs.	48 lbs.	72 lbs.	96 lbs.	120 lbs.	144 lbs.	168 lbs.	192 lbs.	216 lbs.	240 lbs.
6 lbs. 4 oz.	12 lbs. 8 oz.	18 lbs. 12 oz.	25 lbs.	50 lbs.	75 lbs.	100 lbs.	125 lbs.	150 lbs.	175 lbs.	200 lbs.	225 lbs.	250 lbs.
7 lbs. 8 oz.	15 lbs.	22 lbs. 8 oz.	30 lbs.	60 lbs.	90 lbs.	120 lbs.	150 lbs.	180 lbs.	210 lbs.	240 lbs.	270 lbs.	300 lbs.
8 lbs. 12 oz.	17 lbs. 8 oz.	26 lbs. 4 oz.	35 lbs.	70 lbs.	105 lbs.	140 lbs.	175 lbs.	210 lbs.	245 lbs.	280 lbs.	315 lbs.	350 lbs.
10 lbs.	20 lbs.	30 lbs.	40 lbs.	80 lbs.	120 lbs.	160 lbs.	200 lbs.	240 lbs.	280 lbs.	320 lbs.	360 lbs.	400 lbs.
11 lbs. 4 oz.	22 lbs. 8 oz.	33 lbs. 12 oz.	45 lbs.	90 lbs.	135 lbs.	180 lbs.	225 lbs.	270 lbs.	315 lbs.	360 lbs.	405 lbs.	450 lbs.
12 lbs. 8 oz.	25 lbs.	37 lbs. 8 oz.	50 lbs.	100 lbs.	150 lbs.	200 lbs.	250 lbs.	300 lbs.	350 lbs.	400 lbs.	450 lbs.	500 lbs.

From a table prepared by Katharine Flack for the New York State Department of Mental Health Nutrition Service; reprinted by permission.

Appendix Table 9. Conversion Chart of Volume Measures for Recipes in 25-Portion Increments

Instructions

1. Locate the column that corresponds to the original yield of the recipe you wish to adjust. For example, let us assume your original sour cream cookie recipe yields 300 cookies. Locate the 300 column.

2. Run your finger down this column until you come to the amount of the ingredient required (or the amount closest to this figure) in the recipe you wish to adjust. Say that your original recipe for 300 cookies required 2-1/4 C. fat. Run your finger down the column headed 300 until you come to 2-1/4 C.

3. Next, run your finger across the page, in line with that amount, until you come to the column that is headed to correspond with the yield you desire. Suppose you want to make 75 cookies. Starting with your finger at the 2-1/4 C. (in the 300 column), slide it across to the column headed 75 and read the figure. You will need 1/2 C. + 1 T. fat to make 75 cookies from your recipe.

4. Record this figure as the amount of the ingredient required for the new yield of your recipe. Repeat steps 1, 2, and 3 for each ingredient in your original recipe to obtain the adjusted measure needed of each for your new yield. You can increase or decrease yield in this manner.

5. If you need to combine two columns to obtain your desired yield, follow the above procedure and add together the amounts given in the two columns to get the amount required for your adjusted yield. For example, to find the amount of fat needed to make 550 cookies (using the same basic recipe as above) locate the figures in columns headed 500 and 50 and add them. In this case they would be 3-3/4 C. plus 6 T., and the required total would be 1 qt. + 2 T. fat.

6. The figures in Appendix Table 9 are given in measurements that provide absolute accuracy. After you have made yield adjustments for each ingredient, you may round off odd fractions and complicated measurements. For example, you can safely round off to 1 qt. the amount of fat needed in the recipe for 550 cookies.

Portions												
25	50	75	100	200	300	400	500	600	700	800	900	1000
1/4 t.	1/2 t.	3/4 t.	1 t.	2 t.	1 T.	1 T. + 1 t.	1 T. + 2 t.	2 T.	2 T. + 1 t.	2 T. + 2 t.	3 T.	3 T. + 1 t.
1/4 t. (r)	1/2 t. (r)	1 t. (s)	1-1/4 t.	2-1/2 t.	1 T. + 3/4 t.	1 T. + 2 t.	2 T. + 1/4 t.	2-1/2 T.	2 T. + 2-3/4 t.	3 T. + 1 t.	3 T. + 2-1/4 t.	4 T. + 1/2 t.
1/4 t. + 1/8 t.	3/4 t.	1 t. + 1/8 t.	1-1/2 t.	1 T.	1-1/2 T.	2 T.	2-1/2 T.	3 T.	3-1/2 T.	4 T.	4 T. + 1-1/2 t.	5 T.
1/2 t. (s)	3/r t. (r)	1-1/4 t. (r)	1-3/4 t.	1 T. + 1/2 t.	1 T. + 2-1/4 t.	2 T. + 1 t.	2 T. + 2-3/4 t.	3-1/2 T.	4 T. + 1/4 t.	4 T. + 2 t.	5 T. + 3/4 t.	5 T. + 2-1/2 t.
1/2 t.	1 t.	1-1/2 t.	2 t.	1 T. + 1 t.	2 T.	2 T. + 2 t.	3 T. + 1 t.	4 T.	4 T. + 2 t.	5 T. + 1 t.	6 T.	6 T. + 2 t.
1/2 t. (r)	1 t. + 1/8 t.	1-3/4 t. (s)	2-1/4 t.	1-1/2 T.	2 T. + 3/4 t.	3 T.	3 T. + 2-1/4 t.	4-1/2 T.	5 T. + 3/4 t.	6 T.	6 T. + 2-1/4 t.	7-1/2 T.
1/2 t. + 1/8 t.	1-1/4 t.	2 t. (s)	2-1/2 t.	1 T. + 2 t.	2-1/2 T.	3 T. + 1 t.	4 T. + 1/2 t.	5 T.	5-1/2 T.	6 T. + 2 t.	7-1/2 T.	8 T. + 1 t.
3/4 t. (s)	1-1/4 t. + 1/8 t.	2 t. (r)	2-3/4 t.	1 T. + 2-1/2 t.	2 T. + 2-1/4 t.	3 T. + 2 t.	4 T. + 1-3/4 t.	5-1/2 T.	6 T. + 1-1/4 t.	7 T. + 1 t.	8 T. + 3/4 t.	9 T. + 1/2 t.
3/4 t.	1-1/2 t.	2-1/4 t.	1 T.	2 T.	3 T.	1/4 C.	5 T.	6 T.	7 T.	1/2 C.	1/2 C. + 1 T.	1/2 C. + 2 T.
1 t. + 1/8 t.	2-1/4 t.	1 T. + 1/4 t. + 1/8 t.	1-1/2 T.	3 T.	1/4 C. + 1-1/2 t.	1/3 C. + 2 t.	1/4 C. + 3-1/2 T.	1/2 C. + 1 T.	1/2 C. + 2-1/2 T.	3/4 C.	3/4 C. + 1-1/2 T.	3/4 C. + 3 T.
1-1/2 t.	1 T.	1-1/2 T.	2 T.	1/4 C.	1/4 C. + 2 T.	1/2 C.	1/2 C. + 2 T.	3/4 C.	3/4 C. + 2 T.	1 C.	1 C. + 2 T.	1-1/4 C.
1-3/4 t. + 1/8 t.	1 T. + 3/4 t.	1 T. + 2-1/2 t. + 1/8 t.	2-1/2 T.	1/4 C. + 1 T.	1/4 C. + 3-1/2 T.	1/2 C. + 2 T.	3/4 C. + 1/2 T.	3/4 C. + 3 T.	1 C. + 1-1/2 T.	1-1/4 C.	1-1/4 C. + 2-1/2 T.	1-1/2 C. + 1 T.
2-1/4 t.	1-1/2 T.	2 T. + 3/4 t.	3 T.	1/3 C. + 2 t.	1/2 C. + 1 T.	3/4 C.	3/4 C. + 3 T.	1 C. + 2 T.	1-1/4 C. + 1 T.	1-1/2 C.	1-1/2 C. + 3 T.	1-3/4 C. + 2 T.

2-1/4 t. + 1/8 t.	1 T. + 2-1/4 t.	2 T. + 1-1/2 t. + 1/8 t.	3-1/2 T.	1/4 C. + 3 T.	1/2 C. + 2-1/2 T.	3/4 C. + 2 T.	1 C. + 1-1/2 T.	1-1/4 C. + 1 T.	1-1/2 C. + 1/2 T.	1-3/4 C.	1-3/4 C. + 3-1/2 T.	2 C. + 3 T.
1 T.	2 T.	3 T.	1/4 C.	1/2 C.	3/4 C.	1 C.	1-1/4 C.	1-1/2 C.	1-3/4 C.	2 C.	2-1/4 C.	2-1/2 C.
1 T. + 1 t.	2 T. + 2 t.	1/4 C.	1/3 C.	2/3 C.	1 C.	1-1/3 C.	1-2/3 C.	2 C.	2-1/3 C.	2-2/3 C.	3 C.	3-1/3 C.
2 T.	1/4 C.	1/4 C. + 2 T.	1/2 C.	1 C.	1-1/2 C.	2 C.	2-1/2 C.	3 C.	3-1/2 C.	1 qt.	1 qt. + 1/2 C.	1-1/4 qt.
2 T. + 2 t.	1/3 C.	1/2 C.	2/3 C.	1-1/3 C.	2 C.	2-2/3 C.	3-1/3 C.	1 qt.	1 qt. + 2/3 C.	1-1/4 qt. 1/3 C.	1-1/2 qt.	1-1/2 qt. + 2/3 C.
3 T.	6 T.	1/2 C. + 1 T.	3/4 C.	1-1/2 C.	2-1/4 C.	3 C.	3-3/4 C.	1 qt. + 1/2 C.	1-1/4 qt. + 1/4 C.	1-1/2 qt.	1-1/2 qt. + 3/4 C.	1-3/4 qt. + 1/2 C.
1/4 C.	1/2 C.	3/4 C.	1 C.	2 C.	3 C.	1 qt.	1-1/4 qt.	1-1/2 qt.	1-3/4 qt.	2 qt.	2-1/4 qt.	2-1/2 qt.
1/4 C. + 1 T.	1/2 C. + 2 T.	3/4 C. + 3 T.	1-1/4 C.	2-1/2 C.	3-3/4 C.	1-1/4 qt.	1-1/2 qt. + 1/4 C.	1-3/4 qt. + 1/2 C.	2 qt. + 3/4 C.	2-1/2 qt.	2-3/4 qt. + 1/4 C.	3 qt. + 1/2 C.
1/3 C.	2/3 C.	1 C.	1-1/3 C.	2-2/3 C.	1 qt.	1-1/4 qt. + 1/3 C.	1-1/2 qt. + 2/3 C.	2 qt.	2-1/2 qt. + 1/3 C.	2-1/2 qt. + 2/3 C.	3 qt.	3-1/4 qt. + 1/3 C.
1/3 C. + 2 T.	3/4 C.	1 C. + 2 T.	1-1/2 C.	3 C.	1 qt. + 1/2 C.	1-1/2 qt.	1-3/4 qt. 1/2 C.	2-1/4 qt.	2-1/2 qt. + 1/2 C.	3 qt.	3-1/4 qt. + 1/2 C.	3-3/4 qt.
6 T. + 2 t.	3/4 C. + 4 t.	1-1/4 C.	1-2/3 C.	3-1/3 C.	1-1/4 qt.	1-1/2 qt. + 2/3 C.	2 qt. + 1/3 C.	2-1/2 qt.	2-3/4 qt. + 2/3 C.	3-1/4 qt. + 1/3 C.	3-3/4 qt.	1 gal. + 2/3 C.
1/4 C. + 3 T.	3/4 C. + 2 T.	1-1/4 C. + 1 T.	1-3/4 C.	3-1/2 C.	1-1/4 qt. + 1/4 C.	1-3/4 qt.	2 qt. + 3/4 C.	2-1/2 qt. + 1/2 C.	3 qt. + 1/4 C.	3-1/2 qt.	3-3/4 qt. + 3/4 C.	1 gal. + 1-1/2 C.
1/2 C.	1 C.	1-1/2 C.	2 C.	1 qt.	1-1/2 qt.	2 qt.	2-1/2 qt.	3 qt.	3-1/2 qt.	1 gal.	1 gal. + 2 C.	1 gal. + 1 qt.
1/2 C. + 1 T.	1 C. + 2 T.	1-1/2 C. + 3 T.	2-1/4 C.	1 qt. + 1/2 C.	1-1/2 qt. + 3/4 C.	2-1/4 qt.	2-3/4 qt. + 1/4 C.	3-1/4 qt. + 1/2 C.	3-3/4 qt. + 3/4 C.	1 gal. + 2 C.	1-1/4 gal. + 1/4 C.	1-1/4 gal. + 2-1/2 C.
1/2 C. + 4 t.	1 C. + 2 T. + 2 t.	1-3/4 C.	2-1/3 C.	1 qt. + 2/3 C.	1-3/4 qt.	2-1/4 qt. + 1/3 C.	2-3/4 qt. + 2/3 C.	3-1/2 qt.	1 gal. + 1/3 C.	1 gal. + 2-2/3 C.	1-1/4 gal. + 1 C.	1-1/4 gal. + 3-1/3 C.
1/2 C. + 2 T.	1-1/4 C.	1-3/4 C. + 2 T.	2-1/2 C.	1-1/4 qt.	1-3/4 qt. + 1/2 C.	2-1/2 qt.	3 qt. + 1/2 C.	3-3/4 qt.	1 gal. + 1-1/2 C.	1-1/4 gal.	1-1/4 gal. + 2-1/2 C.	1-1/2 gal. + 1 C.
2/3 C.	1-1/3 C.	2 C.	2-2/3 C.	1-1/4 qt. + 1/3 C.	2 qt.	2-1/2 qt. + 2/3 C.	3 qt. + 1-1/3 C.	1 gal.	1 gal. + 2-2/3 C.	1-1/4 gal. + 1-1/3 C.	1-1/2 gal.	1-1/2 gal. + 2-2/3 C.
1/2 C. + 3 T.	1-1/4 C. + 2 T.	2 C. + 1 T.	2-3/4 C.	1-1/4 qt. + 1/2 C.	2 qt. + 1/4 C.	2-3/4 qt.	3-1/4 qt. + 3/4 C.	1 gal. + 1/2 C.	1 gal. + 3-1/4 C.	1-1/4 gal. + 2 C.	1-1/2 gal. + 3/4 C.	1-1/2 gal. + 3-1/2 C.
3/4 C.	1-1/2 C.	2-1/4 C.	3 C.	1-1/2 qt.	2-1/4 qt.	3 qt.	3-3/4 qt.	1 gal. + 2 C.	1-1/4 gal. + 1 C.	1-1/2 gal.	1-1/2 gal. + 3 C.	1-3/4 gal. + 2 C.
3/4 C. + 1 T.	1-1/2 C. + 2 T.	2-1/4 C. + 3 T.	3-1/4 C.	1-1/2 qt. + 1/2 C.	2-1/4 qt. + 3/4 C.	3-1/4 qt.	1 gal. + 1/4 C.	1 gal. + 3-1/2 C.	1-1/4 gal. + 2-3/4 C.	1-1/2 gal. + 2 C.	1-3/4 gal. + 1-1/4 C.	2 gal. + 1/2 C.
3/4 C. + 4 t.	1-2/3 C.	2-1/2 C.	3-1/3 C.	1-1/2 qt. + 2/3 C.	2-1/2 qt.	3-1/4 qt. + 1/3 C.	1 gal. + 2/3 C.	1-1/4 gal.	1-1/4 gal. + 3-1/3 C.	1-1/2 gal. + 2-2/3 C.	1-3/4 gal. + 2 C.	2 gal. + 1-1/3 C.
3/4 C. + 2 T.	1-3/4 C.	2-1/2 C. + 2 T.	3-1/2 C.	1-3/4 qt.	2-1/2 qt. + 1/2 C.	3-1/2 qt.	1 gal. + 1-1/2 C.	1-1/4 gal. + 1 C.	1-1/2 gal. + 1/2 C.	1-3/4 gal.	1-3/4 gal. + 3-1/2 C.	2 gal. + 2-1/2 C.

(r) = slightly rounded.
(s) = scant.

Portions												
25	50	75	100	200	300	400	500	600	700	800	900	1000
3/4 C. + 2 T. + 2-1/2 t.	1-3/4 C. + 4 t.	2-3/4 C. + 1/2 t.	3-2/3 C.	1-3/4 qt. + 1/3 C.	2-3/4 qt.	3-1/2 qt. + 2/3 C.	1 gal. + 1-2/3 C.	1-1/4 gal. + 1-1/3 C.	1-1/2 gal. + 2 C.	1-3/4 gal. + 1-2/3 C.	2 gal. + 1-1/3 C.	2-1/4 gal. + 1 C.
3/4 C. + 3 T.	1-3/4 C. + 2 T.	2-3/4 C. + 1 T.	3-3/4 C.	1-3/4 qt. + 1/2 C.	3 qt. + 1/4 C.	1 gal.	1 gal. + 3-3/4 C.	1-1/4 gal. + 3-1/2 C.	1-1/2 gal. + 3-1/4 C.	1-3/4 gal. + 3 C.	2 gal. + 2-3/4 C.	2-1/4 gal. + 2-1/2 C.
1 C.	2 C.	3 C.	1 qt.	2 qt.	3 qt.	1 gal.	1-1/4 gal.	1-1/2 gal.	1-3/4 gal.	2 gal.	2-1/4 gal.	2-1/2 gal.
1-1/4 C.	2-1/2 C.	3-3/4 C.	1-1/4 qt.	2-1/2 qt.	3-3/4 qt.	1-1/4 gal.	1-1/2 gal. + 1 C.	1-3/4 gal. + 2 C.	2 gal. + 3 C.	2-1/2 gal.	2-3/4 gal. + 1 C.	3 gal. + 2 C.
1-1/2 C.	3 C.	1 qt. + 1/2 C.	1-1/2 t.	3 qt.	1 gal. + 2 C.	1-1/2 gal.	1-3/4 gal. + 2 C.	2-1/4 gal.	2-1/2 gal. + 2 C.	3 gal.	3-1/4 gal. + 2 C.	3-3/4 gal.
1-3/4 C.	3-1/2 C.	1-1/4 qt. + 1/4 C.	1-3/4 t.	3-1/2 qt.	1-1/4 gal. + 1 C.	1-3/4 gal.	2 gal. + 3 C.	2-1/2 gal. + 2 C.	3 gal. + 1 C.	3-1/2 gal.	3-3/4 gal. + 3 C.	4-1/4 gal. + 2 C.
2 C.	1 qt.	1-1/2 qt.	2 qt.	1 gal.	1-1/2 gal.	2 gal.	2-1/2 gal.	3 gal.	3-1/2 gal.	4 gal.	4-1/2 gal.	5 gal.
2-1/4 C.	1 qt. + 1/2 C.	1-1/2 qt. + 3/4 C.	2-1/4 qt.	1 gal. + 2 C.	1-1/2 gal. + 3 C.	2-1/4 gal.	2-3/4 gal. + 1 C.	3-1/4 gal. + 2 C.	3-3/4 gal. + 3 C.	4-1/2 gal.	5 gal. + 1 C.	5-1/2 gal. + 2 C.
2-1/2 C.	1-1/4 qt.	1-3/4 t. + 1/2 C.	2-1/2 qt.	1-1/4 gal.	1-3/4 gal. + 2 C.	2-1/2 gal.	3 gal. + 2 C.	3-3/4 gal.	4-1/4 gal. + 2 C.	5 gal.	5-1/2 gal. + 2 C.	6-1/4 gal.
2-3/4 C.	1-1/4 qt. + 1/2 C.	2 qt. + 1/4 C.	2-3/4 qt.	1-1/4 gal. + 2 C.	2 gal. + 1 C.	2-3/4 gal.	3-1/4 gal. + 3 C.	4 gal. + 2 C.	4-3/4 gal. + 1 C.	5-1/2 gal.	6 gal. + 3 C.	6-3/4 gal. + 2 C.
3 C.	1-1/2 qt.	2-1/4 qt.	3 qt.	1-1/2 gal.	2-1/4 gal.	3 gal.	3-3/4 gal.	4-1/2 gal.	5-1/4 gal.	6 gal.	6-3/4 gal.	7-1/2 gal.
3-1/4 C.	1-1/2 qt. + 1/2 C.	2-1/4 qt. + 3/4 C.	3-1/4 qt.	1-1/2 gal. + 2 C.	2-1/4 gal. + 3 C.	3-1/4 gal.	4 gal. + 1 C.	4-3/4 gal. + 2 C.	5-1/2 gal. + 3 C.	6-1/2 gal.	7-1/4 gal. + 1 C.	8 gal. + 2 C.
3-1/2 C.	1-3/4 qt.	2-1/2 qt. + 1/2 C.	3-1/2 qt.	1-3/4 gal.	2-1/2 gal. + 2 C.	3-1/2 gal.	4-1/4 gal. + 2 C.	5-1/4 gal.	6 gal. + 2 C.	7 gal.	7-3/4 gal. + 2 C.	8-3/4 gal.
3-3/4 C.	1-3/4 qt. + 1/2 C.	2-3/4 qt. + 1/4 C.	3-3/4 qt.	1-3/4 gal. + 2 C.	2-3/4 gal. + 1 C.	3-3/4 gal.	4-1/2 gal. + 3 C.	5-1/2 gal. + 2 C.	6-1/2 gal. + 1 C.	7-1/2 gal.	8-1/4 gal. + 3 C.	9-1/4 gal. + 2 C.
1 qt.	2 qt.	3 qt.	1 gal.	2 gal.	3 gal.	4 gal.	5 gal.	6 gal.	7 gal.	8 gal.	9 gal.	10 gal.
1-1/4 qt.	2-1/2 qt.	3-3/4 qt.	1-1/4 gal.	2-1/2 gal.	3-3/4 gal.	5 gal.	6-1/4 gal.	7-1/2 gal.	8-3/4 gal.	10 gal.	11-1/4 gal.	12-1/2 gal.
1-1/2 qt.	3 qt.	1 gal. + 2 C.	1-1/2 gal.	3 gal.	4-1/2 gal.	6 gal.	7-1/2 gal.	9 gal.	10-1/2 gal.	12 gal.	13-1/2 gal.	15 gal.
1-3/4 qt.	3-1/2 qt.	1-1/4 gal. + 1 C.	1-3/4 gal.	3-1/2 gal.	5-1/4 gal.	7 gal.	8-3/4 gal.	10-1/2 gal.	12-1/4 gal.	14 gal.	15-3/4 gal.	17-1/2 gal.
2 qt.	1 gal.	1-1/2 gal.	2 gal.	4 gal.	6 gal.	8 gal.	10 gal.	12 gal.	14 gal.	16 gal.	18 gal.	20 gal.
2-1/4 qt.	1 gal + 2 C.	1-1/2 gal. + 3 C.	2-1/4 gal.	4-1/2 gal.	6-3/4 gal.	9 gal.	11-1/4 gal.	13-1/2 gal.	15-3/4 gal.	18 gal.	20-1/4 gal.	22-1/2 gal.
2-1/2 qt.	1-1/4 gal.	1-3/4 gal. + 2 C.	2-1/2 gal.	5 gal.	7-1/2 gal.	10 gal.	12-1/2 gal.	15 gal.	17-1/2 gal.	20 gal.	22-1/2 gal.	25 gal.
2-3/4 qt.	1-1/4 gal. + 2 C.	2 gal. + 1 C.	2-3/4 gal.	5-1/2 gal.	8-1/4 gal.	11 gal.	13-3/4 gal.	16-1/2 gal.	19-1/4 gal.	22 gal.	24-3/4 gal.	27-1/2 gal.
3 qt.	1-1/2 gal.	2-1/4 gal.	3 gal.	6 gal.	9 gal.	12 gal.	15 gal.	18 gal.	21 gal.	24 gal.	27 gal.	30 gal.
3 qt. + 1 C.	1-1/2 gal. + 2 C.	2-1/4 gal. + 3 C.	3-1/4 gal.	6-1/2 gal.	9-3/4 gal.	13 gal.	16-1/4 gal.	19-1/2 gal.	22-3/4 gal.	26 gal.	29-1/4 gal.	32-1/2 gal.

3-1/2 qt.	1-3/4 gal.	2-1/2 gal. + 2 C.	3-1/2 gal.	7 gal.	10-1/2 gal.	14 gal.	17-1/2 gal.	21 gal.	24-1/2 gal.	28 gal.	31-1/2 gal.	35 gal.
3-1/2 qt. + 1 C.	1-3/4 gal. + 2 C.	2-3/4 gal. + 1 C.	3-3/4 gal.	7-1/2 gal.	11-1/4 gal.	15 gal.	18-3/4 gal.	22-1/2 gal.	26-1/4 gal.	30 gal.	33-3/4 gal.	37-1/2 gal.
1 gal.	2 gal.	3 gal.	4 gal.	8 gal.	12 gal.	16 gal.	20 gal.	24 gal.	28 gal.	32 gal.	36 gal.	40 gal.
1 gal. + 1 C.	2 gal. + 2 C.	3 gal. + 3 C.	4-1/4 gal.	8-1/2 gal.	12-3/4 gal.	17 gal.	21-1/4 gal.	25-1/2 gal.	29-3/4 gal.	34 gal.	38-1/4 gal.	42-1/2 gal.
1 gal. + 2 C.	2-1/4 gal.	3-1/4 gal. + 2 C.	4-1/2 gal.	9 gal.	13-1/2 gal.	18 gal.	22-1/2 gal.	27 gal.	31-1/2 gal.	36 gal.	40-1/2 gal.	45 gal.
1 gal. + 3 C.	2-1/4 gal. + 2 C.	3-1/2 gal. + 1 C.	4-3/4 gal.	9-1/2 gal.	14-1/4 gal.	19 gal.	23-3/4 gal.	28-1/2 gal.	33-1/4 gal.	38 gal.	42-3/4 gal.	47-1/2 gal.
1-1/4 gal.	2-1/2 gal.	3-3/4 gal.	5 gal.	10 gal.	15 gal.	20 gal.	25 gal.	30 gal.	35 gal.	40 gal.	45 gal.	50 gal.
1-1/4 gal. + 1 C.	2-1/2 gal. + 2 C.	3-3/4 gal. + 3 C.	5-1/4 gal.	10-1/2 gal.	15-3/4 gal.	21 gal.	26-1/4 gal.	31-1/2 gal.	36-3/4 gal.	42 gal.	47-1/4 gal.	52-1/2 gal.
1-1/4 gal. + 2 C.	2-3/4 gal.	4 gal. + 2 C.	5-1/2 gal.	11 gal.	16-1/2 gal.	22 gal.	27-1/2 gal.	33 gal.	38-1/2 gal.	44 gal.	49-1/2 gal.	55 gal.
1-1/4 gal. + 3 C.	2-3/4 gal. + 2 C.	4-1/4 gal. + 1 C.	5-3/4 gal.	11-1/2 gal.	17-1/4 gal.	23 gal.	28-3/4 gal.	34-1/2 gal.	40-1/4 gal.	46 gal.	51-3/4 gal.	57-1/2 gal.
1-1/2 gal.	3 gal.	4-1/2 gal.	6 gal.	12 gal.	18 gal.	24 gal.	30 gal.	36 gal.	42 gal.	48 gal.	54 gal.	60 gal.
1-1/2 gal. + 1 C.	3 gal. + 2 C.	4-1/2 gal. + 3 C.	6-1/4 gal.	12-1/2 gal.	18-3/4 gal.	25 gal.	31-1/4 gal.	37-1/2 gal.	43-3/4 gal.	50 gal.	56-1/4 gal.	62-1/2 gal.
1-1/2 gal. + 2 C.	3-1/4 gal.	4-3/4 gal. + 2 C.	6-1/2 gal.	13 gal.	19-1/2 gal.	26 gal.	32-1/2 gal.	39 gal.	45-1/2 gal.	52 gal.	58-1/2 gal.	65 gal.
1-1/2 gal. + 3 C.	3-1/4 gal. + 2 C.	5 gal. + 1 C.	6-3/4 gal.	13-1/2 gal.	20-1/4 gal.	27 gal.	33-3/4 gal.	40-1/2 gal.	47-1/4 gal.	54 gal.	60-3/4 gal.	67-1/2 gal.
1-3/4 gal.	3-1/2 gal.	5-1/4 gal.	7 gal.	14 gal.	21 gal.	28 gal.	35 gal.	42 gal.	49 gal.	56 gal.	63 gal.	70 gal.

From a table prepared by Katharine Flack for the New York State Department of Mental Health Nutrition Service; reprinted by permission.

Appendix Table 10. Conversion Chart of Volume Measures for Recipes in 8- and 20-Portion Increments

Instructions

1. Locate the column that corresponds to the original yield of the recipe you wish to adjust. For example, let us assume your original custard sauce recipe yields 24 portions. Locate the 24 column.

2. Run your finger down this column until you come to the amount of the ingredient required (or the amount closest to this figure) in the recipe you wish to adjust. Say that your original recipe for 24 portions requires 1-1/2 T. cornstarch and 1-1/4 qts. milk. Run your finger down the column headed 24 until you come to 1-1/2 T. (for cornstarch) and then 1-1/4 qts. (for milk).

3. Next, run your finger across the page, in line with that amount, until you come to the column that is headed to correspond with the yield you desire. Suppose you want to make 64 portions. Starting with your finger at the 1-1/2 T. (in the 24 column), slide it across to the column headed 64 and read the figure. You will need 1/4 C. cornstarch for 64 portions. Repeat the procedure starting with 1-1/4 qts. in the 24 column; tracing across to the 64 column, you find you will need 3-1/4 qts. + 1/3 C. milk.

4. Record this figure as the amount of the ingredient required for the new yield of your recipe. Repeat steps 1, 2, and 3 for each ingredient in your original recipe to obtain the adjusted measure needed of each for your new yield. You can increase or decrease yield in this manner.

5. If you need to combine two columns to obtain your desired yield, follow the above procedure and add together the amounts given in the two columns to get the amount required for your adjusted yield. For example, to find the amount of cornstarch needed for 124 portions of pudding (using the same basic recipe as above) locate the figures in columns 60 and 64 and add them. In this case they would be 3 T. + 2-1/4 t. plus 1/4 C., and the required total would be 7 T. + 2-1/4 t.

6. The figures in Appendix Table 10 are given in measurements that provide absolute accuracy. After you have made yield adjustments for all ingredients you can round off awkward fractions and complicated measurements. In our example of increasing from 24 to 64 portions, you can round the adjusted amount of milk to 3-1/4 qts. without upsetting proportions. The total amount of cornstarch in that example need not be rounded off, since it can be measured easily (1/4 C.).

Portions													
8	16	20	24	32	40	48	56	60	64	72	80	88	96
*	*	1/8 t. (s)	1/8 t.	1/8 t. (r)	1/4 t. (s)	1/4 t.	1/4 t. (r)	1/4 t. (r)	1/4 t. (r)	1/4 t. + 1/8 t.	1/2 t. (s)	1/2 t. (s)	1/2 t.
*	1/8 t. (r)	1/4 t. (s)	1/4 t.	1/4 t. (r)	1/2 t. (s)	1/2 t.	1/2 t. (r)	1/2 t. (r)	3/4 t. (s)	3/4 t.	3/4 t. (r)	1 t. (s)	1 t.
1/4 t. (s)	1/4 t. (r)	1/2 t. (s)	1/2 t.	3/4 t. (s)	3/4 t. (r)	1 t.	1-1/4 t. (s)	1-1/4 t.	1-1/4 t. (r)	1-1/2 t.	1-3/4 t. (s)	1-3/4 t. (r)	2 t.
1/4 t.	1/2 t.	1/2 t. (r)	3/4 t.	1 t.	1-1/4 t.	1-1/2 t.	1-3/4 t.	1-3/4 t. (r)	2 t.	2-1/4 t.	2-1/2 t.	2-3/4 t.	1 T.
1/4 t. (r)	3/4 t. (s)	3/4 t. (r)	1 t.	1-1/4 t. (r)	1-3/4 t. (s)	2 t.	2-1/4 t. (r)	2-1/2 t.	2-3/4 t. (s)	1 T.	1 T. + 1/4 t.	1 T. + 3/4 t.	1 T. + 1 t.
1/2 t. (s)	3/4 t. (r)	1 t.	1-1/4 t.	1-3/4 t. (s)	2 t.	2-1/2 t.	1 T. (s)	1 T. + 1/8 t.	1 T. + 1/4 t.	1 T. + 3/4 t.	1 T. + 1-1/4 t.	1-1/2 T.	1 T. + 2 t.
1/2 t.	1 t.	1-1/4 t.	1-1/2 t.	2 t.	2-1/2 t.	1 T.	1 T. + 1/2 t.	1 T. + 3/4 t.	1 T. + 1 t.	1-1/2 T.	1 T. + 2 t.	1 T. + 2-1/2 t.	2 T.
1/2 t. (r)	1-1/4 t. (s)	1-1/2 t.	1-3/4 t.	2-1/4 t. (r)	1 T. (s)	1 T. + 1/2 t.	1 T. + 1 t.	1 T. + 1-1/4 t. + 1/8 t.	1 T. + 1-3/4 t.	1 T. + 2-1/4 t.	1 T. + 2-3/4 t.	2 T. + 1/2 t.	2 T. + 1 t.
3/4 t. (s)	1-1/4 t. (r)	1-3/4 t. (s)	2 t.	2-3/4 t. (r)	1 T. + 1/4 t.	1 T. + 1 t.	1 T. + 1-3/4 t.	1 T. + 2 t.	1 T. + 2-1/4 t.	2 T.	2 T. + 3/4 t.	2 T. + 1-1/4 t.	2 T. + 2 t.
3/4 t.	1-1/2 t.	1-3/4 t. (r)	2-1/4 t.	1 T.	1 T. + 3/4 t.	1 T. + 1-1/2 t.	1 T. + 2-1/4 t.	1 T. + 2-1/2 t.	2 T.	2 T. + 3/4 t.	2-1/2 T.	2 T. + 2-1/4 t.	3 T.
3/4 t. (r)	1-3/4 t. (s)	2 t.	2-1/2 t.	1 T. + 1/4 t. (r)	1 T. + 1-1/4 t.	1 T. + 2 t.	1 T. + 2-3/4 t. (r)	2 T. + 1/4 t.	2 T. + 3/4 t.	2 T. + 1-1/2 t.	2 T. + 2-1/4 t.	3 T.	3 T. + 1 t.
1 t. (s)	1-3/4 t. (r)	2-1/4 t. (r)	2-3/4 t.	1 T. + 3/4 t. (s)	1 T. + 1-1/2 t.	1 T. + 2-1/2 t.	2 T. + 1/2 t.	2 T. + 3/4 t.	2 T. + 1-1/4 t.	2 T. + 2-1/4 t.	3 T.	3 T. + 1 t.	3 T. + 2 t.
1 t.	2 t.	2-1/2 t.	1 T.	1 T. + 1 t.	1 T. + 2 t.	2 T.	2 T. + 1 t.	2-1/2 T.	2 T. + 2 t.	3 T.	3 T. + 1 t.	3 T. + 2 t.	1/4 C.

1-1/2 t.	1 T.	1 T. + 3/4 t.	1-1/2 T.	2 T.	2-1/2 T.	3 T.	3-1/2 T.	3 T. + 2-1/4 t.	1/4 C.	1/4 C. + 1-1/2 t.	1/4 C. + 1 T.	1/3 C. + 1/2 t.	1/3 C. + 2 t.
2 t.	1 T. + 1t.	1 T. + 2 t.	2 T.	2 T. + 2 t.	3 T. + 1 t.	1/4 C.	1/4 C. + 2 t.	1/4 C. + 1 T.	1/3 C.	1/3 C. + 2 t.	1/3 C. + 4 t.	1/3 C. + 2 T.	1/2 C.
2-1/2 t.	1 T. + 2 t.	2 T. + 1/4 t.	2-1/2 T.	3 T. + 1 t.	1/4 C. + 1/2 t.	1/4 C. + 1 T.	1/3 C. + 1/2 T.	1/3 C. + 2-3/4 t.	1/3 C. + 4 t.	1/4 C. + 3-1/2 T.	1/2 C. + 1 t.	1/2 C. + 3-1/2 t.	1/2 C. + 2 T.
1 T.	2 T.	2-1/2 T.	3 T.	1/4 C.	1/4 C. + 1 T.	1/3 C. + 2 t.	1/4 C. + 3 T.	1/4 C. + 3-1/2 T.	1/2 C.	1/2 C. + 1 T.	1/2 C. + 2 T.	1/2 C. + 3 T.	3/4 C.
1 T. + 1/2 t.	2 T. + 1 t.	2 T. + 2-3/4 t.	3-1/2 T.	1/4 C. + 2 t.	1/3 C. + 1/2 T.	1/4 C. + 3 T.	1/2 C. + 1/2 t.	1/2 C. + 2-1/4 t.	1/2 C. + 4 t.	1/2 C. + 2-1/2 T.	2/3 C. + 1 T.	3/4 C. + 2-1/2 t.	3/4 C. + 2 T.
1 T. + 1 t.	2 T. + 2 t.	3 T. + 1 t.	1/4 C.	1/3 C.	1/3 C. + 4 t.	1/2 C.	1/2 C. + 4 t.	1/2 C. + 2 T.	2/3 C.	3/4 C.	3/4 C. + 4 t.	3/4 C. + 2-1/2 T.	1 C.
1 T. + 2-1/4 t.	3 T. + 2-3/4 t.	1/4 C. + 1-1/4 t.	1/3 C.	1/4 C. + 3 T.	1/2 C. + 2-1/2 t.	2/3 C.	3/4 C. + 1/2 T.	3/4 C. + 4 t.	3/4 C. + 2 T.	1 C.	1 C. + 5 t.	1 C. + 3-1/2 T.	1-1/3 C.
2 T. + 2 t.	1/3 C.	1/3 C. + 2 T.	1/2 C.	2/3 C.	3/4 C. + 4 t.	1 C.	1 C. + 2-1/2 T.	1-1/4 C.	1-1/3 C.	1-1/2 C.	1-2/3 C.	1-3/4 C. + 4 t.	2 C.
3 T. + 1-3/4 t.	1/3 C. + 5 t.	1/2 C. + 2-3/4 t.	2/3 C.	3/4 C. + 2 T.	1 C. + 5-1/2 t.	1-1/3 C.	1-1/2 C. + 1 T.	1-2/3 C.	1-3/4 C.	2 C.	2 C. + 3-1/2 T.	2-1/4 C. + 3 T.	2-2/3 C.
1/4 C.	1/2 C.	1/2 C. + 2 T.	3/4 C.	1 C.	1-1/4 C.	1-1/2 C.	1-3/4 C.	1-3/4 C. + 2 T.	2 C.	2-1/4 C.	2-1/2 C.	2-3/4 C.	3 C.
1/3 C.	2/3 C.	3/4 C. + 2 t.	1 C.	1-1/3 C.	1-2/3 C.	2 C.	2-1/3 C.	2-1/2 C.	2-2/3 C.	3 C.	3-1/3 C.	3-2/3 C.	1 qt.
1/3 C. + 4 t.	3/4 C. + 4 t.	1 C. + 2 t.	1-1/4 C.	1-2/3 C.	2 C. + 4 t.	2-1/2 C.	2-3/4 C. + 2-1/2 T.	3 C. + 2 T.	3-1/3 C.	3-3/4 C.	1 qt. + 2-1/2 T.	4-1/2 C. + 4 t.	1-1/4 qt.
1/3 C. + 5-1/4 t.	2/3 C. + 3-1/2 T.	1 C. + 5-1/4 t.	1-1/3 C.	1-3/4 C. + 1-1/4 t.	2 C. + 3-1/2 T.	2-2/3 C.	3 C. + 2 T.	3-1/3 C.	3-1/2 C. + 2-1/2 t.	1 qt.	4-1/4 C. + 3 T.	4-3/4 C. + 2 T. + 1 t.	1-1/4 qt. + 1/3 C.
1/2 C.	1 C.	1-1/4 C.	1-1/2 C.	2 C.	2-1/2 C.	3 C.	3-1/2 C.	3-3/4 C.	1 qt.	1 qt. + 1/2 C.	1-1/4 qt.	1-1/4 qt. + 1/2 C.	1-1/2 qt.
1/2 C. + 2-1/4 t.	1 C. + 5-1/4 t.	1-1/3 C.	1-2/3 C.	2 C. + 3-1/2 T.	2-2/3 C.	3-1/3 C.	3-3/4 C. + 2 T.	1 qt. + 2-1/2 T.	4-1/4 C. + 3 T.	1-1/4 qt.	1-1/4 qt. + 1/3 C.	1-1/2 qt. + 5 t.	1-1/2 qt. + 2/3 C.
1/2 C. + 4 t.	1 C. + 3 T.	1-1/3 C. + 2 T.	1-3/4 C.	2-1/3 C.	2-3/4 C. + 1-1/2 T.	3-1/2 C.	1 qt. + 4 t.	1 qt. + 1/4 C. + 2 T.	1 qt. + 2/3 C.	1-1/4 qt. + 1/4 C.	5-1/2 C. + 3 T.	1-1/2 qt. + 1/4 C. + 2-1/2 T.	1-3/4 qt.
2/3 C.	1-1/3 C.	1-2/3 C.	2 C.	2-2/3 C.	3-1/3 C.	1 qt.	1 qt. + 2/3 C.	1-1/4 qt.	1-1/4 qt. + 1/3 C.	1-1/2 qt.	1-1/2 qt. + 2/3 C.	1-3/4 qt. + 1/3 C.	2 qt.
3/4 C.	1-1/2 C.	1-3/4 C. + 2 T.	2-1/4 C.	3 C.	3-3/4 C.	1 qt. + 1/2 C.	1-1/4 qt. + 1/4 C.	1-1/4 qt. + 2/3 C.	1-1/2 qt.	1-1/2 qt. + 3/4 C.	1-3/4 qt. + 1/2 C.	2 qt. + 1/4 C.	2-1/4 qt.
3/4 C. + 1-1/4 t.	1-1/2 C. + 2-3/4 t.	1-3/4 C. + 3 T.	2-1/3 C.	3 C. + 2 T.	3-3/4 C. + 2 T.	1 qt. + 2/3 C.	5-1/4 C. + 3 T.	5-3/4 C. + 1-1/2 T.	1-1/2 qt. + 1/4 C.	1-3/4 qt.	1-3/4 qt. + 3/4 C.	2 qt. + 1/2 C. + 1 T.	2-1/4 qt. + 1/3 C.
3/4 C. + 4 t.	1-2/3 C.	2 C. + 4 t.	2-1/2 C.	3-1/3 C.	1 qt. + 2-1/2 T.	1-1/4 qt.	5-3/4 C. + 1 T.	1-1/2 qt. + 1/4 C.	1-1/2 qt. + 2/3 C.	1-3/4 qt. + 1/2 C.	2 qt. + 5 T.	2-1/4 qt. + 3 T.	2-1/2 qt.

*The amount cannot be measured accurately without introducing error.
(r) = slightly rounded.
(s) = scant.

Portions													
8	16	20	24	32	40	48	56	60	64	72	80	88	96
2/3 C. + 3-1/2 T.	1-3/4 C. + 1-1/4 t.	2 C. + 3-1/2 T.	2-2/3 C.	3-1/2 C. + 1 T.	4-1/4 C. + 3 T.	1-1/4 qt. + 1/3 C.	1-1/2 qt. + 1/4 C.	1-1/2 qt. + 2/3 C.	1-3/4 qt. + 2 T.	2 qt.	2 qt. + 3/4 C. + 2 T.	2-1/4 qt. + 3/4 C. + 1/2 T.	2-1/2 qt. 2/3 C.
2/3 C. + 1/4 C.	1-3/4 C. + 4 t.	2-1/4 C. + 2 t.	2-3/4 C.	3-2/3 C.	4-1/2 C. + 4 t.	1-1/4 qt. + 1/2 C.	1-1/2 qt. + 1/4 C. + 3 T.	1-1/2 qt. + 3/4 C. + 2 T.	1-3/4 qt. + 1/3 C.	2 qt. + 1/4 C.	2-1/4 qt. + 2-1/2 T.	2-1/2 qt. + 1-1/2 T.	2-3/4 qt.
1 C.	2 C.	2-1/2 C.	3 C.	1 qt.	1-1/4 qt.	1-1/2 qt.	1-3/4 qt.	1-3/4 qt. + 1/2 C.	2 qt.	2-1/4 qt.	2-1/2 qt.	2-3/4 qt.	3 qt.
1 C. + 4 t.	2 C. + 2-1/2 T.	2-2/3 C. + 2 t.	3-1/4 C.	1 qt. + 1/3 C.	5-1/3 C. + 4 t.	1-1/2 qt. + 1/2 C.	1-3/4 qt. + 1/3 C. + 1/4 C.	2 qt. + 2 T.	2 qt. + 2/3 C.	2-1/4 qt. + 3/4 C.	2-1/2 qt. + 3/4 C. + 1-1/2 T.	2-3/4 qt. + 3/4 C. + 3 T.	3-1/4 qt.
1 C. + 5-1/4 t.	2 C. + 3-1/2 T.	2-3/4 C. + 1/2 T.	3-1/3 C.	4-1/4 C. + 3 T.	5-1/2 C. + 1 T.	1-1/2 qt. + 2/3 C.	1-3/4 qt. + 3/4 C.	2 qt. + 1/3 C.	2 qt. + 3/4 C. + 2 T.	2-1/2 qt.	2-3/4 qt. + 2 T.	3 qt. + 1/4 C.	3-1/4 qt. + 1/3 C.
1 C. + 2 T. + 2 t.	2-1/4 C. + 4 t.	2-3/4 C. + 2-1/2 T.	3-1/2 C.	1 qt. + 2/3 C.	5-3/4 C. + 1 T.	1-3/4 qt.	2 qt. + 3 T.	2 qt. + 3/4 C.	2-1/4 qt. + 1/3 C.	2-1/2 qt. + 1/2 C.	2-3/4 qt. + 1/2 C. + 2 T.	3 qt. + 3/4 C. + 1-1/2 T.	3-1/2 qt.
1 C. + 3-1/2 T.	2-1/4 C. + 3 T.	3 C. + 1 T.	3-2/3 C.	4-3/4 C. + 2 T.	1-1/2 qt. + 2 T.	1-3/4 qt. + 1/3 C.	2 qt. + 1/2 C. + 1 T.	2-1/4 qt. + 2-1/2 T.	2-1/4 qt. + 3/4 C.	2-3/4 qt.	3 qt. + 1/4 C.	3-1/4 qt. + 1/4 C. + 3 T.	3 qt. 2-2/3 C.
1-1/4 C.	2-1/2 C.	3 C. + 2 T.	3-3/4 C.	1-1/4 qt.	1-1/2 qt. + 1/4 C.	1-3/4 qt. + 1/2 C.	2 qt. + 3/4 C.	2-1/4 qt. + 1/4 C. + 2 T.	2-1/2 qt.	2-3/4 qt. + 1/4 C.	3 qt. + 1/2 C.	3 qt. + 1-3/4 C.	3 qt. + 3 C.
1-1/3 C.	2-2/3 C.	3-1/3 C.	1 qt.	1-1/4 qt. + 1/3 C.	1-1/2 qt. + 2/3 C.	2 qt.	2 qt. + 1-1/3 C.	2-1/2 qt.	2-3/4 qt. + 1/3 C.	3 qt.	3 qt. + 1-1/3 C.	3 qt. + 2-2/3 C.	1 gal.
1-2/3 C.	3-1/3 C.	1 qt. + 2-1/2 T.	1-1/4 qt.	1-1/2 qt. + 2/3 C.	2 qt. + 1/4 C. + 1 T.	2-1/2 qt.	2-3/4 qt. 2/3 C.	3 qt. 1/2 C.	3-1/4 qt. 1/3 C.	3-3/4 qt.	1 gal. + 2/3 C.	1 gal. + 2-1/3 C.	1-1/4 gal.
2 C.	1 qt.	1-1/4 qt.	1-1/2 qt.	2 qt.	2-1/2 qt.	3 qt.	3-1/2 qt.	3-3/4 qt.	1 gal.	1 gal. + 2 C.	1-1/4 gal.	1-1/4 gal. + 2 C.	1-1/2 gal.
2-1/3 C.	1 qt. + 2/3 C.	5-3/4 C. + 1-1/2 T.	1-3/4 qt.	2-1/4 qt. + 1/3 C.	2-3/4 qt. + 2/3 C.	3-1/2 qt.	1 gal. + 1/3 C.	1 gal. + 1-1/2 C.	1 gal. + 2-2/3 C.	1-1/4 gal. + 1 C.	1-1/4 gal. + 3-1/3 C.	1-1/2 gal. + 1-2/3 C.	1-3/4 gal.
2-2/3 C.	1-1/4 qt. + 1/3 C.	1-1/2 qt. + 2/3 C.	2 qt.	2-1/2 qt. + 2/3 C.	3-1/4 qt. + 1/3 C.	1 gal.	1 gal. + 2-2/3 C.	1-1/4 gal.	1-1/4 gal. + 1-1/3 C.	1-1/2 gal.	1-1/2 gal. + 2-2/3 C.	1-3/4 gal. + 1-1/3 C.	2 gal.
3 C.	1-1/2 qt.	1-3/4 qt. + 1/2 C.	2-1/4 qt.	3 qt.	3-3/4 qt.	1 gal. + 2 C.	1-1/4 gal. + 1 C.	1-1/4 gal. + 2-1/2 C.	1-1/2 gal.	1-1/2 gal. + 2 C.	1-3/4 gal. + 2 C.	2 gal. + 1 C.	2-1/4 gal.
3-1/3 C.	1-1/2 qt. + 2/3 C.	2 qt. + 1/3 C.	2-1/2 qt.	3-1/4 qt. + 1/3 C.	1 gal. + 2/3 C.	1-1/4 gal.	1-1/4 gal. + 3-1/3 C.	1-1/2 gal. + 1 C.	1-1/2 gal. + 2-2/3 C.	1-3/4 gal. + 2 C.	2 gal. + 1-1/3 C.	2-1/4 gal. + 2/3 C.	2-1/2 gal.
3-2/3 C.	1-3/4 qt. + 1/3 C.	2-1/4 qt. + 2-1/2 T.	2-3/4 qt.	3-1/2 qt. + 2/3 C.	1 gal. + 2-1/3 C.	1-1/4 gal. + 2 C.	1-1/2 gal. + 1-2/3 C.	1-1/2 gal. + 3-1/2 C.	1-3/4 gal. + 1-1/3 C.	2 gal. + 1 C.	2-1/4 gal. + 2/3 C.	2-1/2 gal. + 1/3 C.	2-3/4 gal.
1 qt.	2 qt.	2-1/2 qt.	3 qt.	1 gal.	1-1/4 gal.	1-1/2 gal.	1-3/4 gal.	1-3/4 gal. + 2 C.	2 gal.	2-1/4 gal.	2-1/2 gal.	2-3/4 gal.	3 gal.
1 qt. + 1/3 C.	2 qt. + 2/3 C.	2-1/2 qt. + 3/4 C. + 1-1/2 T.	3-1/4 qt.	1 gal. + 1-1/3 C.	1-1/4 gal. + 1-2/3 C.	1-1/2 gal. + 2 C.	1-3/4 gal. + 2-1/3 C.	2 gal. + 1/2 C.	2 gal. + 2-2/3 C.	2-1/4 gal. + 3 C.	2-1/2 gal. + 3-1/3 C.	2-3/4 gal. + 3-2/3 C.	3-1/4 gal.

1 qt. + 2/3 C.	2-1/4 qt. + 1/3 C.	2-3/4 qt. + 2/3 C.	3-1/2 qt.	1 gal. + 2-2/3 C.	1-1/4 gal. + 3-1/3 C.	1-3/4 gal.	2 gal. + 2/3 C.	2 gal. + 3 C.	2-1/4 gal. + 1-1/3 C.	2-1/2 gal. + 2 C.	2-3/4 gal. + 2-2/3 C.	3 gal. + 3-1/3 C.	3-1/2 gal.
1-1/4 qt.	2-1/2 qt.	3 qt. + 1/2 C.	3-3/4 qt.	1-1/4 gal.	1-1/2 gal. + 1 C.	1-3/4 gal. + 2 C.	2 gal. + 3 C.	2-1/4 gal. + 1-1/2 C.	2-1/2 gal.	2-3/4 gal. + 1 C.	3 gal. + 2 C.	3-1/4 gal. + 3 C.	3-3/4 gal.
1-1/4 qt. + 1/3 C.	2-1/2 qt. + 2/3 C.	3 qt. + 1-1/3 C.	1 gal.	1-1/4 gal. + 1-1/3 C.	1-1/2 gal. + 2-2/3 C.	2 gal.	2-1/4 gal. + 1-1/3 C.	2-1/2 gal.	2-1/2 gal. + 2-2/3 C.	3 gal.	3-1/4 gal. + 1-1/3 C.	3-1/2 gal. + 2-2/3 C.	4 gal.
1-1/2 qt. + 2/3 C.	3-1/4 qt. + 1/3 C.	1 gal. + 2/3 C.	1-1/4 gal.	1-1/2 gal. + 2-2/3 C.	2 gal. + 1-1/3 C.	2-1/2 gal.	2-3/4 gal. + 2-2/3 C.	3 gal. + 2 C.	3-1/4 gal. + 1-1/3 C.	3-3/4 gal.	4 gal. + 2-2/3 C.	4-1/2 gal. + 1-1/3 C.	5 gal.
2 qt.	1 gal.	1-1/4 gal.	1-1/2 gal.	2 gal.	2-1/2 gal.	3 gal.	3-1/2 gal.	3-3/4 gal.	4 gal.	4-1/2 gal.	5 gal.	5-1/2 gal.	6 gal.

From a table prepared by Katharine Flack for the New York State Department of Mental Health Nutrition Service; reprinted by permission.

Appendix Table 11. Sources of Food Service Information

American Gas Association, 1515 Wilson Boulevard, Arlington, Virginia 22209.
American Home Economics Association, 2010 Massachusetts Avenue, N.W., Washington, D.C. 20036.
American Hotel and Motel Association, 888 Seventh Avenue, New York, New York 10019.
American Institute of Baking, 400 East Ontario Street, Chicago, Illinois 60611.
American Meat Institute, 59 East Van Buren Street, Chicago, Illinois 60605.
American Spice Trade Association, 350 Fifth Avenue, New York, New York 10001.
Blue Goose Inc., 332 East Commonwealth, Fullerton, California 92632.
California Avocado Advisory Board, 4533-B MacArthur Boulevard, Newport Beach, California 92660.
California Prune Advisory Board, World Trade Center, San Francisco, California 94111.
California Raisin Advisory Board, 2111 East Dakota Avenue, Fresno, California 93726.
Cling Peach Advisory Board, 1 California Street, San Francisco, California 94111.
Coffee Brewing Center, Pan-American Coffee Bureau, 1350 Avenue of the Americas, New York, New York 10019.
Florida Celery Advisory Board, 4401 East Colonial Drive, Orlando, Florida 32814.
Florida Citrus Commission, P.O. Box 148, Lakeland, Florida 33802.
National Association of Meat Purveyors, 120 South Riverside Plaza, Chicago, Illinois 60606.
National Canners Association, 1133 20th Street, N.W., Washington, D.C. 20036.
National Dairy Council, 111 North Canal Street, Chicago, Illinois 60606.
National Live Stock and Meat Board, 36 South Wabash Avenue, Chicago, Illinois 60603.
National Restaurant Association, 1530 North Lake Shore Drive, Chicago, Illinois 60610.
National Sanitation Foundation, School of Public Health, University of Michigan, Ann Arbor, Michigan 48106.
National Turkey Federation, 111 East Hitt, Mount Morris, Illinois 61054.
Rice Council for Market Development, 3917 Richmond Avenue, Houston, Texas 77027.
Sunkist Growers, 14130 Riverside Drive, Sherman Oaks, California 91403.
United Fresh Fruit and Vegetable Association, 777 14th Street, N.W., Washington, D.C. 20005.
Wheat Flour Institute, 14 East Jackson Boulevard, Chicago, Illinois 60604.

Note: Additional source of information are the cooperative extension departments of state universities and food producers and purveyors.

Appendix 2. Canadian Food-grading System

Food grading started in Canada shortly after the turn of the century when grades for apples, previously established only for export, were made applicable on the home market. Today we have grades for butter, cheddar cheese, instant skim milk powder, eggs, fresh and processed fruits and vegetables, honey, maple syrup, meat, and poultry.

Foods are graded according to national and provincial standards established by legislation. The Canada Department of Agriculture works in close cooperation with industry in developing the national standards. The word "Canada" in the grade name on the package or product means that the food is graded and packed in Canada in accordance with federal standards. The word "Canada" may not be used in a grade name on imported foods sold in their original containers, or on products not subject to federal grading regulations.

Before beef can be graded it must pass health inspection. Health-inspected meat and poultry products from plants registered with the Department's Health of Animals Branch are marked with the round Canada Approved or Canada inspection legend, which means the foods are wholesome but does not indicate that they are graded.

Federal grade standards apply to food exports, to imported foods of a kind produced in Canada, and to foods shipped from one province to another. Canada Department of Agriculture inspectors are responsible for enforcing federal grade standards.

The grading of foods produced and sold within a province is a provincial responsibility. However, where grade standards have been established under provincial authority, Canada Department of Agriculture inspectors collaborate with the provinces in enforcing provincial regulations.

Dairy Products

Creamery print butter and all packaged instant skim milk powder are graded and marked accordingly on the wrapper. Though grading of cheese for retail trade is not compulsory, most bulk cheddar cheese is graded, and sometimes it is sold by grade in consumer packages. All commercial packages of butter, cheddar cheese, and skim milk powder intended for interprovincial or export trade are sampled for composition and graded.

Grades

Butter and cheddar cheese	Instant skim milk powder
Canada First Grade Canada Second Grade Canada Third Grade Below Canada Third Grade	Canada First Grade

Canada Second Grade, Canada Third Grade, and Below Canada Third Grade butter and cheddar cheese are not usually available in retail stores.

Basis for Grades. Grades depend on the following:

Butter	Cheddar cheese	Instant skim milk powder
flavor	flavor	color
texture	texture	flavor
incorporation of moisture	color	odor
color	closeness	fat content
salting	finish	moisture content
packaging		bacterial content
		solubility
		sediment

Grading and Inspection. Federal dairy inspectors grade butter, cheddar cheese, and skim milk powder. The grade of creamery print butter may be declared by the manufacturer, but inspectors check the butter in creameries, warehouses, and retail outlets for accuracy of grading, composition, and weight. They also check the composition of cheddar cheese, process cheese, imported specialty cheeses, ice cream, and instant skim milk powder at wholesale and retail levels, and issue inspection certificates covering shipments of graded dairy products for interprovincial and export trade.

Most provinces have adopted legislation that is concurrent with federal grading regulations, but federal inspectors assign grades to the various products. Provincial dairy inspectors supervise the grading of raw milk and cream for use in manufactured products. Provincial legislation sets standards for pasteurization of fluid milk and cream and controls sanitation of these products.

Eggs

Eggs in the shell are sold by grade in all provinces. Grade marks must be shown on cartons and bulk displays in retail stores. All shell eggs that are imported, exported, or shipped from one province to another must be graded.

Grades

Canada Grade	Weight of each egg
A1 Extra Large Size	at least 2¼ ounces
A1 Large Size	at least 2 ounces
A1 Medium Size	at least 1¾ ounces but less than 2 ounces
A1 Small Size	at least 1½ ounces but less than 1¾ ounces
A Extra Large Size	at least 2¼ ounces
A Large Size	at least 2 ounces
A Medium Size	at least 1¾ ounces but less than 2 ounces
A Small Size	at least 1½ ounces but less than 1¾ ounces
A Peewee Size	less than 1½ ounces
B	at least 1¾ ounces
C	(not specified)
Cracks	(not specified)

Canada Grade C and Canada Grade Cracks are not usually available in retail stores.

Basis for Grades. Eggs are graded on:

—weight
—cleanliness, soundness, and shape of shell
—shape and relative position of yolk within the egg, as viewed during candling
—size of air cell, an indicator of freshness
—presence of abnormalities, such as meat and blood spots

Grading and Inspection. A producer may grade his own eggs or have them graded at an egg-grading station registered with the Canada Department of Agriculture. Registered egg-grading stations must meet certain operating and sanitation requirements. Federal agricultural inspectors spot-check both producer premises and egg-grading stations to ensure that accurate grading is being done under sanitary conditions.

Federal agricultural inspectors check quality of eggs periodically at wholesale distributors, retail stores, restaurants, hospitals, other institutions, and military camps.

All provinces have regulations based on the federal grade standards for shell eggs. Federal agricultural inspectors are responsible for enforcing provincial legislation.

Fresh Fruits and Vegetables

Most Canadian fruits and vegetables grown in large quantities are sold by grade. Not all provinces require grading of the same fruits and vegetables, though all have regulations covering some. Provincial grades are similar to the federal grades outlined below, which are compulsory for interprovincial and export trade.

Grades

Fruit or vegetable	Grades
Apples	Canada Extra Fancy Canada Fancy Canada Commercial or Canada Cee or Canada "C"
Pears	Canada Extra Fancy Canada Fancy or Canada No. 1 Canada Commercial or Canada Cee or Canada "C" or Canada Domestic
Cherries	Canada No. 1 Canada Domestic Canada Orchard Run
Apricots Crabapples Cranberries Grapes Peaches Plums Prunes Rhubarb (field)	Canada No. 1 Canada Domestic
Blueberries Cantaloupes Strawberries	Canada No. 1
Carrots Parsnips	Canada No. 1 and Canada No. 1— Cut Crowns Canada No. 2
Onions	Canada No. 1 and Canada No. 1— Pickling Canada No. 2
Potatoes	Canada No. 1 and Canada No. 1— Large Canada No. 2
Celery	Canada No. 1 and Canada No. 1— Heart Canada No. 2
Asparagus Beets Brussels sprouts Cabbages Cauliflowers Cucumbers (field or greenhouse) Head lettuce Tomatoes	Canada No. 1 Canada No. 2
Rutabagas Sweet corn	Canada No. 1

Apples

Apples must have a minimum diameter of 2¼ inches to meet federal standards. However, in certain years a 2-inch minimum is permitted for red and red-striped varieties of Canada Extra Fancy and Canada Fancy grades with 20 percent more color than normal color standards. Some provinces permit the sale of apples of some varieties in the size range of 2 to 2¼ inches provided they have Extra Fancy color.

Potatoes

Sizes for potatoes are as follows:

Canada No. 1	2¼ to 3½ inches in diameter for round varieties 2 to 3½ inches in diameter for long varieties
Canada No. 1—Large	3 to 4½ inches in diameter
Canada No. 1—Small	1½ to 2¼ inches in diameter
Canada No. 1—New Potatoes	Before September 16 each year, new potatoes with a minimum diameter of 1-7/8 inches (both round and long varieties) may be graded Canada No. 1

Canada No. 2	1¾ to 4½ inches in diameter, with at least 75 percent of the lot having a diameter of 2 inches or larger

Basis for Grades. Fresh fruits and vegetables are graded on:

—uniformity of size and shape
—minimum and maximum diameter
—minimum length
—color
—maturity
—freedom from disease, injury, and other defects and damage
—cleanliness
—packaging

Grading and Inspection. Producers or packers grade their own fruits and vegetables. All products bearing federal grade names must meet grade and label specifications and must be in standard packages. All produce in bulk displays must meet grade specifications if a grade is declared. Bulk displays of apples must also indicate the variety when the grade is marked.

Federal fruit and vegetable inspectors check grades of fruits and vegetables at packing and shipping points and inspect and certify shipments for export. Grades are also checked by federal retail inspectors in food stores.

Ontario and Quebec have their own inspectors who collaborate with federal inspectors in checking grades of produce grown and sold in the province as well as that coming into the province. In the other provinces, where no provincial inspectors are appointed, federal inspectors check the grades of fruits and vegetables.

Processed Fruits and Vegetables

Most processed fruits and vegetables are sold by grade in Canada. About 95 percent of the production in every province is from plants registered for federal inspection and grading. Only federally registered plants may ship their products from one province to another or for export outside of Canada.

Nonregistered plants are not permitted to use a Canada grade name on their products. Sale of such products must be confined to the province in which they were produced.

Imported fruit and vegetable products for which grades are established must carry a grade mark, and they must meet the federal grade standard set out in the regulations for those products. Imported fruit and vegetable products cannot have Canada as part of their grade name when sold in original containers.

Grades

Product	Grades
Canned fruit Canned vegetables	Canada Fancy Canada Choice Canada Standard
Canned apple juice Canned tomato juice Frozen fruit Frozen vegetables Dehydrated fruit Dehydrated vegetables	Canada Fancy Canada Choice

If a product fails to meet the lowest prescribed grade for it, yet is sound, wholesome, and fit to eat, it must be marked "Sub Standard." Products so labeled are not usually found in stores.

Basis for Grades. Processed fruits and vegetables are graded on:

—flavor and aroma
—color
—tenderness and maturity
—uniformity of size and shape
—consistency
—appearance of liquid media
—freedom from defects and foreign matter

Grading and Inspection. Processors grade their own products. Federal fruit and vegetable inspectors check the accuracy of their grading before labeling and shipping, and again in wholesale warehouses. Certificates of grade are issued on request. Grades are also checked by retail inspectors in food stores in cities across Canada.

In Quebec and the Maritimes, provincial inspectors see that provincial regulations are carried out in any processing plants not registered in those provinces for federal inspection and grading service.

Honey

Honey produced for sale in Alberta, British Columbia, Manitoba, Ontario, and Saskatchewan must be graded and classified as to color, except when sold directly to consumers at an apiary. All honey for export, and extracted honey in consumer containers of 8 pounds or less for interprovincial trade, must be graded and color-classified.

Grades and Color Classes. Color of honey does not affect grade, but is an indication of flavor; usually, the darker the honey, the stronger the flavor.

Grades: Canada No. 1, Canada No. 2, and Canada No. 3

Color classes: White, Golden Amber, and Dark

Canada No. 2 and Canada No. 3 are not usually available in retail stores.

Honey that is wholesome but fails to meet Canada No. 3 requirements is marked "Sub Standard."

Basis for Grades. Honey is graded on:

—flavor
—freedom from foreign material
—keeping quality

Grading and Inspection. Honey is graded and color-classified by the packer.

Federal fruit and vegetable inspectors check grades and color classifications claimed at retail, wholesale, and manufacturing levels and certify honey shipments for export trade. Federal retail inspectors also check honey in food stores in most large Canadian cities.

Canada Department of Agriculture inspectors are responsible for checking grades and color classifications of honey produced and sold within Alberta, British Columbia, Manitoba, and Saskatchewan. In Ontario, federal and provincial inspectors share this responsibility.

Maple Syrup

Maple syrup must be graded if it is to be sold in Quebec, but in other provinces grading is at the option of the packer. Grading is not compulsory for interprovincial or export trade. However, federal grades have been established, and products bearing a grade mark must meet the requirements laid down for composition and labeling.

Artificial maple products must bear the manufacturer's name and address, a list of ingredients, and the words "artificially maple flavored."

Grades. Canada Fancy, Canada Light, Canada Medium, and Canada Dark.

Quebec has an additional grade, Amber C, between Canada Medium and Canada Dark.

Basis for Grades. Maple syrup is graded on:

—color
—flavor
—freedom from fermentation
—percentage of solids

Grading and Inspection. Packers grade their own maple syrup except for that sold to companies or cooperatives in the Province of Quebec, which must be graded by provincial inspectors.

Federal fruit and vegetable inspectors check grades when declared, inspect for purity and proper labeling of maple syrup and artificially maple-flavored table syrups, and check composition of maple products at all levels of trade. On authority of the Quebec Department of Agriculture, they also assist provincial inspectors in checking grades and administering composition standards in Quebec.

Meat

Health Inspection. Health inspection by a federal meat inspector is necessary before meat can be moved in interprovincial or international trade. Inspection of meat bought or sold within the province in which it is slaughtered is the responsibility of the province.

Any meat plant in Canada that applies and meets the requirements may receive inspection service provided by the Meat Inspection Division of the Health of Animals Branch, Canada Department of Agriculture. In inspected plants, federal veterinarians examine meat animals before and after slaughter to ensure that all diseased or otherwise unwholesome meat is condemned as unfit for human consumption. Approved meat and meat products are stamped, tagged, or labeled with the official inspection legend—a round stamp bearing a crown in the center and, around the crown, the words "Canada Approved" or "Canada," plus the registered number of the plant. This stamp does not indicate quality or grade, but means that the food is fit for human consumption.

Some small plants not registered for federal inspection operate under provincial health inspection regulations, and in some areas medical health officers inspect meat at local or municipal levels. However, only meat inspected by federal inspectors in registered plants is stamped with the official inspection legend.

Grading. Animals slaughtered in packing plants under Meat Inspection Division, Health of Animals Branch, or provincial inspection are graded by inspectors of the Canada Department of Agriculture, Livestock Division. Beef, veal, and lamb carcasses are graded for producer payment and consumer information, but hog carcasses are graded only for producer payment.

Depending on provincial or municipal legislation, some cattle, hogs, and lambs are slaughtered in plants that do not meet the federal Health of Animals Branch requirements for inspection service. A small portion of these plants are approved for grading of hogs and lambs to provide the basis of payment to producers.

Grading is voluntary except in provinces that have passed grading legislation. British Columbia and Ontario have beef-grading regulations similar to federal regulations, and Alberta, Saskatchewan, Manitoba, and Ontario have branding regulations. In Saskatchewan, all lamb carcasses sold in Regina, Moose Jaw, Saskatoon, and Prince Albert must be grade-stamped under provincial legislation. Grading of carcasses produced and sold within each of these provinces is done by Canada Department of Agriculture officers.

Beef is usually sold by grade, and in some areas consumers may buy graded lamb and veal. Pork is not sold by grade in retail stores. A carcass of beef, when grade-stamped once on each major primal cut, must then be ribbon-branded with a continuous ribbonlike mark in a color indicating grade. The ribbon brand is applied in such a way that it appears on each primal and most retail cuts.

There are nine quality grades for beef and five for veal and lamb. The main grades available in retail stores are:

Grade	Color of ribbon brand mark
Canada A	red
Canada B	blue
Canada C	brown
Canada D	black

The main lamb grades available in retail stores are: Canada Choice, Canada Good, Canada Commercial, and Canada Utility.

Beef. All youthful carcasses are cut between the eleventh and twelfth ribs to expose the Longissimus dorsi muscle and permit the grader to make quality assessments and measure the fat *at a precise point* on the 'rib eye.' There are four fat levels in grades Canada A and Canada B.

Canada A—From youthful animals. The lean is firm, fine grained, and of a bright red color, and has at least slight marbling. The fat covers most of the exterior surface and is white to reddish amber in color.

Fat levels for Canada A

Warm carcass weight *(pounds)*	1	2 *(inches)*	3	4
300-499	.20-.30	.31-.50	.51-.70	over .70
500-699	.20-.40	.41-.60	.61-.80	over .80
700 and up	.30-.50	.51-.70	.71-.90	over .90

As an example, a 550-pound carcass having all the quality factors for Canada A, and 0.5 inches fat at the 'eye' between the eleventh and twelfth ribs would be graded and stamped Canada A2.

Canada B—From youthful animals. The lean is moderately firm with color ranging from bright red to medium dark. The texture of the flesh may be somewhat coarse and the exterior fat may range from white to pale yellow. Marbling is not necessary. Fat levels for Canada B grade are similar to those for Canada A, except that minimum fat for level 1 is reduced by 1/10 inch, that is, .10 instead of .20, .20 instead of .30.

Canada C, Class 1—From youthful to intermediate age animals, including young cows and heifers of intermediate age, as well as youthful steers and heifers below 300 pounds carcass weight and those having below the minimum fat for Canada A or B. The lean can range in color from bright red to medium dark; the fat, from white to pale yellow.

Canada C, Class 2—Age same as Class 1. May be deficient in muscle development. The lean can range in color from bright red to dark; the fat, from white to lemon yellow. The texture of the flesh may be coarse.

Canada D—From mature cows and steers. Classes 1 to 4 are divided according to muscle development and quality, with Canada D4 having the lowest proportion of lean meat to bone. Canada D4 also includes excessively fat carcasses that would otherwise qualify for Canada C.

Canada E—Does not appear in retail stores. This grade is used mainly for manufacturing meat products.

Poultry

Grading of dressed and eviscerated poultry is compulsory for wholesale trade and sale in retail stores in most major cities. The grade mark is prominently indicated on a metal breast tag on fresh poultry or printed on the bag for frozen poultry. All eviscerated poultry that is imported, exported, or shipped between provinces must be graded and health inspected. All imported dressed and eviscerated poultry must meet equivalent Canadian grade standards.

Health Inspection. Health inspection is the responsibility of federal veterinarians stationed in eviscerating plants approved and registered by the Health of Animals Branch, Canada Department of Agriculture. Poultry found wholesome in plants operating under federal government inspection has the Canada Approved or Canada inspection legend on the tag, bag, or insert.

Grades

Grade	Color of tag
Canada Grade Special	purple
Canada Grade A	red
Canada Grade B	blue
Canada Grade Utility	blue
Canada Grade C	yellow
Canada Grade D	brown

Canada Grade Special, Canada Grade C, and Canada Grade D are not usually available in retail stores.

Basis for Grades. Poultry is graded on:

—conformation, meaning presence of deformities that affect appearance or normal distribution of flesh, for example, a crooked keel bone

—flesh, meaning distribution and amount on the carcass

—fat covering, meaning distribution and amounts in specific areas

—dressing, meaning presence of defects such as discoloration, tears, pinfeathers, bruises, or other blemishes.

Grading and Inspection. Poultry may be processed and graded by producers registered to handle only their own products or at registered commercial poultry processing plants. Both types of registered premises must comply with strict operating and sanitation requirements. Federal agricultural inspectors check frequently to ensure that accurate grading is being done under strict sanitary conditions.

Periodic inspections of grade quality are made by federal agricultural inspectors at wholesale distributors, holding freezers, retail stores, restaurants, hospitals, other institutions, and military camps.

All provinces except Ontario have legislation that complements the federal regulations for grading and inspection of poultry. Federal agricultural inspectors are responsible for enforcing provincial legislation.

Glossary

In any trade, profession, or skill, a knowledge of the terminology is considered important to the performance of the tasks and an understanding of the procedures. The following terms are those most often used in food preparation procedures. Although not all-inclusive, this glossary is designed to give the reader a good working vocabulary. For any unfamiliar terms not included here, the reader is advised to refer to a culinary dictionary.

acrolein: a substance that is irritating to the eyes and nose, released as a by-product when fat is broken down by excessive heat.

aging: as applied to meat, notably beef, the process of holding the cut under refrigerated conditions for approximately nine days to improve its taste and tenderness (higher quality beef is often aged for longer periods); as applied to ice cream, the hardening process carried out after the ice cream is mixed and removed from the freezer.

agneau: French word for "lamb."

a la: French term for "in the style of."

a la carte: food items that are priced separately on a menu and usually prepared to order.

a la king: prepared in a cream sauce with mushrooms, green peppers, and pimientos.

a la mode: served with ice cream on top; refers to pies and cakes.

al dente: giving some resistance to the bite; usually refers to pasta products.

allemande: white sauce with egg yolks.

allumette: cut in matchstick form; usually refers to potatoes.

ambrosia: fruits and coconut in a combination dessert.

amino acids: nitrogen-based organic substances that make up proteins.

amylopectin: a starch molecule that has a many-branched chain form.

amylose: a starch molecule with a single, long, straight chain.

anchovy: a small, herring-type fish used in salads, buffets, and appetizers.

angel food cake: a white cake without fat that uses egg whites as leavening.

anglaise: French word for "English."

antipasto: an Italian appetizer course.
aspic: a protein-based gel from meat or poultry.
au: French word for "with."
au gratin: often used to mean "with cheese," but technically means prepared with a white sauce, covered with crumbs, and baked in the oven until brown.
au jus: with natural juices.
au lait: with milk.
au naturel: in simplified form or with minimum seasoning.
bacteria: organisms that can cause fermentation or spoilage of foods; pathogenic types cause diseases in man.
bain-marie: a hot water bath for keeping foods hot.
bake: to cook by dry heat without the addition of moisture.
baked alaska: an ice cream and cake dessert that is covered with meringue and browned in an oven.
baking powder: a chemical leavening agent that generates carbon dioxide when mixed with moisture and heated.
baking soda: sodium bicarbonate, which generates carbon dioxide for leavening products when mixed with an acid food.
barbecued: served with a barbecue sauce or cooked over an open fire.
baste: to pour drippings over a food as it cooks in order to keep its surface moist.
batter: a mixture of solid and liquid ingredients with a pouring consistency.
bavarian: a chilled dessert made with gelatin and whipped cream.
béarnaise: a sauce made with egg yolks, butter, and tarragon.
beat: to manipulate a mixture rapidly in order to incorporate air and make it smooth.
béchamel: a rich cream sauce.
beef: meat from bovine animals one year of age or older.
Bercy: a brown sauce with shallots and wine.
beurre: French word for "butter."
bind: to mold together.
biscuits: small shapes of quick bread made with baking powder.
bisque: a thickened soup made from shellfish.
blanc: French word for "white."
blanch: to partially cook or scald an item in boiling water in order to aid in removing the skin.
blend: to mix two or more ingredients.
boeuf: French word for "beef."
boil: to cook in water at 212 degrees Fahrenheit.
bombe: a dessert made in a special mold from a mixture of ice creams.
bonne femme: prepared in a simple fashion.
Bordellaise: a brown sauce with wine flavoring.
borsch: a beet soup usually served cold with sour cream.
Boston brown bread: a dark, sweet bread that is steamed.
Boston cream pie: a two-layered cake filled with whipped cream or custard and coated with powdered sugar on top.
bouillabaisse: a soup made with a mixture of finfish and shellfish.
bouillon: a rich stock; usually refers to beef stock.
bouquet garni: a cheesecloth bag in which seasonings are held during the preparation of liquid items, so that the herbs are easy to remove.
bouquetiere: served with vegetables.
braise: to prepare by browning, adding liquid, and cooking at simmering temperatures.
bran: the outer layer of a grain.
breading: a covering of bread crumbs applied to an item after it has been dredged with flour and coated with egg wash.
brioche: a sweet dough.
brochette: skewered and broiled.
broil: to cook by direct exposure to a heat source.
buffet: a displayed table of foods.
buns: small shapes of sweetened or unsweetened dough.
butter: the spread obtained by churning cream.
buttercream icing: an uncooked, rich icing containing powdered sugar and fat.
butterscotch: a flavor obtained from butter and brown sugar.

cake: a baked product obtained from a leavened batter that may or may not contain fat.
Calorie: a unit of heat energy that measures foods as fuel.
Canadian bacon: the smoked loin of pork in compact style.
canapé: an appetizer served on toast, bread, or crackers.
candy: to cook food in sweetened syrup.
caper: a bud seasoning.
capon: a male chicken that has been castrated for better weight and tenderness.
caramelized: refers to dry sugar; heated until it becomes dark in color.
carbohydrates: starches and sugars found in food; they provide four Calories per gram.
carbon dioxide: a gas obtained by fermentation of yeast or by the action of soda and an acid, and used to leaven baked products.
casserole: a heavy dish; also food baked and served in a casserole dish.
caviar: sturgeon roe.
cayenne: a hot red pepper.
champignons: French word for "mushrooms."
chantilly: containing cream.
chateaubriand: tenderloin of beef sliced at the table.
chaud: French word for "hot."
cheesecake: a dessert made of a base with a filling of cheese, eggs, and milk.
chiffonade: vegetables finely chopped.
China cap: a strainer in a cone shape.
chives: onion sprouts with a mild flavor.
chop: to divide into small pieces.
choux paste: a dough made of eggs, fat, water, and flour, used to make cream puffs.
cloche: a bell-shaped glass used to cover food for service.
coagulate: to harden protein by heating or beating
coat: to cover the surface of an item with another substance.
coddle: to cook in water below the boiling point.
compote: a combination of fruits.
condiments: food accompaniments.
consommé: a clear, strong soup.
coq: French word for "chicken."
cottage cheese: the curd of soured milk.
court bouillon: a combination of vinegar or wine, water, onions, celery, carrots, and herbs, used to poach fish.
cream: (noun) the fat part of milk; (verb) to mix until smooth; to incorporate air while mixing sugar and fat in cake preparation.
cream cheese: the curd of soured cream pressed until smooth.
creole: a method of preparation in which the food is usually highly seasoned and contains tomatoes, onions, and green peppers.
crepe: French word for "pancake."
croissant: a hard-crusted crescent-shaped roll.
croquettes: a combination of foods shaped into patties bonded together with a heavy white sauce, and then breaded and deep fat fried.
croutons: cubes of toasted bread used in soups and salads.
crullers: long and twisted doughnuts.
cube: to cut into small square pieces or chunks.
curry: a strong East Indian mixed seasoning.
custard: a mixture of eggs, milk, and sugar that is baked or cooked over water.
cut: to divide with a knife; also to mix fat into dry ingredients with cutting motion.
cutlet: a thin piece of meat or poultry, usually boneless.
Danish pastry: a sweet roll made from flaky yeast dough with fat rolled into layers.
deep fat fry: to cook in hot fat; to French fry.
deglaze: to add water to a pan used for roasting to remove the crusted cooking juices.
demi: French word for "half."
demiglacé: a reduced brown stock.
deviled: highly seasoned, for example with tabasco sauce and pepper.
dice: to divide into small cubes.
dissolve: to mix a solid into a solution.
docking holes: holes made in dough to enable it to bake smoothly.
dough: a thick, flour-based product used for breads and rolls.

doughnut: a sweetened dough leavened by yeast or baking powder that is cooked in deep fat.

dredge: to coat the surface with a dry ingredient, such as flour.

drippings: the juices extracted from meats that have been roasted.

duchess potatoes: potatoes that are whipped, mixed with eggs, and piped through a pastry tube; often used to garnish a planked food item.

du jour: French term for "of the day."

dust: to sprinkle an item or a surface with flour or sugar.

éclair: a cream puff made in a long shape.

eggs Benedict: poached eggs served with ham or Canadian bacon on an English muffin and topped with hollandaise sauce.

emulsification: the blending of fat and water into a stable solution.

entrée: the main part of the meal; usually refers to the meat or meat substitute dish.

enzyme: a substance in a living organism that causes changes in organic substances.

escalloped: *see* scalloped.

espagnole: a dark brown sauce.

essence: a concentrated juice; usually refers to meat juices.

extract: an essence of fruits or spices.

farci: French term for "stuffed."

farinaceous: made from a flour mixture.

fermentation: the chemical process that produces carbon dioxide.

filet or fillet: a boneless piece of meat or fish (the fish cut is usually spelled fillet).

flambé: flamed.

Florentine: prepared or served with spinach.

flour: the ground meal of a grain.

foam: an egg and sugar mixture beaten to incorporate air.

fold: to mix or blend without disturbing the incorporated air; also to double one part over another part such as in pastry or omelets.

fondant: a low-moisture sugar syrup that is cooled to prevent large crystal formation.

fondue: a cheese product.

formula: a recipe.

Francaise: French style.

Frenched: having the meat and fat scraped from the ends of the bones; refers to chops or legs of veal or lamb.

French knife: a cook's knife with a broad, slightly curved blade and a pointed tip.

fricassee: to braise; usually refers to poultry.

froid: French word for "cold."

fromage: French word for "cheese."

fry: to cook in hot fat.

garde-manger: a cold meat man; also a pantry.

garnish: to decorate.

gateau: French word for "cake."

gelatin: a protein extractive from the meat, bones, or horns of animals.

gelatinization: the thickening of starch when it is heated in liquid.

giblets: the gizzard, heart, and liver of poultry.

glacé: coated with sugar; also frozen.

glaze: a glossy coating.

gliadin: one of the two proteins in flour that make up gluten.

glucose: corn syrup, a simple sugar.

gluten: the elastic substance that is made when wheat flour is mixed with water.

glutenin: one of the two proteins in flour that make up gluten.

graham flour: whole wheat flour.

grate: to rub against a rough sharp surface in order to divide finely.

grill: to broil or cook on a griddle.

gumbo: a dish containing okra.

herbs: the leaves of plants used for seasoning.

hollandaise: a vinegar, egg, and butter sauce.

homogenized: made one consistency.

hors d'oeuvres: small appetizers.

hydrogenated: refers to fat; treated with hydrogen to make it more solid.

invert sugar: a mixture of dextrose and levulose, made by breaking sucrose with an acid or enzyme.

Italienne: Italian style.

julienne: cut in fine strips.

kabob: meat or vegetable cubes roasted on a skewer.

kneading: the folding and stretching process that develops gluten in a flour mixture.

lactose: a milk sugar.
lait: French word for "milk."
lard: (noun) hog fat; (verb) to insert strips of fat into lean meat.
leavening: raising a food by air, steam, or carbon dioxide, in order to make it lighter.
légumes: French word for "vegetables."
levulose: a simple sugar found in honey and fruits.
lyonnaise: sautéed with onions.
macaroon: a cookie made from coconut and/or almond paste with egg whites and sugar; it contains no flour.
macédoine: a mixture of fruits or vegetables.
maitre d'hotel: (noun) the head of the dining room staff; (adjective) prepared with butter, lemon juice, and parsley.
Manhattan clam chowder: clam chowder with tomatoes.
marengo: with mushrooms and tomatoes; refers to chicken.
marinate: to soak an uncooked item in a sauce or acid mixture.
mayonnaise: a salad dressing with eggs, oil, and vinegar.
melba toast: a thin slice of toasted bread.
meringue: frothy beaten egg whites and sugar.
meunière: sautéed in browned butter and served with wine and lemon juice; usually refers to fish.
middlings: wheat endosperm ground into particles during milling.
mince: to chop finely.
mincemeat: a mixture of raisins, apples, beef suet, and spices.
minestrone: an Italian vegetable soup.
minute steak: a thin steak usually tenderized for ease in cooking and eating.
mirepoix: a mixture of chopped vegetables used to flavor roasts.
mix: to combine ingredients.
mold: a metal container in which foods are shaped or chilled; also an aerobic organism that aids in aging cheese and meats but also causes spoilage of food.
mongole: a soup with tomatoes, peas, and other vegetables.
mornay: a cream sauce with eggs and Parmesan cheese.
mousse: a frozen dessert containing whipped cream or egg whites and flavorings.
mozzarella: a soft Italian cheese.
muffin: a small quick bread.
mulligatawny: a soup containing chicken, rice, vegetables, and curry.
newburg: a cream sauce with wine and paprika, used with seafood.
noir: French word for "black."
O'Brien: prepared with green peppers and pimientos.
oeuf: French word for "egg."
panaché: made of mixed foods of contrasting colors.
panbroil: to cook uncovered in a hot pan without added fat.
panfry: to cook in a hot pan in a small amount of fat.
papilloté: cooked in paper.
parboil: to partially cook in water.
pare: to remove the skin or outer surface with a knife or utensil.
parfait: a combination of ice creams of different colors and/or liqueurs, served in a tall glass.
Parisienne: cut in small round balls; refers to vegetables or fruits, such as potatoes or melons, cut with a Parisienne cutter.
pasteurized: heated to between 140 and 180 degrees, depending on the length of time for which it is held, to kill bacteria.
pastry bag: a bag with a metal tip, used to decorate cakes or for piping foods to create a better display.
paté: a paste.
peel: (noun) a flat wooden implement used to remove hot products from ovens; (verb) to remove the skin.
petit: French word for "small."
petits fours: small cakes that are iced and decorated.
pH: an indicator of acidity, with a range from 1 to 14 (acid to alkaline).
pie: a dessert with a pastry bottom.
pilaf: rice cooked in a small amount of stock.
pimiento: a sweet pepper.

piquant: with a sharp seasoning or flavor.

plank: to cook on a wooden plank; refers to meat or fish.

poach: to cook in water under the boiling point.

poisson: French word for "fish."

Polonaise: with hard boiled eggs and bread crumbs.

polysaccharide: a complex carbohydrate form, such as starch.

pomme: French word for "apple."

pomme de terre: French word for "potato" (literally, "apple of the earth").

popover: a steam-leavened quick bread.

poulet: French word for "chicken."

proof: to let dough ferment in a warm area.

puff pastry: a dough with fat rolled in for extra flakiness.

puree: a thick pulp of sieved or mashed food.

quick breads: bread products that are chemically leavened.

rafted: cleared or clarified by coagulated protein of egg and ground beef, which forms a "raft" as it floats to the top of a stock.

ragout: a stew.

reduce: to lower the volume by evaporation during cooking.

render: to remove fat from tissue.

rissolé: oven-browned.

roast: to cook with dry heat in an oven.

roe: the eggs of fish.

rope: the bacterial growth in bread dough.

rouge: French word for "red."

roux: a fat and flour mixture used to thicken soups and sauces.

Russian dressing: a dressing made of mayonnaise, chili sauce, and lemon juice.

sauce: a thickened liquid accompaniment to a food item.

sauté: to cook in a small amount of fat.

scald: to heat to a point just below the boiling temperature.

scaling: dividing batter or dough according to weight.

scalloped: cut into thin slices; also baked with cream sauce.

score: to cut slits in the surface of a food, to increase its tenderness.

sear: to brown the surface.

shirred: baked with butter; usually refers to eggs.

shred: to divide into small, narrow strips.

sift: to pass through a strainer or sieve, to make light.

simmer: to cook slowly just below the boiling point.

skewer: a metal shaft on which food is fastened for cooking.

slice: to cut with a knife or machine into narrow flat pieces.

smother: to cook in a covered container.

soufflé: a puffed food leavened by egg whites and baked.

sous chef: the assistant to the head chef.

steam: to cook in contact with water vapor.

steep: to let a food stand in liquid in order to extract its flavor and color; usually refers to tea.

stew: to cook in water just below the boiling temperature.

stock: the liquid in which meat, fish, or poultry has been slowly cooked for maximum extraction of its flavor.

straight flour: flour milled from all parts of the wheat kernel except the bran.

suet: beef fat.

sweetbreads: the thymus gland of a calf or veal animal.

Swiss steak: a less tender cut of beef that is braised and served in a heavy gravy.

syneresis: the weeping of liquid from a gel.

table d'hote: a complete meal offering for a single price.

tempering: the process of adjusting the temperature of an ingredient.

torte: a small, decorated cake.

toss: to combine by a lifting and dropping action.

tripe: the stomach of a beef animal.

truffle: a mushroom type of fungus used as a garnish.

viande: French word for "meat."

vichyssoise: a potato soup that is creamed and served cold.

Vienna bread: a bread with a heavy, crisp crust.

vin: French word for "wine."

wash: a liquid that is brushed on the surface of an item; it is a component of the breading process; also a thickening agent, such as a white wash of flour and water.

whip: to beat rapidly in order to incorporate air.

yeast: a plant that causes fermentation and gives off carbon dioxide; it is used to leaven products.

zwieback: a twice-toasted bread.

Bibliography

Altshuler, Susan, and Finklestein, Barry. "Seven Ways Researchers Are Increasing Your Profit." *The Florida Restaurateur,* June 1987, pp. 24-25.

"A Is for Apple? No, Atemoya." *Time,* Aug. 11, 1986, pp. 61-62.

Amendola, Joseph. *The Baker's Manual.* New York: Ahrens Book Company, 1956.

Andrew's, Helen. *Food Preparation.* New York: McGraw-Hill Book Company, 1967.

Applied Cookery. Washington, D.C.: Department of the Navy, 1955.

Armbruster, Gertrude, and others. *Let's Eat Poultry.* Cornell Extension Bulletin no. 971. Ithaca, N.Y., 1957.

Armour Fresh Meat Study Guide. Chicago: Armour and Company, 1962.

Baking Handbook. Washington, D.C.: Department of the Navy, 1958.

Bean, Russell. "New Ovens Give School Food Service a Versatile Tool." *School Food Service Journal,* March 1987, pp. 82-83

"The Big Shift in Americans' Diets." *U.S. News and World Report,* April 30, 1984, p. 20.

Breithaupt, Herman, *Commercial Cooking.* Detroit: Chadsey High School, 1962.

Brody, Jane E. "America Leans to a Health Diet." *New York Times Magazine,* Oct. 13, 1985, p. 32.

Bull, Sleeter. *Meat for the Table.* New York: McGraw-Hill Book Company, 1951.

Burtis, Jean, and others. *How to Cook Lobsters.* Test Kitchen Series no. 11. Washington, D.C.: Department of the Interior, 1957.

———. *How to Cook Shrimp.* Test Kitchen Series no. 7. Washington, D.C.: Department of the Interior, 1952.

"Career Paths." *Nations Restaurant News,* Jan. 1986.

Casola, Matteo. *Successful Mass Cookery and Volume Feeding.* New York; Ahrens Book Company, 1969.

Clawson, Augusta. *Equipment Manual.* New York: Ahrens Book Company, 1959.

Coffman, J.P. *Introduction to Professional Food Service.* Chicago: Institutions Magazine, 1968.

Conner, William. *Food and Beverage Merchandising.* Ithaca, N.Y.: Cornell University, 1958.

Cooking Meat in Quantity. Chicago: National Live Stock and Meat Board, no date.

Culinary Art and Traditions of Switzerland. Vevey: Nestle, 1986.

Cuts of Meat. Agricultural Research Bulletin no. 7. Chicago: Swift and Company, no date.

Dana, A. *Kitchen Planning for Quantity Food Service.* New York: Harper and Brothers, 1949.

Directory of Hotel, Restaurant and Institutional Schools. Washington, D.C.: Council on Hotel, Restaurant and Institutional Education, 1972.

"The Doctors' Diet." *Redbook,* June 1984, p. 130

Downs, Anthony. "Market Trends in Food Service." *Cornell Hotel and Restaurant Administration Quarterly,* May 1969, pp. 5-16.

"Dram Shops." *Restaurant Business,* Sept. 20, 1985, p. 124.

Durocher, Joseph. "Combination Ovens." *Restaurant Business*, June 10, 1987, pp. 198-200.

Eaton, William V. "Microwave Ovens Do and Don'ts." *The Florida Restaurateur*, May 1986, pp. 14-15.

Essentials of Good Table Service. Ithaca, N.Y.: Cornell University, 1971.

"Ethnic Spices." *Restaurant Hospitality*, June 1987, p. 61.

Facts about Coffee. Publication no. 117. New York: Coffee Brewing Center, Pan-American Coffee Bureau, no date.

Faulkner, Elizabeth. "The Food Service Contractor and Corporate Culture." *Restaurants and Institutions*, May 9, 1984, pp. 239-242.

Fay, Clifford T., Jr., and others. *Managerial Accounting for the Hospitality Service Industries.* Dubuque, Iowa: William C. Brown Company, 1971.

"FDA May Target Vegetables in Bacteria Investigation." *Nations Restaurant News*, Oct. 20, 1986, p. 67.

Fitch, Natalie K., and others. *Foods and Principles of Cookery.* New York: Prentice-Hall, 1948.

Fleck, Henrietta. *Introduction to Nutrition.* New York: Macmillan Company, 1971.

Fleck, Henrietta, and others. *Modern Diet and Nutrition.* New York: Dell Publishing Company, 1955.

Florida School Lunch Sanitation and Safety. Bulletin no. 33-F. Tallahassee: State of Florida, 1965.

Folsom, LeRoi A. *Instructor's Guide for the Teaching of Professional Cooking.* Chicago: Institutions Magazine, 1967.

——, ed. *The Professional Chef.* Chicago: Institutions Magazine, 1967.

Food Marketing Handbook. New York: Extension Service, State Colleges of Agriculture and Home Economics, New York, New Jersey, and Connecticut, no date.

"Food Poisoning—How to Avoid the 10 Worse Types." *Good Housekeeping*, Sept. 1983, pp. 212-213.

Food Preferences of Men in the U.S. Armed Forces. Chicago: United States Army, 1958.

Food Purchasing Guide for Group Feeding. Washington, D.C.: Department of Agriculture, 1965.

Food Service Industry Pocket Factbooks, 1983-1987. Washington, D.C.: National Restaurant Association.

Food Service Sanitation Manual. Washington, D.C.: Department of Health, Education, and Welfare, 1962.

Fowler, Sina F., West, Bessie, and others. *Food for Fifty.* New York: John Wiley and Sons, 1971.

Fresh Facts about the Fresh Fruit and Vegetable Industry. Washington, D.C.: United Fresh Fruit and Vegetable Association, 1962.

"Future Foods, A Taste of What's to Come." *Changing Times*, May 1983, pp. 89-91.

Garrett, Alfred B., and others. *Essentials of Chemistry.* Boston: Ginn and Company, 1951.

A Guide to Spices. Chicago: National Restaurant Association and American Spice Trade Association, no date.

Haines, Robert G. *Food Preparation in Hotels, Restaurants and Cafeterias.* Chicago: American Technical Society, 1968.

Handbook of Food Preparation. Washington, D.C.: American Home Economics Association, 1954.

Hawkes, Alex D. *A World of Vegetable Cookery.* New York: Simon and Schuster, 1968.

Hayes, Kirby M., and others. *Frozen Foods in Food Service Establishments.* Food Management Program Leaflet no. 2. Amherst, Mass.: University of Massachusetts, no date.

Hill, Bob. "What Microcomputers Should Do for You." *National Restaurant Association News*, Jan. 1985, pp. 25-26.

How to Buy Cheddar Cheese. Home and Garden Bulletin no. 128. Washington, D.C.: Department of Agriculture, 1967.

How to Buy Fresh Vegetables. Home and Garden Bulletin no. 143. Washington, D.C.: Department of Agriculture, 1967.

How to Buy Instant Nonfat Dry Milk. Home and Garden Bulletin no. 140. Washington, D.C.: Department of Agriculture, 1967.

Huebener, Paul. *Gourmet Table Service.* Rochelle Park, N.Y.: Hayden Books, 1968.

Hughes, Osee, and others. *Introductory Foods.* New York: Macmillian Company, 1970.

Hunter, Beatrice. "Food for Thought." *Consumer Research Magazine*, Nov. 1983, p. 8.

Hunter, Mildred B., and others. *Cake Quality and Batter Structure.* Agricultural Experiment Station Bulletin no. 860. Ithaca, N.Y.: Cornell University, 1950.

Ice Cream Information Sheet. Chicago: National Dairy Council, no date.

Jones, Jeanne. "New Culinary Concept—Lighter, Healthier Menus." *Lodging*, June 1986, pp. 26-27.

Keister, Douglas C. *How to Increase Profits with Portion Control.* New York: Ahrens Book Company, 1957.

Kerr, Rose G. *Basic Fish Cookery.* Test Kitchen Series no. 2. Washington, D.C.: Department of the Interior, 1950.

Kerr, Rose G., and others. *How to Cook Oysters.* Test Kitchen Series no. 3. Washington, D.C.: Department of the Interior, 1950.

Klippstein, Ruth. *A Food Value Wheel.* Home Economics Extension Leaflet no. 25. Ithaca, N.Y.: Cornell University, no date.

Kotschevar, Lendal H. *Quality Food Purchasing.* New York: John Wiley and Sons, 1961.

—. *Standards, Principles and Techniques in Quantity Food Production.* Berkeley, Calif.: McCutchan Publishing Corporation, 1964.

Kotschevar, Lendal H., and others. *Food Service Layout and Equipment Planning.* New York: John Wiley and Sons, 1961.

Lamalle, Cecile. "Food Trends." *Restaurant Hospitality,* Sept. 1986, p. 16.

Lecos, Chris. "The Growing Use of Irradiation to Preserve Foods." *FDA Consumer,* July/Aug. 1986, pp. 12-15.

Lefler, Janet. *Canapés, Hor d'Oeuvres and Buffet Dishes.* New York: Ahrens Book Company, 1963.

Leist, Joyce, ed. *Dietitian's Manual.* New York: American Gas Association, no date.

"The Liability Crisis." *National Restaurant Association News,* April, 1986, p. 7.

Lippert, Joan L. "6 New Foods You'll Be Eating in 1999." *Health,* Jan. 1982.

Little, J.H., and Norman, Nancy. "Kitchen 2001." *Canadian Hotel and Restaurant,* Jan. 1986, pp. 23-24.

Longree, Karla, and others. *Sanitary Techniques in Food Service.* New York: John Wiley and Sons, 1971.

Lowenberg, Miriam E. *Food and Man.* New York: John Wiley and Sons, 1968.

Lukowski, Robert F., and others. *Using Storage in Food Service Establishments.* Food Management Program Leaflet no. 4. Amherst, Mass.: University of Massachusetts, no date.

Lundberg, Donald, and others. *The Management of People in Hotels, Restaurants, and Clubs.* Dubuque, Iowa: William C. Brown Company, 1964.

—. *Understanding Cooking.* New York: Radio City Books, 1967.

Marshall, Anthony. "It's Time Hoteliers Paid More Attention to AIDS Crisis." *Hotel and Motel Management,* March 30, 1987, pp. 17-18.

"Property Pays $6 Million for Not Screening Employee." *Hotel and Motel Management,* April 1985, p. 8.

McWilliams, Margaret. *Food Fundamentals.* New York: John Wiley and Sons, 1966.

Manual of Sanitation Aspects of Installations of Food Service Equipment. Ann Arbor, Mich.: National Sanitation Foundation, 1968.

Meat Carving Made Easy. Chicago: National Live Stock and Meat Board, no date.

Meat Reference Book. Chicago: American Meat Institute, 1960.

Menu Pricing. Chicago: Swift and Company, no date.

Milk Information Sheet. Chicago: National Dairy Council, 1965.

Miller, A. T., and others. *Care and Handling of Prepared Frozen Foods.* Food Management Leaflet no. 9. Amherst, Mass.: University of Massachusetts, no date.

Miller, Bryon. "A Year of Surprises." *New York Times Magazine,* Dec. 8, 1985, pp. 139-140.

Minno, Maurice, P., and others. "Restaurant Budgeting." *National Restaurant Association News,* Nov. 1984, pp. 21-24.

Modern Sandwich Methods. Chicago: American Institute of Baking, 1964.

Morr, Mary L., and others. *Introductory Foods: Laboratory Manual of Food Preparation and Evaluation.* New York: Macmillan Company, 1970.

National Sanitation Standards no. 3. Ann Arbor, Mich.: National Sanitation Foundation, 1953.

Nutritive Value of Foods. Home and Garden Bulletin no. 72. Washington, D.C.: Department of Agriculture, 1964.

Osterhaug, Kathryn, and others. *How to Cook Clams.* Test Kitchen Series no. 8. Washington, D.C.: Department of the Interior, 1953.

"Outbreak of Salmonellosis Linked with Drug Resistant Salmonella." *Restaurants and Institutions,* May 28, 1986, p. 26.

Peckham, Gladys, C. *Foundations of Food Preparation.* New York: Macmillan Company, 1969.

Pest Prevention. Technical Bulletin. Chicago: National Restaurant Association, 1970.

Pollack, Andrew. "Flavor Fresh from the Lab." *St. Petersburg Times,* June 25, 1987, p. 8A.

"A Primer to Parasites." *Seafood Leader,* Winter 1986, pp. 44-48.

"Profile of American Hospitality Industry." *National Culinary Review,* Dec. 1986, pp. 6-7.

Profits with Pork. Chicago: National Live Stock and Meat Board, no date.

"Putting the Brakes on Drunken Driving." *Cornell Hotel, Restaurant and Institutions Quarterly,* Aug. 1985, p. 100.

Quantity Meat Recipes. Chicago: National Live Stock and Meat Board, no date.

"Raw Oyster Feast Fatal." *Clearwater Sun,* July 23, 1987, p. 10A

Recipes and Menus for All Seasons. Chicago: John Sexton and Company, no date.

"Reconnaissance." *Restaurants and Institutions,* Sept. 12, 1984, April 17, 1985, and May 28, 1986.

"The Restaurant Industry in 1990." *Current Issue*

Report. Washington, D.C.: National Restaurant Association, 1985.

Rice in Food Service. Houston: Rice Council of America, 1972.

Roasting Frozen Meat. Chicago: National Live Stock and Meat Board, no date.

Robey, Dorothy M., and others. *How to Cook Crabs.* Test Kitchen Series no. 10. Washington, D.C.: Department of the Interior, 1956.

Roth, Walter. "The Changing Role of Chefs." *National Culinary Review,* Dec. 1985, pp. 9-10.

Sanitary Food Service. Cincinnati: Department of Health, Education, and Welfare, 1969.

Sanitation of Food Service Establishments. Ames, Iowa: State Department of Health, 1962.

Seafood Leader Buyers' Guide. 1987.

Schneider, Nicholas F., and others. *Commercial Kitchens.* New York: American Gas Association, 1962.

Shimizu, Holly H. "Do Yourself a Flavor." *Consumer,* April 1984.

Simeons, A.T.W. *Food: Facts, Foibles, and Fables.* New York: Funk and Wagnalls Publishing Company, 1968.

Simkins, Mary. "New Secrets for Fresher Food." *Social Issues Resources Service,* Vol. 3, Art. 96, 1986.

Smith, E. Evelyn. *A Handbook on Quantity Food Management.* Minneapolis: Burgess Publishing Company, 1955.

Stevenson, Gladys, and others. *Introduction to Foods and Nutrition.* New York: John Wiley and Sons, 1960.

The Story of Beef. Chicago: American Meat Institute, 1959.

The Story of Pork. Chicago: American Meat Institute, no date.

"Survey Finds Widely Varying Attitudes on No Smoking Sections." *The Florida Restaurateur,* May 1987, p. 29.

Sweetman, Marion D., and others. *Food Selection and Preparation.* New York: John Wiley and Sons, 1954.

Terrell, Margaret E. *Professional Food Preparation.* New York: John Wiley and Sons, 1971.

Terry, Ken. "Why is DOE for Food Irradiation?" *Nation,* Vol. 244, No. 5, Feb. 7, 1987, p. 142.

Today's Dairy Foods. Chicago: National Dairy Council, 1969.

Treat, N., and others. *Quantity Cookery.* Boston: Little, Brown and Company, 1967.

USDA's Acceptance Service for Meat Products. Marketing Bulletin no. 47. Washington, D.C.: Department of Agriculture, 1970.

USDA's Acceptance Service for Poultry and Eggs. Marketing Bulletin no. 46. Washington, D.C.: Department of Agriculture, 1969.

USDA's Yield Grades for Beef. Marketing Bulletin no. 45. Washington, D.C.: Department of Agriculture, 1968.

"Vaccine May Prevent Food Poisoning." *St. Petersburg Times,* June 28, 1987, p. 4A.

Walker, J. Earl. "The Amateur Scientist." *Scientific American,* Vol. 256, No. 2, Feb. 1987, pp. 134-138.

Welch, John M. *Analyze Your Food Cost.* Circular no. 723. Columbia, Mo.: University of Missouri, 1960.

West, B. B., and others. *Food Service in Institutions.* New York: John Wiley and Sons, 1966.

Wilkinson, Jule. *The Preparation Kitchen.* Chicago: Institutions Magazine, 1968.

Wood, Adelaine. *Quantity Buying Guide.* New York: Ahrens Book Company, 1957.

Wright, Carlton E. *Food Buying.* New York: Macmillan Company, 1962.

Wrisley, Albert L. *Using Storage Controls to Simplify Determination of Daily Food Costs.* Food Management Leaflet no. 5. Amherst, Mass.: University of Massachusetts, no date.

Zaccarelli, Brother Herman. "The Food Service of the Future Is Knowing When to Purchase Equipment." *Culinary Review,* April 1983, p. 21.

Zarrow, Susan. "Health Rating America's New Foods." *Prevention,* Vol. 36, No. 11, Nov. 1984, pp. 72-76.

Index